UNDERSTANDING
ŚAṄKARA
Essays by Richard De Smet

UNDERSTANDING ŚAṄKARA

Essays by Richard De Smet

Edited by
IVO COELHO

MOTILAL BANARSIDASS PUBLISHERS
PRIVATE LIMITED • DELHI

First Edition : Delhi, 2013

ISBN: 978-81-208-3613-6

MOTILAL BANARSIDASS
41 U.A. Bungalow Road, Jawahar Nagar, Delhi 110 007
8 Mahalaxmi Chamber, 22 Bhulabhai Desai Road, Mumbai 400 026
203 Royapettah High Road, Mylapore, Chennai 600 004
236, 9th Main III Block, Jayanagar, Bangaluru 560 011
Sanas Plaza, 1302 Baji Rao Road, Pune 411 002
8 Camac Street, Kolkata 700 017
Ashok Rajpath, Patna 800 004
Chowk, Varanasi 221 001

Printed in India

by RP Jain at NAB Printing Unit,
A-44, Naraina Industrial Area, Phase I, New Delhi–110028
and published by JP Jain for Motilal Banarsidass Publishers (P) Ltd,
41 U.A. Bungalow Road, Jawahar Nagar, Delhi-110007

CONTENTS

III. REVIEWS

APPENDICES

PREFACE

After *Brahman and Person* (2010), I am happy to be able to present another collection of the essays of the late Prof. Richard De Smet (1916-1997), this time in the area of his chief specialization, Śaṅkara research.

In the first place, my gratitude to all those who have given permission to reprint the articles in this volume. Detailed acknowledgements will be found at the beginning of each article, but here I feel obliged to thank very specially the Rectors of De Nobili College, Pune, first Fr Oscar Rozario and then Fr Keith Abranches, for their graciousnessness and encouragement.

A very large number of people have collaborated in the present work, and I am happy to acknowledge their help:

Archbishop Felix Machado, Bishop earlier of Nashik and now of Vasai; Msgr. Markus Solo of the Pontifical Council for Interreligious Dialogue; Arul Jeevan, SJ, Librarian of Jnana Deepa Vidyapeeth, Pune; Errol D'Lima, SJ, Librarian of De Nobili College, Pune; and Banzelão Teixeira, Peter Gonsalves, Tino Fernandes, Jason Coelho, Sahayadas Fernando and Thumma Vijay Prathap Reddy for help with bibliographical research.

Bernard Britto, Edward Pereira, Nazareth Denis and Shyju Babykutty for help with secretarial work: without them this book would hardly have been possible at all.

Banzelão Teixeira once again for his inestimable service of proof-reading.

My young nephew Amish Coelho for the cover design, which alludes appropriately to Śaṅkara's frequent use of the definition of a lotus through *sāmānya* and *viśeṣa*—"this kind of lotus is blue, big, sweet-smelling" (*nīlaṃ mahat-sugandhy-utpalam-iti*)—in order to contrast it with *Brahman* which cannot be defined by genus and species.

Michael Fernandes, Provincial of the Salesians of Don Bosco, Mumbai, and the community of Don Bosco Nashik for the support and space I have enjoyed while engaged in this work.

A special word of thanks to Prof. S. Panneerselvam, Dean, Dept. of Philosophy, University of Madras, who had graciously consented to write a Foreword, but which, due to problems of logistics, I had to forego. Prof. Panneerselvam knew Fr De Smet personally, and esteemed him to the extent of regarding him as one of the Advaitins of India.

As this collection of essays centred around the great Śaṅkarācārya is offered to the public, I would like to pay homage also to Fr De Smet, himself an unforgettable *guru*. May his work continue to bear fruit, and, indeed, play its part in leading us onward—together!—to the Ultimate Shore. For is it not part of the effort to at least indicate what cannot be expressed? *Tal-lakṣyate na tū'cyate*! We are, as De Smet himself used to say, like little children throwing stones at mangoes high up in the tree: the stones may not reach the mangoes, but they do go some way in their direction.

Ivo Coelho, SDB
15 August 2011
Divyadaan: Salesian Institute of Philosophy, Nashik

INTRODUCTION

Among Richard De Smet's chief contributions to indology and to interreligious dialogue are his clarifications regarding the personhood of the *para Brahman* and his rejection of the illusionist and acosmist interpretation of Śaṅkara's *advaita*.[1] Long unavailable to the general public in an easily accessible manner, De Smet's essays on the first topic were, in 2010, brought together under the title *Brahman and Person*.[2] His essays on the second topic are now being brought together in the present collection. While I have tried to include all items dealing principally and directly with De Smet's interpretation of Śaṅkara, there are two significant exceptions: the doctoral dissertation, and the Śaṅkara chapter of his 'Guidelines in Indian Philosophy.'[3] The reason is mundane: they were simply too large to be included in a collection of essays, and deserve independent publication.[4]

The essays in the present collection have been divided into three sections: studies, comparative and dialogical efforts, and reviews. Within each section, however, the order is chronological. An appendix contains three unpublished manuscripts from De Smet's early years. The present introduction will not attempt to give an account of all these items, but will focus simply on a single issue: De Smet's interpretation of Śaṅkara's alleged acosmism. Interestingly, we will see that De Smet's rejection of the *māyāvāda* interpretation of Śaṅkara is to be found not in his doctoral dissertation, but only in essays dating from 1964.

1. Early Position

Three facts from De Smet's early years are significant for his lifelong interest in Śaṅkara: his chancing upon a French article on Advaita while still a 16 year-old schoolboy in Belgium;[5] the light shed upon this article by a much-loved Jesuit teacher in school;[6] and an immersion into Indian thought already during his

Jesuit novitiate, especially through the writings of Pierre Johanns, one of the great lights of the so-called 'Calcutta School' of indology.[7]

The fact that De Smet entered the Belgian province of the Jesuits was another important factor in his vocation as indologist. The Calcutta mission was the responsibility of the Belgian province, and it was to this mission that De Smet was assigned after the completion of his philosophical studies. Calcutta was the place of Brahmabandhab Upadhyay, whose seemingly failed endeavours at a rapprochement between Hinduism and Christianity had borne fruit in an unexpected manner in the work of William Wallace, SJ (1863-1922).[8] Under Upadhyay's influence, Wallace became convinced that Christianity had to be Indianized if it had to gain a successful hearing in Bengal. It was Wallace who persuaded the Belgian province to dedicate gifted men to the study of Indian texts. Johanns and Dandoy[9] were fruits of this vision. These Jesuits "produced a durable synthesis of Catholicism and Hinduism.... The 'Bengal School,' which these came to be clubbed under, was the lasting contribution to India of Father William Wallace."[10]

De Smet thus arrived in Calcutta at a moment of significant activity and ferment. In 1922 Dandoy and Johanns had founded *The Light of the East*, a monthly directed to the Hindu intelligentsia as an instrument of interfaith reflection and dialogue. In 1919, Dandoy had published *An Essay in the Doctrine of the Unreality of the World in the Advaita.*[11] In 1932 he published *L'ontologie du Vedānta: Essai sur l'acosmisme de l'Advaita.*[12] Johanns' chief work was *To Christ through the Vedānta*, published first as a series of articles in *The Light of the East* (1922-34) and later in book form in French.[13] Other lights were R. Antoine and P. Fallon, Sanskritists and founders of the dialogue centre in Calcutta named Shanti Bhavan.[14]

De Smet recalls that the theology courses in St Mary's Kurseong, which he began probably in June 1946, were 'India-oriented,' and that there was even a seminar on the relationship of the world to the Absolute according to Śaṅkarācārya. His earliest statements on Śaṅkara are, in fact, two essays from this period: "Upadhyay's Interpretation of Śaṅkara" (Ascension Day, 1949) and "A Note on Śaṅkara's Doctrine of Creation" (13 June 1949).[15] His comments on Upadhyay indicate that he is already seeing similarities between Śaṅkara and the Christian teaching on creation:

> Instead of ridiculing *Māyā* as he had done before when Śaṅkara's statement of the unreality of the world seemed to his mind to be absolute and therefore to lead to a vague theopanism, he henceforward adopted it, identifying it, more faithfully to Śaṅkara's tenets, with the transcendental relation of the creature to the Creator, or the "*creatio passive sumpta*" of the Schoolmen.[16]

He is sharply critical instead of Fr Hegglin, who had taken Upadhyay to task, contending that "Śaṅkara's theory was in truth that absurd conception of the absolute unreality of all creatures".[17] Hegglin, says De Smet, "himself held a very unrefined conception of Creation" and was "a perfect rationalist, unable to grasp that our own mode of knowing can in no way be attributed to God. His conception of God was at bottom that of a Super-man, not of a transcendent God."[18] It is Śaṅkara rather than Hegglin who is much closer to the truth:

> It is however an undeniable fact for Śaṅkara as for us that we ourselves and the world are existing. What is the meaning of this existence? Being (*sattā*) is indeed the one characteristic feature of the world as well as of *Brahman* (*B.S.Bh.* 2, 1, 6), but they are irremediably distinct and different because existence in the creatures cannot receive the attributes of absolute substantiality and infinity as in *Brahman*. Created existence is only an image, a reflection of the absolute existence, and as such a dependent participation, not an existence by right.[19]

However, De Smet recognizes that to speak of participation is to 'neatly delineate' the 'what' of the mysterious relationship between the Absolute and the world, but not yet its 'how.' And Śaṅkara's way of suggesting it, which is different from the Christian one, is that of *māyā*:

> In the parts of his works which provide such hints, the notion of *Māyā*, which incidentally is hardly to be found in the Upaniṣads, is given prominence. The word itself conveys the idea of glamour, illusion, dazzle and by using it Śaṅkara wishes to stigmatize our congenital error of believing ourselves and the world to be self-sufficient beings while compared with the Infinite Being, the only adequate measuring rod of all beings, we are like nothing.

> Hence to say that the world is Māyā means that the world has no right to exist; it is not absolute but contingent being and entirely dependent on the Supreme.[20]

And again:

> Śaṅkara therefore does not say that our phenomenal world is a world of dreams but that compared with the absolute being of God it is in a relation of unreality analogous to the relation of unreality of the dreams when compared to the objects of the waking state.[21]

This extremely positive judgment of Śaṅkara is confirmed in conclusion:

> We have patiently followed up the direction pointed out to us by Upadhyay towards the great Vedantin and we have discovered a doctrine which, more than the teachings of the Greek philosophers, provides an intellectual body for the Christian Spirit.[22]

The essay on Śaṅkara's doctrine of creation largely confirms this interpretation and attitude. Śaṅkara's doctrine is neither monism nor theopanism but Advaita, non-dualism: he denies the existence of anything apart from *Brahman*.[23] *Vivartavāda* is Śaṅkara's way of rejecting *pariṇāmavāda* or change in *Brahman* as material cause of the world. About *māyā*, instead, De Smet is now more circumspect:

> The doctrine here hinted at of *Māyā* as a tentative explanatory theory of the 'how' of the creation has been explained elsewhere and moreover we do not wish to give it an importance and a prominence which are not to be found in Śaṅkara's writings; it is but a complementary theory and its value is one of suggestion rather than of assertion.[24]

The concluding estimation of Śaṅkara is once again very positive: "Simultaneously to exalt man up to asserting that he is a reflection of God, and to humiliate him down to stressing that he is only a reflecting participation and as nothing in himself, this is indeed Śaṅkara's imperishable greatness."[25]

By 1952 we find De Smet working on his doctoral thesis on the theological method of Śaṅkara. The chief merit of the dissertation is to have demonstrated that Śaṅkara was not a pure philosopher but rather a *śrutivādin*, and that the doctrine of indirect signification (*lakṣaṇā*),[26] already recognized by O.

Lacombe, plays a central role in Śaṅkara's theological method.[27] But despite the influence of Upadhyay that we have noted above, the dissertation does not really arrive at a clear rejection of the acosmist interpretation of Śaṅkara. This might be explained perhaps by the fact that neither the Calcutta School[28] nor Lacombe had themselves arrived at such a rejection.

Johanns, for example, notes that Śaṅkara's chief 'positive' doctrine is the absolute independence of God: God is self-existent and unrelated to the world, and there is no real *pariṇāma* or evolution of *Brahman*, but only a *vivarta*, the illusion of an evolution. The *Śruti* teaching that God is not only efficient but also material cause implied that there was a real self-evolution of God, and this Śaṅkara could not accept: for if God has passed over completely into the world, then he no longer subsists in himself; and if he has passed over partially into the world, then there is a split in the divine nature, and God loses his simplicity. "This Śaṃkara refused to admit to be possible. He consequently denied the reality and even the possibility of the world."[29] Johanns quotes here his colleague Dandoy: "And it is the glory of the Advaita that alone among the Vedānta systems, it has maintained, even at the cost of the reality of the world, the true notion that the Self-Subsistent is absolutely unchangeable, without modes or accidents."[30] Johanns concludes: "Śaṃkara was so convinced of the truth of his positive doctrine that for its sake, he gave up the belief that men will give up last—the belief in the existence of the world of sense."[31]

If Johanns and Dandoy—regretfully perhaps—acknowledge that Śaṅkara was an acosmist, Lacombe is less clear. He seems to hesitate to call Śaṅkara an idealist, if by idealism is meant the primacy of thought over being, and also admits that Śaṅkara vigorously refuted the idealisms that preceded him.[32] But, like Johanns, he does talk, and repeatedly, about Śaṅkara's doctrine of *vivarta* or illusory transformation. He notes that Śaṅkara admits both the real transformation of the cause into the effect (*pariṇāmavāda*) and illusory transformation (*vivartavāda*), but that he does not put them on the same level. From the point of view of the effect, it is *satkāryavāda* or *pariṇāmavāda* that is valid; but from the point of view of the cause, it is *satkāraṇa*- or *vivartavāda* that is valid. But the former can be seen clearly only on the basis of the latter. One has to mount from the effect to the cause, from a lesser to a greater reality, in order to return to the effect and to be able to say to it: 'You do not exist as effect, you are nothing but your cause.'[33]

A similar ambiguity seems to mark De Smet's own position in his doctoral dissertation. He recognizes that Śaṅkara abides by the principle of *abādhitatva*: only what is never contradicted is real. He knows that, on the basis of this principle, Śaṅkara distinguishes three degrees of reality: the utter unreality (*atyantābhāva*) exemplified by the son of a barren mother; the utter Reality (*paramārtha sattā*) of that which is never contradicted; and in between all the objects of possible and actual secular (*laukika*) experience, which are either *prātibhāsiki sattā*, those things contradicted by waking experience, or *vyāvahāriki sattā*, the things of waking experience which are themselves contradicted from the standpoint of the *paramārtha sattā*. Thus he is aware that the objects of the second degree are false and yet not absolutely non-existent: they are objects of the *pramāṇas*, the correct means of truth, and are neither existent nor non-existent (*sad-asad-vilakṣaṇa*).[34] They cannot be called real in the strict sense. Still, it is as particular that particular objects are unreal. Supreme Knowledge destroys the individuality of things, the particular forms, by negating the limits they put upon Reality and reabsorbing them into the partless Being. "But, it cannot be said that the whole of our secular knowledge is thus destroyed; no, the *samānādhikaraṇa*, the substratum common to both the true and the erroneous ideations which constitute every ordinary judgment, remains after the discrimination has taken place and shines in the splendour of Being itself from which it is now known as non-different."[35] Thus even a pure illusion, such as a mirage, is never a mere imagination of the mind, but depends upon the reality of its substratum, the desert, on which the imagined water is superposed.[36] The mirage has, of course, no reality apart from the surface of the desert. There obtains a non-reciprocal relation between Cause and effects: the Cause is the *ātman* of its effects; the effects are nothing *apart from it*.[37] The Cause is *anya*; they are *ananya*. "*Ajñāna* consists in nothing else than the belief in the absolute reality of the effect **independently from** its cause."[38] And again: secular knowledge has a legitimacy of its own within the sphere of duality which it creates. This world receives its consistency from the immanent presence of its basis, *sat*, affirmed in every cognition and pervading all. Thus, on account of the omnipresence of this self-luminous substratum, the world is not a mere absurdity.[39]

Despite this rather nuanced treatment of the reality and unreality of the world, however, in his conclusion De Smet refers to Śaṅkara as an acosmist, though, in the light of his disquisition on the use of language, he finds this acosmism "less paradoxical and, even, more acceptable":

> On the contrary, the world and all worldly beings are validly said to be *sat*, *vastu*, etc., if these terms are used in their primary and ordinary sense (*vyavahārika*), but no longer when they are taken in their secondary and full sense (*paramārthika*). And the language of Śaṃkara being always of the latter kind when he speaks *paramārthataḥ* (from the supreme standpoint), the acosmism of his *advaitavāda* becomes less paradoxical and, even, more acceptable.[40]

In sharp contrast, on the question of pantheism De Smet betrays no ambiguity: Śaṅkara is, in his opinion—and here again he is following Johanns and Dandoy—no pantheist at all.[41]

The ambiguous attitude regarding Śaṅkara's acosmism continues to be reflected in De Smet's writings of the immediate post-doctoral period. Thus in "Towards Re-orienting Indian Philosophy" of 1956, he regards the *vivartavāda* of Śaṅkara's disciples as a distinct advance on the master's position, and even thinks that this theory will help work out a more adequate expression of the causality of *Brahman*:

> In the wake of his own effort, his disciples elaborated *vivartavāda* which is surely a more adequate, though still imperfect, theory of the total causality of the independent Absolute. It is, in my opinion, at the level of this formulation that our attempt to find an improved expression of it should take its departure.[42]

Again, in "Indian Contribution to General Metaphysics" of 1961, after summarizing Śaṅkara's position on the ontological status of worldly realities (the terms being, true, meaningful, valuable cannot be applied to anything but the permanent and uncaused pure Consciousness; w.r.t. the absolute Being everything else, insofar as it is independently affirmed, is a mere *upādhi*), he concludes:

This is the view of Śaṅkara which is at least preferable to the pure pantheism of Rāmānuja.[43]

Later in the same paper, speaking of *tādātmya* De Smet says:

But when we come to the Upaniṣads, we find many expressions and assertions which incline heavily towards an affirmation of pure identity, together of course with others which emphasize distinction between Brahma and his effects. We further notice that reflection has now shifted from eschatology to downright ontology.

Hence, it is not surprising that the first great systematic advaitin, Śaṅkara, choses [sic] the term '*tādātmya*' to express the intimate invariable relationship of changing beings with the unchanging Brahma. This term can sometimes be translated as 'identity', but etymologically it means 'having that as one's own *ātmā*'. Hence, it possesses a certain ambiguity which allows it to become one of the chief technical terms of a system which itself is not without ambiguity, *since it seems to oscillate between sheer acosmism and a theory of ontological participation with a strong bent towards apophatism.* Śaṅkara affirms with all due emphasis that 'the effect has its *ātmā* in the cause, but not the cause in its effect' (*Ved. Sūt. Bh.*, 2, 1, 9) and thus *tādātmya* is not a reciprocal relationship such as pure identity would be.[44]

And yet he is able to say: "the relationship of *tādātmya* between every being and *Brahman* is its relationship of total ontological dependence upon Brahma."[45] A subsequent discussion indicates, in fact, that he is already on his way to negating his earlier remark about the preferability of *vivartavāda*. "The followers of Śaṅkara," De Smet tells us, "have tried to clarify more and more this *tādātmya*... mostly by elaborating technically the theory of *vivarta*." Śaṅkara himself tended to avoid the term *vivarta*, because it was connected with the *bhedābheda* theory that he emphatically rejected. Even when he uses the term '*vivartate*' in *B.S.Bh.* 1, 3, 39, he puts it in the mouth of his opponent. The term he accepts is *pariṇāma*, because it is found in Bādarāyaṇa's *Sūtra*, but at the same time he rejects *pariṇāmavāda*, because *Brahman* is absolutely without change. Still, he uses many examples and comparisons "in order to make it clear that the mode of causality which is suitable to Brahma does in no way detract from his complete transcendence, simplicity, unchangeability and freedom, and neither implies, as does *pariṇāmavāda*, any univocal community of being between changing beings as such and their total Cause."[46]

"It is this intention of Śaṅkara which his disciples have correctly perceived and tried to translate through unambiguous terms."[47] Sureśvara still works with comparisons, engages in a polemic with Sāṁkhya *pariṇāmavāda*, and never uses the term *vivarta* in connection with Advaita. Padmapāda is the first Advaitin who relates *vivarta* to his own system. "Padmapāda distinguishes *vivarta* from *pariṇāma* and *vikāra*, but under the influence of Śabdādvaita gives it the meaning of an external manifestation which, though objective, is yet somehow illusory; he thus unwillingly [unwittingly?] paves the way for the future *māyāvādins*."[48] Prakāśātman, commenting on Padmapāda, defines *vivarta* in opposition to *pariṇāma*, and insists on the fact that the self-manifesting Cause remains absolutely unchanged by the *vivarta* process of self-manifestation. Vimuktātman avoids giving a definition of *vivarta*, and fully introduces the term *māyā* into Advaita, and so assimilates Advaita to its chief enemy, the pure *māyāvāda* of the Buddhists. He also makes fashionable the term *anirvacanīya*, which becomes an excuse to avoid delving deeply into the mystery of finite existence. "Yet, besides refuting *Dvaita*, he strongly rejects the pure identity of *Brahman* and world as implied in the Śabdādvaita theory of *Bhedābheda*."[49] Vācaspatimiśra does not contribute anything new. Sarvajñātman sees that no theory can measure up to the reality of the mystery. *Pariṇāmavāda* is a first approach; it is cancelled by *vivartavāda*, which is itself cancelled by a perfect intuition that completely sublimates causality as a conception. As for Prakāśānanda, he practically returns to the Buddhist position which Śaṅkara had so strenuously opposed:

> Prakāśānanda hardens this interesting view and his monism (rather than non-dualism) seems to Dasgupta "surprisingly similar to the idealism of Vāsubandhu." Indeed, his *dṛṣṭi-sṛṣṭi*, which is quite alien to Śaṅkara's Advaita, eliminates all forms of ontological causality, and he expressly states that *vivartavāda* is a mere pedagogical device.[50]

2. Rejection of the *Māyāvāda* Interpretation

By 1964—interestingly, in a joint publication with other members of the Calcutta School—De Smet arrives at a clear rejection of the 'current interpretation' of Śaṅkara as acosmist.[51] Helpfully, he summarizes this current interpretation as follows:

(1) *Satyam Brahma, jagad mithyā*:[52] the world is *māyā*, a purely illusory manifestation of *Brahman*, caused by *Avidyā*; Advaita means strict monism and implies acosmism; the statements of identity are to be taken literally. (2) The causal self-modification of *Brahman* into the world is illusory (*vivarta*). (3) The *jīvātman* is really identical with *Brahman*; in the state of *avidyā*, it identifies itself as a finite principle of consciousness, activity and passivity; senses and body are mere *upādhis* or superimpositions due to Nescience.[53] He follows this up with a remark about Śaṅkara's radically valuational perspective (in the course of which, for the first time, he makes use of capital letters, something which he will eventually popularize):

> In order to overcome the distorting simplicity of this interpretation, we should try to place ourselves within the special perspective of Śaṅkara himself. His was a teaching of wisdom, trying to ascertain values, and his language was meant to serve his purpose of evaluating realities. Hence, his key-distinction between what is primary and what is secondary. The primary is usually expressed in positive terms: for instance, *sat* means the unchanging real or the REAL, i.e., *Brahman*, whereas *asat*, when said of the world, means the changing real or un-REAL.[54]

De Smet's point is that Śaṅkara did not regard it as his task to talk about the ontological status of the world. The rest of the article does not really make an argument challenging the current interpretation, but is content to substantiate the valuational perspective.[55] The rejection of pantheism in the conclusion is not new, except for the explicit reference to Johanns: "Fr P. Johanns used to say that pantheism was not only foreign to the doctrine of Śaṅkara but had been clearly refuted by him. But his language kept to such heights that the lower genius of many a pseudo-disciple and, more commonly, of the neo-Vedāntins of to-day could not keep pace with him and they have turned his transcendentalism into an unpalatable brand of pantheism."[56]

"*Māyā* or *Ajñāna*?" (1966) is an important step in De Smet's interpretation of Śaṅkara.[57] Even in his own estimation he regards his highlighting of the low frequency of *māyā* in Śaṅkara's works as one of the three steps in his definite rejection of the *māyāvāda* interpretation of Śaṅkara, the other two being his demonstration that Śaṅkara was a *śrutivādin* who had recourse to the indicative power of words, and his reliance solely on the genuinely authentic works of Śaṅkara.[58] The points made in the 1966 article may be summarized as follows: Śaṅkara favoured *ajñāna* or *avidyā* over *māyā*; in the *B.S.Bh.*, for example, the ratio of *ajñāna/avidyā* to *māyā* is 10:2. Further, *ajñāna* is used as a precise technical term of the system, being clearly defined as *adhyāsa*, superimposition, while *māyā* is still an ordinary term with various meanings, none of which has yet been privileged: (1) deception; (2) magic; (3) marvellous power of the Lord.[59] Śaṅkara never attributed any causal character to *māyā* in the sense of magic. Given that his authoritative texts were influenced by Sāṁkhya and spoke of cosmic causality in terms of self-modification (*pariṇāma*), Śaṅkara felt obliged to retain the term while modifying its meaning. Thus the point of the comparisons using *māyā* in the sense of magic was to help understand how *Brahman* remains unchanged and unaffected by his creation. Śaṅkara was aware that the comparisons had been used by some Buddhists in order to deny any reality of the mundane beings, but he explicitly rejected their teaching, asserting that those things of which we are aware in our waking state are never negated in any state. (*B.S.Bh.* 2, 2, 29).[60] The article ends by explaining the process by which *māya* and *vivarta* were introduced into the Śaṅkara school;[61] this is largely a reproduction of the discussion of 1961, but De Smet no longer sees the disciples as having "correctly perceived" the intention of the master and as having made attempts to translate it "through unambiguous terms."[62] What he does say instead is that, while Śaṅkara favoured the terms *ajñāna* or *avidyā*, "his later disciples diffused his teaching as an authentic form of *māyāvāda* and it is as such that it met with strong opposition from diverse quarters."[63]

De Smet's 'Guidelines in Indian Philosophy' bear the date 1968 but contain an interesting development, which might be explained by the fact that these notes for students were composed over a period of time up to 1975.[64] In ch.10 on the Mīmāṃsā Darśana, De Smet classifies Śaṅkara among the idealists, together with Śūnyavāda, Vijñānavāda and the Śaṅkarian school.[65] In ch. 11 on the Vaiśeṣika Darśana he registers a dissatisfaction with Śaṅkara's notion of *tādātmya*. Both Bhaṭṭa and Śaṅkara, De Smet notes, rejected the Vaiśeṣika *padārtha* called *samavāya* (a necessary relation of inherence) on the grounds that it is an entity between entities and would thus lead to infinite regress.

> But the *tādātmya* or *bhedābheda* by which they have replaced it lead to other insurmountable difficulties or at least cannot be a final answer. All this demonstrates how unfortunate it is that Indians did not discover the full authentic theory of relation, especially that it can be either logical or real (ontological) and that it must not therefore necessarily be ontological in order to give rise to a true judgment.[66]

By the time he comes to the philosophy of Śaṅkara in ch. 15, however, he has arrived at an interpretation that is not different from the one found in the 1964 article in *Religious Hinduism.* His summary of Gauḍapāda's teaching is already indicative in the way it blames this earlier Vedāntin for the acosmistic interpretation of Śaṅkara:

> With regard to the universe, Gauḍapāda is an uncompromising acosmist and *śūnyavādin*; with regard to the appearance of this universe, he is a *māyāvādin* like the Vijñānavādins. As to the absolute *Vijñāna*, it is not a respository-consciousness [sic] (*ālaya-vijñāna*) but a substantial *Svayam-jyoti* as in the Upaniṣads. However, his theory ruthlessly simplifies the complexity of Upanishadic teachings to which Śaṅkara will do better justice. Because of him, the teaching of the latter has unfortunately often been interpreted in an acosmistic way.[67]

Ch. 15 of the 'Guidelines' is perhaps De Smet's most substantial treatment of Śaṅkara. It notes that Śaṅkara's authentic teaching is not easy to uncover because (1) most of his authentic writings are *bhāṣyas* rather than systematic treatises; (2) his vocabulary, which he wants conformed to his texts, is inadequate to his true thought (e.g., he uses Sāṁkhya *pariṇāma* while rejecting *pariṇāmavāda*); (3) his followers modified his teaching by simplifying it, introducing new emphases, and even re-Sāṁkhyanizing it; this influences the modern interpreters; (4) many unauthentic *bhāṣyas* have been attributed to him, most especially the *Māṇḍ. Up. Bh.* which expands the doctrine of Gauḍapāda.[68] As for De Smet, he takes the following as genuine: the *B.S.Bh.*; the *Bhāṣyas* on the 9 Upaniṣads (*Bṛh. Ār. Up.*, *Chānd. Up.*, *Taitt. Up.*, *Ait. Up.*, *Muṇḍ. Up.*, *Praśna Up.*, *Kaṭha Up.*, *Kena Up.*, *Īśa Up.*); the *Bh. Gītā Bh.*; and the *US*. He notes, however, that the authenticity of the *US* in whole or part is doubted by some scholars.[69]

De Smet goes on to present Śaṅkara's Brahmavāda in three ways: the way of causality, the way of transcendental analysis (or *ātmā-jñāna*), and the way of the exegesis of the *mahāvākyas* through the *lakṣaṇā*-method. It is worth going into the way of causality at some length, because of its clear rejection of the *māyāvāda* interpretation of Śaṅkara. This way deals with Śaṅkara's modification of the Sāṁkhya *satkāryavāda*; his retention of the *pariṇāma* language of *Śruti* while rejecting *pariṇāmavāda* by appealing to comparisons often borrowed dangerously from Mahāyāna; and his adoption of the term *tādātmya*. Where in ch. 11 De Smet was ambiguous about *tādātmya*, here he is clearly positive and appreciative. *Tādātmya* is the non-reciprocal relation between the supreme Cause and its effects. "We must obviously interpret this as meaning that *tādātmya* from effect to cause is a real and necessary relation, but from cause to effect it is only logical and contingent. The ground which founds this twofold relation-and-correlation is not in the cause but in the effect; it is the very existence of the effect as distinct from its cause."[70] The effects are characterized by a total ontological dependence on the Cause: without the Cause, they would not be. *Brahman*, on the other hand, is totally independent: it creates freely, not out of any need or want, with no help either of external materials or of instruments but by mere intention and totally out of itself, yet without internal modification or acquisition of any real external relation. It is immanent, since it is not only *nimitta*- but also *upādāna-kāraṇa*. But it is also transcendent: though causing, it remains unmodified and absolute.

> The effects are neither parts, nor modifications, nor modes, nor conditions, nor accidents of *Brahman*, nor relata implying a real relation of *Brahman* to themselves. This does not mean that they are not real or being in our primary sense of the term *sat* (with a small *s*) for they are not absolutely Non-being (*Asat* with a capital *A*) like the 'son of a barren woman' and other impossibilities. But in the supreme sense (*paramārthataḥ*) of the term, *Brahman* alone is *Sat* (with a capital *S*) and they are a-*Sat*. Thus, says Śaṅkara, they cannot be defined either as *Sat* or as *Asat* (*sad-asad-vilakṣaṇa*) though they are 'existent effects' (*sat-kārya*) (KAUBh 2, 3, 13).[71]

Once again De Smet makes use of capital letters to illustrate the relationship between *Brahman* and its effects, but now with explicit notice. It is worth quoting De Smet's summary *in extenso*:

> When treating of the transcendence of the causal *Brahman*, Śaṅkara often appeals to the following comparisons: magician and his magic; dreamer and his dreams; water and foam; mirage and illusory water; rope and illusory snake; cosmic space and jar-space; sun or moon and their reflections; etc. These comparisons, if taken literally as adequate parallels of the relation between *Brahman* and the universe, would imply that the world is illusory (acosmism) and that Śaṅkara deserves the accusation made against him by Madhva that he is "a hidden Buddhist" (*prachanna Bauddha*). There would be no real difference between him and Gauḍapāda.
>
> But Śaṅkara does not fail to make it clear that comparisons are valid only insofar as they illustrate the precise point under issue. The point of the above comparisons is to show that 'abaleity'[72] is the mark of all effected beings. They are totally dependent on their Cause; they cannot exist, endure or act apart from their Cause any more than illusions can appear independent of their ground and support. The comparisons further show that *Brahman*, despite its Causing, remains as unmodified as any ground of illusion.
>
> We must remember that Śaṅkara finds it besides his duty to provide the quite valid (within its limitations) cosmology or psychology available from *pratyakṣa* and *anumāna*. His role is exclusively to teach the metempirical, scriptural truth about beings. This is the truth of their ontological, total dependence upon the absolute and immutable *Sat*, which they are not (neither as parts, modes or states) though they appear to be, but without which they are not. They are *sat* in the common sense of the term but this assertion must be purified of its apparent self-sufficiency by saying that they are *a-Sat*. Then the paradox of a *sat* which is *a-Sat* must be lifted through the understanding that their being is a received being, dependent, caused, contingent, unfounded in itself but grounded on an Other which is yet their own *Ātman*, inner basis, support, ruler and lord.[73]

Without going into detail, we might note that the second section of the way of causality deals with various arguments for the existence of *Brahman* that De Smet finds in Śaṅkara's writings. As for the second and third ways, they consist of the analysis of various *mahāvākyas*—chiefly *Tattvamasi* and *Satyam Jñānam Anantam Brahma*—by means of *anvaya-vyatireka* or *jahadajahallakṣaṇā*, as already outlined in the doctoral dissertation. Thus the way of *ātmā-jñāna* or transcendental analysis reveals that the Inner *Ātman* is somehow immediate and evident in the notion of 'I,' but, due to an innate lack of discrimination, is taken for the body, inner sense, *jīvātman*, etc. It is thanks to *Śruti* that the pure Subject is unveiled in its true nature as the *Ātman* of the enjoyer and knower. But what is this enjoyer or knower or agent? The answer of *US* 18 is that it is the reflection of the *Ātman* in the ego-sense (*aham-kartṛ*). What is the ontological status of this reflection? It is a property neither of the face nor of the mirror. It is not a property of both. Neither is it an independent reality, since it depends entirely on a certain relation between face and mirror. Hence it is unreal. But if the three are discriminated—*Ātman*, reflection, reflector—it is possible to interpret *Tattvamasi* through *lakṣaṇā,* since the primary meaning of *tvam* will refer to the *ābhāsa* mistakenly taken for the Witness, whereas the secondary and supreme meaning will refer to the pure Witness free of all superimposition.[74]

3. Causality and Creation

It should have become evident by now that the way of causality represented in the 'Guidelines' is really a discussion of creation. This becomes more readily evident in a series of articles in the 1970s, chiefly "Śaṅkara and Aquinas on Creation" (1970) and "Origin: Creation and Emanation" (1978).[75]

The 1970 article is an interesting effort to interpret Aquinas by means of Śaṅkara and vice versa. We are told that both teachers regard God / *Brahman* as the omniscient, omnipotent Cause of the universe, and that for both, the relationship between the two is non-reciprocal. Aquinas reserves the term creation to designate divine causation of the world, but can define it only by borrowing terms from the realm of finite causality on the basis of analogy. Thus he proceeds in three steps: confused affirmation, which corresponds to *adhyāsa*; purification or negation (*apavāda*); and elevation (*paramārthāpatti*).[76] As for Śaṅkara, he regards *Brahman* as the one total Source of the universe. As such, it is both *upādāna-* and *nimitta kāraṇa*. As *upādāna-kāraṇa*, it contains all *nāma-rūpas* virtually, in the manner of future effects; the manifestation of these *nāma-rūpas* involves no modification or diversification in the partless *Ātman*. As *nimitta-kāraṇa*, *Brahman* creates by intelligent decision. This intelligent

Source is universally immanent in real existents, but the being of the latter is wholly relative. When creating, the *Ātman* needs no instruments, and is not impelled by needs and wants. The relation of effects to Cause is *tādātmya*, the "constant ontological dependence which implies the pervading causal presence of *Brahman* in all other beings."[77]

The 1978 article reworks the above discussion into a single treatment of creation. It contains an extensive treatment of the moment of purification (*apavāda*) in which De Smet affirms that there is no independent pre-existence of the created, no need of pre-existing matter, instruments or demiurge, nor of a temporal beginning of creation, etc. Most relevant for our purposes is the section 'As participated being, the creature is non-Being,' in which De Smet asks about the ontological weight and positivity of finite existents. "There are interpretations of Śaṅkara's Vedānta which view it as an acosmism and attribute only illusory being to all effects. What is the verdict of Śaṅkara himself?"[78] In answer he resorts once again to the use of capital and small letters. On the ordinary level, effects and their Cause are beings (*sat*). But *Brahman* transcends its effects so much that compared to them it is non-being (*a-sat*). This consideration is the root of apophatism. But *Brahman* is not absolute Non-being (*atyanta Asat*). It non-being (*a-sat*) only because it is absolute Being (*atyanta Sat*). Compared to it, creatures are non-Being (*a-Sat*), although they are not absolute Non-being (*Asat*). They are *Sad-Asad-vilakṣaṇa*, unable to be denoted either by *Sat* or *Asat* if these terms are taken in their supreme sense. Thus Śaṅkara "is a radical valuationist who measures everything to the absolute Value, the *Brahman*, and declares its unequality to it rather than the degree of its participation in it. This manner of speaking is legitimate but has led many into acosmistic interpretations of his doctrine."[79] Thomas, instead, prefers the language of participation. A participated being is in its own deficient way what the Absolute *Esse* is without restrictions. This *Esse* is not a logical genus but the ontological Reality of God. Its participations are not parts nor accidents, complements, or developments of it.[80]

Śaṅkara considers effects as *upādhis* of *Brahman*. But like any *upādhi* they need the constant support of this total cause which pervades them intimately without any loss of transcendence. This is why *upādhis* are comparable to magical illusions which do not affect the magician while depending entirely on their power; the appearance of their independent subsistence is due to the spectator's ignorance. "This comparison together with the concept of *upādhi* does away with pantheism and preserves nevertheless the central notion of the creatures' total dependence on their Creator."[81]

We might pause to note also that in "Śaṅkara Vedānta and Christian Theology" (1980) De Smet reveals that his use of capitals is borrowed from Pessein whose *Vedānta Vindicated* had drawn the approval of eminent scholars like Radhakrishnan and S. Vedanta Aiyengar.[82] Thus *Avidyā* may consist in (1) considering the world as *a-sat* (like a mirage); this is the position of the Buddhists, and is refuted by Śaṅkara; (2) considering the world as *Sat*, existing in its own right, independent and underived; this is the position of Sāṁkhya and Vaiśeṣika, and is equally rejected by Śaṅkara; (3) identifying the world with the soul alleged to be all-pervading, or with *Brahman*; this is the error of pantheism; (4) failing to see *Brahman* as the *Ātman* / Ground of every derived reality, and seeing it only as Absolute, excluding even the possibility of derived existence: this is the error of acosmism. "Some interpreters have fallen into the one or the other error. This is due to their failing to clarify the language of Śaṅkara as done by Pessein."[83]

4. The Mature Interpretation of the Final Years

4.1 Three levels of language

"Spiritual Values of Advaita Vedānta and Social life" (1986) is one of De Smet's best explanations of how Śaṅkara is neither pantheist nor acosmist. De Smet points out that there is, in Śaṅkara's writings, an intercrossing of three manners of language rather than three degrees of reality: (1) *vyavahāra* language, (2) Vedānta or upaniṣadic language, and (3) the language of the exegete, the *śrutivādin*.[84] In *vyavahāra* language the conscious ego (*aham*, *tvam*) is the integrator which unifies our mental and corporeal reality. In Vedānta language, it is unreciprocally identified with That (*tat*), the innermost *Ātman*. In the *śrutivādin's* language, it is shown to designate directly the conscious ego, but as image of That, and thus indirectly to indicate That as its own supreme *Ātman*.[85]

De Smet explains further that the term *tādātmya* "is not an accessory and extrinsic relationship but one that is ontologically constitutive of those beings. Hence, if it is omitted from our conception of them, the latter is inadequate and thus, if I may say so, metaphysically false though it may be physically correct far as it goes."[86] "These authentic explanations together with the whole theory of *upādhi* stand in direct opposition to any pantheistic interpretation Śaṅkara's *advaitavāda*. He always upholds the *Brahman's* perfect transcendence and he does this with particular sharpness when he explains that the allegedly real relations of *Brahman* to the cosmos are only *upādhis* (just as St Thomas Aquinas declares that they are only logical relationships)."[87]

In "Forward Steps in Śaṅkara Research" (1987), after repeating the above explanation about the three levels of language, and after adding a note on the ambivalence of upaniṣadic pairs of terms (such as *Sat* / *a-Sat*; *Vidyā* / *a-Vidyā*) which can be understood either as plain contraries (*Sat* / *Asat*) or else as contradictories (*Sat* / *a-Sat*), De Smet concludes: once we realize that the threefold distinction is not ontological but linguistic and conceptual, we become free of the difficulties that have plagued Śaṅkara interpretation in medieval and modern times.[88]

4.2 *Radhakrishnan's interpretation of Śaṅkara*

De Smet's 1989 articles on Radhakrishnan are not only models of generosity and charity but also masterly expositions of his own interpretation of Śaṅkara. In the first article, he begins by pointing out that one of the reasons for Radhakrishnan's acosmist interpretation of Śaṅkara is his acceptance of the authenticity of the *Māṇḍ. Up. Bh.* whose author seems to have deliberately Vedanticized an acosmism of Buddhist origin. But H. Jacobi has said that the author of the *Māṇḍ. Up. Bh.* cannot be the same as that of the *B.S.Bh.*, V. Bhattacharya has argued against its traditional attribution to Śaṅkara, and after Radhakrishnan's composition of his *Indian Philosophy*, Belvalkar, Lacombe, Renou rejected its genuineness. Mayeda, on the other hand, accepted its authenticity, having examined it in the light of the linguistic criteria determined by Hacker; but De Smet remains doubtful.[89]

Radhakrishnan fails to note that Śaṅkara had sedulously avoided *māyāvāda* because it was the label of Buddhist schools; he rejected Buddhism in all its forms.[90] Again, Radhakrishnan recalls Śaṅkara's teaching regarding *avidyā*, but fails to see that, before their truth can be intuited, the correct meaning of the *mahāvākyas* has to be discovered through an exegesis which leads beyond the primary meaning of their terms to their supreme meaning. Further, he does not see fully that none of the five types of *mahāvākyas* can be cancelled: negative, superlative, cosmos-relational, ego-relational, and essential.[91]

In his second presentation of Śaṅkara's teaching, Radhakrishnan does base his exposition on the *mahāvākyas*. However, he does not pay sufficient attention to the definition of *Vidyā* as the opposite of all forms of superimposition, and to the exegetical principle that all *mahāvākyas*, including the *yataḥ* type, are infallible only as to their purified and elevated meaning. So he continues to misunderstand divine causality and Śaṅkara's teaching regarding the double form of *Brahman*, *nirguṇa* and *saguṇa*.[92]

Again, Radhakrishnan does admit that the world is not absolutely unreal, that it is not *Asat* or nothing, and that it has empirical existence, which is quite different from the eternal being of *Brahman*. De Smet points out, however, that Śaṅkara, relying on the Indian theory of primary and secondary meanings of terms according to their contexts, is far more precise: *Brahman* is *paramārthataḥ Sat*, real in the supreme sense of the term; the son of a barren woman is *paramārthataḥ Asat*, unreal in the supreme sense; the world is *Sad-Asad-vilakṣaṇa*, it cannot be characterized as Real or Unreal in the supreme sense.[93]

Yet again, since the world is neither real nor unreal, Radhakrishnan says it is *anirvacanīya*, and that causation applies only to the realm of phenomena. De Smet observes that the restriction of causation to the realm of phenomena goes back to the Buddhist Dharmakīrti (c. 600-660); Śaṅkara does not appropriate it anywhere. Further, does Śaṅkara say the world is *anirvacanīya*? Bhartṛhari and Maṇḍanamiśra use the phrase *sadasadbhyām anirvacanīya*. Śaṅkara uses only *tattvānyatvābhyām anirvacanīya*, that which cannot be described as 'that' or 'other than that,' and this only of the world as objective potentiality in *Brahman*. Śaṅkara would never call the world indefinable, since he has defined it positively as totally effect and negatively as *Sad-Asad-vilakṣaṇa*.[94]

But is the world of the nature of *mithyā*? The world as known by the ignorant, yes. But as known in *Vidyā*, it is not false but true in the manner of an effect totally dependent on *Sat*. Ordinary *vyavahāra* thinking lacks this metaphysical perspective and implies *dvaita*; it has to be sublated by Advaita speech and thinking. This does not mean the world is phenomenal; Buddhist *māyāvāda* is completely rejected by Śaṅkara; rather, the ontological status of the world is a dependent one. It is *a-Sat*, but still *sat* and not *Asat*.[95]

4.3 The conception of vākya *as controlling the interpretation of* Śruti

A new element is De Smet's insight that the variations in the Vedāntic interpretations of the *Śruti* are a function of different conceptions of *vākya* (sentence / proposition) and understanding. This development seems to be first recorded in 1994, in "The Presuppositions of Jaimini and the Vedāntins" and "Śaṅkara on Meaning and Truth."[96] It is the subject of a lecture of the same year, entitled "The Vedāntins' Diverse Conceptions of *Vākya* (Sentence) as Responsible for the Diversity of their Interpretations of the Same Scriptures," which I have been unable to trace, but which is probably well represented anyway in the Jaimini piece. It brings De Smet's central insights to bear on Śaṅkara's texts in a way that is old and yet refreshingly new.[97]

The "Jaimini" article, then, proposes that diverse—and extra-textual—conceptions of *vākya* are responsible for the diversity of interpretations of *Śruti* such as those of Śaṅkara, Rāmānuja, Madhva and Vallabha.[98] Most especially, it is the understanding of understanding or intellection that is the determining factor. Thus it is Śaṅkara's rejection of the naive realist mirror theory of understanding that governs his understanding of the *mahāvākyas*.[99]

The normal understanding is that speech mirrors reality, and that there is one-to-one correspondence between a word and its objective ground. Sentences are complex expressions indicative of a plurality of objective grounds. But *Brahman* is ontologically free of such plurality; how then can it ever be signified by any sentence? Śaṅkara's reply is that the intellect is not a mirror but a synthesizer. "The intellect considers as a unitary whole [the plurality of words or other data it receives]" (*samasta-pratyavamarśinī-buddhiḥ*) (*B.S.Bh.* 1, 3, 28).[100] This is the heart of Śaṅkara's conception of intellection. The intellect does not consider a sentence as a duplicate of reality but as a sequence of signs. Whether these are descriptive or otherwise expressive, merely indicative or allusive, it unifies all their syntactical significations so that they converge into a unitary understanding. Interpreting and any act of understanding is an active process which results in the single flash of knowledge finally attained.[101]

These insights may be found incorporated into "Śaṅkara's Non-Dualism (*Advaitavāda*) (1997)," which is a thorough reworking of the 1964/68 version of the *Religious Hinduism* article.[102] We might recall that the 1964 version was De Smet's first statement of his rejection of the *māyāvāda* interpretation of Śaṅkara; fittingly, the 1997 version is his last substantial statement of his interpretation of Śaṅkara.

5. Conclusion

Our brief investigation has uncovered a certain development in De Smet's interpretation of Śaṅkara, which we might summarize as follows.

In the early essays of 1949, we find De Smet, under the influence of Upadhyay, assimilating Śaṅkara's teaching to the Christian doctrine of creation (properly understood), and regarding *māyā* and *vivartavāda* as Śaṅkara's ways of holding on to the unchangeability of *Brahman* as well as to the participated and entirely dependent existence of the world. Śaṅkara is, for him, neither monist nor 'theopanist' (a variation of 'pantheist'). In his doctoral dissertation De Smet continues to reject a pantheist interpretation of Śaṅkara, but, despite several positive indications, holds on to the standard reading of Śaṅkara as an acosmist—most probably under the influence of Johanns and Dandoy. The strength of the dissertation lies in its unambiguous affirmation of the *śrutivāda* nature of Śaṅkara's method, and the outlining of the nature of this method, together with its constitutive antinomies which, however, De Smet finds Śaṅkara himself addressing in more than one manner—see the way of transcendental deduction, transcendental analysis, and the exegesis of the *mahāvākyas* by means of *anvaya-vyatireka* or *jahadajahallakṣaṇā*.

In the works of the immediately succeeding period, we find De Smet continuing to regard Śaṅkara as acosmist. It is only in 1964 that we have a first indication of a decisive rejection of the 'current' *māyāvāda* interpretation of Śaṅkara. This is confirmed by the 1966 article proposing that *māyā* is not a technical term in the *B.S.Bh.*, and that it was introduced in a systematic manner only by certain members of the post-Śaṅkara school. The 'Guidelines in Indian Philosophy' reflect a certain ambiguity, but by the time De Smet arrives at the chapter on Śaṅkara, he is clearly affirming his new interpretation of Śaṅkara as non-dualist rather than monist, and as upholding the entirely relative reality of the world in complete ontological dependence on the supreme *Brahman-Ātman*. The long discussion of the causality of *Brahman* contained in these notes is expanded and further enriched by a pair of articles on creation in the following years that draw from both Śaṅkara and Thomas Aquinas, finding—as in his early articles of 1949—a surprising degree of similarity in the thinking of these great teachers on what is no doubt one of the most difficult points in the history of human reflection.

The articles of the 1980s and 1990s consolidate De Smet's interpretation of Śaṅkara. Special mention might be made of his popularization of Pessein's use of capitals to explain the paradoxes of upaniṣadic language. It is interesting that despite his reported appreciation of Pessein's attempt, Radhakrishnan himself was not able to put aside an acosmist reading of Śaṅkara, as De Smet shows at length. In my own reading, I was surprised to note that Radhakrishnan is clearly familiar with Śaṅkara's distinction between distinction between the absolute unreality of the son of a barren woman, the *prātibhāsika* reality of a mirage, and the *vyāvahārika* reality of the world of empirical things, and that he also takes issue with the translation of *māyā* as illusion. Despite all this, however, he is not able to cut himself off completely from the language of *vivarta* and illusion.[103] My impression is that, after almost a half century of De Smet's rejection of the *māyāvāda* reading of Śaṅkara, Radhakrishnan's position remains representative of the majority of Śaṅkara scholars.

On a more general note, we must record a certain change of tone in De Smet's approach to Śaṅkara, from the earlier rather ready criticisms (as fideist, for example,[104] or as unable to make place for the truly supernatural[105]) to greater and greater appreciation, as is implied by the development we have been tracing, and as should hopefully become evident to anyone reading the essays in the present collection.

Again, there is the question of originality. Clearly some of De Smet's key insights—his rejection of the pantheistic reading of Śaṅkara; Śaṅkara's use of the method of indirect indication; the relative infrequency of Śaṅkara's use of *māyā*; the use of capitals to designate the differences between three levels of language; the personhood of the *para Brahman*—have been borrowed from people like Lacombe, Hacker and Pessein. Despite this, what De Smet said of Thomas Aquinas is probably applicable in some way to his own work: he synthesized what he borrowed into an interpretation of Śaṅkara that is, in the end, quite different from the ones he found in his sources. But more work would have to be done to substantiate this remark.

In the area of interreligious dialogue, I venture to say that we still have to go a long way before either side of the dialogue begins to take seriously De Smet's proposal that, while Śaṅkara is no monist *māyāvādin*, Christianity is itself non-dualist.[106]

My hope is that the present collection might serve to bring De Smet's interpretation of Śaṅkara once more into the public sphere, and to set in motion a new retrieval of the authentic doctrine of one of India's greatest masters. It is all too easy to dismiss De Smet's efforts as eisegesis, as a wrong-headed reading of Aquinas into Śaṅkara, but we must keep in mind that there is really no presuppositionless viewpoint, as people like Heidegger and Gadamer have brought so forcefully to our notice.[107] One reads from where one is, and the work of the scholarly community consists not in facile and global dismissals but in painstaking and punctual engagement with differing views and, eventually, viewpoints. Such engagement will surely have to take into account multiple points in De Smet's reading of Śaṅkara: that he (Śaṅkara) is a *śrutivādin* rather than a pure philosopher; that therefore his focus is on the *mahāvākyas* of the Upaniṣads; that he uncovers the supreme meanings of these great sayings by using a method that was already well-established in his time, the method of *anvaya-vyatireka* or indirect indication; that he favours the epistemological terms *ajñāna* / *avidyā* rather than the ontological term *māyā*, and that the latter can hardly be said to be a technical term of his system; that he knows very well that whatever the status of the world of our experience, it is not the *atyanta Asat* or nothingness of the son of a barren woman; that he understands the *tādātmya* relation between *Brahman* and the world as non-reciprocal, and that this is a vital element in the proper understanding of the *upādhi* nature of the world; that he is a radical valuationist whose sole aim is to help the aspirant attain the supreme realization, rather than a philosopher desirous of proposing a comprehensive view that might include a cosmology, an anthropology, an ethics. In addition, there is the thorny question of the genuine works of Śaṅkara, for much depends on whether or not an interpreter decides to accept a work like the *Māṇḍ. Up. Bh.* as authentic. Here, in my opinion, there opens up a space for the proposal of the philosopher-theologian-economist Bernard Lonergan, whose generalized method or hermeneutics is an interesting way of handling the implications of the fact that our most persistent and radical disagreements and conflicts lie in the realm of our radical and fundamental options.[108]

Notes

[1] See J. Vattanky, "Fr. Richard De Smet, S.J.: Friend, Scholar, Man of Dialogue," *Vidyajyoti: Journal of Theological Reflection* 71/4 (2007) 251, 254, and Bradley J. Malkovsky, "Introduction: The Life and Work of Richard V. De Smet, S.J.," *New Perspectives on Advaita Vedānta: Essays in Commemoration of Professor Richard De Smet, S.J.*, ed. Bradley J. Malkovsky (Leiden / Boston / Köln: Brill, 2000) 13.

[2] *Brahman and Person: Essays by Richard De Smet*, ed. Ivo Coelho (Delhi: Motilal Banarsidass, 2010).

[3] Richard V. De Smet, 'The Theological Method of Śaṃkara' (Rome: Pontifical Gregorian University, 1953), unpublished. Richard V. De Smet, 'Guidelines in Indian Philosophy' (Pune: De Nobili College, 1968-1975), cyclostyled notes for students. The 'Guidelines' are being serially published in *Divyadaan: Journal of Philosophy and Education* (see the Introduction and chs. 1, 2 and 3.1 in **20** [2009] 259-282, 467-472 and **21** [2010] 257-289 respectively) and will hopefully also be published separately. But other items do contain important and relevant matter: see, e.g., 'Indian Contribution to General Metaphysics' (1961), typescript, Collected Papers B, 342-360 = DNC 73/DES/COL 342-360, published as "Indiens Beitrag zur allgemeine Metaphysik," *Kairos* (Salzburg) **3/4** (1961) 161-182; "Patterns and Theories of Causality," *Essays in Philosophy presented to Dr. T. M. P. Mahadevan on his 50th Birthday* (Madras: Ganesh, 1962) 347-367; and "Some Governing Principles of Indian Philosophy," *The Philosophical Quarterly* (Amalner, India) **35**/4 (1963) 249-258 and *Philosophy Today* **9**/3-4 (1965) 192-199.

[4] In one of his last letters, De Smet had given permission for the publication of an updated and edited version of his thesis to George McLean, who worked with Malkovsky towards this end. The publication (indicated in Malkovsky 8, note 11) is still awaited. As for the 'Guidelines,' see note 3 above.

[5] R. De Smet, 'The Trajectory of My Dialogical Activity' (autobiographic text for Bradley J. Malkovsky, Rome, 23 April 1991, unpublished) 1. Also "Forward Steps in Śaṅkara Research" 173 below.

[6] De Smet, 'The Trajectory of My Dialogical Activity' 1.

[7] De Smet, 'The Trajectory of My Dialogical Activity' 1. For biographical details regarding Johanns (1882-1955), see Sean Doyle, *Synthesizing the Veda: The Theology of Pierre Johanns, S.J.* (Oxford: Peter Lang, 2006).

[8] Doyle 123-126.

[9] Georges Dandoy (1882-1962). See Doyle 126ff.

[10] Udayan Namboodiry, *St Xavier's: The Making of a Calcutta Institution* (New Delhi: Viking/Penguin Books India, 1995) 116.

[11] Calcutta: Catholic Orphan Press, 1919.

[12] Paris, 1932.

[13] *Vers le Christ par le Vedānta*, 2 vols. (Louvain: Museum Lessianum, section philosophique, 1932-33). The original essays from *The Light of the East* were published in book form, with the encouragement of De Smet, as *To Christ through the Vedānta: The Writings of Reverend P. Johanns, S.J.*, 2 vols., ed. Theo de Greeff (Bangalore: The United Theological College, 1996).

[14] De Smet, 'The Trajectory of My Dialogical Activity' 4.

[15] R. De Smet, "Upadhyay's Interpretation of Śaṅkara" = Appendix 1 below; and "A Note about Śaṅkara's Doctrine of Creation" = Appendix 2 below.

[16] De Smet, "Upadhyay's Interpretation of Śaṅkara" 455 below.

[17] De Smet, "Upadhyay's Interpretation of Śaṅkara" 455 below.

[18] De Smet, "Upadhyay's Interpretation of Śaṅkara" 455, 456 below.

[19] De Smet, "Upadhyay's Interpretation of Śaṅkara" 456 below.

[20] De Smet, "Upadhyay's Interpretation of Śaṅkara" 457-458 below.

[21] De Smet, "Upadhyay's Interpretation of Śaṅkara" 459 below.

[22] De Smet, "Upadhyay's Interpretation of Śaṅkara" 461 below.
[23] De Smet, "A Note about Śaṅkara's Doctrine of Creation" 463, 471, 482 below.
[24] De Smet, "A Note about Śaṅkara's Doctrine of Creation" 480 below.
[25] De Smet, "A Note about Śaṅkara's Doctrine of Creation" 483 below.
[26] De Smet, 'The Theological Method of Śaṃkara' 290. It was this chapter that De Smet chose for the obligatory publication of an 'extract': see "Langage et connaissance de l'Absolu chez Çaṃkara" = ET ch. 1 below. In "Śāṅkara Vedānta and Christian Theology" 393 below, De Smet claims this as his contribution to the Advaitin-Christian dialogue, while also admitting that it was Lacombe who first assimilated Śaṅkara's use of *lakṣaṇā* to the medieval doctrine of analogy (ibid. 385).
[27] De Smet, 'The Theological Method of Śaṃkara' 292. See also "Śāṃkara Vedānta and Christian Theology" 385 below. I recall De Smet saying that this discovery was at first resisted, and then quietly accepted, by important Indologists and passionate Vedāntins such as the renowned T.M.P. Mahadevan; but this claim would need to be properly researched.
[28] In his preface to his dissertation (iv), De Smet acknowledges his debt to the 'Calcutta School of Catholic Indologists,' making mention of W. Wallace, P. Johanns, G. Dandoy, M. Ledrus, J. Bayart, C. Bulcke, P. Fallon and R. Antoine. His bibliography includes the works of many of these.
[29] Johanns, *To Christ through the Vedānta* 1:9.
[30] Dandoy, *An Essay on the Doctrine of the Unreality of the World in the Advaita* (Calcutta: Catholic Orphan Press, 1919) 56, cited in Johanns 1:9. Dandoy's *L'ontologie du Vedānta: Essai sur l'acosmisme de l'Advaita* (1932) seems to be a translation, by Jacques Maritain, of *The Doctrine of Unreality....* Both Maritain and Olivier Lacombe contributed commentaries at the end of the work.
[31] Johanns, *To Christ through the Vedānta* 1:9.
[32] O. Lacombe, *L'Absolu selon le Vedānta: Les notions de Brahman et d'Ātman dans les systèmes de Çankara et de Rāmānoudja* (Paris: Geuthner, 1937) 57 note 1.
[33] Lacombe 56-58.
[34] De Smet, 'The Theological Method of Śaṃkara' 38-43.
[35] De Smet, 'The Theological Method of Śaṃkara' 47-48.
[36] For the whole paragraph, see De Smet, 'The Theological Method of Śaṃkara' 44-48.
[37] "The total cause is, no doubt, radically independent from its effects, but the world of the effects is essentially dependent on its cause: 'The effect has its self in the cause, but not the cause in its effect'; the relation between the two is not reciprocal." *B.S.Bh.* 2, 1, 8; De Smet, 'The Theological Method of Śaṃkara' 56.
[38] De Smet, 'The Theological Method of Śaṃkara' 55.
[39] De Smet, 'The Theological Method of Śaṃkara' 72. De Smet's exposition of Śaṅkara's refutation of Buddhism (in ch. 11 of the dissertation) also seems to imply that the world cannot simply be considered unreal. "To all this Śaṃkara

replies: the non-existence of external things cannot be maintained because we are conscious of the existence of external things." See ibid. 318-319.

[40] De Smet, 'The Theological Method of Śaṃkara' 344.

[41] De Smet, 'The Theological Method of Śaṃkara' 264-266.

[42] R. De Smet, "Towards Re-orienting Indian Philosophy: Hints from a Thomist," *The Philosophical Quarterly* **29**/4 (1957) 196.

[43] De Smet, 'Indian Contribution to General Metaphysics' 348.

[44] De Smet, "Indian Contribution to General Metaphysics" 352, emphasis added.

[45] De Smet, 'Indian Contribution to General Metaphysics' 355-356.

[46] De Smet, 'Indian Contribution to General Metaphysics' 353.

[47] De Smet, 'Indian Contribution to General Metaphysics' 353.

[48] De Smet, 'Indian Contribution to General Metaphysics' 353.

[49] De Smet, 'Indian Contribution to General Metaphysics' 353-354.

[50] De Smet, 'Indian Contribution to General Metaphysics' 354. The Dasgupta quotation is from *A History of Indian Philosophy* (Delhi: Motilal Banarsidass, 1975) **2**:19. Vāsubandhu was an Indian Buddhist scholar-monk, and one of the main founders of Indian Yogācārà.

[51] See R. De Smet, "Śaṅkara's Non-Dualism (*Advaitavāda*) (1964/68)" = ch. 3 below. The earlier version of this article (1958) has no indications of this rejection of the current interpretation of Śaṅkara: see R. De Smet, "The Great Hindu Theologies: 1. Shankara's Advaita or Non-Dualism," *Hinduism, A Course by Letter*, Lesson XVIII (October 1958) 1-15.

[52] This is not from Śaṅkara but from the *Bālabodhini*, a later work falsely attributed to him, as De Smet informs us in "Śaṅkara's Non-Dualism (*Advaitavāda*) (1997)" 306 below.

[53] De Smet, "Śaṅkara's Non-Dualism (*Advaitavāda*) (1964/68)" 84-85 below.

[54] De Smet, "Śaṅkara's Non-Dualism (*Advaitavāda*) (1964/68)" 85 below.

[55] In fact, this part of the article is a carryover from the 1958 version: see De Smet, "Shankara's Advaita or Non-Dualism" (1958) 5-13.

[56] De Smet, "Śaṅkara's Non-Dualism (*Advaitavāda*) (1964/68)" 94 below = "Shankara's Advaita or Non-Dualism" (1958) 14. The 1958 version speaks of "a repulsive" brand of pantheism.

[57] R. De Smet, "*Māyā* or *Ajñāna*? A Textual Analysis" = ch. 6 below.

[58] R. De Smet, "From the Vedas to Radhakrishnan" 295-297 below.

[59] De Smet, "*Māyā* or *Ajñāna*?" 122-126 below.

[60] De Smet, "*Māyā* or *Ajñāna*?" 123 below.

[61] De Smet, "*Māyā* or *Ajñāna*?" 126-128 below.

[62] De Smet, 'Indian Contribution to General Metaphysics' 353.

[63] De Smet, "*Māyā* or *Ajñāna*?" 122 below.

[64] De Smet provides a 1968-1975 date in his 'Bibliography of Fr. Richard De Smet, SJ,' 9 November 1993 (25 pp. typescript, unpublished) item II B/16.

[65] De Smet, 'Guidelines' 221.

[66] De Smet, 'Guidelines' 231.

[67] De Smet, 'Guidelines' 277.

[68] De Smet, 'Guidelines' 278. In 1975 he calls the *Māṇḍ. Up. Bh.* an "extremely doubtful" work (see Review of M. Piantelli, *Śaṅkara e la rinascita del Brāhmanesimo* 415 below) and in 1989, against the authority of Radhakrishnan and Mayeda, he once again rejects it ("Radhakrishnan's Interpretation of Śaṅkara" 210-211 below). Finally, in 1994, he notes that the most thorough rejection of the authenticity of the *vivaraṇa* is by Thomas E. Wood (see "From the Vedas to Radhakrishnan" 296 below).

[69] De Smet, 'Guidelines' 287.

[70] De Smet, 'Guidelines' 292. See Sara Grant, *Śaṅkarācārya's Concept of Relation* (Delhi: Motilal Banarsidass, 1999). In an article of 1980 De Smet says: "It [*tādātmya*] is the tightest kind of unity, short of pure identity, since it subjects the whole being *qua* being to the total Cause which penetrates it most intimately as the Plenitude imbibes the totality of each one of its participations. ("Love versus Identity," *Indian Philosophical Quarterly* 7/4 [July 1980] 525)

[71] De Smet, 'Guidelines' 294-295.

[72] 'abaleity': derivative of the Latin *ab alio* = from another.

[73] De Smet, 'Guidelines' 296.

[74] De Smet, 'Guidelines' 305-306.

[75] R. De Smet, "Śaṅkara and Aquinas on Creation" = ch. 23 below. R. De Smet, "Origin: Creation and Emanation" = ch. 26 below.

[76] De Smet, "Śaṅkara and Aquinas on Creation" 345-347 below.

[77] De Smet, "Śaṅkara and Aquinas on Creation" 351 below.

[78] De Smet, "Origin: Creation and Emanation" 376 below.

[79] De Smet, "Origin: Creation and Emanation" 376-377 below.

[80] De Smet, "Origin: Creation and Emanation" 377 below.

[81] De Smet, "Origin: Creation and Emanation" 377 below .

[82] The reference is to J.F. Pessein, *Vedānta Vindicated or the Harmony of Vedānta and Christian Philosophy* (Trichinopoly: St Joseph's Industrial School Press, 1925). Pessein is mentioned once again in the bibliography at the end of "Śaṅkara's Non-Dualism (*Advaitavāda*) (1997)" = ch. 20 below. He is absent, however, from the bibliography of De Smet's doctoral dissertation.

[83] De Smet, "Śāṃkara Vedānta and Christian Theology" 386 below.

[84] De Smet, "Spiritual Values of Advaita Vedānta and Social Life" 162-163 below

[85] De Smet, "Spiritual Values of Advaita Vedānta and Social Life" 165 below.

[86] De Smet, "Spiritual Values of Advaita Vedānta and Social Life" 165 below.

[87] De Smet, "Spiritual Values of Advaita Vedānta and Social Life" 168 below.

[88] R. De Smet, "Forward Steps in Śaṅkara Research" 187-188 below. See also "The Buddha, Meister Eckhart and Śaṅkarācārya on 'Nothing'" 202 below: the current and widespread interpretation is that Śaṅkara is an acosmist who asserts that there is only one true Reality, the *Brahman*-Ātman, and that all else, whether selves or bodies, is illusory. But much recent work has been done by a few scholars who interpret Śaṅkara by Śaṅkara (De Smet uses this phrase of himself in "From Catholic Theology to Śāṅkara Vedānta and Return with Fr. F.X. Clooney" 399 below) and thus reach a new interpretation.

[89] De Smet, "Radhakrishnan's Interpretation of Śaṅkara" 210-211 below.

[90] De Smet, "Radhakrishnan's Interpretation of Śaṅkara" 211 below.
[91] De Smet, "Radhakrishnan's Interpretation of Śaṅkara" 215 below.
[92] R. De Smet, "Radhakrishnan's Second Presentation of Śaṅkara's Teaching" 233-234 below.
[93] De Smet, "Radhakrishnan's Second Presentation of Śaṅkara's Teaching" 237 below.
[94] De Smet, "Radhakrishnan's Second Presentation of Śaṅkara's Teaching" 237-238 below.
[95] De Smet, "Radhakrishnan's Second Presentation of Śaṅkara's Teaching" 239 below.
[96] R. De Smet, "The Presuppositions of Jaimini and the Vedāntins" = ch. 17 below. R. De Smet, "Śaṅkara's Perspective on Meaning and Truth" = ch. 16 below.
[97] This is perhaps an exemplification of Bernard Lonergan's insight that cognitional theory governs epistemology and metaphysics, and that a good grasp of the three is an invaluable aid in interpretation. See Lonergan, *Insight: A Study of Human Understanding*, Collected Works of Bernard Lonergan 3, ed. F.E. Crowe and R.M. Doran (Toronto: University of Toronto Press, 1992) 553-554.
[98] However, in "Śaṅkara's Perspective on Meaning and Truth" 269 below—published the same year—De Smet says that he is inclined to believe that Śaṅkara's conception of *vākya* is derived from *Śruti*.
[99] On this point, see I. Coelho, 'Retrieving Good Work: De Smet on Śaṅkara,' paper presented at the 37th Annual Lonergan Workshop, "Reversing Social and Cultural Decline 'in a Friendly Universe'," 20-25 June 2010, Boston College, Boston, to be published in a forthcoming issue of *Lonergan Workshop*.
[100] Correcting De Smet's reference to *Taitt. Up. Bh.* 2, 3.
[101] De Smet, "The Presuppositions of Jaimini and the Vedāntins" 279-280 below.
[102] De Smet, "Śaṅkara's Non-Dualism (*Advaitavāda*) (1997)" = ch. 20 below.
[103] S. Radhakrishnan, tr. and intr., *The Brahma Sutra: The Philosophy of the Spiritual Life* (London: George Allen & Unwin, 1960) 33, 137-138.
[104] See De Smet, 'Indian Contribution to General Metaphysics' 357; "Śaṅkara's Non-Dualism (*Advaitavāda*) (1964/68)" 94 below; 'Guidelines' 309.
[105] See De Smet, 'Indian Contribution to General Metaphysics' 342, 360; "Śaṅkara's Non-Dualism (*Advaitavāda*) (1964/68)" 94 below.
[106] See a very good statement of Christian non-dualism in R. De Smet, "*Advaitavāda* and Christianity" = ch. 24 below. See also I. Coelho, "Fr. Richard V. De Smet (1916-97): Reminiscences," *Divyadaan: Journal of Philosophy and Education* 8/1 (1997) 3-15.
[107] In this connection, see T.S. Rukmani who, after a study of three articles, rejects De Smet's interpretation of Śaṅkara as fatally coloured by his Christian prejudices. In support of an 'objective' and 'non-prejudiced' interpretation, she cites what she believes is Gadamer, but is in fact quite the opposite of Gadamer's well-known position that prejudices are the key to understanding. It turns out that her long 'Gadamer quote' is actually David Linge reporting

Schleiermacher, Dilthey and the neo-Kantians in his introduction to Gadamer's *Philosophical Hermeneutics* (Berkeley: University of California Press, 1977). See T.S. Rukmani, "Dr Richard De Smet and Sankara's Advaita." *Hindu-Christian Studies Bulletin* **16** (2003) 19.

[108] Lonergan, *Method in Theology* (Toronto: University of Toronto Press, 1990) ch. 10: Dialectic. See also I. Coelho, 'Person and Subject in Lonergan: A Methodical Transposition,' paper presented at the 36th Annual Lonergan Workshop, "Ongoing Collaboration in the Year of St Paul," 21-26 June 2009, Boston College, Boston (to be published in *Lonergan Workshop*), in addition to "Retrieving Good Work: De Smet on Śaṅkara" mentioned above (see note 99).

I. STUDIES

1

LANGUAGE AND KNOWLEDGE OF THE ABSOLUTE ACCORDING TO ŚAṄKARA[1]

1. Introduction

Towards the end of the dominance of the Buddhist heresy,[2] Śaṅkara (788-820 or 826 AD) effected a doctrinal reform that established him in the history of Indian thought as the most important and genial restorer of Brahmanic orthodoxy.

His commentaries on the principal Upaniṣads, the *Bhagavad Gītā*, and the *Vedānta Sūtras* (basic manual of the Mīmāṃsakas or ritualist exegetes) formed a corpus which has remained, up to our day, the highest authority after the Vedic scriptures for its adepts, and, for its adversaries, at once an ideal of exegesis and a body of doctrine irritating for its high logic and monolithic consistency.

As for the doctrine of non-dualism (Advaita) to which Śaṅkara reduced the whole teaching of the sacred tradition (*Śruti*), it also acquired such a preponderance that, willingly or unwillingly, all subsequent theologians of Brahmanism were obliged to situate and differentiate their systems with respect to it, and even the non-Vedic elements that contributed to the formation of Hinduism were not able to integrate themselves independently of the non-dualist perspective.

All the same, this doctrine is disconcerting. The paradox of its acosmism makes it inhuman and almost irrational. And the most authoritative expositions of the last hundred years have hardly been able to lessen the scandal. The Neo-Vedānta that is so popular these days not only does not help in understanding it, but even denatures it into an unassimilable and superficial pantheism. In trying to popularize it, it succeeds only in watering it down and devaluing it in the eyes of serious thinkers.

In order to rediscover it in its original integrity we must return to the Master, submit to his point of view, and rediscover his primary intention by studying his aim, method and the means he used.

This is what we have attempted to do recently in a work entitled 'The Theological Method of Śaṃkara.'[3]

Śaṅkara appeared to us there as a Vedic theologian in the most technical sense of the term. The basis of his teaching is faith which he attributes without reserve to the non-human (*apauruṣeya*) and infallible testimony of the Brahmanic tradition called Veda or sacred Knowledge and which consists essentially of the four Vedas, the Brāhmaṇas, the Āraṇyakas and about 14 Upaniṣads. This faith, of which he himself had the complete experience up to the supreme intuition, he proposes to expound for his disciple and to elevate him also to the direct and full experience of absolute Knowledge. His theological enterprise (*Brahmajijñāsā*) consists in making the disciple adhere to this saving Knowledge by eliminating all the obstacles impeding clear vision, until the revealed truth alone shines and illuminates the inmost depths of the spirit.

This elimination normally proceeds by steps that are successive and integrative. First comes a propaedeutic whose aim is to calm the passions and put the aspirant in such a spiritual disposition that no worldly solicitation can disturb the *élan* of his *fides quaerens intellectum*. Once this disposition has been attained, the master (*guru*) makes him listen to the Scriptures and leads him through an appropriate pedagogy to grasp its essential message. Towards this end he employs the tried and tested methods of classical exegesis (*pūrva mīmāṃsā*), adapted however to his particular goal. Once the central mystery of the sacred doctrine has thus been revealed, exegesis follows and confirms this revelation by a systematic demonstration of the harmony (*samanvaya*) that this mystery and it alone confers on all the Vedic texts. This harmony satisfies the faith which must evidently reject every exegesis that is incapable of supporting it, because it cannot accept contradiction at the heart of a testimony that it considers infallibly truthful. But man is not merely faith, he is also intelligence, and, after faith has been reassured and convinced that the mystery proposed to it as essential is truly revealed and supported by all the texts that it considers infallible, it remains to persuade the intelligence that this mystery is in perfect conformity with its own evidences. This is the task of the next stage which examines and refutes all the objections that have been raised or that could possibly oppose the truth of the primordial mystery. This defence of the faith makes use of two types of arguments: scriptural arguments, where the decisive element is a recourse to the sacred texts or to the truths and principles deriving from it, and properly rational arguments that destroy the objection by recourse to the laws proper to reason, and especially the principle of non-contradiction.

So the scriptural exegesis determines the object proper to faith, the harmonising exegesis establishes its intrinsic coherence, and the rational defence assures its extrinsic coherence and renders it impervious to doubt and objection. After this, the field is open for the effort of recollection which makes the disciple pass from the stage of notional adherence to that of lived experience and direct illumination. This is accomplished by means of the yogic practice of concentration on the formula (*mantra*) of the revealed mystery and continuous and unwavering contemplation of its truth.

By itself, this *yoga* can well prepare the spirit for the direct intuition (*sākṣātkāra*) but cannot properly cause it. Its proper function is to destroy the last vestiges of complexity which still oppose the vision of the supreme simplicity; but this vision is as different from all that precedes it as the waking state is from the world of sleep and of dream; it is in fact nothing other than consciousness perfectly awoken to its ontological reality and, no more than this reality is the result of human creation, can it be itself the result of theological effort.

All direct relation of cause to effect being thus negated between theological inquiry and its result, we must ask about the value that such a radically impotent discipline can claim. Beyond this difficulty the very doctrine of Śaṅkarian non-dualism forces the one who elucidates it to push this critique further and to question himself about the very nature of a theological science that presents itself as culminating in a truth that negates it as a science.

This non-dualism, in fact, posits as real Being only the "Reality-Knowledge-Infinite" that designates indifferently the terms *Brahman* and *Ātman*. And it admits nothing as real Knowledge except the absolutely exhaustive and incomplex intuition of this supreme Being. Every form of consciousness that distinguishes itself from this intuition is considered ignorance, just as every form of being that distinguishes itself from *Brahman-Ātman* is considered unreal. Now it is clear that theological science considered in itself, independently of the supreme illumination in which it is expected to culminate, lacks the perfect simplicity that characterizes absolute Knowledge. Its source, revelation (*Śruti*), consists in a multiplicity of texts, its master-formulas are complex propositions, its elaboration is done through the discursive intelligence of man, and though it might well tend all through its development to the simple unity of intuition, that intuition cannot arise except in an experience that is heterogeneous and destructive of all discourse, and therefore of all theological science. How then can Śaṅkara pretend to lead man to the absolute Knowledge by means of an inquiry (*jijñāsā*) that regards itself and all its elements as ignorance and unreality?

Such is the fundamental antinomy of his theological enterprise: all complex knowledge is heterogeneous to Knowledge and deserves to be called nothing more than ignorance, and yet a form more or less of ignorance, the *Brahmajijñāsā*, that is to say theological inquiry conducted under the guidance of a Master, can lead to true Knowledge.

To resolve this antinomy, Śaṅkara proposed a doctrine of transcendental illumination, comparable to that of St Augustine, that explains how all finite consciousnesses are supremely clarified by the infinite Consciousness and are therefore, at their very source, in direct communication with the absolute Reality.

He has also made use of a transcendental analysis of human knowledge to demonstrate that in every one of his cognitive experiences man implicitly affirms the absolute Being through and beyond his explicit particular affirmations. It follows that at the very heart of these 'acts of ignorance' that are complex judgements, simple Knowledge is constantly exercised even when it is not lived as an exclusive and beatifying experience.

In the end Śaṅkara had recourse, at the decisive moment of his exegesis, to the theory of implication (*lakṣaṇājñāna*) or the theory of knowledge by indirect signification. This theory permits, through the very means of the inadequate terms of certain propositions, to pass to knowledge of the transcendent and undifferentiated identity that they signify indirectly. It attributes therefore to certain 'forms of ignorance,' i.e., to certain Vedic propositions that discursively define the Absolute, a power of transcendent signification that allows him who understands them to negate from the object indicated the complexity that they explicitly signify and to apprehend in them the ontological simplicity that they can signify only implicitly but nonetheless positively. In fact this third element of the solution also indicates a passage from 'ignorance' (*avidyā*, *ajñāna*) to the true Knowledge (*Vidyā*, *Jñāna*). It permits also to better interpret the trenchant differences in the Śaṅkarian vocabulary about the notions of knowledge and ignorance, of reality and unreality, etc., and so to attenuate their rigour.

Without occupying ourselves any further in this article about the first two elements of the solution of this fundamental antinomy of Śaṅkarian theology, we propose to study in detail this theory of implication or analogy that is central to the Śāṅkarian interpretation of the Veda. We will see that it is as general as our theology of analogy and that, even if he was not a strict theologian of the Veda, Śaṅkara was able to use it to constitute a general metaphysics that was more complete and less disconcerting than his *advaitavāda* (doctrine of non-dualism) established on the narrow base of the Brahmanic scriptures.

* * *

Every philosophical or theological system that claims to demonstrate that man is capable of knowing the absolute Reality that transcends it totally while being intimately immanent to it, is forced to explain how the inherent anthropomorphism of language can be surmounted and how certain combinations of ordinary words arranged in the form of propositions can signify and indicate in some positive fashion this transcendent Being that, strictly speaking, is inexpressible. The medieval

Scholastics, for example, developed the theory of different meanings (univocal, analogous and equivocal) that can form the terms of a proposition and applied it to the knowledge of God.

A similar theory responds to the same necessity in the doctrine of Śaṅkara. This is the theory of the knowledge by implication (*lakṣaṇājñāna*) or indirect signification.

Already at work in the esoteric speculations of the Brāhmaṇas, it received its first elaboration at the hands of the ancient Grammarians and Exegetes. Its influence is felt in the Sāṁkhya system and in the different Buddhist schools. The distinction of different meanings of which the same term can be the vehicle in different contexts belongs thus, at the end of the eighth century AD, to the ordinary arsenal of the Indian schools. The originality of Śaṅkara is to put this distinction at the service of his exegesis and to establish in fact that a certain valid knowledge of the Transcendent is possible, already before the supreme intuition, beginning from concepts, derived from the world of empirical objects, and through the medium of language.

He never stops to expose systematically the different categories of contextual meanings, because he has the right to suppose them known to the readers of his time, but many of his disciples, for example, Dharmarāja Adhvarīndra in his elementary but clear treatise, the *Vedānta Paribhāsa*, filled up this lacuna in his writings.

2. The Semantic Polyvalence of Words

Apart from proper names (*nāmadheya*) that, strictly speaking, can designate only a single individual, substantives, adjectives, and also in some way verbs, are common or generic. They express abstract concepts applicable to several individuals. In other words, they denote concrete universals (*ākṛti*) that, in each individual, constitute this particular common thing (*sāmānya*) that is found in all the individuals of the same genus (*jāti*).

Now this common essence exists in each individual in a different manner. Language itself cannot fulfil its proper function if it is incapable, while expressing the general concept, to indicate also the particular mode, the individual difference that concretises it in each case.

On the other hand, when it comes to characterising the supreme Reality that transcends every empirical reality and does not fit into any genus (*ajāti*), the concepts employed will be not only inadequate but even mendacious if language is not able to confer on the words that express them a new power that allows them to indicate in some fashion the properly ineffable mode according to which the perfect Being realizes these concepts.

We must therefore study the different resources of language and highlight not only its natural power of direct expression but also its powers of suggestion, of secondary indication, of indirection signification.

It is by the intervention of modifiers, such as negations, adjectives, adverbs, by the mutual determination of terms of the same proposition, by the reciprocal influence of the propositions of the same text, in short, by the exigencies of their whole context that words acquire powers of signification that far surpass their simple power of expression.

According as it is considered in isolation or within a context, a word can acquire two types of meanings: either a direct and explicit sense, or different indirect meanings implied (*lakṣita*) by the context.[4]

The direct meaning (*śakya*) or proper power (*śakti*) is the primary denotation (*mukhya*) of words in relation to the concrete objects they express.[5] This meaning is direct (*sākṣāt*), that is to say, obvious (*avyavahita*, not hampered), immediate (*parokṣāt*), not figurative (*agauṇa*).[6] It is therefore the normal sense that one attributes to words when one defines them apart from any precise context, for example, in view of constituting the dictionary of a language. Words can evidently maintain this meaning within a given context, but it is also possible that the latter can modify it into one or other of the secondary senses of which a word is capable.

It can happen that a writer, contrary to general usage, calls the primary sense of a word that one of its many senses that is closest to its etymological origin, or again, that represents to the highest degree the notion expressed by this word. Thus Śaṅkara considered, for example, "that a *Brahmavid* (knower of *Brahman*) is a *Brāhmaṇa* (a member of the highest caste) in the primary sense (*mukhya*) of the term; earlier, the brahmanic nature of this term did not exist except in a figurative sense (*gauṇa*)."[7] Such a practice is the principal source of the ambiguity of the Śaṅkarian vocabulary. According as he accepts current usage (*vyavahāra*) as the principal term of reference, or else searches this term in the metaphysics of the Vedic revelation (*paramārtha*), Śaṅkara attributes to words primary values that are very different. Terms such as being, reality, knowledge, goodness, *brahman*, *ātman*, etc., have an ordinary usage and, according to this, it is only secondarily and analogically that they apply to the Absolute; they have also a Vedic usage, or at least an advaitic one, and, according to this usage, it is to the Absolute that they apply in the first place, and also, most often, exclusively; their application to empirical objects is therefore merely secondary, or even unreal and false because, as Śaṅkara puts it, it is then a result of false attribution or superimposition (*adhyāropa*, *adhyāsa*). The interpreter of the writings of the Master of Advaita must constantly take into account this particularity of his vocabulary because its consequences are very important for the understanding of his doctrine.

The secondary (*gauṇa*) or implicit (*lakṣita*, *lakṣya*) meanings of a word are the meanings, different from the primary sense, of which it becomes the carrier in virtue of the different contexts in which it is introduced.

When classified according to the degree of complexity of the mental operation required by their apprehension, one obtains the following division:

1. simple implication (*kevalalakṣaṇā*),
2. complex implication, or implication mediated by a primary implication (*lakṣitalakṣaṇā*).[8]

In simple implication, the relation of the secondary sense to the primary sense is direct (*sākṣātsaṁbandha*). For example, in the expression "the village on the Ganges," which means "the village on the bank of the Ganges," the relation on which one bases oneself is that which exists in reality between the Ganges and its bank and which is obviously direct.[9]

In complex implication, the relation of the secondary sense to the primary sense is indirect (*aparokṣāt*). For example, in the figurative expression "you are a lion," which means "you are remarkably courageous," implication is not possible except through the intermediary of the abstract and general notion of the nature of a lion that is itself derived from the concrete perception of individual lions and indicated (*lakṣita*) through the direct meaning of the word 'lion.' For the understanding of the phrase demands a passage, imperceptible no doubt but real, through the notions lion, leonine nature, courage.[10]

One can also classify the secondary senses according to their similarity to the primary sense. When it is a question of implication strictly speaking and not of pure equivocation, the retention of the primary sense through the secondary sense is always effective under some aspect but it involves different degrees.

According to this relation of similarity between the secondary sense and the primary sense, implication can be of three types:

1. *ajahallakṣaṇā*, non-exclusive implication (of the primary sense);
2. *jahallakṣaṇā,* exclusive implication (of the primary sense);
3. *jahadajahallakṣaṇā*, implication at once exclusive and inclusive (of the primary sense).[11]

In the first (*ajahallakṣaṇā*), the primary sense is maintained *in toto* but the context modifies it accidentally, restricting it or specifying it, by means of the syntactic function devolving to it. For example, in the phrase "it is the red that runs," which means "it is the red horse that runs," the adjective 'red' is used substantively and it is the context that clarifies this usage.

This sort of implication that maintains the univocal sense of the terms is frequent in the ordinary usage of language which refers solely to empirical objects. But it is of no use to us when it is a question of speaking with exactitude about metempirical reality.

In exclusive implication (*jahallakṣaṇā*), the relation between the secondary sense and the primary sense exists only thanks to a resemblance that is purely accidental or totally metaphorical. The poets use for example the word '*dvirepha*,' literally 'double R,' in the sense of bee, because the word '*bhramara*,' which means 'bee,' contains twice the letter R.

The anagogic meditations, so numerous in the Upaniṣads, are ordinarily based on such implications. For example, the sacrificial horse is contemplated as Prajāpati because one finds a certain exterior analogy between its physical parts and the aspects or powers of this mythological figure;[12] the bricks called *yājusmati* that form part of the construction of the altar of sacrifice of the *Agnihotra* are contemplated as the 360 oblations of the year, then as the *prajāpati* or god of the year, because they are also of the number 360;[13] the god of the wind (*Vāyu*) is contemplated as *Prāṇa* (vital breath, life) because the wind and the breath both have the power to fade or pull away by themselves;[14] etc. The utility of such secondary meditations is purely pedagogic; they do not reveal the truth but they do dispose the heart towards it by purifying it and teaching it to recollect itself.[15]

In exclusive-inclusive implication (*jahadajahallakṣaṇā*), the secondary sense substantially maintains the notion currently expressed by the word but changes its normal application or the mode of actuation, etc.

For example, someone cries, "My dress is burnt!" while it is only a part of the dress that is burnt. Using thus the whole for the part, saying "my dress" instead of "that part of my dress," is to use the word 'dress' beyond its normal usage but in a way permitted by language and without necessarily falling into equivocation, because the context (visual, gestures, etc.) can clearly suggest the way in which the word is being used.

This example is rudimentary. There are other cases when the implication rests on the distinction between the notion expressed by the primary sense of a term and the different possible modes according to which this notion can be concretely realised.

Every time, for example, that the Vedic revelation (*Śruti*) attempts to define the absolute Being in a language that is not exclusively anthropomorphic, the correct understanding of such definitions calls for recognition of this kind of exclusive-inclusive implication (*jahadajahallakṣaṇā*). We will soon see how Śaṅkara proceeds in the exegesis of these fundamental texts of the Upaniṣads.

To the different secondary senses studied up to now, we must add the suggested sense (*vyangyārtha*) which the Rhetoricians (*Alankāraśāstrin*) make much of. It is purely metaphoric and does not rely on the primary sense except according to the laws of poetic logic. It is therefore not used in Vedāntic theology, and neither in the systems of the Logicians (*Nyāya*).

Apart from these different senses, a word cannot be used except in a false or illusory sense (*mityārtha*), which rests on an error of apperception or of judgment, whereas it must be understood well that "the idea obtained from one of the legitimate secondary senses (*gauṇapratyaya*) is not a false idea (*mithyāpratyaya*), because the significative power of the secondary senses is based [not on error] but on the awareness that this is a legitimate manner of speaking."[16]

Before continuing with this study we propose the following table that summarizes the notions exposed so far:

> *PADĀRTHA* (meaning of words)
>
> I. *Mukhya* (primary sense), also called *śakya* (direct power) or *vācya* (immediate expression) or *abhideya* (simple denotation)
>
> II. *Gauṇa* (qualified or secondary sense), also called *lakṣya* or *lakṣita* (indicated, implied);
> A. — 1) *kevalalakṣya* (simply, directly implied)
> 2) *lakṣitalakṣya* (implied indirectly, i.e. through a primary implication), also called *gauṇya* (figurative)
> B. — 1) *ajahallakṣya* (including the primary sense);
> 2) *jahallakṣya* (excluding the primary sense);
> 3) *jahadajahallakṣya* (exclusive and inclusive of the primary sense at the same time)
>
> III. *Vyangya* (suggested, purely metaphorical).
>
> IV. *Mithyā* (illusory, false).

3. The Meaning of Propositions (*vākyārtha*)

Language is ordinarily composed not of words but of propositions (*vākya*), where the terms combined condition each other reciprocally, and of phrases, where the propositions in their turn are united according to relations of coordination or subordination. The meaning of these propositions and phrases does not consist in a simple totalising juxtaposition of the individual meanings of their terms but in a whole (*anvaya*) that takes up and transcends the set of these individual meanings. It is this transcendent sense that demands in certain cases that we understand some or even all the terms of a proposition not according to their expressed meaning but in a secondary sense to be determined each time according to the indications of the context, and which is therefore implied (*lakṣita*).

About the meaning of propositions (*vākyārtha*) it must also be said that it is implied by the syntactic presentation of their terms and by the whole context of the discourse. "The meaning of a proposition," writes Vācaspati, "is the common intention of the set of its terms; this is because each of these terms, while expressing its particular sense, tends to manifest the meaning of the proposition that is thus secondarily implied or indicated (*lakṣita*) by all the terms of the set."[17]

In a proposition, there is the presence, ordinarily explicit, of the verb (*kriyā*) that operates the synthesis (*anvaya*) of the individual terms.

There is a controversy between the two great schools of Exegesis (Mīmāṃsaka), the school of the Prābhākaras and that of the Bhāṭṭas, about the way in which the mind (*buddhi*) apprehends this synthesis. Without entering into details, themselves extremely interesting, of this dispute, we recall here that the Bhāṭṭas hold that the memory of words cannot by itself account for our knowledge of their synthetic meaning, as their opponents would have it, but that it is the intelligence (*buddhi*), aided no doubt by the memory, that constructs, from the individual meanings evoked by each word, the synthetic sense of the proposition. In this question as in others, Śaṅkara and his school adopted the position of the Bhāṭṭas.

The conditions of this constructive apprehension are three:

1. The affinity of the ideas expressed by the words;
2. The syntactic proximity (*āsatti*) of the words;
3. The knowledge of the intention of the author of the discourse (*tātparyajñāna*).[18]

The first consists of two elements:

a) *ākāṁkṣā* (expectation), that is to say the incompleteness of each word taken in isolation and its expectation of a complement of meaning from the other words; for example, the word 'gives' calls for a direct complement.

b) *yogyatā* (capacity), that is to say the corresponding aptitude of each word to complete the meaning of words which are syntactically united to it.

The second condition, the syntactic proximity (*āsatti*), is temporal in spoken language, spatial in written language. It is this that enables the knowledge of which words must be combined together in order to form a proposition.

The third, the knowledge of the intention of the author of the discourse, is obtained either directly, from the immediate context, or, in case of doubt, by an attentive consideration of the universe of discourse, its introduction, its conclusion, etc.

It presupposes the truthfulness of the author. According to the Advaitins, such veracity is one of the postulates of language. Of itself, a discourse demands to be believed. It is only because of elements extrinsic to discourse that in certain cases the hearer has the right to doubt its truth. Faith (*śraddha*) is the spontaneous and normal response to testimony (*śabda*); doubt is secondary and anormal; it justifies itself only by appealing to grounds different from testimony itself.

The Buddhists, the Jains and certain Vaiśeṣikas claimed that testimony (*śabda*) cannot be considered an autonomous source of true knowledge (*pramāṇa*), because one can never place faith in it independently of an induction (*anumāna*) about the veracity of its author.

The Mīmāṃsakas and the Advaitins on the contrary defended the independence of testimony as a specific source of valid knowledge (*prāmāṇya*), showing the absence of grounds for such a generalised scepticism since the spontaneous reaction of every man, including the sceptic, is to have confidence in the one who speaks, doubt arising only later and for reasons extrinsic to the nature of language.

The three conditions indicated above, which are inherent to language, suffice thus to assure a correct understanding of its statements (*śabdabodha*) and to distinguish it from the apprehension of successive words by simple memory, as well as from the type of knowledge that results from an induction (*anumāna*).

According to the Mīmāṃsakas, a proposition (*vākya*) is the statement of a relational synthesis (*saṁsarga* or *saṁbandha*) between the subject, called *viśeṣya* (*determinandum*, term to be differentiated) or *uddeśya* (subject of the relation), and the predicate, called *viśeṣaṇa* (*determinans*, differentiator, attribute) or *vidheya* (term related to the subject, qualifier).

This theory is rejected by Śaṅkara and his school for its lack of generality. There are, in fact, propositions whose intention is not to determine the subject by means of a relation (*saṁbandha*) of action, of qualification, etc., but to express the strict identity (*tādātmya*) of subject and predicate. Such are the judgments of identification or even the definitions of perfect Being which are not relational definitions by genus and specific difference, because the perfect Being is beyond any genus. These propositions are not '*saṁsargāvayāhi*' (relational) but '*akhaṇḍārthaka*,' that is to say that their subject is designated as an undivided absolute (*akhaṇḍa*) and not as the term of a relation.

Let us examine, for example, the judgment of identification that presents itself in Sanskrit in the form: "this is that Devadatta." The term 'this' here designates Devadatta as apprehended within present time and space, while the term 'that' designates the same man as present in memory such as he was apprehended in the past. As for the synthesis operated by the verb 'is,' it means merely that the two opposing determinants, 'this' and 'that,' are identical, (we will soon, in fact, indicate their difference), not that the one specifies the other (as the adjective 'blue' specifies the substantive 'lotus' in the definition, "this is a blue lotus"). It does not mean further that Devadatta, insofar as determined by 'this,' is exactly the same insofar as determined by 'that.' But it signifies identity despite the differences indicated by these two terms, differences that are only informative references from which the identifying synthesis as such abstracts.[19]

We will soon see that when it is a question of identifying the perfect Being this abstraction becomes pure and simple negation, because in this case all difference is fictitious and its expression rests only on the anthropomorphism inherent to our manner of conceiving and speaking, but not however to our power of affirming.

4. The Apophatism of Theological Language

According to the Upaniṣads, the Absolute cannot be attained by any of the ordinary means of knowing (*pramāṇas*), such as sense perception, induction, comparison, postulation, human testimony. In the ordinary sense of the words 'to know' and 'to express,' it can be neither known nor expressed.

> There, the eye cannot reach,
> Nor speech, nor intellect (*manas*).
> We do not know, we do not understand
> How to teach it.
>
> For it is different from the known
> And beyond the unknown....[20]
>
> Words recede from it
> Together with the intellect (*manas*), without having attained
> The Joy of *Brahman*.[21]

According to Śaṅkara, "only that which can present itself to the senses as an object can be known."[22] It is therefore evident that "the principle of knowing in the knower certainly cannot be known, any more than the principle of burning in fire can itself be burnt."[23]

In order to understand this position well we must understand that the *manas* (a term we have rendered inadequately by 'intellect') is that which the Indians call the internal organ (*antaḥkaraṇa*) of knowing and that it is merely a *material* sense, although more subtle than the external senses, and not a purely spiritual faculty. It is therefore not possible for it to reach pure subjectivity. Human knowing can *know* only that which the external senses and the *manas* can *objectify* (*viṣayīkriyanti*) and the *Brahman-Ātman* "is a subject (*dharma*) too subtle (*aṇuḥ*) to be apprehended as object (*viṣaya*)."[24]

Every time therefore that the *Brahman* seems to be apprehended by the senses or the *manas*, it is merely mendacious, because these cannot manifest it except as bound to the *upādhis* or fictitious attributes that hide its true nature.[25]

However the *Brahman* is not absolutely unknowable because the true testimony of the *Śruti* can indicate it (*lakṣayati*) and faith can recognize it:

> 'This is He,' thus they recognise
> The Supreme and indescribable *Brahman*.[26]

Further, if it cannot be known (*cintayita, viṣayīkṛta*) as an object (*viṣaya*), it is not impossible however that it be 'realized,' apprehended as immediate (*sākṣāt*) through the direct intuition (*sākṣātkāra*) that is the goal envisaged by the whole theological effort (*Brahmajijñāsā*), and, in this sense, which is superior more than secondary, it can be known (*vidita*), seen (*dṛṣṭa*,[27] *īkṣita*), and is knowable (*jñeya*).

This knowledge is possible because, in every act of knowing, the knower is immediately apprehended as thinking subject (*pramātṛ*)[28] without having necessarily to be objectified, and because the *Brahman* is the *Ātman*, that is to say, the Absolute of the knowing subject, the supreme Witness (*sākṣin*), the Illuminator of every knowing, whose essence is intelligence (*cicchaktisvarūpamātra*).[29]

"There is no other way of knowing the Absolute of the self.... When the *Brahman* is known as the Absolute of the subject of all the states of consciousness (*pratyayapratyagātmatayā*), then it is truly known (*matam*)."[30]

It is not therefore by presenting it to us as an object that the *Śruti* reveals to us the *Brahman*, but in urging us to turn away completely from the universe of empirical objects and to concentrate on the absolute of subjectivity with which we communicate without ceasing through our finite ontological subjectivity (*jīvātman*), but whose exigencies for action (*karman*) distract us without respite.

With the aid of *Śruti*, the master (*guru*), who is full of compassion for his pupil immersed in ignorance, brushes away indefatigably the spontaneously (*naisargika*) objectifying representations[31] of the supreme Subject and distinguishes it from all the *upādhis* or fictitious attributes. "That," he repeats, "which cannot be expressed by words, but by which every word is expressed, know that as *Brahman*."[32] "Once every definition of that which is in reality indefinable, without distinction, supreme and harmonious has been brushed away, the idea that the *Brahman* is the *Ātman* is taught by the Veda in the passages such as: 'It is the Word of the word, the Eye of the eye, the Spirit of the spirit, etc.,' 'The *Brahman* is Knowledge, Bliss,' etc."[33]

The function of Vedic testimony is therefore at once negative and positive. It is apophatic and kataphatic. "The *Śruti* serves only to eliminate the alien attributes superimposed on the *Ātman* [on the absolute Subject of the subject] and never makes known that which is never unknown."[34] But at the very heart and by means of this elimination, it designates and *indicates* (*lakṣayati*) with words the Ineffable that no word can express (*vācayati*).

Since all words emerge from the world of experience, it is clear that it is never according to their direct sense that they can be instruments of such a designation of the metempiricial Transcendent, but either according to their secondary 'exclusive-inclusive' sense (*jahadajahallakṣyārtha*), and therefore by their partial negation (*bhāgalakṣaṇā*), or by their purely negative form, where nothing of what they express can designate the Absolute. Apophatism is therefore inherent in the language of revelation (*Śruti*).

The purely negative descriptions of *Brahman*[35] do not offer any difficulty of interpretation. But to say of *Brahman* that it is 'not this, not this' ('*Neti, neti*')[36] or to say that "the *Ātman* is silence,"[37] is no more than removing the false representations that one has spontaneously made of it. The advantage of this purely negative way (*apavādamārga*) is simply propaedeutic. It is necessary but not sufficient.

Our study must therefore concentrate on the Śaṅkarian interpretation of some Vedic texts whose intention is to designate and indicate positively the very nature of the *Brahman-Ātman*.

5. The Rules of Recourse to the Implied Sense (*lakṣyārtha*)

It is not the syntactic unintelligibility (*na anvayānupapatti*) of these texts that forces the exegete to have recourse to implication, but the unintelligibility of their direct sense (*tātparyānupapatti*).[38]

Grammatically, in effect, these propositions are correct, but the meaning that they offer at first sight is a philosophical nonsense.

For example, the affirmation "*Tattvamasi*" ("That [the total Being] thou art") expresses a relation of identity between 'that' and 'thou' that, for the grammarian, does not present any difficulty. But what intelligibility, in the eyes of the philosopher, could the apparently affirmed identity of the Absolute and the finite individual possibly have? He is therefore forced to consider the context to discover there the general intention and, in this light, to determine that which is really indicated (*lakṣita*) by the direct statement (*Śruti*).

Any reason other than the impossibility of understanding a proposition according to the direct sense of its terms is insufficient to justify recourse to implication. Now, "this must always be justified."[39] For the first rule of the exegete is to keep to the literal (*Śruti*) sense in all the cases where it is possible: "to abandon the direct sense of a word of the revealed text in order to substitute it with an imagined sense is an error of method (*anyāyyatvāt*), unless a higher reason demands it";[40] "every time there is a doubt between the directly expressed meaning (*śruti*) and a simply implied meaning (*lakṣaṇā*), the first ought to be preferred."[41]

Besides, "the secondary senses always depend on the primary sense."[42] The latter therefore always merits attentive consideration and should never be abandoned except when there is no other way.

When the direct sense is impossible, the exegete must allow the context (*prakaraṇa*) to guide him in order to determine according to which of the different possible secondary senses the text must be understood. This rule is traditional in the Mīmāṃsā school[43] and Śaṅkara subscribes to it entirely.[44]

However, the context can be insufficient to clarify the sense of a text. In this case we must refer to the general sense (*artha*) of the doctrine, as it is expressed in the whole section, or even in the ensemble of revealed texts whose unity of meaning is a postulate of Śaṅkarian theology.[45] This rule, equally traditional,[46] is adopted without discussion by Śaṅkara.[47]

In sum, that which must guide above all the work of exegesis is the principle of coherence. Contradiction cannot be maintained in any part of the revealed texts.[48] It is because of this that the elucidation of a particular passage cannot be correct unless it confirms and is confirmed by not only the immediate context but also its extended context, and even the totality of the testimony of the *Śruti*.

6. The Mental Operation Characteristic of Implication

When two contrary facts, related to the same subject, appear to us indubitably as simultaneous, our spirit does not rest until it has discovered a third fact that explains this simultaneity and resolves this contrariety.

For example, corpulence and prolonged fasting are incompatible; if therefore I observe that my neighbour is vigorous even though he always fasts during the day, I am led to postulate that he eats during the night. In the same way, being alive and being absent from every place are incompatible; if therefore, when visiting my neighbour who I know is alive, I do not find him at home, I conclude immediately that he is elsewhere.

These rudimentary examples are traditionally used in the Indian schools to explain this particular source of valid knowledge (*pramāṇa*) that iṣ *arthāpatti*.

The term *arthāpatti* is a composite of *artha* (fact, sense) and *āpatti* (result, conclusion); it means the affirmation of the existence of a fact or of a meaning until then unknown, on the basis of facts or of meanings that are known and mutually contrary, or better, on the basis of the exigence of meaning of these facts or meanings: *arthād arthāpatti*. We can therefore translate it as assumption, postulation, transcendental deduction, as the case may be.

One sees immediately that such a rational operation derives from the principle of non-contradiction. This is because the latter is the law of thought and of being that, faced with incompatible facts, the spirit is legitimately led to posit the existence of a single fact that can reconcile them. This fact may not be easy to determine and error is always possible, but this difficulty cannot invalidate the operation itself, because its legitimacy comes from the principle of non-contradiction that one cannot deny without positing it by that very act.

In its exercise, this operation must conform to the principle of economy and thus postulate nothing that is not strictly needed for reconciling the facts that are apparently contradictory.

The school of the Logicians (Nyāya) claimed to reduce *arthāpatti* to a special form of the Indian syllogism (*anumāna*), i.e., the *vyatireka nyāya* or syllogism by exclusion. According to them, our first example should be expressed thus: daytime fasting and vigorous health exclude one another, unless one eats at night; now my neighbour fasts during the day and is in vigorous health; therefore he eats at night.

But who cannot see that the major of such a syllogism is nothing but an expression of the principle of *arthāpatti* and therefore presupposes it?

Also the school of the Bhāṭṭas, followed again on this point by Śaṅkara, rejects this form of *anumāna* because of its begging of the question.

For the same reason, it rejects also the contrary claim to reduce all *anumāna* to *arthāpatti*. There is no sense in saying, for example, that "to see smoke on the hill and to see no fire there, are incompatible facts, unless there is there an unseen fire," unless one supposes that "wherever there is smoke, there is a fire," which is precisely an expression of the principle of *anumāna*.

Arthāpatti is therefore a mental operation that is perfectly distinct and completely legitimate.[49]

It is traditionally divided into *dṛṣṭārthāpatti* or postulation on the basis of facts of experience (facts that are seen: *dṛṣṭārtha*) and *śrutārthāpatti* or postulation on the basis of oral or written testimony (*śrutārtha*). This second sort of postulation is the only one that interests us here.

The incompatibility that it aims to resolve can be operative in verbal expressions (*abhidāna*) or in the realities that they directly signify (*abhihita*). It is this latter case that is most frequent in the Vedāntic texts.

The *śrutārthāpatti* consists in discovering the hidden sense of an apparently contradictory position by postulating for each of its terms the only secondary sense that allows the reconciliation of all of them, according to their reciprocal or contextual implications.

Its usage is constant in Śaṅkarian exegesis and often explicit.[50]

7. The Exegesis of the Vedāntic Identifications of the Absolute[51]

No word, we have seen, can adequately express the Absolute, but language does possess mysterious powers that allow it to signify it indirectly, to point it to the searcher (*parabrahmabhāvin*). It is thus that the Upaniṣads indicate it by formulas such as: "*Tadeva Brahma iti*," ("This only is *Brahman*, thus"), "*Tadātma iti*" ("This is the *Ātman*, thus"), etc.

"The use of the participle '*iti*' (thus, yes) after the word '*ātman*' means that absolutely speaking the word and the concept '*ātman*' are unable to represent objectively the reality of the *Ātman*."[52] The word '*iti*,' by indicating that the formula is merely analogical, that the Reality intended is merely 'like' (*iti*, thus) what its terms express directly, safeguards us from the illusion of believing that we are dealing here with an adequate expression of the supreme Reality.

The use of different names, i.e., '*Brahman*' and '*Ātman*' is another sign of the transcendence of this Reality and the inability of our concepts to express it directly. It would be an error to rely on their direct sense and to believe that the supreme Reality is twofold like the words that signify it.

"We know that the words *Brahman* and *Ātman* signify one only reality (*sāmānādhikaraṇyāt*)."[53]

"The purpose of all the Upaniṣads is to show that the *Ātman* is not different from the supreme *Brahman* (*ātmanaḥ parabrahmatva*)".[54]

It is by their mutual rapport that the terms '*brahman*' and '*ātman*' require us to pass, by the method of exclusion (*apavāda*), to their implied sense:

"The terms '*ātman*' and '*brahman*' qualify each other, There is no difference between them: the *Ātman* is the *Brahman* and the *Brahman* is the *Ātman*. But the term '*brahman*' excludes the limited self (*ātman*) immersed in the body, [because this finite self is not *great* as the objects signified by the word '*brahman*' which comes from the root *bṛh*, to make grow, to make big], and the term '*ātman*' excludes the sun and other manifestations which, [because of their *greatness*,] are contemplated as *brahman*; [it excludes them because they are not *conscious* like the objects signified by the word *ātman*, i.e., self, spiritual principle]. It is thus that is established the idea that *Brahman* is the Self of all, Vaiśvānara, and our Self."[55]

The Upaniṣads indicate to us this absolute unity of the *Brahman* and the *Ātman* (*Brahmātmaikatva*) by means of identifying formulas such as "*Tattvamasi*" (That thou art),[56]

"*Ahaṁbrahmāsmi*" (I am *Brahman*),[57] "*Etadātmā Brahma iti*" (This *Ātman* is the *Brahman*, thus),[58] etc. They must be understood like any other proposition of identification of the type "This is that Devadatta."

In the *Chānd. Up*., Uddālaka, the father of Śvetaketu, leads his son, by a series of progressive but inadequate identifications, to the true identification of the Absolute, which he expresses in these terms: "Now, that which is the most subtle essence, in which all this finds its Self (*ātman*); that is the true Reality (*satyam*); that is the Self (*ātman*); *that thou art*, O Śvetaketu."[59]

It is by referring to the context and to parallel passages that Śaṅkara explains this proposition: "That thou art (*Tattvamasi*)."

"The term 'that'," he writes, "means that which in the immediate context has been called Being (*sadākhya*), the most subtle essence (*aṇimāṇubhāva*), the root of the world (*jagato mūlam*). The world, because it is *sadātmā*, i.e., because it has Being like the *Ātman*, [as the supreme conscious principle], is *aitādātmya*, i.e., identical with that, [excluding, naturally, its finitude and its imperfections], and "has no other Witness than that."[60] This cause (*kāraṇa*) of the world is true, absolutely real (*paramārthasat*). It is, in fact, as pure Reality alone (*vastumātrarūpeṇa hi*) that it includes all the differentiated realities of the world (*viśeṣaṇāni vyāpnoti*). It is when it is perceived thus in its proper form of Reality (*evaṁ... svena vasturūpeṇa gṛhyamāno*) that it becomes total (*kṛtsno... bhavati*)."[61]

"It is because of this that it is in fact the *Ātman* of the world, i.e., its own most intimate form (*pratyakṣasvarūpam*), its reality itself (*satattvam*), its truth (*yāthātmya*). In fact, the term *ātman* without any qualifying prefix is dedicated by usage (*nirūḍhatvāt*) to express the deepest self (*pratyagātmani*)."[62]

One sees here how the implication (*lakṣaṇā*) required by the context for the understanding of the proposition "*Tattvamasi*" excludes (*jahat*) from the term '*tat*,' and from the term '*ātman*' that it replaces, all the imperfect connotations that are inherent to them in ordinary usage and includes (*ajahad*), while elevating to the absolute, the essential notion represented by these terms.

In the same way, the term 'thou' (*tvam*) must be purified and elevated to the absolute degree. "It designates directly the individual (Śvetaketu) who, although he is qualified to listen [to the Veda], pondering [its sense] and awaiting the knowledge [perfect and intuitive], had not, till he was instructed by his father, apprehended the true nature of his own Self, as Being, Self of all, distinct from all the aggregates of causes and effects, (that is to say, from bodies and senses), which are merely its reflections. Now, instead, enlightened by his father, he has understood by means of the teaching '*Tattvamasi*' that 'I am Being itself'.... Because the result effected by this proposition is the exclusion of the idea that the Self is the [finite self] that acts and enjoys. This exclusion is accomplished by the proposition by the mere fact that the two notions [of the perfect Self and of the self implied in empirical action] are contradictory."[63]

We have seen, in fact, that it is only the impossibility of the direct meaning of the terms that forces us to have recourse to their indirect signification. Now it is clear that if the proposition "*Tattvamasi*" were to be understood in its primary sense to mean: "You, Śvetaketu, son of Uddālaka, as such, you are that, the Absolute of the world," we would be reduced to absurdity. In order to really understand it, we should therefore, through an *arthāpatti*, determine the implied sense and understand it in the following way: "*That*, i.e., the world in its true reality, i.e., as seen in its Cause which is the absolutely perfect Reality of its reality, *you*, i.e., the infinitely perfect and spiritual Absolute of this self that you know yourself to be, *you are that*," or, in other words: "The Absolute transcendent and immanent to the objective world and the Absolute transcendent and immanent to the subject are the same true Absolute."

It remains to determine the meaning of the verb 'are' (*asi*).

> Should we not say that it means a simple fictitious attribution destined to orient anagogically the meditation (*sampad*), as in the proposition: 'The sun is the *brahman*'?
>
> *Response*:—No, because the proposition '*Tattvamasi*' is entirely different (*vākyavailakṣaṇyāt*) from the propositions like 'the sun is the *brahman*.' In the latter, because of the particle '*iti*' (thus) with which it ends, the brahmanity or absoluteness in the direct sense of the term (*sākṣātbrahmatva*) is not taught (*na gamyate*), because the sun is a sensible form, etc.... while, [in our proposition,] the fact that the Thou is the *Ātman* of being (*sadātmabhāva*) is declared without any restriction (*niraṅkuśam*; note, in fact, the absence of the participle '*iti*' in '*Tattvamasi*').[64]

Objection:—This assertion can be metaphorical (*gauṇa*) as in the expression: 'You are a lion'...

Response:—No, because all metaphorical contemplation (*upacāravijñāna*) is illusory (*mṛṣātvāt*). Now, here, [in the section to which our text belongs,] it is first taught, by the examples of the clay, fire, etc., that the true Real (*satyam*) is Being, one, without a second (*sadekamevādvitīyam satyamityupadeśāt*), and then that from this knowledge comes deliverance (*mokṣa*), and this cannot be true if the declaration of identity were metaphorical and therefore false.

Obj.—The phrase could be nothing but an eulogy (*stuti*).

Resp.—No, for, on the one hand, Śvetaketu is not an object of adoration (*anupāṣyatvāt*) and, on the other hand, it is not praise of Being to declare it identical to Śvetaketu. One does not praise a king by calling him a servant. It is not appropriate to restrict to one sole point the Being that is the *Ātman* of all, because that would be like saying to an emperor that he is lord of a village.

Apart from these three ways, there is no other way of interpreting the proposition, except to declare the identity of 'Thou' with the 'Self' of Being.

Besides, if the object of this text were merely an anagogical meditation, the literal sense of other texts would be equally impossible, texts which declare that 'he who has a master, knows,' that 'the delay for him is merely so much,' etc.[65] ... Now, all the propositions of the Upaniṣads are subordinate to the teaching of this particular proposition (*sarvopaniṣadvākyānām tatparatayaivopekṣayāt*).

Obj.—But if the *Ātman* is Being, how is it that one does not know one's own self (*Ātman*)?

Resp.—This does not affect our position at all. The animate beings (*prāṇa*) are not aware at all that they are a vital entity (*jīva*), an active and passive principle, distinct from the composite of body and senses. How can they in these conditions realize that their *Ātman* is Being itself? ...[66]

It follows from all this that what the proposition does is to deny that the notion of *ātman* corresponds to that vital self (*jīva*) that is merely a product, unreal [because it is not real in the absolute sense of the word] and qualified [to carry out the rites].[67]

The development of the exegesis of this text, which he considers the heart of the Upaniṣads, has shown Śaṅkara very conscious of his method of interpretation by *jahadajahallakṣaṇā* (implication at once exclusive and inclusive of the primary sense) or, according to the terminology of his disciple Sadānanda, by *bhāgalakṣaṇā* (indication by a part [*bhāga*] only of the primary sense).[68]

This method makes the mind pass through three phases:

1) a phase of still confused affirmation (*adhyāropa*); the proposition presents the positive notions directly signified by its

terms, at the same time that there appears the impossibility of retaining entirely this direct signification;

2) a phase of negation (*apavāda*), during which the finite and imperfect mode according to which these notions are realised by their primary objects is definitively excluded ('*neti neti*': it is not thus, it is not thus);

3) a phase of elevating transmutation (*lakṣaṇā*) which results in affirming the perfect identity in a single subject of the notions expressed by the terms, but this time according to the supreme mode of actuation which is proper to them in this absolutely perfect subject.

The implication which allows this correct understanding of a proposition such as "*Tattvamasi*" does not therefore reject the notions themselves expressed by the direct sense of its terms; consequently, it is not a *jahallakṣaṇā*; but it cannot however conserve them according to the same mode signified by this direct expression, because their perfect identity would be thus impossible: consequently neither is it an *ajahallakṣaṇā*. It is therefore a question of *jahadajahallakṣaṇā* or *bhāgalakṣaṇā*, since on the one hand, from the ensemble of the primary sense of the terms, something is retained (*ajahad*), that is to say, the very ideas which they express, and, on the other hand, something is rejected (*jahad*), that is to say, the imperfect mode according to which they express them.

Such an implication does not result in rendering the proposition tautological, because tautology supposes the identity of the direct sense of the terms of a proposition. Now, in our case, there is a conflict between the terms thus understood and it is only in overcoming this conflict by recourse to their indirect sense that the mind can accept the perfect identity that the proposition affirms.[69]

Rāmānuja, the foremost adversary of Śaṅkarian non-dualism, has brought out well this method of *jahadajahallakṣaṇā* and, before rejecting it (mistakenly, we think), has given an excellent resumé that confirms our explanations.[70]

The disciples of Śaṅkara have generally understood this method as we have done. However Prakāśātman in his *Vivaraṇa* and Sarvajñātma Muni on many occasions have proposed a different explanation.[71] On the other hand, Sureśvarānanda in his *Vārttika* and Sarvajñātma Muni in his *Saṅkṣepaśārīraka* 1, 169, support exclusive implication (*jahallakṣaṇā*), in keeping with their personal theory according to which the *Ātman* is believed to be identical to Ignorance (*avidyā*), which, clearly, is not good Śaṅkarian orthodoxy.

Finally, a late Advaitin, Dharmarāja, claims that "the exegesis by implication that the Master has done of the text '*Tattvamasi*' must be understood as a purely accommodating explanation (*abhyupagamavādena*)."[72] But he is aware of the novelty of his interpretation[73] that depends on a not very felicitous modification that he has made to the classic theory of the semantic polyvalence of words.

8. The Exegesis of the Vedāntic Definitions (*lakṣaṇa*) of the Absolute

"The intention of the texts of Vedānta is twofold: some aim to make known the true nature of the supreme Self, [these are its definitions: *lakṣaṇa*,] others to teach the unity of the supreme Self and the [absolute] Self of knowledge (*vijñānātmanaḥ paramātmaikatva*)."[74]

Before explaining the proposition "*Tattvamasi*" which is of the second type, let us explain the principal examples of the first type.

The term '*lakṣaṇa*' and the term '*lakṣaṇā*' are visibly related. They come from the same root which means: to show, indicate, designate. The first means: direct indication, definition; the second: indirect indication, determination by the implied sense.

There are two types of definition (*lakṣaṇa*):

1) *svarūpalakṣaṇa*, definition by the proper form of the object to be defined; this is also called *viseṣalakṣaṇa*, because it defines the object by establishing its specific attributes. We will see that, from this point of view, it is of two types.

2) *taṭasthalakṣaṇa*, definition of the object by reference to something that is not essential to it but neutral or alien (*taṭa*); it is also called *upalakṣaṇa*, because it defines its object by relating it to fictitious or accidental attributes (*upādhis*). .

For example, to define someone as the son or brother or friend of such a one, is to supply a valid indication about him and is often sufficient in practice, even when this rapport of relationship or friendship is accidental to him and does not define by his personal essence. Even to define a man as a magician, or an object as the cause of such an illusion, is to define them extrinsically (*taṭa*), by their imagined rapport to a purely fictitious effect (*upādhi*) that one mistakenly attributes to them, and yet such a definition is valid since it allows us to recognize clearly the man or the object in question.

The first type of definition, the *svarūpa* or *viśeṣalakṣaṇa*, is of two sorts:

a) The first is of the type: "This is a blue lotus." This is the definition by genus and specific difference. It implies a real complexity in the object that is the basis of this distinction between genus and specific difference.[75] The rapport that, in this type of definition, unites the attributes to the substantive, is not therefore pure identity but a qualified identity that manifests a relation of subordination of the specific difference to the genus.

b) The second is *nirapekṣa*, non-relational, because it excludes such a relation. It is also called *akhaṇḍārthaka*, because it has for object (*artha*) a simple being, absolutely without distinction (*akhaṇḍa*).

Despite its appearance, it is not a definition by genus and specific difference, because simple Being is beyond such a distinction. It would be therefore erroneous to take it literally; one must, on the contrary, strive to discover the only sense possible which is implied (*lakṣya*) by the ensemble of its terms. The simple Being, in fact, cannot be expressed directly by a chain of subordinate concepts, but only indicated, indirectly signified, by a series of coordinated concepts. Every one of its concepts must be represented entirely since partial representation of a being without parts and without essential distinction (*akhaṇḍa*) can only indicate an error. On the other hand, the poverty and the inadequateness inherent in every conceptual representation of perfect Being forces us to multiply its concepts in such a way that, multiplying our conceptual aims we succeed in converging in some way on the inexpressible riches of the pure Perfection.

At the beginning of the *Vedāntasūtra*, the *Brahman* is defined by a *taṭastha* or *upalakṣaṇa* like "That from which [proceed] the origin, [the subsistence and the dissolution] of this [world]."[76]

Śaṅkara transforms this extrinsic definition into a *svarūpalakṣaṇa*, commenting on it thus: "This omniscient and all-powerful Cause from which, etc."[77] This transformation is legitimate because this *sūtra* is a direct recall of *Taitt. Up*. 3, 1 whose immediate context (especially 3, 6) supplies the elements of this intrinsic definition; further, similar Vedāntic passages confirm it as well-founded.

It is by the method of exclusive-inclusive implication (*jahadajahallakṣaṇā*) that we must elucidate the definition thus transformed.

The terms of the primitive formula suffice to indicate quite exactly the supreme Being but not to define it, properly speaking, since they designate it as the total Cause of the world, which it is not necessarily and by nature. The terms added by Śaṅkara indicate on the contrary its true nature and allow us to attain the true sense implied by the complete definition. They indicate in fact an Absolute of knowledge and of power that cannot but be independent of the fact that it posits or does not posit in being a reality even as imposing as our universe. This fact is neutral (*taṭa*) or inessential to the nature of this Absolute, because the creation of a necessarily limited effect such as this universe cannot condition perfect omniscience and omnipotence.

In order to understand this definition, we must therefore negate as inessential the creative relation that it seems to affirm as essential, (this is the phase of *apávāda* or negation), then elevate to the supreme degree the notions of knowledge and power that its terms directly denote and identify them in the absolute.

The object of such a definition is not therefore to teach us that the *Brahman* is the Creator of the universe, but to indicate to us its true essential nature. "All the passages," Śaṅkara says to us, "that concern the creation of the world, have only a single aim, to make us know *Brahman*."[78] "The essential object of such passages is to propose to us knowledge of the *Ātman*; they are therefore merely *arthavāda*, i.e., passages subordinate to the 'great sayings' (*mahāvākyāni*)... because no fruit [such as *mokṣa* or final deliverance] can be drawn from the knowledge of the fact or of the details regarding creation."[79] "If one were to take literally the Vedic accounts of creation, one would fall into contradiction. For it is said, for example, that the Lord meditates, although he has no internal sense (*manas*), that he creates, although there is no previous material, that he draws man from the water and fashions him, that he enters into the cranium, etc."[80] "Further, these accounts do not agree among themselves about the order of the things created. But they agree about the Creator. They describe him consistently as omniscient, Lord of all, Self (*Ātman*) of all, without a second."[81]

The text: "Now his name: Reality of reality (*satyasya satyam*)"[82] is equally a *svarūpalakṣaṇa* constituted on the basis of a *taṭasthalakṣaṇa*. In effect, according to the explanations of Śaṅkara, to name the *Brahman* Reality of reality, is to make him known in relation to his two forms, his subtle form (*amūrta*), i.e., his proper essence, and his gross form (*mūrta*), (i.e., his form reflected in his effects), which constitutes the world with the five elements and their modifications, etc. "It is because of their relative reality that the elements and their modifications are called 'reality' (*satyam*), but what the text signifies is that through this relative reality the knowledge of the absolute Reality is attained."[83] It is in fact by starting from our empirical knowledge of the realities of this world that we can make for ourselves an approximate idea of the absolute Reality. Such an idea or representation is principally negative and we observe in fact that "it is by elimination of these *upādhis* [called 'reality'] that the *Śruti* means to define negatively the nature of *Brahman*, repeating: '*neti neti*' (not thus, not thus)."[84]

The definition of *Brahman* as "the internal Moderator (*Antaryāmin*) of the earth, of water, etc., [i.e., of the five elements and their modifications, that constitute the universe], your own immortal *Ātman*,"[85] is of the same type as the preceding and must be interpreted according to the same method, considering as an *upādhi* to be excluded from the essence of *Brahman* its expressed relation to the world and to the 'I.' His immediate context, as Śaṅkara explains, leads us in fact to use this *jahadajahallakṣaṇā*: "It is never seen by the eyes of the body, but, being immanent to the eye as the essence of sight (*dṛṣisvarūpa*), it is the Witness. It is never heard, but being the power of hearing that never fails (*aluptaśravaṇaśakti*), it is the Hearer immanent in every ear. It is never thought (*amata*), but it is the Thinker, the power of thinking that never fails (*aluptamananaśakti*) and it is immanent to all the organs of thought (*manas*). It is never known, apprehended in a definite manner like colour, pleasure, etc., but it is the One that knows, the power of knowing that never fails, and it is immanent in all intelligences."[86]

The definition: "It being only, one, without a second (*Sadeva... ekamadvitīyam*)"[87] also calls for a purification and an elevation of its terms in order to be correctly understood.

According to its direct sense, the term *ekam* (one) intends to say: first in the series of numbers. Here, its modification by the restrictive particle '*eva*' (only) and its connection with the purely negative term '*advitīyam*' (non-dual) as well as the seemingly restrictive term '*sadeva*' (being only), should lead us to abandon partially this direct sense so as to understand '*ekam*' of the Being that is outside all series and transcends all numeric qualification. "What we learn from this text," writes Śaṅkara, "is that Being really cannot be reduced to numeric qualification, and it expresses itself in this manner only because it refers to the notions of being, unity and non-duality which its context proceeds to discuss."[88]

Śaṅkara's conclusion is that "since the element common to all these definitions of *Brahman* is pure consciousness (*cinmātra*),[89] it is understood that the proper essence of *Brahman* is consciousness (*citsvarūpatā*) and it is thus that all these definitions state one and the same thing (*iti... ekavākyatā*)."[90]

We pass now to the elucidation of a proper definition or *svarūpalakṣaṇa* of *Brahman*, that of *Taitt. Up.*: "*Satyam, jñānamanantam brahma*" ("The *Brahman* is Reality, Knowledge, Infinite").[91]

Although it is a matter of *svarūpa* and *viśeṣa*, i.e., although it defines *Brahman* by the attributes that constitute its own essence, it nonetheless requires in its turn the purification that must remove from its terms their natural reference to *upādhis* that, for us, serve as their basis (it is in fact a non-relational definition, *nirapekṣa*) and the elevation that must change their proper mode into that of the object that they mean to define (because this object is *akhaṇḍa*, absolutely simple).

Let us listen to Śaṅkara explaining to us how the connection of the terms of this definition makes us pass by the negative way to the true meaning that they imply:

> In this definition of *Brahman*, the three words '*satyam*,' '*jñānam*,' '*anantam*' state the specific attributes (*viśeṣaṇārthāni*) of the substantive (*viśeṣyasya*) *Brahman*.... Thus differentiated by these words, the *Brahman* is distinguished from all other substantives. [It is thus a definition, because,] in effect, it is when a thing is known in this way that it is distinguished from all other things, as when we speak of 'a big, blue, sweet-smelling lotus.'
>
> *Obj.*—A substantive cannot be specified by an attribute unless it can be specified equally by an attribute that is quite different, as for example the lotus which can be pink or blue or of some other colour. It is only when there are many substances belonging to the same genus and each can be distinguished by a distinct attribute that such attributes have a sense, but not when there is only a single thing, unique in its genus, because such a thing cannot be specified by another attribute. Now, just as there is only one sun that we see, so also there is only one *Brahman*; there are no other *Brahmans* by which it can be distinguished. This case is therefore not similar to that of the blue lotus. [The objection amounts to saying therefore that there is only one type of definition properly speaking, the one by genus and specific difference, and that consequently *Brahman* cannot be defined, because it is unique and does not fall under any genus.]
>
> *Resp.*—No, [it is a question here of a definition of *Brahman*], because these epithets are destined [by the *Śruti*] to define it. Your objection does not apply therefore to this case.
>
> *Obj.*—Why?
>
> *Resp.*—Because the principal object of these attributes is to define *Brahman*, and not simply to state its distinctive qualities.
>
> *Obj.*—What is the difference between definition and object defined, on the one hand, and specific attributes and specified object on the other?
>
> *Resp.*—We will explain it to you. The specific attributes can distinguish an object only from other objects that belong to the same genus (*samānajātiyebhya eva*), whereas a definition aims at distinguishing a thing from all other things (*sarvata eva*), as when we say that '*ākāśa* is the mother-substance of space.' [The general notion of definition extends thus to other cases than the more particular notion of definition by genus and specific difference.] And we have said that the proposition '*satyam*, etc.' is destined to define [the *Brahman*, therefore to distinguish it from all else].
>
> [But what is therefore the syntactic situation of the terms of this definition?]
>
> The words '*satyam*,' etc. are not subordinated among themselves (*na parasparaṁ saṁbadhyante*) because they are destined to define something else [i.e., the *Brahman*, and not a genus, as in the case of the proposition: 'this is a blue lotus,' where the qualifier 'blue' is subordinated to the generic substantive 'lotus,' which it specifies].

Consequently, each of these attributive terms is independent of the others and relates directly to *Brahman*, in the following fashion: *Brahman* is Reality, *Brahman* is Knowledge, *Brahman* is Infinite." [As we have said earlier, this is the only way that the attributes can relate to the subject in an *akhaṇḍārthaka* and *nirapekṣa lakṣaṇa*, i.e., in a definition which does not involve a relation (*nirapekṣa*) among its attributes, because its subject is not intrinsically composite (*akhaṇḍa*)].

Let us come to the meaning of '*satyam.*'

That whose essence, i.e., the form that allows knowledge of it, does not change, that is '*satyam*' (true, real, from which real as such, true reality). Its opposite is '*anṛtam*' (not-true, not-real, false). The mutability implies therefore falsity, unreality.... It is thus established that '*satyam*' means '*sadeva*' (being only), and the expression '*satyam... brahma*' thus distinguishes the *Brahman* from all changing things (*vikārānnivartayati*).

Obj.—But it follows from this that the *Brahman* is the primordial causal substance (*pradhāna*), and thus the creative agent (*kartṛ*), and that therefore it is a thing (*vastutvāt*), it is bereft of intelligence (*acidrūpatā ca*), as the clay [which is the material cause (*pradhāna*) of the jars and other objects of pottery].

Resp.—It is to respond to this objection that it is said that '*Brahman* is Knowledge (*... jñānam... brahma*)'.

The term '*jñānam*' signifies act of knowing (*jñāpti*), consciousness (*avabodha*). It means the ontological perfection (*bhāvasādhana*) [of knowing], and not the fact of being the author of acts of knowing (*na tu jñāṇakartṛ*). In effect, it is the correlation between the terms '*satyam*' and '*anantam*' that determines the *Brahman*, and the true reality and infinity are incompatible with the fact of being the author of acts of knowing. For, being the subject of change by fact of being the author of acts of knowing, how could [the *Brahman*] be the true Reality and the Infinite? That, in effect, is infinite that cannot be divided into anything else, and, if the *Brahman* is a knower, it is divided into act of knowing and the known, and cannot be infinite....

Obj.—But when we say that the *Brahman* is knowledge, that means that it is finite, because we find that all knowing in this world is finite.

Resp.—It is to respond to this objection that it is said that '*Brahman* is infinite.'

Obj.—One may object that, since [as it appears from your explanations] the terms '*satyam*, etc.' are used with the sole aim of denying the attribution of [their contraries] '*anṛtam*, etc.' to *Brahman* which is their subject, they do not make it known like [the definitions which we admit make known] the lotus, etc. Consequently, the proposition '*satyam*, etc.' is as void of sense (*śūnyārtha*) as the following phrase: 'Having bathed in the water of a mirage and crowned with a garland of celestial flowers, this son of a sterile woman goes out, armed with a bow made of the horn of a hare.' [The objection amounts to saying that only the definition by genus and specific difference is admissible, because, beyond it, one is reduced to using propositions so apophatic that they say nothing about the object to be defined and cannot therefore claim the title of definitions.]

Resp.—No, because the proposition '*satyam*, etc.' is a definition. We have already said that despite the fact that they are determinatives, the terms '*satyam*, etc.' are meant to define *Brahman*. On the other hand, it is only when the object to be defined is inexistent (*śūnye hi lakṣye*) that the definition is void of sense (*anārthakam*). Consequently, since this proposition is meant to be a definition, we believe it is not void of sense.

[And here is how this is possible:] while they differentiate [their subject from all that is not that subject], the terms '*satyam*, etc.' preserve their own sense (*svārtha*), [they are not therefore purely negative], because when they are totally void of sense [words] cannot determine (*niyantṛtva*) [a subject]. But, if these terms preserve their proper sense, they are capable by this sense of determining (*niyantṛtva*) their subject *Brahman*, [by distinguishing it] from all other subjects whose attributes are incompatible with their proper sense. [The sense of the terms of the proposition is therefore *ajahad* (inclusive), since they retain the essential notion expressed by their primary sense. However, it is also *jahad* (exclusive), because, according to the doctrine of the preceding paragraphs, their coordination itself excludes from each of them the imperfect mode inherent in their primary sense.]

Further, the word '*Brahman*' [that designates the subject] is equally meaningful by its own sense. The word '*anantam*' [which is purely negative] specifies it by denying of it all finitude. But the words '*satyam*' and '*jñānam*' determine it in virtue of their proper sense [which is positive]. [This explanation makes precise the contribution of each of the terms to the positive whole that constitutes the teaching of the proposition, in showing how, by its mere presence, the term '*Brahman*' transforms them, without making them lose their original signification. The objections that follow allow Śaṅkara to explicitate further the positive information that the definition supplies.]

Obj.—Against the interpretation of '*jñānam*' as 'pure Knowledge,' one can object that, since it is clear from other texts of the *Śruti* that the *Brahman* is the very essence of the knower (*vedituḥ svarūpaṁ brahma*), we must say that it posits acts of knowing (*ātmā jñāteti prasiddham*).... It is thus false to say that the *Brahman* is the Knower (*jñāptirbrahmetyayuktam*) since it is the agent of knowing. But efficient causality implies impermanence [because it implies an essential relation to the effect, and thus an ontological dependence].

And suppose that the word '*jñānam*' understood in the sense of 'act of Knowing' (*jñāpti*) expresses the ontological form (*bhāvarūpatā*) of *Brahman*, in this case also it follows that it is impermanent and dependent, because the products depend on their makers (*dhātvarthānām kārakāpekṣatvāt*) and that knowledge [which you say that *Brahman* is,] is a product (*jñānam ca dhātvarthaḥ*)....

Resp.—This objection is faulty because it [knowledge] is called a product only after a manner of speaking (*kāryakopacārāt*) when in fact it does not exist apart from the essence (*svarūpavyatirekena*) [of the Self]; [it is, in effect, this essence itself, and not an accidental attribute]. Knowledge, being the very essence of the Self, is not distant from it (*na tato vyatiricyate*); that is why it is permanent.

Obj.—However, the transformations (*pariṇāminyāḥ*) which are characteristic (*lakṣaṇāyāḥ*) of the ***upādhi buddhi***, i.e., of intelligence as a faculty, while it undergoes the action of sight and of the other senses which present it with sensible objects (*cakṣurādidvarairviṣayakāreṇa*), and that are manifested by signs such as words, etc., are objectifications of the consciousness of the self (*te ātmavijñānasya viṣayabhūta utpadyamānā eva*) and are all impregnated by this consciousness of the self (*ātmavijñānena vyāptā utpadyante*). Consequently, as appearances or manifestations of the consciousness of the self, and expressed by the word '*vijñāna*' (differentiated knowledge), they are merely effects of the self (*dhātvarthabhūtā ātmano eva*), its properties (*dharmāḥ*), the forms of its development (*vikriyārūpāḥ*).

Resp.—This is what the ignorant imagine. But the consciousness of *Brahman* is as inseparable from its essence (*brahmasvarūpāvyatiriktam*) as the light is from the sun and the heat from the fire. It is truly its essence (*svarūpameva tat*). It does not depend on any other cause because its own essence is eternal.

Because it transcends all conditions (*sarvabhāvānām ca tena vibhakta*) of space and time, and is itself the Cause of space, time, etc., and in virtue of its extreme subtleness (spirituality), nothing is different from it (*na tasyānyad*), nothing is unknown, nothing is far from it (*viprakṛṣṭam*) in the past as in the present and the future.

That is why the *Brahman* is omniscient, as is said in *Śvet. Up*. 3, 19, and, according to another revealed text (*Śruti*), 'the Knowledge of the Knower is without intermittence (*viparilopa*) because it is indestructible (*avināśitvāt*) since they do not constitute a pair (*na tu taddvitīyamasti*).' Consequently, since the proper essence of the Knower is not a thing apart [from itself] and since it does not depend on efficient causes, etc., it is established that *Brahman* is permanent, even though its essence is Knowledge, and [it is established that] the Knowledge is not a product (*dhātu*), because its nature is not an operation (*tadkriyārūpatvāt*), and, at the same time, it does not signify 'agent of knowledge.'

That is why the *Brahman* is not expressed directly (*vācyam*) by the word '*jñānam*,' and yet, by this word that expresses originally its reflection (*tadavabhāsavācakena*), i.e., the attribute of intelligence presented as an object (*buddhidharmaviṣayeṇa*), it is signified indirectly (*tallakṣyate*) but not directly expressed (*na tūcyate*). [And, if it is not directly expressed,] it is because it is bereft of attributes, such as genus (*jāti*), etc., [i.e., quality, action, relation,] which are the basis of the usage of the words (*śabdapravṛttihetu*).

In the same way also, [it is signified indirectly, and not expressed directly] by the word '*satyam*,' because the proper form of *Brahman* is bereft of all internal distinction. By the expression '*satyam... brahma* (the *Brahman* is Reality),' it is signified indirectly (*lakṣyate*) by means of the word '*satyam*' whose primary object is the universal '*sattā*,' i.e., the existence common to all external things (*bāhyasattāsāmānyaviṣayeṇa satyaśabdena*). But the *Brahman* is not expressed directly (*vācyam*) by the word '*satyam*.'

Thus, by the fact of their mutual coordination (*itaretarasaṁnidhānāt*), the words '*satyam*, etc.' determine one another (*anyonyaniyamyaniyāmakāḥ santaḥ*) and it is in virtue of this active and passive determination that they exclude the primary sense expressed by the words '*satyam*, etc.' (*satyādiśabdavācyāttānnivartakaḥ*) and take on the secondary sense that indirectly defines *Bràhman* (*brahmano lakṣaṇārthaśca bhavantīti*).

Thus is safeguarded the ineffability of *Brahman* (*avācyatvam*) in accord with the *Śruti*[92] and the impossibility of expressing it directly by a proposition (*avākyārthatvam ca*) of the type: 'this is a blue lotus'.[93]

In his sub-commentary, Sāyaṇa takes up once again this doctrine of the definition of *Brahman* by the secondary sense of words:

"The terms of this definition," he writes, "while conserving their essential signification, arrive at indicating the nature of the Supreme while excluding [from their primary sense] all that is alien to that nature and rejecting thus the ignorance that is the root of all illusions. 'Reality' and the other words employed here have a particular sense only in the measure that they serve to eliminate particular notions, such as 'unreality.' And once this elimination has taken place, each of these words indicate only the essential nature of *Brahman* which is not therefore a complex thing, expressible (*vākya*) by a combination of words related among themselves."

Sāyaṇa goes on to explain the secondary semantic power of a definition of the type studied:

"Although," he says, "the relation subject-attributes that the definition contains explicitly is not real, nonetheless it makes us enter into the knowledge of the true nature of *Brahman*, in the same way that a reflection, although false in itself, leads us to the knowledge of the real object, or a dream in which we see a feminine figure is a sign that something good is going to come to us. And it is in the measure that the triple attribute ['*satyam*, etc.'] procures for us a true knowledge of the real nature of *Brahman* that it constitutes a definition of *Brahman*."

Further, Sāyaṇa and Ānandagiri remark, in their sub-commentaries on this text of the *Taitt. Up*. 2, 1, that the cause of the *arthāpatti*, thanks to which we discover the implied sense of the terms of the definition, is the incompatibility of the direct sense of these terms '*satyam*, etc.' with the nature of the subject to be defined, such as is manifested by their immediate context and the whole of the teaching of the *Śruti*.

The commentary of Śaṅkara and the sub-commentaries of his disciples have therefore allowed us to retrieve, but from the text this time, all the essential notions which we had first studied abstractly while exposing the theory of the semantic polyvalence of words. It is clear that this theory is central to the theology of Śaṅkara, who applies it uniformly in his exegesis of all the 'great sayings' (*mahāvākyāni*) of the *Śruti*.

"It is," writes Sāyaṇa, "according to the principle that has been adopted in the elucidation of the proposition '*Brahman* is Reality, etc.' that we must construct, as each forming an independent definition, expressions such as: '*Brahman* is Knowledge and Bliss,'[94] 'Self-luminous (*svayaṁ-jyotiḥ*),'[95] 'The Beyond is Fullness (*pūrṇamadaḥ*),'[96] etc. Consequently, it is under this relationship [i.e., the function common to them of defining *Brahman*,] that we must unify the terms 'Bliss,' etc., and consider them together, according to the rule established in the *Vedāntasūtra* 3, 3, 11-13."

"It is because the common illusions concerning the nature of *Brahman* are many and must all be rejected, that its definitions are also many. [We have also seen that its definition in *Taitt. Up.* 2, 1 makes use of three terms in place of one so as to eliminate the false representations of *Brahman* that objections raised in the commentary have detailed, and that one term alone would not have been able to destroy them all.] But it does not follow that the *Brahman* is of different species. It is in fact as undifferentiated (*nirviśeṣa*) that all these definitions designate it in the last analysis."[97]

On the subject of these different definitions Śaṅkara repeats, for his part, that they are capable of indicating, of signifying indirectly the *Brahman*, but incapable of representing it directly by the primary sense of its terms (*tallakṣyate na tūcyate*):

"Of this Self-Bliss, completely undifferentiated and absolutely one, as *Taitt. Up*. 2, 8 has defined it, 'all words recede without having attained it,' that is to say, all words, all designations (*abhidhānāni*) whose objects are only representable things (*savikalpavastuviṣayāṇi*), such as substances (*dravya*), etc., although they are also employed by the Masters (*prayoktṛbhiḥ*) in the teaching of the undifferentiated and one

Brahman, in view of manifesting it (*prakāśanāya*), [and rightly so,] because to it also applies the universal notion of 'being something' (*vastusāmānyāt*), [all words, says Scripture,] recede without having attained it, that is to say, are incapable of representing it clearly (*aprakāśya*), they lose their own power (*svasamarthyāddhīyante*)."[98] And they should lose it, because, explains Sāyaṇa, the idea of a word engenders in the mind a form, a representation, and cannot therefore attain *Brahman* that is nothing but consciousness [without forms]." If therefore we can define the Absolute in some way, it still remains always ineffable.

9. Conclusion

Having wanted to present only an objective exposition of the Indian theory of the semantic polyvalence of words and Śaṅkara's use of it in his Vedic theology, we have not made a comparative study. But our readers who are more familiar with the medieval theory, and especially the Thomist theory of the univocal, analogical and equivocal senses of words and the role that it plays in Christian theology, will themselves make the necessary comparisons.

The problem that we placed before ourselves was to find out how a *Brahmajijñāsā*, i.e., a quest of the Absolute that was also an intellectual inquiry and a conversion and a transformation of the whole man, was compatible with a doctrine that affirms that the Absolute is the only Real in the supreme sense of the word and its Knowledge the only truth, while it considers every changing being as un-Real and all complex knowledge as non-Knowledge (*ajñāna*). It seems, in effect, that, if it is thus, there is no means, not even the *Śruti*, of passing from non-Knowledge to absolute Knowledge. For all teachings, including those of *Śruti*, are of the same type as those of our finite knowledge.

Besides the doctrine of transcendental illumination and that of the transcendental analysis of knowing that we have not been able to expose, the doctrine of the secondary powers of words that Śaṅkara has exposed and used in his commentaries contributes a quasi-solution to our problem.

It shows, in effect, how the *Śruti*, whose infallibility is affirmed by faith, can confer on words that it uses to indicate the absolute Real a superhuman power, or more exactly, if we permit the expression, a 'meta-verbal.' power. Doubtless, it is of the nature of language to possess powers of suggestion and of indication that go beyond its immediate power, but it is because it is infallible that *Śruti* guarantees the truth of a verbal definition of the Absolute based on these secondary powers of language. Of itself, language can merely aim approximately at such a high object. The power of signifying comes to it, in truth, from elsewhere, and it is because of this that we call it 'meta-verbal.'

One could ask whether there is really need of an infallible revelation to confer on language this power of faithfully signifying the true nature of the Absolute, but Śaṅkara always holds that the *Śruti* is the sole source of valid knowledge concerning the Absolute.

We have said that this theory contributes only a quasi-solution to our problem. The theological knowledge that it allows us to acquire remains in effect notional and therefore complex. As such, it is far from being equivalent to Knowledge itself and one cannot call it knowledge in the supreme sense of the term. The disciple who has obtained it has not yet therefore emerged from Ignorance.

Attentive to this difficulty, Śaṅkara, following the Upaniṣads, proposes for him a method of recollection and prolonged meditation, inspired by Yoga, which should normally allow him to attain the direct intuition (*sākṣātkāra*) of that which he as yet knows only conceptually. This intuition, because it is vision (*darśana*), is a direct experience, a 'realization' that is impervious to doubt and absolutely simple.

As for its genesis, one cannot say that it depends causally on the theological enterprise (*Brahmajijñāsā*). For if there exists a dependence of the one on the other, it is purely extrinsic. The only possible effect of theological effort is the elimination of the obstacles that are opposed to this intuition, but the truth that essentially constitutes the vision is eternal, it cannot be created by research, it can only be apprehended. Just as the eyes do not create the object that they see, so the well-prepared mind of the disciple does not create the Absolute that it suddenly intuits. The direct experience that he has can only be an awakening (*avabodha*), an illumination, and, just as the waking state is different from sleep and dream, so Knowledge is different from every form of ignorance. Dream visions can become as close as possible to the clear view of the waking state, it cannot however be that the latter is the pure homogeneous development of the former, for it is always necessarily of a different nature from them. It is the same for the most refined theological knowledge and for the lived Knowledge of the supreme intuition.

The crucial moment of passage from the one to the other remains therefore unexplained. For Śaṅkara, it is a fact, and, since some have attained this experience, it is possible that others can repeat it. He maintains on the other hand that, despite his tangible and strongly proved orthodoxy, the theology that he proposes cannot directly cause this experience, although it alone is capable of preparing adequately the mind of man.

The whole effort of Śaṅkara concludes thus with an admission of radical incapacity. However the Vedic faith transcends this admission and the experience can annul it. But, on the plane of concepts, according to Śaṅkara himself, there is no radical justification of this theology.

* * *

Bibliographical note

We have cited the Upaniṣads and their commentary by Śaṅkara according to the following edition: Śaṅkara, *Upaniṣadbhāṣyam*, ed. in two volumes by H.R. Bhagavat, 2nd ed. (Poona: Ashtekar, 1927 and 1928); the *Bhagavadgītā* and its commentary by Śaṅkara in the edition *Śrīmadbhagavadgītāśrīśaṅkara... bhāṣyena sahitā*, critically ed. D.V. Gokhale, 2nd rev. ed. (Poona: Oriental Book Agency, 1950); the *Vedāntasūtra* and its commentary by Śaṅkara: *Brahmasūtraśaṅkarabhāṣyam*, ed. Mahadeva Shastri Bakre and rev. W.L. Shastri Panshikar, 3rd ed. (Bombay: Nirnaya Sagar Press, 1934); its sub-commentary by Vācaspati Miśra, the *Bhāmati*, is also contained in this edition.

The *Kārikā* of Gauḍapāda is cited according to the edition: *The Āgamaśāstra of Gauḍapāda*, ed., tr. and annotated by Vidhushekhara Bhattacharyya (Calcutta University, 1943); the *Mīmāṃsā Sūtra: Pūrvamīmāṃsāsūtra* (of Jaimini), ed. (ch. 1-3) by G. Jha, *Sacred Books of the Hindus*, vols. 10-11 (Allahabad, 1911); the *Vedāntaparibhāṣā* of Dharmarāja Adhvarīndra, ed. S.S.S. Shastri (Adyar, Madras, 1942); the *Siddhāntabindu* of Madhusūdana, English tr. P.M. Modi (Bhavnagar, 1929, 2nd ed. 1938).

Notes

[1] [Richard De Smet, "Langage et connaissance de l'Absolu chez Çaṃkara," *Revue Philosophique de Louvain* **52** (3e séries / 33) (February 1954) 31-74. This reworking of part of chapter 9 of De Smet's doctoral dissertation, 'The Theological Method of Śaṃkara' (Rome: Pontifical Gregorian University, 1953) served, together with the Table of Contents and Bibliography of the dissertation, as the 'extract' required by the University. Translated by Ivo Coelho, and published here with permission of *Revue Philosophique de Louvain* / Peeters Publishers and De Nobili College, Pune.]

[2] Buddhism, born in India about 500 BC, attained its apogée under King Kaniska between 78 and 102 AD, and then, from the sixth century, began to weaken and fall into decadence, till its almost complete disappearance between 800 and 1000 AD. Still, it survived sporadically up to the twelfth century, and even later in the old Bengal, where a degenerate form of Buddhism, Tantrāyāna, enjoyed popular favour under the dynasty of the Pāla kings.

[3] Presented to the Faculty of Philosophy of the Pontifical Gregorian University for the degree of Doctor of Philosophy (June 1953). [The dissertation has not been published to date, but has enjoyed wide circulation in 'roneotyped' form among students and Indologists. See also above, "Introduction" note 4.]

[4] *Vedānta Paribhāṣā* 4, 12.

[5] *Vedānta Paribhāṣā* 4, 13.

[6] *Bṛh. Up. Bh.* 3, 4, 1, p. 184.

[7] *Bṛh. Up. Bh.* 4, 4, 23, p. 305.

[8] *Vedānta Paribhāṣā* 4, 20.

[9] *Vedānta Paribhāṣā* 4, 21.

[10] *Vedānta Paribhāṣā* 4, 22.

[11] On these three types of implication, cf. D.M. Datta, *The Six Ways of Knowing* (London: Allen & Unwin, 1932) 283ff.

[12] *Bṛh. Up. Bh.* 1, 1, 1, p. 4.

[13] *Bṛh. Up. Bh.* 1, 5, 2, p. 82.

[14] *Chānd. Up. Bh.* 4, 3, 1-3.

[15] Cf. *Chānd. Up. Bh.* Introd. at 1, 1. *Āgamaśāstra* or *Gauḍapāda Kārikā* 3, 14-16, 23, etc.

[16] *Bh. Gītā Bh.* 18, 66.

[17] *Bhāmati* commenting *B.S.Bh.* 1, 1, 4.

[18] Cf. *Vedānta Paribhāṣā* 4, 2-10.

[19] Cf. Datta 307-312.

[20] *Kena Up.* 1, 3.

[21] *Taitt. Up.* 2, 4.

[22] "*Yaddhi vedyaṁ vastu viṣayībhavati tatasthu veditum śakyam.*" *Kena Up. Bh.* 2, 1, p. 85.

[23] *Kena Up. Bh.* 2, 1, p. 86.

[24] *Kaṭha Up. Bh.* 1, 21, cf. also 1, 20; *Kena Up. Bh.* 1, 3, p. 82; *Taitt. Up. Bh.* 4; *B.S.Bh.* 1, 1, 4, pp. 78, 80.

[25] Cf. *Kena Up. Bh.* 2, 1, p. 86; *Bṛh. Up. Bh.* Introd. at 1, 1, p. 3; *B.S.Bh.* 1, 1, 4, p. 87; 3, 2, 23, p. 657; *Taitt. Up. Bh.* 2, 6, p. 369; etc.

[26] *Kaṭha Up*. 5, 14.
[27] *B.S.Bh.* 3, 2, 24.
[28] *Bh. Gītā Bh*. 2, 18.
[29] Cf. *Kena Up. Bh*. 2, 4.
[30] *Kena Up. Bh.* 2, 4.
[31] Cf. *B.S.Bh.* Introd. at 1, 1, pp. 9-10.
[32] *Kena Up. Bh.* 1, 5.
[33] *Kena Up. Bh.* 1, 5, p. 84.
[34] *Bh. Gītā Bh*. 2, 18.
[35] See, for example, *Bṛh. Up*. 2, 3, 6; 3, 9, 26; *Kaṭha Up*. 2, 14; *Muṇḍ. Up*. 2, 14.
[36] *Bṛh. Up*. 2, 3, 6.
[37] *B.S.Bh*. 3, 2, 17.
[38] *Vedānta Paribhāṣā* 4, 30.
[39] *B.S.Bh*. 1, 4, 11, p. 311.
[40] *Bṛh. Up. Bh*. 1, 4, 10, p. 58; the same in *B.S.Bh.* 1, 1, 4, p. 63.
[41] *B.S.Bh.* 3, 1, 22, p. 616; 4, 2, 1, p. 855, the same rule is cited for the adversary without being rejected by Śaṅkara; cf. also *B.S.Bh.* 2, 4, 2, p. 567; *Bṛh. Up. Bh*. 1, 3, 1, p. 17; etc.
[42] "*Mukhyāpekṣatvācca gauṇatvasya*": *Bṛh. Up. Bh*. 1, 3, 1, p. 18.
[43] Cf. *Mīmāṃsāsūtra* 1, 4, 9; 2, 3, 24; 3, 3, 11; applications ibid. 2, 4, 1; etc.
[44] Cf. *B.S.Bh.* 1, 4, 9, p. 307; etc.; applications in *Bṛh. Up. Bh*. 1, 3, 21, pp. 30-31; 1, 5, 2, p. 79; etc.
[45] Cf. *B.S.* 3, 3, 1, 4-5; *Praśna Up. Bh*. 4, 5; etc.
[46] Cf. *Mīmāṃsāsūtra* 1, 4, 30; compare ibid. 2, 3, 16.
[47] Cf. *B.S.Bh*. 1, 1, 1, p. 40; 2, 3, 17, p. 527; *Kena Up. Bh*. 4, 8; etc.
[48] Cf. *Bṛh. Up. Bh*. Introd. at 3, 2, 1, p. 170; 4, 3, 6, p. 237; 4, 3, 7, p. 240; *Muṇḍ. Up. Bh*. Introd. at 1, 1, 1; *B.S.Bh.* 2, 2, 25, pp. 462-463; etc.
[49] On the general theory of *arthāpatti*, see Datta 231-239, and C. Kunhan Raja, in Indian Philosophical Congress, 16th Session.
[50] Cf. *Bṛh. Up. Bh*. Introd. at 3, 3, 1, pp. 177-178; 4, 3, 34, p. 274; *Bh. Gītā Bh*. 18, 67; etc.
[51] [This title in the doctoral dissertation reads: The Exegesis of the Vedic *Advaita*- or Identity Statements. See 'The Theological Method of Śaṃkara' 260.]
[52] "*Yastvātmaśabdasya itiparaḥ prayogaḥ ātmaśabdapratyayayoḥ ātmatattvasya paramārthato 'viṣayatvajñāpanārtham*": *Bṛh. Up. Bh*. 1, 4, 7, p. 54.
[53] *Bṛh. Up. Bh*. 1, 4, 10, pp. 153 and 160.
[54] *Bṛh. Up. Bh*. 2, 3, 6, p. 135.
[55] *Chānd. Up. Bh*. 5, 11, 1, pp. 235-236.
[56] *Chānd. Up*. 6, 8, 7.
[57] *Bṛh. Up*. 1, 4, 10.
[58] *Bṛh. Up*. 2, 5, 19.
[59] *Chānd. Up*. 6, 8, 7.
[60] *Bṛh. Up*. 3, 8, 11.

[61] *Bṛh. Up. Bh.* 1, 4, 7, p. 49.
[62] *Chānd. Up. Bh.* 6, 8, 7, pp. 265-266.
[63] *Chānd. Up. Bh.* 6, 16, 3, pp. 275-276.
[64] Compare the same argument in the *B.S.Bh.* 4, 1, 3, pp. 832-833.
[65] Compare the same argument in *B.S.Bh.* 2, 1, 14, p. 376.
[66] Compare *Bh. Gītā Bh.* 13, 15.
[67] *Chānd. Up. Bh.* 6, 16, 3, pp. 276-277.
[68] *Vedāntasāra*, text and tr. M. Hiriyanna (Poona: Oriental Book Agency, 1929) 10.
[69] The study of *B.S.Bh.* 4, 1, 3, pp. 832-833 will only confirm these explications. See also *Vedāntasāra*, pp. 3-4 and 7.
[70] Cf. *Śrībhāṣya*, Bombay Sanskrit and Prakrit Series, LXVIII (Bombay, 1914) pp. 19-21 and 59.
[71] Cf. Madhusūdan, *Siddhāntabindu*, tr. P.M. Modi (Bhavnagar, 1929; 2nd ed., 1938) pp. 111-118.
[72] *Vedānta Paribhāṣā* 4, 28.
[73] Cf. *Vedānta Paribhāṣā* 4, 26-27: "*iti sampradāyikaḥ. Vayantu brūmaḥ....*" (Thus say the traditionalists. But we, we say....).
[74] *B.S.Bh.* 1, 3, 25, p. 246.
[75] [The French text is defective here because of the repetition of a line and the probable omission of another:

> a) La première est du type: "Ceci est un lotus bleu". C'est
> tinction entre genre et différence spécifique. Le rapport qui, dans
> l'objet une complexité reèlle qui est le fondement de cette dis-
> tinction entre genre et différence spécifique. Le rapport qui, dans
> cette sorte de définition, unit les attributs au substantif, n'est donc
> pas l'identité pure mais une identité qualifiée que manifeste la
> relation de subordination de la différence specifique au genre.

Fortunately, we are in possession of the original typescript (available in the JDV library, Pune, S6/SM391, accession no. 74410) which reads:

> a) La première est du type: "Ceci est un lotus bleu". C'est la définition par genre et différence specifique. Elle implique dans l'objet une complexité réelle qui est le fondement de cette distinction entre genre et différence spécifique. Le rapport qui, dans cette sorte de définition, unit les attributs au substantif, n'est donc pas l'identité pure mais une identité qualifiée que manifeste la relation de subordination de la différence spécifique au genre.]

[76] *B.S.* 1, 1, 2.
[77] *B.S.Bh.* 1, 1, 2.
[78] *B.S.Bh.* 1, 4, 14, p. 319.
[79] *Ait. Up. Bh.* Introd. at 2, 5.
[80] *Ait. Up. Bh.* Introd. at 2, 5.
[81] *B.S.Bh.* 1, 4, 14, p. 318. Cf. also *Bṛh. Up. Bh.* 1, 4, 7, p. 48; *Taitt. Up. Bh.* 2, 6; *Siddhāntabindu* (tr. Modi), p. 118.

[82] *Bṛh. Up.* 2, 3, 6.
[83] *Chānd. Up. Bh.* 7, 17, 1, p. 293.
[84] *Bṛh. Up. Bh.* Introd. at 2, 3, 1.
[85] *Bṛh. Up.* 3, 7, 3-23.
[86] *Bṛh. Up. Bh.* 3, 7, 23.
[87] *Chānd. Up.* 6, 2, 1.
[88] *Chānd. Up. Bh.* 7, 24, 1, p. 295.
[89] In his magisterial work, *L'Absolu selon le Vedānta* (Paris: Geuthner, 1937) pp. 118-119, O. Lacombe has justified this translation of '*cinmātra*' as 'pure consciousness.'
[90] *Chānd. Up. Bh.* 8, 14, 1, p. 333.
[91] *Taitt. Up.* 2, 1.
[92] *Taitt. Up.* 2, 4 and 2, 7.
[93] *Taitt. Up. Bh.* 2, 1, pp. 356-359.
[94] *Bṛh. Up.* 3, 9, 28.
[95] *Bṛh. Up.* 4, 3-9.
[96] *Bṛh. Up.* 5, 1, 1.
[97] Cf. *B.S.* 3, 2, 11-21.
[98] *Taitt. Up. Bh.* 2, 9, p. 383.

2

THE FUNDAMENTAL ANTINOMY OF SRĪ ŚAṄKARĀCĀRYA'S METHODOLOGY[1]

1. Śaṅkara is a guru, not a private researcher; he is the transmitter of an authoritative sacred tradition, not an independent philosopher; he is a theologian, not a purely rational inquirer. The manner of his teaching supposes that he himself has thoroughly grasped the entire doctrine which he exposes. It even seems to imply that he has mystically realized the truth of the doctrine, although he never refers explicitly to such an experience as his own, but only as the experience of *Ṛṣis* and other enlightened men as testified by the *Śruti* (cf. his *Bhāṣya* on *B.S.* 4, 1, 15; also 2, 1, 14; 4, 1, 19; and on *Bṛh. Up*. 1, 4, 7). He holds that "the *Brahman* should be understood through the traditional teaching of preceptors and not by reasoning, disquisition, mental power, learning, austerities, ritual sacrifices, etc." (*Kena Up. Bh.* 1, 4). "No knowledge can prove effective, except that alone which is imparted by those who have realized the truth" (*Bh. Gītā Bh.* 4, 34). Indeed, the whole endeavour of Śaṅkara consists in imparting to his disciple that meaning of the *Śruti* and *Smṛti* which he considers as alone true.

2. Such a teaching is called *Brahmajijñāsā*, i.e., enquiry prompted by the desire of knowing *Brahman* or the Absolute. As such, it is not an enquiry performed by the *guru* for his own account (because the *guru* is 'he who knows,' and he who knows is beyond any 'desire of knowing'), but it is a pedagogical enquiry performed by the *guru* in front of, and for the sake of, the disciple; it is a 'method' in the Greek sense of the term. This enquiry supposes a certain number of conditions in the *śiṣya* or disciple who has to be qualified not only morally (cf. the four moral prerequisites listed in *B.S.Bh.* 1, 1, 1), but also according

to *varṇa* and *āśrama*, and the conjunction of these prerequisites is, as a matter of fact, so rare that, according to Śaṅkara, there is "but one in a thousand" (*Bṛh. Up. Bh.* 4, 4, 12), "but one among many that attains *Jñāna*, as experience shows" (*Bh. Gītā Bh.* 13, 2).

3. Once, however, such a qualified disciple is found, the enquiry can proceed according to the three traditional steps: *śravaṇa*, *manana*, *nididhyāsana*, i.e., hearing or instruction, reflection and inward concentration on the meaning proposed by the *guru*. This threefold progress is entirely under the direction or supervision of the *guru*, but it is in *śravaṇa* that he is most active. The first of his functions in *śravaṇa* is, of course, to inculcate to his *śiṣya* the letter of the *Śruti*, but the second and most important is to communicate to him the true meaning of the sacred texts, while the third is to answer convincingly all possible objections raised against this meaning and the fourth to manifest directly its inner rationality and consistency. His methodical teaching is therefore essentially exegetical, dogmatic and apologetical. In short, it is a complete *mīmāṃsā* and it technically corresponds to what we, Christians, call a theology or rational science of the revealed Word about God. This general agreement in method between Catholic theology and Śaṅkara's *Brahmajijñāsā* is striking, but it raises no question about any possible influence or dependence of the one upon the other or vice versa, because such a method is but the natural way of proceeding in any endeavour to bring out scientifically the hidden meaning of any testimony believed by its adherents to be infallible; moreover, this agreement in method is but general and covers real dissimilarities which, however, I cannot expose in this paper.

4. However brief it is, this outline of the intention and method of Śaṅkara's teaching is sufficient to my purpose which is to manifest the antinomies arising from the conjunction of such a method and intention with the Absolute doctrine of Advaita. The object of this doctrine is the Absolute and revelation of its true nature. According to Śaṅkara, it cannot be known through any *pramāṇa* except the non-human (*apauruṣeya*) and, hence, infallible testimony (*Śabda*) of the *Śruti*. The gist of this testimony is that there is but one absolute Reality, which can indifferently be called *Brahman* or *Ātman*, or

Brahman-Ātman and which is repeatedly designated or defined (*lakṣyate*), not however adequately expressed (*na tūcyate*), (for this distinction, cf. *Taitt. Up. Bh.* 2, 1), through the 'great sayings' (*mahāvākyāni*) or *Vedānta statements* properly so called, such as "*Tattvamasi*," "*Satyam jñānam anantam brahma*," etc. Whatever else appears to the unenlightened man to be reality is not absolutely so, but is *sadasadvilakṣaṇa*, i.e., different from both Reality and Unreality. Hence, all the evidence of the senses and the intellect, which, according to Śaṅkara, naturally (*naisargikaḥ*) attribute absolute reality to their objects, is ultimately to be discarded as untruth, since the *Śruti* testimony contradicts it, while no superior *pramāṇa* can ever contradict the *Śruti* itself. The ultimate *anubhava* or *sākṣātkāra* is but the supreme confirmation of this testimony in the form of an immediate and entirely self-evident intuition of the truth of its meaning.

5. The paradox of Śaṅkara's teaching is that it is meant to lead the disciple from the unreal sphere of duality to the intuition of absolute non-duality and to do this with the help of means which all imply duality. On the one hand, the master spring of his undertaking is the desire of knowing perfectly the non-dual *Brahman* (*Brahmajijñāsā*), on the other hand, he himself tells us that "there can be no desire in the subject matter of the knowledge of *Brahman*, for it is the oneness of everything" (*Bṛh. Up. Bh.* 1, 5, 2). Further, the whole *Śruti*, even its essential part, the *Vedānta statements*, is intrinsically dualistic, since it is language; and besides, it is a *pramāṇa*, a means of valid knowledge, and all *pramāṇas* imply multiplicity, since they imply the threefold distinction of knower, object known, and means of knowing. It is even limited in its function as *pramāṇa*; indeed, Śaṅkara tells us that "the Śruti is a *pramāṇa* only because it serves to eliminate the superimposition (on the self) of attributes other than the Self but not because it would reveal what is never unknown" (*Bh. Gītā Bh.* 2, 18). The *ekamevādvitīyam Brahmātmā*, to which the supreme *Jñāna* or *samyagdarśana* is identical, is the ever existing reality and no means can bring it about. Śaṅkara affirms emphatically and repeatedly this powerlessness of any means with regard to the supreme *Vidyā*; still, his teaching is a painstaking endeavour to help the disciple to reach it, in which no possible means is

neglected, either exegetical or logical or ascetical. The rules of Jaimini's *mīmāṃsā* are recast, the theory of *lakṣaṇā* or indirect implication is consistently applied to the interpretation of the Vedānta statements, the ancillary function of *pramāṇas*, such as perception and the various forms of reasoning, is utilized to the utmost, virtues and *yoga-sādhanas* are appraised and given a function in *Brahmajijñāsā*, in short, Śaṅkara musters to his purpose all the resources of his culture and of his own personality. Still, he asserts over and over again that all these means are *avidyā* and that the *Śruti* "leads to the highest goal of man not with, but without, the help of any means, for otherwise there would be contradiction all around" (*Bṛh. Up. Bh.* 2, 4, 1).

6. The conflict between the *advaita* doctrine which he always upholds vigorously and the very process of *Brahmajijñāsā* to which he relentlessly devotes the marvellous powers of his mind ought to be exposed in its many aspects, but it can be summed up in the following antinomy: whatever is not the perfectly simple realization of the Absolute is not *vidyā*, but *avidyā*, hence, *Brahmajijñāsā* itself and all its means are *avidyā*; now, no form of *avidyā* and no combination of any privileged forms of it can ever cause *vidyā*, which is ever existing and can never be caused; and still, *Brahmajijñāsā* is painstakingly undertaken and proposed to the disciple as if it were the real means of extinguishing *avidyā* and thus causing the manifestation of *vidyā*. Of this antinomy Śaṅkara was fully conscious, as witness numerous passages of his writings, and he conscientiously endeavoured to solve or at least to reduce it, without however compromising on any of his fundamental convictions. This endeavour has resulted in three theories, which form an important part of the methodology scattered in his writings, and which I shall now expose as briefly as possible.

7. The only way of reducing the antinomy is to show that secular knowledge is not so completely *avidyā* as the *advaita* doctrine seems to imply and that, if not in its expression, at least in its exercise, it posits *vidyā* itself which is therefore immanent to it. The first way of manifesting this immanent presence of *vidyā* to ordinary knowledge is to proceed to a transcendental analysis of this knowledge. Such an analysis is found especially in *Bh. Gītā Bh.* 2, 16 and in *Chānd. Up. Bh.* 8, 5, 4, and is hinted

at or referred to in many other passages. In his commentary on *Gītā* 2, 16, Śaṅkara writes as follows:

> In every case, (i.e., in every existential assertion), there is perception of a twofold knowledge: that of being (*sat*) and that of non-being (*asat*). That is *sat* which is the object of a knowledge which does not fail; that is *asat* which is the object of a knowledge which fails. The division between *sat* and *asat* standing (thus) in dependence of knowledge, a twofold knowledge is in every case perceived by all with reference to the same substratum—not as in (the case of) 'a blue lotus'—but as in (the existential expressions) 'the existing jar,' 'the existing cloth,' 'the existing elephant.' Thus, in every case. In this twofold knowledge, the knowledge of the jar, etc. fails, as it has been shown. But not the knowledge of '*sat*.' Therefore, the object of the knowledge of a jar, etc. is unreal, because it fails; whereas the object of the knowledge of '*sat*' (is) not (unreal), since it does not fail.... The knowledge of '*sat*' has for its exclusive object the attributive (*sat*) ... (It is objected that) the knowledge of '*sat*' also is not perceived once the jar is destroyed. (The answer is,) no, for that is due to the absence of a substantive. Since the knowledge of '*sat*' has for its object the attributive, what could its object be once the attributive becomes impossible in the absence of the substantive? But (the non-perception of '*sat*') is not due to the absence of its own object. (It is further objected that) in the absence of substantives such as 'jar,' etc. the unity of substratum is not fitting. (The answer is,) no, for unity of substratum is perceived even in the absence of one of the two, as in the case of a mirage, etc. (when we say,) 'this is water.' Therefore there is no existence of '*asat*,' i.e., of body, etc. and pairs, which have a cause. Similarly, of '*sat*,' i.e., of the *ātman*, there is no non-existence (*abhāva*), because, as we have said, it never fails.

Of course, men do not ordinarily pay attention to this ever-present consciousness of being, still it is present in, and constitutive of, every affirmation and it can be grasped through reflexive analysis. But not only the consciousness of being is immanent to every secular judgment, but also the consciousness of self: "the inner self is not non-object in the absolute sense of the term, for it is the object of the notion of 'I' (*asmatpratyaya*) and it is well known to exist because it is directly apprehended" (*B.S.Bh.* 1, 1). "The self is unknown to nobody... in the form, 'I am' (*ittham aham*) (*Bh. Gītā Bh.* 2, 18). "To try to teach what the consciousness of the self is like is unnecessary, inasmuch as it is invariably apprehended in association with all objects of perception which are set up by *avidyā*. *Brahman* is self-evident; we have only to eliminate what is falsely ascribed to *Brahman* by *avidyā*. *Brahman's* remoteness is such only for the unenlightened who do not discriminate" (*Bh. Gītā Bh.* 18, 50). "Since any object of cognition is apprehended through cognition, cognition is quite as immediately known as pleasure, etc. It is not a thing which one seeks to know. It is self-revealed. And therefore, also, is the cognizer self-revealed" (*Bh. Gītā Bh.* 18, 50). Hence, every ordinary cognition, though it is *avidyā*, implies the direct knowledge of being (*sat*), *ātman*, and *jñāna* which, when seen as one, constitute the supreme *vidyā*. There is therefore a link or a kind of passage between *avidyā* and *vidyā*.

8. We go a step further in the reduction of the antinomy through the theory of transcendental illumination. This is again the outcome of reflexive analysis of secular knowledge. Consciousness itself (*caitanya*), which is always present in any such knowledge, cannot be explained, except as rooted in, and dependent upon, something which must be called transcendent and absolute Consciousness. Either, indeed, individual consciousness is immediately grasped as infinite or it postulates the infinite *caitanyajyotiḥ* from which it receives its own illumining power, for there is no limit to the illuminative power of our consciousness, and, unless we accept infinite regress, we must posit "the illuminer of everything as itself not illumined by anything else" (*Bṛh. Up. Bh.* 4, 3, 7). "The light of consciousness is the illuminer of the *manas*, because it is its controller, being the source of its light. The inner self being the innermost of all objects, the *manas* cannot move towards it, but it is able to think only when it is illumined by the light of consciousness residing inside. Hence, knowers of *Brahman* declare that the *manas* with all its functions is thought, is the object of, is pervaded by, this (supreme consciousness). Hence, one should know that the self of the *manas*, the internal cognizer, is the *Brahman*" (*Kena Up. Bh.*1, 6.). Further texts ought to be adduced to make this theory plain, but the little I have said is sufficient to indicate that here again ordinary knowledge, although it is *avidyā*, bears an intrinsic relation to *vidyā* which is a necessary condition of its possibility.

9. Not only ordinary knowledge, but language, which is its sign, and which, being essentially discursive, seems to be at loggerheads with Advaita, possesses some intrinsic powers of signification according to which it can be reconciied with it. These powers are called *lakṣaṇā* or indirect signification as

opposed to *abhidhā* or direct expression. *Lakṣaṇā* or *lakṣyārthas* are all those variations of meaning which terms come to signify according to their various relations with other terms in the same sentence and with the proximate and remote context of this sentence, and which are somewhat different from their direct and express meaning as recorded, for instance, in dictionaries. The theory of indirect signification is of paramount importance for Śaṅkara because it is only through recourse to this theory that he can correctly interpret the *Vedānta statements*, which, according to him, constitute the directly and independently authoritative part of the *Śruti*. In explaining these statements, Śaṅkara very carefully exposes how the primary meaning of their terms is to be not entirely discarded, but purified and elevated in such a way as to apply to the Absolute whose mode of Being is utterly different from the mode of being of the finite and impermanent objects from which we derive the concepts of these terms. This treatment is *jahadajahallakṣaṇā*, i.e. *lakṣaṇā* such that it, at the same time, somehow includes the primary or proper sense (*svārtha*) of the terms and somehow excludes it. The secondary meaning arrived at through this process is the *paramārtha* or supreme meaning of these terms. What has it in common with their primary meaning? The 'what' which both signify, but not the 'how' of this signification. In other terms, it is, for instance, that which we usually understand by 'reality' which is signified of the Absolute, when the *Śruti* says that *Brahman* is *satyam*, but this statement of the *Śruti* means that *Brahman* is reality in a way utterly different from that of those objects which we apprehend as realities. How can we grasp *Brahman's* specific way of being? As long as we remain in *Brahmajijñāsā*, we can grasp it only negatively, that is to say, by discarding successively all other possible ways of being, but it is only in *sākṣātkāra* or immediate intuition that this knowledge can become entirely positive. This short account of *Brahmalakṣaṇājñāna* again shows an intrinsic relation between ordinary knowledge and the supreme *vidyā*. Since the *lakṣaṇā* used by Śaṅkara is not *jahat* (exclusive of the primary meaning), but *jahadajahat*, it builds a bridge between ordinary knowledge, deemed as *avidyā*, and the pure *vidyā*. It similarly asserts some kind of ontological community of being between the objects of this world taken as such and the supreme Being.

10. Thus, through these three theories the fundamental antinomy of which I have spoken is certainly reduced to a great extent, but not completely discarded. Śaṅkara, indeed, would not and probably could not negate either of the two assertions of this antinomy. Still, the very existence of his *Brahmajijñāsā* and especially the three theories which I have exposed, actually destroy the absoluteness of their opposition. The question, therefore, may be put whether complete consistency would not require some complete revision and re-working of his synthesis which would successfully eliminate the antinomy entirely and simultaneously preserve all those precious insights of the doctrine, which belong to *philosophia perennis*.

Notes

[1] ["The Fundamental Antinomy of Śr[ī] Śaṃkarācārya's Methodology" was a lecture given at the Philosophical Association, 24 August 1954 (1 p. + 1 p. summary + 7 pp, cf. Typescript, Collected Papers A, 23-31 = DNC 73/DES/COL). The paper was subsequently published in *Oriental Thought* (Nashik) **2**/4 (Oct. 1956) 1-9. Having been unable to trace the rights holders of *Oriental Thought*, this is reprinted here with kind permission of De Nobili College, Pune.]

3

ŚAṄKARA'S NON-DUALISM (*ADVAITAVĀDA*) (1964/68)[1]

The restoration of upaniṣadic Brahmanism was the work of the Vedānta school, whose basic text was the *Brahma-sūtra* compiled by Bādarāyaṇa to harmonise the teachings of the Upaniṣads. Of the first Vedāntins we know hardly more than a few names. But the masterful commentary written by Śrī Śaṅkarācārya on that *Sūtra* as well as his commentaries on nine Upaniṣads and on the *Gītā* together with some minor works set such a high standard of rigorous teaching that they immediately commanded the whole further development of the Vedānta school.

The dates of his life are uncertain. After exploring the whole question again during the last ten years, specialists now agree to place him in the eighth century AD and more probably in the second half of that century. A Śaiva Brahmin, he was probably born at Kāladi (Malabar) and spent many years in the monastery which he founded in Śṛṅgeri (Mysore). He is generally reported to have died relatively young either in Kedarnāth (Himālaya) or perhaps in Kāñcī. The other traditional details of his life are legendary.

What set him above all previous Vedāntins was his success in synthesising for the first time the elements of pure wisdom scattered in the Upaniṣads and, through selection, adaptation or downright rejection, relating to that synthesis the variety of contrasting currents and doctrines which we described in chapter 3.[2] Before him, this variety had engendered bewilderment and scepticism or a sort of resigned conformism. This situation had been aptly summarised in *Mahābhārata*, Vana-parvan, 312, 115:

Tārko 'pratiṣṭhāḥ śrutayo vibhinnāḥ
Naiko ṛṣir yasya vacaḥ pramāṇam
Dharmasya tattvam nihitaṁguhāyām
Mahājano yena gataḥ sa panthaḥ.

Reasoning is unstable and sacred texts diverge;
There is not one Sage whose word carries authority;
The essence of Religion is kept bound in a cave;
Where goes the great number, there is the present way.

1. The Current Interpretation of Śaṅkara's Teaching

The young saṇnyāsiṇ who was to release the essence of Religion from the cave of confusion appeared around 750 AD endowed with the best gifts which nature and *sādhanā* could provide: metaphysical genius, faultless acumen, dexterous logic, incomparable erudition and unshakable faith. Because of his exclusive faith in *Śruti* he was to be a *Śrutivādin* and his writings would be commentaries (*bhāṣya*) following the order of his basic texts, rather than systematic treatises. Due to his readiness to accommodate himself to the traditional modes of thought, he would use the predominantly Sāṁkhya language of speculation and fail to create new terms to express his novel conceptions. Finally, the greatness of his name would induce paler imitators and even opponents to ascribe to him hundreds of spurious works which would not influence his immediate disciples but would falsify the interpretation of his doctrine by later followers.

On account of these three main factors: unsystematic presentation, inadequate vocabulary, influence of spurious works, there has arisen in India an interpretation of Śaṅkara which distorts his authentic teaching but has unfortunately been accepted by many. According to this current interpretation, the chief tenets of *Advaitavāda* (Non-Dualism) are the following:

(1) *Satyam Brahma, jagad mithyā*: *Brahman* alone is real, the world is false. The world is *māyā*, i.e., a purely illusory manifestation of *Brahman*, caused by transcendental Nescience (*Avidyā* or *Ajñāna*). Hence, *advaita* means strict monism and implies acosmism. The statements of identity, such as "Verily, this whole world is *Brahman*" (*Sarvam khalv-idam Brahma*), or

"I am *Brahman*" (*Aham Brahmāsmi*), must be understood literally as they stand.

(2) *Brahman* is the material cause of the world; this seems to imply that it is a sort of unconscious stuff which becomes modified according to the variety of "names and forms". But this causal self-modification is illusory (*vivarta*).

(3) *Brahman* is *nirguṇa*, which should be translated 'impersonal.' Hence, there is no real possibility of establishing interpersonal relationships with it.

(4) The *jīvātman* which, in the state of *avidyā*, appears to itself as a finite principle of consciousness, activity and passivity, is really identical with *Brahman*, the *Ātman* of all. Senses and body are mere *upādhis* or superimpositions due to Nescience. The *Śruti*-revelation of Advaita is alone capable of freeing (*mokṣa*) the *jīvātman* from the bond of Nescience. It cancels all other evidence and its realisation is absolute Bliss.

2. Śaṅkara's Key-Distinction between Primary and Secondary

In order to overcome the distorting simplicity of this interpretation, we should try to place ourselves within the special perspective of Śaṅkara himself. His was a teaching of wisdom, trying to ascertain values, and his language was meant to serve his purpose of evaluating realities. Hence, his key-distinction between what is primary and what is secondary. The primary is usually expressed in positive terms: for instance, *sat* means the unchanging real or the REAL, i.e., *Brahman*, whereas *asat*, when said of the world, means the changing real or un-REAL.

The first of the four qualifications laid down by Śaṅkara for the study of Vedānta is "the capacity to discriminate between eternal and impermanent realities" (*nityānityavastuviveka*) (*B.S.Bh.* Introd.). The guru should train his disciple to recognise *parā* from *aparā vidyā* (perfect from imperfect knowledge), *satya* from *māyā* (truth from illusion), *sat* from *asat* (unchanging from changing being), *ananta* from *anta* (infinite from finite reality), *kāraṇa* from *kārya* (cause from effect), *viṣayin* from *viṣaya* (subject from object), *ātman* from *deha* (spirit from body), *bhūman* from *alpa* (great from small), *guru* from *laghu* (important from insignificant), *śreya* from *preya* (excellent from pleasant) and, generally, *mukhya* from *gauṇa* (primary from secondary).

"As the flamingo (according to Indian folklore) sifts milk from water, so the wise man sifts the excellent from the merely pleasant, going mentally all around these two objects, examining them closely, weighing their respective importance or futility; and having distinguished them, he chooses the excellent alone on account of its superiority" (*Kaṭh. Up. Bh.* 2, 2).

3. Its Systematic Application

3.1 The primacy of true knowledge

The tradition upholds four ends of man (*puruṣārtha*): *artha* (material possessions), *kāma* (love-enjoyment), *dharma* (morality), and *mokṣa* (emancipation from *saṃsāra*). Which one do you say is the chief end of man?—It is undoubtedly *mokṣa* for it alone eliminates all pain and dissatisfaction; this is the teaching of all followers of *Śruti* (*śrutivādins*).

Very well, but *Śruti* opens two ways to *mokṣa*: ritual action (*karma*) and knowledge (*jñāna*); further, *Smṛti* speaks of *yoga*, *niṣkāma karma*, and *bhakti*. Which then is the right way?—Knowledge is really the way. Rites are inefficient; save perhaps as a remote preparation. Even selfless activity can only induce favourable dispositions. True knowledge alone can dispel ignorance, which is the root of all misery. *Yoga* is useless except insofar as it disciplines the inner man for the advent of knowledge. As to *bhakti*, it should be understood as complete self-surrender and devotion to truth, not to any anthropomorphic deity.

3.2 The primacy of Śruti

I grant that truth is to be our goal, but how shall we reach it? So many opposed theories are proposed that it is well-nigh impossible to select anyone among them.—This should not confuse you. There are at your disposal six different *pramāṇas* or sources of valid knowledge: sense-perception (*pratyakṣa*) and its negative counterpart, non-observation (*anupalabdhi*), three forms of reasoning, *anumāna*, *upamāna*, *arthāpatti*, and finally testimony (*śabda*); with their help you can criticise those theories and discover the truth.

Are all those *pramāṇas* equally reliable and final?—No. We, Vedāntins, consider the first five *pramāṇas* as secondary, and only the last one as primary, at least in the form of *Śruti*. Sense-perception is primary in time but not in truth-value; though superior to dream-knowledge, it can yet err, as witness the many cases of illusory perception, and, besides, it is only concerned with passing, contingent realities. Reasoning suffers from the same defects since it depends upon perception. As to testimony, it is of two kinds; *pauruṣeya* and *apauruṣeya*, i.e., it either originates from an individual witness (*puruṣa*) or it does not. *Smṛti*, for instance, is mere human tradition and its authority is therefore defective, for men are fallible. But *Śruti* (i.e., the Vedic and Brahmanic scriptures, especially the Upaniṣads) is entirely free from dependence upon individual authors; hence, it is absolutely infallible and its authority is supreme.

Does '*Śruti*' not mean 'that which has been heard,' and does' it not therefore depend upon the individual *ṛṣis* from whom it was heard for the first time?—No, that dependence is merely apparent. In its essence, *Śruti* is but the eternal word (*śabda*) identical with the omniscient consciousness of the supreme *Ātman*; the variety of its words should not deceive us for that is merely accidental. The privilege of the *ṛṣis* is to have 'seen' it directly, on account of the purity of their intellect; thus they were 'seers,' not intermediary 'revealers.'

If *Śruti* is what you say, what then should be our trust in the rest of our traditional literature?—The writings of Buddha, Jina and the Materialists deserve no trust at all since, being *nāstikas*, these authors reject and even oppose *Śruti*. We must combat by all the means at our disposal their pernicious influence. As to the *āstikas*, who pay either lip-homage or heartfelt allegiance to *Śruti*, our duty is to evaluate their writings in the light of *Śruti*. We shall thus sift away the errors which mar our Epic, Purāṇic, legal and linguistic literature as well as our Vaiśeṣika, Sāṁkhya, Nyāya, Yoga, Mīmāṃsa and even Vedānta *darśanas*. What in them is conformed to *Śruti*, we shall retain as ancillary to our quest.

Will any complete work escape unscathed this purifying progress? Hardly any but the *Bhagavad-Gītā*, a gem of such purity that it rightly deserves the name of authoritative *Smṛti*. But even though authoritative a *Smṛti* can at best be secondary and subservient to *Śruti*.

3.3 The primacy of transcendental experience

But surely the primacy of *Śruti* must be taken on faith and faith cannot be our chief reliance? Faith, indeed is not valid unless it is rationally justified.—We shall not fail to satisfy this request. Indeed, our inquiry is to proceed in three steps: *śravaṇa* (hearing), *manana* (reasoning), *nididhyāsana* (realising). In the first step we shall not only listen to and memorise the sacred texts, but also discover their meaning and their mutual harmony. The second step is purely rational: using all the resources of dialectics, we shall refute all possible objections against that ascertained meaning and establish our final conclusion (*siddhānta*). The third, to which the first two are of course ancillary, is a personal process of assimilation unimpeded by any remaining doubt. It should culminate in a divinelike intuition (*anubhava*) which renders the intellect absolutely conformed to the absolute Reality indicated by the texts. Thus Vedic faith, which at first was a mere reliance on the intuition of the *ṛṣis*, becomes fully validated at the very moment when it turns into that final transcendental experience.

3.4 The primacy of monastic renunciation

What means should I take to reach this wonderful experience?—Strictly speaking, there exist no 'means' as such, for the word 'means' is used in reference to effects to be accomplished, but Reality, being ever present to us, is not to be accomplished. Its discovery is a sheer awakening, similar to our being aroused from sleep to waking knowledge. Yet, just as there are degrees from deep sleep to light slumber, so also do we find ourselves in distant or close proximity to that final awakening, according to our caste, state of life, character and inner dispositions.

Where then is the most apt disposition to be found?—Among castes, the chief one is the *Brāhmaṇa* for the Brahmin alone is fully entitled to Vedic study. Among the states of life the most suitable is that of the wandering monk, and of all orders of monks, the highest is that of the *Paramhaṃsas* (great Swans), whose renunciation is so complete that they hardly cling at all to anything transient. The *Gītā* fully confirms this supremacy of *saṅnyāsa* or renunciation as a disposition to *anubhava*. Yet, do not forget that dispositions are not means and, therefore, absolutely speaking, realisation may dawn upon any man independently of his caste, sex or state of life.

3.5 The primacy of jñāna-kāṇḍa

Śruti consists of two sections: *karma-kāṇḍa*, the concern of Mīmāṃsakas, which centres around sacrificial activity, and *jñāna-kāṇḍa*, the domain of Vedāntins, whose interest is theoretical knowledge. Is there a link of dependence between these two?—No. The *jñāna-kāṇḍa* stands alone in its independence. The *karma-kāṇḍa* is not even conditional or dispositive; it had better be left out altogether, for it is only suited to householding, which is not a state of life adequate for the obtaining of *mokṣa*. Yet, the rules of interpretation elaborated by the Mīmāṃsakas will be useful to us on condition that we correct them and adapt them to our own purpose.

3.6 The primacy of the indicative assertions in jñāna-kāṇḍa

According to those rules we should place our texts into two main categories: first, the injunctions (*codana*); second, the accompanying texts (*arthavāda*), which are subservient to the first. Can we accept this distinction as valid?—No we should really reverse it. Let our own distinction be that between *artha* and *arthavāda*. The manifold of *Śruti* centres around indicative assertions which point directly to its proper object (*artha*); these are accompanied by declaratory assertions (*arthavāda*), such as introduction, preparatory discussions, closer and closer approximations, praising comments, mnemonic mantras, and even those injunctions to which Mīmāṃsakas have given the first place. *Arthavādas* have but a secondary, pedagogical importance, whereas primacy should be given to the indicative propositions.

3.7 The primacy of the propositions indicating Brahman

Are there also diverse kinds of indicative propositions? Yes some designate only natural entities, such as the basic elements (*mahābhūta*), the sun, the moon, or nature itself (*prakṛti*) ; others designate finite beings, such as men or gods, or only the conscious principle in them (*jīvātman*), or their senses (*indriya*), etc. All such propositions are secondary and should not be given ultimate value for their concern is only with dependent and passing realities, which can very well be known through perception and the other *pramāṇas* apart from *Śruti*. "It is not in *Śruti* that we should seek for the means of obtaining the desirable and avoiding the undesirable in matters coming within the range of experience for this double end can be attained with certainty through perception and inference" (*Bṛh. Up. Bh.* Introd.). Neither is it the function of *Śruti* to inform us about the manifestations (of the world), its formation and similar topics. For we neither observe nor are told by *Śruti* that the welfare of man depends on those matters in any way. Nor have we any right to assume such a thing, because... *Śruti* itself declares that all the passages setting forth the creation, etc. are subservient to the purpose of teaching *Brahman*" (*B.S.Bh.* 1, 4, 14). Further, "it is nowhere the purpose of *Śruti* to make statements regarding the conscious principle in the living beings (*jīvātman*). From ordinary experience the *jīvātman*, which, in the different bodies, is joined to the internal organs and other adjuncts (*upādhi*), is known to everyone as agent and enjoyer and, therefore, we must not assume that it is what *Śruti* aims at setting forth. But the Lord, about whom ordinary experience tells us nothing, is to be considered as the special topic of all texts of *Śruti*" (*B.S.Bh.* 1, 3, 7). Indeed, "*Śruti* is an authority only in matters not perceived by means of perception and other ordinary *pramāṇas*. A hundred *Śrutis* may declare that fire is cold or dark; still, they possess no authority in that matter" (*Bh. Gītā Bh.* 18, 66). Hence, those propositions alone which directly refer to *Brahman* possess primacy and independent authority.

3.8 The primacy of the 'great sayings'

Do all such propositions stand on the same level?—No, for *Śruti* moves on two different planes: that of inadequate knowledge (*avidyā*), which is congenital to the enquirer, and that of adequate knowledge (*vidyā*), to which it purposes to awaken him. Hence, in order to orient his mind towards *Brahman* it sometimes refers to the latter as conceived by *avidyā*, namely, as qualified by mundane realities or as particularly well imaged in some of them. But, beyond such inadequate pointers, its 'great sayings' (*mahā-vākya*) are given us as true definitions (*lakṣaṇa*) of *Brahman*.

Which statements come under the category of 'inadequate pointers'?—Those statements which, in a restricted sense of the term, are called '*vidyās*' and which, for the purpose of meditation (*upāsanā*) identify *Brahman* with such particular realities as ether, light, the inner 'space' in the heart, the '*puruṣa*' in the pupil of the eye or in the sun, the *manas* or inner sense, a symbolic word such as '*oṃ*,' a particular deity, or even the Lord (*Īśvara*) anthropomorphically conceived. In particular there are many instances of the last example and we must speak a little more about them, because they can more readily be taken as true definitions instead of mere symbolic pointers and thus mislead the enquirer. Whereas a true definition should point to *Brahman* as *nirguṇa*, i.e., as pure simplicity of being, intelligence and bliss, these statements represent *Brahman* as *saguṇa* and to that extent they are false. Indeed, what they directly say is not only that there exists a supreme Lord, but that he is endowed with (*sa*–) secondary characters (*guṇa*), such as qualities, powers, desires activities, bodies, etc. This imagining of a sort of glorified *rājā* may have pedagogical usefulness but, taken literally, it leads into error. It should be taken as a mere inadequate pointer ancillary to, and destined to be superseded by, the true definitions of *nirguṇa Brahman*, which alone are adequate and, hence, primary.

3.9 The primacy of the svarūpa-lakṣaṇas

Are those adequate definitions also of different degrees of validity?—Indeed, we should actually distinguish three kinds of

Brahma-lakṣaṇas: the relational, the negative and the essential definitions.

What do you mean by 'relational definition'?—First of all, let us attend to the term 'definition,' for it is but an approximate rendering of our term '*lakṣaṇa*.' *Lakṣaṇa* comes from the root '*lakṣ*,' which simply means 'to point, to indicate.' In the realm of mundane realities, *lakṣaṇas* can expressive, but when we deal with God, they can only be indicative, for no finite concept or word can really express the infinite Being. Now a relational *lakṣaṇa* points to its object as to an existent which it merely determines by reference to something else which is more immediately known. In many cases such relationship is intrinsic to the object pointed out but in the case of *Brahman* no relationship to anything of the world can be said to be intrinsic. Just as riverbanks (*taṭa*) are not the river but lie alongside of it (*taṭastha*), so also the relationships of *Brahman* to the world lie, as it were, alongside of it and are really alien to it. This is why relational *Brahma-lakṣaṇas* are called *taṭastha-lakṣaṇas*.[3]

If this is the case, I understand that you must at once deny them to that extent to which they are misleading.—Exactly. And this is the function of our negative or '*neti neti*' *lakṣaṇas*. They point to *Brahman* by excluding from it all unsuitable predicates.

Thus they narrow down our search but where can we find what we really seek, namely, such positive *lakṣaṇas* as to enlighten us about the proper nature of *Brahman*?—In those passages of *Śruti* which contain what we call '*svarūpa-lakṣaṇas*,' i.e., direct indications of the proper form (*svarūpa*) of *Brahman*. They tell us, for instance, that *Brahman* is "reality, knowledge, infinite," "intelligence only," "bliss," etc. These are the topmost rungs of the *Śruti*-ladder of indications. It is to them that all our previous steps have led us.

*3.10 The primacy of the highest meaning (*paramārtha*)*

You said earlier that no possible definition can really express *Brahman*. How then can we know it with the help of those *svarūpa-lakṣaṇas*?—Through a process of interpretation which we call *lakṣaṇā*, and which takes us beyond the ordinary meaning of their terms to their most elevated, supra-mundane meaning (*paramārtha*). In this process we move along a threefold ascending path through causality (*hetubhāva*), negation (*apavāda*) and elevation (*paramārtha-lakṣaṇā*), according to the suggestions of the context. Thus, for instance, when we try to understand the passage "*Brahman* is reality, knowledge, infinite" (*Taitt. Up*. 2, 1), the term 'reality' is first understood according to its primary meaning (*mukhyārtha*), as it applies to material realties, such as clay, bodies, etc., but the context makes it clear that it is not in that sense that it applies to their Cause. Indeed, the term 'knowledge' is there to warn us that *Brahman* is not inert, unconscious reality but a conscious existent. Again, we might understand the term 'knowledge' in its mundane sense and think that *Brahman* has knowledge as a quality but the term 'infinite' forces us to deny this and to understand that it simply is knowledge and reality in the most elevated sense of those terms. Similarly, other passages teach us that it is bliss, power, etc. The important passage, "*Tattvamasi*" (That thou art), which occurs in *Chānd. Up*. 6, 8, 6ff, is to be understood in the same fashion: '*tat*' does not stand for any world-entities but for the root-cause of the world, '*tvam*' does' not stand for the individual 'thou' as such but for the root cause of the knowing subject, and the identity signified by '*asi*' is the pure identity of the one universal Cause, known indifferently as *Parabrahman* or *Paramātman*.

4. Appraisal

On the basis of *Śruti* worked out according to a theological method of which faith is the animating principle and reasoning the ancillary instrument, Śaṅkara has given us a still incomplete, yet correct, doctrine of God. As for a corresponding philosophy of man and the world, we should not search for one in his writings, for he explicitly considered that as secondary and did not mean to produce one. What he had to say on the subject of man and the world was merely consequential upon what he meant to say about God, and is expressed for the most part in negative or relative terms.

He said this: that man and the world cannot be truly comprehended apart from, and independently of, God, for they depend entirely upon him as upon their total cause; that since they are totally his effects, they are nothing by themselves, yet by him they are in their own imperfect way what he is in his own most perfect way; and that, therefore, they are neither sheer non-being nor being in the highest sense of the term (*sad-asad-vilakṣaṇa*). He thus spoke of them in a language which confines itself to using terms in their purest sense, a language which St Augustine, St Bonaventure and St Thomas Aquinas used also, but which they refused to employ exclusively for it can mislead the untrained mind. Fr P. Johanns used to say that pantheism was not only foreign to the doctrine of Śaṅkara, but had been clearly refuted by him. But Śaṅkara's language kept to such heights that the lower genius of many a so-called disciple and more commonly, of the neo-Vedāntins of today could not keep pace with him, and they have turned his transcendentalism into an unpalatable brand of pantheism. When he said that this universe is to God as the creations of our dreams are to the world of our awakened mind, as the illusions of the juggler are to concrete reality, and as a mirage is to the desert, they understood him to say that the world is absolute *māyā*, i.e., sheer illusion, thus forgetting that comparisons are meant to reach their object through a process of purification and elevation. When he said that "we are *Brahman*," they neglected his subtle but correct interpretation by precise *lakṣaṇā* and simply endowed our finite self with divinity, an error which he had been most emphatic in refuting, since for him the essence of *avidyā* is to superimpose finiteness upon God and divinity upon the finite.

However, though sincere study can eliminate such gross misrepresentations of Śaṅkara's teaching, this would not be sufficient to permit us to incorporate it into the body of our own Christian teaching. We should first correct certain fundamental wrong views which have crept into his largely correct doctrine: his radical fideism, which made him reject as impossible a purely rational demonstration of the existence and true nature of God; his conception of *Śruti* as a transcendent yet natural succour of human reason; his ignorance of the possibility of a supernatural plane of divine initiative and elevation by grace; his consequent misconception of supreme intuition (*anubhava*) as an achievement well within the natural power of man, rather than as a pure self-gift of God, undue and inaccessible to our unaided, effort; the confusion which he failed to remove between identity through knowledge and identity through nature; the imprecision of his theory of divine causality, which is to be praised in that it maintained both the absolute freedom and transcendence of God and his intimate immanence in the effects which he originates, preserves and directs, but which borrowed its terms from the inadequate doctrine of Sāṁkhya and thus failed to present itself in a technical garb of its own, which could have preserved it from alterations and falsifications.

Once set right on such points the doctrine of Śaṅkara ought to be completed by a fully positive philosophy of man and nature and crowned by an adequate philosophy of religion. Thus it should be possible to bring to perfection the task to which Fr P. Johanns had so heartily devoted himself in his *To Christ through the Vedānta*.[4]

Notes

[1] [R.V. De Smet, "Śaṅkara's Non-Dualism (Advaita-Vāda)," *Religious Hinduism: A Presentation and Appraisal*, ed. R. De Smet and J. Neuner, 2nd rev. ed. (Allahabad / Mumbai: St Paul Publications, 1964) 52-62. Reprinted with kind permission of St Pauls, Mumbai.

The text remains unchanged in the 3rd rev. ed. (Allahabad: St Paul Publications, 1968) 80-96. For the text of the substantially revised 4th ed., see below, chapter 20.

The first three and a half pages of the 'first' edition—"Lesson XVIII: The Great Hindu Theologies: 1. Śaṅkara's Advaita or Non-Dualism," *Hinduism: A Course by Letter* (October 1958) 1-16—are different, and read as follows:

> **Introduction.** In his *History of Ancient Vedānta*, published in Japanese (*Prācīna-Vedānta-Vāda*, Vol. I, 1950; II, 1951; III, 1955), Hajime Nakamura, at the end of a thorough enquiry, places Śaṅkara somewhere during the first half of the eighth century AD. Renou and other specialists have approved this conclusion which unfortunately does not yet give us the satisfaction of quoting quite precise dates. The details of Śaṅkara's life are as problematical but his decisive influence in the restoration of orthodox Brahmanism is incontestable.
>
> What sets him above all previous Vedāntins is his success in systematizing for the first time, through selection, adaptation and downright rejection, the whole material of religious and philosophical literature accumulated in India during a period of over 1500 years. (See Lesson I, pp 5-8; Lesson II, pp. 1-6).
>
> **The Main Currents of Pre-Śaṅkara Literature**
>
> The difficulty of Śaṅkara's task will be seen if we recall briefly the many heterogeneous trends to which this literature had given expression:
>
> —the polytheism of the Vedas;

—the literalism of the Brāhmaṇas and their magic conception of the efficacy of sacrificial rites;
—the symbolism of the Āraṇyakas;
—the inner search of the Upaniṣadic thinkers for supreme Being (*Parabrahma*) or supreme Spirit (*Paramātmā*); their first elaboration of the themes of *karma* and rebirth; and their deeper answers to the mystery of life;
—the atheistic but very ethical puritanism of Mahāvīra Jina;
—the emphasis laid by Gautama Buddha on the allied conceptions of *saṃsāra* (the stream of ever renewed existences) and *karma* (the chain of actions determined by previous actions and determining further activities which maintain the course of *saṃsāra*); his disregard for metaphysical questions; and his pointing out a way (*mārga*) to *mokṣa* (liberation in the form of *nirvāṇa* or complete emancipation from *saṃsāra*) through the practice of meditation (*dhyāna-yoga*) and monastic morality;
—the unrelenting development by Buddhist philosophers of a destructive kind of dialectics which led their various schools from Phenomenalism to absolute Voidism (*śūnya-vāda*) by way of a sharp criticism of all normal presumptions concerning activity, knowledge and existence;
—the traditionalism of the *Dharma-sūtras* and *smṛtis*, such as *Manu-smṛti* and other codes of customs, rights and duties, and the refinement of the technique of interpretation of legal texts;
—the 'theism' of the *Bhagavad-Gītā*, which tends to reconcile the desire of the masses for a personal cult (probably stirred up by the impact of the personalities of Buddha and Jina) and their conservative attachment to Brahmanism, by merging together the upaniṣadic *Brahmātmā* and the mythical figure of Kṛṣṇa into a *Bhagavān* to whom a cult of *bhakti* (personal devotion) may be rendered;
—the new doctrine of selfless activity (*niṣkāma-karma*) proposed by the same *Bhagavad-Gītā*, which infuses the detachment of monastic morality into the ethics of a society of castes ruled by their respective dharma; (see Lesson V, pp. 7-8; Lesson VI, pp. 1-2; Lesson XV)
—the rules of interpretation compiled by Jaimini in his *Mīmāṃsā-sūtra*, which is especially focussed upon the solution of all problems regarding *dharma*; and the development by its chief commentators, Śabara, Prabhākara and Kumārila Bhaṭṭa of the atheistic philosophy implied in the theory of *karma*;
—the succinct harmonization by Bādarāyaṇa in his *Brahma-sūtra* of the main Vedānta texts concerning the nature and mutual relationship of world, souls and *Brahma*;
—the pluralism of Kaṇāda's *Vaiśeṣika-sūtra*, which reduces all reality to six categories, the chief of which comprises the nine kinds of substances, namely, four varieties of atoms, ether, time, space, souls and minds, while it significantly omits any mention of a supreme *Brahma*;

—the dualism of Īśvarakṛṣṇa's *Sāṁkhya-kārikā*, which posits two irreducible categories: the self-evolving material *Prakṛti* and the category of *puruṣa*, which comprises the many 'centres of awareness';
—the exacting logic and the conceptualistic realism of Gotama's *Nyāya sūtra*, and their easy association with a theistically modified Vaiśeṣika pluralism;
—the mental discipline of Patañjali's *Yoga-sūtra*, which aims at stabilizing the activities of the mind (*citta-vṛttinirodha*) in order to redintegrate the *puruṣa* in its original isolation (*kaivalya*) from *prakṛti*; (see Lesson IX)
—the hedonistic materialism of Lokāyatikas, Cārvākas, and other Nāstikas (unbelievers), who follow their mythical founder Bṛhaspati in his rejection of castes, *dharma*, and authoritative scriptures;
—the penetrating speculations on language by Grammarians, Rhetoricians and Exegetes; in particular, their upholding of the eternity of words (*śabda*), which strengthens the belief of *Śrutivādins*, originates a peculiar form of Vedānta (Śabdādvaita) developed by Bhartṛhari, and influences the esoteric current of *Tantra*, a complex system of ideas, mantras and rites, which constitutes the worship of Durgā, the consort and *Śakti* (power) of Śiva; (concerning *Tantra*, Lesson IV, pp. 8-9)
—the cult of devotion (*bhakti*) of Vaiṣṇavite, Śaivite and other sects which, by using exhaustively the suggestions of Epics and Purāṇas, exploit fully the concepts of *avatāra* (phenomenal manifestation of God) and *bhagavān* (God conceived as owning a body by which He is individualized); they popularize their anthropomorphic theism by means of devotional hymns and psalms, sung in the centres of pilgrimage; these sects will have their greatest expansion after the time of Śaṅkara but he may have heard about some of the sixty-three Śaivite 'saints' (*Nāya Nār*) and twelve Vaiṣṇavite 'deep' sages (*Āḷvār*), the apostles of this *bhakti*-movement; (see Lessons XVI-XVII).
—finally, the syncretist attempts, much influenced by Buddhism, of such early Vedāntins as Bhartṛprapañca, Gauḍapāda and the anonymous author of *Yogavāsiṣṭha*; in particular, their *bhedābhedavāda*, a doctrine which teaches that *Brahma* is both different and non-different from the world and thus fails to overcome the error of pantheism.

The effect upon the Indian people of such a jungle of diverse tendencies growing side by side could be nothing else but bewilderment, scepticism or resigned conformism. The situation is aptly summarized in the well-known stanza:

...

Then Śaṅkara appeared: his unshakable faith, metaphysical genius, faultless acumen, dexterous logic and peerless erudition made him fully equipped for the tremendous task of restoring Brahmanism in its pristine purity.

Seizing upon a very simple distinction often hinted by the Upaniṣads he used it as a clearing tool to set in order the Indian domain of thought.]

[2] [The reference here is to De Smet, ch. 3: Ancient Religious Speculation, *Religious Hinduism* (1964, 1968).]
[3] [In this paragraph, the original text reads mostly *lakṣaṇā*, which I have corrected to *lakṣaṇa*.]
[4] [Originally published in *The Light of the East*. Now available as *The Writings of P. Johanns: To Christ through the Vedānta*, ed. Theo de Greeff (Bangalore: United Theological College, 1996).
The version of October 1958 (see note 1 above) contained the following bibliography:
The Vedānta-sūtras with the Commentary of Śaṅkarācārya, tr. G. Thibaut, Sacred Books of the East, vols. XXXIV and XXXVIII, Oxford, 1890 and 1896.
Bṛhadāraṇyakopaniṣad with Śaṅkara's Bhāṣya, tr. Swami Madhavananda, 3rd ed., Almora, 1950.
Upadeśasāhasrī, text and tr. Swami Jagadananda, 2nd ed., Madras, 1949.
G. Dandoy, SJ, *An Essay on the Doctrine of the Unreality of the World in the Advaita*, [Catholic] Orphan Press, Calcutta, 1919.
P. Johanns, SJ, *To Christ through the Vedānta*, a series of articles in *The Light of the East*, Vol. I, III, IV, V, and XIII, Calcutta.
P. Johanns, SJ, *A Synopsis of 'To Christ through the Vedānta': I—Śaṅkara*, Pamphlet no. 4 of The Light of the East series, Calcutta, 1930.]

4

THEOLOGICAL METHOD AND VEDĀNTA[1]

Professor C.T. Kenghe has been kind enough to criticize in the last issue of *Oriental Thought* (III, 2-4, pp. 35-50)[2] my article on "The Fundamental Antinomy of Śaṅkarācārya's Methodology," published in the October 1956 (II, 4, pp. 1-9)[3] issue of the same Quarterly. I have read his comments with interest and instruction and I sincerely agree with much of what he said in them. However, since I also feel that he has misunderstood and, consequently, misrepresented several of my statements, it is likely that I had expressed them in too concise a way. That misunderstanding occurred mainly with regard to my introductory paragraphs in which I had sketched, much too briefly, the *śrutivāda* nature of the *Ācārya's* method of teaching, and pointed out its equivalence with the method of the Catholic theologians.

I think it, therefore, advisable to re-state that part of my article in its true light and proportion.

* * *

"The importance of the study of methodology for the proper understanding of philosophy can never be exaggerated." (C.T. Kenghe, *Oriental Thought* III. 2-4, p. 202)

Methodology is the study of the process through which a piece of knowledge, especially such bodies of systematized knowledge as constitute the various sciences, becomes established as true in a human intellect.

Any such process starts from a well-ascertained point of departure, in order to reach a definite point of arrival, following a way (*meta hodon*, hence, *met-hodos*, method) precisely orientated from the one to the other. The methodology of a science is, therefore, the study of its starting-point, its method, and its aim or point of arrival.

The term 'method' is often enlarged so as to cover both starting-point and point of arrival as well as the passage from the one to the other (i.e., the 'method' in the stricter sense of the term). Following this usage, philosophers say that it is the method, rather than the subject-matter, which specifies the various sciences. Indeed, the same object, e.g., the human body, can be studied according to various methods so that we have, for instance, a chemistry, a geometry, a physiology, an aesthetics, a philosophy, etc., of the same human body. This, however, does not mean that any object whatsoever can be a subject-matter for all the sciences, but that the subject-matter of a science consists only in that or those objects which lend themselves to being considered according to the particular method of that science.

The question comes now whether the term 'philosophy' is but a common label pinned on the corpus of all sciences or at least on a certain group of some of the sciences, or whether it is the proper name of one particular science. History tells us that both usages have been and still are to some extent current.

In its broadest sense, 'philosophy' denotes the human pursuit of wisdom (*jijñāsā*, or more precisely *puruṣārtha-jijñāsā*). Wisdom means true knowledge of the supreme end of man and of the fitness of means to conduce to it. Thus understood, it is clear that philosophy is equivalent to the study of all possible subjects according to all possible methods for it must consider all possible ends and means from all possible standpoints. This is the most frequent usage of the word from Pythagoras to Aristotle, although Plato had already distinguished mathematics and history from philosophy. The mediaeval schoolmen further distinguished supernatural theology from philosophy but retained the latter word to designate the generality of the other sciences they were pursuing, apart from history. And this broad meaning has endured through Bacon and Descartes down to the nineteenth century and even, exceptionally, to our own days. It allows us, when we do not wish to be very precise, to use such phrases as 'Indian philosophy,' 'Christian philosophy,' or such other non-technical manners of speaking as are exemplified in Prof. Kenghe's passage quoted above or in the quotation from Aurobindo Ghose which he included in his article, pp. 38-39.

However, it is more frequent nowadays to restrict the meaning of the term 'philosophy' so as to render it equivalent to the term 'metaphysics,' an equivalence which is not entirely out of step with the practice of Aristotle himself. Indeed, feeling the need for such a restriction, he had called 'First Philosophy' that peculiar science which he treated in those of his writings which his editor, Andronicos of Rhodes (first century BC), placed after his treatises on 'Physical Philosophy' (*meta ta physica*, hence, as is well known, the more common term, 'Metaphysics').

The object assigned by Aristotle to this First Philosophy or Metaphysics is 'the existent as existent' (*Metaphysics* III, 1, 1003a21; V, 1, 1026a31; etc.). And, since the science of such an object requires the knowledge of its ultimate causes, he defines metaphysics as "the theoretical science of the first principles and causes" (*Metaphysics* I, 2, 982b9-10). But, whether they are many or one, it is obvious that those first causes must be transcendent, immutable and, therefore, divine realities, and that the First Philosophy may rightly be called Theology (*Brahmajijñāsā*). Hence, there are three theoretical or speculative sciences: mathematics, physics, and what we may call theology. It is obvious that if the divine is present anywhere, it is in things which exist separately and are immutable, and that the highest science must deal with this highest genus; so that the speculative are the highest of the sciences, and 'theology' the highest of all these.... But if there is an immutable substance, the science which deals with it must be primary and be the 'First Philosophy.' And because it is primary it is universal, and is therefore concerned with the existent *qua* existent, i.e., with its essence and with the properties which pertain to it *qua* existent. (*Metaphysics* V, 1, 1026a18-32)

As far as Aristotle is concerned, the term 'theology' is synonymous with 'First Philosophy' or what has been called afterwards 'Metaphysics.' It is a purely rational and, hence, independent science. But with the advent of Christianity a new sort of science of God appears in Asia, North Africa and Europe. It is first called '*Gnosis*' (*jñāna*), then 'Sacred Theology,' and later on 'Revealed or Supernatural Theology.' The Christian scholars distinguish it carefully from the Aristotelian 'Theology' or 'First Philosophy,' and especially from that part of metaphysics which is concerned with God, the Absolute and the

First Cause, and which Leibniz was the first to call 'Theodicy.' Revealed theology is rational for it is a real science developed by reason, but it is not purely rational for it depends essentially on a supra-rational starting point, namely, the divine and therefore infallible testimony (*śabda*) made known to mankind by Christ and His disciples. It is not supposed to supplant natural theology, but to complement this science which it presupposes and subordinates to itself.

As a science based on an infallible testimony, it belongs to a common genus with Muslim *Kalām* and *Śruti-Mīmāṃsā* since the latter two are also developed on the basis of a testimony held by their adherents to be infallible and concerned essentially with the Absolute. The method of these three sciences is similar in all essentials, and this essential unity of their method entails the unity of their genus. Whether we call this genus 'theology' or '*mīmāṃsā*' or some other name is a mere question of terminology upon which it should not be difficult to come to an agreement.

In order to characterize this method, we must define its starting-point, its rational process, and its aim.

The starting-point of all such sciences should be a supra-rational and infallible testimony, received as such by an intellectual act of faith. It should therefore be possible rationally to ascertain its credibility, though all claims for a perfect evidence of its contents in the light of unaided reason are obviously irrelevant. Such testimony is rightly called '*apauruṣeya*' in the sense that it is not mediated through the agency of a finite individual characterized by fallibility. It is up to each tradition to attempt to prove in its own way the absence of such a fallible mediation in the very constitution of its basic testimony.

The aim pursued in the systematic study of that testimony is perfect wisdom (*samyag-jñāna*), which cannot be attained short of a perfect knowledge of the divine Absolute. "The direct object of the desire (which animates *Brahmajijñāsā*) is a knowledge culminating in full apprehension (*avagatiparyantam jñānam*)." (*B.S.Bh.* 1, 1, 1) In other words, "that knowledge which discriminates Brahma and discards nescience, terminates in intuition (*anubhavāvasānam*)." (*B.S.Bh.* 2, 1, 4). Christian theology is in perfect agreement with these texts insofar as it also places its ultimate aim in a blissful intuition of the divine essence.

It also acknowledges that no human means by themselves alone, and therefore not even theological activity itself, can produce that intuition. Yet, when it is completely sincere and animated by a pure love for its end, it is the most proximate disposition towards it, and the most worthy pursuit to which man can devote himself.

This pursuit is now to be described. It is a rational pursuit, yet it actually begins with an abdication by reason of any claim for self-sufficiency in the matter of Supreme knowledge. Indeed, reason begins here with an act of faith in the exclusive authority of a given testimony concerning the proper nature of the Transcendent. "The transcendent highest Brahma can be fathomed by means of *Śruti* only, not by mere reasoning." (*B.S.Bh.* 2, 1, 31) This is the Augustinian first movement of "*crede ut intelligas*": belief is the gateway to intellection. But it immediately implies the second movement of "*fides quaerens intellectum*": faith is to be transcended into intellection. For, even though it yields to faith, reason cannot renounce its own nature, hence, it naturally tends to assimilate, i.e., to render fully intelligible to itself that testimony which it has received on faith. The various steps of this process towards full intellectual assimilation follow logically from both the nature of reason and of the testimony which it trusts.

They are clearly proposed in *Bṛh. Up*. 2, 4, 5: "It is by the vision of the *Ātmā*, through hearing, reflection, and understanding, that all this is known." Taking this as a statement of method, Śaṅkarācārya explains: "The *Ātmā* should *first* be heard of from teacher and from the infallible tradition, it should *afterwards* be reflected upon through logical reasoning, it should *then* be pondered on, steadfastly concentrated upon. Thus, indeed, it becomes seen: when these initiatory steps (*sādhanā*), *viz*. hearing, reflecting, concentrating (*śravaṇa-manana-nididhyāsana*), have been gone through. When these three are combined, then the true vision of the uniqueness of Brahma is brought about successfully, not otherwise, viz. by hearing alone." (*Bṛh. Up. Bh.* 2, 4, 5)

The Christian tradition prescribes the same threefold *sādhanā*. "The word of God," writes St Ambrose, "begins to grow in our soul when it is received, increases while it is rationally understood, and comes to maturity when it is fully grasped and assimilated." These three steps, *viz. susceptio* (*śravaṇa*), *intellectio* (*manana*), and *comprehensio* (*nididhyāsana*) constitute one process entirely necessary to him who pursues perfect wisdom. The slightly different Augustinian triad: *fides*, *intellectus*, *visio* (belief, intellection, vision), is taken by all the medieval theologians as well as the Christian theologians of today, as the blue-print of their method, and is explained in the words of St Bonaventure as: *credere*, *intelligere credita*, *videre intellecta* (to believe, to understand what you believe, to come to see what you have understood).

The supreme vision of which the Christian theologians speak is not considered by them as realizable in this life, though the possibility in this life of the highest kind of mysticism is acknowledged by all. Śaṅkarācārya, on the contrary, admits the possibility of the supreme intuition in this very life, though never as produced by means of any *sādhanā*, not even of *Brahmajijñāsā*. It simply cannot be mediated by any means whatsoever. His explicit authority for such an admission is never (at least to my fallible knowledge) his own experience, but that of *ṛṣis* and other enlightened men as testified by the *Śruti* (for references cf. my previous article).[4] Yet, it appears to be implicit *in the very manner of his teaching* that he had reached that supreme illumination. Hence, the suitability of the method of *Brahmajijñāsā* did not concern him directly but only *indirectly*, insofar as he chose to be a teacher, whereas it *directly* concerned his disciples. It is for them and as a teacher that he wrote: "What the first *sūtra* proposes is an *exegesis* of the propositions of the Vedānta, *served by* irrefutable arguments, and having the supreme good as its *aim* (*vedānta-vākya-mīmāṃsā tad-virodhi-tark'opikāraṇa niḥśreyas-prayojanā prastyuyate* (*B.S.Bh.* 1, 1, 1).

The term *mīmāṃsā* is here used in its strict sense, equivalent to *śravaṇa*. It designates the direct study of the text (the Ambrosian *susceptio*) so as to grasp its exact significance (*artha*). It is of course more than a mere process of hearing and the *Ācārya's* words: "not by hearing alone" are echoed by John Moschus, the Abbot, when he warns his disciples lest they take "lovers of words for true lovers of wisdom" and "esteem clever talk above meditation, silence and tranquillity." *Mīmāṃsā* is an intellectual process which uses the rationally devised rules of all linguistic and literary interpretation, suitably recast according to the nature of the sacred text. Of such a text or set of texts the very infallibility requires that its significance should be grasped as internally *one*. This harmony (*samanvaya*) is perceived through a process of comparison which establishes the correct reference to each other of primary and secondary statements. Its result may be confirmed by recourse to mediated (*pauruṣeya*) traditions (*Smṛti*). This recourse is not necessary but helps to produce in the seeker's mind a solid conviction regarding the significance of the *apauruṣeya* testimony. In the wielding of the traditional *pramāṇas* or rules of interpretation the teacher does, of course, not act as a mere mechanical transmitter of unchangeable solutions; for, even apart from recasting those rules if he deems it necessary, he must exercise true sagacity and originality in deciding about their application to each particular case.

But it is in his second step, called *manana* (*intellectio* in the Ambrosian terminology), that his originality is displayed at its best. The higher his metaphysical insight and the keener his logical acumen, the more perfectly he will be able to manifest the intelligibility of the *artha* ascertained in his first step. This manifestation has two complementary aspects: it must, first, emphasize the inner rationality of that *artha*; and, secondly, it must confront it with all possible objections inspired from the other *pramāṇas* so as to show that it can never be contradicted. When both inner rationality and complete non-contradiction (*abādhitatva*) are secured, full credibility, the end of *manana*, is obtained.

However, full credibility is not yet direct evidence of vision. It is simply the necessary and sufficient condition of the third step, called *comprehensio* or *nididhyāsana*. Because *manana* has removed all doubt and contradictions, the aspirant has now attained a state of complete tranquillity. This state is not empty but calmly illumined by the full radiance of the ascertained truth. The intellect, whose nature is to imbibe truth, can now allow itself to be thoroughly penetrated by the supreme truth till it reaches perfect coincidence or conformity (*anubhava*), characterized by immediacy (*pratyakṣatva*).

In spite of the brevity of the above exposition I feel confident that no Vedāntin will be tempted to deny any of its essential assertions regarding the method of the Vedānta. As to the method of Catholic theology, I did not bring forth all the many references that are relevant to it, but I can say that methodology is one of the most accurately ascertained domains of that theological science and that I have presented it faithfully.

It should then be admitted that both Vedānta and Catholic theology belong to the same genus, namely, both are sciences of a testimony believed to be infallible. Yet, they differ specifically: Vedānta is the science of *Śruti*, and its subject-matter coincides with the subject of what the West calls metaphysics (the Aristotelian 'first philosophy') or, at least, theodicy. Catholic theology is the science of the Jewish revelation culminating in Christ, and its subject-matter is complementary to, and therefore distinct from, the subject of metaphysics. It is, indeed, concerned with a truth inaccessible to unaided reason, though supremely desirable to it: the mysterious truth concerning the proper reality of God, the Absolute, and the free initiative of His goodness towards man and the world, which are His free creation. It is obvious that such truth is the secret of God and is, therefore, inaccessible to reason apart from a direct communication by God.

In their relation to reason, Vedānta and Christian theology agree to a large extent. Both consider that they are the work of reason, but not of purely autonomous reason. Both consider that unaided reason is valid in its own domain, which is not the domain of perfect truth by which the universal Cause and, therefore, all its effects are known exactly as they are (*yāthātmya*). Both consider that the ordinary *pramāṇas* can be ancillary to *Śruti* and serve reason in its theological enquiry; "indeed, the comprehension of Brahma is completed by the full determination, *consequent on discussion*, of the significance of the sentences (of the infallible testimony) (*vākyārtha-vicārṇādhyavasāna-nivṛtti hi brahm'āvagatiḥ*); but it is not completed by the other *pramāṇas* such as inference, etc. (*n'ānumān'ādi-pramāṇ'āntara-nivṛtti*)." (*B.S.Bh.* 1, 1, 2) It is, therefore, as an assisting means (*sahāyatyena*) that logical argumentation (*tarka*) is allowed by Scripture, namely, as a means of confirming (*dāḍhadhārya*) the meaning ascertained through *śravaṇa*. When discussing the opinions *on his own subject* of *nāstika*, i.e., of people who reject his infallible *śabda*, the Vedānta teacher or the Christian theologian will naturally use those (*pramāṇas*) only which they accept, but even then his argumentation will only be for the sake of corroborating the scriptural assertions, not for proving them independently of his infallible authority.

Where Vedānta and Christian theology disagree as to their relation to reason is regarding the proper domain attributable to unaided reason. For Christian theology it is possible for human reason independently of Christian revelation, to develop a valid metaphysics, including a valid theodicy, although this theodicy is to be completed by that revelation. In other words, it is possible apart from revelation to obtain through reasoning the metaphysical certainty of the existence of the supreme Cause and a true but very imperfect knowledge of its true nature. This incomplete knowledge can then be raised to perfection by divine revelation culminating in direct experience. The mutual complementarity of natural reason and supernatural revelation is thus faultless.

For Vedānta, on the contrary, no such complementarity appears, at least at first sight, to exist between *Śruti* and reason left to itself. The domain of the latter is limited to the range of *pratyakṣa* and the three kinds of reasoning, to which may be added the *pauruṣeya śabda* of *itihāsas*, *purāṇas* and other more valuable *smṛtis*. And this domain is said to be ruled entirely by *avidyā*, in such a way that even though a certain knowledge of the existence of Brahma is possible within it, our knowledge of its nature is always fraught with superimposition (*adhyāsa*) and, hence, erroneous. *Śruti*, then, whose object is *vidyā*, cannot be said to be the complement of unaided knowledge for it has simply to supersede it, at least insofar as metempirical reality is concerned. Moreover, *Śruti* itself, and the very process of *Brahmajijñāsā*, belong to the realm of *avidyā* because they are *pramāṇas*. For as the *Ācārya* explains in his Introduction to *B.S.*: "it is preceded by superimposition that all activities, either profane or Vedic, dependent on sources and objects of knowledge, are developed, and also all scriptural teachings, whether they are concerned with injunctions and prohibitions, or with final release" (*adhyāsa puraskṛtya sarve pramāṇa-*

prameya-vyavahārā laukikā vaidikāśca pravṛttā sarvāṇi ca śāstrāṇi vidhi-prativedha-mokṣa-parāṇi)." Hence, not only the *karmakāṇḍa* but even the *jñānakāṇḍa* of *Śruti* presupposes *avidyā* and does not function as a *pramāṇa* apart from it.

This is the situation responsible for the antinomy which was the concern of my previous article. The term antinomy simply means apparent contradiction, without yet deciding whether this contradiction is real or not. After the contradiction which I have pointed out appeared to me on the basis of the facts mentioned in my previous paragraph (and more at length in the article referred to), I have tried to reduce it by a recourse to some important features of the *Ācārya's* teaching and method. However, even with their help, that reduction has remained incomplete so far. If anyone is ready to consider without any prejudice the terms of that antinomy, and succeeds in displacing it entirely, he will deserve my utmost gratitude.

Since I have made my terminology clear in the body of this article, I may now present a few conclusions which will provide the answer to Prof. Kenghe's criticism:

(1) As far as his method is concerned, Śrī Śaṅkarācārya is not an independent philosopher or pure metaphysician, notwithstanding the fact that the subject-matter of his science is essentially identical with that of rational metaphysics or 'first philosophy.'

(2) The term 'theology' may be used to designate the genus of his science, provided it be understood correctly and applied with all due accommodations.

(3) The term 'Hindu theologian' may therefore be used as an equivalent for *śrutivādin*, *Uttara-mīmāṃsaka*, or *Vedāntin*. Hence, it is correct to say that the *Ācārya* is "the transmitter of an authoritative sacred tradition," a phrase which should not be disfigured into "nothing else but a transmitter of a tradition like a mechanical radio-transmitter."

(4) The fact that his science is theological prevents him from being original as to his starting-point (the sacred text), but far from precluding originality of insight and method, it rather demands it. I may add that, to my mind the *Ācārya* is by far the most original of all Vedāntins.

(5) Neither does it make his science esoteric, but rather directed *de jure* to all men.

(6) However, as a matter of fact, the *Ācārya* requires some definite dispositions in the aspirant. Indeed, the reading of the Veda (and, therefore, birth in one of the three upper castes) is the common antecedent of both Mīmāṃsās. As to the special antecedent of Uttaramīmāṃsā, it consists in the four well-known *sādhanas*; "these being present, it is possible, either before or after *dharma-jijñāsā*, to desire to know Brahma, and to know it; but not otherwise (*na viparyaye*)."(*B.S.Bh.* 1, 1, 1) Let us notice that they are required both for desiring to know, and for knowing *Brahma*, and are said to be not only a sufficient condition for knowing *Brahma* (*teṣu hi satsu... śakyate brahma... jñātum*), but even a necessary one (*na viparyaye*). Now, the second of those *sādhanas* is "*ihāmutrārtha-bhogavirāga*," a renunciation which can hardly be said to exist but in the four *āśramas*, and, at its best, but in the state of *bhikṣācārya*. However, *virāga* is more an inner disposition than an external status; hence, it is possible to say, at least in a secondary sense (*kayācid guṇavṛttyā*), that a man with a fire (*sāgni*), i.e., householder, is a true *saṁnyāsin* and *yogin* if he has renounced all desire for fruits of actions (*karma-phala-saṅkalpa-saṁnyāsāt*), according to *Bh.G.Bh.* 6, 1. Considered as external status, *varṇa* and *āśrama* do not therefore condition *Brahmajñāna* in the same necessary way as the four internal *sādhanas*. But the latter are its necessary and sufficient condition. Hence, if it is true, "as experience shows," that there is "but one among many that attains *jñāna*," (*Bh.G.Bh.* 13, 2) it must be because that condition is not present in more people. And this happens in spite of the fact that, *de jure*, *Brahmajijñāsā* is open to all (cf. *Bṛh. Up. Bh.* 4, 4, 8; *Taitt. Up. Bh.* 1, 11; *B.S.Bh.* 3, 4, 38; *Bh.G.* 10, 32; etc.), though this is not true of *Brahmajijñāsā* understood strictly as *Śruti-mīmāṃsā* (cf. *B.S.Bh.* 1, 3, 38 aptly quoted by Prof. Kenghe).

(7) With regard to the relation of *Brahmajijñāsā* to human reason, we observe in the first place that the validity within their own sphere of the *pramāṇa* other than *apauruṣeya śabda* is never challenged; in the second place, their ancillary competence within the process of *Brahmajijñāsā* is fully acknowledged; in the third place, the other *darśanas* are acceptable, even in what they say concerning the proper object of *Śruti*, insofar as that conforms to the *artha* of *Śruti*. Besides, *Brahmajijñāsā* is the work of *manas*, though *Brahmajijñāsā* itself is not a mental

action: *na mānasī kriyā*; cf. *B.S.Bh.* 1, 1, 4. Hence *Brahmajijñāsā* is as much a rational science as Christian theology but, like it also, it is neither independent philosophy nor a purely rational science. Both also recognize that the supreme experience cannot be produced by them for it transcends reason and all its means. Yet what they do is extremely valuable for it is a progressive removal of all ignorance.

(8) Despite the fact that those two sciences belong to the same genus on account of the similarity of their method, we should not think that their respective teachings are identical, though to the well-informed these teachings do appear to have much in common. Incidentally, I do not see how Bradley can be considered a valid source for ascertaining the Christian notion of God.

(9) As to the nature of *Śruti*, I fail to see how the *Ācārya* could endorse Prof. Kenghe's assertion that the *Śruti* "contains important metaphysical achievements of great ancient thinkers and seekers of truth," for such a view simply turns *Śruti* into *pauruṣeya śabda*, and *Brahmajijñāsā* into an effect of human effort. We know, on the contrary, that *Brahmajijñāsā* can in no sense effect *jñāna* but is only undertaken by disciples *as if it were* a means causing the manifestation of knowledge.

(10) It is, indeed, for the disciples alone that *Brahmajijñāsā* functions as a means, not for the *guru*; for to be a perfect *guru*, one must have transcended the whole sphere of means. It is also at the level of the disciple only that the antinomy which I have pointed out may appear; for the *Brahmavid* stands beyond the reach of all antinomies.

Notes

[1] [First published in *Oriental Thought* (Nashik) 4/1-2 (Jan.-Apr. 1960) 20-35. See also the typescript, Collected Papers A, 167-179, and DNC 73/DES/COL/167-179. Having been unable to trace the rights holders of *Oriental Thought*, this is reprinted here with kind permission of De Nobili College, Pune.]

[2] [C.T. Kenghe, *Oriental Thought* (Nashik) 3/2-4 (1957) 35-50.]

[3] [See above, ch. 3.]

[4] [See above, ch. 3.]

5

THE LOGICAL STRUCTURE OF '*TATTVAMASI*' ACCORDING TO SUREŚVARA'S *NAIṢKARMYA SIDDHI*[1]

The importance of the distinction between primary and secondary meanings for the understanding of Śaṅkara's exegesis of "*Tattvamasi*" and other *mahāvākyas* is fast becoming recognized by those scholars who take the trouble of reading all the authentic writings of the great *Āçārya* and of studying the works of his immediate followers.

Thus, for instance, Professor Louis Renou writes in a recent article:

> What is the Śaṅkarian Vedānta but a total adherence to the letter and the spirit of the 'great propositions' contained in the Upaniṣads? The initial principle is that these propositions must necessarily teach the Absolute as the sole reality and assimilate to it the immaterial Self which resides within each human being. However, it is patent that most upaniṣadic propositions make use of both images and fiction. Does it then follow that they are lacking in authority, that they belong to a category of discursive knowledge? No; rather they express the supreme truth but on an implicit plane; they use the artifices peculiar to ordinary language in order to achieve this truth on another level. Since the Absolute is not designated by a direct term (and how could it be?), everything that serves to evoke it necessarily belongs to a secondary and implicit semantics. The Śaṅkarian Vedānta is based on a certain ambiguity arising from the language.[2]

To take another example, Professor A.C. Mukerji, in an article published about the same time, emphasizes "the '*advaita*' distinction between the adjective (*viśeṣaṇa*) and what is known as *lakṣaṇā*." He rightly considers that this distinction between the expressing and the indicating power of terms "has saved its exponents from one of the disastrous and far-reaching fallacies of thought."[3]

One of the first post-Śaṅkara exponents of this distinction was Sureśvara. He was a direct pupil of Śrī Śaṅkarācārya and the references to Bhagavan Pūjyapāda (as he usually called his spiritual Teacher) which we find in his writings constitute, together with those of Padmapāda, the only really trustworthy personal information we have about the great Vedāntin.

"The individuality as well as the charm of Sureśvara consists largely in the vehemence with which he insists on the full purity of the doctrine of Advaita."[4] His *Naiṣkarmya Siddhi* reiterates many verses of the *Upadeśasāhasrī* of Srī Śaṅkara and contains clear echoes of his *Gītā Bhāṣya*; this is a first indication that he follows his master very closely. A comparative study of their respective teachings can further show that they differ very little. There are, however, according to Mr. A.J. Alston, three peculiarities of doctrine in the *Naiṣkarmya Siddhi* which deserve mention. The first is a refinement which tends to uphold pure *naiṣkarmya*: "The injunction (i.e., 'he should meditate only on the Self') can only be a restrictive (*niyamavidhi*: this is Śaṅkara's opinion) or a negative one (*parisaṅkhyāvidhi*: this is the alternative opinion preferred by Sureśvara) for we can meditate on the highest Self only when the not-self has already been excluded from view" (*NS* 1, 88). The second is Sureśvara's peculiar treatment, in certain passages only, of the concept of *ahaṁkāra*. He treats it as the most subtle modification of the *manas*, the nodal point where consciousness is inserted into the empirical personality and, therefore, the last element to be transcended in *Brahmajijñāsā*. The third peculiarity of Sureśvara's doctrine is his insistence on the magic power (*mahiman* or *mahimā*) of the *mahāvākyas* when pronounced by a genuine *guru* to an attuned pupil. The presence of this power cancels the need for a final *manovṛtti* to destroy nescience.[5]

The third book of the *Naiṣkarmya Siddhi* explains the meaning of the cardinal text "That thou art." This explanation of the grammatical and logical structure of that text prepares the pupil immediately for the solemn hearing of the formula of his *guru*. It is itself preceded by the well-known discipline destined to purify his mind and qualify him for *Brahmajijñāsā*, and more and more immediately by the discursive reflection which, proceeding according to the method of agreement and difference (*anvaya-vyatireka*), should lead him to discriminate the permanent from the impermanent (*nityānityavastu-viveka*) "Without reasoning (*anvaya* and *vyatireka*) there is no understanding of the meaning of the (great) sentences, and without this, nescience cannot be destroyed" (*NS* 2, 9). Sureśvara emphasizes this role of reasoning and considers it as usually indispensable, but he also stresses that this function is purely ancillary. Indeed, because the inferences merely establish the existence (of the *Ātman*), they do not reveal the meaning of the (great) sentences" (*NS* 3, 57).

The meaning of *Tattvamasi* is strictly *akhaṇḍārthaka*: its reference is to the absolutely simple Reality. Any exegesis of it which would result in a final residue of duality is therefore inappropriate.

For instance, we should reject all *samuccaya* views, even if they are proposed by such Vedāntins as Brahmadatta or Maṇḍana Miśra. The first falls into line with the Mīmāṃsaka insofar as he holds the view that the Upaniṣads like the *karmakāṇḍa* of the Veda are essentially injunctive in character, their injunction being about symbolic meditation, variously termed *prasaṃkhyāna*, *bhāvanā*, or *upāsanā* (*NS* 1, 67). Accordingly, such assertive propositions as *Tattvamasi* are merely subsidiary (*arthavāda*) to the corresponding injunction *Ātmetyevopāsīta* (*Bṛh. Up.* 1, 4, 7). They do not bring about final release directly through the knowledge they convey, but rather through the special conviction which is generated by *prasaṃkhyāna* and which improves upon ordinary knowledge. This improved knowledge is entirely the result of the creative work of the meditator. But, replies Sureśvara, "the spiritual conviction (*bhāvanā*) amassed through repeated meditation cannot bring *all saṃsāra* to an end, for in this case the cessation of *saṃsāra* is a result, due to the generation of that spiritual conviction and, as such, it cannot be eternal" (*NS* 3, 91). Besides we should remember that the truth of knowledge depends upon the reality of its object (*vastutantram*) and not upon the effort of the knower.

Maṇḍana Miśra incurs the same criticism insofar as his teaching agrees with that of Brahmadatta in upholding *bhāvanā* arising from repeated meditation (*abhyāsa*). He, indeed, holds that "the knowledge 'I am *Brahman*' generated by the upaniṣadic sentences is relational (*saṃsargātmaka*) and hence does not penetrate to the real nature of the *Ātman*. But this is no fault, for in the case of one who meditates as continuously as the Ganges flows, another kind of knowledge arises which does not consist of a propositional meaning (*avākyārthātmakam*), It is this latter knowledge alone which eradicates all the darkness of nescience." (*NS* 1, 67)

Against this position Sureśvara upholds the immediacy and the finality of the knowledge generated by the *mahāvākyas* and rejects as misapprehension the accusation that they are relational:

> The knowledge derived from the *Śruti* demolishes nescience... at a single stroke. Hence there can be no association between the two (i.e., between knowledge and action even in the form of repeated meditation). (*NS* 1, 67)

> In sentences like, 'verily the ether in the jar is the ether in the sky,' we point [not to a subject qualified by its predicate but] to a reality not directly expressed in the words of the sentence, [namely, to the ether unlimited by jar or sky]. So in sentences like 'That thou art' we *immediately* receive knowledge beyond the expressed meaning of the sentence. (*NS* 3, 9)

> And if the meanings of the words are understood but the spiritual experience does not arise, it will not help to invoke purely imaginary injunctions to generate a different knowledge [through repeated pondering]. For there is no other meaning to be understood but [that conveyed by the sentence itself]. (*NS* 3, 119)

> And again, what need of action [such as symbolic meditation] has the one who has experienced successively the five *kośas* and rejected them as non-*Ātman*, and understood the meaning of 'I am *Brahman*' [according to the discipline of the *Taittirīya Upaniṣad*]?
>
> If scriptural texts do not promote correct knowledge of the subject they refer to simply being heard (under the proper conditions), can *Śruti* be regarded as authoritative at all?
>
> If an objector (such as Maṇḍana Miśra) says, 'Man knows through symbolic meditation (*prasaṃkhyāna*)'—then how can the word be teaching the truth? 'We hold that knowledge derived from words is mediate and indirect (*parokṣa*),' the objector replies, 'but that it becomes intuitive conviction of reality through *prasaṃkhyāna*.'
>
> If his reason and the words do not produce correct and immediate (*aparokṣa*) knowledge in the first place, independently of that (symbolic meditation), how can they produce right knowledge later merely by being repeated? (*NS* 3, 121-124)

We can conclude this controversy in the words of A.J. Alston: "For Sureśvara *Brahmajñāna* is achieved through a discipline (*Brahmajijñāsā*) that has two stages. First comes *anvaya* and *vyatireka* on the basis of the *Śruti* texts, key and subordinate, and on one's own experience. Then, when this been brought to the point where one is certain of the unreality of all the non-*Ātman*, a final *mahāśravaṇa* (solemn hearing of the texts) serves to transport the pupil beyond the realm of empirical cognition altogether. The second stage of the discipline is thus brief, though Sureśvara regarded it as absolutely necessary."[6]

Since, according to Sureśvara, the first stage excludes *upāsanā* as leading to an *avākyārthātmaka* knowledge, we are brought back to the necessity of understanding the proper *vākyārtha* of the great propositions. Since the Reality they signify is absolutely simple, their meaning cannot be relational even though taken at their face-value such statements do not appear different from common relational statements. We should then understand in some peculiar sense, presently to be determined.

Should we call them identity-statements? This appellation would be ambiguous since strict identity is a reciprocal relation (if A is identical with B, then B is identical with A) whereas the *tādātmya* relation which exists between '*aham*' and '*Brahma*' or between '*tvam*' and '*Tat*' is surely not reciprocal. For "the effect," says Śaṅkara, "has its *Ātman* in the cause, but not the cause in its effect" (*B.S.Bh.* 2, 1, 9).

It would be better then to call the *mahāvākyas* identifying or identification-statements. An identification-statement can be understood as indicating an identity even though its terms are not strictly identical when taken in their direct and primary meaning. In the sentence "This is that Devadatta," the term 'this' denotes directly 'this grown-up individual in front of me,' whereas the term 'that Devadatta' denotes directly 'that boy Devadatta who was my classmate in school,' but my intellect strips them of their *upādhis* or accessory connotations in order rightly to understand their essential identity. This or a similar process of purification conditions the right apprehension of any identifying statement.

Accordingly, Sureśvara has proposed two *prima facie* different treatments of the *mahāvākyas*. The first proceeds through a negation of the formal connotation of the subject-term;

the second discovers the correct but secondary meaning (*lakṣyārtha*) of both terms through *lakṣaṇā*. Let us call them the negation-process and the *lakṣaṇā*-process.

The negation-process is of the type "This snake is but a rope," "That stump is but a man," etc. Verbally, such statements refer to a snake or a stump, but actually to a rope or a man. Similarly, the *Śruti*-statement "I am *Brahman*" is found to mean the exact opposite of its verbal or primary denotation. It has the logical structure of an affirmative proposition involving a concealed negation.

> If the opponent says that the 'I' must be non-different [from the supreme *Ātman*] on account of the *Śruti*-text 'I am *Brahman*,' we reply that, as in the case of 'I am fair,' not all statements made about the 'I' really refer to it. The sentence 'I am *Brahman*' actually denies the 'I.'
>
> The notion of 'I' is negated completely by the rise of the notion 'I am *Brahman*,' just as the notion of the stump of a tree is negated by the notion of man in the sentence 'That stump is a man.' (*NS* 2, 28-29)

> The term 'I' indicates [the innermost *Ātman*] in the same way as the term 'snake' indicates the rope. Indeed, it is only by excluding [the primary notion of] 'I' that the meaning of the sentence is known, for that which it indicates is really the supporting abode of the 'I.' (*NS* 3, 27)

> When a man wishes to dispel the erroneous notion of other, he first conforms his speech to that erroneous notion as if it were a fact and then he informs him that 'it is not so.' It is in the same way that statements like 'Thou art That' [apparently affirming what they actually deny] dispel nescience.
>
> [In the case of one who takes a post for a man] one does not remove the idea 'man' by merely repeating [as if to the sky or with reference to another substratum] 'post... post... post.' One cannot remove the erroneous idea 'man' without first conforming to it (and saying, 'that man is not a man but a post').
>
> The word 'thou' is used only to conform to the [ignorant] standpoint of the hearer, and hence the state of being a limited (*jīva*) subject to pain is not inculcated [by the proposition but only apparently referred to]. If [the sentence 'That thou art'] were a plain assertion, then indeed there would result a contradiction [between 'That' and 'thou,' and the sentence would be as absurd as the assertion 'horse is cow']. But between what is really affirmed ['That'] and what merely repeats [the ignorant notion, as does the word 'thou' used as a mere concession to the hearer], there is no conflict. Conflict, indeed, may be expected only when the two terms [subject and predicate identified in a sentence] are understood according to their primary and proper sense (*svapradhāna*), [since in that case the sentence would identify things which are really different]. But the two terms [of our

> sentence] are not denoting their own [specific] universal (*sāmānya*), therefore they do not conflict.
>
> Not tied to the [specific] universal [contained by their direct meaning], not used to express anything limited such as the *Śruti* wishes ultimately to avoid, the terms 'That' and 'thou' are emancipated (from their primary and empirical meaning). Hence, they can coalesce without any contradiction. (*NS* 3, 73-75)

The above quotations show that in working out the negation-process we must of necessity develop the more complete *lakṣaṇā*-process. The first merely emphasises the negating phase of the second. It is but a part of the latter and there is therefore no adequate distinction between the two processes.

The *lakṣaṇā*-process has three phases. The first is the moment of *adhyāropa* or superimposition, when the sentence is understood according to its direct verbal import as asserting the identity of the individual ego (*jīvātman*) or at least, following Sureśvara, of the ego-sense (*ahaṁkāra*) with the Supreme *Ātman*. Next comes the phase of *apavāda* or negation; the pupil prepared through his training in *anvaya-vyatireka* realizes that "this 'I' or 'ego-sense,' which can be dismissed as non-*Ātman* through reasoning according to *anvaya* and *vyatireka*, is not the thing that is really referred to in texts like 'I am *Brahman*,' since, if it were, the 'I' and the '*Brahman*,' as subject and predicate of a proposition implying identity, would find that identity in being the non-*Ātman*! Evidently the word 'I' is used in a special sense and not in the ordinary one" (*NS* 2, 54). The pupil therefore denies the primary sense of 'I.' Yet he does not, like the Buddhist, deny all meaning to the word 'I,' but seeks for a secondary meaning (*gauṇī* or *lakṣaṇā vṛtti* or *lakṣyārtha*) which will destroy the incongruity of the *āropita* understanding and establish the compatibility of 'I' with its predicate '*Brahman.*' The nature of this predicate governs his search and leads him to the most elevated meaning (*paramārtha*) of the term 'I,' i.e., '*Paramātman.*' This is the third phase of the process, the *paramārtha-lakṣaṇā* or assumption of the supreme meaning. The pupil at last realizes that, *paramārthataḥ*, i.e., according to the supreme meaning of its terms, the sentence "I am *Brahman*" really means "My *Paramātman* is *Brahman*." Thus he discovers the *tādātmya* relation that exists between the limited 'I,' as an effect, and its innermost yet transcending Cause, *Brahman* as *Paramātman*.

Sureśvara explains this *lakṣaṇā*-process at length throughout the *Naiṣkarmya Siddhi*. A few quotations will give us his thought in his own words:

> Since the meaning of the word 'I' [in this sentence] is to denote the innermost *Ātman*, it ought to be explained by means of those secondary meanings which *lakṣaṇā* can bring about (*prasiddha-lakṣaṇā-guṇa-vṛttibhiḥ*).
>
> 'I knew nothing' said the one who rose from deep sleep. Hence, just as we speak of the burning iron [figuratively to indicate the fire that burns in the iron, the *Śruti* uses] the term 'I' to indicate the *Paramātman*.[7]
>
> Because [the ego-sense] is interior [to everything else but the supreme *Ātman*], because it is extremely subtle, and because it imitates the vision of the *Ātman*, for these [three] reasons, all other notions are discarded and the [*Paramātman*] is indicated figuratively by the ego-notion (*ahaṃ-vṛttyo-'palakṣyate*).
>
> And again the supreme Self is indicated by the ego-notion since the ego-sense cannot exist without the *Ātman*; it would immediately dissolve if the *Ātman* were withdrawn, and it rests on no other support but the *Ātman*. (*NS* 2, 54-56)

> When a man understands texts like 'Thou art That' in their correct sense as 'I am *Brahman*,' then 'I' and 'mine' are destroyed and he no longer treads the path of words and mind.[8]
>
> Indeed, the very moment he grasps the very meaning of 'That' in the meaning of 'thou,' he comprehends that which cannot be *directly* conveyed by any sentence (*avākyārthatām*) and wanders no longer on the path of words and mind. Why is this so? The reason is as follows:[9]
>
> The word 'That' means the perfect Reality; the word 'thou' means the innermost *Ātman*. Through these [secondary meanings], the primary meanings of those terms, namely, 'suffering jīvahood'[of 'thou'] and 'non-ātmahood' [of 'That'] are rejected, just as in the sentence 'the lotus is blue'[the term 'lotus' rejects non-lotushood and the term 'blue' rejects non-blueness].
>
> He who thus reasons through *anvaya* and *vyatireka* reaches through the sentence the real meaning which stands beyond the expressive power of any sentence (*vākyād-evā-'vākyārtham pratipadyate*).
>
> The relation between a subject and a predicate that qualifies it (*viśeṣaṇa-viśeṣyatā*) consists in expressing jointly the same object (*sāmānādhikaraṇyam*), whereas the relation between the meanings of the terms ['thou' and 'That'] and the innermost *Ātman* is that of indirect indicators and indirectly indicated (*lakṣya-lakṣaṇa-saṃbandhaḥ*). (*NS* 3, 1-3)[10]

Just as in sentences like, 'verily the ether in the jar is the ether in the sky,' we attain to a reality not directly expressed in the words of the sentence (*avākyārtha*), namely [the ether unlimited by jar or sky], through a rejection (*vyāvṛtteḥ*) [of the jar-ether directly expressed by the subject and of the sky-ether directly expressed by the predicate], so also [in sentences like, 'That thou art'], we immediately (*sākṣāt*) receive knowledge beyond the expressed meaning of 'That' and 'thou.'

How can that Reality which stands beyond the direct reach of any sentence be conveyed by a sentence composed of a subject qualified by a predicate?[11]

The fact that the reality indicated by 'thou' is not the suffering *jīva* is conveyed by the term 'thou' being qualified as *Brahman* through the word 'That'; and the fact that the reality indicated by 'That' is the innermost (*Ātman*) is conveyed by the presence of the word 'thou' in apposition to the term 'That.'[12]

Thus the relation of qualifying predicate and qualified subject is explained away by understanding the terms as indirect indicator and indirectly indicated.[13]

The intelligence and interiority of the *Ātman*, which is firm as a mountain peak, are natural to it, and not accidental characteristics introduced from without (*animittam*). The *Ātman* is the cause of the awareness [of the intellect] and of the interiority [of the ego-sense]. This is why it is indicated indirectly (*upalakṣyate*) as 'knower' and as 'I.' (*NS* 3, 9-11)

Not tied to the universal [contained by their direct meaning], not used to express anything limited such as the *Śruti* wishes to ultimately avoid, the words 'That' and 'thou' are emancipated [from their empirical meanings] and hence can without contradiction coalesce....[14]

The meaning of both terms is the same *Ātman*, void of duality and perfectly self-transparent. There is no non-dual [*Brahman*] without the *Ātman*; there is no *Ātman* without that Eternal Consciousness [which is *Brahman*].

The notion of 'other' conveyed by the word 'That' must be rejected, as in the case of the word 'thou' I must similarly reject the identification of 'I' with the inward [ego-sense] since the *Ātman* is other than [that ego-sense].[15]

'That' when placed in apposition to 'thou' negates individuality and plurality as meanings of the latter; and 'thou' can stand in apposition to 'That' only if the latter has been shorn of its meaning of 'otherness.'[16]

Non-duality and subjection to *saṃsāra* are mutually incompatible, as also are the quality of 'otherness' and the *Ātman*. Subjection to *saṃsāra* and 'otherness' are negated by 'That' and 'thou' respectively, but only by implication (*prāsaṅgikam*).

Because the implied meaning of both 'That' and 'thou' [viz. *Brahman-Ātman*] is that end of man which is unknown, yet can be heard [from the *Śruti*], it contradicts [the surface meanings of] those words, without however cancelling their proper meaning. [In other words, this is a case of what is known technically as *jahad ajahal lakṣaṇā*]. (*NS* 3, 75-80)

> The 'I' is like pure consciousness; it also resembles the *Ātman* in being more inward than anything but the *Ātman*; for these reasons and others already mentioned (cf. 2, 56 cited above) the *Ātman* is indicated by the word 'I.'[17]
>
> If the transcendent Seer could be indicated indirectly[18] by the notions of those objects that belong to the thou-realm of objectivity (*yuṣmad-arthābhiḥ*), He would be 'non-*ātman*,' and all the teaching of the *Śruti* would be vain.
>
> Indeed, it is only through a fractional part (*guṇa-leśena*) of the primary meaning of the term 'I' that the *Ātman* is indicated indirectly (*lakṣyate*), after all reference to the individual self either as subject or object has been discarded. The *Ātman* is not directly named by the word 'I.'
>
> Why? Because words can apply only to things that have characteristics—such as relations, qualities, or activities—or else to things that can be subsumed under universal concepts (*jāti*), or else that can be named through universally accepted convention. Not one of these conditions is fulfilled by the *Ātman*. Therefore it cannot be named.
>
> Then how can right knowledge ensue from the words 'I am *Brahman*'?
>
> To attain that to which no means applies, a means is found by a false route: it is because it is our own inmost *Ātman* that, if suitably disciplined, we can know it through the secondary meaning (*guṇavṛttyā*) of words [such as 'I' or 'thou']. (*NS* 3, 100-104)[19]

> That 'interiority,' partless and unborn, which the *Śruti* teaches in emphatic tones in the passage 'that which, though not seeing [in deep sleep], yet sees' (*Bṛh. Up*. 4, 3, 23), that infinite, which nothing precedes or follows, that is indicated indirectly by the word 'thou' (*tvamā tad-upalakṣyate*). (NS 4, 39)[20]

These texts need no further comment. They express clearly a firm doctrine which is one of the highest points reached by metaphysical reflection. Sureśvara and his master Śrī Śaṅkarācārya developed it as an ancillary requirement of the testimonial science of *Brahmajijñāsā*. In the wake of Aristotle's distinction of the various meanings of terms, St Thomas Aquinas and other Christian thinkers have also developed it in equivalent terms to serve their own testimonial science, Christian theology. However, they also upheld its value as an independent piece of metaphysical knowledge, apart from its ancillary function in theology. Indeed, it essentially demonstrates the logical (or metalogical) structure of any proposition that purports to indicate correctly the supreme Existent. Hence it is not to be wondered that this doctrine will always attract philosophers as the sweetest flowers attract the eager honey-bee. In a letter which he sent to

Professor Russell to correct Russell's appreciation of the *Tractatus*, Wittgenstein wrote:

> The main point is the theory of what can be expressed (*gesagt*) by propositions—i.e. by language (and, what comes to the same, what can be *thought*) and what cannot be expressed by propositions, but only shown (*gezeigt*); which, I believe, is the cardinal problem of philosophy....[21]

Notes

[1] [First published in Proceedings of the Indian Philosophical Congress (1960) 51-61. Reprinted in *The Philosophical Quarterly* (Amalner) **33**/4 (1961) 255-265, and published here with kind permission of De Nobili College, Pune, having had no response from *The Philosophical Quarterly* despite several reminders. See also "The Logical Structure of 'Tattvamasi' according to Sureśvara's Naiṣkarmya-Siddhi," Poona: De Nobili College, typescript of 12 pp, Collected Papers, Part B, 244-256, and DNC 73/DES/COL 244-256.]
[2] Louis Renou, "The Enigma in the Ancient Literature of India," *Diogenes* **29** (Spring 1960) 40.
[3] A.C. Mukerji, "Idealistic Trends of Contemporary India," *The Philosophical Quarterly* **32** (July 1960) 119.
[4] A.J. Alston, "Introduction," *Naiṣkarmya Siddhi of Śrī Sureśvara*, tr. A.J. Alston (London: Shanti Sadan, 29 Chepstow Villas, W. 11, 1959) i.
[5] Cf. Alston, "Introduction" i-ii.
[6] Alston, note on *NS* 3, 40, p. 140.
[7] [This paragraph is from the typescript: see Collected Papers B, 244-256 = DNC 73/DES/COL 244-256. Missing in the published versions.]
[8] [From typescript; missing in the published versions.]
[9] [From typescript; missing in the published versions.]
[10] [From typescript; missing in the published versions.]
[11] [From typescript; missing in the published versions.]
[12] [From typescript; missing in the published versions.]
[13] [From typescript; missing in the published versions.]
[14] [From typescript; missing in the published versions.]
[15] [From typescript; missing in the published versions.]
[16] [The typescript reads: "has been shorn of its meaning 'other.']
[17] [From typescript; missing in the published versions.]
[18] [directly?]
[19] [The last 3 paragraphs are not indented in the printed versions; we are following here the typescript.]
[20] [From typescript; missing in the published versions.]
[21] Quoted in G.E.M. Anscombe, *An Introduction to Wittgenstein's Tractatus* (London: Hutchison, 1959) 161.

6

MĀYĀ OR *AJÑĀNA*? A TEXTUAL ANALYSIS[1]

Whether Advaita is to be presented in terms of *māyā* or of *ajñāna* is surely a matter of considerable importance. *Ajñāna* is a state of the mind which is relevant to epistemology whereas *māyā* appears as an ontological category whose status is so ambiguous that it baffles our understanding and is *anirvacanīya*, unaccountable. Now it is well known (though not always attended to) that Śrī Śaṅkarācārya favoured the term *ajñāna* or *avidyā*, but his later disciples diffused his teaching as an authentic form of *māyāvāda* and it is as such that it met with strong opposition from diverse quarters. The question, therefore, arises whether these disciples were sufficiently faithful to their *ādiguru* or perverted his teaching. A complete investigation of the text of that school would be necessary to answer fully that question but a rapid enquiry into the *Brahma-Sūtra-Bhāṣya* will already provide a strong indication of the mind of Śaṅkara.

In this fundamental text, the ratio of frequency of the terms *ajñāna* (or *avidyā*) and *māyā* is 10 against 2. Besides, *ajñāna* is constantly used as a precise technical term of the system (being clearly defined as *adhyāsa*, superimposition), while *māyā* is still an ordinary term with various significations, none of which has yet been privileged. It will be interesting to trace this variety of meanings through the text.

1. In the general sense of deception, it comes in *B.S.Bh.* 2, 3, 6 together with *alīka* (untruth) and *vañcana* (deceit): "Nor can Vedic affirmations about things be viewed, like ordinary human statements, as mixed up with deception, untruth and deceit." In this passage, *māyā* bears no special reference to Advaita.

2. Another sense of *māyā* in ordinary language is *magic*, which is a special form of deception for the sake of entertainment. Magic does not deceive the magician, who knows all about the trick he performs, but only the spectator who looks on without understanding it. Apart from this *ajñāna* in the viewer, it cannot be magic. When the viewer overcomes his ignorance, his illusion vanishes in the sense that his interpretation of the facts is replaced by the authentic one, not in the sense that he would now deny the genuine existence of those facts. Magic can, therefore, serve as an apt comparison to explain what happens in us as observers of the cosmic display. We first attribute to all mundane entities, including ourselves, an independence and absoluteness which is truly illusory; but the world is not the cause of this misapprehension but only its subject-matter and occasion; indeed, no magic can ever be in its own right a cause of illusion, otherwise it would produce it even in the magician. This is why Śaṅkara, unlike some of his followers, never attributes any causal character to *māyā* in the sense of magic illusion. The reality which underlies the illusion is genuine in its own way and he who truly knows the world knows it as an effect of *Brahman* endowed with a reality which is totally relative to, dependent on, and constantly sustained by the fullness of Reality which is its inner (*upādāna*) and efficient (*nimitta*) cause. What is contradicted by true knowledge is not the particular kind of real existence proper to the world, but only the independence and absoluteness attributed to it by the ignorant. When Śaṅkara used magic as a comparison to illustrate his theory, he knew that the same comparison had been used much more radically by some Buddhists in order to deny any reality of the mundane beings and he explicitly rejected their teaching. He himself made it quite clear that magic cannot stand apart from an underlying reality as its subject matter but he did not consider illusion as causally produced by it since the weakness of our understanding is a sufficient explanation of it.

The comparison itself comes in such passages as *B.S.Bh.* 1, 1, 17: "*Īśvara* differs from *vijñānātman*... in the same way as the real juggler who stands on the ground differs from the illusive juggler, who, holding in his hand a shield and a sword climbs up to the sky by means of a rope." Or *B.S.Bh.* 1, 3, 19: "The aim [of this *śārīraka-śāstra*] is to show that the only one highest Lord, ever unchanging, who is knowledge by essence (*vijñāna-dhātuḥ*) appears as manifold due to *avidyā* (*avidyayā*), just as the magician [appears in different shapes] due to magic (*māyayā*)." In *B.S.Bh.* 2, 1, 21, Śaṅkara first reminds us that "every person who has produced some tangible effect remembers that he has been the cause of it." Then, rejecting the opponent's thesis that the embodied *ātman* is the cause of the world, he says: "as the magician easily retracts, whenever he likes, the magic which he had projected forth, so the embodied *ātman* also would be able to retract this creation, but it cannot even reabsorb its own body." In *B.S.Bh.* 2, 1, 28, he notes that magic does not affect the magician: "[Not only in dreams] but in ordinary life too multiform creations, elephants, horses and the like are seen to exist in gods, etc., and magicians without interfering with the unity of their being." In *B.S.Bh.* 2, 2, 29, he emphasises that the realities which are the subject-matter of our perceptive illusions are undeniable: "The things of which we are conscious in a dream are negated by our waking consciousness.... In an analogous manner, the things of which we are conscious when under the influence of a magic illusion, and the like, are negated by our ordinary consciousness. Those things, on the other hand, of which we are conscious in our waking state, such as posts and the like, are never negated in any state" (this reply is directed against Buddhist *vijñānavāda*).

The purpose of the comparisons just recorded is to help us understand how *Brahman* as the creative Lord remains unchanged and unaffected by his creation which the ignorant falsely interprets as a self-modification and diversification of the Absolute. Of this creation the Lord is the immanent and total Cause, not however as an unconscious *upādāna*, but as that primary *upādāna* which, being conscious, creates and retracts by will and is, therefore, simultaneously *nimitta kāraṇa*. The last quotation reminds us that the effects of the Lord have a reality of their own which is easily misapprehended but can never be negated in any state.

These comparisons were generally introduced by *iva*, *yathā* or *-vat*. In other cases, *māyā* is the common term in comparative compounds of the *karma-dhāraya* or apposition type, such as *saṃsāra-māyā* (*B.S.Bh.* 2, 1, 9), *svapna-darśana-māyā* (ibid.), *nāmarūpa-māyā* (*B.S.Bh.* 2, 2, 2), etc. The terms *māyāmātra*, *māyāmaya*, on the other hand, when they appear in such passages as *B.S.Bh.* 3, 2, 3, do surely not mean "made out of *māyā* [as from a material cause]" but clearly indicate that such things as the creations of dream (*B.S.Bh.* 3, 2, 3), or even the world as manifested to our ignorance, i.e., the *prapañca* (*B.S.Bh.* 3, 2, 4), are not real, *paramārthataḥ*, namely, in the supreme sense of the term. Unlike later Advaitins, Śaṅkara refuses to identify *māyā* with an alleged material out of which illusory existences would be woven. The one passage (*B.S.Bh.* 1, 4, 3) where he identifies *avyakta* with *māyā* refers to another topic. He teaches there that a previous stage of the world as causal potentiality of the Lord must necessarily be admitted and that it is rightly denoted by the term *avyakta*, undeveloped. This undeveloped principle is identical with the Lord and "is sometimes spoken of as *māyā*; so, for instance, 'Know then *Prakṛti* is *māyā*, and the great Lord he who is affected with *māyā*' (*Śvet. Up.* 4, 10). For *māyā* is properly called undeveloped or unmanifested since it cannot be defined either as that which is or that which is not." Even in this passage, which is dominated by the terminology of the Upaniṣad, Śaṅkara does in no way set up *māyā* as a sort of *upādāna-kāraṇa* distinct from the Lord but simply explains how the effects are virtually contained in their one *upādāna*, the Lord himself.

3. The third frequent meaning of *māyā* is "marvellous power [of the Lord]." Since the time of the *Ṛg Veda*, the term *māyā* has had a 'propitious' as well as an 'unpropitious' meaning. The propitious *māyā* is the creative power attributed especially to Viṣṇu, the *Vaiṣṇavi māyā* as Śaṅkara calls it in his *bhāṣya* on the *Bhagavad-Gītā*. It is in this sense, as opposed to its unpropitious meaning as illusion, that *māyā* is used about half of the times when the term comes up in *Brahma-sūtra-bhāṣya*, for instance, in, such passages as *B.S.Bh.* 1, 1, 20 where the highest Lord is said to be *māyāmayam rūpam*, one whose form is full of creative power. This is the active counterpart of the passive causal potentiality (*avyakta-māyā*) of *B.S.Bh.* 1, 4, 3 referred to above. *Brahman* possesses the 'great creative power,' namely, is *mahāmāyā* as well as *sarvaśakti* and *sarvajña* (*B.S.Bh.* 2, 1, 37 and 2, 2, 4); for "the highest *Ātman* is characterised by non-activity inherent in his own nature, and, at the same time, by moving power inherent in his *māyā* or creative energy"

(*svarūpa-vyapāśrayaṁ audāsinyaṁ māyāvyapāśrayaṁ ca pravartakatvam*: *B.S.Bh.* 2, 2, 7).

To return to statistical evidence, it now appears that for every 10 times that the term *ajñāna* is used in the *Brahma-sūtra-bhāṣya* the ratio of 2 which belongs to the term *māyā* is to be divided about equally between its propitious meaning as 'creative power' and its unpropitious meaning as 'illusion.' Even in this sense *māyā* functions almost exclusively as a comparative term and not as a technical term of Śaṅkara's system.

The reason why he had recourse to this and many other comparisons is to be looked for in the terminological situation of his school in his own time. The authoritative texts of this school, namely, the Upaniṣads, the *Brahma-sūtra* and, secondarily, the *Bhagavad-gītā*, were couched in terms of early Sāṁkhya when there was question of cosmic causality, especially the term *pariṇāma* (self-modification). Due to the sacredness of those texts, Śaṅkara had himself to use *pariṇāma* but he was also determined to 'de-sāṁkhyanise' it. While holding in common with Sāṁkhya that the effects pre-exist in their immanent cause (*satkāryavāda*), he strongly denied that the latter was a sort of material that could be transformed and diversified by its own progenitive energy; the divine and purely spiritual *Upādāna* is a Fullness which no causality could alter or render complex. Therefore, while using *pariṇāma* he modified its Sāṁkhya meaning with the help of comparisons. The comparisons taken from the domain of magic and perceptive illusion, which were frequent in Buddhist writings but several of which were also found earlier in Brāhmanic writings, were especially apropos since they pointed at the unchanged nature of the maker and of the ground of the illusion as well as at the utterly dependent and relative nature of their apparent effects and at the almost inevitable misapprehension of the latter by ignorant observers.

In order to designate this transformed theory of *pariṇāma*, Śaṅkara could not use the term *vivarta* which then belonged to Śabdādvaita, a theory inacceptable to him, or to Maṇḍana Miśra, who identified it with *pariṇāma* understood in a Sāṁkhya sense. Gauḍapāda himself, though he had used constantly *māyā* instead of *ajñāna*, had systematically avoided *vivarta*.

The introduction into the Śaṅkara school of the *vivarta* and *māyā* terminology can be recorded briefly:

Sureśvara still works with comparisons. He and Toṭaka develop a sharp polemic against Sāṁkhya *pariṇāmavāda* and free the absolute Cause from any appearance of real relationship to its effects by which it would be modified. Neither they nor their opponents use the term *vivarta* in connection with Advaita but those among them who use it do it only when they refer to Śabdādvaita.

Padmapāda is the first Advaitin who relates this term to his own system, probably under the influence of his study of Śabdādvaita, either in the writings of Maṇḍana Miśra or more directly in those of Bhartṛhari. Padmapāda distinguishes *vivarta* from *pariṇāma* and *vikāra*, but under the influence of Śabdādvaita gives it the meaning of an external manifestation which, though objective, is yet somehow illusory; he thus unwillingly[2] paves the way for the future māyāvādins.

His commentator, Prakāśātman, insists in his definition of *vivarta* as opposed to *pariṇāma*, upon the fact that the self-manifesting Cause remains absolutely unchanged and unaffected by the *vivarta* process of self-manifestation.

Vimuktātman avoids giving a definition of *vivarta*. He fully introduces the term *māyā* into Advaita; this introduction tends inevitably to assimilate Advaita to its chief enemy, the pure *māyāvāda* of many Buddhists. He is also responsible for making fashionable the term *anirvacanīya*, which becomes an excuse for avoiding delving deeply into the mystery of finite existence. Yet, besides refuting *Dvaita*, he strongly rejects the pure identity of *Brahman* and world as implied in the Śabdādvaita theory of *Bhedābheda*.

Vācaspatimiśra witnesses to this development but fails to contribute anything new to it.

Sarvajñātman perceives clearly that no theory can measure up perfectly to the reality of the mystery which it may be brought up to explain. The value of any such theory is purely pedagogical. *Pariṇāmavāda* can serve as a first approach to be cancelled by *vivartavāda*, but *vivartavāda* is itself to be ultimately cancelled by a perfect intuition (*paripūrṇadṛṣṭi*) which completely sublimates causality as a conception (*kāraṇa-kārya-dhi*).

Prakāśānanda hardens this interesting view and his monism (rather than non-dualism) seems to Dasgupta "surprisingly similar to the idealism of Vāsubandhu."[3] Indeed, his *dṛṣṭi-sṛṣṭi*, which is quite alien to Śaṅkara's Advaita, eliminates all forms of ontological causality, and he expressly states that *vivartavāda* is a mere pedagogical device.

These indications add their historical evidence to the results of our textual analysis. Both together provide a negative answer to our initial question, whether Śaṅkara exposed his doctrine in terms of *māyā* and whether it is right to designate his system as *māyāvāda*.

Notes

[1] [First published as "*Māyā* or *Ajñāna*?" *Indian Philosophical Annual* **2** (1966) 328-335. Reprinted as "*Māyā* or *Ajñāna*? A Textual Analysis," *Indian Ecclesiastical Studies* **9**/2 (1970) 80-84, and published here with permission of the same.]

[2] [Perhaps this should read 'unwittingly.']

[3] S. Dasgupta, *A History of Indian Philosophy* (Delhi: Motilal Banarsidass, 1975) **2**:19. [Vāsubandhu was an Indian Buddhist scholar-monk, and one of the main founders of Indian Yogacara. In vol. 1 of his *History*, Dasgupta gives his dates as 420-500 AD, but in vol. 2 he corrects himself to 280-360 AD: see **2**:19 note 2.]

7

QUESTIONING VEDĀNTA[1]

In this contribution to the Seminar on "Advaita Vedānta and Western Thought," I intend to apply to Vedānta a critical consideration made by St Thomas Aquinas about early Greek philosophy and thereby to question Śaṅkara's treatment of supreme intuition and, more radically, at least one position of a whole group of his modern interpreters.

St Thomas Aquinas once gave a bird's eye view of early Greek philosophy as a development governed by the postulate, "the like is known by the like," till the overthrow of the latter by Aristotle. This postulate may, correctly enough, be understood as expressing the rule of intellectual discovery when it infers the nature of a new object from its similarities with another object previously known (as in *upamāna*). But, according to him, it was understood in a different way by the Presocratics. The likeness which they took for granted was between the known and the knower. For them, knowledge implied an essential similarity or basic identity between the objects and the subject and *vice versa*. Now, it was obvious to them that objects were material, made as they were of the elements, earth, water, air and fire; hence, for the first of those philosophers, the subject too was to be considered as material. Even when Heraclitus noticed the *logos* as the power in the knower which relates and binds the fleeting moments of knowledge, he understood it as being of the same nature as the fire which brings about the moving consistency of the flux of the objective world. And when Parmenides noticed the indeterminacy, oneness and infinity of pure thought, he projected them upon the object of thought which he conceived as strictly monistic being. Indeed, if mind coincides with being, the modes of the mind must be the modes of being and vice versa. Thus also the first Atomists attributed to their atoms love and hatred, the force of attraction and repulsion which they had experienced on the mental plane.

For Socrates, on the other hand, and soon for Plato, it became evident that knowledge was radically intellectual, spiritual, and consequently they declared its objects to be essentially *eidos* or *eideai*, idea (from the root *oid-* or *vid-*), matter being only a degradation or shadow of idea and corresponding to *doxa*. Thus they continued to adhere to the old postulate. Aristotle was the first to see that "whatever is received takes in its receiver the mode of that receiver." For instance, objects as received (actively) by the intellect of a man take on the mode of being of that intellect and are thus found there in the form of ideas. But the ideas of things are, as received by matter, materialized so that they constitute physical existents. Thus it is no longer true for Aristotle that the modes of thinking are the modes of being, or *vice versa*. Physical objects are not composed of genus and difference which are but modes of our mental representations of them, but of prime matter and substantial form which are the inner co-principles of their real essence. Accordingly, Aquinas will say that the whole universe may be considered either in its actual reality, and then it is complex, material, changing, etc., or in its potentiality as possible in the divine All-power, or also as divinely known by its Creator, and in these two cases it must be said to be identical with the divine Essence or *Esse*. This, by the way, is the *satkāryavāda* of Aquinas as stated in his *De Potentia* 3, 16, 24.

Taking our cue from Aristotle and St Thomas we may now wonder whether Indian philosophy, including Vedānta, has not been governed unknowingly by the wrong postulation of a one-one relation between thinking and being. This would not be astonishing since knowledge is often conceived as the result of a process of *bimbapratibimba* in the mirror-like *buddhi*. Indications are not lacking that this is perhaps what did indeed happen. To take first a rather gross instance, Vaiśeṣika did range *sāmānya* and *viśeṣa* among its scheme of ontological *padārthas*. Though it did say that they are *buddhy-apekṣa*, it gave them a realistic interpretation in the manner of all Realists faced with the problem of the status of universals. Similarly many Mīmāṃsakas imagined a realm of subsistent *sphoṭas* not unlike Plato's realm of ideas. Others ontologised the *akṛtis*. Even the term *nāma-rūpa* which refers directly to speech and perception was very early given a realistic interpretation.

Our questioning becomes more central when we examine the influence of meditational introversion and *yoga* upon philosophical doctrines. These methods are essentially ascensional and abstractive. They draw man away from the concreteness of sense-objects and *mano-vṛttis* towards the upper indeterminacy of pure consciousness. Or they ascend from the concrete *nāma-rūpas* of the universe towards their more and more internal causes. Internal causes form a ladder of *upādānas* or *ātmans* whose highest rung is the *Parabrahman* or *Paramātman*. Every step, says Śaṅkara, is marked by higher subtleness, greatness, interiority and transcendence. Whether the ascension goes from objects to pure consciousness or from effects to supreme inner cause, its end and goal is a point of supreme abstraction. Infinite and indeterminate, it is figuratively spoken of as *ākāśa*. Transcending the agitation of desires and passions, it is called peace or also isolation, *kaivalya*, and beyond the *guṇas* (*nirguṇa*). Undifferentiated, void of forms (*nirākāra*) and qualities (*nirguṇa*), ineffable, uncompounded, (*asaṁskṛta*), it is interpreted by the Buddhists, especially of Mahāyāna, as Void, *Śūnya*. However, apprehended differently as most subtle inner cause, highest concentration of energy and consciousness, it is interpreted by Brahmavādins as Fullness (*Pūrṇa*), Reality-Knowledge-Infinite (*Satyam-jñānam-anantam*), Bliss (*Ānanda*).

The diversity of these interpretations, from Buddhistic *śūnya* to Sāṁkhya *puruṣa* to Vedāntic *Pūrṇa*, may make us wonder about the exact nature of the experience (*anubhava*) which they claim to express. The question may be put in this way, is it ontological or gnoseological, is it the experience of Reality or the experience of the highest state of consciousness? Is it a synthetic experience of Reality and Consciousness at their highest level, or does it imply projection from mode of consciousness unto degree of reality? In other terms, are not the ontologizing interpretations unknowingly governed by the pseudo-principle that the like is known by the like, and that the modes of knowing are the modes of being?

Indeed, the very process of yogic meditations suggests that it might be so for it consists in a gradual isolation of consciousness from its concrete and finite forms. In its Buddhistic form, we are told that the meditating man can reach gradual stages of deliverance (*vimokkha*) among which the following are of interest: First, by passing beyond any conception of matter, sensation and multiformity, he attains the state of mind in which the only idea present is the infinity of space (*ākāśānañca*). On this follows a stage in which the infinity of intellect (*viññānānañca*) is alone present. The next stage is reached when there is nothing at all present to the mind (*akiñcaññāyatana*). Then is achieved the stage when neither the presence nor the absence of ideas is specifically present (*nevasaññānāsaññāyatana*). Finally is attained the state where there is suppression of both sensation and idea (*saññāvedayitanirodha*). In Patañjali's *Yogasūtra* 1, 51, we find a similar teaching concerning *nirbīja samādhi*, the seedless state of consciousness in which all objects and modifications of the mind are suppressed (*nirodha*).

For Śaṅkara, meditation (*nididhyāsana*) consists in "grasping the teaching relating to Knowledge (*vidyā-śravaṇa-grahaṇa*), holding it (*dhāraṇa*) and repeating it mentally (*abhyāsa*)" (*Taitt. Up. Bh.* 2, 1). With its culmination, *samādhi*, it constitutes *dhyānayoga* "which is the most immediate means to *Vidyā*" (*Bh. Gītā Bh.* 5, 27), "the highest form of *yoga*; it consists in abiding constantly in the *Ātman*, bearing in mind that the *Ātman* is all and nothing else is absolutely existent" (ibid. 6, 25.) This *dhyāna* surely resembles that of Patañjali and the Buddhists. It culminates in the same *nirodha* of objects, sensations, ideas and all reflections of consciousness and in the same purity of consciousness. However, this consciousness is not a *śūnyam* but a *pūrṇam*. It is *paramārthataḥ sat*. This is an interpretation of the supreme *dhyāna*-experience about which we may wonder whether the above mentioned pseudo-principle is not at work in it. Indeed, the latter can work in two ways. If the modes of being are the exact counterparts of the modes of knowledge, then the extreme purity of consciousness in the state of complete *nirodha* may be interpreted either as implying a radical emptiness of being—this is the śūnyavādin's position—or as implying that being is supremely pure and transcendent and, in that case, pure being and pure consciousness can be identified as the one *Ātman* or *Brahman*—this is Śaṅkara's interpretation which recovers the truth of *Taitt. Up*. 2, 1, 1: *Satyam-jñānam-anantam-Brahm'eti*.

But this is an interpretation which seems to go beyond the experience itself. It seems to read into the experience something imported from outside it, namely, from the *Śruti*-assertion of the ontological nature of the *sākṣin* as Fullness. The experience of pure consciousness in the state of *nirodha*, even if it proceeds from the *Śruti*, '*neti*, *neti*,' does not suffice to justify that interpretation. Śaṅkara himself says it in *Upadeśasāhasrī* 18, 125:

> If in this context you maintain that [there is] a negation [of all else other than the *Ātman*, which] proceeds through the sole authority of the *Śruti*, [*neti neti*,] we reply that in that case a mere void would result, as there would be no [previous] ascertaining (*prasiddhi*) of the witness.

Sarvajñātma Muni confirms this in *Samkṣepa Śārīraka* 1, 255: "The false appearance of a snake arising from ignorance of a rope cannot be cancelled by mere negation not preceded by a positive cognition of the rope. And similarly, the pain of transmigration proceeding from ignorance of the inmost *Ātman* cannot be cancelled by the mere notion 'it is not so' (*neti*) arising from the *Śruti* [*neti neti*] without previous positive apprehension of *Brahman*."

Śaṅkara appears to reject in the above quotation the doctrine of Maṇḍanamiśra in *Brahma Siddhi*, p. 157: "What then is taught by the *Śruti*? [Merely] the non-existence of the universe."[2] Śaṅkara continues:

> If you answer [that one could infer the *ātman*-nature of pure consciousness] by saying, 'thou art conscious: how couldst thou be the [non-conscious] body?' we reply, 'No, for [the *Ātman* as pure consciousness] is not established [thereby, or previously].' This argument [also] proceeds through negation of what is contradictory [to the *Ātman* as pure consciousness]. It would be valid only if pure consciousness were already established through some other proof. (*US* 18, 127)

> [Further,] if someone were to say, 'the witness affirms its own self-existence because consciousness is immediately evident (*aparokṣa*),' we reply that in that case the witness ought to affirm itself even in the case of the *Śūnyavādin*. (*US* 18, 127)

It appears, therefore, that for Śaṅkara the mere experience of pure consciousness, unprepared by *śravaṇa* and *manana* upon the *Śruti* positive characterisations (*lakṣaṇa*) of the *Ātman*, could lead no further than the apprehension of *śūnya*. Its positive interpretation as experience of the *Ātman* required to be supported by another *pramāṇa*, namely, the *śabda* of *Śruti*, or, more precisely, such *mahāvākyas* as *Tattvamasi* and the definitions of *Brahman*. What is the reason for this insufficiency of the experience of pure consciousness so long as it is not prepared, informed and supported by *śabda*?

My suggestion is that Śaṅkara, without formulating the postulate "like is known by like," views knowledge within its perspective and remains influenced by the simile of *buddhi* as mirror. If the modes of knowledge and reality coincide, then when the mode of knowledge is purity it mirrors nothing and the mode of reality can only be *śūnya*.

In opposition to this theory of coincidence, its reversal which I have traced to Aristotle conceives that knowledge is in every state polarized on being. Being, in all its instances, is always independent of knowledge; its modes are simply its own. Knowledge, on the other hand, does in its dynamic search for being pass through many modes which are the forms of its approaches of being. The link of knowledge with being is the very orientation of its dynamism ever focusing upon being and thus ever affirming it, if not explicitly, at least through the constant aiming of its very *élan* towards it. This link is not representational as in the static mirror-theory of knowledge. The dynamism of knowledge goes beyond any representation just as it goes beyond the empirical, the changing, the finite, the limited, the imperfect. Thus from its very inception it obscurely affirms Being in its fullness, infinite, permanent, absolute. An implicit assertion of the Absolute is exercised in all the explicit assertions performed by a human knower and pervades the whole dynamism of his knowledge. In short, human knowledge is oriented by nature towards being or reality. The nature of its highest aim is measured by the scope of its pursuit. The range of this scope is unlimited since our quest goes ever beyond, and is unsatiated by, any reality marked by finiteness or limitation of any kind. Hence, the only goal that can satiate our appetite for knowledge is the Absolute grasped as Fullness. This is the theory of Aquinas, developed on the basis of Aristotle and exposed anew in the light of Kant by the greatest (to my mind) of contemporary Thomists, Joseph Maréchal.

Śaṅkara himself tried to overcome the defects of the theory of knowing, which he had inherited, in several ways. First of all, in his Commentary on *Bh. Gītā* 2, 16, "*Nāsato vidyate bhāvaḥ*," he instituted a transcendental analysis of judgement. First, he defined being (*sat*) as "that object whose knowledge never fails" and nonbeing (*asat*) as "that object whose knowledge fails"; thus, he writes, "their division stands in dependence of knowledge." He, then, therefore, analyzed knowledge, i.e., more precisely, judgement, the assertion of an existent object, such as, 'this is a jar,' 'this is a cloth,' 'this is an elephant,' (*san-ghaṭaḥ, san-paṭaḥ, san-hasti*) and as opposed to 'blue lotus' (*nīl'otpalavat.*) "Now, in every judgement," he says, "all men are aware of a double knowledge (*buddhi*) with reference to the same substratum, namely, *sat* and such subjects as *ghaṭaḥ, paṭaḥ*, etc. Of these two *buddhis*, the second happens eventually to fail since jars, etc., pass away, but the first, the *sad-buddhi*, does never fail. It is present even when the judgement deals with illusory objects like the water of a mirage." From this he concludes that the various subjects of judgements which are effects and mutable and whose knowledge fails, are *asat*; but "of being (*sat*) there is no inexistence or absence, because, as we have said, it never fails anywhere.... Being designates *Brahman*... and non-being designates whatever changes and has a cause."

In this analysis, we can find at least the first point of the Thomistic analysis, namely, that the immutable Being is somewhat affirmed in every judgement, even in false judgements, as the radical object of the existential copula. That judgement is anchored in the Absolute as in its one Pole and Goal, is discovered by Śaṅkara as well as by St Thomas. But he does not explain this by a theory of knowledge dynamism. Rather, he conceives it through the *Śruti* assertion of the *Ātman* as *Sākṣin*. The *Ātman* is the immutable Being ever present to the judging intellect, as he says in the same commentary. St Thomas equally holds that God, the divine Absolute, is the ever-present Illuminer of our intellects but this might not suffice to explain the intentionality of our intellects apart from a clear awareness of their dynamism.

In another important passage, namely, in his commentary on *Kaṭha Up*. 2, 3,12, Śaṅkara comes back upon that permanent anchoring of *buddhi* in *sat*:

> Although [*Brahman*] is devoid of all differences, yet, since it is arrived at as the root of the world, it indeed exists, because the elimination of effect terminates in existence or Is-ness (*astitva*). Indeed, this effect [the world] when thus followed along the ascending series of its more and more subtle [inner causes] leads ultimately to the simple awareness of *sat*. Even when through the elimination of objects, the *buddhi* itself becomes eliminated, it is at that moment big as it were with the embryo *sat*. For *buddhi* is our instrument in ascertaining the truth of both *sat* and *asat*. If the world had no cause, this effect being transfused with *asat* only would at every step be grasped as non-being only. But in fact it is not so; it is, on the contrary, grasped at every step as being only, just as jars, etc., which are the products of clay, etc., are perceived as permeated with clay, etc.

We see here again how *buddhi* is related to being (*sat*) by its very nature. When it is in connection with *asat*, it asserts being in it and through it. When it regresses from that *asat*, which is effect, "along the ascending series of its more and more subtle" inner causes or *ātmans*, it is all the time pregnant with being. And when, in the state of complete *nirodha*, it eliminates even itself, being is as it were born, manifested in its fullness. However, the link of *buddhi* with *sat* is static, not dynamic, even though it is affirmed on the side of objects, as pervading effects and their inferior inner causes.

For Aquinas, it is dynamic on the side of objects though static on the side of the subject where God stands as absolute Illuminer. In any case, absolute being is for him also found through a regression from effects to Cause and through finally going beyond the intellective soul itself:

> To That which transcends everything we ascend, as much as we can, by a threefold way and relation, namely, through an elimination of all things, through an elevation above all things, and through attaining the Cause of all things. This is why God is known in all things and yet beyond and without all things. Thus He is known through knowledge and through ignorance, inasmuch indeed as [for us, men, in this life] this is to know God, namely, to be clearly aware that we do not yet know what He is. And this 'knowledge through ignorance' is most divine because it is attained by a supra-mental union which takes place when our mind [*mens*: intellective soul] leaves all things and then dismisses itself also. Then it is united with the light that is above all lights and illumined by the inscrutable abyss of

Wisdom. (*Commentary on Dionysius's 'Concerning the Divine Names'* 7, 3, n. 731-732)

Thus in Aquinas too the ascent to the absolute Being requires a complete *nirodha* but here also it has been preceded by a *pramāṇa* which has established a supreme Positivity above the whole series of effects and causes which It sustains. This *pramāṇa* is a whole metaphysical enquiry. In Śaṅkara it is the whole exegetical enquiry upon the *śabda* of *Śruti*. It includes, of course, *manana* and, in that sense, a metaphysical enquiry. Yet, it is essentially testimonial.

The status of *Śruti* as *śabda* requires a justification since it is said to be *apauruṣeya* and eternal and thus independent and self-standing in contradistinction from the other *pramāṇas* though not in contradiction with them. The Mīmāṃsakas had their own justification for it and Śaṅkara refined it. But contemporary Vedāntins rarely accept it and rather hold that the authority of *Śruti* is validated by the ultimate experience (*anubhava*) to which it conduces. But if it is so and if at the same time we hold with Śaṅkara that this *anubhava* is bound to be merely 'śūnyavādic' unless it is preceded by another and independent *pramāṇa*, we are in a quandary. Indeed, *Śruti* would be justified by that *anubhava* and the latter in turn would for its positive content be justified by *Śruti*. This is an antinomy which is incident to the stand of modern Vedāntins though not of Śaṅkara. It deserves, I think, to be grasped, discussed and, hopefully, solved.

To sum up: This paper recalled, first, the influence of the postulate "like is known by like" upon the Greek philosophers up to Plato; then, its overthrow by Aristotle who established that known and knowledge have each their own mode though knowledge endows the known with its own mode. The said principle was, then, found to have played a similarly governing role in Indian philosophy. This was examined further with regard to the interpretation of the supreme experience of *dhyāna*, which is śūnyavādic in Buddhism but brahmavādic in Vedānta. Śaṅkara was shown to have perceived the difficulty of establishing the brahmavādic interpretation on the sole basis of the *dhyāna*-experience, and to have demanded a previous *prasiddhi* by *Śruti*. This indicates that he was himself unknowingly accepting the consequences of the above postulate. Thomas Aquinas, on the contrary, had developed a theory of the dynamism of knowledge which preserved him from that difficulty. Through this theory he could pass by a continuous movement and without recourse to the authority of a testimony from ordinary knowledge to his equivalent of the *dhyāna*-experience. Śaṅkara overcame for the essentials the consequences of the similarity postulate, mainly through his transcendental analysis of judgment. Modern Vedāntins, on the other hand, have to face the antinomy which arises if *Śruti* is validated by the supreme *anubhava* and the latter by *Śruti*.

Notes

[1] [Lecture at the Seminar on 'Advaita Vedānta and Western Thought,' August 1971, Centre of Advanced Study in Philosophy, University of Madras, Madras. Published as "Questioning Vedānta," *Indian Philosophical Annual* 7 (1971) 97-105, and reprinted here with kind permission.]

[2] [*Brahmasiddhi by Maṇḍanamiśra and commentary by Sankhapāni, with introduction, appendices and indexes*, ed. S. Kuppuswami Sastri, Madras Government Oriental Series, 4 (Madras: Government Press, 1937) 157. Now available as a reprint by Sri Satguru Publications, Delhi, 1984.]

8

CHINKS IN THE ARMOUR OF *AVIDYĀ*[1]

Scripture declares that the Ātman, although eternally unchanging and uniform, reveals itself in a gradual series of beings and so appears in forms of various dignity and power.

(*B.S.Bh.* 2, 1, 14)

There is the story of that horseman who, at night and in a thick fog, rode unknowingly across a frozen lake. On reaching the other side he found an inn where exhausted he went to sleep for a long time. When he woke up, the sun was high in the sky and had melted the ice into scummy water. On seeing this the man got so frightened that he collapsed.

And there is the story of Modern Man who started so confidently on his journey towards progress only to find himself today in the midst of a disintegrating world, his values shattered and his self struck with existentialistic despair.

Would the Vedāntin be right after all? Is the scientific world of our reliance a mere crust of ice upon an abyss of nothingness? Are all the advances of modern knowledge nothing but waves upon waves of sheer nescience?

But modern man easily brushes aside such questions as absurd and such parables as irrelevant. For even though our progress is no unmixed blessing and our science is quite shortsighted, the tree of modern knowledge is vigorous and its fruits are mostly nutritious or curative. And if we turn to Śaṅkara, the Vedāntin, his pessimism may be doubted for he often confirmed the capacity of secular knowledge to achieve man's goals within its own domain, simply condemning its pretension to deal equally well with metaphysical questions regarding the metempirical nature of reality and man's supreme goal. His calling it *avidyā* (or rather *a-Vidyā*) only did away with this pretension and set it down as totally inferior to *Vidyā*, the saving knowledge grounded on the testimony of the Upaniṣads.

Yet, *a-Vidyā* does not easily accept to climb down and to acknowledge *Vidyā's* claim to sovereignty. Especially in its modern expansion it is well-armoured and combative. Instruments of observation and refined methods of experimentation give it access to the inner structures of biological life and physical reality. The psychical itself is open to its investigation. And there seems to be no limit to the illumining power of its purely rational enquiry. It stands strong and well-entrenched whereas religions, metaphysics, mysticism and revelational wisdoms, including Vedānta, appear disabled and disspirited.

However, to my mind, this is a false prospect arisen from a condition of cold war between *a-Vidyā* and *Vidyā*. So long as we oppose them to each other in either-or fashion, they appear as irreconcilable foes and the strength of the one seems to imply the weakness of the other. But if for warlike opposition we substitute peaceful dialogue we shall discover beyond their undeniable heterogeneity a surprising amount of mutuality, complementarity and concurrence, *Vidyā* permeating *a-Vidyā* and the latter providing helps towards the advent of *Vidyā*. There will appear chinks in the armour of *a-Vidyā*, not only as points of weakness but as apertures shining with the bright presence of *Vidyā* in the very texture of *a-Vidyā*. In discerning them we shall be guided mainly by Śaṅkarācārya.

At the outset, let us recall his two important definitions of *Sat* and *a-Sat* (Being and non-Being), on the one hand, and of *Vidyā* and *a-Vidyā*, on the other hand. The first is found in his *Gītā-Bhāṣya* 2, 16 in the course of his transcendental analysis of any affirmation of the type, 'this is a pot' (*san ghaṭaḥ, iti*). Although concerned with a single substratum, such affirmation is always twofold (*dve buddhi*) since it bears simultaneously upon 'existent' (*sat*) and upon a concrete object such as a pot (*ghaṭa*). Now, whereas in its second respect it varies and can fail, in its first respect it is constant and unfailing (*tayoḥ buddhyoḥ ghaṭādibuddhiḥ vyabhicarati, na tu sadbuddhiḥ*). Hence, the definition: "*Sat* is that, the affirmation of which is constant" (*yadviṣayā buddhiḥ na vyabhicarati, tat sat*) and "*asat* is that, the affirmation of which is inconstant" (*yadviṣayā buddhiḥ vyabhicarati, tat asat*). *Sat* is thus defined here in Platonic fashion as the absolutely permanent, that which never falls under the scope of negation but is, on the contrary, affirmed in some way in every judgment. As such, it can only be the absolute Being and, since it is the fixed Pole of the affirming intellect, it must be its innermost *a priori* and supreme *Ātman*, namely, the self-effulgent Light (*svayam jyoti*) of pure Consciousness (*Cinmātra*), the radical Subject (*Viṣayin*) and transcendent Witness (*Sākṣin*). The variables associated with it, whether empirical objects, subjects or acts of cognition, constitute the sphere of the non-permanent, hence, of non-Being, *a-Sat*. This sphere comprises the whole changing universe, the subject-matter of all mundane knowledge both ordinary and scientific. What opposes it to *Sat* is not unaffirmability (for it is affirmable) but only its changeableness. Thus *Sat* and *a-Sat* are not contradictories (like *Sat* and *Asat*, the utterly non-existent and impossible) but contraries. More precisely, they stand, says Śaṅkara, in the relation of cause and effect. For just as a pot can never be apprehended apart from (*vyatirekeṇa*) its immanent substrate, clay, so also the changeable can never be affirmed apart from the unchangeable *Sat*; and how to interpret this dependence in affirmability otherwise than as the total dependence of the effect on its immanent cause and ontological support?

What happens now in the judgment? Since we cannot affirm its subject (*viśeṣya*), namely, the pot or any such object, independently of the existential predicate (*viśeṣaṇa*), we superimpose it upon *Sat* and vice-versa. Thus it takes on as it were the properties of *Sat*, its beingness, constancy, solidity, independence, etc., and in turn *Sat* becomes endowed as it were with the properties of *a-Sat*, its plurality, changeability, materiality, etc. Potness or any other kind of name-and-form (*nāma-rūpa*) seem to be the differentiating predicates (*viśeṣaṇa*) of *Sat* while they are only external adjuncts (*upādhi*) superimposed on it and masking it. This leads us straight to Śaṅkara's definition of *a-Vidyā*.

First, the illusions and errors of ordinary experience provide him with the general notion of superimposition (*adhyāsa*) as "the apparent presentation of the attributes of one thing in another thing" (*anyasyānyadharmāvabhāsatā*: *B.S.Bh.* 1, 1, 1). Then, he applies it to the case of the judgment which exhibits a "mutual superimposition of the Self and the non-Self" (*atmānātmanoritaretar-ādhyāsaṃ*: *B.S.Bh.* 1, 1, 1). This superimposition, located in the judicative assertion and "thus defined, wise men consider to be *a-Vidyā*, and the ascertainment of the proper nature of the Real (*vastusvarūpa*) by discriminating it from the un-Real, they call *Vidyā*" (*B.S.Bh.* 1, 1, 1). Therefore, the *a-Vidyā* which Śaṅkara wishes to dissipate is a case apart from the trivial errors of perception, etc. and this I have meant to convey through my use of capital letters. It is not a limited and contingent accident of perception but a pervading feature of all human knowledge short of *Vidyā*. "In this world," says Śaṅkara, "it is the natural (*naisargika*) procedure," innate to our undiscriminative mode of knowing. It can thus be identified with it so that we should label as *a-Vidyā* all ordinary knowledge, all scientific achievements and even the Upaniṣads in the discursivity of their text though not in their meaning (cf. *Muṇḍ. Up. Bh.* 1, 1, 4-6).

Discursive, undiscriminated knowledge, although it is *a-Vidyā* in the special sense of Śaṅkara's definition, is not *avidyā* in the ordinary sense of error. Indeed, "it results from *pramāṇas* (means of procuring valid knowledge) and the object of the *pramāṇas* is reality as it exists" (*yathābhūtavastuviṣayam*: *B.S.Bh.* 1, 1, 4). It may not penetrate down to the radical difference between *Sat* and *a-Sat* and perceive its reals (*sat*) as un-Real (*a-Sat*) but its constant horizon is *sattā*, reality, *astitva*, 'is-ness.' "Between *Brahman* and the world, there is at least one characteristic in common": *sattā*" (*B.S.Bh.* 2, 1, 8). The awakening to the true Self will reveal that this commonness is due to the sovereign causality of this Self within the universe of its effects but, in the meantime, it gives ontological weight and truth-value to discursive knowledge. "Before the awakening to the true Self, every cognition is real in regard to its own object" (*Chānd. Up. Bh.* 8, 5, 4).

This is why *a-Vidyā* is not simply dismissed as if it were sheer absurdity (*Avidyā*) like the nonsensical stanza quoted by Śaṅkara:

> Having bathed in the water of a mirage,
> Crowned with sky-flowers,
> This son of a barren woman goes

Armed with a bow made of a hare's horn.
(*Taitt. Up. Bh.* 2, 1)

It actually constitutes the field throughout which Śaṅkara exercises his discriminating analysis under the guidance of upaniṣadic *Vidyā*. Being naturally pervaded (*vyāpta*) by *Vidyā*, illumined by pure Consciousness, it is made cognitive by its light and reflects it in all its partial truths. "The light of Consciousness is the illuminer of the mind (*manaso avabhāsakam*) because it is its controller (*niyantṛtvāt*), being the source of its light. The inner *Ātman* being the innermost of all objects, the mind cannot move towards it. Rather the mind itself is able to think only when it is illumined by the light of Consciousness residing inside it. Hence, knowers of *Brahman* declare that the mind with all its functions is made into thought (*matam*), made into a cognizing subject (*viṣayīkṛtam*), as pervaded by (*vyāptam*) this inner *Ātman*" (*Kena Up. Bh.* 1, 6).

Due to this kind of osmosis between *Vidyā* and *a-Vidyā*, the latter provides the principle of contradiction so often appealed to by Śaṅkara, the principle of the *cogito ergo sum* owing to which the Self is never unknown to exist, though its nature remains undiscerned and which is brandished by Śaṅkara as his main weapon against Buddhist *anātmavāda* (denial of all self), the principle of retortion by which he ridicules self-stultifying statements, the principle of the self-validity (*svataḥprāmāṇya*) of knowledge, the prohibition of infinite regress (*anavasthā*) in hierarchical chains of causes or middle terms, and other principles of reason. These are all at work in the vast field of human knowledge circumscribed as *a-Vidyā*.

Again, due to the same osmosis, *a-Vidyā* unfolds itself as propelled by an intellectual dynamism, a desire for knowing (*jijñāsā*), which spurs it on from lesser to greater realities and opens it up beyond its own limited reach to the achievement procured by *Vidyā*. *Jijñāsā*, indeed, is a constitutive teleology whose ultimate aim is *Brahman*, the absolute *Sat*, to be apprehended as *Ātman* in a most comprehensive intuition (*avagatiparyanta*: *B.S.Bh.* 1, 1, 1). It impels the mind within the horizon of *sattā* from sense-perception to rational disquisition, from the apprehension of external forms to the disclosure of the whole hierarchy of internal and universal forms (*B.S.Bh.* 1, 1, 11 quoting *Ait. Ār.* 3, 2, 1), from effects to the ascending series of their more and more internal causes or *ātmans* (*Kaṭha Up. Bh.* 1, 3, 10-11), from the ephemeral to the longer-lasting, etc.

In this teleological search, *a-Vidyā* is constantly evaluative. The lowest judgment is already an act of transcending the sense data in terms of being. The in-built norm—due to the presence of *Vidyā*—of intellectual valuation is ontic permanence (*avyabhicāritva*), uncontradictedness (*abādhitatva*). In the measure in which a thing appears to be durable, it is accepted as satisfying *jijñāsā*; in the measure in which it appears transitory, it is transcended and *jijñāsā* seeks beyond it for its total fulfilment. This is an unceasing process of discrimination (*viveka*) which is found to be at work, though often fallibly, in every man even before he eventually turns for help to the Upaniṣads. Indeed, Śaṅkara states that the first prerequisite for upaniṣadic schooling is "discrimination between eternal and non-eternal reality" (*nityānityavastuviveka*: *B.S.Bh.* 1, 1, 1). Man's endowment of *viveka* gives him a privileged status among living beings and makes him alone directly capable of liberation from transiency and *a-Vidyā* (cf. *Taitt. Up. Bh.* 2, 1). It can be educated and become effective to turn his natural *jijñāsā* into that 'desire for liberation' (*mumukṣutva*) which is the fourth qualification required for Vedāntic schooling. This is not a new desire but only the explicit and proper focusing of the human *jijñāsā* which will not relent its drive till it is satiated in the blissful grasp of the Infinite (*Chānd. Up. Bh.* 7, 23-24). Its effect is to make man so disposed that he is ready to seek beyond the limits of his own intellectual acquisitions and put his faith in such a verbal testimony as the upaniṣadic *Śruti* which promises perfect liberation. It is thus from within *a-Vidyā* and through the very dynamism which animates it that he aspires definitely towards *Vidyā*.

It is also due to the infinite dynamism immanent in *a-Vidyā* that man has discovered the degrees of being and the possibility of a Maximum. This is imbedded in language which uses words on various levels of meaning. Detached words have a one-level, primary meaning (*mukhyārtha*), which their definition circumscribes, but when used contextually, in sentences, they put on different-level, secondary meanings (*lakṣyārtha*). Some words, like being, bliss, knowledge, etc., whose definition does not debar infinity, can even take on a supreme meaning (*paramārtha*) and serve the need of indicating the absolute goal of intellectual dynamism.

Śaṅkara made excellent use of this feature of speech, especially in his exegesis of the 'great sayings' of *Taitt. Up*. 2, 1: "*Brahman* is Reality, Knowledge, Infinite" (*satyam jñānam anantam Brahma*) and *Chānd. Up*. 6, 8-16: "That thou art" (*tat-tvam-asi*). The truth-meaning of such statements pertains to *Vidyā* but through their sentential structure they still belong to *a-Vidyā* according to Śaṅkara. They bridge the gap between the two. While unable, of course, to express directly and comprehensively the ineffable *Brahman*, they yet manage to indicate it correctly as definitions of its proper essence (*svarūpa-lakṣaṇa*) because of the *paramārtha* of their terms. Through them, says Śaṅkara, "that [*Brahman*] is indicated [or defined] but not expressed" (*tallakṣyate na tūcyate*: *Taitt. Up. Bh.* 2, 1). His exegesis remains apophatic and thus bears the mark of *a-Vidyā*.

The whole thrust of Śaṅkara's teaching is to exalt *Vidyā* and make us pass beyond *a-Vidyā* but he is ever aware of the kinship between *a-Vidyā* and *Vidyā* which remains hidden to the man of *a-Vidyā*. Witness again his theory of the one Seer of the two sights, the one transitory and the other eternal: "through this unfailing, eternal sight which is his essence and is called the self-effulgent light, the Seer of sight always sees the other, transitory sight whether in dream as impression or in the waking state as idea" (*Bṛh. Up. Bh.* 1, 4, 10). "It is only as inhabited by the energy of *Brahman* that the eye and other faculties have the power of seeing and so forth" (*Bṛh. Up. Bh.* 4, 4, 18). "Man discerns only through the *Ātman* which is of the nature of consciousness and is altogether distinct from the aggregate (of the senses, etc.) just as it is by fire that a metal burns" (*Kaṭha Up. Bh.* 4, 3). The immanence of the absolute Witness (*Sākṣin*) grounds the whole efflorescence of *a-Vidyā* on *Vidyā* itself, giving it a derived effulgence, an induced dynamism and an infinite capacity to use with discernment the various *pramāṇas* and explore the nature of all things in this vast universe.

This active curiosity of *a-Vidyā*, its hope (*āśā*: *Chānd. Up. Bh.* 7, 14, 1) of penetrating to the very essence of things (for truth is *vastu-tantra*, depending on things themselves) leads it to metaphysical questions. But it is prone to answer them erroneously or, at least, to trust as final its inadequate insights, because it spontaneously superimposes on the still unknown its memory of the already known. This is why it is in need of a radical conversion by which it will cease to trust itself and begin to rely on the *Śruti* under the guidance of an expert Vedāntin guru. Once converted, the man of *a-Vidyā* will be led along the path of interiority blazed by the 'great sayings' to the innermost *Ātman* which is the Ground of *a-Vidyā* and along the path of transcendence to the absolute *Sat* of which all *a-Sat* is but a reflection and an *upādhi*, including his own finite self (cf. *US* 18, 27-39).

Scriptural *Vidyā* cancels *a-Vidyā* insofar as the latter is erroneous in its pretensions of independence, self-sufficiency, perfect reliability and metaphysical finality. But insofar as *a-Vidyā* is accurate within the limits of its own *pramāṇas*, admits the inadequacy and revisability of its own achievements and obeys the teleology of a dynamism which opens it to the possibility of becoming healed and perfected by a *pramāṇa* superior to its own, it is not exactly abolished but fulfilled by *Vidyā*.

I have tried to show something which is only a side object of Śaṅkara's teaching, namely, the hidden kinship of *a-Vidyā* with *Vidyā*. But it is not to be belittled for, as he says, "it is from [the relative reality of] the objects [known by *a-Vidyā*], such as breath and so forth that is obtained the discriminative knowledge of that which is True Reality in the supreme sense of the term" (*prāṇa-viṣayāt-paramārtha-satya-vijñānābhimānāt*: *Chānd. Up. Bh.* 7, 17, 1).

Notes

[1] ["Chinks in the Armour of Avidyā," *Knowledge, Culture and Value. Papers Presented in Plenary Sessions, Panel Discussions and Sectional Meetings of World Philosophy Conference [Golden Jubilee Session of the Indian Philosophical Congress] Delhi, Dec. 28, 1975—Jan. 3, 1976*, ed. R.C. Pandeya and S.R. Bhatt (Delhi: Motilal Banarsidass, 1976) 77-84.]

9

CONTEMPLATION IN ŚAṄKARA AND RĀMĀNUJA[1]

1. Contemplation in Śaṅkara

1.1 The nature of contemplation

One of the terms used by Śaṅkara to designate contemplation is *vijñāna* as distinguished from preparatory *jñāna*. "*Jñāna*," he says, "is the enlightenment (*avabodha*) regarding *Ātman*, etc. as obtained from the *śāstra* and the *ācāryas*," i.e., the still theoretical knowledge obtained with the help of the teachers through the scriptural-philosophical discipline of Vedānta. But "*vijñāna* is the experience of that (*tad-anubhava*) in its specificity (*viśeṣataḥ*) (*Bh. Gītā Bh.* 3, 41). More precisely, it consists in converting into one's own experience (*sv'ānubhava-karaṇam*) the knowledge obtained from the science (*Bh. Gītā Bh.* 6, 8; 7, 2; 9, 1).

The experiential enlightenment, this realization of the Reality which theoretical truth can only point to in abstract fashion and fails to present vividly, cannot be entered into at will and without preparation. The *sv'ānubhava-karaṇa* presupposes the perfect possession of the śāstric *jñāna*. Mysticism here claims no independence from scientific theology. It is but the third stage in the threefold process of *Brahma-jijñāsā* (Theology, the enquiry prompted by the desire of knowing the *Brahman*) which begins with *śravaṇa*, the exegetical mastering of the upaniṣadic texts, and *manana*, the rational establishing of their doctrine beyond all doubts and objections.

Indeed, so long as the mind is still ridden with doubts and has not yet surmounted all real or imaginable objections against the truth on which *śravaṇa* has focussed it, it has not reached the calm and stability required for the third stage, namely the stage of *nididhyāsana* or *yoga*-like concentration which is to give birth to *vijñāna*. It must be in peaceful and uncontestable possession of the theoretical truth before it can assimilate it existentially and make it its own vivid awareness.

Śaṅkara's conception of faith (*śraddhā*) as pervading the triple process and especially its third stage points clearly to this. Faith, he says, "is the conviction held in a peaceful mind that it is like that," namely, that the *śāstra* teaching regarding the *Brahman* as innermost *Ātman* is uncontroversially true (*citta-prasāde āstikya-buddhiḥ*); such a faith precedes and initiates all the efforts of man towards his Goal" (*Muṇḍ. Up. Bh.* 2, 1, 7). "When there is faith, the mind becomes concentrated upon the subject which it desires to comprehend, and then due comprehension follows" (*Chānd. Up. Bh.* 6, 12, 2). And perfect faith is no longer a merely intellectual assent but a surrender of the whole mind; it is *buddhi* coupled with *bhakti*; more precisely, it is *āstikya-buddhir-bhakti-sahitā*, "conviction of existence / of the *Brahman-Ātman* / accompanied with devotion" (*Bṛh. Up. Bh.* 3, 9, 21). *Bhakti* here, as elsewhere in Śaṅkara, even when he comments on the *Gītā*, is intellectual love rather than volitional affection: it is *niṣṭha-jñāna*, steadfast knowledge, undisturbed intellectual commitment. Note that it is not yet *vijñāna* but the accomplished *jñāna* which conditions it.

The process of *vijñāna* or contemplation consists in *dhāraṇā* (retention) and *abhyāsa* (repetition) tending towards *samādhi* (enstatic absorption). This is *dhyāna-yoga*, the highest form of knowledge, which consists in abiding constantly in the *Ātman*, bearing in mind that the *Ātman* is all and nothing else is really Existent" (*Bh. Gītā Bh.* 6, 25). Is this process to be performed once only till it terminates in sudden illumination, or is it to be repeated again and again as suggested by the term *abhyāsa*? In a long discussion (*B.S.Bh.* 4, 1, 1-2), Śaṅkara accepts reluctantly the sheer possibility of the first alternative but, on scriptural and observational grounds, he asserts the second as the norm. We may recall that a similar discussion developed among the Mahāyāna schools of Buddhism which led to the Chinese Ch'en and the Japanese Zen schools holding the first position.

Another discussion, more important to Śaṅkara, concerned the admixture or not of elements of *manana* within the process of *nididhyāsana*. It has been pointed out already that for Śaṅkara this assimilative concentration on the truth already heard, discussed and unreservedly accepted is unmixed with *manana*. The opposite view was held by the Prasaṃkhyānavādins, comprising Bhartṛprapañca, Maṇḍana Miśra and, later on, Vācaspati Miśra (all householders, not *saṅnyāsins*). They upheld *prasaṃkhyāna*, i.e., prolonged meditation mixed with reasoning and even worship rituals. Śaṅkara, in his conviction that *dhyāna-yoga* stands beyond reasoning and also that action, even ritual action, can only impede salvation (*mukti*), opposed them repeatedly, for instance in *US* 18, 9-21, 105-108, 199, 222.

The typical *yoga* nature of *dhyāna* raised another doubt. Could not any *yoga* independent of *Śruti* (here the Upaniṣads and their *mahāvākyas* or 'great sayings') lead to the illumination as well as *nididhyāsana*? Every *dhyāna-yoga*, indeed, is *citta-vṛtti-nirodha*, i.e., a withdrawing from all mental modifications, an emptying of their diversity. But let us remark that by itself such an emptying reveals nothing but its emptiness. Hence, it has lent itself to the greatest diversity of interpretations. The Buddhists interpret it strictly as *śūnya*, void, the Yoga-Sāṁkhyas as *kaivalya*, the isolation of the individual *puruṣa* or pure spirit, the Vedāntins as *Ātma-anubhava*, the realization of the universal Spirit, etc. Such a conflict of interpretations shows that yogic emptiness does not bear with it its own interpretation. For Śaṅkara, therefore there can be no reliance in an independent *dhyāna-yoga*. The type he upholds must be preceded and conditioned (*pūrvaka*) by a positive ascertaining (*prasiddhi*) of the transcendent *Ātman* as *Pūrṇa* (the Full). This is arrived at under the guidance of the *Śruti* in the two previous steps (*śravaṇa* and *manana*), and not only by the negative teaching of the upaniṣadic *neti neti* ('not thus, not thus'), as Maṇḍana Miśra thinks, but by the positive one of *Tattvamasi* ('That thou art') and similar *mahāvākyas* (*US* 18, 124-127). We see here clearly that even *nididhyāsana* is strictly śrutivādic, i.e., grounded in scripture. We see also that its apophatic nature is pervaded by the apophatic-kataphatic teaching of this scripture.[2]

In short, the type of contemplation taught by Śaṅkara is a process of *vijñāna* quite distinct from, but conditioned by, scriptural *jñāna*; an efflorescence of faith; a repeatable plunging into *dhyāna-yoga*; an emptying of the mind but around a focusing on Brāhmic Fullness; and a personal appropriation of the scriptural truth in the register of intuitive experience (*svānubhava-karaṇa*). Even Śaṅkara cannot avoid here the active term *karaṇa* but he would reject any idea that *nididhyāsana* is a *karma*, an active modification, or open to an intrusion of *karma*, whether ritual or epistemic. It is the repose of the pacified intellect "big, as it were, with the embryo '*Sat*' (Existent)" (*Bh. Gītā Bh.* 2, 16) and silently receiving its irradiation in undistracted focusing on this *Sat* which is *Cit*, absolute Consciousness. We may, indeed, adapt to this context the pregnant expression '*patiens divina*' (enjoying the divine) and even '*docibilis Deo*' (in the intellectual sense of 'submitting eagerly to being taught by God').

1.2 The role of divine grace

Is this eager passivity a bathing in God's grace? Are its antecedent stages, *śravaṇa* and *manana*, undertaken through man's effort unaided or aided merely by the external grace of the *guru*? Or should we rather say that the whole process of *Brahmajijñāsā* is initiated and constantly sustained by divine grace?

In his commentary on the *Bhagavad Gītā*, Śaṅkara clearly suggests that we should:

> Out of mercy, anxious as to how they may attain bliss, I dwell in their internal organ (*antaḥkaraṇa*), which is the abode of the *Ātman*, and destroy the darkness of ignorance—i.e., that illusory knowledge which is caused by the absence of discrimination—by the lamp of wisdom, the lamp of discrimination, which is fed by the oil of devotion (*bhakti-prasāda*), fanned by the wind of earnest meditation on Me, furnished with the wick of right intuition, purified by the cultivation of chastity and other virtues, held in an internal organ completely detached from all worldly concerns, placed in the wind-sheltered nook of that *manas* which is withdrawn from all sense-objects and untainted by attachment

and aversion, and shining with the light of right knowledge generated by the constant practice of concentration and contemplation. (*Bh. Gītā Bh.* 10, 11)

We may then be surprised to find that Śaṅkara, when commenting on *Kaṭha Up.* 2, 23 or *Muṇḍ. Up.* 3, 2, 3 which speak clearly of divine election and grace, explains them in such a way as to eliminate any affirmation of divine grace. It may be because he finds the language of grace anthropomorphic and tending towards a dualism of parallel entities, viz., God, grace and man.

At other times, however, Śaṅkara does not refuse to "assume that salvation is effected by discerning knowledge (namely, advaitic contemplation: *vijñānena*) caused (*hetukena*) by His grace (*tad-anugraha*), because scripture teaches it" (*B.S.Bh.* 2, 3, 41), i.e., "by the attainment of knowledge caused by the grace of the Lord (*īśvara-prasāda-jñāna-prāptya eva*)' (*Bh. Gītā Bh.* 2, 39).

In conceiving of divine grace Śaṅkara remains faithful to the primary type of grace in India. This is not the favour of a powerful monarch to one of his subjects but the *guru's* compassionate communication of knowledge to his ignorant pupil. The divine *Guru*, however, is the inner Teacher, the indwelling *Ātman*, uttering no words, sending forth no special inspiration, but simply self-effulgent at the centre of the mind (*manas*) and thus "illumining the mind (*manaso avabhāsaka*)" (*Kena Up. Bh.* 1, 6). This illumination is constitutive of man and his mind and derives from the mind to all the other senses. But the mind which bears its reflection (*ābhāsa*) in the form of the ego (*aham*) (*US* 18, 27-33) is normally outward-bound and diffracts it into external knowledge which is but *a-Vidyā*. However, there exists eternally the *Vidyā*-repleted *Śruti* which is, as it were, the externalized Consciousness of the *Ātman* (cf. *Taitt. Up. Bh.* 2, 3). To those who are qualified for it, the human *gurus* give access to it so that it functions as the external divine grace in the form of Word (*Śabda*). Under its teaching, the mind is turned inward and focused on its very Source, the self-effulgent *Cit.* Thus comes about the conjunction of the divine external grace, the *Śabda*, with the self-subsistent inner

Grace, the *Cid-Ātman*, and saving Knowledge (*Vidyā*) blazes forth.

1.3 The goal of contemplation

The goal of contemplation is *Vidyā* or, more precisely, *parā Vidyā*. This is the perfect knowledge of the absolute *Brahman* as our innermost *Ātman*. As perfect, it culminates in intuitive apprehension (*avagati-paryanta*: *B.S.Bh.* 1, 1, 1). It is the fulfilment of the desire of knowing *Brahman* (*Brahmajijñāsā*), the end of a threefold process, the "one goal" (*ek'āyana*: *Bṛh. Up. Bh.* 2, 4, 11) of man; yet it is not something to be effected. Its so-called means are not means of production; what they do is simply to remove the veil of passions and ignorance which hides its eternal actuality:

> The knowledge of the *Ātmā*-consciousness is not 'an effect to be obtained' in as much as it is invariably apprehended / in every cognition / as that illumining Consciousness / which is distinct from all forms of objects set up by ignorance.... *Brahman* is self-evident: we have only to eliminate what is falsely ascribed to *Brahman* by *a-Vidyā*. (*Bh. Gītā Bh.* 18, 50)

This elimination is effected on the conceptual plane through *śravaṇa* and *manana*, and on the level of existential interiority by contemplation in *nididhyāsana*:

> In the matter of *parā Vidyā*, the aim is accomplished simultaneously with the realization of the import (*artha*) of the texts for there is nothing here / to be done / except becoming centred on the sole knowledge of the meaning revealed by the mere words. (*Mund. Up. Bh.* 1, 1, 6).

Finally, there is a problem which has divided the Śaṅkarites regarding the psychological nature of the substitution of *a-Vidyā* by *Vidyā*. Does this imply a final and perfecting modification of the mind (*mano-vṛtti*) or is it the evanescing, itself illusory, of all illusion? The answer to this question commands a radical choice between two interpretations of Śaṅkara's teaching: the utterly acosmistic and the not so acosmistic one. Śaṅkara himself provides texts favouring either the first or the second explanation and has, therefore, left this important question undecided.

2. Contemplation in Rāmānuja

2.1 The nature of contemplation

While Rāmānuja does not fail to teach a *jñāna-yoga* aiming at *ātma-jñāna* (self-knowledge) and which has more affinity with Sāṁkhya than with Advaita, his more influential and characteristic teaching is that of *bhakti-yoga* to which even that *jñāna-yoga* is leading. The opening sentence of his *Srībhāṣya* reveals its centrality:

> May my *buddhi* or *jñāna* blossom into *bhakti* or devotion to *Brahman* or Srīnivāsa whose nature is revealed in the Upaniṣads as the self that, out of the *līlā* or sport of love, creates, sustains and reabsorbs the whole universe with a view to saving the *jīvas* or souls which seek his love. (*Srībhāṣya* 1, 1, 1)

The path of *bhakti* begins with seven *sādhanas* or means which for lack of time but not of importance I must abstain from explaining. They pave the way to *upāsanā*, the life of worshipful meditation through which the love of God is cultivated to the utmost. The chief practice of this *Brahmopāsanā* is *dhyāna*, the continuous process of mental one-pointedness (*ekāgra-cittatā*) on *Brahman* as the one Lord. It is to be practised daily till the moment of death. It is defined as "ceaseless remembrance of the Lord, uninterrupted like the flow of oil from one vessel to another" (*taila-dhāra-vad avicchinna-smṛti-saṃtāna-rūpa*: *Śrībhāṣya* 1, 1, 1 and see *Bh. Gītā Bh.* 9, 34). It makes use of the technique of the eight stages of *yoga*. In virtue of its intensity and repeatedness, this reflection gradually changes into a likeness of vision (*darśana-samānākara*). Thus it turns into a direct presentation (*pratyakṣatā*) of the Lord to the intellect and imagination, of the contemplator. This is possible, it seems, because the *Brahman* of Rāmānuja is not the Śaṅkarian *nirguṇa Brahman* from which all words, concepts and imagination recede, unable to attain it, but the complex *viśiṣṭa Brahman*, infinite and transcendent Spirit, no doubt, but with an infinite number of differencing attributes, perfect qualities, modes which are its cosmic bodies and even an eternal body of its own which is of unsurpassable beauty, adorned with incomparable clothes, jewels and weapons, and situated in a celestial abode of unrivalled delight where the perfect female *Śrī* and a retinue of worshipful servants are at its constant service. Such a complex *Brahman* in which all the perfections of spirit and matter are displayed in uppermost glory is not inaccessible to our conceptual intellect and our aesthetic imagination. This is why contemplation can turn into direct intuition (*sākṣātkāra*).

The attitude of the contemplator (*upāsaka*) is derived from an upaniṣadic passage which Rāmānuja explains literally:

> He who, dwelling within the self, is different from the self, whom the self does not know, *of whom the self is the body*, who rules the self from within, He is thy Self, the Inner Ruler (*Antaryāmin*) immortal. (*Bṛh. Up.* 5, 22, Mādhyaṃdina recension)

This teaches that the human soul is a body (*śarīra*) of the Lord who is in turn its internally ruling Soul (*śarīrin*). Body is defined by Rāmānuja as "any substance that an intelligent entity (*cetana*) is able completely to control (*niyantum*) and to support (*dhārayitum*) for his own purposes, and the essential nature of which is entirely subservient (*śeṣatā*) to that intelligent entity (*Srībhāṣya* 2, 1, 9). Or, briefly, "the body of a being is constituted by that, the nature, substance and activity of which depend on the will of that being" (*Śrībhāṣya* 2, 1, 8). And Rāmānuja pursues: "In this sense, then, all conscious and non-conscious beings together constitute a body of the Supreme Person" (*Śrībhāṣya* 2, 1, 9).

The *upāsaka*, therefore, is directed to stand before the Lord as an obedient body, a conjoined instrument, a totally dependent subordinate, but also to glorify in this status, to cherish it, since it is not a matter of his or the Lord's arbitrary choice but the truth of his nature. As in Śaṅkara, salvation here also consists in recovering the eternal truth of one's being. Recovering it with delight is a matter of *jñāna*, knowledge, but of *jñāna* turning into *bhakti* (*bhakti-rūp'āpanna-jñāna*).

Since the object of this knowledge is not simple but *viśiṣṭa*, the *upāsaka* can focus on it through a variety of types of contemplation called *Brahma-vidyās*. There are 32 *Brahma-vidyās* described in the Upaniṣads. For instance, the Lord may be contemplated as *Sat*, the Existent without a second, as *Bhūman*, the Infinite, as *Satya*, Truth, as *Jñāna*, Knowledge, as *Ānanda*, Bliss, as *Amalatva*, purity, as *Bhuvana-sundara*, of Form

Beautiful, as *Antaryāmin*, Inner Ruler of the soul, etc. Besides, the *Bhagavad Gītā* and the *Purāṇas*, especially the *Viṣṇu Purāṇa*, provide a wealth of contemplations on the Lord in his *avatāras* (descents) where he appears singularly as *Parama Karūṇika* (Supreme Commiserator) and *Suhrit* (Friend). This variety explains why the term *smṛti* (remembrance) is used in the definition of *dhyāna*.

2.2 The role of grace and love in contemplation

Through these *vidyās*, the *upāsaka* comes to recognize the redemptive will of his *Śeṣin* or *Svāmin* (Principal or Master), who is his Saviour (*Rakṣaka*). In him alone he takes his refuge (*śaraṇa-gati*). From pure self-effort he expects nothing but from his Lord he awaits all goods, including *bhakti* itself and finally *mukti* (salvation). He remembers the statement of *Kaṭha Upaniṣad* which is clear and conclusive: "It is not by study or reflection that *Brahman* is realized; whom He chooses, unto him He reveals his form." This is the theme of divine election which Śaṅkara avoided. Rāmānuja develops it in the wake of the *Bhagavad Gītā*. For him it is true that the Lord chooses his friends whom he saves. But to be chosen one must be choice-worthy. He is worthy who is an incipient *bhakta* (devotee) presenting to his Lord the eight-petalled lotus of non-violence, kindness, patience, truth, self-control, austerity, inwardness and knowledge. At times, though, it seems that this very beginning of *bhakti* is itself a divine gift but the question of priority between God's grace and man's first love is never clearly decided.

Under God's grace and through the practice of dhārmic duties allied with the reiteration of *upāsanā*, loving devotion turns into self-surrender (*ātma-nikṣepa*) and affection (*sneha*) into *prītī* or *preman* (self-forgetting love). The *jñānin* (knower) becomes a *prapanna bhakta* (surrendered devotee). He lives and has his being in divine love.

But the Lord himself seeks the *jñānin* and sees him as His very life and self, in accord with *Bh. Gītā* 7, 17-18. Love inverses paradoxically the *śeṣin-śeṣa* relationship. The Lord abdicates as it were his principality (*śeṣitva*) and subordinates himself in love to his very subordinate. His *saulabhya* (accessibility) triumphs over his *paratva* (supremacy). There is now only the reciprocity of love. The Lord adapts himself to the devotional needs of men. Overpowered by his compassion (*dayā*), he descends into their world (*jīva-loka*) in *avatāra*-forms of saviourship. Thus he builds a *sopana*, a ladder, between his supreme abode (*parama-pada*) and the *Kṣirabdhi*, or world of men, along which he descends so that his elected devotees may ascend. He who is the end (*upeya*) makes himself the means (*upāya*).

2.3 The goal of contemplation

Mukti, release, is the consummation of this communing love of *bhakta* and *Bhagavān* through which the *bhakta* attains to the perfect nature of the Highest Person without, however, losing his individuality of a subordinate. The individual self recovers his own eternal form, true and full. He becomes free from all evils, such as sin and nescience, which obscured him and made him miserable. "Intelligence, bliss and the other essential qualities of the soul which were obscured and contracted by his *karma*, expand and thus manifest themselves when the bondage due to *karma* passes away and the soul approaches the Highest Light" (*Srībhāṣya* 4, 4, 3).

In *mukti*, the self in blissful communion with the Lord knows itself in its true nature. "And this true nature consists in this that the souls have for their Inner Self the Highest Self while they constitute the body of that Self and hence are modes (*prakāra*) of it" (*Srībhāṣya* 4, 4, 5).

Does the released soul enjoy all divine powers? "Freed from all that hides its true nature, it possesses the power of intuitively beholding the pure *Brahman*, but it does not possess the power of ruling and guiding the different forms of motion and rest belonging to animate and inanimate nature" (*Srībhāṣya* 4, 4, 17). "Because it is of such a nature that it essentially depends on the Lord, the equality with the Lord which the released soul may claim does not extend to the world-ruling energies" (*Srībhāṣya* 4, 4, 20).

Concluding his doctrine of *mukti*, Rāmānuja writes:

> We know from Scripture that there exists a supreme Person whose nature is absolute bliss and goodness, who is antagonistic to all evil, who is the

> cause of... the world, ... who is an ocean of kindness..., who is immeasurably raised above all possibility of any one being equal or superior to him.... And with equal certainty we know from Scripture that the supreme Lord, when pleased by the faithful worship of his devotees... frees them from the influence of nescience..., allows them to attain to that supreme bliss which consists in the direct intuition of His own true nature, and after that does not turn them back into the miseries of *saṃsāra*.... For He Himself has said..., 'I regard him as my very self' (*Bh. Gītā* 7, 17). (*Śrībhāṣya* 4, 4, 22)

Thus, Rāmānuja says, "everything is settled to satisfaction" (*iti sarvam samānjasam*) (*Srībhāṣya* 4, 4, 22).

Notes

[1] [First published as "Contemplation in Śaṅkara and Rāmānuja," *The Living Word* **83**/3 (1977) 199-210. Reprinted in *The Divine Life* **40**/6-7 (1978) 176-179, 210-212, and in *Prayer and Contemplation*, ed. C. Vadakkekara (Bangalore: Asian Trading Corporation, 1980) 209-220. Reprinted here courtesy De Nobili College, Pune, having had no replies either from *The Living Word* (Carmelgiri, Aluva) or from Asirvanam Benedictine Monastery (Anchepalya, Bengaluru) despite several requests.]

[2] [This argument is exposed at greater length in "Questioning Vedānta" = ch. 7 above.]

10

SPIRITUAL VALUES OF ADVAITA VEDĀNTA AND SOCIAL LIFE[1]

As India moves towards the end of the twentieth century we feel that our traditional hierarchy of human values (*artha*, *kāma*, *dharma*, *mokṣa*) threatens to topple upside down so that the materialistic values become preponderant at the expense of the spiritual and religious goods of man. Only forty years ago, the French scholar Jean Herbert could still write:

> The dominant concern of the 'average Hindu' is not the material problems (food, professional status, social rank, luxury, salary, retirement, health, speed of transportation, security of investments, etc.), nor the social matters (politics, class struggle, level of prices, industrialization, financial market, philanthropy, etc.), nor even the artistic interests (books, theatre, films, music, painting, etc.). It is of a purely spiritual order (existence and nature of God, search for a *guru*, methods or meditation and *yoga*, etc.). All the rest is only of secondary or accessory importance.[2]

It was the time of Mahatma Gandhi, Rabindranath Tagore, Sarvepalli Radhakrishnan and Aurobindo Ghosh. They kept the mind of even the man in the street focused on ideals and spiritual pursuits. Nowadays such pursuits are no longer a general obsession of the Indian people. Religious beliefs are often questioned. The young are being turned towards more earthly achievements. And their parents are so full of anxieties for mere survival that they have but little time for higher concerns.

When seeking explanations for such a mutation one must, of course, put forth modernization and secularization, the prestige of scientific achievements, the pressures of social conflicts and the hope of achieving here on earth a very much needed liberation: a liberation from social inequality and all types of alienation[3]. But, besides these, there appears to exist a growingly explicit dissatisfaction with, and often a turning away from, the exclusive spiritualism of the dominant religio-philosophical traditions of India, more pointedly, with the alleged acosmism of Advaita Vedānta.

It is around this latter point that I shall centre my reflections. Unless we can show that *advaitavāda* is not necessarily the theory of acosmism, the *māyāvāda*, which it has repeatedly been said to be, it will prove ever more to be a stumbling block to our contemporaries. In attempting to do this I shall naturally turn to Śaṅkarācārya. And unavoidably, I shall first have to recall some basic positions of the Master.

1. Difference between *vidyā* and *a-vidyā*, *Vidyā* and *a-Vidyā*

"Knowledge (*jñāna*), writes Śaṅkara, results from the different *pramāṇas*, i.e., the sources of valid knowledge, and the objects of the *pramāṇas* are the existent things as they are in reality (*yathā-bhūtavastu-viṣayam*) (*B.S.Bh.* 1, 1, 4). It is their total objectivity, their *yāthātmya*, which knowledge must focus upon if it is to be true. Its grasping turns *jñāna* into *pramā* or *vidyā*, correct knowledge.

This term *yāthātmya* is important. By itself it suggests the possibility of a succession of increasing approximations. The conformity implied by *yathā* (as, like) can be more or less partial before it is complete. Hence, we have various depths of correct knowledge or *vidyā*. If I perceive an object which is far and indistinct, my knowledge is objective but too generic. It can become increasingly specific and even individual but still remain external, a knowledge by external characteristics. Perhaps it can arrive at grasping internal and even essential characteristics. Further, it can possibly ascertain the outer and even the inner relations of that object to other objects, especially its ontological dependence on its causes, proximate, mediate and even ultimate. Thus by degrees of approximation our knowledge may progress towards full conformity with the total objectivity, *yāthātmya*, of realities as they are ontologically (*yathā-bhūta-vastu*).

It is to be noted that, according to the Śaṅkarians, each such approximation is sublated (*bādhita*)—Hegel would say, *aufgehoben*—by the next and closer ones. Thus cancelled by enrichment, it loses its provisional finality and is deemed non-knowledge, *a-vidyā*, in comparison with the richer one. However it is not simply abolished but rather integrated into the closer approximations.

In connection with this, we must recall Śaṅkara's way when he deals with views different from his own. Those that contradict his view of Vedānta are thoroughly criticised and rejected; but those that are not inconsistent with it are allowed to be held or even given room within his methodically established conclusions (*siddhānta*). He states this clearly in *B.S.Bh.* 2, 1, 3, and in 2, 4, 12 he accepts a point of doctrine from Yoga Darśana on the ground, he says, of the axiom, "if another doctrine is not inconsistent with our own it becomes an accompaniment of our own" (*paramatam-apratiṣiddham-anumatam-bhavati*).

But we must now consider another way in which statements may detract from the full *yāthātmya*. They may ignore its deepest core, namely, the *advaita* truth that "the *Brahman* is the supreme *Ātman* of all contingent beings" and yet present themselves as final. In this sense, all the so-called true statements of ordinary knowledge and, we can say, of our positive sciences, are, in the language of Śaṅkara, *a-Vidyā*, i.e., deficient with regard to, and even opposed to, *Vidyā*, the ultimate Knowledge. This is because they are statements implicitly superimposed with finality, self-sufficiency, absoluteness whereas these qualities belong only to the *advaita* statements.

Superimposition, *adhyāsa* or *adhyāropa*, is a key-notion in Śaṅkara's writings. Here is how he explains it:

> All the definitions of superimposition agree insofar as they represent *adhyāsa* as the apparent presentation of the attributes of one thing in another thing.... This *adhyāsa*, thus defined, learned men consider to be *a-vidyā*, and the ascertainment of the proper nature of a reality by discriminating it from [the attributes superimposed on it] they call *vidyā* (*B.S.Bh.* Introduction)

Applying these definitions to the whole domain of knowledge, he divides it into two spheres, the sphere of the notions of 'I' and the sphere of the notions of 'non-I,' i.e., of the subject (*viṣayin*) and of the object (*viṣaya*) and, hence, of consciousness and unconsciousness whose natures are as opposed as light and darkness. Due to this opposition neither their natures nor their attributes can be mutually identified.

> Hence, it follows that it is falsehood (*mithyā*) to superimpose (*adhyāsa*) upon the Subject, whose sphere is the notion of 'I' and whose essence is Consciousness (*cid-ātmaka*), the object, whose sphere is the notion of 'non-I,' as well as its attributes; and vice versa to superimpose the Subject and the attributes of the Subject on the object. In spite of this, it is on the part of man an innate (*naisargika*) procedure... [to commit such mutual superimpositions] thus coupling the Real and the un-Real (*Sat* and *a-Sat*) (*B.S.Bh.* Introduction)

> It is in the wake of this mutual *adhyāsa* of *Ātman* and non-*Ātman*—which is designated as *a-Vidyā*—that there proceed all empirical usages (*vyavahāra*) of the world relating to correct knowledge and its sources (*pramāṇa*) as well as the sacred teachings even those concerned with liberation (*mokṣa*). (Ibid.)

> [This is because all the processes of knowing, acting and undergoing joy or suffering are unable to operate unless] the I-notion of the ego-sense (*ahaṁkara*) be superimposed on the Inner *Ātman* (*pratyag-ātman*) which is the Witness (*sākṣin*) of all its modification and vice versa the Inner *Ātman*, the All-Witness, be superimposed on the inner organ (*antaḥkaraṇa*), the senses and so on. In this way there goes on this beginningless, endless and innate *Adhyāsa*, which appear in the form of wrong conception, which impels agentship and enjoyership, and which is observed by everyone. (Ibid.)

Of course it is observable to everyone only in the form of wrong conception. To interpret this observation in the light of the above scheme of two spheres is the long task which Śaṅkara then undertakes. His conviction that the sphere of the I-notion has a Centre which is absolute Consciousness (*Cit*), perfect Existent (*Sat*) and, as to the knower, innermost *Ātman* (*Pratyagātman*) and universal Witness (*sarva Sākṣin*), is an insight of the Upaniṣads which Śaṅkara takes as the cornerstone of his teaching but which is not a commonplace of observation. In its presented formulation it is strictly a teaching of Advaita Vedānta although it is held equivalently by dominant systems of Christian thought. St Thomas Aquinas, for instance, distinguishing definition and total conception, says that to define 'man' as 'rational animal' is to give a quite correct definition but that no total conception of man would be correct if it ignored or denied his creaturely dependence on the absolute God who is his sole ultimate Cause, Preserver, providential inner Guide and Illuminer. As such, in the words of St Augustine, God is "more interior to man than man's innermost, and superior to man's uppermost" (*intimior intimo meo et superior summo meo*).[4] Augustine himself speaks of the world with its pretension of self-sufficiency and capacity to beatify man as *mendacium magnum*, a great lie.[5] Such writers are substantially aware of the *a-Vidyā* which Śaṅkara defines as man's innate procedure to superimpose the *Ātman* and its attributes on the non-*Ātman* and vice versa the non-*Ātman* and its attributes on the *Ātman*. Yet, within their uncompromising doctrine of the transcendence and immanence of the absolute and simple Deity, they integrate a positive conception of man and the universe.

Is Śaṅkara really bound to refuse any such integration? Or is he simply rejecting the other Indian systems of his time because they were actually built up on the universal superimposition he diagnoses? Is he not, as he says, considering that his only task as a *śrutivādin*, an interpreter of the Upaniṣads, is to put forth with utmost emphasis the first class truth that the supreme *Brahman* is the innermost *Ātman* of all, and leaving to others the task of establishing second class truths concerning man and world? Or should we point to a choice of language, namely, his choice of a language of extreme opposites, *Vidyā*, *a-Vidyā*, *Sat*, *a-Sat*, etc., with no legitimate status for intermediary terms? Let us try to understand the language of Śaṅkara.

2. The Linguistic Cribwork of Śaṅkara's Writings

Foundational to Śaṅkara's writings there is an intercrossing, a cribwork of three manners of language: the mundane *vyavahāra* language; the Vedānta or upaniṣadic language; and the language of its exegete, the *śrutivādin*. Let us, to start with, consider how the term *sat*, being, is used with different values:

	Vyavahāra	*Vedānta*	*Śrutivādin*
1.	I am *sat* (a being) The jar is *sat*.	*Neti neti* (not so, not so). *Brahman* is *a-sat*. *Brahman* is *Sat*.	*Brahman* is other than any *sat* because it is *paramārthataḥ Sat* (Being in the most elevated sense). And any *sat* is *a-Sat*.
2.	Only the 'son of a barren woman' and other impossibles are *Asat* (*paramārthataḥ*).		I agree that no existent man, jar, etc., is *Asat*. They are *Sad-Asad-vilakṣaṇa* (not definable by '*Sat*' or '*Asat*' in the perfect sense of these terms).
3.	But what am I apart from such comparison with *Sat*?	You are *San-mūla* (having *Sat* as your root).	Any consideration of you apart from your Root, *Brahman*, would be false. *Brahman* is your innermost total Cause apart from which nothing of you can exist.
4.	But I am a living self (*jīvātman*) autonomously.	*Brahman* is your *Ātman*, your *parama pratyag-Ātman* (supreme inner *Ātman*). It is the supreme *Ātman* of all.	The reflective pronoun '*ātman*' serves to designate you and whatever is interior to you. Thus there is a ladder of *ātman* in you. Ascend it and find that each higher one is "more subtle, more causal and more interior."[6] The higher-most *Ātman* is subtlest Consciousness, sovereign Cause of your being and innermost *Ātman*.
5.	But effects exist in themselves apart from their shaping cause (*nimitta-kāraṇa*).	All this is *Brahman* (*sarvam idam Brahma*). That you are (*Tat-tvam-asi*).	*Brahman* is not only your shaping Cause but also your internal reality-giving Cause (*Upādāna*) in which you exist in unreciprocal identity (*tādātmya*), as is to be explained.

It will be clear from the above presentation in parallels that Śaṅkara in explaining the paradoxical statements of the Upaniṣads has recourse to the conception of various senses of terms which was well-known in his time. From the ordinary commonsense meaning of some terms he ascends to their most elevated meaning (*paramārtha*). There are transcendental terms like *sat*, *ātman*, *vidyā*, etc. which can be infinitized because their proper meaning (*svārtha*) is neutral with regard to finitude or infinity. Naturally the process of infinitizing them implies a step of negation of all their finite connotations. Once thus purified and elevated to infinity, they can be predicated not only of *Brahman* in itself but also of *Brahman* as causally innermost in us and even of ourselves as totally penetrated by our constitutive Cause. Thus the Upaniṣads say, "I am *Brahman*," "That thou art." To people unused to such paradoxical sayings Śaṅkara explains them especially well in his *US* 18.

3. The Meaning of *Tattvamasi* and Unreciprocal Identity (*Tādātmya*)

The statement "That thou art" seems to refer to our human self as ordinarily apprehended and simply to identify it with the Absolute. It would be a cause of reciprocal identity: I am *Brahman*, *Brahman* is me. But how could an ignorant, suffering, sinful ego be identical with That whose essence is *satyam-jñānam-anantam* (Reality-Knowledge-Infinite)? Yet it is true, says Śaṅkara, that our conscious ego is the door (*dvāra*) by which we have access to the true import of this saying. (*US* 18, 110)

It is the door because of its close similarity with That, the *Brahman* which is absolute Consciousness. Indeed, it is its mirror-reflection (*ābhāsa*) in the ego-sense:

> The ego which says 'I' and 'mine' (*abhimānakṛt*) is the ego-sense (*ahaṁ-kartṛ*) which, always standing in proximity to that [absolute Awareness], acquires a reflection of it. Hence, there arises the dual complex of *Ātman* and *ātmiya* (what pertains to *Ātman*) which is the sphere of 'I' and 'mine.' (*US* 18, 27)

> Only when there is a reflection (*ābhāsa*) of the inner Witness can such words [as 'I' and 'thou'] by referring to the reflection indicate the Witness indirectly. They cannot designate the Witness directly in any way. (*US* 18, 29)

> The reflection of a face is different from the face, since it conforms to the mirror; and in turn the face is different from its reflection, since it does not

conform to the mirror. The reflection of the *Ātman* in the ego-sense is comparable to the reflection of a face, while the *Ātman* is comparable to the face and, [therefore,] different [from its reflection, the conscious ego]. And yet the two remain undiscriminated [by the ignorant]. (*US* 18, 32-33)

Let us note Śaṅkara's unambiguous statement that the conscious ego and the *Ātman*-Consciousness are different. The ego is not *Vastu*, Reality in the full sense. By the whole of itself it is a reflection, a similitude (like all effected beings) but the closest, an image of the perfect *Vastu*. It does not designate but it indicates it indirectly. A door is to be crossed and leads beyond itself. An image by the whole of itself refers to the face it reflects. It is deceptive only to the ignorant who takes it for the face owing to its very similarity with it. This is the most deceptive case of mutual superimposition.

To understand "That thou art" we have, therefore to pass up to the supreme meaning (*paramārtha*) of 'thou' through a process of purification which this time operates on our common conception of our own ego. In *vyavahāra* language, the conscious ego is the integrator which unifies (*ekīkaroti*, cf. *Bṛh. Up. Bh.* 4, 3, 7) our whole mental and corporeal reality. In Vedānta language, it is (unreciprocally) identified with 'That,' the innermost *Ātman*. In the *śrutivādin's* language, it is shown to designate directly that conscious ego but as the image of That and, thus, indirectly to indicate That as its own supreme *Ātman*.

The term '*tādātmya*,' in its usage by Śaṅkara, means exactly 'the relation of having That (*Tat*) as one's own supreme *Ātman*.' It applies to every finite reality in reference to its Cause, *Brahman*. It is not an accessory and extrinsic relationship but one that is ontologically constitutive of those beings. Hence, if it is omitted from our conception of them, the latter is inadequate and thus, if I may say so, metaphysically false though it may be physically correct as far as it goes.

Let us examine six notions implied by *tādātmya* as used by Śaṅkara.

(1) *Unreciprocality*: The inner cause (*upādāna*) is the (*ātman*) of its effects; the effects are not the *ātman* of their causes.

Names-and-forms [= finite entities] in all their states have their [innermost] *Ātman* in *Brahman* alone, but *Brahman* has not its *ātman* in

> them. (*Taitt. Up. Bh.* 2, 6, 1) Despite the 'non-otherness' (cf. 4) of effect and [inner] cause, the effect is not the *ātman* of the cause but the cause is the *ātman* of the effect. (*B.S.Bh.* 2, 1, 9)

(2) *Dependence*: This is intrinsic and total because it is ontologically constitutive.

> It is an accepted principle even in the world that an effect is intimately dependent (*anuvidhāyin*) on its inner cause. (*Bṛh. Up.* 1, 5, 14) The doctrine that the embodied *ātman* has *Brahman* as its *Ātman* does away with the independent own existence of this embodied *ātman*... and likewise with the independent existence of the entire world of mundane experience. (*B.S.Bh.* 2, 1, 14)

(3) *Non-separateness*: This is an application of the principle that between the effect and its inner cause (*prakṛti*) there is non-separation, ... non-division (*abheda*)." (*B.S.Bh.* 2, 3, 6)

> If the [inner] cause were to be dissolved, the effect too could no longer exist; but we may assume a continued existence of the cause although the effect is destroyed. (*B.S.Bh.* 2, 3, 14)

(4) *Non-otherness*: What this term denies is otherness strictly understood, i.e., mutual foreignness, heterogeneity, extrinsicity, ontological unrelatedness, as between the nine eternal substances of the Vaiśeṣikas or the *prakṛti* and *puruṣa* of the Sāṁkhyas. Śaṅkara explains non-otherness (*ananyatva*) as 'non-existence apart from (*vyatirekeṇa abhāvaḥ*)' and Vācaspati explains, "We do not say that *ananyatva* is 'non-distinction' but that it excludes 'division' (*bheda*)." (*Bhāmati* 2, 1, 14)

> It is impossible even within hundreds of years, ever to bring about an effect which is other than its [inner] cause. The root-cause (*mūlakāraṇa*), by appearing like an actor in the form of this or that effect up to the last effect of all, thereby becomes the basis for all current notions and terms concerning mundane experience. (*Bhāmati* 2, 1, 18) There exists in the past, present or future, not one thing simply other than the *Ātman*, simply non-*Ātman*, separated [from it] by space or time, utterly subtle, disconnected and remote. (*Taitt. Up. Bh.*.2, 6, 1)

> A thing which is other serves as an element of limitation with regard to that than which it is other because when the intellect is busy with the one it detaches itself from any other. That by which a thing is circumscribed serves as the limit of its notion. For instance, the notion of cowness is contradicted by the notion of horseness in such a way that horseness

excludes cowness and the latter is limited by it. Such limitation is seen to exist also in the case of the distinct substances [of Vaiśeṣika]. The *Brahman* is not other in such a fashion, since it is not subject to limitation by exclusion on the part of other substances (*Taitt. Up. Bh.* 2, 1)

The upaniṣadic words '*neti neti*' eliminate from *Brahman* any difference due to limiting adjuncts (*upādhi*). These two words refer to a quid devoid of any such distinctive characteristics as name, form, action, alterity (otherness), species or quality. (*Bṛh. Up. Bh.* 2, 3, 6)

(5) *Distinction*: Effects are always transcended ontologically by their inner cause and thus inferior to, and distinct from, it.

If absolute equality were insisted on, the relation of [inner] cause and effect would be annihilated.... This relation is based on the fact that there is present in the cause an excellence [which is absent from the effect]. (*B.S.Bh.* 2, 1. 6)

(6) *Manifestative extrinsic denomination*: An actor's dress and make-up manifest him but only by extrinsic denomination, say, as a prince. His princehood is not an intrinsic attribute (*viśeṣaṇa*) but only an *upādhi*. An *upādhi* (from *upa* + *ā* + *dhi*, to put upon) or external adjunct is an extrinsic denominator. It never manifests the intrinsic nature of a being but it yet manifests this being by reference to objects, roles, etc. which are extrinsic to it but linked with it in some characteristic way. The ignorant takes such superimposed denominators for authentic *viśeṣaṇas*; the discriminator knows them as mere *upādhis*. A second mistake of the ignorant is to think that when some entity is said to be an *upādhi* of a given subject, something has been said about the intrinsic nature of that entity. On the contrary, it has simply been said that it manifests that subject through extrinsic denomination. In short, *upādhi* never says anything intrinsic whether of the subject or of the entity that manifests it.

We must keep this in mind when we wish to understand what Śaṅkara means when he says that the cosmic effects are *upādhis* of *Brahman* and that relations such as causality, inner ātmanhood witnessing, inner guidance, etc., are mere *upādhis* in the case of *Brahman*. He himself asks, what is the difference between the absolute immutable *Brahman* and the *Brahman* related to the world and apparently qualified by the effects of its causality?

It is only a difference due to *upādhis*. Intrinsically there is neither difference nor identification for the [allegedly] two *Brahmans* are by nature the [one] pure Intelligence, homogeneous like a lump of salt.... Therefore:

(1) [the 'great saying'] *neti neti* (not such, not such) designates the *Brahman* unaffected by *upādhis*, which is beyond the grasp of speech and mind, undifferentiated and one;

(2) when it is [extrinsically] related to such *upādhis* as body and organs, which are characterized by non-Knowledge, it is called 'transmigrating individual *ātman*';

(3) when its *upādhi* is the power of eternal and unlimited Knowledge, it is called inner Ruler (*Antaryāmin*) and Lord (*Īśvara*);

(4) the same *Ātman* as by nature transcendent, absolute and pure is called the immutable and supreme *Ātman*;

(5) in the same way, by upādhic connection with the bodies-and-organs of Hiraṇyagarbha, the 'undifferentiated,' the gods, the species, the individuals: men, animals, disembodied spirits, etc., the *Ātman* assumes [through superimposition], those particular names-and-forms. (*Bṛh. Up. Bh.* 3, 8, 12)

So long as one does not realize in this [*neti neti*] way this *Ātman* which has been described, so long does one accept the *upādhis*... as one's very *Ātman* and, considering through *a-Vidyā* the *upādhis* as intrinsic to the *Ātman*, one transmigrates under the influence of *a-Vidyā*, desire and action. (*Ait. Up. Bh.* 2, 1—Introduction)

These authentic explanations together with the whole theory of *upādhi* stand in direct opposition to any pantheistic interpretation of Śaṅkara's *advaitavāda*. He always upholds the *Brahman's* perfect transcendence and he does this with particular sharpness when he explains that the allegedly real relations of *Brahman* to the cosmos are only *upādhis* (just as St Thomas Aquinas declares that they are only logical relationships). Śaṅkara is more concerned with upholding divine transcendence than with rejecting acosmism but such a rejection is implicit in passages like the following:

In the same way as the *Śruti* speaks of the origin of the cosmos from *Brahman*, it also speaks of *Brahman* as subsisting apart from its effects.

This appears from the passages which point to the difference between cause and effect...; further from the passages which describe the unmodified *Brahman* as abiding in the heart; and from those which declare that the *jīvātman* is united with the Existent (*Sat*)...; moreover the possibility of *Brahman* becoming the object of sense-perception is denied, whereas its effects can be perceived by the senses. For these reasons the existence of the unmodified *Brahman* has to be admitted.... That which is alleged to be a break in *Brahman's* nature [on account of its causality] is imagined through *a-Vidyā*.... By this purification—which is imagined through *a-Vidyā*... not definable as either *Sat* or *Asat*—*Brahman* becomes the basis of all that goes on in the guise of transformation, etc. , while in its absolutely true form it at the same time remains untransformed and untouched by anything that goes on in the cosmos.... Nor is there any reason to find fault with the doctrine that there can be a manifold creation in the one *Ātman* without destroying its character. (*B.S.Bh.* 2, 1, 25-28)

4. Conclusion

I have been trying to situate the language of extreme opposites which Śaṅkara adopts in the wake of the *Śruti*. It is the language of supreme meanings (*paramārtha*), which I conveyed by letters, as in *Sat*, *Asat*, *a-Sat*, etc. When elevated to their *paramārtha*, words are no longer descriptive but merely indicative of the perfect Reality. This language presupposes the language of primary meanings (*mukhyārtha*) on whose levels words are descriptive of finite realities. Between these two languages, there is a semiotic tension because the supremacy of the *paramārtha* presses the *mukhyārtha* to abdicate its pretension of finality and to accept to become measured up by the *paramārtha* standard. This is demanded because Truth, short of which there is no liberation, has to be in complete conformity (*yāthātmya*) to reality beyond even scientific descriptions, explanations and all approximations.

Our ordinary and even scientific view of man and world is condemned as falsehood only insofar as it lacks this abdication of finality, this total relativization and this acceptance to be transmuted by integration with the upper level view that man and world are ontologically rooted in and 'Ātmanized' by the absolute *Brahman*.

What follows from accepting this is neither pantheism nor acosmism but a correct metaphysical situating of man and world in, and in comparison with, their *Ātman*. As rooted in It, they are totally effects in *tādātmya* relation with It, i.e., dependent, non-separated, non-other, distinct and also *upādhis* manifesting it by extrinsic denomination. In comparison with It, they are its similitudes and the conscious ego, in particular, is its image by reflection (*ābhāsa*). Ontologically, they are *Sat-kāryas*, existent effects (*Kaṭha Up. Bh.* 2, 3, 13) totally caused by *Brahman* as *Sat* and *Cit*. The Knowledge (*Vidyā*) that the latter is thus the Innermost *Ātman* of all (*sarva-Ātman*) does not reject them to the nothingness of *Asat*; it simply takes away the *a-Vidyā*-born superimpositions upon them of the attributes of *Sat*: independence, monadic self-sufficiency, absolute self-subsistence, etc. This interpretation may appear novel but I have endeavoured to ground it in the *Ācārya's* own authentic writings from which I derived it. It permits the spiritual values to shine in more genuine brightness and it eliminates the hoary objection that Advaita Vedānta is a stumbling-block in the pursuit of the values of social life. These values, though subordinate, will appear genuine.

Appendix

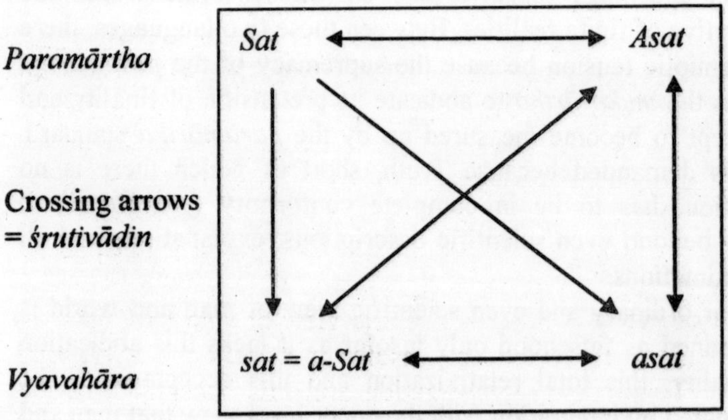

As an appendix I have given above the *semiotic square* of tensional opposition and reconciliation of the three languages found at work in Śaṅkara's commentaries.

Definitions:

a) *Sat* = Being, i.e., being in the most elevated sense of the term.

b) *Asat* = Non-being, the extreme opposite of being, namely that which not only is not but can never be, the impossible.

c) *sat* = being, i.e., any finite being.

d) *a-Sat* = non-Being, i.e., the same finite being when, properly known as rooted in its inner Cause, *Sat*, it is found to be unequal to it (*a-Sat*). As such it manifests It but only as an extrinsic denominator (*upādhi*).

e) *asat* = any delimiter of a *sat* through otherness (*anyattva*). In its own right it is also *sat* / *a-Sat*.

Interrelationships:

1) *Sat* and *Asat* are opposed by mutual contradiction. This opposition is merely epistemological since *Asat* has no ontological value.

2) *Sat* and *sat* or *asat* are not opposed either by contradiction or contrariety or mutual delimitation, but only distinct as Cause and effects by the contrast of superiority and inferiority. Indeed, they have in common the holistic perfection *sattā* (beingness, or *astitā*: is-ness); but *sattā* belongs to *Sat* by absolute right and to *sat* and *asat* by the relative right of having received it causally.

3) *Sat* is absolutely transcendent even in causing.

4) *Sat* is, however, innermostly immanent to *sat* and *asat* owing to its causing them totally by a causality which is free and leaves the Cause unaffected in any way by it. This immanence and this causality are, therefore, mere *upādhis* of *Sat*.

5) *sat* and *asat* are not intrinsic parts or modes or accidents or attributes or bodies of the partless and immutable *Sat*. But they are integrally its effects and similitudes and *upādhis*.

6) *sat* and *asat* are imbued with *sattā* because *Sat* is their supreme *Ātman*; which is to say that their relation to It is

tādātmya with its six characteristics: unreciprocality, dependence, non-separateness, non-otherness, distinction, and manifestative extrinsic denomination.

7) *sat* and *asat* are, therefore, not reciprocally identical with *Sat*; hence, they are *a-Sat*.
8) *sat* and *asat* are opposed contradictorily to *Asat* as particular positives over against the altogether negative. That is to say, they are non-*Asat*.
9) Hence, they are *Sad-Asad-vilakṣaṇa*, i.e., not characterizable by either of the superlatives *Sat* and *Asat*.

Similar semiotic squares may be drawn up around such terms as *Ātman*, *Vidyā*, etc.

Notes

[1] [First published in *Indian Philosophical Annual* **18** (1985-86) 1-15, and reprinted here with kind permission.]

[2] Jean Herbert, "Védantisme et vie pratique," *Mélanges sur l'Inde* (Paris: Cahiers du Sud, 1941) 150-184, at 151.

[3] [The text reads 'inalienation'.]

[4] St Augustine, *Confessions* 3, 6, 11.

[5] He also calls it 'vapor' (*The City of God* 7), 'smoke' and 'wind' (*Commentary on the Gospel according to John* 10.2). These comparisons must be understood in the light of his *Discourse on Psalm 134, 4*: "God is Being to such a degree that in comparison with him those things which have been made are not. If we do not make that comparison, we say that they are, because they are from Him; but compared to Him, they are not, because true Being is immutable Being—which he alone is."

[6] *Kaṭha Up. Bh.* 1, 3, 10-11.

11

FORWARD STEPS IN ŚAṄKARA RESEARCH[1]

Fifty-five years ago, when I was a 16 year-old school boy in Belgium, I happened on a French article on Advaita. There was much question in it of *Brahman* and *Ātman* but I could find no clear explanation of these terms. For months I puzzled over them until light came from the titular of our terminal class of humanities, Fr René Debauche. Such was my first introduction to Śāṅkara Vedānta. I pursued on my own the exploration of the various types of Vedānta until I came to India in 1946. The interpretations of Śaṅkara by S. Radhakrishnan and others, which had appeared since around 1920, did not seem to represent correctly the *Ācārya's* thought. I would have to study Sanskrit and ponder the very text of his authentic works. This I was doing in Calcutta when in 1950 I attended for the first time a session of the All-India Philosophical Congress, its Silver Jubilee session presided by its chief founder, the prestigious Professor Dr Sarvepalli Radhakrishnan. After then graduating with a doctoral dissertation entitled 'The Theological Method of Śaṃkara,'[2] I began in 1954 my regular teaching in Poona. In that same year, I attended the Kandy session of our IPC of which soon afterwards I became a life-member. As such I have presented many a paper treating of some aspect of the doctrine of Śaṅkara.

Now you have asked me to deliver in this session the Pratāp Seṭh Vedānta lecture. It is an honour for which I am deeply grateful. It is also a task which I undertake with joy despite my declining memory and weakened sight but with a consciousness of being little worthy of it.

Indeed, such a lecture ought to advance scholarship in the field of Vedānta whereas I can only present to your critical hearing the chief steps forward which I made in my unrelenting study of Śaṅkara and which I perhaps wrongly consider to be true advances.

1. Śaṅkara: Strictly an Interpreter of the *Jñāna-kāṇḍa* of the *Śruti*

I first considered it important to ascertain the intention of Śaṅkara and the specific nature of his teaching, i.e., the *pramāṇa* in the authority of which he had made his doctrinal assertions. Was he a *śrutivādin*, according to the long-favoured opinion, or was he a rational philosopher in the manner of most of the modern philosophers of the West, as asserted persuasively by Radhakrishnan and many who sided with him? There was no doubt that Śaṅkara was a master of reasoning but was he relying on independent reasoning or on reason aided by testimony?

Soon the evidence from his own writings concerning his purpose, his *pramāṇa* of reliance, and the nature of his method became forceful:

> We begin the study of the Vedānta-texts in order to get free from the wrong notion which is the cause of all evil and to attain thereby the knowledge of the absolute unity of the [supreme] Self. (*B.S.Bh.* Introd.)

> The import of the *Śruti* is the demonstration that the *Ātman* is the supreme *Brahman*: in this only the aim of all the Upaniṣads is exhausted. (*Bṛh. Up. Bh.* 2, 3, 6)

> It is only with the help of the *Śruti* that this exceedingly deep *Brahman* can be fathomed, not of reasoning. (*B.S.Bh.* 2, 1, 31)

So much for his purpose and his reliance on the *Śruti*. He further explains the latter (1) with regard to *Ātman*, (2) with regard to *Brahman*:

(1) As to the *Ātman*, "is it not the object of perception? No, because we observe an actual conflict of opinions regarding the very existence of any *Ātman* connecting the body of this birth and the body of another birth, since this is denied by the Lokāyatikas and the Buddhists. In spite of the idea of 'I,' the Vaināśika [Buddhists] really profess the inexistence of any *Ātman* different from the body.

"Neither is the existence of an *Ātman* provable by inference, because no relation to another birth is perceived. We do not deny that the Mīmāṃsakas [e.g. Śabara in *M.S.Bh.* 1, 1, 5[3]] and the Vaiśeṣika-Naiyāyikas [e.g. *V.S.* 3, 2, 4-21[4]] have proposed such inferences. But it was while actually following in the footsteps of the *Śruti* and finding there the empirical grounds of their inferences. They fancy that the idea of 'I' and the other grounds of inference, which are Vedic only, do originate from their own thought, and so they declare that the *Ātman* is knowable through perception and inference whereas in fact it is only so through the Vedic word." (*Bṛh. Up. Bh.* Introd.)

(2) As to the *Brahman*, it is clear from the Upaniṣads that it transcends the whole empirical realm and has no ontological relation to its own effects. Hence, it cannot be grasped by perception or established by inference (since *anumāna* depends on *pratyakṣa*) and is not even expressible by words (since words primarily refer to substances which belong to a *jāti* and to their actions, qualities and relations while the *Brahman* stands beyond all categories; cf. *Bh. Gītā Bh.* 13, 13).

In modern times we often seek in Śaṅkara for an unlimited philosophy complete with ontology, cosmology, epistemology, psychology, ethics but Śaṅkara's teaching is limited to the transcendent Reality and the transcendental relations to it of the universe of things and selves.

"The *Śruti* is an authority in transcendental matters, in matters lying beyond the bonds of human knowledge, i.e., beyond perception and reasoning, but not in matters lying within the range of perception, etc.

"A hundred *śrutis* may declare that fire is cold or dark; still, they possess no authority in the matter. Thus we should in no way attach to *Śruti* a meaning which is opposed to other *pramāṇas* or to its own declarations." (*Bh. Gītā Bh.* 18, 66).

In particular, "it is not in *Śruti* that we should seek for the means of attaining the desirable and avoiding the undesirable in matters coming within the range of experience and ascertainable through perception and inference." (*Bṛh. Up. Bh.* Introd.)

And "it is nowhere the purpose of *Śruti* to make statements regarding the *jīvātman*, since from ordinary experience the latter is known to everyone as the agent and experiencer.

"But the Lord, about whom ordinary experience tells us nothing, is to be considered as the special topic of all *Śrutis.*" (*B.S.Bh.* 1, 3, 7)

Neither is it the function of the *Śruti* to inform us about the manifestation [of the world], its formation and similar topics upon which the welfare of man depends in no way. The *Śruti* itself declares that passages setting them forth are but subservient to the purpose of teaching *Brahman.*" (*B.S.Bh.* 1, 4, 14)

Thus Śāṅkara Vedānta is a transcendental doctrine grounded strictly in the *Śruti*. It exists side by side but without compromise with the non-transcendental sciences. It asserts their limited validity. It completes them by the addition of its own dimension and perspective without substituting for them.

However, it corrects them eventually by opposing their pretended metaphysics and substituting for it its own *Śruti*-founded metaphysics. For instance, Nyāya-Vaiśeṣika operates within its proper bounds of perception and inference when it develops an analysis of the world of effects in terms of its categories (*padārtha*) but, due to the insufficiency of its acceptance and grasp of the *Śruti pramāṇa*, it has added to that an *Īśvaravāda* or theology which posits God as a mere correlative of his effects. Indeed, he is not subsistent Fullness but a *viśeṣa ātman*, a special *ātman* characterized by omniscience and freedom and the *partial* omnipotence of combining the eternal substances and other *padārthas* into an organized universe. Such a God pales when compared to the transcendent Existent (*Sat*) which is the cause not only of the structure but of the very reality of its effects.

As to the *method* of Śaṅkara's metaphysics, it is directly derived from Yājñavalkya's statement: "Verily, O Maitreyī, it is the *Ātman* that should be seen, heard about, reflected on and meditated upon." (*Bṛh. Up.* 2, 4, 5) Of the three steps here clearly demarcated: hearing, reflecting and meditating (*śravaṇa, manana, nididhyāsana*), the second one should retain our attention.

Manana signifies the whole endeavour of reason to penetrate the import of the *Śruti*. To borrow a phrase from St Anselm, it is 'faith seeking understanding.' Its overall principle is harmony (*samanvaya*), the conviction held in faith by all Vedāntins that the meaning of the *Śruti* is homogeneous and excludes contradiction between any of its statements. The first task of the teacher is to study and eventually to correct the traditional analysis of the *Śruti* into meaning-units centred on a great saying (*mahāvākya*) which itself is subserved by ancillary sayings (*arthavāda*). Understanding each *mahāvākya* is properly the scriptural rational task. One or more *prima facie* interpretations are brought forth, then the teacher ascertains the correct interpretation and establishes it into a firm conclusion (*siddhānta*). He does this through *samanvaya Śruti* passages, support from *Smṛti* passages, and extensive rational discussion. Ideally, *manana* should be continued as long as doubts remain and all other plausible opinions have not been debarred.

This critical enquiry constitutes the prior ascertaining (*pravṛtti*) which Śaṅkara requires before the third step be undertaken (*US* 18, 125 and 126). It is the ascertaining of a positive content, namely the existence and nature of the Witness (*Sākṣin*), by *manana* on the great saying "That thou art." Without it, *nididhyāsana* would result in mere void (*śūnya*):

> If you say, 'what is prescribed here by the authority of the scriptural word ['*neti neti*'] is negative meditation (*nivṛtti*),' [the answer is,] 'the Witness not having been positively established (*aprasiddhatvāt*), a mere void (*śūnya*) would result'. (*US* 18, 125).

Śaṅkara is here countering Maṇḍana Miśra (*Brahma Siddhi* p. 157: "What then is taught by *Śruti*? [Only] the non-existence of the universe") who was driven to attribute final authority solely to the *mahāvākya* "It is not so" and other negative *Śrutis* because he did not believe that positive speech, being dualistic, could express the non-dual Absolute. For Śaṅkara, speech could be indicative (*lakṣ–*) where it could no longer be expressive (*vac–*) and, therefore, he could hold that "That thou art" and other positive *mahāvākyas* did provide the positive ascertaining which, he thought, must precede and give substance to *nididhyāsana*.

This is confirmed by his definition of the state of enlightened faith (*śraddhā*) which the aspirant must have reached at the end of *manana*. Faith, he says, is "the awareness of positive existence held in the pacified mind" (*citta prasāde āstikya buddhi*) (*Māṇḍ. Up. Bh.* 2, 1, 7). The mind is now at peace, having cleared off all doubts, but it is focused upon the non-dual Existent.

This focusing is *nididhyāsana*: it consists in grasping the Knowledge which has been heard (*vidyā-śravaṇa grahaṇa*), holding it (*dhāraṇa*) and repeating it mentally (*abhyāsa*)" (*Taitt. Up. Bh.* 2, 1). With its culmination, *samādhi*, it constitutes *dhyāna yoga* "which is the most immediate means to *Vidyā*" (*Bh. Gītā Bh.* 5, 27), "the highest form of *yoga*; it consists in abiding constantly in the *Ātman*, bearing in mind that the *Ātman* is All and nothing else is Existent" (ibid. 6, 25). In this work at least, he defines it as *vijñāna* contrasted with *jñāna*: "*jñāna* means the enlightenment (*avabodha*) regarding *Ātman*, etc. as obtained from the *śāstras* and the *ācāryas* [thus this fruit of *manana* is still abstract and general]; *vijñāna* is the experiencing of that (*tad-anubhava*) in its specificity (*viśeṣataḥ*)" (ibid. 3, 41). It means "turning into personal experience (*sv'ānubhava karaṇa*) the knowledge obtained from the science" (ibid. 6, 8; 7, 2; 9, 1). Let us notice that, contrary to some modern presentations, Śaṅkara's teaching does not start from experience; he starts from the *Śruti*, which he thinks is authorless (*apauruṣeya*), and terminates hopefully into experience.

Hopefully, I say, because achievement here does not mean the automatic conclusion of a dialectical process. There hovers over it an uncertainty which situates the role of divine grace. In Śaṅkara's most authoritative work, he says: we must "assume that liberation is effected by a discerning (*vijñānena*) caused by His grace (*tad-anugraha-hetukena*) because Scripture teaches it" (*B.S.Bh.* 2, 3, 41), i.e., "by the attainment of knowledge caused by the grace of the Lord" (*Īśvara-prasāda-nimitta-jñāna prāptyā eva*) (*Bh. Gītā Bh.* 2, 39).

2. A Quest for Supreme Values

Phenomenologically, the teaching of the *Ācārya* appears as a quest for supreme values rather than a systematic work of rational speculation. His very first requirement for the aspirant is "the capacity to discriminate between eternal and transient realities." (*B.S.Bh.* Introd.) And his very language is a language of discernment and evaluation. His aim, however, is not to establish a hierarchy of all possible values but in every mixture to discern the most excellent and to set aside all the rest whatever be its relative value. He formulates this *key-distinction* as follows:

"As the wild goose [according to Indian folklore] sifts milk from water, so the wise man sifts the excellent from the mere pleasant, going mentally all around these two objects, examining them closely, weighing their respective importance or futility; and having distinguished them, he chooses the excellent alone on account of its superiority." (*Kaṭha Up. Bh.* 2, 2)

It is possible to expose the whole teaching as a Value seeking spiral of successive siftings and choices. It would start naturally with a selection of the supreme end of man.

1. Of the four ends of man, liberation alone is to be selected.

2. Of the two ways, ritual action and knowledge, knowledge alone is to be chosen.

3. Of the six sources of knowledge, *śabda* (word) is primary.

4. Among all words, only the authorless word of *Śruti*.

5. And in *Śruti* the knowledge section alone must be our reliance.

6. Out of the manifold of these texts, we must pick up the sentences which convey knowledge, namely, the indicative assertions.

7. And from the sequences of assertions choose those which appear to be 'great sayings' around which ancillary sentences are organized.

8. Those 'great sayings' refer in various ways to the *Brahman-Ātman*. Out of all objects, be interested in this *Brahman* alone. It is conveyed by them as by diverse definitions (*lakṣaṇa*). We must take them all in combination because they complete one another by correcting in turn some aspect or trend of our innate ignorance.

9. The negative definitions of the *neti neti* type posit the *Brahman* as exempt of all finitude and exceeding the primary scope of all words and concepts. Thus they assert its absolute transcendence and exorcise our mind from all temptation of pantheism. They root us in apophatism by excluding the *Brahman* from the *expressive* power of mind and speech. They are fundamentally normative and must remain subjacent to our correct understanding of the affirmative definitions.

10. The superlative definitions posit the *Brahman* not as a relative maximum (such as the *Īśvara* of Nyāya) but as the absolute Maximum beyond any commensuration with mundane entities. It is *Pūrṇa*, the Fullness of all illimitable perfections, and thus the most desirable, the supreme Value. This definition must be grasped in coordination with the *neti lakṣaṇa*. Thus the *Brahman* is simple (*akhaṇḍa*) in its very *pūrṇatā*. It is intensive Fullness (not fullness by conglomeration). Hence, it is *nirguṇa*, qualityless, not by deprivation but by superessentiality. Neither the *Sāṁkhya* conception of *guṇas* as three internal tensors of *Prakṛti* nor the Nyāya distinction between substance and accidents finds any application in it. It is homogeneous (*ekarasa*) Goodness. The superlative mode of speech does not express this maximality (for there is no mundane instance of it) but it can *point* it out with vigour and precision.

11. The causal and other relational definitions (*upalakṣaṇa* or *taṭastha-lakṣaṇa*) posit the *Brahman* as the Root (*mūla*) of the universe and all its entities, the total Cause of their being and moving. The risk of misinterpretation here is anthropomorphism. Indeed, causality is a feature of our world which we constantly experience. We risk therefore superimposing upon divine causality the modalities of the causal activity of nature and man. This is why we must approach these definitions with a mind imbued with the previous teaching of negativity and maximality. *Brahman*'s causality is total. As the master-cause, *Brahman* produces out of nothing but its Fullness the whole reality as well as the structure and the dynamic development of the universe. It is its *upādāna*, i.e., its substantive or reality-giving cause, without being subject to such mutability (*pariṇāma*) as characterizes the *upādāna-kāraṇas* of our mundane experience. It is also the *nimitta-kāraṇa* or ordaining cause without having any need of pre-existing materials, calculation, tools or wants to fulfil. In its universal causality, the *Brahman* is absolutely free and immutable.

Its causality is so pervasive and ontologically total that it is the innermost *Ātman* of every single entity. This is not any of the lower *Ātmans* or *puruṣas* which the Upaniṣads enumerate but the *Paramātman* which presides causally over, and, for instance, illuminates every sentient being.

As relations from *Brahman* to the world, causality, immanence, ātmahood and the associated fact of being the Lord, the Illuminer, the Witness, the Goal, etc. appear to add something extrinsic to the absolute Essence. But we know that the *Brahman* is transcendent and unchangeable Fullness. Hence, these relations cannot be ontological but logical only. They are not intrinsic attributes (*viśeṣaṇa*) but extrinsic denominators (*upādhi*). Similarly, in regard to *Brahman*, all its effects are *upādhis*. The relational *lakṣaṇas* are true in what they affirm, not in the manner of affirming it. What they affirm is the communicativity of the changeless Absolute but they affirm it in terms of our experience of ontological relations. A mind steeped in the teaching of *neti neti* and *pūrṇa* can receive their message without being misled by its modality.

But if one fails to correct his first grasp of them, he is led to believe in the qualified *Brahman* (*saguṇa*). This notion points to the *Brahman* but inadequately and incorrectly still. It is propaedeutic and thus useful on the way, especially for meditations of what the Upaniṣads call the *vidyā* type, but finally we must reach beyond them. Just as we must reach beyond the three sovereign forms of Brahmā, Viṣṇu, Śiva and beyond *a*, *u*, *m*, to the *turīya* solely intended by the syllable *auṁ*.

12. "That thou art" (*Tattvamasi*) and its equivalent "I am *Brahman*" (*aham Brahm'āsmi*) are cardinal 'great sayings' expressing the *tādātmya* relation between the knower/agent and *Brahman*. In this case, *tādātmya* is not reciprocal identity, as in "I am my parents' first son," but the unreciprocal relation of "having *Tat* as one's *Paramātman*." In *Upadeṣasāhasrī* 18, Śaṅkara explains particularly well what is this 'I' which is the subject of that relation:

> The appropriator (*abhimāna kṛt*, that says 'I' and 'mine') is the ego sense (*aham kartṛ*) which always stands in proximity to this [*Ātman* which is pure Awareness, *upalabdhi*] and acquires a reflection of It (*tad ābha*). Hence, there arises the [undiscriminated] complex of the *Ātman* and what relates to It (*ātmīya*) which is the sphere of 'I' and 'mine.' (*US* 18, 27)
>
> Only when there is a reflection (*ābhāsa*) can words [such as *aham*, *tvam*], referring to the internal Vision indicate (*lakṣayeyuḥ*) [the *Ātman* Witness] but in no way designate Him directly. (*US* 18, 29)
>
> It is because the ego sense bears a reflection of the *Ātman* that it is designated by words pertaining to the *Ātman*; just as words pertaining to

> fire are applied to torches, etc. but not directly (*na añjasā*) since their direct referent [fire] is other.
>
> The reflection (*ābhāsa*) of a face is different from the face since it conforms to the mirror; and in turn the face is different from its reflection since it does not conform to the mirror.
>
> The reflection of the *Ātman* in the ego-sense is comparable to the reflection of the face. As in the case of the face the *Ātman* is other (*anya*), says the tradition, and the two [*Ātman* and *ābhāsa*] are indeed likewise undiscriminated [by the ignorant]. (*US* 18, 31, 33)

Why this lack of discrimination? Because of the similarity, closeness and intimate dependence of the reflection-ego upon its Prototype. But it is also on account of this proximity of the *jīvātman* to the *Paramātman* that *Tattvamasi* can be effective, the *ābhāsa* serving as the door (*dvāra*: *US* 18, 110) across which the mind can reach to the supreme *Tat*. This is why Śaṅkara can use the method of *anvaya vyatireka* (agreement and difference) to explain that sentence. If we wish to understand him we must remember the rule of Diṅnāga that words placed 'in apposition'[5] restrict one another's meaning (e.g., in 'black horses,' 'black' excludes all non-blacks including non-black horses, and 'horses' exclude all non-horses even if they are black).

> Because the words '*tvam*' and '*Sat*' (for '*Tat*') refer to one and the same entity, they function like the words 'black' and 'horses.' Through being brought into apposition with the word '*Sat*' which expresses absence of pain, the word '*tvam*' [loses its reference to anything connected with pain and] is left with the meaning '*Sat*.' And similarly through being set in apposition with a word signifying 'inmost self' (*pratyag-ātman*), the word '*Sat*' [is left with the meaning 'inmost Self']. (*US* 18, 170-171)

> Without giving up their own meaning (*svārtha*) the words *tvam* and *Tat*/*Sat* convey a specific (*viśiṣṭa*) meaning. And they lead to immediate awareness (*avagati*) of the inmost *Ātman*. Apart from this meaning, there can be no other one which would not result in a contradiction. (*US* 18, 173)

Let us notice Śaṅkara's innovative application of the *anvaya-vyatireki* method. It is equivalent to the *jahad-ajahal-lakṣaṇā* method employed explicitly by one of his direct disciples, Sureśvara. It is used to understand a 'great saying' which is true (since *Śruti* is infallible) and yet cannot be true according to the primary meaning (*mukhyārtha*) of its terms. One must then seek for their secondary meaning as suggested by the context (*lakṣyārtha*) which, in this case, can only be their supreme meaning (*paramārtha*). This seeking progresses through *apavāda* or *vyatireka* which, in the light of *neti neti*, excludes all the finite objects denoted by the *mukhyārtha*: to that extent the *lakṣaṇā* is *jahat*, exclusive. But it preserves the proper notion (*svārtha*) of the terms: hence, it is *ajahat*, inclusive. It is then possible, in a final step, to elevate the two *svārthas* to their highest possible value and thus accede to their common *paramārtha* (*anvaya* in the light of *Pūrṇa*). The logical link between primary and supreme meaning is the *svārtha* but dynamically what sets the process into motion is the suggestion that *jīvātman* is a reflection of the supreme *Ātman* and thus in *tādātmya* relation with it.

Tādātmya is not peculiar to the *jīvātman* but is the founding relation which imbues all effects of *Brahman*. It has the following characteristics.

(a) *unreciprocality*: "Names and forms in all their states have their *Ātman* in *Brahman* alone, but *Brahman* has not its *Ātman* in them." (*Taitt. Up. Bh.* 2, 6, 1)

(b) *dependence*: "It is an accepted principle even in the world that an effect is intimately dependent (*anuvidhāyin*) on its cause." (*Bṛh. Up. Bh.* 1, 5, 14)

(c) *indwelling*: "All the created beings abide within the *Puruṣa* ; for every effect rests within its cause." (*Bh. Gītā Bh.* 8, 22)

It is also called *non-separation, non-division*: "An effect is non-separate (*avyatirikta*) from its cause." (*Bṛh. Up. Bh.* 1, 6, 1) "The non-separation of the two is possible only if the whole aggregate of things originates from the one *Brahman*. And we understand from the Veda that this affirmation can be established only on the principle that between the substantive cause and its effect there is non-separation, ... non-division (*abheda*)." (*B.S.Bh.* 2, 3, 6)

(d) *non-otherness*: To be 'other' the effect would have to be utterly foreign, heterogeneous and ontologically independent from its cause. But "there exists in the past, present or future not one thing simply other than the *Ātman*, simply non *Ātman* separated by space or time, utterly subtle, disconnected and remote." (*Taitt. Up. Bh.* 2, 6, 1) "The effect is non-other than the

Cause, i.e., it has no existence / essence apart from the Cause (*vyatirekenā 'bhāvaḥ*)" (*B.S.Bh.* 2, 1, 14)

Vice versa, "the *Brahman* is not other in such a fashion [namely, as circumscribed by delimitators, as 'cowness' is delimited by 'horseness,' etc.], since it is not subject to limitation by exclusion on the part of other substances." (*Taitt. Up. Bh.* 2, 1) *Brahman* is described through *neti neti* "by means of the elimination of any difference due to limiting adjuncts (*sarvopādhi-viśeṣā-'pohena*); the two words [*neti neti*] refer to a quid devoid of any such distinctive characteristics as name, form, action, alterity, species or quality." (*Bṛh. Up. Bh.* 2, 3, 6)

(e) *distinction*: "If absolute equality were insisted on, the relation of cause and effect would be annihilated.... This relation is based on the fact that there is present in the cause an excellence [which the effect is lacking. On the other hand, they are similar, since] one characteristic feature, namely existence (*sattā*) is found in ether, etc. as well as in *Brahman*" (*B.S.Bh.* 2, 1, 6)

(f) *extrinsic denominativity*: how the effects are not ontological adjuncts but *upādhis* of *Brahman* has been explained above. It does not mean that they are illusions for they have *sattā*.

But how can this assertion of the ontological reality of the effects be reconciled with the fact that his doctrine is said to be a form of *māyāvāda*?

I cannot take up here the whole question of *māyā* in Śaṅkara. I have done it elsewhere.[6] Suffice it to say that in the largest number of instances Śaṅkara uses *māyā* in the traditional sense of 'extraordinary power' and uses it in the sense of 'magic' or 'product of magic' in a quite limited number of cases only. These cases are to be understood in reference to his theory of *avidyā* (nescience), a term ubiquitous in his writings. *Avidyā* is superimposition (*adhyāsa*) either of the properties of the Absolute on the relative beings or vice versa. In *avidyā*, we misapprehend things and persons as independent subsistents and the *Brahman* as changing and appearing in manifold forms. Now the aim [of the *Śārīrakaśāstra*] is to show that the only one highest Lord, ever unchanging, whose essence is knowledge, appears as manifold due to nescience (*avidyayā*), just as the magician due to magic (*māyayā*)." (*B.S.Bh.* 1, 3, 19) As usual, magic is brought in only as a point of comparison. It makes us understand both the source of illusion (our ignorance) and the magician's free mastery and unchangingness. Historically, the mutation of Śaṅkarism into *māyāvāda* took place only with Vimuktātman.

The relational definitions have by now been sufficiently explained. It is time to pass on to the best, the essential definitions.

13.[7] The essential definitions (*svarūpa-lakṣaṇa*) are of the type: "the *Brahman* is Reality, Knowledge, infinite" (*satyam jñānam anantam Brahm'eti*). (*Taitt. Up*. 2, 1, 1) Śaṅkara treats it according to the method we have already seen at work:

(a) The defining terms stand in coordination, not in subordination since *Brahman* is exempt from genus and difference; hence, "each term is independently connected with the term *Brahman*." But "by virtue of their mutual contiguity they are controlled by, and controlling, one another, and thus they exclude (*nivartaka*) from that [*Brahman*] the express meaning (*vācyārtha*) of *satyam*, etc. and become the indicatives (*lakṣaṇārtha*) of *Brahman*." However, they "certainly do not lose their proper meaning (*svārtha*)." Thus the process of interpretation is *jahad-ajahal-lakṣaṇā*.

(b) The *svārtha* of SATYAM is being, ontological truth, stable reality. "Its primary denotation (*mukhyārtha*) is existence as common to all external things." But its connection with JÑĀNAM excludes materiality, and its connection with ANANTAM excludes all finitude.

(c) The *svārtha* of "JÑĀNAM is knowing (*jñāpti*) awareness (*avabodha*) .... Its primary denotation consists of whatever is appropriated by the *buddhi* (organ of intellection) and expresses (*vācaka*) the reflection (*ābhāsa*) of that [*Brahman*]." But here, "because it determines *Brahman* along with SATYAM and ANANTAM," it must be understood in its supreme sense as unrestricted actuality of its root *jña*–; for "it is *bhāva sādhana* [a Pāṇinean expression meaning the sole root without declensional endings such as nominative, etc.]." Any such ending would introduce the distinction of knower, knowing, knowable whereas "that which is ANANTAM is not divided from anything." Indeed, *Bṛh. Up*. 4, 3, 30 says: "There is no discontinuity (*viparilopa*) between the Knower and his Knowledge on account of his indestructibility."

(d) Thus, by the *paramārtha* of SATYAM and JÑĀNAM, "the *Brahman* is indicated but not expressed (*tal-lakṣyate na tū 'cyate*)."

"So, in agreement with... *Taitt. Up.* 2, 7 ["It is unexpressed (*anirukta*)], it is established that *Brahman* is inexpressible (*avācya*) and that, unlike the blue lotus [defined through *jāti* and *viśeṣa*], it is not the object of any expressive sentence." (All quotations from *Taitt. Up. Bh.* 2, 1, 1)

This is the way along which Śaṅkara led his pupil to the supreme Value, "the Goal of him who stands knowing It" (*Bṛh. Up.* 3, 9, 28). Through the negative definitions he has raised his mind above all the empirical, through the superlative focused him on the transempirical Absolute Fullness, through the relative, especially *Tattvamasi*, and the essential definitions he has established within him the positive contents without whose ascertaining (*prasiddhi*) the pupil would have nothing to appropriate and experience in *nididhyāsana*.

3. An Intercrossing of Three Levels of Language

The previous section has shown that we must distinguish in Śaṅkara's writings three levels of language rather than three degrees of reality, for their distinction depends on man's approach to reality through the *pramāṇas* rather than on reality itself (*vastu*).

1. Ordinary (*vyavahāra*) language. It is circumscribed by the first two *pramāṇas*, sense-perception and inference. It embraces the *mukhyārthas* (primary meanings) of all terms and their classification and definitions. It provides the basis starting from which the other two levels of language are elaborated, chiefly by absolutization, revision and negation.

2. Upaniṣadic language. It is circumscribed in the *jñāna kāṇḍa* of the *Śruti*. It is focused on the metempirical and metaphysical. It absolutizes words whose denotation is such that they can be unlimited: words such as *sat*, *jñāna*, *ātman*, *Brahman*, *satya*, *vidyā*, *asti*, etc. As absolutized, such terms are often, by convention, written with an initial capital: *Sat*, *Jñāna*,

Ātman, etc. They are thus maximalized, which is also done by using them in the superlative mode.

As maximalized, they lend themselves to a simple dialectic of Yes/No opposition in the form of *Sat / a-Sat*, *Asti / Nāsti*, *Vidyā / a-Vidyā*, etc. This gives rise to the paradoxes of the Upaniṣads. They arise from the ambivalence of the negation of a term which can result either in its contrary (*Sat / Asat*) or in its simple contradictory (*Sat / a-Sat*) and the two are not phonetically distinguished. Now, compared to *Sat*, any *sat* is *a-Sat*, but it is not *Asat* (like 'the son of a barren woman'); yet, it sounds as if it was.

This manner of speech is not exclusive to the Upaniṣads. Jesus, for instance, employs it in the following episode: A young man ran to him and asked, 'Good master, what must I do to have eternal life?' Jesus replied, 'Why do you call me good? One alone is Good: God.'

It will help to present this matter in the form of a diagram:

<table>
<tr><td>Positive
ABSOLUTE</td><td colspan="2">Negative
OPPOSITES</td></tr>
<tr><td rowspan="2">Sat</td><td>Contradictories
→</td><td>Contrary</td></tr>
<tr><td>a-Sat</td><td>Asat</td></tr>
</table>

3. Śaṅkara's commentatorial language. It is the three-step ladder by which he makes us ascend from ordinary to upaniṣadic language: the three steps are (a) *adhyāsa* (superimposition), at which it is seen that so long as the terms of a 'great saying' are taken in their primary sense, it is stultified; (b) *apavāda* (negation) by which all the finite connotations or modalities of those terms are eliminated; (c) *paramārtha-lakṣaṇā* (indication by the supreme sense) by which the *svārtha* of each term is elevated to infinity and thus becomes a proper indicative of the maximal Value and Being, the *Brahman-Ātman*.

Once we realize that the threefold distinction is not ontological but linguistic (and conceptual), we become free from the difficulties which have plagued the interpretation of Śaṅkara in late-medieval and modern times.

4. The Intellectual Dynamism of Srī Śaṅkarācārya

Let me finally draw your attention to one feature in Śaṅkara's profile by which he stands out among Indian thinkers. It is his presupposition that human intelligence is dynamic and interpretative rather than static and mirror-like. It is interpretative because "the intellect has the power of considering as a whole" (*samasta-pratyavamarśinī buddhi*: *B.S.Bh.* 1, 3, 28)[8] the successive data of the senses which it synthesizes and judges. It is dynamic because it is driven by a constitutive desire to know (*jijñāsā*) which is not limited to finite realities but reaches beyond them to the supreme Reality.

The *Śruti* makes this desire explicit and directs it clearly to *Brahmajijñāsā*, the "quest to know *Brahman*," so as to reach the supreme goal of man (*parama puruṣā'rtha*).

Jaimini had defined *puruṣārtha* as "that object to which human desire is inherently attached because it cannot be disconnected from it." (*M.S.* 4, 1, 2[9]) As inherent, it need not (though it may) be enjoined. (*M.S.* 4, 1, 3) The desire for "the perfect good" (*niḥśreya*) is radically the desire for immortality (*amṛtatvam icchan*: *Kaṭha Up. Bh.* 4, 1), for final release (*mumukṣutva*: *B.S.Bh.* 1, 1, 1), whose precise "object is the inmost *Ātman*" (*pratyagātmā-viṣayā jijñāsā*: *Kena Up. Bh.* 1, 1). This paramount desire of the intellect tends to know the supreme Reality in the best manner possible:

> The direct object of the said desire is a knowledge culminating in an intuitive penetration (*avagati paryantam jñānam*), desires having reference to fruits. Knowledge, indeed, constitutes the means (*pramāṇa*) by which *Brahman* is desired to be intuitively comprehended (*avagatum iṣṭam*). For this direct comprehension of *Brahman* is the end of man (*Brahmā-'vagati hi puruṣārtha*) since it extirpates completely that which is bad, namely, Nescience, etc., the seed of the entire *saṃsāra*. (*B.S.Bh.* 1, 1, 1)

> The knowledge which discerns *Brahman* and discards Nescience terminates in experience (*anubhavā-'vasānam*). (*B.S.Bh.* 2, 1, 4)

It is because intelligence is tensed by its inner dynamism upon the highest Object that it can pursue it along the *lakṣaṇā* indications of the 'great sayings' beyond any expressed meaning of words. Its intentionality breaks through the limits of effability to rush into the domain of the ineffable. It frees it from the dual structure of sentences to ascend through *lakṣaṇā* to the *Paramārtha*. Thus freed, it is full with faith (*śraddhā*) as *āstikya-buddhir-bhakti-sahitā*: "an assurance of its existence which devotion accompanies." (*Bṛh. Up. Bh.* 3, 9, 21)

What is the relation of other human longings to this uppermost desire? On the one hand, they are subsumed by it since "it is for the love of the *Ātman* that husband, wife, sons, etc. are dearly loved." (*Bṛh. Up. Bh.* 2, 4) On the other hand, no one is qualified for *Brahmajijñāsā* unless "he renounces all desire to enjoy objects whether here or hereafter." (*B.S.Bh.* 1, 1, 1) Hence, negation (*apavāda*) is not only a step in the dialectic but affects, as *nivṛtti* or *saṅnyāsa* (renunciation), the whole quest of man for immortality.

Yet, here also, just as the *svārtha* was preserved, what is positively valuable in each desire is preserved to be exalted in the obtention of the uppermost Fruit:

> The knower of *Brahman* enjoys all desires, all delights procured by desirable objects, without exceptions. Does he enjoy sons, heavens, etc. alternately as we do? No, he enjoys all delectable things simultaneously, as amassed together in a single moment, through a single perception, which is eternal like the light of the sun, which is non-different from the essence of *Brahman*, and which we have described as Reality-Knowledge-infinite.... He enjoys all things by that *Brahman* whose nature is omniscience. (*Taitt. Up. Bh.* 2, 1, 1)

Notes

[1] [Pratap Seth Endowment Lecture on Śaṅkara Vedānta, delivered at the 62nd Session of the Indian Philosophical Congress, University of Kashmir, Srinagar, 6-9 June 1987. First published in *Darshana International* (Moradabad, India) **26**/3 (1987) 33-46. Reprinted here with permission of De Nobili College, Pune, having had no reply from *Darshana International* despite several reminders.]

[2] ['The Theological Method of Śaṃkara' (Rome: Pontifical Gregorian University, 1953). See also "Introduction," note 3 above.]

[3] [Śabara, *Mīmāṃsā-Sūtra-Bhāṣya.*]
[4] [Kaṇāda, *Vaiśeṣika-Sūtra.*]
[5] [Correcting 'in opposition.']
[6] R. De Smet, "*Māyā* or *Ajñāna*," *Indian Philosophical Annual* (Madras) **2** (1966) 220-225 [= ch. 6 above].
[7] [Corrected from '12.']
[8] [Corrected from *Taitt. Up. Bh.* 2, 3.]
[9] [Jaimini, *Mīmāṃsā-Sūtra.*]

12

THE BUDDHA, MEISTER ECKHART AND ŚAṄKARĀCĀRYA ON 'NOTHING'[1]

This essay has three parts, as indicated in its title. The three doctrines it inquires into are Buddhism, especially early Buddhism, Eckhart's mysticism, and Śaṅkara's non-dualism. I hope to show that the negativism which is one of their marks is not only linguistic but also perspectivistic and experiential.

1. The Negativism of Siddhārtha Gautama Śākya (*muni*), the *Buddha*

Prince Siddhārtha left his family and renounced his princely status and functions at the age of 29 (probably in BC 537 according to Lamotte) after discovering the sorrowful nature of life. Determined to find the remedy against this existential sorrow (*duḥkha*) he first practised *yoga* but the passing trances induced by *yoga* failed to satisfy him. Then, for six years, he subjected himself to extreme forms of austerity (*tapas*) but all in vain. Finally, renouncing all conventional practices, he took his station at Bodh-gayā under a banyan-tree and determined to puzzle out the mystery of existence simply by persevering meditation. On a memorable night, he attained the perfect illumination (*bodhi* or *sambodhi*) which made him truly enlightened (*buddha*). He was 35 years old and would preach his doctrine through the whole region of the middle-Ganga for 45 years.

1.1 A possible reconstruction of the sambodhi

The Buddha never narrated directly the details of the event of his enlightenment. And scholars have been chary of crossing beyond the limits of his indirect indications. But a process of intuitiveness grounded in the Buddhist texts may perhaps, daringly but hopefully lead us to a plausible reconstruction of that central event. It appears to have developed in several steps.

1.1.1 Ascertaining the nature of duḥkha: *Duḥkha*, the contrary of *Sukha*, happiness, is frustration and its consequent unhappiness, sorrow, suffering; it is disease in the etymological sense of disease. Common experience is enough to see that it imbues every surge of the dynamism of life, as the Buddha was to point out in his first sermon (cf. *Samyutta-nikāya, V Mahā-vagga* 420):

> Birth is sorrow; old age is sorrow; sickness is sorrow; death is sorrow; getting what is not desired is sorrow; losing what is loved is sorrow; failing to get what is desired is sorrow. In short the five objects of attachment are sorrow.

If these are the manifestations and extent of the disease, what is its cause or, more precisely, its constant antecedent?

> It is the thirst (*tṛṣṇā*), which tends to rebirth, combined with pleasure and lust, finding (passing) pleasure here and there: the thirst for pleasure, the thirst for existence, the thirst for non-existence.

Thus sorrow is in every case consequent upon thirst or desire (the genetic conditions of birth and the pathogenic agents of sickness are ignored). Attention and analysis are now directed to desire and its products.

1.1.2 Analyzing my dynamic dispositions (saṃskāra): At whatever moment I consider myself, I find that I am characterized by dispositions of many sorts. These are arising, passing away or becoming permanent. This entails that they are products, resulting 'con-fections' (*saṃskāra*), conditioned (*saṃskṛta*).

By what are they conditioned?

This is not difficult to see if we observe the establishing of habits, those permanent dynamic dispositions for acting. Such *saṃskāras* become established from the spontaneous or systematic repetition of similar actions. Each action in succession leaves behind an imprint or trace (*vāsanā*) which is as it were reinforced by the succeeding ones. Once sufficiently reinforced, it may be called a seed (*bīja*).

From such *bījas* or *vāsanās* arise further actions more and more stereotyped. Their development and maturation has the form of discrete bits of action and trace in series. The temporal contiguity of those bits gives the impression of permanence and continuity and we speak of permanent dispositions.

Such series go from action to action. Hence they are not static but dynamic. They are, as it were, imbued with desire or, better, desire is itself a *saṃskāra* which results from, and presides over, them. This becomes more acceptable if we can say that desire and, in some collective sense, those series are beginningless.

Let us note that the bits that make up such series are never exactly identical but only similar. Hence, the series are not marked by uniformity but by variability.

1.1.3 Generalizing: What I have found to be the state or affairs for permanent dispositions or habits must be the case for all my dispositions. Together they make up what at any moment I appear to be, my phenomenal essence (*bhāva*). I am not a permanent substance (*dravya*) but a bundle of dispositions (*saṃskāra*). They are not my 'second nature' but simply my nature (*svabhāva*).

But *saṃskāras* issue forth from action (*karma*). Action is as it were their mother. Now I know from empirical experience that the child is similar in nature to his mother. And what characterizes *karma*? Momentariness. Even if I have the impression that an action lasts for some time, I can analyse it into a temporal series of similar bits of action.

But then I must say that my *bhāva* is not truly permanent but is, at every instant, momentary. As a flame gives the impression of being continuous and permanent yet is nothing but a series of successive oxidations, so also my ego (*aham*), this individual (*pudgala*), gives a similar impression but is nothing but an aggregate of chains of *karmas* and *saṃskāras*. It is not a true *ātman*, not a subsistent self that could survive after death.

> What is called mind, or thought, or consciousness, is produced and disappears in a perpetual revolving of day and night. Just as, O monks, a

monkey sporting in a wood seizes now a branch and then another, so also what is called mind or thought or consciousness is produced and vanishes in a perpetual passing from day to night. (*Samyutta Nikāya* II: 94-95)

What we call person (*pudgala*) has no more self than a chariot which is a mere aggregate of parts (cf. *Samyutta Nikāya* I:135 and *Milinda-panha* 2, 1, 1). It is a mere 'burden-taking' (*bhāra-hāra*), the burden being the five aggregates (*skandha*) of physical forms (*rūpa*), sensations (*vedanā*), perceptions (*saṃjñā*), mental constructions (*saṃskāra*) and forms of consciousness (*vijñāna*). It is like a flame fed by oil:

As a flame, blown out by the wind, disappears and cannot be named, even so the recluse when released from name and body, disappears and cannot be named.
He who has disappeared, is he non-existent?
No measuring is there of him that has disappeared, whereby one might know of him that he is not; when all qualities are removed, all modes of speech are removed also. (*Sutta-nipāta* 1075-6)

The doctrine thus arrived at is the doctrine of *pudgala-nairātmya* which rejects the assertion that what we call and perceive as a person (*pudgala*) implies metaphysically a substantial *ātman*, a permanent principle of its coherence and continuity. The Buddha's understanding of the term *ātman* is most probably akin to that of the Materialists (who denied it) and the Jainas or Pre-Jainas (who asserted it) rather than to that of the upaniṣadic Sages.

A critical remark is to the point here. Logic tells us that generalization from *some* to *all* is risky and often leads to fallacy; it is at the most conjectural, a hypothesis which cannot lead to firm conclusions. Now, if my reconstruction is plausibly correct, the Buddha took this daring step. His initial analysis extended only to some dispositions, those obviously arising from repeated action; then he extrapolated its results to the whole field of dispositions, many of which stand beyond the limits of introspective observation.

Of course, he could know nothing of modern genetics which establishes a fundamental field of genes as radical originators of the primary dispositions of the living existents; action and the dispositions arising from it can only be secondary.

Within his generalized perspective, the question of the origin of the series of action-trace-*saṃskāra* and of desire could be only a false question: there was no necessity at any time that a particular antecedent should be self-standing and first, or that a sufficient condition of another type—say, a divine creator—should be assumed as 'prime mover.' The understretching series (*santāna*) of an individual's existence could only be beginningless.

Hence, the doctrine of rebirth: any particular birth is a rebirth preceded by an indefinite sequence of prior births.

1.1.4 Extending this view to all substances: The analogy that exists between all categories of living beings inclines to extending to them all the results obtained by the meditator with regard to his own existence. Moreover, the denial of substance weakens the specific variety of the living species. Their variety is only phenomenal. No leap is required in the transition from one to the other. Yet, there is no true continuity but only contiguity between the death of one form and its rebirth as another form.

The Buddha does not seem to have devoted special attention to non-living substances or pseudo-substances. He simply formulated the celebrated summary sentence: *sarvam duḥkham, sarvam anityam, sarvam anātman* (all things are sorrow, all are impermanent, all are devoid of *ātman*). The Hinayāna schools puzzled over that problem, especially as to the status of the alleged substance, space (*ākāśa*), which they declared to be non-conditioned (*asaṃskṛta*) and thus, unexplainably, *hors série*.

Some further precisions may have been arrived at by the Buddha in the course of his *bodhi*.

All the residue of his analysis, namely, the minimal items which Hinayāna will call *dharmas*, are *anitya* and *anātman*. They are not a self and do not belong to a self (*pudgala-nairātmya*). But they have a *svabhāva* ('own being') and specific characters (*lakṣaṇa*). They are conditioned (*saṃskṛta*) and conditioning as antecedents and consequents. They have an arising (*utpāda*) and a cessation (*nirodha*).

Are these random events?

It is likely that the Buddha discovered that same night the basic answers to this question: No, they are not random events but occur in succession according to a law of *pratitya-samutpāda* (sequential or dependent co-arising). Canonical texts most often agree that it has twelve limbs (*aṅga*).

This law is their manner of being (*tathatā*) in the form of if a, then b; if b, then c; etc.

1.1.5 Discovering the way to nirvāṇa: Such are the *dharmas* of transient existence, such is sorrow and such is its origin. Desire, thirst, is inveterate and unquenchable. Can there be a complete cessation of it?

Yes, because desire is not a substance nor a force but only a *saṃskāra*, a temporal *santāna* of minimal moments of desire which may be beginningless but may come to a stop.

> Now this, O monks, is the noble truth concerning the cessation of sorrow: the extinction of thirst through the complete destruction of desire, its abandonment, forsaking, release, non-attachment.

And there is a sure way that leads to this destruction of desire. One can starve it from its falsely attractive goals as one becomes more and more convinced, through meditation and concentration, of the insubstantiality of things and even self and, accordingly, starts behaving in a renounced fashion.

> But there is a non-born (*ajāta*), a non-produced (*abhūta*), a non-made (*akṛta*), a non-confectioned or non-conditioned (*asamskṛta*): the *Nirvāṇa*. It is the refuge (*śaraṇa*) of the beings that are born, produced, made, confectioned.
>
> Now this, O monks, is the noble truth concerning the cessation of sorrow: it is the noble Way of the Eight [Rightnesses], namely, right view, right intention, right speech, right action, right livelihood, right effort, right mindfulness, right concentration.
>
> When, monks, in those four noble truths my due knowledge and insight [...] became well-purified, then, monks, [...] I attained the highest complete enlightenment. This I recognized. [...] This is the doctrine that whatever is liable to origination is all liable to cessation.

1.2 The neg-ontology of the Buddha

From the above it should be clear that such ontological terms as *bhāva* (essence or being), *jana*, *pudgala* (individual), *dravya* (substance) are voided of any legitimate application, save that *dharmas* are said to have a *svabhāva* (even this will be denied by

Nāgārjuna). They are reduced to the status of collective terms whose reference is not a unitary substance.

How is this emptying of ontological meaning to be understood?

It will be helpful first to consider the pre-Buddha usage, for instance, in the Hymn of Creation (*Ṛgveda* 10, 129) which says:

> There was not the non-existent nor the existent then.... Was there water, unfathomable, profound (*gahanaṃ gambhīram*)?

Here, the existent (*sat*) and the non-existent (*asat*) do not jointly constitute the totality of the cosmos. There is something more primeval, antecedent to *sat* and *asat* and which is not determined but only alluded to as an ocean, unfathomable, profound. This, as R. Robinson points out,[2] is reminiscent of the *Aggi-Vacchagotta-sutta*:

> Freed from denotation by form ... is the *Tathāgata*, Vaccha, he is deep (*gambhīra*), immeasurable (*appameyya*), unfathomable (*duppariyogāho*) as is the great ocean. (*MN* 1, 487, trans. 166)

Robinson continues: "The stock canonical passage on being and non-being is the *Kaccāyana-ovāda, Saṃyutta* 122, 15: "This world, Kaccāyana, usually bases [its view] on two things: on existence and non-existence. Now he who with right insight sees the uprising of the world as it really is, does not hold with the non-existence of the world. But he who with right insight sees the passing away of the world as it really is, does not hold with the existence of the world.... Everything exists: this is one extreme. Nothing exists, this is the other extreme. Not approaching either extreme, the *Tathāgatha* teaches you a doctrine by the middle [way]: Conditioned by ignorance activities come to pass, etc., etc."

The passage defines existence and non-existence as contraries and absolutes. As absolutes, they cannot be predicated within the field of change: what passes away is absolutely speaking neither existent nor non-existent. Its case is like that of scents, which are neither colourful nor non-colourful, of sounds, which are neither tasty nor non-tasty, etc. Only a non-conditioned permanent self-subsistent, such as an *ātman*, could be asserted to be existent; but *sarvam anātman*.

The Buddha "does not approach either extreme," his teaching stands clear of the ontological language as he has limited it. Its field is the middle region of what for a brief moment "arises and ceases." The *dharmas* that arise and cease are neither existent nor non-existent.

But what about their complete cessation, *nirvāṇa*?

This is the deep, unfathomable, unmeasurable. To speak of it, only a negontological language can help. It is the *nirodha-dhātu*, the domain of cessation, which is non-spatial, imperceptible, immutable (*acyuta-sthāna*) Such a negontological language is grounded in the *yoga* experience where consciousness (*vijñāna*) recedes beyond the realm of desires (*kāma-dhātu*) into the realm of non-form (*arūpa-dhātu*) and then into the realm of cessation (*nirodha-dhātu*) (*Dirgha-Nikāya* 111, 215), otherwise called *dharma-dhātu*, the realm of the true doctrine.

This is not absolute nothingness. And it is not a universal *Ātman*. It is the transcendent state of completely cooled, peaceful (*śānta*) consciousness (*vijñāna*). As such it is the supreme value, the aim of the desire for liberation, the 'other shore' (*pāra*). It cannot be objectified, it is not a thing, it cannot be spoken about in terms of the ontological language as viewed by the Buddha.

But it is viewed by him in a *valuational perspective*. He focuses men's minds upon it as upon the only genuine Value, the supreme best (*pāramita*), the immortal (*amṛta*) that is to be reached. It is the 'full of merits' (*arhant*) who reaches it once he 'has become fully excellent' (*brahmabhūta*). What he reaches is health, the end of *duḥkha*.

If we accept as fact this valuational perspective of the Buddha, the paradox of his emphatic rejection of the ontological language may appear less puzzling, and we shall have hit upon a new opening for dialogue with the Buddhists.

2. The Apophatism of Meister Eckhart

Negativism (but not agnosticism) is one of the chief themes of Eckhart's teaching and preaching.[3] It marks his belonging to the Dominican school initiated by St Albert the Great and St Thomas Aquinas. The latter, breaking away from the simplified neo-platonism of the Augustinian tradition (in which Henry of Ghent goes to the extreme of postulating an immediate evidence of the divine essence in every intellectual apprehension), give emphasis to the apophatism taught by Pseudo-Dionysius and to the distance which separates the divine mystery from what human reason can grasp of it.

Eckhart's apophatism pertains to a precise epistemology. It is centred on our access to the ultimate truth in every intellective activity. Intellective thinking develops around objective 'intelligible forms' or ideas which Albert and Thomas connect (as participations) with the creative Idea in the divine Word or second Person of the Trinity. The whole theme of divine ideas, which was Augustinian, is elaborated by Thomas chiefly through appeals to Dionysius. For Eckhart, the notion of the constant dependence of mind on the creative Idea as ultimate measure of being and truth is of central importance.

This measuring reference animates our intellectual dynamism towards the plenitude of intelligibility of the divine Word and subsumes all the intelligible forms that preside over our knowing. It does not provide immediate evidence concerning the absolute Being but it polarizes the intellect and creates a noetic tension towards that plenitude of intelligibility in which the manifold intelligibles find their reconciling unity. As the pole and supreme ideal of our intellect, the creative Idea is immanent to it from its beginning, before any concrete intellection, *ante rem*, says Albert, *a priori*, as its constitutive necessary condition, as its radical 'pre-conscious,' as an overall power (*virtus*) prior to the soul's faculties (*potentiae*).

Ontologically, this power (*kraft*, *virtus*) is the ungrounded *ground* (*grunt*) of the soul, its very rooting in the ontological fullness of its creator:

> The soul receives its being (*sein*) immediately from God; this is why God is nearer to the soul than the latter is [to itself]; this is why God is in the ground (*grunt*) of the soul with his whole divinity. (DW I, 162)

> God by his nude essence which is above any naming enters and penetrates the nude essence of the soul which too is without a proper name and is deeper than its faculties, intellect and will. And, (after saying this concerning the creation of the soul, I must add that the same is true as regards its deification by sanctifying grace:) the soul is the hamlet that Jesus enters by an entering which concerns its being rather than its acting and by which he endows the soul with divine being and God-conformity

> (*esse divinum et deiforme*) by grace; for the latter concerns essence and being (*esse*) according to 1 Cor 15, 10: "it is by the grace of God that I am what I am." (LW I Théry 258)

Dynamically, this ontological grounding of the soul in God is to be viewed as an illumining: the ground is then called light (*licht*) or spark (*vunkelin*). Since it is the very 'lighting up,' the effection of the soul as intellective essence, it is, Eckhart dares to say, the "uncreated and uncreatable 'part' of the soul" (DW I, 197-198)

As we have seen, this creative lighting up of the soul provides it with no immediate vision but with the pole of its dynamism and the criterion of its measurings.

It is in virtue of it that the soul begins to discern the ontological weight and imperfection of all its objects, including its own self. It measures them to the One for the created universe is *universus* 'turned toward the One' (LW III, 447). We are not far here from Plotinus (e.g., *Enneades* 6, 9).

2.1 The objects of Eckhart's negativism

The primary object of Eckhart's negativism is the self. St Thomas taught him the disparity between the evident awareness of our self and the difficulty to discern the nature of the soul which demands "a diligent and subtle search" (*S.Th.* I, 87, 1; I, 77, 1, 7). Eckhart, with the theme of the ground / light / spark of the soul which remains occult and recondite, amplifies this application of negativism. The deepest recess of the soul is beyond evidence, unknown, without proper name, as God himself is beyond any name. It is "neither this nor that," "neither here nor there," it has no being of its own. But it is there identified with the absolute One "in the night... in the silence where nothing speaks to the soul." (DW II)

This intellectual apophatism regarding the soul entails an ethical negativism of ascetical renunciation and purification. This is Eckhart's doctrine of spiritual poverty and self-stripping:

> This is an ethical teaching which trains man to renounce all things, to become naked and poor, to entertain no love for earthly things if he truly wishes to be a disciple of Jesus and to love God without measure and without any limiting self-claim. (LW I, Théry 258)

This denial is a condition for a positive attainment. The soul must be free of earthly affections in order to pierce through to God in whom it finds through his grace its genuine Self (DW II, 31, 5 s).

This is not simply a dialectical sublation of whatever is not God but a substitution of the Word's creative idea, of Christ's viewing, for the merely human habit of viewing.

> Whoever sees God becomes aware that all creatures are nothing. In comparison to another creature a creature is beautiful and is something; but if one compares it to God, it is nothing (DW I, sermon 69). We must take our station in eternity, raised above time (DW I, 78). I say more: if the soul wants to discover God, it must also forget itself and lose itself (DW I, sermon 69, 222).

The second point of application of apophatism is God. The teaching of Albert and Thomas, inspired from Dionysius (and the Bible) and confirmed by Maimonides, had inaugurated the "famous and knotty problem" of the divine names. It had emphasized the ineffability of God and the inadequacy of all our speech, derived as it is from the created world only. Names like Being, Sage, Good or Intelligence, Goodness, etc. do not express but merely allude to God for they conceal him under a mode which is not his.

Even the name 'God' must be transcended, says Eckhart. Thomas was of a similar opinion but more cautious. Eckhart distinguishes 'God' and 'Godhead' and favours the latter because it evokes the 'hidden God' of Dionysius and Isaiah, whereas the first is still essentially referring God to the creatures.

For him, the only name worthy of God is Being / Existent as suggested by *Exodus* 3, 14: "I am who am." He rejects a contemporary theory that divine nature is, first, Being, and only consequently, Intelligence / Thought. The reduplication of 'am' in the Exodus formula must suggest, he explained, that the divine Being is reflective and, thus, is essentially Consciousness / Intelligence. (Eckhart does not use those nouns but the corresponding verb '*Intelligere*' just as in the case of Being, '*Esse*.') Compatible with the fullness of this '*intelligere*,' the notion of pure Being, '*esse nudum*' with its connotation of negativity of any limit is particularly suitable for designating God for it is called for by the intellective reflexivity in virtue of which God is intimately present to himself and the creatures he causes to well up from the fullness of his *Esse-Intelligere*.

What he says about the need to go beyond the trinity of divine Persons is more puzzling as uttered by a man of deep Christian orthodoxy. But the immediate context shows that he simply wants to purify the number three from its undesirable connotation of ontological multiplicity in order to discern the absolute ontological unity of the divine Persons. (DW III, 437, 11)

To conclude, Eckhart's negativism is essentially a high instance of intellective and epistemological asceticism, though it also entails a thorough ethical asceticism. It displays itself at that point where metaphysics merges with mysticism. It leads, thanks to unitive grace, to the incarnate Word in whom and by whom all things and, first of all, the self receive their authentic meaning.[4]

3. The Negativism of Śrī Śaṅkarācārya

The current and widespread interpretation of Śaṅkara is that he simply an acosmist who asserts that there is but one true Reality, *Brahman-Ātman*, and anything else, whether selves or bodies, is illusory.

But much work has been done in recent years by a few scholars who have applied themselves to read the very text of his authentic writings and to "interpret Śaṅkara by Śaṅkara." They have thus reached a new interpretation of which the following may give some idea.

3.1 The linguistic crib-work of Śaṅkara's writing

Śaṅkara is a *śrutivādin*, an exegete of the Vedānta Scriptures. His writings present an intercrossing, a crib-work, of 3 languages:

1. the utilitarian (*vyavahāra*) mundane and ordinary language;
2. the language of extremes (*paramārtha*) which is characteristic of the 'great sentences' (*mahā-vākya*) of the Vedānta;

3. his own hermeneutical language by which he bridges over the two and aims at reconciling them, i.e., the *śrutivāda* language.

The language of extremes uses terms like *sat* (being/existent), *ātman* (self, the reflexive pronoun), *vidyā* (knowledge), *kāraṇa* (cause), etc. only "in their most elevated sense" (*paramārthataḥ*). To indicate this, I shall write them with an initial CAPITAL letter, as in *Sat*, *Ātman*, etc. Since in Sanskrit terms are negatived by an initial privative *a* or *an*, the contraries of those terms will be written as *a-Sat*, *an-Ātman*, *a-Vidyā*, etc. A brief discussion of the 'being or non-being' problem can now be presented as follows:

VYAVAHĀRA	*VEDĀNTA*	*ŚRUTIVĀDA (ŚANKARAVĀDA)*
I am *sat*, i.e., a being: likewise, a jar or any other thing is *sat*.	But the *Brahman* is "not thus not thus" (*neti, neti*) and is hence non-being (*a-sat*). Because the *Śruti* says, It is *Sat*.	*Brahman* is other than any *sat*, because It is *paramārthataḥ Sat*, Being in the most elevated sense of the term. And in comparison with it, any *sat* is *a-Sat*.[5]
But only such impossible things as 'the son of a barren woman' are *A-sat* (*paramārthataḥ*).		What you say is true. No man, jar, etc. is *A-sat*. They stand in the middle between *Sat* and *A-sat*. They are *Sad-Asad-vilakṣaṇa*, 'not to be defined in terms of the absolutes *Sat* or *A-sat*.'
Then in which terms should I be defined?	You are *Sanmūla*, rooted in *Sat*. All finite beings (*sat*) have *Brahman* as their [ontological] Root (*Mūla*).	To apprehend yourself apart from your Root, *Brahman*, is the greatest falsehood. It is the wrong knowledge (*a-Vidyā*)[6] which Vedānta alone can eradicate. *Brahman* is your innermost total Cause (*Kāraṇa*) apart from which (*tad-vyatirekeṇa*) no effect subsists.
But I am a 'living self' (*jīvātman*), autonomous, self-subsistent.	No, *Brahman* is your *Ātman*, your supreme inner *Ātman* (*parama pratyag-Ātman*). It is *sarv'Ātman*, *Ātman of all*.	There is a hierarchy of selves: bodily self, life self, sensory self, intellective self, *jīvātman* and topping them all, the highest self. Each self (*ātman*) is "more subtle, more causal, more inner" than the one that precedes it. The highermost *Ātmaṅ* is 'Reality / Knowledge / infinite' (*Satyam Jñānam-anantam*).

How can the *Brahman* be my Self? I am other than my Cause.	You are distinct but non-other (*an-anya*). That thou art (*Tat-tvam-asi*). All this is *Brahman* (*sarvam-idam Brahma*).	If the *Brahman* were simply your assembling Cause (*nimitta-kāraṇa*), you would, indeed, be other than It. But It is, besides, your substrative Cause (*upādāna-kāraṇa*), That 'from which' (*yataḥ*) effects issue forth as realities (*sat*, though *a-Sat*).[7] Hence, it is impossible for an effect to be simply other than It, i.e., foreign, extrinsic, remote, heterogeneous. It is from Its Fullness (*Pūrṇa*) that you are.
If the *Brahman* is such a cause of its effects, it is modified and relativized by them. Then it is not the Absolute.	The *Brahman* is *satyasya Satyam*, the Real of the real. But owing to Its Fullness, It is forever *Kūṭastha*, 'standing immutable like a peak.'	Any relation from *Brahman* to Its effects is not an added reality but an *upādhi*, an extrinsic denominator. It belongs to our manner of conceiving, not to Its Reality.

3.2 The tādātmya relationship

Between the reals and the Real, there is a relation called *tādātmya*. In its ordinary sense, it means 'identity' but here it must be taken in its etymological sense, 'having That as one's *Ātman*.' According to Śaṅkara's explanations, it has the following properties:

1. *Unreciprocality*: "Names-and-forms (finite reals) in all their states have their *Ātman* in *Brahman* alone, but *Brahman* has not Its *Ātman* in them." (*Taitt. Up. Bh.* 2, 6, 1)
2. *Dependence*: "The doctrine that the *Brahman* is the *Ātman* of the embodied *ātman* does away with the independent own existence of the embodied *ātman*." (*B.S.Bh.* 2, 1, 14)
3. *Non-separateness*: "Between the effect and its substrative cause there is non-separation, ... non-division." (*B.S.Bh.* 2, 3, 6)
4. *Non-otherness*: Śaṅkara explains this *an-anyatva* as 'no-existence apart from' (*vyatirekeṇa abhāvaḥ*) and says,

"There exists in the past, present or future, not one thing simply other than the *Ātman*, simply non-*Ātman*, separated by space and time, utterly subtle, disconnected and remote." (*Taitt. Up. Bh.* 2, 6, 1)

5. *Distinction*: "Absolute equality would annihilate the relation of cause and effect.... There is in the cause an excellence." (*B.S.Bh.* 2, 1, 6)
6. *Extrinsic denominativeness*: Effects are not intrinsic qualifiers (*viśeṣaṇa*) but extrinsic denominators (*upādhi*) of *Brahman*; likewise the relations of *Brahman* to the universe. "The great saying, *neti neti*, designates the *Brahman* unaffected by *upādhis*." (*Bṛh. Up. Bh.* 3, 8, 12) "The alleged break in *Brahman's* nature (on account of Its Causality) is imagined through *a-vidyā*." (*B.S.Bh.* 2, 1, 28)

The above suffices to suggest that attention to what Śaṅkara does in his writings can eliminate both misinterpretations, pantheism and acosmism. The negativity of many of his statements is a matter both of language and of perspective. As an exegete of Vedānta he is driven to use a threefold language; and as a Vedāntin, he has to view everything from the perspective of the transcendent Absolute.

4. Conclusion

Language and perspective are linked. At least, this is so in the three cases we have considered.

The Buddha's perspective is analytical and empirical in a large sense including his *dhyāna* or *yoga* experiences. Its field is the flux of the immediate present as consequent upon the past and conditioning the future. He analyzes it into minimal bits appearing in a sequence of contiguity which never amounts to a continuity. Thus he dissolves the notion of *bhāva* (being) and denies substances and *ātmans*. Hence, he negatives the ontological language and tends to promote a language of pure dynamism in terms of desire, action and *saṃskāra*, and their cessation. But is such a language really possible?

Meister Eckhart takes his perspective from the Bible and from the highly metaphysical standpoint of his teachers, Albert and Thomas, already shaped up into 'negative theology' by the influence of Dionysian apophatism. But he emphasizes and enlarges some central insights of Thomas; for instance, Thomas had written: "As causally possible in its divine Cause, as well as known by God, the creature *is* the divine Essence." Eckhart centres on this doctrine as permanently valid for it reflects the creative Idea of the divine Word.

Hence, our knowledge of the creature, if it is to be really true, must reflect this creative Idea for, of itself, the creature is nothing whereas, as immanent to the creative Idea, it is the very divine Essence.

On the other hand, such a knowledge-reflection can only be apophatic and mystical for no human speech, no concept derived from our experience of the finite, can be adequate to expressing that immanence which coincides with the Essence and Unity of Fullness of the Creator. At this depth of darkness, the 'spark' alone can shine.

Śrī Śaṅkarācārya's perspective is likewise taken from Scriptures which provide him with the very viewpoint of the Absolute. This explains the interplay of three manners of language in his writings. He weaves them on by means of superlatives and negatives. We must not focus on these negatives apart from the superlatives.

Thus he strains the possibilities of human language but, in so doing, he drives us to an apophatic theology which opens directly onto *Vidyā*, the perfect and saving Knowledge. Was this not the blissful goal of the upaniṣadic prayer?

Oṃ. Asato mā Sad-gamaya,
Tamaso mā Jyotir-gamaya,
Mṛtyor-mā-'mṛtam gamaya.
Om Śānti, śānti, śāntiḥ.
Oṃ. From the un-Real, lead me to the Real.
From darkness, lead me to Light,
From death, lead me to the Immortal.
Om. Peace, peace, peace.
(*Bṛh. Up*. 1, 3, 28)

Notes

[1] Paper presented at the San Diego conference of NEW ERA on 'God: the Contemporary Discussion (29 December 1986 – 4 January 1987). [First published in *The Journal of Religious Studies* (Patiala) **17**/2 (1989) 56-69, and reprinted here with permission.]

[2] Richard Robinson, "Some Methodological Approaches to the Unexplained Point," *Philosophy East and West* **22** (1972) 320.

[3] The almost terminated Critical Edition of Eckhart's Works (Stuttgart: Kohlhammer) comprises: *Latin Works* (LW), vols. I-V; *German Works* (DW), vols. I-III, Sermons 1-86 and vol. V Treatises.

[4] On all this, cf. Ed. H. Weber, "Mystique parce que theologien: Maitre Eckhart," *La Vie Spirituelle* (Paris: Éditions du Cerf) **136**/652 (1982) 730-749.

[5] [Correcting the textual *a-sat*.]

[6] [Correcting the textual *a-vidyā*.]

[7] [Correcting the textual *a-sat*.]

13

RADHAKRISHNAN'S INTERPRETATION OF ŚAṄKARA[1]

My first acquaintance with Dr S. Radhakrishnan was at the celebration of the silver jubilee of the All-India Philosophical Congress in 1950. He had been its chief founder and the first chairman of its executive committee. A tall figure in immaculate white dress and turban, he was addressing the delegates in the chaste English of his flowing prose.

What struck me then was the character of his utterances. No ratiocination, no dialectic, no supporting argument, but the assertions of a sage sparsely adorned with apt quotations. Later, I would find that he had written, "philosophy is not so much a conceptual reconstruction as an exhibition of insights." His speech obeyed his bent towards universalism and ethical values. Its substance was Advaita Vedānta but these two inclinations he seemed to derive from Jesus and the Buddha.

These first impressions were to be enriched on later occasions. The last time I heard him was at Simla, on 20 October 1965 when he opened the Indian Institute of Advanced Study and inaugurated our seminar on 'Religion and Society.' His inaugural speech was a curious distillation of Vedānta convictions and Christian beliefs. Starting from the upaniṣadic "Lead me from the unreal to the real," the Buddha's quest of the beyond of old age, sickness and death, and the Christian "He has risen from the tomb," he went on to say:

> If life has significance, we must have something which is exempt from death, and which makes us feel there is a deathless element in all. This reality must be Being, it must have intelligence and purpose and freedom to choose. You may call it *saccidānanda,* being, intelligence and freedom.

Further, after new quotations from the Upaniṣads, the Gospel and the Qur'an, he said:

> Every religion says *deho devālaya namaḥ*. The *deha*, the body, must be regarded as *devālaya*. *Jīva* which is *sanātana* is something which is eternal in character. If we overlook that spirit, that spark of the Divine which we all have, we will become bound to things, ideas and abstractions, we will lose real creativity. Unless you are able to feel that there is some element in you which is trans-objective, you are not a true man. It is the human individual who has to realize that God is the spark in him. It is he that has to take into account his own creativity, his own freedom. It is possible for the human individual to make this world a better one, because the human individual is the image of the Divine.[2]

These abstracts from his Simla speech of 1965 show some chief convictions which Radhakrishnan entertained in the final years of his brilliant career, and around which he had shaped his long life. They were a blend—not a conceptual synthesis—of Śāṅkara Vedānta, the Gospel, the Qur'an and the Buddha's quest. They were the living core of his own philosophy.

But, besides developing his own philosophy, he had equipped himself with a personal knowledge of "the great masters of thought, ancient and modern, Eastern and Western"[3] and, especially from 1917, had undertaken to become an expert historian of Indian philosophy.

While preparing to write his *Indian Philosophy*, he was aware of the high degree of objectivity and impartiality such a task would demand but he soon keenly felt the difficulty of reconciling faithfulness with the historical data and with the subjectivity required in interpreting them:

> The writer may at times allow his personal bias to determine his presentation.... His work at best will be a personal interpretation and not an impersonal survey.... There is also the danger that we are inclined to interpret ancient systems in a manner acceptable to modern minds.... Often a sense of hero-worship exalts the classical thinkers above the level of history.... I tried not to overstate any case or indulge in personal dislike for its own sake.... Intellectual unselfishness or humility is the mother of all writing, even though the writing may relate to the history of philosophy.... In all philosophical interpretation, the right method is to interpret thinkers at their best, in the light of what they say in the moment of their clearest insight.... I am aware of the limitations of the comparative method which can either be a bane or a blessing.... If systems of philosophy are themselves determined by historical circumstances, there is no reason why

> the method adopted in historical interpretation should not take into account the needs and conditions of the age.[4]

Thus knowing the difficulties which he felt and faced up to, we can try to emulate his humility if not his critical acumen in examining his historical presentation of the teaching of Srī Śaṅkarācārya.

Among the many similar attempts made during the last hundred years, his is truly outstanding. Besides the continuous charm of its style, it has the qualities of great scholarship: completeness and clarity of information, penetrating intelligence, courage to face thoroughly all the difficulties of interpretation, and a faultless balancing of admiration and impartial criticism.

However, as he knew well, every interpretation, even the most painstaking, is dated and subject to revision. My task, as I understand it, is to try to question his reconstruction for the sake of even greater faithfulness to Śaṅkara. I shall not "look for fleas in the lion's mane" but take up a few main themes worth re-examining and about which an interpretation different from his own may come closer to the authentic mind of Śaṅkara.

In the mid-twenties, when Radhakrishnan was composing his *Indian Philosophy*, a certain consensus existed among scholars about which works attributed to Śaṅkara by tradition were genuine, doubtful or spurious. Radhakrishnan let himself be guided by this consensus but made use of some doubtful works. However, this point is important only with regard to the *Māṇḍūkyopaniṣad Bhāṣya* whose author appears to have deliberately 'Vedāntized' an acosmism of Buddhist origin. Could this author be the same as the author of the *Brahmasūtra Bhāṣya*? H. Jacobi had denied the possibility in 1913 but T.R. Chintamani refuted his argument in 1924 and tried, ineffectively, to answer Jacobi's various objections.[5] The question was taken up again by V. Bhattacharya who argued extensively against its traditional attribution at the Third Oriental Conference (Madras, 1924) [and] in his contribution to the *Sir Asutosh Mookerjee Silver Jubilee Volume* (Calcutta, 1925).[6] Apparently, he did not convince Radhakrishnan, who accepted the authenticity of the work. In consequence there is an emphasis on acosmism in his interpretation of Śaṅkara's *māyāvāda*.

It is relevant to mention that S.K. Belvalkar (in 1929), Lacombe (in 1937), Renou (in 1945) did not accept the *Bhāṣya* as a work of Śaṅkara.[7] In 1967, however, Dr Sengaku Mayeda subjected it to a new examination in the light of linguistic criteria determined by P. Hacker. He concluded that the *Bhāṣya* is authentic.[8] Nevertheless, I remain doubtful about its authorship and would not accept that it should determine my interpretation of Śaṅkara.

Radhakrishnan surely tried to abide by his determination "to interpret thinkers at their best, in the light of what they say in the moments of their clearest insights"[9] but he could not free his mind completely from the pervasive influence of the current interpretation of Śaṅkara in terms of *vivarta* and illusionistic *māyāvāda*.

Now Śaṅkara himself had avoided the term *vivarta* because it belonged to the Śabdādvaita conception of *bhedābheda* with which he disagreed strongly. The term he used was *pariṇāma*, imposed on him by the *Śruti* texts upon which he commented, but he carefully de-Sāṁkhyanized it by asserting the unchangeability of the *Brahman*. The term *vivarta* was later introduced into Śāṅkara Vedānta as a technical term by Padmapāda with a connotation of illusionism. Prakāśātman avoided this in his definition which properly stressed that the absolute is unaffected by the process of its manifestations. But Vimuktātman compromised this understanding with trends of *māyāvāda* and made fashionable the term *anirvacanīya* which had not been a technical term of Śaṅkara for *māyā*.

As to the term *māyāvāda*, Śaṅkara had sedulously avoided it because it was the label of schools of Buddhist thought with which he did not want to be identified; besides, he rejected Buddhism in all its forms. Again, under the pressure of the texts he commented on he had used the term *māyā* in at least three diverse senses and, whenever its sense was magic, then only for the sake of comparison. He had not defined it as a technical term of his system as he did *avidyā*. It was the responsibility of later Advaitins to adopt it as a technical but indefinable term. As to causal *māyā* it will be considered presently.[10]

There exists a function of our faculty of knowing which we feel is more penetrating, less mediated, more satisfactory than the ordinary operations of reason. We call this intuition, insight, and at times, experience. Through it, well-gifted minds feel the solution to a problem before any explicit reasoning. This capacity is reinforced by training and expertise. There are more than a few men and women who possess a sort of spontaneous sense of truth and of the true values. Life teaches them that their insights are not all lucky guesses, however, and that they must check by reasoning what is found wanting. Still, such insights are valuable as working hypotheses or, in matters difficult to investigate, intimations of wisdom, adumbrations of the religious mysteries, assurances that the universe is holistically meaningful.

Radhakrishnan was abundantly gifted with this faculty. And the sort of early religious education he received had given it vigour. Early on he acquired a number of convictions from which he would never depart. Therefore, he was delighted when he found that:

> According to the Upaniṣads there is a higher power which enables us to grasp the central spiritual reality.... Man has the faculty of divine insight or mystic intuition, by which he transcends the distinctions of intellect and solves the riddle of reason.[11]

Thus, he seems to say, this capacity is found in every man. But his next sentence speaks only of 'chosen spirits': "The chosen spirits scale the highest peak of thought and intuit the reality."[12] This is closer to Śaṅkara's opinion, which restricts such actual intuition either to Madhucchandas and other *ṛsis* who are said to 'find' or 'see' the eternal Veda in the beginning of the *kalpa* or to the very few (of the intent aspirants "one in a thousand" only: *Bh. Gītā Bh.* 13, 2) who reach the blissful intuition of the *Brahman-Ātman*. The idea that the few are 'chosen spirits' is supported by *Kaṭha Up.* 1, 2, 23 or *Muṇḍ. Up.* 3, 2, 3 and Śaṅkara's commentary on them and his recalling that "the liberating discrimination is caused by the Lord's grace because *Śruti* teaches it" (*B.S.Bh.* 2, 3, 41). But, for Radhakrishnan, this is an *ad hoc* answer to an illegitimate question.

But I am afraid there is a deep discrepancy between Śaṅkara and his interpreter as to the place and availability of Vedāntic intuition. Radhakrishnan, in his effort to de-mythologize Vedānta, appears to imply that the Advaita intuition stands in simple continuity to the kind of intuition accessible to us when unaided by *Śruti*: "The Vedas contain truths which man could by the exercise of his own faculties discover, though it is to our advantage that they are revealed."[13] This is an opinion akin to that of a St Thomas Aquinas in Christianity but it would not be ratified by Śaṅkara. Radhakrishnan expresses this opinion as the very conclusion of chapter 22 in which he recalls much of the doctrine of Śaṅkara on the role of *Śruti* but without transmitting the full vigour of his unambiguous position.

Śaṅkara held that *Śruti* is the only reliable *pramāṇa* or source of truth concerning the *Brahman*. The *Śruti* has to be investigated by reason but no independent search by unaided reason can win the truth which *Śruti* alone can yield. Reasoning is here powerless unless it first accepts the authority of the *Śruti* and then acts as its handmaid to manifest its intelligibility. Śaṅkara's *Brahmajijñāsā* is a strong form of *Śrutivāda* and is similar to the scripture-bound theology of Christianity or Islam.

But Radhakrishnan tells us in his very introduction that the "austere intellectualism [of the Advaitism of Śaṅkara], its remorseless logic, which marches on indifferent to the hopes and beliefs of man, its relative freedom from theological obsessions, make it a great example of a purely philosophical scheme."[14] This interpretation put me off in 1949 as I already knew Śaṅkara enough to realize it would lead me astray. But it contributed to my decision to investigate thoroughly Śaṅkara's scripturo-theological method and the scientific specificity of his enquiry into the *Brahman* as supreme *ātman* of all.

The trouble with Radhakrishnan as an historian is that he was mixing another aim with the proper aim of historical writing. He wanted to give philosophical respectability to traditional Indian thought and especially to Vedānta by presenting them in terms of the monistic and ethical idealism which he found to be their valuable core. In a response published in *Mind* in April 1926 to the critics of his method of approach he said:

> The historian of philosophy must approach his task, not as a mere philologist or even as a scholar but as a philosopher who uses his scholarship as an instrument to wrest from words the thoughts that underlie them. A mere linguist regards the views of ancient Indian thinkers as so many fossils... and from his point of view any interpretation which makes them alive and significant is dismissed as far-fetched and untrue. A philosopher, on the other hand, realizes the value of the ancient Indian

> theories... and treats them not as fossils but as species which are remarkably persistent.... It is the task of creative logic... to piece together the scattered data, interpret for us the life they harbour and thus free the soul from the body.... [The historian] must pay great attention to the logic of ideas, draw inferences, suggest explanations and formulate theories which would introduce some order into the shapeless mass of unrelated facts.[15]

This is an able self-defence but the free scope it gives to 'creative logic' threatens to obfuscate the first concern of the historian which is to discover the authentic significance and aliveness of the ancient writings within their own historical context, rather than to creatively enforce upon them interpretations which show their relevance to us today. Radhakrishnan presents us with most of what Śaṅkara said but usually ends with what he wants him to have said. Adopting a critical reflection made about his 1918 book *The Philosophy of Rabindranath Tagore*, one could remark that the non-expert cannot tell when Śaṅkara's thought ends and Radhakrishnan's begins. A further remark is that Radhakrishnan's concern for reinterpretation appears to have hampered his search for Śaṅkara's own intelligibility.

At the very outset of his commentary on *Brahma Sūtra* Śaṅkara very carefully defines the notion of *avidyā*, for it is in the light of this definition that his enquiry is due to proceed. As a general term, *avidyā* is a type of superimposition, namely, the mental superimposition of the nature and characteristics of one thing upon another and vice versa. The special case which retains all the attention of Śaṅkara is the innate *avidyā*, which superimposes the non-*ātman* and its characteristics on the supreme *ātman* and the other way around. It imbues all our judgements until the *Śruti* enlightens us about it and dissipates it entirely. This very ceasing is the reaching of its contrary, *vidyā*, i.e., the intuitive realization of the *Brahman-Ātman* beyond any distorting superimposition. This is not simply a matter of substituting intuition for the conceptual discourse of the intellect but of the mind opening itself to a non-mental source of truth, a *śabda*, the word of *Śruti* inherited from the past (*āgama*): "The *Brahman* is to be obtained by the mind fully instructed by the teacher and scripture (*ācāryāgamā-saṁskṛtena manasā*)" (*Kaṭha Up. Bh.* 2, 1, 11).

This seems not to have been retained solidly by Radhakrishnan because he belittles the sovereignty of *Śrutivāda*. But, of course, he does not fail to abundantly recall Śaṅkara's teaching regarding *avidyā*.[16] Only he does not seem to have sufficiently perceived what it entails: namely, that the whole process of *Brahmajijñāsā* is epistemological, intra-logical; it is a purgation of the mind and of language by way of enlightening 'great sentences' (*mahāvākya*). Before their truth can be intuited, their correct meaning has to be discovered through an exegesis which leads beyond the primary meaning of their terms to their supreme meaning (*paramārtha*). Only on this level of signification can they abolish *avidyā*. As Śaṅkara says in *Upadeśasāhasrī* (18, 125-6) this is a positive ascertainment (*prasiddhi*) which must be done before the *svānubhava-karaṇam* (to use his term in *Bh. Gītā Bh.* 6, 8; 7, 2; 9, 1), the "turning it into one's own experience," can be undertaken fruitfully.

The *mahāvākyas* can be grouped into five categories: negative (*neti neti* type), superlative (*pūrṇam* type), cosmos-relational (*yataḥ* type), ego-relational (*tattvamasi* type), and essential (*satyaṃ jñānam-anantam* type). They are complementary. None of them can be cancelled since each is an integral part of the faultless meaning of the *Śruti*. This does not seem to have been fully seen by Radhakrishnan, as we shall now see.

Radhakrishnan, following in the footsteps of some post-Śaṅkara advaitins, appears to think that the teaching of *janmādyasya yataḥ* (*B.S.Bh.* 1, 1, 2) is not final because it relates the *Brahman* to the world as its total cause, and to *Brahman*, relation can only be *upādhi*. This reason is insufficient. Let us examine more closely how Śaṅkara treats this topic.

First of all, here and elsewhere he unrestrictedly affirms the universal causality of *Brahman*. Traditionally, two types of cause were usually referred to: the *upādāna kāraṇa* or reality-giving cause, and the *nimitta-kāraṇa* or structure-giving cause. "*Brahman* is to be acknowledged as the *upādāna* as well as the *nimitta-kāraṇa*... at the same time... one without a second.... The *ātman* is thus the *nimitta-kāraṇa* because there is no other ruling principle, and the *upādāna* because there is no other substance from which (*yataḥ*) the universe could originate" (*B.S.Bh.* 1, 4,

23). This is the first debunking of *avidyā* in this matter. Indeed, what are the superimpositions made by *avidyā* here?

They consist of attributing to *Brahman* in diverse ways the characteristics of mundane causality. According to our experience, any cause is:

a) Either *upādāna* or *nimitta*; Śaṅkara says, the one *Brahman* fulfils both functions.

b) *Upādāna* implies materiality and transformation (*pariṇāma*); Śaṅkara: these are not essential since what it denotes is simply reality-giving. *Brahman* gives reality (originates, etc.) but not through any self-transformation: "Like the magician... or the dreamer... He is not touched [by the differences of his effects]" (*B.S.Bh.* 2, 1, 9). "The *Śruti* teaches that he is absolutely changeless (*kūṭastha*)' (*B.S.Bh.* 2, 4, 20). Neither has the *Brahman* to be material in order to be *upādāna*: "These *nāma-rūpas* [the names-and-forms that he also calls *ākṛtis*], which are identical with the *ātman* in their unmanifested state [i.e., when they pre-exist in the fullness of the cause in the manner of 'future': *bhāviṣyena rūpeṇa*] can become the materials (*upādāna-bhūte*) of the manifested universe. Hence, it is not incongruous to say that the omniscient one creates the universe by virtue of its oneness with the materials, namely, names-and-forms which are identical with itself" (*Ait. Up. Bh.* 1, 1, 2).

c) *Upādāna* and its effects pertain to a common genus (*jāti*) and are, therefore, univocal. This is not necessary. *Brahman*, the transcendent *upādāna*, escapes the reach of all conceptual categories and words, whether *jāti*, difference, species, quality, action or relation: "The *Brahman* is not other in such a fashion [namely, as circumscribed by delimitation, in the manner in which 'cowness' is delimited by 'horseness,' etc.] since it is not subject to limitation by exclusion on the part of other substances" (*Taitt. Up. Bh.* 2, 1, 1). Between *Brahman* as *upādāna* and its effects, surely there is a certain similarity, but not a univocality; a non-difference (*abheda*) and non-otherness (*ananyatva*) but not equality: "If absolute equality were insisted on, the relation of cause and effect would be annihilated.... This relation is based on the fact that there is present in the cause an excellence [which is lacking in the effect. On the other hand, they are similar since] one characteristic feature, namely *sattā* [existence-reality] is found in ether, etc. as well as in *Brahman*." (*B.S.Bh.* 2, 1, 6) In order to be other than its *upādāna*, the effect would have to be utterly foreign, and ontologically independent from it. But "there exists in the past, present or future not one thing simply other than the *ātman*, simply non-*ātman*, separated by space or time, utterly subtle, disconnected and remote [from it]" (*B.S.Bh.* 2, 1, 6). Further, "the effect is intimately dependent (*anuvidhāyin*) on its *upādāna*" (*Bṛh. Up. Bh.* 1, 5, 14); "every effect abides within its cause" (*Bh. Gītā Bh.* 8, 22), "is non-separate from it (*avyatirikta*)" (*Bṛh. Up. Bh.* 1, 6, 1). Indeed, 'the non-separation of the two is possible only if the whole aggregate of things originates from the one *Brahman*. And we understand from the Veda that this affirmation can be established only on the principle that between the *upādāna kāraṇa* and its effects there is non-separation.... non-division (*abheda*) (*B.S.Bh.* 2, 3, 6).

d) A *nimitta-kāraṇa* has to be intelligent but also corporeal, for it must have a body with hands, etc. if it is to move, organize, rule, etc. "That whose nature is pure intelligence cannot move anything!—A thing which is itself devoid of motion (*pravṛtti-rahita*) can nevertheless move other things (*pravartaka*). The magnet, itself devoid of motion, yet moves iron; and colours as well as the other objects of the senses, although themselves devoid of motion, produce movements in the eyes and the other organs of the senses. So the Lord also, who is immanent in all, the *ātman* of all, all-knowing and all-powerful can, even though himself devoid of motion, move the universe" (*B.S.Bh.* 2, 2, 2).

e) But a *nimitta-kāraṇa* needs some extraneous help. "The absolutely complete power of *Brahman* does not require to be supplemented by any extraneous help" (*B.S.Bh.* 2, 1, 24), not even by a demiurge or intermediary Lord "because outside *Brahman* the *upādāna* there is no other ruling principle, for the *Śruti* says, that prior to creation, *Brahman* was one only, without a second" (*B.S.Bh.* 1, 4, 23). "Its high power is revealed as manifold, as inherent, acting as force and knowledge" (*B.S.Bh.* 2, 1, 24). That which is intelligence itself needs no helper to pattern and rule the world intelligently.

f) An intelligent cause has a purpose corresponding to a need and a desire. Creation, being an intelligent causing, has a purpose (*artha*), namely, *loka-saṁgraha*, the orderly cohesion of the world and thus the welfare of living beings (*Bh. Gītā Bh.* 3,

24), but it intends no fruit (*phala*) that would quench a desire of the creator. Whatever desire we might imagine the creator to entertain is already reality in his ontological fullness: *Brahman* is *satyakāma*, *āptakāma*.

g) The intelligent creator-lord must be *saguṇa*, qualified by endowments which are secondary additions to his substance, e.g. creative intentions and relationships such as lordship, etc. Therefore, he cannot be the absolute *Brahman* which is *nirguṇa*. This is a common opinion, also espoused by Radhakrishnan, but which still represents an *avidyā* view. It is true, says Śaṅkara, that due to his "absolutely complete power" the supreme *ātman* creates "like gods, etc. who, without availing themselves of any extraneous means, produce palaces, etc. by their mere intention which is effective in consequence of those beings' peculiar power" (*B.S.Bh.* 2, 125). But "how are these [creative volitions] found in *Brahman*? As essentially reality knowledge, and as pure in virtue of being their own *ātman*" (*Taitt. Up. Bh.* 2, 6, 1).

As to the relations induced in *Brahman* by his being the universal cause (causality and its various forms, omniscience, omnipotence, lordship, witnesshood, etc.) they are not real additives to its essence but mere extrinsic denominators (*upādhi*). According to Śaṅkara, we cannot express but only indicate the essence of *Brahman*: *tal-lakṣyate na tū-'cyate* (*Taitt. Up. Bh.* 2, 6, 1). We do this in two ways: either through intrinsic denominators (*viśeṣaṇa*), such as *satyam*, *jñānam*, etc. (*Taitt. Up. Bh.* 2, 6, 1) or through extrinsic denominators (*upādhi*). These are qualifying it by reference to diverse *nāmarūpas* or larger features of the world which, as limited, can only be adjuncts external to it and thus *upādhis*. *Avidyā* considers them as intrinsically qualifying *Brahman*, this is the mistake corrected by Śaṅkara when he declares them to be mere *upādhis*. He does not deny the universal causality, lordship, etc. of *Brahman*—for they are logically entailed by the true fact of the world's ontological dependence upon it—but only that they affect the simplicity of its essence: "The Lord's lordship, omniscience, omnipotence, etc. all depend on the limitations due to the adjuncts... in reality none of these qualities belong [as a *guṇa*, an additive to the substance] to the *ātman* whose nature is cleared by right knowledge [the corrective of *avidyā*] from all adjuncts whatever" (*B.S.Bh.* 2, 1, 14).

Is there, then, no ontological difference between *Brahman* as cause and *Brahman* as absolute?

> The difference is [only logical as it is] due to *upādhis*. Intrinsically there is neither difference nor identification for the [alleged] two *Brahmans* are by nature the pure Intelligence, homogeneous like a lump of salt.... Therefore, *neti neti* designates the *Brahman* unaffected by *upādhis*, which is beyond the grasp of speech and mind, undifferentiated and one... when its *upādhi* is the power of eternal and unlimited knowledge, it is called inner ruler and lord (*Īśvara*); the same *ātman* as by nature transcendent, absolute and pure is called the immutable and supreme *ātman* (*Bṛh. Up. Bh.* 3, 8, 12).

The following quotations sum up this matter:

> So long as one does not realize in this way this *ātman* which has been described [by *neti neti*], so long does one accept the *upādhis*... as one's proper *ātman* and, considering through *avidyā* the *upādhis* as intrinsic to the *ātman*, one transmigrates under the influence of *avidyā*, desire and action (*Ait. Up. Bh.* 2, 1). It is on this *Brahman* which is absolutely Being (*Sat*) that all the worlds... are fixed during origination, subsistence and dissolution. Nothing whatsoever, no modification, transcends that *Brahman* (*Kaṭha Up. Bh.* 2, 3, 2).

Thus, Radhakrishnan's view that the doctrine of divine causality and lordship is only a product of logic, "The Vedas give us the highest logical approximation to the truth."[17] In writing this he seems to have been influenced by Deussen whom he quotes: "Strictly viewed, this *aparā vidyā* is nothing but metaphysics in an empirical dress." That this is to be superseded by the monistic insight of intuition, is not sustained by Śaṅkara. The latter does not attribute to our logic the teaching of the *mahāvākya*, *janmādyasya yataḥ*, nor does he cancel it as ultimately invalid. He only clears from all possible anthropomorphism (or, as he says, superimposition) our understanding of it. And he does it, not by inducing in us an intuition, but in the light of the other 'great sayings' *neti neti* and *satyam jñānam-anantam*.

Causality and lordship imply power (*śakti*). We have already quoted Śaṅkara speaking of the special "excellence" of the universal cause, of "the absolutely complete power of *Brahman*," of its "high power acting as force and knowledge." Indeed, when we understand that the non-dual *Brahman* is full (*pūrṇa*) being, since it is reality-knowledge-infinite, we grasp immediately that by its very essence it is inherently capable of giving reality and intelligent structure to any kind of universe it decides to freely create. Yet this power is so unique that we have no way of imagining or representing it; we can only indicate it by terms which in our experience designate various sorts of extraordinary power. One of those terms is *māyā*, used once in the sense of 'creative power' (in *Bṛh. Up*. quoting *Ṛg Veda*) and once (in *Śvet. Up*. 4, 9-10) where it is said that "*prakṛti* is *māyā* and the *māyin* is the Great Lord." It is also used once (in *Praśna Up*. 1, 16), not however as denoting a kind of power, but a vice, deceitfulness, which is said to be absent from the stainless Brahma-world. A third meaning of *māyā*, magic, the extraordinary and deluding power of the magician, had moreover found a scope in Buddhist lore as a useful comparison. Śaṅkara also found it useful for comparison but to illustrate his own point which was that the *māyin* is not affected by his own magic, and his effects are totally dependent on him.

Radhakrishnan laboured much over the doctrine of *māyā* which, he says, "is the chief characteristic of the Advaita system". The doctrine holds that the world is unreal. Then "what is the relation between the real *Brahman* and the unreal world? For Śaṅkara, the question is an illegitimate one, and so impossible of answer."[18] In this Radhakrishnan interprets the rather few passages of Śaṅkara that speak of *māyā* in the light of posterior commentaries, which on occasion put questions and develop a doctrine of *māyā* much beyond what the *ācārya* had said. The chapter is intricate and demands a critical examination sentence by sentence. Since this cannot be done here, the following corrective suggestions are proposed.

An 'extraordinary power' is difficult to comprehend; it is puzzling, eludes our grasp, and thus connotes our ignorance. Both the power displayed by the magician and its effects are misapprehended, appearing different from what they are. *Māyā*, in the writings of Śaṅkara, is the *Brahman*'s power similarly misapprehended by our innate *avidyā*. Anthropomorphism and chrematomorphism affect our erroneous viewing of it and its effects, and projects upon them all kinds of superimpositions. Because it is the original matrix, it is called *prakṛti* and Śaṅkara has to take care that it be not identified with the Sāṁkhya *prakṛti*, *pradhāna* or *avyakta* ('undeveloped') (*B.S.Bh*. 1, 4, 3 seq.). Both of them presuppose that the effects pre-exist as possible 'futures' (*bhāviṣya*) in their cause (*satkāryavāda*), but the two systems understand this differently: "We admit only a previous state [of the world] dependent on the highest Lord, not an independent state" (*B.S.Bh.* 1,4, 3). But even this formulation is still tinged with *avidyā* for it imagines a state of potentiality prior to production as if the 'absolutely complete power of *Brahman*' proceeded through phases. "That causal potentiality is of the nature of *avidyā*... it is of the nature of an illusion; it is a universal sleep..." (*B.S.Bh.* 1, 4, 3). And neither is there really a process in which the supreme cause would be engaged (as men are engaged) in the process of production: *Brahman* is not an artisan (*kartṛ*). As Radhakrishnan says, "the Absolute always abides in its own nature."[19] In spite of the fact that the texts Śaṅkara comments on use no other term than *pariṇāma* to designate causation, he eliminates all idea of a transformation of the *Brahman*-cause: "the passages about *Brahman* modifying itself into the form of this world are merely to be applied as means for the cognition of the absolute *Brahman*... changeless" (*B.S.Bh.* 2, 1, 14). He had said elsewhere that "the 'names-and-forms' are identical with the *ātman* in their unmanifested state" (*Ait. Up. Bh.* 1, 1, 2); here he refers to them as *avidyā* and conceives them as "germinal principles of evolution called *nāma-rūpa*, whose essence is *avidyā*; upon them depend omniscience, etc. [understood as *guṇas* of *Brahman*]." (*B.S.Bh.* 2, 1, 14)

Radhakrishnan examines many other superimpositions wrought by *avidyā* upon the idea of the causal power of *Brahman*, but he fails to distinguish the 'absolutely complete power of *Brahman*' from our misunderstandings of it and is inclined to reject the teaching of *Brahman*'s causality. Yet the strength of this teaching and of his own philosophical sense prevents him from taking this fatal step and he prefers to say both that *māyā* is incomprehensible and that:

> If *Brahman* is to be viewed as the cause of the world, it is only in the sense that the world rests on *Brahman*, while the latter is in no way touched by it, and the world which rests on *Brahman* is called *māyā* [and] the principle assumed to account for the appearance of *Brahman* as the world is also called *māyā*.[20]

The first part of this statement deserves highlighting. Radhakrishnan is convinced that *māyā* can only be conceived as an endowment of the Lord, and the Lord only as the *saguṇa Brahman*, which alone is the cause. He affirms this despite of having mentioned[21] that *Īśvara* is pure being (*san-mātram*: being only). For him, this conception of the causal Lord of *māyā* is a product of logic. He writes, "there is a gap between the intuited *Brahman* which is devoid of logical determinations and the conceived *Brahman* which is the productive principle".[22] We see here how his distinction between a logical conception and intuition, which he superimposed upon Śaṅkara's own unitary understanding of his testimonial science (*śabda-śāstra*), leads him to write:

> The criticism that Śaṅkara leaves us with an unbridgeable chasm at the summit of things, between the *nirguṇa Brahman* of which nothing can be said and the *saguṇa Brahman* which embraces and unifies all experience, is due to a confusion of standpoints.[23]

Radhakrishnan says that not the *nirguṇa Brahman* but the *saguṇa* is properly God and personal God. Since terms like 'person,' 'personality,' etc. are absent from the vocabulary of Śaṅkara, we could neglect this opinion. But it is important to notice that Radhakrishnan's understanding of these terms differs from the meaning they traditionally had in Christianity since coined in the fourth century AD and since Boethius fixed it with precision around 500 AD. The traditional meaning of 'person' is 'intellectual subsistent.' This entails no limitation of 'intellectuality'; it can be finite or infinite; Christianity applies it to the three of the divine Trinity as well as to human or angelic beings. It does not demand a real distinction of subject and object, or of knower-knowing-known-knowledge in every person. In the Christian God there is no such distinction any more than in the *nirguṇa Brahman*. The latter is thus 'personal' as well as the first.[24]

Radhakrishnan, following a recent usage which began in the nineteenth century with Hegel, uses the term as modelled on the human person, the individual, whose knowing depends on external objects opposed to him as subject. It is this inferior type of personality which he applies anthropomorphically on the *saguṇa Brahman* and which he can obviously not apply to the *nirguṇa*. He would only be right if 'person' had to be either anthropic or anthropomorphic. He says:

> *Īśvara* is not pure consciousness (*caitanya*) but a self-conscious personality.... Knowledge, self-consciousness and personality are possible only if there are objects. Omniscience (*sarvajñatva*) characterises God.... *Brahman*, whose nature is knowledge, becomes a knower when he is confronted with an object to be known. Śaṅkara agrees with Rāmānuja and Hegel in thinking that a not-self remains an integral element of personality.[25]

This formulation has proved to be a great hindrance in inter-religious dialogue.

For Śaṅkara, language—which is the same for *Śruti* as for mundane usage (*vyavahāra*)—is structured in accordance with the manner of our sensitive-rational knowing. By its means, we can express (*vac*) the objects of our mundane awareness in terms of noun, quality, verb, relational prepositions, etc. Thus we can define (set aside from all the rest and properly characterize) a certain type of flower as a "big, blue, sweet-smelling lotus".[26]

But the *Śruti* has to speak of the transmundane, the *Brahman* which stands beyond any category of genus, difference, species, action (as process), quality or relation (as endowments), and thus beyond the expressive power of speech. How can it nevertheless do it with correctness and precision? This is a question of primary importance to a *Śrutivādin* (a scripturalist) and to which Radhakrishnan seems to have paid no great attention.

The *Śruti* and the *Śrutivādin* rely on the second-level power of language, the power to indicate (*lakṣ*) what it cannot express. According to the context, words become significative even when they are used beyond their primary area of signification, their *gocara*, but within their range of similarity. For most words, this is possible not according to their denotation but only according to their connctations. Their indicative capacity is only metaphoric and thus extrinsic. As metaphors (*upacara*), many words are used in the *Śruti* to indicate the power, majesty, greatness, all-pervasiveness, etc. of the *Brahm*an. They are inappropriate for defining its essence but Śaṅkara explains their anagogic function: how they help the meditator to focus upon the supreme reality.

Fortunately, some words like 'being' or 'reality,' 'knowledge,' 'self,' etc. whose denotation (what he calls the 'proper meaning' or *svārtha*) is not restricted by any limitation of materiality or finitude, can be infinitized. Their indicative power can then be intrinsic. This happens in such essential definitions (*svarūpalakṣaṇa*) of *Brahman* as: *satyam jñānam-anantam brahm'-eti* (*Taitt. Up. Bh.* 2, 1), i.e., "*Brahman* is reality-knowledge-infinite." Śaṅkara explains how these terms lead us to disengage their *svārtha* from materiality and finiteness and to elevate them to their highest reach. The second term *jñānam* disengages the first *satyam* from the material mode of being, and the third *anantam* infinitizes them both, thus elevating them to their supreme level of proper signification. It is thus according to their supreme, and yet intrinsic, meaning (*paramārthataḥ*) that such words can indicate properly the transcendent Essence. This Essence is defined but not expressed (*tal-lakṣyate na tū-'cyate*). Thus, even in his highest claim, Śaṅkara remains a 'negative theologian,' an apophatic. This smoothens the sharp edge of his propositional theology and saves it from being rationalistic (like the doctrine of Hegel, which seems to have unduly fascinated Radhakrishnan).

Any theological talk about the transcendent requires this recourse to extreme senses. To a man who had called him "good master," Jesus said "why do you call me good? Only one is good, God." Indeed, in such extreme senses, positive words can apply only to God. This is why Śaṅkara says that the *Brahman* alone is being, i.e., *paramārthataḥ sat*, and all the rest is non-being (*asat*). It is, however, not non-being (*asat* in the supreme sense), i.e., an impossibility such as the son of a barren woman. Indeed, it is an effect of *sat* and shares in *sattā* (real existence) but it is *sad-asad-vilakṣaṇa*, unable to be defined by either *sat* or *asat* in their supreme senses. Creatures are real in as much as totally dependent effects can be. They are not real as *avidyā* imagines them, as autogenic, self-supported, self-sufficient monads.

Radhakriṣhnan made a most searching enquiry in all the authentic (and some unauthentic) writings of Śaṅkara. But he wanted so much to present him as a rational and independent philosopher that he did not appreciate his essential scripturalism. He secularized Śaṅkara's faith-reliance on the *Śruti* as a recourse to intuition, and thus failed to recognize the exact place of intuition as pursued by *Brahmajijñāsā*: hopefully at the end of the protracted work of hermeneutics (with its three well-known phases: *śravaṇa, manana, nididhyāsana*[27]). Opposing intuition to logic, he saw the latter at work, where Śaṅkara sees only superimpositions made by *avidyā*; Śaṅkara limits the theological competence of the logical mind but never belittles the solidity of its principles and its capacity to integrate the *vidyā* offered by a reliable testimony such as the *Śruti*. Thus Radhakrishnan did not fully escape the pitfalls of which he was aware. He indulged 'a personal bias' and decided to interpret an ancient system in terms acceptable to modern minds. Under pressure of his 'creative logic' he somewhat curtailed his 'philologist's task' of perfectly reconnoitring Śaṅkara's own conception of *Brahmajijñāsā*. He misapprehended Śaṅkara's conviction that *avidyā* can be overcome only by the teaching of the 'great sayings,' that these work in complementarity and that none of them is to be sublated; that their terms, such as cause, self, reality, etc. are significant only in their supreme sense, beyond all anthropomorphism but still within apophatism; that this level of signification is attainable only by way of painstaking hermeneutics (demanding not only acumen but also ascetical virtues which I failed so far to mention); that its realization in intuitive manner depends on divine grace.[28]

Notes

[1] [First published in *Radhakrishnan Centenary Volume*, ed. G. Parthasarathi, D.P. Chattopadhyaya (Delhi: Oxford University Press, 1989) 53-70. Reprinted here with permission of Oxford University Press, Delhi.]

[2] S. Radhakrishnan, ["Religion And Society,"] *Transactions of the Indian Institute of Advanced Study* **1** (1965) 39-42 *passim.*

[3] S. Radhakrishnan, "Fragments of a Confession," *Radhakrishnan Reader*, ed. P.N. Rao, K. Gopalaswami and S. Ramakrishnan (Bombay: Bharatiya Vidya Bhavan, 1969) 22.

[4] Radhakrishnan, "Fragments of a Confession" 24-27 *passim.*

[5] [H. Jacobi, "On Māyāvāda," *Journal of the American Oriental Society* **33** (1913) 52 note 2. T.R. Chintamani, "Śaṅkara—The Commentator on the Māṇḍūkya Kārikās," *Proceedings of the Third Oriental Conference* (Madras, 1924) 419-421.]

[6] [V. Bhattacharya, "Śaṅkara's Commentaries on the Upaniṣads," *Sir Asutosh Mookerjee Silver Jubilee Volume*, vol. III, part 2 (Calcutta, 1925) 103-110.]

[7] [S.K. Belvalkar, *Shree Gopal Basu Mallik Lectures on Vedānta Philosophy*, pt. 1 (Poona, 1929) 218. O. Lacombe, *L'Absolu selon le Vedānta* (Paris: Geuthner, 1937) 23 seems to accept Belvalkar's list of the authentic works of Śaṅkara, but he is not beyond making reference to the *Māṇḍ. Up. Bh*: see ibid. 168-169.]

[8] For bibliographical references, see Sengaku Mayeda, "On the Author of the *Māṇḍūkyopaniṣad* and the *Gauḍapādīya-Bhāṣya*," *The Adyar Library Bulletin* **31-32** (1967-68) 73-94.

[9] Radhakrishnan, "Fragments of a Confession" 26.

[10] See my "*Māyā* or *Ajñāna*," *Indian Philosophical Annual* **2** (1966) 220-225 [= ch. 6 above].

After writing the present paper, I happened to read Sengaku Mayeda's introduction to his critical edition of Śaṅkara's *Upadeśasāhasrī* (Tokyo: The Hokuseido Press, 1973) [*Śaṅkara's Upadeśasāhasrī*, 2 vols., tr. and ed. S. Mayeda (Delhi: Motilal Banarsidass, 2006)]. I found in it an authoritative confirmation of some of the main points of my understanding of Śaṅkara. I summarize it as follows:

i) *Avidyā* in *B.S.Bh.* is identical with innate *mithyā-jñāna* (false knowledge) rather than being the material cause from which the latter would originate. Śaṅkara considers it to be a psychic affection (*kleśa*) rather than a cosmic power (*śakti*). The 'state of nescience' (*avidyāvasthā*) is opposed to the 'state of the supreme goal' (*paramārthāvasthā*). The effects of *avidyā* are not denoted by terms like *upādāna-kāraṇa* or *prakṛti* but by *adhyāropa, nimitta, bīja, kṛta* and such like. *Avidyā* is not called *anādi* (beginningless) like eternal substances but is an attribute of *saṃsāra* (the world of change). Unlike later Advaitins, Śaṅkara neither analyzes it in detail nor calls it *anirvacanīya*.

ii) *Avyākṛte nāmarūpe*, the unevolved names-and-forms, are according to *B.S.Bh.* the seeds or primary 'materials' of the world in conformity with *Chāṇḍ Up.* 6, 3, 2; 8, 14, 1. They are the eternal *ākṛtis* or forms comprised in the fullness of the *Brahman's* essence. As such they are *tattvānyatvābhyām anirvacanīya* (not expressible as 'this' or 'other than this'). Contrast this with the *avidyā / māyā* of later Advaita which is said to be *sadasadbhyām anirvacanīya* (not expressible as 'being' or 'non-being').

iii) *Māyā*: the frequency of *māyā, nāmarūpa* and *avidyā* in *B.S.Bh.* is in the proportion of 2:7:10. Śaṅkara never calls his doctrine *māyāvāda*. Compared to the primary terms *Brahman* or *Ātman*, *māyā* is of quite secondary importance. Most frequently, *māyā* means 'creative power' and very rarely 'fraud'; when it means magic, it is usually a term of comparison (as signified by *yathā*, *iva*, *–vad*). Such comparisons are made to suggest either the case of the causing or the illusoriness of the effect (as perceived through superimposition by the spectator) or the fact that, like the magician, the *Ātman* is unaffected by his creating.

iv) *Īśvara* is a frequent term of Śaṅkara writings. In *B.S.Bh.*, (*param*) *brahma(n)* and *paramātman* are interchangeable with *Īśvara*.

v) *Ānanda* (bliss): Śaṅkara characterizes the *Brahman* as *ānanda* only when the texts he interprets force him to mention it. The appellation *saccidānanda* is posterior to Śaṅkara.

vi) *Vivarta*: this term does not come at all in *B.S.Bh.* The latter makes use of the verbal form *vivartate* and its participle *vivartamana* but with no illusionistic connotation.

[11] S. Radhakrishnan, *Indian Philosophy* (London, 1929) **1**:176.

[12] S. Radhakrishnan, *Indian Philosophy* (London, 1929) **2**:515.

[13] Radhakrishnan, *Indian Philosophy* **2**:518.

[14] Radhakrishnan, *Indian Philosophy* **2**:445.

[15] Radhakrishnan, *Indian Philosophy* **1**:671-672. [From the 'Appendix: Further Consideration of Some Problems,' which first appeared as "*Indian Philosophy*: Some Problems," *Mind*, New Series **35**/138 (1926) 154-180.]

[16] Radhakrishnan, *Indian Philosophy* **2**:505 seq.

[17] Radhakrishnan, *Indian Philosophy* **2**:519.

[18] Radhakrishnan, *Indian Philosophy* **2**:565-574.

[19] Radhakrishnan, *Indian Philosophy* **2**:567.

[20] Radhakrishnan, *Indian Philosophy* **2**:573-574.

[21] Radhakrishnan, *Indian Philosophy* **2**:546.

[22] Radhakrishnan, *Indian Philosophy* **2**:561.

[23] Radhakrishnan, *Indian Philosophy* **2**:561.

[24] See my "Is the Concept of Person Congenial to Śaṅkara Vedānta?" *Indian Philosophical Annual* **8** (1972) 199-205 [= *Brahman and Person: Essays by Richard De Smet*, ch. 8].

[25] Radhakrishnan, *Indian Philosophy* **2**:556.

[26] Radhakrishnan, *Indian Philosophy* **2**:490, note 4: "An attribute (*viśeṣaṇa*) is an invariable distinguishing feature, as blueness in a lotus. A limitation (*upādhi*) is separable, distinguishable feature, as the red flower standing in the vicinity of a crystal which seems to be red owing to its presence."

[27] Śaṅkara wrote in *Bṛh. Up. Bh.* 11, 4, 10 that "*Śruti* is *pratyakṣa* (immediate knowledge)". The term *pratyakṣa* designates (i) sense-perception, especially through sight or through the other outer senses, (ii) mental perception through the inner sense, as in Yoga, (iii) the perfect intuition (*sākṣātkāra*) which is the goal of *Brahmajijñāsā* based on *Śruti*. This is an important reason why *Śruti* is called *pratyakṣa*—rather than because it was 'seen' by the *ṛṣis*. But the main reason is because, like sense-perception, it is direct and independent: "The fundamental texts about *Brahman* produce instruction as their immediate result, just as information regarding the sense-objects ensues as soon as the objects are approximated to the senses" (*B.S.Bh.* 1, 1, 1). "With regard to the matter stated, the authority of the Veda is independent (*nirapekṣam*), just as the light of the sun is the direct means of our knowledge of form and colour". (*B.S.Bh.* 2, 1, 2)

[28] Two complementary studies may be consulted with profit: Ram Pratap Singh, "Radhakrishnan's Substantial Reconstruction of the Advaita of Śaṅkara," *Philosophy East and West* **16** (1966) 5-32 [see excerpts in "Śaṃkara and Radhakrishnan," *Radhakrishnan Reader: An Anthology*, ed. K.M. Munshi, R.R. Diwadkar, P. Nagaraja Rao, K. Gopalaswami, and S. Ramakrishnan

(Bombay: Bharatiya Vidya Bhavan, 1969) 615-628]; and the unattributed criticism at the end of Rao et al., *Radhakrishnan Reader* (Bombay, 1969) [607-614 = "(Editors') Introduction," *Radhakrishnan: Comparative Studies in Philosophy Presented in Honour of His Sixtieth Birthday*, ed. W.R. Inge, L.P. Jacks, M. Hiriyanna, E.A. Burtt, and P.T. Raju (London: Allen & Unwin / New York: Humanities Press, 1951, 1968) 9-15.]

14

RADHAKRISHNAN'S SECOND PRESENTATION OF ŚAṄKARA'S TEACHING[1]

Radhakrishnan's first integral exposition of Śaṅkara's writings formed ch.8 of Vol. II of his *Indian Philosophy*. On the occasion of the international seminar which took place in Delhi on February 14-17, 1989, to honour his birthday centenary, I made of it a critical study which has now been published as ch. 7 of the *Radhakrishnan Centenary Volume*.[2]

Some twenty years later, he wrote his second presentation of Śaṅkara which I now wish to study in similar fashion. It is ch. 13A of the first volume of *History of Philosophy Eastern and Western*, 1952. The idea of preparing such a wide ranging book had first been mooted by the great educationist Maulana Abul Kalam Azad who had become Minister of Education in the first cabinet of independent India. It was received with enthusiasm by Radhakrishnan who shared the same intercultural horizon and felt that such a work would "demonstrate the unity of human aspirations which transcend geographical and national limitations and perhaps lead to a better international understanding."[3] He became the Chairman of its Editorial Board and accepted to write the chapter on Śaṅkara.

In this chapter his intellectual generosity is immediately revealed in his initial declaration that "we have to harmonize the two sets of statements" in the Upaniṣads, the one that identifies *Brahman*, individual soul and world, and the other which distinguishes them.[4] But he will not come back upon this declaration to substantiate it.

1. Gauḍapāda and Śaṅkara

In *Indian Philosophy* he had laid importance on the *Māṇḍūkya-Kārikā-bhāṣya* whose attribution to Śaṅkara was and still is controverted. Here, he speaks only of the *Māṇḍūkya-Kārikā* which is Gauḍapāda's "attempt to combine in one whole the negative logic of the Mādhyamikas with the positive idealism of the Upaniṣads."[5] Radhakrishnan is clearly in sympathy with this grandguru of Śaṅkara because he could accept Buddhistic doctrines when they were not in conflict with his own Advaita. He says, "his liberal views enabled him to accept doctrines associated with Buddhism and adjust them to the Advaita design."[6]

However, he does not fail to sort out the differences between Gauḍapāda and Śaṅkara: The first holds the unreality of the external objects of perception and links them with the objects seen in dream, thus welcoming the subjectivism associated with *Vijñānavāda*. But "Śaṅkara is anxious to free his system from that subjectivism." Further, Gauḍapāda integrates the nihilism of Nāgārjuna and declares that the subject is as unreal as the object; he denies the validity of causation and the possibility of change, hence of both bondage and liberation; he traces the empirical world to *avidyā* or, in Nāgārjuna's idiom, to *saṁvṛti* and he declares the highest state to be beyond the reach of the predicates of existence, non-existence, both or neither. On the contrary, "Śaṅkara used every device to defend his belief in the reality of a transcendental non-dual *Brahman*.... There is considerable measure of similarity between Śaṅkara's view and Buddhist doctrine. Śaṅkara used some of the reasonings made familiar by the Buddhist dialectic in support of his non-dualism. [But] there is no doubt that Śaṅkara's views are a straightforward development of the doctrines of the *Upaniṣads* and the *Brahma-sūtra*."[7]

This is a well-balanced appreciation. Regrettably, however, he adds a remark which echoes the assertions of some scholars of his time but which more recent buddhology would reject: "Unfortunately we are inclined to forget that Buddhism also developed on the foundations which were already laid in the Upaniṣads. The two tendencies of the Vedānta and Buddhism are parallel developments out of common background."[8] Actually, none of the traditions which specialists consider as probably close to the time of the Buddha would suggest that he knew anything about the Upaniṣads.

2. The Sources of Śaṅkara's Doctrine

Regarding this topic, Radhakrishnan's interpretation remains ambiguous. To this section he gives the title, 'Authority, Intuition, Reason,' which already weakens the exclusive reliance of Śaṅkara on the *Śruti*. Then he begins it with the declaration, "In the interpretation of texts, Śaṅkara is faithful to the spirit of the teachings of the Upaniṣads rather than to their letter."[9] This affirmation is supported with a quotation from *Taitt. Up. Bh.* 1, 2, 1 in which Śaṅkara speaks of the primacy of the meaning (*artha*), a term more precise than 'spirit.' Then he says, "He claims for his views not only the authority of the Scriptures but also intrinsic reasonableness and direct experience."[10] He no longer says, as in *Indian Philosophy* **2**:445, that reliance on this intrinsic reasonableness makes Śaṅkara's non-dualism "a great example of a purely philosophical scheme." But he still considers scriptural authority, intrinsic reasonableness and direct experience as "three different types of knowledge," as he writes in the next sentence. And, nevertheless, he still tends to consider the *Śruti* as if it were intuition since "only direct experience can bring us into contact with reality."[11] Did Śaṅkara not write in *Bṛh. Up. Bh.* 11, 4, 10 that "*Śruti* is *pratyakṣa*"? And did he not say that *Śruti* is what the primordial seers 'saw' or 'heard'? And that the enquiry into *Brahman* is *avagati-paryanta*, culminating intuitive penetration? But these statements concerning origin and goal do not mean that the enquiry-process is itself imbued with intuition. So long as he is enquiring he does not yet experience. And yet the *Śruti* is *pratyakṣa* objectively, in itself, as Śaṅkara explains in *B.S.Bh.* 1, 1, 1: "The fundamental texts about *Brahman* produce instruction as their immediate result, just as information regarding the sense-objects ensues as soon as the objects are approximated to the senses." The simile he uses in 2, 1, 2 points even more clearly to *pratyakṣatā* as an objective quality of *Śruti*: "With regard to [the *Brahman*] the authority of the Veda is independent (*nirapekṣa*), just as the light of the sun is the direct means of our knowledge of form and colour."

Radhakrishnan knows and refers to this text but he still seems to think that *Brahmajijñāsā* is intuitive all along and not only in its very termination.

3. The Role of Ignorance in *Brahmajijñāsā*

When interpreting an author it is perhaps advisable to pay attention to his manner of presenting and justifying his undertaking. Śaṅkara, before embarking on *Brahmajijñāsā*, makes us realize a congenital (*naisargika*) procedure of our mind which he says is caused by wrong knowledge (*mithyā-jñāna-nimitta*): that of superimposing the Self and its attributes upon the Non-Self and vice versa. Then he defines carefully 'superimposition' in general, explains the terms of this remarkable case of superimposition, and defends the reasonability of asserting it as a fact. And he concludes: "this superimposition thus defined, learned men consider to be *avidyā*."

Obviously, these men are learned in the Brahma-knowledge derived from the *Śruti*. And it is the *Śruti* alone which reveals the metaphysical dimension of this superimposition. Its opposite, they call *vidyā*. This they define as "the ascertainment of the true nature of that which is [the Self] by means of the discrimination of that [non-Self]. "Since this is *vidyā* in a supreme sense, I may be allowed the convention that I shall write it with a capital as *Vidyā* and its opposite as *a-Vidyā* (whereas *Avidyā* would mean complete absence of any knowledge). *Vidyā* can be obtained only from the *jñāna-kāṇḍa* of the *Śruti*, namely, the Upaniṣads in their great sayings (*mahāvākya*).

It is by grasping firmly the correct meaning of the *mahāvākyas* that the desired discrimination takes place. Basically, this happens through the first part of *Brahmajijñāsā* which is *śravaṇa*; it has then to be confirmed rationally through *manana*; and finally appropriated in *nididhyāsana*. Such is the whole process which leads to the perfect ascertainment which one desires to attain. But let us note that *śravaṇa*, its first step, is itself a complex process of purification and elevation: the terms of the *mahāvākyas* that refer to the Self have to be purified of all their empirical and finite connotations and their radical denotation (*svārtha*) thus purified has to be elevated to the supreme degree. Thus one attains their supreme sense (*paramārtha*) beyond any superimposition.

It is not in this way that Radhakrishnan's exposition proceeds. Of *a-Vidyā* he speaks only on p. 280 while writing about the *jīva* (misconceived individual). What he says sums up only the first part of the Śaṅkarian text which I have just exposed. He does not seem to have found there the whole profile of Śaṅkara's undertaking. When earlier[12] he begins to describe the tenets of Śaṅkara, he quickly says that "Śaṅkara interprets the Scripture, argues the case and holds that *Brahman* is an object of intuition." Then without attending to the process that may hopefully lead to that intuition, he rushes to describe the latter.

4. The Role of the Great Sayings (*Mahāvākyas*)

Still he bases his exposition of *Brahman* on the *mahāvākyas*. From the pedagogical standpoint, these may be said to form a hierarchy of five types which point to the *Brahman* in mutual control and complementarity:

1. the *neti neti* (not thus, not thus) type, which points to it as free from any superimpositions;
2. the *pūrṇam* (full) type, which points to it as supremely perfect Reality;
3. the world-relational *yataḥ* (that from which) type, which points to its paramount and universal causality of the world;
4. the ego-relational *Tattvamasi* (that thou art) type, which points to it as the innermost and uppermost *Ātman* of the knower and doer;
5. the *satyam-jñānam-anantam* (reality-knowledge-infinite) type, which does not[13] express but indicates correctly the inexpressible essence of the *Brahman-Ātman*.

Under these five types can be ranged all the great sayings which comprise the essential teaching of the Upaniṣads. All of them are thus infallible. None of them can be sublated by any of the other ones.

(1) and (2) are normative for the interpretation of the other three. (1) prescribes that we purify their terms from all anthropomorphisms and other superimpositions. (2) prescribes

that we elevate their purified terms to their supreme degree of signification.

Radhakrishnan, although he does not clarify these principles which pervade the exegesis of Śaṅkara, turns spontaneously, first, to the *neti neti* passage which, he says, "tells us that *Brahman* is absolutely non-empirical."[14] Then he turns to the second, "ultimate reality, for Śaṅkara, is fullness of being"[15] and to the third, "this universe has its root in being (*san-mūla*), has its basis in being (*sad-āśraya*), and is established in being (*sat-pratiṣṭha*).[16] Finally, inverting the above suggested order, he first brings forth the essential definition, "the ultimate reality is being and consciousness"[17] and then the fourth, "ultimate reality, though it transcends all distinctions of subject and object, is not wholly unknown to us for it is our very self.... *Ātman* is not the subject (*pramātṛ*) but it is the basis of the subject-object distinction.... What appears as not-self (*anātma-vastu*) has its being in the self. It is *bhūta-vastu* which we have only to acknowledge. *Brahman* is being (*sat*), consciousness (*cit*), and bliss (*ānanda*)."[18]

This turning to the *mahāvākyas* and in that order reveals in Radhakrishnan an essential scripturalism (*śrutivāda*) which, in his haste to focus on intuition, he scarcely deigns to avow.

However, not paying enough attention to the above-recalled definition of *Vidyā*[19] as the opposite of all forms of superimposition on *Brahman*, and the exegetical principle that all the *mahāvākyas*, including the *yataḥ* type, are infallible only as to their purified and supremely elevated meaning, he continues after many to misunderstand the assertion of divine causality and Śaṅkara's teaching regarding the double form of *Brahman*, *nirguṇa* and *saguṇa*.

He writes: "The supreme *Brahman* when viewed as the creator and governor of the universe is said to be *sa-guṇa Brahman* or the personal God (*dvi-rūpam hi brahmāvagamyate, nāma-rūpa-vikāra-bhedopādhi-viśiṣṭam, tad-viparītam sarvopādhi-varjitam*)."[20]

This quotation, which he leaves untranslated, comes from Śaṅkara's commentary on the *Vedānta Sūtra* 1, 1, 11. There he first concludes that the Vedānta-texts which he has exhibited under the first eleven *sūtras* are capable of proving, and have finally settled, that the all-knowing *Brahman* is the general cause of the world, and further, "that all the Vedānta-texts whatever maintain an intelligent cause." Then he puts the question, "What reason is there for the subsequent part of the Vedānta-sūtras?" He replies with the words quoted by Radhakrishnan: "*Brahman* is apprehended under two forms; in the first place, as qualified by limiting conditions owing to the multiformity of the changes of names-and-forms; in the second place as being the opposite of this, i.e., free from all limiting conditions whatsoever." He does not then say, like Radhakrishnan, "Both are valid forms of *Brahman*."[21] Rather he explains that the *Śruti* presents this double form of *Brahman* "according as it is the object either of knowledge or of Nescience" and that, therefore, "an enquiry will have to be undertaken into the meaning of the texts, in order that a settled conclusion may be reached concerning that knowledge of the *Ātman* which leads to instantaneous release." Finally, he already announces that the texts which connect *Brahman* with *upādhis* (limiting adjuncts) present it as an object of devout meditation (*upāsanā*) whereas those which present it as free from *upādhis* present it as the object of Knowledge.

Much later on, in 4, 3, 14, he puts the question, "But are there really two *Brahman*s, a higher one and a lower one?—Certainly they are two, for Scripture declares this." Then, he brings forth the expected objection, "This distinction of a higher and a lower *Brahman* stultifies the scriptural texts asserting non-duality.—Not so, we reply. The objection is removed by the consideration that names-and-forms as *upādhis* are due to Nescience."

We conclude that the highest form of *Brahman* is fully valid, as pertaining to Knowledge, but the lower form is ineffective for leading to Knowledge; it has validity only as a meditational device, says Śaṅkara, "whose fruit falls within the sphere of *sàṃsāra*, Nescience having not as yet been discarded."

Radhakrishnan makes the further assertion, "We have the interaction between the two (*nir-guṇa* and *sa-guṇa Brahman*) which is the cosmic process gradually realizing the values of spirit in its upward ascent from nothingness to the kingdom of God under *divine* (underlined by him) inspiration and influence."[22] This cannot properly be grounded in the writings of Śaṅkara.

5. The Status of the World

In this section Radhakrishnan makes a number of important assertions which derive from Śaṅkara but sometimes distort his teaching:

(a) "We deny only the existence of the world apart from or independent of *Brahman*."[23]

(b) "God is sometimes represented as the creator of the universe and *māyā* is then treated as the power or *Śakti* through which he creates. In this sense God is the material as well as the efficient cause of the universe."[24] Actually, it is not God or the lower *Brahman* who is thus cause in two ways. What Śaṅkara affirms is this: "*Brahman* [absolutely understood as in 1, 1, 2 before the distinction of the two *Brahman*s which begins to be made only from 1, 1, 12] has been defined as that from which there proceeds the origination, sustentation and retractation of this world.... This definition comprises alike the relation of substantive causality (i.e., of *upādāna*, the reality-providing cause, which need not be 'material') ... and the relation of operative causality (of the *nimitta-kāraṇa*, the structure-providing cause which gives shape and order and, hence, needs to be intelligent) .... The *Ātman* is the operative cause, because there is no other ruling principle, and the *upādāna kāraṇa* because there is no other substance from which the world could originate." (*B.S.Bh.* 1, 4, 23) Let us notice that in this *sūtra* both Bādarāyaṇa and Śaṅkara assert here the total sufficiency of *Brahman*'s causality which excludes all other proposed causes, especially unconscious ones like *prakṛti* or atoms. Later, in 2, 1, 14, Śaṅkara will purify the notion of *upādāna* as applied to *Brahman* by excluding from it *pariṇāma* in the sense of modification of the cause: "A number of passages, by denying all modifications of *Brahman*, teach it to be absolutely changeless (*kūṭastha*) .... And, being changeless, *Brahman* cannot be the substratum of varying attributes."

On other occasions Śaṅkara purifies further the notion of *Brahman*'s causality from such superimposition as necessity, dependence on instruments or other helps, desire for a fruit; he elevates it to supereminence as when he speaks of "the absolutely complete power of *Brahman*" (*B.S.Bh.* 2, 1, 24). This power belongs to the highest *Brahman* as Fullness which alone precontains and can reveal all the names-and-forms (cf. *B.S.Bh.* 1, 3, 41). *Brahman* is that Fullness; it has nothing, not even the kind of adjacent and dependent *māyā* or *prakṛti* held by some later Śaṅkarians and, in their wake, by Radhakrishnan.

(c) "*Brahman* with *prakṛti* or *māyā* is *sa-guṇa Brahman* or *Īśvara* comprehending the diversity of souls and objects. *Īśvara* as the lord of all existences is immanent in the cosmic process."[25]

In *B.S.Bh.*, the term *Īśvara* (lord) is, first (chronologically and by full right) attributed to the absolute *Brahman*, the object of *Vidyā*. It refers to the paramount rulership which, as we saw, belongs to the operative side of its total causality. The title of *Īśvara* is also given to the lower *Brahman*, the object of *upāsanā*, but in this case it lacks the sovereign transcendence of the first.[26]

(d) *Brahman* is real (*sat*). The world is not absolutely real but it is not *a-sat* or nothing. The world has empirical existence which is quite different from the eternal being of *Brahman* and absolute non-being.... *Brahman* [is] the basis of the empirical world."[27]

Śaṅkara, relying on the Indian theory of the different meanings, primary and secondary, of terms according to their contexts, expresses this more precisely: *Brahman* is *paramārthataḥ sat*, i.e., real in the supreme sense of the term; the son of a barren woman is *paramārthataḥ asat*, unreal in the supreme sense of the term. The world is *sad-asad-vilakṣaṇa* (I would write *Sad-Asad-vilakṣaṇa*), it cannot be characterized as Real or Unreal supremely understood.

(e) "It is often said that the world is an illusory appearance for Śaṅkara.... The self-existent character of the world persists so long as the knowledge of its rootedness in *Brahman* does not arise. In the state of enlightenment we realize that the world is only a manifestation of *Brahman*.... The world cannot be viewed as either real or unreal. It is inexpressible (*a-nirvacanīya*) .... [As such] it is sometimes called *māyā*.... It is of the nature of *mithyā* and is eternal.... The world rests on *Brahman* as the serpent on the rope and not *Brahman* on the world, not the rope on the serpent. According to Śaṅkara, the whole conception of causation applies within the realm of phenomena.... Causation cannot apply to a being that is essentially non-empirical."[28]

Actually, this restriction of causation to the realm of phenomena goes back to the Buddhist logician Dharmakīrti (c. 600-660). Śaṅkara does not appropriate it anywhere. As to "the self-existent character of the world," Radhakrishnan is right in distinguishing the pre-enlightenment and the enlightenment states. During the first, *a-Vidyā* reigns. Through superimposition of *Sat* on *a-Sat*, the world is viewed as self-existent, independent, eternal, made of monadic beings, intrinsically independent and linked among themselves only by extrinsic relations such as causation. When, thanks to the *mahāvākyas* of *Śruti* we enter into *Vidyā*, such superimpositions vanish like so many illusions and we realize the truth, namely, that the world and its beings are *totally effects*, ontologically and intrinsically dependent upon their total Cause, of which therefore they are imperfect manifestations, varied and graduated according to a scale of excellence, comparable to reflections (*ābhāsa*), distinct but never simply different from *Sat* (how could they since whatever they are is issued forth from it alone?) and constantly rooted in it (*San-mūla*), but in no way affecting this *kūṭastha* through mutation or loss or gain. This is the aspect of *Vidyā* which concerns the world. Since it is true, it can never be sublated but only better and better penetrated and appropriated.

Does Śaṅkara say that the world is *anirvacanīya*? Unlike Bhartṛhari and Maṇḍana Miśra, he never uses the phrase *sad-asadbhyām-anirvacanīya* but only *tattvānyatvābhyām anirvacanīya* for that which cannot be defined either as 'that' or as 'other than that.' And this is never the world but its objective potentiality in *Brahman*. Thus in *B.S.Bh.* 1, 1, 5 the question is put, "What was the object of *Brahman*'s thinking before the creation?" And his reply is, "The object of thinking is unevolved names and forms (*nāmarūpe avyākṛte*) which are not definable as 'that' or 'other' (*tattvānyatvābhyām anirvacanīya*) and which are going to be manifested." But let us note that they are quite definable in terms of reality since he says in *Ait. Up. Bh.* 1; 1, 2: "These *nāma-rūpas*, which are identical with the *Ātman* in their unmanifested state, can become the material elements (*upādāna-bhūte*) of the manifested universe." In *B.S.Bh.* 1, 4, 3, it is the undifferentiated *māyā* which is said to be *tattvānyatva nirūpanasya*, an equivalent expression. In *B.S.Bh.* 2, 1, 27, the phrase is again connected with the unevolved names-and-forms.

As to the world, Śaṅkara would never declare it undefinable since he has defined it as 'totally effect' and negatively as *Sad-Asad-vilakṣaṇa.*[29]

But is not the world "of the nature of *Mithyā*"? The world as known by the ignorant is, indeed, *mithyā*, because the ignorant superimposes upon the real world the nature and characteristics of the absolute Subject or *Sat*. But as known correctly by those who have been properly instructed in *Vidyā*, it is not false but true in the manner of an effect whose totality depends existentially on *Sat*. The ordinary *vyavahāra* thinking and speech lacks this metaphysical perspective and implies *dvaita*; this is why it has to be sublated by the *advaita* speech (of the *Śruti*) and thinking. This *advaita* thinking does not mean that we now apprehend the 'phenomenal nature' of the world. The world is not just phenomenal as in Buddhist *māyāvāda*—so, completely rejected by Śaṅkara[30]—but its ontological status is that of an effect, limited, impermanent, imperfect in being, intelligibility, reliability and finality, totally and constantly dependent on its *Sat*-Cause, but also manifesting it in diverse ways like so many reflections of it. It is *a-Sat* but all the same *sat* and not *Asat*.

(f) "We can never understand how the ultimate reality is related to the world of plurality, since the two are heterogeneous."[31]

This alleged heterogeneousness is denied by Śaṅkara when he asserts the *an-anyatva* (non-otherness) of the contingent beings from their *upādāna* cause. For instance, in *B.S.Bh.* 2, 1, 18: "It is impossible, even within hundreds of years, ever to bring about an effect which be different (*anya*) from its cause." Or in *Taitt. Up. Bh.* 2, 6, 1: "There exists in the past, present or future not one thing other (*anya*) than the *Ātman*, i.e., non-*ātman*, separated [from it] by space or time, utterly subtle, disconnected and remote [from it]."

(g) "*Īśvara's* power of self-expression... is called *māyā*. This energy of *Īśvara* becomes transformed into the *upādhi* or limitation, the unmanifested matter (*avyakta prakṛti*) from which all existence issues."[32]

This is falling back into Sāṁkhya, "our worst enemy" wrote Śaṅkara. He had taken trouble to 'de-Sāṁkhyanize' the language of the *Brahma-sūtra*, for instance, the term '*pariṇāma*'[33] of which he refused the implication of change in the *Brahman* when causing as *upādāna*. Among his followers the *māyāvādins* 're-sāṁkhyanized' his Vedānta and this is what the above statement of Radhakrishnan echoes.

6. The Individual Soul

Radhakrishnan devotes one page to this topic. It is of the same vein as the previous section: a mixture of Śaṅkara's teaching with later advaitism. The chief points of what he writes are these:

"The *jīva* or the individual soul is a composite of self and non-self.... Their wrong identification is the basis of all experience. Through identification with the limitations (*upādhi*) like the internal organ (*antaḥkaraṇa*) the self functions as enjoyer subject to rebirth or bondage.... *Jīva* is the empirical form or manifestation of *Brahman*.... When viewed in its true character... it is the *sākṣin* or the witness self. It is consciousness, pure and simple."[34]

This passage is derived from the end of Śaṅkara's introduction to his *B.S.Bh.* But we may look for further light in *B.S.Bh.* 1, 1, 1: "Everyone is conscious of the existence of [his] self, and never thinks 'I am not'.... But there is a conflict of opinions as to its special nature.... [opinions are exposed of which the last is the opinion of those Vedāntins with whom Śaṅkara agrees.] Others, finally, maintain that the Lord is the *Ātman* of the enjoyer (*atmā sā bhoktur-ity-'pare*)." Elsewhere he says, "the *Ātman* of the knower (*jñātuḥ*)" or "of the doer (*kartuḥ*)"—note the genitive. What is this enjoyer-knower-doer-ego? An elaborate answer is given in the *Upadeśasāhasrī* 18:[35]

"The appropriator (*abhimāna-kṛt*) is the ego-sense (*ahaṁ-kartṛ*) which always stands in proximity to this [*Ātman* which is pure consciousness, *upalabdhi*] and acquires a reflection of it (*tad-ābha*). Hence, there arises that complex [which will have to be discriminated] of the *Ātman* and what pertains to it (*ātmiya*), which is the sphere of 'I' and 'mine'." (*US* 18, 27)

"Only when there is a reflection (*ābhāsa*) [of the inner Witness on the ego-sense] do words [such as *aham, tvam*, by referring to the reflection] indicate indirectly (*lakṣayeyur*) the inner Seer (*pratyagdṛśim*). They cannot designate him directly in any way (*na sākṣāt tan abhidadhyuḥ kathaṃcana*)." (*US* 18, 29) Radhakrishnan did not speak in this second presentation of

Vedānta about the incapacity of words to express *Brahman* according to their primary (empirical) meaning (*mukhyārtha*) and of their capacity, according to their secondary meanings (*lakṣyārtha*), for 'indicating indirectly' the Ineffable on the basis of some similarity to it which is present in its reflections or other manifestations to which they refer primarily. Yet, it is an important contribution to Vedānta exegesis.

"Because the ego-sense bears a reflection of the *Ātman*, it is spoken about in terms of *Ātman* (*ātma-śabdaiḥ*); just as words pertaining to fire are applied to torches and the like though only indirectly and not directly (*parārthatvān-na cā-'njasā*)." (*US* 18, 30-31)

"The reflection of a face is different from the face since it conforms to the mirror; in turn, the face is different from its reflection since it does not conform to the mirror. The reflection of the *Ātman* in the ego-sense is comparable to the reflection of the face, while the *Ātman* is comparable to the face and different from its reflection. And yet (in ordinary thinking and speaking) the two remain undiscriminated." (*US* 18, 32-33a)

He then gives four opinions which attempt to define the ego as *saṃsārin* (migrating from birth to birth) but fail to discriminate correctly the *Brahman-Ātman-Sākṣin*, its reflection and the reflector. (*US* 18, 34-36) The reflection is a property (*dharma*) neither of the face (since it conforms to the peculiarities of the mirror and disappears with its removal whereas the face remains) nor of the mirror (since the latter ceases to contain it when the face is displaced.) Neither is it a property of both (since it is not seen when both are present but improperly placed) (cf. *US* 18, 37-39). But a reflection is also not a reality in its own right (*vastu*) since it entirely depends on a certain conjunction between face and mirror. "And thus it is taught by both the *śāstra* and reason that a reflection is not the reality (*ābhāsa-'sattvam*) [and the reflection of *Sat* in the ego-sense is *a-Sat*, not the Reality]." (cf. *US* 18, 39-43)

If the three are clearly discriminated, it is possible to interpret the *Tattvamasi* teaching through the indicative power (*lakṣaṇā*) of its terms. The primary meaning of *tvam* will be understood to refer to the *ābhāsa* mistakenly taken for the *Sākṣin* superimposed with the agency of the inner sense *buddhi*, but its secondary and supreme meaning will be understood to indicate the pure *Sākṣin* free of all superimpositions. (cf. *US* 18, 50-65)

In this teaching it is through the simile of face-reflection-mirror that Śaṅkara has demonstrated the total dependence of the *jīvātman* on the *Paramātman*, its being conditioned by a material support (*āśraya*, cf. *US* 18, 43a), immediately the inner sense or senses, and the fact that it is not Reality in its own right and that it has to be transcended for it is totally referring to another.

Indeed, it has the positive content of being totally an image of the supreme Self: its form is his own Form (*Svarūpa*). This is why it can be mistaken for Him, but this is why also "this *ābhāsa* is the only door (*dvāra*) through which we can cross from the primary [and empirical] to the secondary [and metempirical] meaning of *tvam*" (*US* 18, 110). This crossing is like an awakening from a painful dream (cf. *US* 18, 186); it is the "experience of the self" (*anubhavā-'tmanaḥ*). (*US* 18, 104) In this experience, the Witness is not 'witnessed' (as if it were an object and needed to be illuminated) but realized as Witness, absolute Subject, pure Consciousness. (cf. *US* 18, 136)

7. *Mokṣa* or Liberation

Śaṅkara affirms further that this realization is liberation and that it can happen even in this life (*jīvan-mukti*). *Mukti* is not a becoming—this would imply that the reflection is an independent entity changing into another—or a becoming clear (a tenet of the Bhāṭṭas), but a 'being known,' being established (*siddhi*) (*US* 18, 137-138) as *Sākṣin* and *Sat* of the *ābhāsa*. Compare "*Ātmā sā bhoktuḥ*" of *B.S.Bh.* 1, 1, 1.

Radhakrishnan gives us equivalently the same teaching on p. 281. But he adds some peculiar notations of his own.

First, he says, "It is wrong to assume (like Deussen whom he rebukes here) that in the state of liberation all plurality is annihilated. To get rid of the ego-sense is not to get rid of all life and existence." This he explains a little later in the following way: "The Absolute consciousness is viewed either as being 'without any limiting adjuncts or as being all the limiting adjuncts.' [He does not mention the source of this quotation.] It becomes the self of all salvation, is *sarvātma-bhāva*."

As to the *jīvan-mukta*, he says that "his life will be one of dedicated service to humanity, which is a spontaneous expression of his realization of the oneness of all." Some of those illumined souls "retain their individualities for fulfilling the functions assigned to them by the supreme Lord (cf. *B.S.Bh.* 3, 3, 32) .... They transform their energies into a living whole which expresses itself through love and power."[36]

8. Conclusion

We may end on this high note of altruism. Its root is in the *Brahma-sūtra* and its commentary but it has the accent of Radhakrishnan.... He had a very altruistic personality and the highest sense of responsibility in discharging the offices entrusted to him. The exposition we have examined was itself an altruistic present he was offering to mankind. In it he was concerned to adapt Śaṅkara's teaching to the comprehension of modern minds. He was not an indologist intent on the most faithful recovery of the *Ācārya's* thinking, unadulterated by that of later and lesser thinkers. But the very ability of his own presentation spurs us to question it and test its reliability. Scholars will agree that this is the best form of homage we can pay a great scholar on his birthday centenary.

Notes

[1] [First published as "Radhakrishnan's Second Presentation of Śaṅkara's Teaching," *Prajna: Kashi Hindu Vishvavidyalaya Patrika* **34** (1989) 83-96. Reprinted here with permission of De Nobili College, Pune, having had no response from *Prajna* despite several reminders.]

[2] G. Parthasarathi and D.P. Chattopadhyaya, *Radhakrishnan Centenary Volume* (Delhi: Oxford University Press, 1989) 53-70.

[3] S. Radhakrishnan, ed., *History of Philosophy Eastern and Western* (London: G. Allen & Unwin, 1952), [vol. 1,] "Editor's Preface" 6.

[4] Radhakrishnan, *History of Philosophy Eastern and Western* 272.

[5] Radhakrishnan 273.

[6] Radhakrishnan 273.

[7] Radhakrishnan 284.

[8] Radhakrishnan 284.

[9] Radhakrishnan 274.

[10] Radhakrishnan 274.
[11] Radhakrishnan 274.
[12] Radhakrishnan 274-275.
[13] [The 'not' is missing in the text, but seems to be required by the sense of the sentence.]
[14] Radhakrishnan 275.
[15] Radhakrishnan 275.
[16] Radhakrishnan 275.
[17] Radhakrishnan 275.
[18] Radhakrishnan 276. We may remark here that the *Saccidānanda* definition of *Brahman* is posterior to Śaṅkara.
[19] [The text reads *aVidya.*]
[20] Radhakrishnan 276.
[21] Radhakrishnan 276.
[22] Radhakrishnan 276.
[23] Radhakrishnan 276.
[24] Radhakrishnan 277.
[25] Radhakrishnan 276.
[26] See Sengaku Mayeda, *Śaṅkara's* Upadeśasāhasrī *critically edited* (Tokyo: Hokuseido Press, 1923), Introduction 38-39 [= 2006 ed. **1**:38-39: see above, ch. 13 note 10.]: "In the *BSBh, (param) brahma(n) and paramātman* are interchangeable with *īśvara.* Even in the case of *upāsanā, aparaṃ brahma, (param) brahma(n)* and *paramātman* may refer to *īśvara.*
[27] Radhakrishnan 277.
[28] Radhakrishnan 277-278.
[29] See Mayeda 32-34 [= 2006 ed. **1**:32-34]; Paul Hacker, "Eigentumlichkeiten der Lehre und Terminologie Śaṅkaras: *Avidyā, Nāmarūpa, Māyā, Īśvara,*" *ZDMG* [*Zeitschrift der Deutschen Morgenländischen Gesellschaft*] **10** (1950) 246-286, reprinted in his *Kleine Schriften* (Wiesbaden: Franz Steiner, 1978) 69-109; and Kiyoshima Hideki, "The Concept of *anirvacanīya* in Early Advaitavedānta," *Acta Asiatica* **57** (Tokyo: The Tōhō Gakkai, 1989) 45-60.
[30] See Daniel H.H. Ingalls, "Śaṅkara's Arguments against the Buddhists," *Philosophy East and West* **3** (1953-54) 291-306.
[31] Radhakrishnan 279.
[32] Radhakrishnan 279.
[33] [The text reads '*parimāṅa.*']
[34] Radhakrishnan 279-280.
[35] Mayeda, *Śaṅkara's* Upadeśasāhasrī *critically edited*, has established the authenticity of *Upadeśasāhasrī* in his introduction.
[36] Radhakrishnan 281.

15

THE CREATIVE WORD IN ŚĀṄKARA VEDĀNTA[1]

At the dawn of the Indian speculation about the origin of the universe, in the latest hymns of the *Ṛg Veda,* we find the idea that the whole comes from the One (*tad-Ekam,* that One: 10, 129) which is its sole and total Cause. But how?

The Vedic hymn-makers take up in turn all the models of causality which their experience suggests without privileging anyone of them. Among these models, we find the productive speech (*vāc*), whether command or sacral formula (10, 125), especially the verbal *brahman* (this is the original Vedic meaning of this term). This verbal *brahman,* the seer of *Atharvaveḍa* 4, 1 will soon eulogize as the "matrix of being and non-being," which seems to mean "of formed reality and its formless elements," i.e., of the entirety of the generated cosmos.

In the Upaniṣads, the sages go much further in their reflection about the creative One which they often name *Brahman* or *Ātman.* The term *Brahman* has by that time gained the meaning of 'ontological Absolute.' It designates the transcendent Being which is the universal Cause. This is why Śaṅkarācārya will link this term with the verbal root *bṛḥ* which has the causative sense of 'to make big,' 'to cause to grow.'

As to the term *ātman*, it is first of all the reflexive pronoun. As such it designates whatever can be referred to by a self-pointing gesture: the global subject, the body or one of its central parts such as the trunk. Further, the 'entities' corresponding to its ontological levels, namely, the physical self, the organic self, the animal self as well as any of its sensing functions, the intellectual self, the individual soul or *jīvātman* and also his supreme Cause since the latter is innermost to him. Let me remark that this goes beyond the normal use of 'self' in English. But the extension of the reflexive pronoun is larger in Sanskrit precisely because the subject is rarely viewed only as a unitary essence but rather generally as a *locus* or meeting-ground of a hierarchy of *ātmans*, each one of which in turn is "more subtle, greater and more interior than his inferior one," as Śaṅkara explains when commenting on *Kaṭha Up.* 1, 3, 10-11. The climax of subtleness, greatness and interiority is the *Puruṣa* or uppermost *Ātman*. The lower *ātmans* are his mere *upādhis* or extrinsic adjuncts; yet, "through the gradual rise of their excellence..., of their gradation as beings (*sat*), they reveal their Uppermost as the supreme *Ātman*, and Being". (*B.S.Bh.* 1, 1, 11) Seeing how the term '*ātman*' is used in such texts should hopefully make it less astonishing that the supreme *Brahman* is called the supreme *Ātman* of every knower and even of every contingent being (*bhūta*).

1. Śaṅkara and the Wishing Word of the All-Maker

Śaṅkara's sole purpose is to explain and harmonize the teachings of the Upaniṣads concerning the *Brahman*, as the *Paramātman* of all. Now this is the One "who is the Maker of these *Puruṣas* [the twelve cosmic lords of *Bṛh. Up.* 2, 1] and of whom this universe is the work". (*Kauṣītaki Up.* 4, 19)

Such a text speaks of the *Brahman* as the All-Maker. As such it is only like the potter who gives shape and beauty to the jar but does not by himself provide its clayish reality. However, like the potter it is intelligent and its productive activity depends on an intellectual and free decision. This 'intelligence' and 'free decision' have, of course, to be understood as modifying in no way the essence of the *Brahman*. Śaṅkara explains on several occasions this aspect of its causality:

> This *Ātman* who, being omniscient by nature, can think without body and thinking organs, being then the only existent, thought, 'Let me now create worlds', and, having thus thought, i.e., considered or visualized these worlds, he created them after that deliberation. (*Ait. Up. Bh.* 1, 1, 2)

> Passages like, 'He wished, may I be many, etc.' show that the *Ātman* is the agent in the independent activity which follows his reflection. (*B.S.Bh.* 1, 4, 24)

Is this activity (*pravṛtti*) a novelty which would add to the essence of the agent, as happens in our own case? Is it a motion which would be an ontological accident to that Substance? Śaṅkara replies, No, and explains how it is possible:

> A thing which is devoid of motion (*pravṛtti-rahita*), for instance, a magnet, can nevertheless be a *pravartaka,* i.e., a mover of other things.... So the Lord also, who is immanent in all, the *Ātman* of all, the all-knower and the all-power, can, although devoid of motion, set the whole world into activity (*B.S.Bh.* 2, 2, 2: *evam pravṛtti-rahito 'pi-īśvaraḥ sarvagataḥ sarvātmā sarvajñah sarva-śaktiś-ca san sarvam pravartayet*).

Let us notice here how carefully Śaṅkara eliminates all accidents, all *guṇas* from the simple (non-complex) divine essence which is nevertheless all-power owing to its ontological fullness. For the same reason, it needs no instrument or other help:

> The absolutely complete power of *Brahman* does not require to be supplemented by any extraneous help...; its high power is revealed as manifold, as inherent, acting as force and knowledge. (*B.S.Bh.* 2, 1, 24)
>
> [He creates] like gods and other such beings who, without availing themselves of any extraneous means, produce palaces, etc. by their mere intending which is effective in consequence of the peculiar power of those beings. (*B.S.Bh.* 2, 1, 25)

The peculiarity of the *Brahman's* power is that it is 'absolutely complete' because the *Brahman* is Fullness. But then how is it possible for it to have desires and wishes and to be impelled by them as we are by ours?

> Desires cannot thus impel the *Brahman*. How then [are they found in it]? As essentially Reality-Knowledge, and as pure in virtue of being their own *Ātman*; and, as such, they do not impel it.... Therefore, the *Brahman* is independent in its volitions; hence, it does not want things as yet unattained. (*Taitt. Up. Bh.* 2, 6, 1)

But does not every agent, even a mad man, act for a purpose?

> We see in everyday life that certain doings of princes or other men of high position who have no unfulfilled desire left have no reference to any extraneous purpose, but proceed from mere sportfulness.... Analogously, the activity of the Lord may be supposed to be mere sport (*līlā*),

> proceeding from his own nature without reference to any purpose.... And if in ordinary life we might possibly, by close scrutiny, detect some subtle motive even for sportful actions, we cannot do so with regard to the actions of the Lord, whose wishes are all fulfilled (*āpta-kāma*), as the *Śruti* says. (*B.S.Bh.* 2, 1, 33)

Of course, although creating is in no way useful to the Lord, it is useful to the creatures since "it is performed for their welfare". (*Bh. Gītā Bh.* 3, 24)

2. The All-Maker as Providing Reality to Its Effects

In the potter-jar model, the potter is the agent 'by which' (*yena*) the jar is shaped up. He need not provide out of his own essence the substantial reality of the jar and remain immanent to it. This is why it is called *nimitta-kāraṇa,* a cause required only 'for the occasion' of the molding of clay into a jar.

The clay is that 'from which' (*yataḥ*) the jar obtains its reality. It is an *upādāna-kāraṇa,* a substantive cause. In this case, it happens to be material but such a cause need not be material. This is why I prefer to call it a 'substantive or reality-providing' rather than a 'material'. cause for the latter appellation is misleading. It is out of itself that a substantive cause provides the reality of an effect and thus inheres in it, preserving its reality until this effect perishes, in which case its reality is reabsorbed into its substantive cause (this, indeed, seems to be the etymological meaning of *upādāna:* the re-collecting or reabsorbing cause). All real effects, therefore, pre-exist in, and if perishable return into their immediate substantive cause and, by way of it, eventually, into the ascending series of its higher and more subtle such causes up to the highest, subtlest and primordial *upādāna-kāraṇa* which itself is uncaused and self-existing (*svayam-bhū*).

The latter is the *Brahman* which, indeed, is defined as "that omniscient, omnipotent Cause from which (*yataḥ*) proceed the origin, subsistence and dissolution of this whole world". (*B.S.Bh.* 1, 1, 2) "There is no other substance from which the world could originate". (*B.S.Bh.* 1, 4, 23) Because it alone is Fullness, it precontains all realities that can possibly be created. How can we approach this mystery?

> In the beginning, before creation, when the differences of names-and-forms were not yet manifested, this world was but the one *Ātman*. (*Ait. Up. Bh.* 1, 1, 1)

As such, the *nāma-rūpas* pre-existed only in a virtual state, "in the form of futures" (*bhāviṣyena rūpeṇa*) explains Śaṅkara (*Ait. Up. Bh.* 1, 1, 2), just as future jars, statues, etc, pre-exist in the malleable substantiality of the lump of clay.

> These *nāma-rūpas*, which in their unmanifested state are identical with the *Ātman*, can become the substantive-causal elements (*upādāna-bhūte*) of the manifested universe. Hence, it is not incongruous to say that the Omniscient creates the universe by virtue of his oneness with those causal elements, namely, names-and-forms, which [in their unmanifested state] are identical with himself. (*Ait. Up. Bh.* 1, 1, 2)

What seems incongruous, however, is that according to this explanation the *Ātman* appears to be a malleable Primary Matter of which the creatures would be integral parts or modifications!

> The case is rather like that of the clever magician who, independent of any materials, transforms himself, as it were (*iva*), into a second man seemingly climbing into space. (*Ait. Up. Bh.* 1, 1, 2)

The point of this comparison is that the All-Maker is not at all changed by his creating. The self-transformation which we imagine him to undergo is as untrue as the one of that magician. This is what the post-Śaṅkaṛa *vivarta* theory has rightly emphasized. The comparison should not be misunderstood as implying that the created world itself is unreal.

The text from which I took the last quotations establishes the complete sufficiency and entire independence of the Creator. He creates even this very material out of

> no independent matter, unreducible to his own Self, such as the *pradhāna* of the Sāṁkhyas or the primordial atoms of Kaṇāda. (*Ait. Up. Bh.* 1, 1, 1)

> What the Scripture calls *ajā*, i.e., the causal matter of the four classes of beings, has itself sprung from the highest Lord. (*B.S.Bh.* 1, 4, 9)

All this could not be asserted if the *Brahman-Ātman* were conceived as primarily Spirit or Knowledge. But for Śaṅkara it is primarily *Sat,* Being, Existent, and, indeed, *paramārthataḥ Sat,*

Being in the supreme sense of the term. Being thus ontological Fullness, it can produce any kind of beings, even the most material universe. What it produces is, indeed, a universe of true beings, issued forth from the truest Being, and constantly inhabited and pervaded by this causal Being:

> The *Ātman* should be realized as Existent (*Sat*), as productive of existent effects (*sat-kārya*), namely, intellect, etc., which will be explained presently. (*Kaṭha Up. Bh.* 2, 3, 13)
>
> *Prāṇa*, the life-Breath, [i.e., the *Ātman* as the Source of life,] is equal to all these bodies of white ants, mosquitoes, elephants, etc. in the sense that it is present in them in its entirety (*kartsyena-parisamāpta*), somehow as cowness is present in each individual cow. But it cannot be merely of the size of those bodies for it is formless and all-pervading. (*Bṛh. Up. Bh.* 1, 3, 22)

Created beings, although issued from, and pervaded by, the absolute Being, are not its attributes; they are as unable to characterize its nature as a mask is powerless to characterize the inner nature of a man. A mask is an *upādhi*, an external adjunct. We must equally say that with regard to the Absolute, creatures are only *upādhis.* Although they are 'from' its Essence, they are not 'of' its Essence. Although they are 'in' It, they are not 'intrinsic' to It. This does not mean that they are unreal, but it excludes any pantheism while affirming clearly non-dualism.

3. The Causality of the Creative Word

Let us now take up an apparent contradiction in the Scripture which Śaṅkara examines in *B.S.Bh.* 1, 3, 28:

> In *sūtra* 1, 1, 2 ("[The *Brahman* is] that from which there is the origin, etc. of this universe") it has been proved that the world originates from *Brahman*; how then can it be said here that it originates from the word?

The answer to this objection is given as follows:

> The origination of the world from the 'word' is not to be understood in that sense, that the word constitutes the substantive cause (*upādāna*) of the world as *Brahman* does; but while there exist the everlasting words, whose essence is the power of denotation in connection with their eternal sense, [namely, the universal forms (*ākṛti* = Gk. *eidos*), i.e., the names-and-forms

> (*nāma-rūpa*) of all the species they denote,] the accomplishment of such individual things as are capable of having those words applied to them is called an origination from those words.

How should we understand the connection between the *Brahman* and the creative words?

> Both *Śruti* and *Smṛti* declare that creation is preceded by the word. For instance, *Bṛh. Up.* 1, 2, 4 declares, 'He with his mind united himself with speech'; and we read in the *Smṛti*, 'In the beginning Maheśvara shaped from the words of the Veda the names-and-forms of all things and the procedure of all actions'.
> Moreover, we all know from observation that anyone when setting about some thing which he wishes to accomplish first remembers the word denoting the thing, and after that sets to work.

This reminds me of a sentence in St Peter Canisius' *Confessions* which runs, "Many were the things... which in those days [of my youth] I *thought* and *desired* and *planned* and *performed*." Śaṅkara suggests that by observing such successive phases of the human procedure of production, we can gain an inkling into the mystery of the *Brahman's* creative causality. We may consider in it the following phases without, however, taking them as a temporal succession:

Phase I: The *Brahman*, in its absoluteness, is the 'mass of knowledge,' the 'fullness' of 'Reality-Knowledge infinite.' As such, this Knowledge comprises the knowledge of all *possible* reflections / similitudes / effects of this *Brahman*. They are precontained, implicit, in the simplicity of its Essence. An explanation given in *Taitt. Up. Bh.* 2, 1, 1 may help us here:

> All delectable objects [are here known] as amassed together in a single moment, through a single perception, which is eternal like the light of the sun, which is non-different from the essence of *Brahman*, and which we have described as 'Reality-Knowledge-infinite', [for it is the essence of] that *Brahman* whose nature is omniscience.

Phase II: Now the *Brahman* freely "*desires*, May I be many," not through an impossible self-dismembering (for its essence is partless), not to complement itself (for it is fullness), not out of need (for it has nothing to desire, being *āptakāma*, *satyakāma*) but gratuitously (as princes exert themselves in sport: *līlā*).

Phase III: Then it '*considers*' among all the possibles the kind of objects it will create, thus, as it were, marking them out, giving them explicitness. In this 'form of futures' they are no longer simply intrinsic to its homogeneous essence but somehow explicit and plural. Hence, we have to consider them as extrinsic *upādhis* of the divine essence.

Phase IV: Finally, the *Brahman* '*intends*' them, by uttering, as it were, the corresponding words [for instance, *bhūr-bhuvaḥ-svaḥ*, earth, atmosphere, sky] and thus creating a whole world by mere intention:

> Just as [according to our legendary myths] gods, manes, primordial sages and other beings of great power, who are all of intelligent nature, are seen to create many and various objects, such as palaces, chariots, etc., without availing themselves of any extraneous means, *by their mere intention*, which is effective in virtue of their peculiar power, [so also the *Brahman*, whose power is absolutely complete, can create a whole universe by his mere intention]. (*B.S.Bh.* 2, 1, 25).

Śaṅkara ends his justification of *sūtra* 1, 3, 28 with the following conclusion:

> We, therefore, conclude that before the creation the Vedic words became manifest in the mind of Prajāpati the creator, and that after that he created the things corresponding to those words.

4. Conclusion

The Indian speculation knew two types of causes, the *upādāna-kāraṇa*, the substantive cause 'from which' the effect obtains its reality, and the *nimitta-kāraṇa*, the efficient cause 'by which' it is shaped up. The principal type of the latter is the intelligent agent whose activity implies a deliberate intention, a creative word.

The *Taitt. Up*. 2, 1 had taught Śaṅkara that the *Brahman* is 'Reality-Knowledge-infinite' (*Satyam-jñānam-anantam*). From this he easily derived its capacity to unite those two types of causality and thus to be the sole universal Cause:

> There is no other substance 'from which' the world could originate.... It is at the same time the shaping cause of the world because outside *Brahman*, the substantive cause, there is no other ruling principle, for Scripture says

that, previously to creating, *Brahman* was one only, without a second. (*B.S.Bh.* 1, 4, 23)

APPENDIX on the Egyptian tradition about the *Creative Word*

Origen, whose name means 'Horus-born,' was probably a Copt. Living in Alexandria, he knew Greek but must have spoken his native language too and known its lore. As a Christian theologian, his particular contribution to theology had to do with the Incarnation, more precisely with the possibility of the involvement of the divine Essence in a human body. It was Origen's thesis that the Divine Word—and it is by the Word that men can be saved and made free—was revealed through the incarnation in Jesus. There was an ancient Egyptian doctrine that it was through knowledge, through the Word, the Speaking, that the universe came into existence. The god who represented this view of Creation was PTAH.

The ancient Egyptians did not, unlike the Vedic poets, put clearly to themselves the question of creation as a change from non-being to being. Probably because there was only one river in their country, the Nile, and they did not know it had a source, they lacked the notion of 'source' as 'originative production of water.' Thus they did not think of an absolute source of being and did not develop a conception of monotheism, but at the most of henotheism (of the sun-disk) with the 'heretical' Pharaoh Akhenaton (Amenophis IV 1365-1347 BC).

Yet, they had myths which explained somehow the 'emerging' of the world in the same way as the land emerged when the yearly Nile flood receded. The most interesting one for us is the 'creation-myth' of Ptah. He is thought which by its mere speaking makes the world arise like a primeval hill out of the ocean of chaos. As to the beginning of individual realities, it was explained in other ways, in stories of men being made out of clay by Ptah or from the tears of Re, etc.

In spite of the many stories which explained 'the first time' as they called it, the Egyptians were not so concerned with this problem as the Babylonians or the Hebrews or the Vedic and post-Vedic Aryans.

Ptah was also the god of art. His temple at Karnak had been built by Thutmose III (1490-1436 BC) of the XVIII dynasty (New Kingdom ca. 1558-1085). There was also found in it a statue of Ptah's partner, the lion-headed Sekhmet, the goddess of war. The tomb of Tutankhamon contained a wooden statue of Ptah, covered with gold except for eyes of inlaid glass and a blue faience cap.

Notes

[1] [First published in *La parola creatrice in India e nel Medio Oriente: Atti del Seminario della Facolta di Lettere dell'Universita di Pisa, 29-31 maggio 1991*, ed. Caterina Conio (Pisa: Giardini, 1994) 91-99. Reprinted here with permission from Fabrizio Serra Editore, current holders of the rights.]

16

ŚAṄKARA'S PERSPECTIVE ON MEANING AND TRUTH[1]

The great *ācārya* Śaṅkara, who flourished in the first half of the eighth century AD, had no other aim in life but knowing the divine Absolute (*Brahman*) through understanding and interpreting the Upaniṣads (which are the speculative part of the Vedic Scriptures or *Śruti*). It is, therefore, not astonishing that Hans-Georg Gadamer's reflections and notions concerning hermeneutics[2] are at home with him. I shall describe his 'hermeneutical situation' but, prior to that, my own at the outset of this piece of writing.

I entered into his writings—which have not ceased to entice my understanding—against the backdrop of my particular 'horizon,' the chief 'prejudices' (assumptions and predispositions) of which were and still are the following: a keen desire to penetrate the core of upaniṣadic thought; a sympathy and readiness to learn, ensouled by the conviction (originally formulated by Pseudo-Ambrosius and often recalled by St Thomas Aquinas) that "whatever is true, by whomsoever it be uttered, is from the Holy Spirit"; an empathy (nurtured by my training in both Jesuit spirituality and Western scholasticism) with Śaṅkara as a renouncer and seeker of the absolute God and as the foremost master among Indian schoolmen as well as a staunch upholder of negative theology.

There was also a suspicion that his teaching had become distorted through its interpretations by late Śaṅkarians and Neo-Vedāntins and a determination to bypass them and endeavour to understand his mind in the light of those writings which the best specialists agreed to consider as authentically his. This has created in me a familiarity which has invigorated my affinity with him.

1. Śaṅkara's Hermeneutical Situation

We have no trustable access to Śaṅkara as a historical personality. The *Śaṅkara Dig-Vijaya* and other 'biographies' are only late garlands of entertaining but fictitious episodes enclosing perhaps a few undiscernible facts. It is from his writings that we must discern his 'prejudices,' not forgetting that such assumptions and beliefs are not necessarily barriers to understanding but rather conditions and enable understanding (as well as misunderstanding). Let me highlight the obvious ones:

(1) *Imperious desire for the excellent alone*. He is deeply aware that what life presents to us is a mixture of values (and disvalues). However, he is not interested in a hierarchy of values but only in the top ones which, he feels, are alone worthy of our wholehearted pursuit:

> As the wild goose (according to Indian folklore) sifts milk alone from a mixture of water and milk, so the wise man sifts the excellent from the mere pleasant, going mentally all around these two objects, examining them closely, weighing their respective importance or futility; and, having distinguished them, HE CHOOSES THE EXCELLENT ALONE on account of its superiority. (*Kaṭha Up. Bh.* 2, 2)

(2) *A life-world of linguisticality*. More than most human beings, Śaṅkara is haunted by language. He speaks and thinks and writes in Sanskrit. His upbringing has been oral. He learned by heart the Vedas and Upaniṣads and mastered their auxiliary disciplines. He displays an incredibly broad erudition in all the philosophical currents, orthodox or heterodox, of a culture which had already produced most of its foundational works. But it is in the 'revelation' (*Śruti*) and, more precisely, in its teachings concerning the *Brahman* that he has 'taken his refuge,' and it is within the tradition of Vedānta that he is fully ensconced. It is in the *Śruti* that he breathes and lives[3] because he trusts it as the infallible source of the only knowledge that can liberate a man from the cycle of rebirths.

> The *Śruti* is an authority in transcendental matters, in matters lying beyond the bonds of human knowledge, i.e., beyond perception and reasoning. (*Bh. Gītā Bh.* 18, 66)

> It is only with the help of the *Śruti* that this exceedingly deep *Brahman* can be fathomed, not of reasoning. (*B.S.Bh.* 2, 1, 31)

(3) *An awareness of the full extent of human ignorance.* There is, he thinks, an inborn transcendental nescience which imbues all our ordinary knowledge and disqualifies it for liberation. He seems to be the first Vedāntin to become clearly aware of this (perhaps indirectly under the influence of Buddhism).

Ignorance (*avidyā*) he defines as "the superimposition of the nature and characteristics of one thing on another and vice versa." When the two things are *Brahman* or Absolute, on the one hand, and the ego or any contingent being, on the other hand, the superimposition is transcendental Ignorance. It is possible and even innate but only known as such in the light of the *Śruti*. Spontaneously, from our earliest age, we attribute to ourselves the monadic autonomy, independence, centrality, excellence and even permanence that pertain properly to the Absolute. This is due, Śaṅkara remarks, to the closeness, intimate dependence and high similarity of the ego to its innermost Self (*Ātman*), the very *Brahman*, of which it is a reflection (*ābhāsa*) in the ego-sense.

> The reflection of a face [in a mirror] is different from the face since it conforms to the mirror; and in turn the face is different from its reflection since it does not conform to the mirror.
>
> The reflection of the *Ātman* in the ego-sense is comparable to the reflection of the face. As in the case of the face, the *Ātman* is other (*anya*) [than the *jīvātman* or ego, which is its reflection and image], says the tradition, and the two [*Ātman* and *jīvātman*] are indeed likewise undiscriminated [by all men so long as they have not been enlightened by the *Śruti*]. (*US* 18, 32-33)

Vice versa, we superimpose upon the *Brahman-Ātman* the characteristics of the ego. It is the supreme Being without any inner difference or secondary endowment (*aviśeṣa*, *akhaṇḍa*, *nirguṇa Sat*) but we reduce it to the realm of 'having' and imagine it as having qualities (*saguṇa*), individuality (as Śiva, Viṣṇu, etc.) and even a body (of glorious *sattva*). Because it is Fullness (*pūrṇam*), "its power is absolutely complete" (*B.S.Bh.* 2, 1, 24), but we imagine it on the model of our own, as requiring pre-existing materials, a preconditioning by *karma* (the traces left by a being's past actions and determining its new birth) and a need for extraneous helps. Further, we imagine that it is only a sort of material substantive cause (in the manner of the *prakṛti* of the Sāṁkhya school) originating the universe through a self-transformation (*pariṇāma*) or only as an intelligent cause (*nimitta-kāraṇa*) which, in virtue of its complete knowledge of the nine eternal substances (taught by the Nyāya-Vaiśeṣika school), can organize them (in the manner of an artisan) into this universe of products. But the truth is that:

> The *Brahman* is to be acknowledged as the substantive (*upādāna*) as well as the efficient Cause (*nimitta-kāraṇa*)... at the same time... One without a second.... The *Ātman* is thus the *nimitta-kāraṇa* because there is no other ruling principle, and the *upādāna* because there is no other substance from which (*yataḥ*) the universe could originate. (*B.S.Bh.* 1, 4, 23)

Thus Śaṅkara discerned in the light of the *Śruti* that all the forms of theism (*Īśvaravāda*) developed up to his time by either the rational philosophers of Nyāya or the theologians of the sects entailed the transcendental superimposition and thus pertained to ignorance.

As to ordinary knowledge, obtained from sense-perception (*pratyakṣa*) and induction from it (*anumāna*), he acknowledged its validity within the limits of its own province. He only objected to our spontaneous attribution to it of finality (whereas it is mainly approximative only) and completeness (whereas it is unable to penetrate the ontological structure of things up to their relation to their supreme Cause, the *Brahman*):

> The *Śruti* is the authority in matters lying beyond the bonds of *pratyakṣa* and *anumāna*, but not in matters lying within their range. (*Bh. Gītā Bh.* 18, 66)

> It is not in *Śruti* that we should seek for the means of attaining the desirable and avoiding the undesirable in matters coming within the range of experience and ascertainable through perception and inference. (*Bṛh. Up. Bh.* Introduction)

> It is nowhere the purpose of the *Śruti* to make statements regarding the ego or *jīvātman* since from ordinary experience the latter is known to everyone as [the knower], the doer and the enjoyer. (*B.S.Bh.* 1, 3, 7)

[We, the Vedāntins,] maintain that the Lord is the [innermost and uppermost] Self of the enjoyer (*Ātmā sā bhoktur-iti*). (*B.S.Bh.* 1, 1, 1)

(4) *An awareness of the unlimited dynamism of our intellect.* Jaimini had already defined those 'goals of man' (*puruṣārtha*) which are not contingent but whose desire is inscribed in our very nature:

A *puruṣārtha* is that object to which human desire is inherently attached because it cannot be disconnected from it. (*Mīmāṁsā sūtra* 4, 1, 2)

For Jaimini the Mīmāṁsaka, there were only three such goals. For Śaṅkara the Vedāntin, there is a fourth one, liberation unto *Brahman*. This *mukti* is so excellent that it sublates the other three goals. The desire for it (*mumukṣutva*) is the most determining disposition for undertaking the study of Vedānta, according to Śaṅkara. (*B.S.Bh.* 1, 1, 1) Because it is the desire for "the most excellent" (*niḥśreyas*), its precise "object is the inmost *Ātman*." (*Kena Up. Bh.* 4, 1) This can only be attained through knowledge. Therefore, the paramount desire of man is to know the *Brahman-Ātman* in the best way possible, i.e., through direct intuition:

The direct object of the said desire is a knowledge culminating in penetrative intuition (*avagati*).... Knowledge, indeed, is the means by which the *Brahman* is desired to be intuitively penetrated (*avagatum iṣṭam*). For this direct intuition of *Brahman* is the end of man (*Brahmāvagati hi puruṣārthaḥ*), since it extirpates completely that which is bad, namely, Ignorance and its sequels which is the seed of the entire round of rebirths. (*B.S.Bh.* 1, 1, 1)

(5) *A self-projection towards the supreme goal through renunciation.* As soon as the supreme *Ātman* was discovered to be the most excellent Reality and, therefore, Goal, a decision was taken which ever since has characterized Hinduism, the decision of shunning all other desires for the exclusive pursuit of that Goal. In the earliest Upaniṣad, the sage Yājñavalkya says:

Once a man has come to know Him, he becomes a 'silent sage" (*muni*). Desiring Him alone as their world, wandering renouncers (*pravrājin*) leave their homes. This is what the men of old knew well, [and knowing it,] they had no wish for offspring. Rising above their desire for sons, their

> desire for wealth, their desire for [exalted] states of being, they wander forth to lead a beggar's life. (*Bṛh. Up*. 4, 4, 22)

Śaṅkara had his life modelled on this upaniṣadic stance and, probably quite early, had committed himself to renunciation (*saṁnyāsa*). Indeed, no one, he thinks, is qualified for the "enquiry inspired by the desire of knowing *Brahman*" (*Brahmajijñāsā*) unless "he renounces all desire to enjoy objects here [in this life] or hereafter [in afterlife] and possesses such [renouncer's] virtues as tranquillity (*sama*), self-restraint (*dama*), etc." (*B.S.Bh.* 1, 1, 1) One is fully qualified when one achieves the most complete degree of renunciation, that of the *paramahaṁsa*, the swan among ascetics.

This complete renunciation is not the extinction of the dynamism of human desire but its exclusive focussing on the supreme *Ātman* and Lord:

> [He will be] without desires... because he will be one to whom all the objects of desire are but the *Ātman* and nothing separate from it exists that could still be desired. (*Bṛh. Up. Bh.* 4, 4, 6)

The complete renouncer does not even rely exclusively on his own capacity for "discerning the eternal from the non-eternal" (*nityānitya-vastu-viveka*) but trusts in divine grace:

> He assumes that liberation is effected by discriminative knowledge (*vijñānena*) caused (*hetukena*) by His grace (*tad-anugraha*), because the *Śruti* teaches it. (*B.S.Bh.* 2, 3, 41)

(6) *A firm belief in the infallibility and inner harmony of the Śruti*. Śaṅkara inherited the belief of both Mīmāṁsā and Vedānta that the *Śruti* had no author—no individual (*puruṣa*), i.e., neither a man nor a god, composed and uttered it originally—and, hence, it is eternal. For the same reason, it is infallible since the factor of possible distortion between the revealed reality and the word revealing it, the *puruṣa*, is absent.

Several theories had attempted to justify this belief. Śaṅkara criticizes them and proposes his own. The most novel part of it is as follows:

> The *mantras* [and the rest of the *Śruti*] are the Consciousness of the *Ātman*, as limited by extrinsic adjuncts (*upādhi*), namely the modifications

> (*vṛtti*) of the inner sense, and as abiding in those *vṛttis* of the inner sense. Thus, of that *Ātman* they are the Knowledge that has neither beginning nor end. (*Taitt. Up. Bh.* 2, 3)

It follows from this that the *Śruti* contains a teaching marked by absence of inner contradiction and unity of purport. *Tat-tu samanvayāt* is the fourth *sūtra* in Bādarāyaṇa's *Brahma-sūtra.*[4] Śaṅkara expands it as "But that [*Brahman* is to be known from the *Śruti*,] because it is connected [with its Vedānta-texts as their purport]." Then, he explains it:

> That all-knowing, all-powerful *Brahman*, which is the cause of the origin, subsistence and dissolution of the world, is known from the Vedānta-part of scripture. How? Because in all the Vedānta texts the sentences construe in so far as they have that [*Brahman*] for their purport. (*B.S.Bh.* 1, 1, 4)

Belief in this kind of connectedness (*samanvaya*) commands a large part of Śaṅkara's exegetical task, namely, the explaining away of the apparent contradictions in the *Śruti*:

> [In our commentary on *sūtras* 1-11,] we have shown that the Vedānta texts exhibited under these *sūtras* are capable of proving that the [*Brahman*]... is the cause... of the world. And we have explained by pointing [under *sūtra* 10] to the prevailing uniformity of view that all Vedānta-texts whatever maintain an intelligent cause. The question might therefore be asked, 'what reason is there for the subsequent part of the *Vedānta-sūtra* [as the chief part is settled already]?'
>
> To this question we reply as follows: *Brahman* is apprehended under two forms: in the first place as qualified by particular extrinsic characteristics (*sopādhika*, whose equivalent is *saguṇa*)...; in the second place as being the opposite of this, namely, as free from all *upādhis* whatever (*nirupādhika*, whose equivalent is *nirguṇa*).... [To illustrate this he quotes here many passages and then says:] All these passages, with many others, declare *Brahman* to possess a double nature, according as it is the object either of Knowledge or of Ignorance. [Therefore, the texts concerning *Brahman* as the object of Ignorance will have their purpose clarified.] And again an enquiry will have to be undertaken into the meaning of the [other] texts, in order that a settled conclusion may be reached concerning the knowledge of the *Ātman* which leads to instantaneous release. (*B.S.Bh.* 1, 1, 11. See further precisions in 3, 2, 21)

Śaṅkara sees well that the *Śruti* appears to be a self-contradictory mixture of anthropomorphic texts side by side with transcendental texts, the two kinds being as opposed as ignorance and knowledge. He will justify their co-presence by a complementarity of distinct purposes. The first are intended for devotion and are somehow propaedeutic to the second for they purify the minds and attune them to the highest quest which the second fulfil.

2. Meaning and Truth

Affirmative sentences are used to convey a significant information to the mind, they mean something, they have a purport. However, apart from their context (close but also remote), they are rarely unambiguous. They offer a plurality of meanings (*artha*) one of which only may be the signified truth (*yāthātmya*). This will be the case normally if the sentences are statements resulting from a *pramāṇa*, a valid source of knowledge, such as perception, inference, testimony (*pratyakṣa*, *anumāna*, *śabda*):

> Knowledge results from the different *pramāṇas* and the objects of the *pramāṇas* are the existent things as they are in reality (*yathā-bhūta-vastu*). (*B.S.Bh.* 1, 1, 4)

(1) *Truth*. This conformity of a knowledge (*jñāna*) whose object (*viṣaya*) is an existent (*vastu*) with its ontological reality (*yathā-bhūta*) is called *yāthātmya*. It turns that knowledge into *pramā*, knowledge of the truth as ascertained through a *pramāṇa*.

Pramāṇas are many (six are generally accepted by Advaitins). Each one has its province, hence, its limits. But they are complementary. By combining them we can obtain a fuller knowledge of reality. If we ignore the need of each *pramāṇa* to be complemented by the others, we may wrongly attribute to a piece of knowledge a finality and completeness which it is lacking. Recourse to a higher *pramāṇa*, especially the *śabda* of *Śruti*, which concerns the ontological core of the existents, will banish that mistake while preserving and integrating the (more superficial but authentic) *pramā* of that piece of knowledge. In Śaṅkara's language, the latter is said to have been sublated (*bādhita*)—Hegel would have said *aufgehoben*—by the deeper knowledge which cancels its erroneous pretention and absorbs its truth. Sublation should not be understood as complete cancellation.

A combined recourse to all the *pramāṇas* available provides completeness of information; focussing on the object provides truth:

> Knowledge depends only on the *pramāṇas* and the reality of the object (*vastu-tantram*)... it does not depend on the will of man, but merely on what really and unalterably exists.
>
> We are to direct our attention to that [reality]. Even when a person is face to face with some object of knowledge, knowledge may either arise or not; all that another person wishing to inform him about the object can do is to point it out to him; knowledge will thereupon spring up in his mind of itself, according to the object of knowledge and according to the *pramāṇas* employed. (*B.S.Bh.* 3, 2, 21)

We know that there is no naked attention. Attention is supported and predisposed by our predispositions, conscious and unconscious. Śaṅkara had his own. We studied the most consequential ones. He was aware of these and let them influence his understanding of the *Śruti* because he had acquired them from his frequentation with it.

(2) *The* Śruti-*truth concerning the* Brahman. There was especially his intellectual dynamism towards the unlimitedly Excellent. It focussed him on that which is "One without a second," "infinite Reality-Knowledge," "supreme," "Full" and hence "not-such, not-such [as finite things]." But That is so great, so transcendent, that it stands beyond the expressive power of language and thought:

> It is that from which words fall back, together with the mind, unable to attain it. (*Taitt. Up.* 2, 4, 9)

Yet Śaṅkara started also with the belief that the *Śruti* can lead to the knowledge of that *Brahman*. How is that possible? It is possible, he discovered, once we realize that through the *Śruti*

> That is indicated (*tal-lakṣyate*) but not expressed (*na tū-cyate*). (*Taitt. Up. Bh.* 2, 1, 1)

Language, indeed, has a further power beyond the expressive one, namely, the indicative. The normal range of language is the finite because it is patterned on our empirical experience of this finite world. The largest number of words express finite essences, qualities, actions, etc., which entail materiality: they cannot be said properly (according to their intrinsic meaning: *svārtha*) of anything infinite or at least spiritual. But there are words, such as being (*sat*), good (*sadhu*), spirit (*cit*), consciousness (*caitanya*), knowledge (*jñāna*), self (*ātman*), cause (*kāraṇa*), etc. whose *svārtha* is neutral to finiteness and infinity though the manner in which we ordinarily use them is finite and to that extent they are expressive. Such words can be raised to infinity without losing their intrinsic meaning; but of course, they then lose their finite mode and thus their direct link with our experience. This is why they cease to express and only indicate.

For instance, whereas we have experienced what it means to be good like a delicious mango, or like a kind parent, or like an able leader, we have no experience of the superlative divine goodness. Therefore, learning that the *Brahman* is superlatively good is not beatifying because it is still but an abstract knowledge; it does not yet fulfil our desire for the direct experience of its Goodness. The whole *Śruti*-teaching regarding the *Brahman* is of this kind: merely indicative, abstract. Yet it is true since the *Śruti* is infallible.

Its truth is available to him alone who interprets and understands its sayings correctly. Let him be constantly attentive to the two basic indications, that the *Brahman* is supreme (*parama*) and unlike this or that contingent being (*neti neti*). In their light he should understand the *Śruti* 'great sentences' (*mahāvākya*), stripping their terms of their finite mode and raising their *svārtha* to the supreme degree (*paramārtha*).

For instance, "*Brahman* alone is *sat*" must be understood as "is Being in the supreme sense of the term (*paramārthataḥ*)," *Brahman* is the *ātman*" as "supreme *Ātman* (*paramātman*)," "That thou art (*tattvamasi*)" as "thou, not the limited individual Śvetaketu, ignorant, suffering, but that which is uppermost within thee, namely, thy supreme *Ātman*, is That Root of all contingent beings, most subtle, infinite, namely, the supreme *Brahman* of the universe"; "It is that from which the universe has its origin, etc." as "It is the one complete (both as *upādāna* and *nimitta*) cause which from its fullness alone (and, hence, as both omnipotent and omniscient) produces, rules and preserves the universe in all its states and modes"; "It is reality-knowledge infinite" as "Its essence is the oneness in simplicity of absolute unlimited Being and knowledge." How does Śaṅkara reach these interpretations? By accepting only that understanding which is homogeneous with both the immediate context and the whole *Śruti* and, in particular, with the clauses "*neti neti*" and "*pūrṇam*" or "*paramam*" of which he never loses sight. Here is an interesting example of such exegesis:

> *Bṛhadāraṇyaka Up.* 2, 3, 1 says, 'Two forms of *Brahman* there are indeed, the material and the immaterial.... Now then the teaching by, 'Not so, not so' (*neti neti*) for there is nothing else higher than this: It is not so.
>
> Here we have to enquire what the object of the negation is.... The doubt arises whether '*neti neti*' negatives both *Brahman* and its two forms or... its two forms only and not *Brahman*. [The easier solution seems to be that the three are negatived or even the *Brahman* alone.] For as *Brahman* transcends all speech and thought, its existence is doubtful, and admits of being negatived. The two cosmic forms, on the other hand, fall within the sphere of perception and inference and can, therefore, not be negatived.
>
> To this we reply. It is impossible that [the three be denied] for this would imply the [Buddhist Nāgārjuna's assertion] of a general Void (*śūnyam*) [which for reasons which he gives here is unacceptable]. Nor can *Brahman* alone be denied; for that would contradict the introductory sentence of this chapter 2, 1, 1. 'Shall I tell you *Brahman*?' ...; besides it would be opposed to definitive assertions such as, 'He is to be apprehended as He is (*asti+iti*)' (*Kaṭha Up.* 2, 6, 13); and would involve a stultification of the entire Vedānta. As to the teaching that *Brahman* transcends all speech and thought it must certainly not be viewed as a denial of existence but... rather as intimating the transcendence of *Brahman*.
>
> The passage under discussion has, therefore, to be understood as follows. *Brahman* is that whose nature is permanent purity, intelligence, and freedom; it transcends speech and mind, does not fall within the category of 'object,' and constitutes the inner Self of all. Of this *Brahman* our text denies all plurality of forms; but *Brahman* itself it leaves untouched....
>
> This passage, we conclude, conveys information regarding the nature of *Brahman* by denying the reality of the forms fictitiously attributed to it [and thus establishing that] the *Brahman* is formless. (*B.S.Bh.* 3, 2, 22)

(3) *The unsatisfactory meanings*. A meaning is an understanding which seems to account properly for the significant content of a text. However, to be relevant a meaning must take into account the whole surrounding context of that text, i.e., the rest of the meaningful unit to which it belongs, and all the corpus of literature of which this unit is a part if that corpus is supposed to provide a homogeneous information, but also the well-established truths derived from the other valid sources of knowledge.

For lack of conformity with this total context, many an interpretation of the *Śruti* will be deemed unsastisfactory. Śaṅkara starts usually his discussion of an *adhikaraṇa* (topic) with a consideration of some among such interpretations which appear to be rooted at least in the proximate context and in some of the 'great sayings' (as we just saw). He calls them *prima facie* opinions (*pakṣa*). He exposes them as fairly as possible (as when he restates some opinions of the sixth century AD Vedāntin Nimbārka whose commentary on the *Brahma-sūtra* has come down to us)[5] one after the other (as *pūrva*, prior, *uttara*, second. etc.) and then criticizes them by exposing their incongruity with the total teaching of the *Śruti* and refuting them also by rational arguments.

When after that he presents and argues solidly for his own interpretation, he may include some aspects of those *pakṣas* which he finds acceptable or, at least, tolerable.

(4) *Śaṅkara's openness to complementary views*. Like most Vedāntins, he considers as man-made and, hence, fallible the whole body of literature called *Smṛti* (tradition) and esteemed highly by most Hindus. But he discerns in it many valuable sayings which he does not hesitate to quote in confirmation of his interpretations. Insofar as a *Smṛti* work is consistent with his understanding of the *Śruti*,[6] he accepts it. For instance, he writes a commentary on the *Bhagavad Gītā* which he manages to interpret in the *advaita* (non-dualistic) mode. When accepting a point of doctrine from Yoga darśana, he explains why by quoting the following axiom:

> If the doctrine of another [scholar or school] is not inconsistent with our own, it becomes an accompaniment of our own (*paramatam-apratisiddham-anumatam bhavati*). (*B.S.Bh.* 2, 4, 12)

3. Consequences of Śaṅkara's Interpretation of the *Śruti*

3.1 Appropriation of this interpretation

On the occasion of a text which makes a distinction between *jñāna* and *vijñāna* (knowledge and discerning knowledge), Śaṅkara says:

> *Jñāna* means the enlightenment regarding the *Ātman*, etc. as obtained from this scientific discipline and the teachers [thus still abstract and public].
>
> *Vijñāna* is the experiencing of that (*tad-anubhava*) as specifically relevant (*viśeṣataḥ*) [to the seeker]. (*Bh. Gītā Bh.* 3, 41) It signifies turning into one's own experience (*sva-anubhava-kāraṇa*) the knowledge obtained from the science. (*Bh. Gītā Bh.* 6, 8; 7, 2; 9, 1)

The *Śruti* is not just interesting speculation. It leads to salvation (through the extinction of Ignorance). It is not simply to be learned but to be personalized, individually appropriated. The teacher mediates it through an exegesis which ceases only when all possible doubts raised by himself and the pupil have been solved through a *siddhānta*, a well-established conclusion. At the end of this exegesis, the pupil should have developed his initial faith (*śraddha*)—which was only a general trust in the *Śruti*—into a faith which Śaṅkara defines as:

> an intellectual conviction that this [teaching] is true, held in the tranquillity of a mind [free of doubts] (*citta-prasāde āstikya buddhiḥ*). (*Muṇḍ. Up. Bh.* 2, 1, 7)

This is the faith born from the exegetical 'prior ascertaining' (*pūrva-prasiddhi*). It precedes the *nididhyāsana*, the yogic focussing of the mind on the truth attained so as to assimilate it in silence so deeply and intimately that it turns—hopefully, under the light of divine grace—into intuitive experience. What sustains the seeker along this final step is the impelling of his *mumukṣutva* (desire for liberation). It perfects his faith into:

> *āstikya-buddhir-bhakti sahitā*: an intellectual conviction that [the *Śruti* teaching] is true, accompanied with focussing devotion. (*Bṛh. Up. Bh.* 3, 9, 21)

3.2 A turning-point for the Vedānta school

Śaṅkara is an important link in the long chain of the Vedānta school originated from the Upaniṣads. Bādarāyaṇa, when codifying it in his *Brahma-sūtra*, had taken account of the variety of contrary interpretations proposed by past teachers. Śaṅkara considers the same opinions and also those of some other teachers whom he mentions as 'another' or 'others' or 'some of ours' or 'the *vṛttikāra*' or more often 'the *pūrvapakṣin*,' a term which can designate many a different thinker but surely for some *sūtras* Nimbārka. Yet, his overall interpretation is so consistent and so successful in its own right that he does not feel the need of supporting it much by appeal to authorities.[7]

This interpretation soon became predominant owing to its all-inclusiveness, coherence, simplicity and the depth and subtlety of its argumentation. In Gadamer parlance, we could say that Śaṅkara's understanding modified the *Śruti so that it could remain the same* and that he gave it a contemporaneity with every present time.

He had let himself be questioned in depth by the text. His interpretation also raised questions which have not ceased to be debated.

4. Conclusion

Śaṅkara's hermeneutics is exemplary for several reasons. First of all, he was aware that an exegesis is conditioned by what Heidegger and Gadamer have called the 'prejudices' of the interpreter. He knew his own chief ones and made use of them as the starting point from which his understanding could advance and his 'horizon' get broadened through his meeting with the 'otherness' of the *Śruti* text and its earlier interpreters' own horizons.

Secondly, his commentaries are free from the obsession to discover 'the intention of the author,' since he had adopted the Mīmāṁsā conception of the *Śruti* as authorless. (But, when dealing with dialogues, he pays primary attention to their introduction and termination which often state clearly the intention of the speakers.) What he endeavours to attain is the *artha*, the true purport of the text itself. Paul Valéry said, "there is no such thing as the meaning of a text." But he was directly concerned with poetical texts whereas the *Śruti* is obviously doctrinal and must have an *artha* which can be found.

Thirdly, Śaṅkara's commentaries offer a constant interplay of meanings and truth. The 'true' understanding is not imposed dogmatically. Probable views are presented, their plausibility is exposed fairly, then their failure to agree with their total context. Next the interpreter's own view is presented, shown to be consistent with the whole context and with earlier 'well-established conclusions' (*siddhānta*) and, finally, argued for through a ratiocination as strict as possible.

The *saṁnyāsa* (renunciation) of both teacher and taught, the religious seriousness of their quest, their attachment to a transindividual tradition, the referring of all ego-claims to the sphere of that Ignorance which is to be superseded, all these characteristics converge toward a bracketing of subjectivity.

Let me end with a parting question. In my study of the non-Śaṅkarian Vedāntins, Rāmānuja, Madhva, Vallabha, Caitanya, I became convinced that their interpretations of the *Śruti* were very much commanded by extra-*Śruti* conceptions superimosed on the *Śruti*, especially distinct 'prejudicial' conceptions of what a sentence (*vākya*) is and of the interrelationships between its terms. Hence, the divergence of their commentaries from one another and from Śaṅkara's. Were the latter also determined by an extra-*Śruti* conception of *vākya* or was this conception itself derived from the *Śruti*, as I am inclined to believe?

Notes

1 [First published in *Hermeneutics, Truth and / or Meaning*, ed. J. Maliekal (Kondadaba: St John's Regional Seminary, 1994) 50-60. Completed 25 February 1992, see ibid. 60. Reprinted here with permission of St John's Regional Seminary.]

2 My references to his *Meaning and Truth* [surely De Smet means *Truth and Method.* 1st ET Garrett Barden and John Cumming (New York: Seabury, 1975), 2nd ET J. Weinsheimer and D.G. Marshall (New York: Crossroad, 1989)] and *Philosophical Hermeneutics*, tr. and ed. David E. Linge (Berkeley: University of California Press, 1976)] will be mainly implicit because another contribution to this volume will be devoted to his ideas. [By "this volume" is meant here

Hermeneutics, Truth and / or Meaning; however, the volume does not contain any article devoted exclusively to Gadamer's ideas.]

[3] Paul Claudel, the French poet who was also a particularly original exegete, was asked by a young lady, "Do you read the Bible much, Mr Claudel?" "Miss," he replied, "I don't read the Bible, I dwell in it."

[4] [*B.S.* 1, 1, 4.]

[5] One of my students, Fr Satyanand, IMS, established solidly the time of Nimbārka in his doctoral dissertation defended before the Sanskrit Department of the Poona University and accepted by it but not yet published. [The dissertation has since been published: see J. Satyanand, *Nimbārka: A Pre-Śaṁkara Vedāntin and His Philosophy* (Varanasi: Vishwa Jyoti Gurukul, 1994).]

[6] He states this clearly in *B.S.Bh.* 2, 1, 3.

[7] George Thibaut who translated the *Vedānta-sūtras* (= *Brahma-sūtra*) with Śaṅkara's commentary for the *Sacred Books of the East* series wrote in his introduction, p. xx: "Śaṅkara does not on the whole impress one as an author particularly anxious to strengthen his own case by appeal to ancient authorities, a peculiarity of his which later writers of hostile tendencies have not failed to remark and criticize."

17

THE PRESUPPOSITIONS OF JAIMINI AND THE VEDĀNTINS[1]

1. Jaimini

Daya Krishna, in his article "Mīmāṃsā before Jaimini,"[2] raised a number of uncomfortable questions regarding the very nature and components of the *Śruti*. Their pertinence is grounded in the validity of Jaimini's *sūtra* concerning the authorlessness and, hence, eternality and infallibility of *Śruti*. Daya Krishna's difficulties might be lightened, if not vanish, were the genesis of these *sūtras* properly retraced. A recent article of M.M. Deshpande on "The Changing Conceptions of the Veda: From Speech-Acts to Magical Sounds"[3] will help us to do just that.

1.1 The pre-Jaimini metamorphoses of the Veda

Speech-acts. The term *veda* does not appear in the *Ṛg Veda* but *vid* (to know, to find) is commonly used. It is supposed that knowledge and speech mirror each other. When a Vedic poet composes a *sūkta*, a hymn, it is a speech-act of praise and invocation of some deity. *Vāk* (speech) is *devī* (*Ṛg Veda* 8, 100, 11) because it praises deities; non-Aryan speech is *adevī*. The poets are often aware that their praise is an action in process. At times they refer to their activity as crafting *brahmans* (potent invocations). Every such crafting is a work of beauty and blessing:

> When, like men cleansing corn flour in a sieve, the wise in spirit have created language, there friends see and recognize the marks of friendship. Their speech retains the imprinted beauty of blessing. (*Ṛg Veda* 10, 71, 2)

In many places the name of a poet remains attached to his creation.

Decontextualized sacral formulas. A sacralization of *brahman* and *vāk* begins when the hymns are decomposed into sacrificial formulas (*yajus*) for utilization in the ritual. For the ritual the causal power of speech is exalted. It is fully reified in the *Atharva Veda*. This leads to a deification of speech (just as of *soma* or *agni*). *Vandanā* (praise) is offered to *vāk*. The godly speech (*devī vāk*) is transformed into the *Vāk Devī*, the Goddess Speech, especially in the *Atharva Veda* and later texts. She has a male correspondent, *Vācaspati / Brahmaṇaspati / Bṛhaspati / Vākpati / Vākpā*, to whom creatorship is also attributed. The climax of deification of *vāk* is reached in *Ṛg Veda* 10, 125 (= *Atharva Veda* 4, 30). This deification gradually decontextualizes the speech-acts of the poets which cease to be acts of communication.

Primordial origination of the Saṃhitās. The *saṃhitās*, the collections, are now appealed to (e.g., *Ṛg Veda* 10, 90) as born from the primordial sacrifice performed by the *devas*. *Bṛh. Ār. Up.* 1, 2, 5 says that the *Prajāpati* first created the three *saṃhitās* and 2, 4, 10 says that they are the outpouring of the breath of the Great Being. *Śata. Brāh.* 9, 5, 1, 18 equates their *trayi vidyā* with *satya*, truth. In *Taitt. Brāh.* 3, 10, 11, 4, the real Vedas are said to be infinite and the known Vedas to be only a handful from them. Again, *Śata. Brāh.* 1, 1, 58, transcending all notions of human sages being authors of Vedic hymns, says that *Ṛg Veda* was born from Agni, the *Yajur Veda* from Vāyu and the *Sāma Veda* from Sūrya.

As to the detached verses used ritually as sacrificial *mantras*, they are now stripped from their original context and sacralized in terms of their ritual application (*viniyoga*). They are said by *Ait. Brāh.* 1, 13 to give perfection of form (*rūpa-samṛddhi*) to the sacrifice:

> That in the sacrifice is perfect which is perfect in form, namely, that the rite as it is performed is concomitantly described by the Vedic verse [which is recited].

Their exegesis in the Brāhmaṇas. However, the archaic Sanskrit of the Vedic prayers thus turned into sacral formulas was hardly understood. In the *Brāhmaṇas*, one notices a tremendous urge to understand their meaning but often in terms of contemporary pragmatic needs. Indeed, it is believed that their correct utterance during the ritual action can "yield all desirable objects" (*Ait. Ār.* 5, 1, 5), of course only to "him who knows thus" (*ya evam veda*). But should he know only the *mantra* to be used in a specific ritual or grasp its real meaning?

Yāska's reply to first criticisms. Around 500 BC, Yāska's *Nirukta* 1, 15 discusses the opinion of Kautsa, an opponent who upholds the meaninglessness of the Vedic stanzas; he is refuted in 1, 16. Kautsa argues, somewhat in the manner of Daya Krishna:

> The order of words in the preserved stanzas is absolutely fixed, unlike the natural language; for some sentences such as 'save him, O plant,' there can be no sensible meaning; several sentences in the Veda are mutually contradictory; and the meaning of many Vedic expressions is obscure beyond recovery.

Yāska answers that the Vedas are meaningful because their words are identical with those of the current spoken language to which Kautsa's objections would also apply. As to their obscurity, he replies that it is not the fault of a pillar if a blind man does not see it.

Let us notice that Kautsa's complaint about the contradiction between some Vedic statements implies that together with the conception of a unified Veda without different authors there had developed the expectation that the sentences of this Veda did not contradict insight into *dharma* by ancient sages:

> There were in remote times sages who had direct intuitive insights into religious duty. By oral instruction, they handed down the hymns to later generations who were destitute of the direct intuitive insight. Generations that came still later, declining in oral transmission, compiled this work, the Veda and the ancillary treatises, in order to comprehend their meaning. (*Nirukta* 1, 20)

Yāska points here to the development in his time of the recitational techniques of preservation of the Vedic text. Soon

Pāṇini would analyse the Vedic as well as the current Sanskrit texts of his days. The following centuries saw the growth of a *mīmāṃsā* school and the diffusion from the third century BC of the *Mīmāṃsā Sūtra* attributed to Jaimini.

1.2 Jaimini and the authorless Śruti

Samiran Chandra Chakrabarti, in his study on *The Paribhāṣās in the Śrautasūtras*,[4] notes that "the *Pūrva-Mīmāṃsā* discusses a much greater number of controversial issues than the *Paribhāṣās* in the *Śrauta-Sūtras* do, and reflects the growing multiplicity of conflicting views. It represents an age of criticism, when ritual had to be defended by logic."

If the age of the *Śrauta-Sūtras* and then of Jaimini is an age of criticism, this is, we know, because of the strong and widespread influence of Buddhism. Jaimini does not name Buddhism but he does answer the Buddhist criticism of the Brahmanic reliance on the Veda via the *Brāhmaṇas*, the *Āraṇyakas* and the *Upaniṣads*.

In particular, this criticism is directed against the very authority of that whole *Śruti*. Francis X. Clooney, in the sixth chapter of his *Thinking Ritually: Rediscovering the Pūrva Mīmāṃsā of Jaimini*,[5] has studied the Buddhist context of the *Pūrva-Mīmāṃsā Sūtra*. For brevity's sake a few quotations are borrowed from it:

> In Ambaṭṭha Sutta of the Dīgha Nikāya, the Buddha deflates the authority of the Brahmin Ambaṭṭha's teacher and rejects the standard appeal to tradition: 'But just so, Ambaṭṭha, those ancient Rishis of the Brahmans, the authors of the verses, the utterers of the verses, whose ancient form of words so chanted, uttered or composed, the Brahmans of today chant over and over again and rehearse, intoning or reciting exactly as has been intoned or recited... though you can say, "I, as a pupil, know by heart their verses," that you should on that account be a Rishi, or have attained to the state of a Rishi—such a condition of things has no existence.'

In the *Tejjiva Sutta*, we see that even the *ṛṣis* themselves lack personal authority to back up their teaching. Two young Brahmins ask the Buddha to resolve their doubt about the Vedic schools. Here the Buddha attributes the differences between the various *śākhās* to the fact that not even the original *ṛṣis* had personal experience to validate their teaching for they had not seen Brahma face to face.

Jaimini sidesteps these and other Buddhist criticisms by asserting that the things the Buddha devalues are of secondary importance. For him, the *ṛṣis* and *śākhās* are merely expounders (*pravaktṛ*) of a complex interrelationship of word, purpose and action (*śabda*, *artha*, *karma*) that pre-exists them and is independent of human authority and creativity. It seems clear that it is to bypass Buddhist criticism that Jaimini impersonalizes the whole *Śruti* by declaring it *apauruṣeya* and eternally self-existent (*Pūrva-Mīmāṃsā Sūtra* 1, 1, 6-23). Clooney remarks that these *sūtras* 1, 1, 6-23 are a separable unit: the theory of the eternity of word is distinct from and not necessary to the theory of authorlessness: 1, 1, 24 could follow straightaway from 1, 1, 5 (p. 32). For Jaimini authorlessness is very important for undermining the ground of the critics. It is the criterion by which he can hold that *Śruti* alone is *śabda-pramāṇa*. *Laukika śabda* is not *pramāṇa* for all human speakers are fallible and non-authoritative. Thus the Buddha *vacana* itself lacks authority. Was this tenet grounded in the *Śruti* itself or only a decision of Jaimini?

1.3 The intrusion of para-textual factors in Mīmāṃsā

This question concerns what Hans-Georg Gadamer calls the 'hermeneutical situation' or the 'horizon' of each interpreter.[6] By this he means the backdrop of what he calls 'prejudices' (in the sense of 'prejudgments'), i.e., the predispositions, inclinations, assumptions, pet-theories of the interpreter by which he may, wittingly or unwittingly, and for good intellection or bad, be influenced in his interpretation of a text. Gadamer has taught us to pay attention to such para-textual factors of understanding and interpretation.

Apauruṣeyatva, authorlessness, is a radical and paradoxical conception of *Śruti* for which there is no real precedent before Jaimini. It brushes aside all ideas of its origination by gods or *Brahman* that have been suggested, as recalled above, at various times. It is an ad hoc solution to the difficulties raised naggingly by Buddhists which has the advantage of simultaneously reducing the teaching of their human founder to the downgraded rank of *pauruṣeya śabda*. It is, therefore, to be understood as a para-textual conception (similar as such to the two interpretative principles singled out by Daya Krishna, p. 107) invented by Jaimini in reaction to an external stimulus. This, of course, relativizes it, allows a certain freedom with regard to it, and relaxes the pressure of Daya Krishna's questioning.

2. The Vedāntins' Diverse Conceptions of *Vākya* (Sentence) as Responsible for their Diverse Interpretations of the Same Scriptures

2.1 Introduction

The question in this part is somewhat ambitious. Can we find out the reason why Vedāntins differ in their interpretation of the one *Śruti* on the basis of the same basic rules of interpretation? Is it a reason grounded in the very *Śruti*, for instance, a radical ambiguity of the texts themselves or is it para-textual?

Rāmānuja's endeavour in *Śrī Bhāṣya* to refute Śaṅkara's method suggests that this reason is para-textual and pre-exegetical and is a different conception of *vākya* (sentence) held by each Vedāntin. We can test this hypothesis by comparing Śaṅkara's conception of *vākya* with that of Rāmānuja and then, at least briefly, that of Madhva and that of Vallabha.

2.2 Śaṅkara

The understanding of what sentences are, what they do and how they do it is central to Śaṅkara's exegesis (*mīmāṃsā*) of the Upaniṣads since he centres each of their meaning-units on a *mahāvākya* (great sentence), usually a definition (*lakṣaṇa*) of *Brahman*. However, before such sentences can be grasped as meaningful, several difficulties are to be surmounted:

First difficulty: the ineffability of Brahman. "In all the Vedānta-texts of *Śruti*, the sentences construe in so far as they have that *Brahman* as their purport." (*B.S.Bh.*1, 1, 4) But *Taitt. Up.* 2, 4 says that *Brahman* is "that from which words fall back, together with the mind, having failed to reach it" and *Taitt. Up.* 2, 7 asserts that "it is unexpressed (*anirukta*)".

Reply: the two powers of sentences. Through the words of the defining sentences, "that [*Brahman*] is indicated but not expressed (*tal-lakṣyate na tū+ 'cyate*)." (*Taitt. Up. Bh.* 2, 1, 1)

Indeed, as is well-known to exegetes since Jaimini, speech has two levels of signification, the *Expressive* (*vac-*) and the merely *Significative* (*lakṣ-*). On the expressive level, words signify according to their primary meaning (*mukhyā+ 'rtha*) and describe mundane realities; their primary sphere, indeed, is our mundane experience for describing which and its objects they have been coined.

But words are limited in number while the world is extremely manifold and its beings varied in their aspects. We cannot have a term for each bit of information we wish to communicate, but language is very supple. If we lack a proper term we can use other terms on the basis of similarity, causality or other connections to at least indicate what we cannot express. This is the indicative level on which words signify according to their indicative meanings (*lakṣyā+ 'rtha*); these meanings are also called *lakṣitā+ 'rtha* because they are 'indicated' by the context.

Second difficulty: the ontological simplicity of Brahman. Granting that *lakṣyārthas* can be informative in their own way, the definitions at least should be done according to class characteristics (*sāmānya* and *viśeṣa*, i.e., genus and difference) and qualities (*guṇa*), etc. But *Brahman* is "one only without a second" and thus transcends all class characteristics; it is *nirguṇa*, not endowed with qualities and other accidents since it is *akhaṇḍa*, ontologically simple and free from such internal distinctions as between substance and accidents. In short, it completely escapes the reach of all categories (cf. *Bh.Gītā Bh.* 13, 13).

Reply: the defining capacity of both viśeṣaṇas *and* upādhis. It is true that in typical definitions, such as 'large blue sweet-smelling lotus' the defining terms are *viśeṣaṇas*, intrinsic characterizers, namely, a constitutive substance, lotus, and its three noticeable accidents, but there exists another type of definition called *taṭastha-lakṣaṇa*, definition by way of something which 'stands alongside' the defined entity. Such extrinsic characterizers are called *upādhi* (from *upa+ā+dhā*, to put upon). They can be objects (for instance the female stage-dress which makes one say, 'Devadatta is the princess') or relations (as in 'Devadatta is our gardener').

A number of definitions of *Brahman* are of this type. All contingent beings are mere *upādhis* (extrinsic pointers) to *Brahman*. The latter is definable as their Cause, *Ātman*, Lord, Witness, etc. but this Causality, *Ātma*hood, Lordship, etc. are only *upādhis* extrinsic to its incomplex Essence:

> The Lord's Lordship, omniscience, omnipotence, etc. all depend upon the limitations due to the *upādhis* which ignorance makes us take as intrinsic, whereas in reality none of these belong as qualities to *Brahman* whose true nature is cleared by true knowledge from all adjuncts whatever. (*B.S.Bh.* 2, 1, 14)

Of the two functions of definitions set out by Śaṅkara in *Taitt. Up. Bh.* 2, 1, 1, namely, (1) differentiating the definable from all other entities, and (2) declaring its essence, these definitions by *upādhis* fulfil only the first, which is the minimal one. Nevertheless, such definitions as "*Brahman* is that from which (*yataḥ*) the universe sprang forth" or "That thou art" are further enlightening because of the relations they imply between the universe or ego and *Brahman*. Besides, the essential definition (*svarūpa-lakṣaṇa*) will fulfil both the first and the second functions.

Third difficulty: the lack of viśeṣaṇas *of Brahman*. The essence of *Brahman* cannot be defined because it transcends all categories and thus all possible intrinsic characterizers.
Reply: There exist terms susceptible of a supreme meaning (paramā+'rtha). The meaning of such terms as 'reality,' knowledge,' 'bliss,' and such like is not restricted to the finite world but is illimitable. In their supreme meaning, they are *viśeṣaṇas* of *Brahman*, characterizing it intrinsically.

However, if used singly, they may give rise to a plurality of mistakes unless the context indicates clearly that their sense is supreme. For instance, one might understand that *Brahman* is *material* reality, or a *piece of* knowledge, or *sensual* bliss, or is composed of a plurality of perfections.

This is why the *Śruti*, in order to obviate this danger, provides definitions such as *'Satyam-jñānam-anantam'* or '*Vijñānam-Ānandam,*' etc. in which such terms are coordinated. The effect of this is explained by Śaṅkara:

> Each term is independently connected with the term *Brahman* but by virtue of their mutual contiguity they are controlled by, and controlling, one another so that they exclude from it the expressive meaning (*vācyārtha*) of *satyam*, etc. and become the indicatives (*lakṣyārtha*) of *Brahman.* [They, however, are not metaphorical but intrinsic indicatives because] they certainly do not thereby lose their proper meaning (*svārtha*). (*Taitt. Up. Bh.* 2, 1, 1)

What happens is that *jñānam* excludes from *satyam* its normal connotation of materiality, and *anantam* (infinite) excludes from *satyam-jñānam* their normal connotation of finitude. As a result the three terms are understood only in their proper but most elevated meaning (*paramārthataḥ*), and the *Brahman* is correctly and properly indicated although it is not expressed.

Fourth difficulty: No sentence can mirror the Brahman. The normal understanding of speech is that it mirrors reality. Each category of words corresponds to a special part of the reality that a sentence is about. Is this not the meaning of *padārtha*, the object (*artha*) of a word (*pada*)? There is a one-to-one correspondence between a word and its objective ground. Now every sentence is a complex expression indicative of a plurality of objective grounds. But the *Brahman* is ontologically free of such or any other plurality. Hence it cannot be signified by any sentence.

***Reply:* *the intellect is not a mirror but a synthesizer*.** "The intellect considers as a unitary whole [the plurality of words or other data it receives]" (*samastapratyavamarṣinī buddhiḥ*) (*B.S.Bh.* 1, 3, 28).[7] This is the heart of Śaṅkara's conception of intellection. The intellect is not a passive receiver but a synthesizer. It does not consider a sentence as a duplicate of reality but as a sequence of signs. Whether these are descriptive or otherwise expressive, merely indicative or allusive, it unifies all their syntactical significations so that they converge into a unitary understanding. Interpreting and any understanding is an active process which results in the single flash of knowledge finally attained,

Because Śaṅkara held this para-textual conception, he was not hampered by such apparent difficulties as we have examined but derived from the plurality of the *Śruti* sentences the doctrine of the utterly simple *nirguṇa Brahman*, a doctrine which was negative theology without being purely apophantic (as Maṇḍana Miśra would have it).

His conception was not a 'naive-realistic' view of intellection but a highly critical theory. He did not receive it from the *Śruti* but surely refined it by using it to interpret the *Śruti*.

2.3 Rāmānuja

No more than Śaṅkara did Rāmānuja approach the *Śruti* with a mind void of preconceived notions and theories. His theory of intellection is actually adopted by him after a careful study of that of Śaṅkara—which could be retrieved in his own words from his *Śrī Bhāṣya* 1, 1, 1—and directed against Śaṅkara's kind of exegesis. He had perceived very precisely the ultimate primary given by the latter to the indicative *lakṣyārtha* over the expressive *mukhyārtha*. This was very different from the role of exception granted to *lakṣaṇā* by Jaimini. Rāmānuja decided to stay closer to Jaimini and to interpret every sentence of the *Śruti*, especially those which he called *śoḍhaka vākya* (which do not all coincide with Śaṅkara's *mahāvākya*), according to the expressive meaning of its terms.

The structure of the sentence mirrors the structure of things. Rāmānuja's theory is grounded in the naive-realistic conviction that the structure of the assertive sentence mirrors and duplicates that of the corresponding reality. Here the notions of *viśeṣa*, difference, and hence of *viśeṣaṇa* are central:

> Every nascent awareness is produced by some distinctive aspect (*viśeṣa*) so that it may be expressed in this way: 'this is such' (*idam ittham*); for it is not possible to apprehend any object of speech (*padārtha*) without a particular configuration, such as a triangular head, dewlap, etc. (*Śrī Bhāṣya* 1, 1, 1)

Thus, in perception, the *idam* element is the *viśeṣya*, the subject standing for the reality to be differenced in its separation (*bheda*) from all others, and the *ittham* element is the *viśeṣaṇa*, the differencing predicate.

This *viśeṣya-viśeṣaṇa* structure is called by the Grammarians *samānādhikaraṇya*, a positional construction. It means "the fact that a plurality of terms, whose use is motivated by a plurality of objective grounds, denote one and the same thing. It aims at making one and the same thing known as differenced (*viśiṣṭa*) by a plurality of differencing terms (*viśeṣaṇa*)." (*Śrī Bhāṣya* 1, 1, 1)

Śaṅkara used the term *viśiṣṭa* as the special *meaning* obtained by the opposition of two terms like black and horse (or *tat* and *tvam* or *satyam* and *jñānam*). But for Rāmānuja it refers to the thing (*vastu*) itself. It is the thing which always presents a "plurality of objective grounds," i.e., a differenced structure. (When his doctrine was originally called *viśiṣṭādvaita*, this was understood for several centuries uniquely as 'non-dualism of the differenced' *Brahman*.) Let us see how this works out in his interpretation of *Tattvamasi*:

> Whether we take the several terms of this definition in their primary sense (*mukhyārtha*), i.e., as denoting qualities [his position] or as denoting modes of being opposed to whatever is contrary to those qualities [Śaṅkara's position], in either case we must need admit a *plurality of causes* [which he understands as *objective* grounds, whereas Śaṅkara understands them as *subjective*, namely, propensities of man to err in diverse directions concerning *Brahman*] for the application of those several terms to one thing. There is, however, this difference between the two alternatives, that, in the former case, the terms preserve their primary meaning, while in the second case, their denotative power depends on the so-called *lakṣaṇā*. This view would, moreover, be in conflict with the *samānādhikaraṇya* notion, as it would not allow of difference of *objective* ground for several terms applied to one thing. (*Śrī Bhāṣya* 1, 1, 1)

The prakārin-prakāra *ontology.* If the above is admitted, no reality (*vastu*) can be simple (*akhaṇḍa*, *nirguṇa*); every *vastu*, including the *Brahman*, can only be complex, internally differenced, a substratum of modes:

> The element which is referred to as *ittham* when a *vastu* is apprehended as 'this is such' is a mode (*prakāra*). (*Srī Bhāṣya* 1, 1, 13)

Its relation to its *prakārin* is of inherence and subservience:

> Class characteristics and qualities inhere in the substance as in their substrate and their final cause (*prayojana*), and they are its modes.... Since a mode depends on its *prakārin*, the cognition of the mode depends on and includes the *prakārin*. From this it follows that a word denoting a mode includes in its denotation the substance having that mode. (*Śrī Bhāṣya* 1, 1, 1)

The śarīra-ātman *ontology*. Let us further see how Rāmānuja arrives at his favourite ontology in terms of body and body owner:

> Just like genus and quality, so substances (*dravya*) also may occupy the position of a *viśeṣaṇa*, in so far namely as they constitute the *body* of something else.... The relation of bodies to the self (*ātman*) is strictly analogous to that of class characteristics and qualities to the substance in which they inhere; for it is the *ātman* only which is their substrate and their final cause and they are modes of the *ātman*. (*Śrī Bhāṣya* 1, 1, 1)

Rāmānuja is aware that this is a quite novel conception for he objects to himself:

> But in ordinary speech the word 'body' is understood to mean the mere body; it does not, therefore, extend in its denotation up to the *ātman*!
>
> Not so, we reply. The body is, in reality, nothing but a mode of the *ātman*.... (*Śrī Bhāṣya* 1, 1. 1)

We can now unfold the full Vedānta scope of his theory:

> As the individual *ātmans* with their body-modes constitute a body of the highest *Ātman* and, hence, are modes of it, the words denoting them ascend in their connotations up to the very highest *Ātman*. And as all intelligent and non-intelligent beings are the mere modes of the highest *Brahman*, and have reality thereby only, the words denoting them are used in *samānādhikaraṇya* with the terms denoting *Brahman*. (*Śrī Bhāṣya* 1, 1, 1)

This may suffice to establish that Rāmānuja differed from Śaṅkara by reason of a theory of intellection which he no more derived from the *Śruti* than Śaṅkara did his own. Both theories come under what Gadamer called the 'prejudices' of the interpreters.

2.4 Madhva

A similar influence of a preconceived theory appears to have determined Madhva's decision to interpret the Upaniṣads in a way definitely different from either that of Śaṅkara or Rāmānuja.

What he saw well is that every assertive sentence posits its *viśeṣya* not only as being but as one, i.e., as undivided in itself and divided from all the rest. He saw further that it is as being that the *viśeṣya* is one. It is not simply by some secondary particularity that every being differs from all others but by its very essence. It is thus radically *sa-viśeṣa*, differentiated.

But he does not seem to have been clearly aware that in so far as a being is inferior in the hierarchy of beings, and thus imperfectly being, it must be in the same ratio imperfectly one, i.e., imperfectly undivided in itself, hence intrinsically complex and imperfectly divided from all others, hence, ontologically related to others. In particular, it is related by a relation of total dependence to that perfect Being which alone can be the Cause of other existents.

If this is seen, then the non-dualism of inferior beings with the transcendent Cause, not only of their structure, but of their very reality, becomes manifest. If it remains ignored, the understanding of the Upaniṣads will be dualistic.

This, it seems to me, is the explanation of the *dvaita* nature of Madhva's doctrine which makes it radically different from the Advaita of either Śaṅkara or Rāmānuja.

2.5 Vallabha

A few words will suffice to give an idea of Vallabha's para-textual conception of *vākya*. They may begin with a recall of the parable of 'The elephant and the blind men of Hindustan.'

There is a whole elephant but each blind man perceives it only partially according to the limited part he is touching. Similarly, for Vallabha, to know is always to know partially. In each sentence of the *Śruti*, or any other sentence, the reality spoken about is the one *Brahman* only but in a limited way, as tree or cow or blade of grass or man or *ātman* or Kṛṣṇa, etc. when no sentence is uttered or thought of, the *Brahman* is concealed. It is like a game of hide and seek, but this game is

Brahman's līlā. It plays it according to alternances of its two powers, *tirobhāva* (concealing) and *āvirbhāva* (displaying).

This analytical conception of *vākya* allows Vallabha to interpret every sentence of the *Śruti* literally and yet to reject any kind of plurality and to uphold his *śuddhā+ 'dvaita* or monistic non-dualism.

3. Conclusion

From the above, the point seems to be settled that the plurality of mutually opposed Vedāntic doctrines arises, not from textual disharmony in the *Śruti*, but from para-textual conceptions of *vākya* according to which each one of the chief interpreters moulded his own interpretation.

Notes

[1] [First published in *JICPR* [*Journal of Indian Council of Philosophical Research*] **11**/2 (1994) 77-87 and reprinted here with kind permission.]
[2] *JICPR* **9**/3 (1992) 103-11.
[3] *Brahmavidya, Adyar Library Bulletin* **54** (1990) 1-41.
[4] (Calcutta: Sanskrit Pustak Bhandar, 1980) 108.
[5] [Vienna: Institut für Indologie der Universität Wien, 1990].
[6] Cf. Gadamer's chief books, *Meaning and Truth* [= *Truth and Method*] and *Philosophical Hermeneutics*.
[7] [Correcting *Taitt. Up. Bh.* 2, 3.]

18

THE DYNAMICS OF CONTEMPLATION ACCORDING TO SAṄKARĀCĀRYA[1]

1. The Desire to Intuit the Divine Essence

What impels the whole process whose last phase is contemplation is 'the desire to know (*jijñāsā*) the *Brahman,*' a desire which will not be satiated unless the intellect reaches a full intuition of the divine Essence. This desire initiates a quest also called *jijñāsā*. It is the paramount desire of the intellect. Śaṅkara does not say explicitly that it is congenital and constitutive of its whole dynamism but he explains it as the desire for 'the end of man' (*puruṣārtha*).

And he probably agreed with the definition given by Jaimini: "*Puruṣārtha* means that object to which human desire is inherently attached because it cannot be disconnected from it" (*Mīmāṁsā Sūtra* 4, 1, 2). Such objects are said to be of four kinds. The fourth one is liberation, immortality, the utmost good, which according to Śaṅkara can only be "the object of the desire to know the innermost *Ātman*."[2]

> The direct object of the said desire is a knowledge culminating in an intuitive penetration (*avagati paryantam jñānam*), desires aiming at fruition. Knowledge, indeed, constitutes the means by which the *Brahman* is desired to be penetrated intuitively (*avagatum*). For this intuition of the *Brahman* is the end of man (*puruṣārtha*) since it extirpates completely that which is bad, namely, Nescience and its sequels which is the seed of the entire fleeting world. (*B.S.Bh.* 1, 1, 1)

> That knowledge which discerns the *Brahman* and discards Nescience terminates in experience (*anubhava*). (*B.S.Bh.* 2, 1, 4)

The divine Godhead, when considered in itself, is called *Brahman*, the Absolute, or at times *Puruṣa*, approximately the Person. In reference to its creaturely effects, especially man, it is called *Ātman* or *Paramātman*, the supreme self. The reflective pronoun, *ātman*, designates the subject, the ego (*aham*). But it has a large range of applications, closer or remote: I can use it to designate my gross body or an important part of it, such as the trunk, or my subtle body, my intellect, my soul or empirical ego, the ultimate subject of my actions and experiences; but I can also—and here Sanskrit differs from English—use it to indicate that *Brahman* which, though it transcends me altogether, is my innermost Ground and Cause, Inner Light and Inner Ruler, my supreme Aim and End. It is my 'Self' but neither my activities nor my passivities are attributable to It.

2. The Starting-Point of the Quest: the Upaniṣads

The quest is not based on some independent metaphysical reflection but on ancient texts whose truth-value is regarded as absolutely faultless. These are the Vedic texts: the four *Vedas*, the *Brāhmaṇas* and, principally, the *Upaniṣads* which are the 'end of the Veda,' the *Vedānta*.

These are difficult, often obscure, texts which have to be approached under the guidance of a master (*ācārya*) faithful to an authoritative commentatorial tradition.

Of the tradition of Advaita (non-dualism) the most ancient commentaries (*bhāṣya*) of Upaniṣads we possess are those written by Śaṅkara probably during the first middle of the eighth century. This paper is an exposition of his teaching.

There is, he says, a basic faith (*śraddha*) which "precedes and initiates all the efforts of man towards his goal." (*Muṇḍ. Up. Bh.* 2, 1, 7)

Through the quest, it leads to a more complete sort of faith which will be defined presently. "When there is faith, the mind becomes concentrated upon the subject which it desires to comprehend and then due comprehension follows." (*B.S.Bh.* 1, 1, 2)

3. The First Two Steps: *Śravaṇa* and *Manana*

The first two steps constitute a discipline of exegesis. Not everyone is qualified to subject himself to it. One must be from one of the upper classes (*varṇa*) and normally a renouncer (*saṅnyāsin*). Besides domination over sense desires, truthfulness, chastity, patience and other ascetic virtues, one must be able to discern (metaphysically) the changeless from the ever changing, the transcendent from the relative, and be haunted by the desire for final release from rebirth into empirical forms of existence. Acceptance by a recognized *ācārya* authenticates such qualifications.

Then begins the first step: *śravaṇa*, hearing. It comprises listening to the texts, repeating and learning them by heart, having them explained linguistically and grammatically, receiving a *prima facie* understanding of them. Then being guided to divide them into meaning-units centred around a 'great saying' (*mahāvākya*) by ancillary sentences (*arthavāda*). Further, realizing that words in a unitary set of sentences have a contextual meaning which may differ from their primary meaning, and that this is bound to be the case of the words making up the 'great sayings' since these point to, unable to express, the Transcendent which stands beyond the reach of the empirical and primary meanings of word.

For instance, Śaṅkara when explaining a 'great saying' of *Taitt. Up.*[3] expands it, first, into:

> *Brahman* is that omniscient, omnipotent Cause from which proceed the origin, subsistence and dissolution of this universe. (*B.S.Bh.* 1, 1, 2)

Then he shows how this perfect and entirely sufficient cause of the totality of contingent beings differs from all the kinds of empirical causes with which we are acquainted. It is, he writes, "the sole substance from which (*yataḥ*) the [reality of the] world could originate.... At the same time it is the shaping Cause (*nimitta-kāraṇa*) of the world because outside *Brahman* as reality-providing Cause (*upādāna-kāraṇa*) there is no other ruling principle, for another Vedic text says that previously to creation the *Brahman* was one without a second." (*B.S.Bh.* 1, 4, 23)

Hence, creation presupposes "no independent matter, unreducible to the *Ātman*, such as the *pradhāna* (prime Matter) of the Sāṁkhyas or the Primordial atoms of Kaṇāda." (*Ait. Up. Bh.* 1, 1, 2) Creation follows upon an intelligent decision: "That *Ātman* who, being omniscient by nature can think without body and thinking organs, being then the only Existent, thought, 'Let me now create worlds,' and, having thus thought, i.e., considered or visualized those worlds, he created them after that deliberation." (*B.S.Bh.* 2, 2, 2) This intelligent volition did not imply any active change (*pravṛtti*) in the *Ātman* himself for "a thing which is devoid of motion (*pravṛtti-rahita*), e.g. a magnet, can nevertheless be a mover (*pravartaka*).... So the Lord also who is innermost in all, the *ātman* of all, the all-knower and the all-power, can although devoid of motion set the whole world into activity." (*B.S.Bh.* 2, 2, 2) Further, "the absolutely complete power of *Brahman* does not require to be supplemented by any extraneous help." (*B.S.Bh.* 2, 1, 24) As to the question whether *Brahman* created in order to satisfy some want, Śaṅkara's response is: "The *Brahman* is independent in its volitions; hence, it does not want things as yet unattained." (*Taitt. Up. Bh.* 2, 6, 1) Indeed, it is *āptakāma*: "the Lord 'whose desires were never unattained,' as the Vedic text says." (*B.S.Bh.* 2, 1, 33)

Another example: In *Chānd. Up.* 6, a young man, Śvetaketu, requests his father to teach him the *Brahman*. In a marvellous piece of catechism, the father takes up a whole series of approaches which together point to the *Brahman* in complementary fashion. Each one of them terminates with the same 'great saying': "This is the *Ātman*; That thou art." *Prima facie*, according to the primary meaning of the term 'thou,' this saying teaches that the boy Śvetaketu or at least his conscious ego or soul is the very *Brahman* which is the *Ātman* of all. But this would be nonsense, says Śaṅkara, for it would imply the contradiction that Śvetaketu whom the Upaniṣad presents as ignorant and unhappy is the Perfect whose essence is "Reality Knowledge infinite" (*satyam-jñānam-anantam*), as defined by *Taitt. Up.* 2, 1. Hence, the term 'thou' is to be taken in a secondary sense, as demanded by the context, and this can only be 'the innermost and absolute Witness (*Sākṣin*) which is the transcendent Consciousness that illumines every empirical thinker.' In another work, Śaṅkara explains that the latter's ego is only a reflection (*ābhāsa*) of that sun-like Consciousness. (*US* 8, 27, 33) In the same work, he sums up the exegesis of *Tattvamasi* (That thou art) after substituting the term *Sat* (Existent) for *Tat* (That); he here makes use of the logician Dinnāga's rule that in a sentence such as 'this is a black horse' the two terms in apposition restrict one another's meaning. Similarly:

> Because the terms *tvam* and *Sat* refer to one and the same entity, they function like the terms 'black' and 'horse'. Through being brought into apposition with *Sat* (the Existent) which expresses absence of misery, *tvam* [loses its connotation of misery and] is left with the meaning of *Sat*. And in the same way through being set in apposition with a word [namely, *tvam*] signifying 'inner self' (*pratyag-ātman*), the term *Sat* [is left with the meaning 'inmost Self.'] ...
>
> Without giving up their own meaning (*svārtha*), the terms *tvam* and *Sat* convey a special (*viśiṣṭa*) meaning. And they lead to the comprehensive knowledge (*avagati*) of the innermost *Ātman*. Apart from this meaning, there can be no other one which would not result in a contradiction." (*US* 18, 170-173)

According to a custom of the Upaniṣads, let me repeat this important conclusion: "Apart from this meaning, there can be no other which would not result in a contradiction."

The second step is *manana*: reflection, the application of one's critical mind (with the help of the *ācārya*) to test the rational value of the explanation of the text provided in the first step. How does it compare with rival explanations (the *pūrvapakṣas*, which Śaṅkara exposes in all their apparent force and then refutes in his commentaries)? Does it resist any objection, any doubt? This investigation is to be pursued until the least shade of doubt has vanished and the rational credibility of the non-dualistic explanation is fully established. Once this is attained, faith flourishes unhindered:

> When in the becalmed mind, the conviction is held that it is [truly as explained], this is faith, *śraddhā* (*citta-prasāde āstikya-buddhiḥ*)." (*Muṇḍ. Up. Bh.* 2, 1, 7)[4]

4. From *Jñāna* to *Vijñāna*

Before passing on to the third step, let me take up an enlightening passage of Śaṅkara's commentary (probably early) on the *Bhagavad Gītā*. In it he explains the meaning (at least in this text) of *vijñāna* (discerning knowledge) as distinct from *jñāna* (knowledge):

> *Jñāna* is the enlightenment (*avabodha*) regarding the *Ātman*, etc. as obtained from the *śāstra* (exegetical discipline) and the *ācāryas* (teachers). [This knowledge is still theoretical and external.]
> *Vijñāna* is the experience of that (*tad-anubhava*) in all its particularity (*viśeṣataḥ*). (*Bh. Gītā Bh.* 3, 41)
>
> [*Vijñāna* consists in] converting into one's own experience (*svā+nubhava-karaṇam*) the knowledge obtained from the science. (*Bh.Gītā Bh.* 6, 8; repeated in 7, 2 and 9, 1)

This knowledge must precede *vijñāna*. It is apophatic, not merely negative. Certainly, no conceptual knowledge can *express* the *Brahman* but most of the 'great sayings' are *positive indicatives* of its Reality. By them, "it is indicated positively but not expressed" (*tal-lakṣyate na tū+cyate*). (*Taitt. Up. Bh.* 2, 1) Śaṅkara had to counter Maṇḍana Miśra who, in his *Brahma-siddhi*, contended on the base of the 'great saying' *Neti neti* (Not so, not so) that the upaniṣadic teaching terminated in apophatism with regard to the *Brahman* and acosmism with regard to the world. Indeed, said Śaṅkara, "if the Witness (the *Brahman* in us) had not been positively established (*aprasiddhatvāt*), a mere void would result." (*US* 18, 125) But, if its positive ascertainment has preceded (*pūrvā prasiddhi*), then the teaching has a positive content, the *Brahman* as *Sat* (Existent), and can be turned into experience.

5. The Third Step: *Dhyānam*, the Assimilative Contemplation

At the end of the teaching comes the time for *yoga*. Provided with a truth-content and freed from all doubts, the mind can now concentrate on this content in *nididhyāsana*. The analysis of this term will enlighten us on the nature of this final step: *āsana* means the squatting *yoga*-posture to be adopted, *dhy* means the intellect which is to fix itself exclusively, *di* with ever-renewed intensity (as implied by this repetitive prefix *di*), *ni*, upon the truth previously ascertained. The simpler term *dhyāna* (earlier much used by Buddhism and which gave *jhāna*, *ch'n*, and *zen*) is also used, it means fixation of the intellect (*dhi/dhy* or *buddhi*), contemplation. It demands a cessation of all mental modifications[5] (in common with all forms of *yoga*) and a positive truth and reality to be concentrated upon (as in all forms of Brahmanic-Hindu and Jain forms of *yoga* but not in Buddhist *dhyāna*). Śaṅkara insists that *yoga*-concentration is useless so long as this positive truth is not yet thoroughly ascertained. It could even be pernicious as in the case of Buddhism, Sāṁkhya and all doctrines incompatible with his own Advaita (non-dualism) (and which he thinks he has definitely refuted) for, assimilated through *yoga*, a false view would root man deeper into Nescience.

The effect of *dhyāna* is not an assimilation of the soul to the Absolute which would connote an ontological transformation. Ontologically, it is already as similar to its Prototype and as non-dual with it as a reflection with the face it images. But it is an assimilation by the mind of the truth established in it by the teaching, an appropriation which may be compared with the digestion of well chewed up food. Single-minded contemplation interiorizes that truth, gives it a vivid, existential evidence which imbues the whole subject and enraptures him. Hopefully it acquires the quality of irresistible immediate experience (*anubhava*), of *vijñāna* as defined above.

Is this the *avagati*, the comprehensive penetrating intuition of the absolute Essence which satiates the inherent desire to know the *Brahman*? And thus the end of Nescience and all its sequels? Śaṅkara admits that liberation can take place in this life (*jivan-mukti*) but apparently not with all its sequels since life continues unto death when liberation can become perfect. However, Śaṅkara more simply says:

> In the matter of the higher Knowledge (*parā Vidyā*), the aim is accomplished simultaneously with the realization of the import of the texts for there is nothing here to be done except becoming centred on the sole knowledge of the meaning revealed by the mere words. (*Muṇḍ. Up. Bh.* 1, 1, 6)

This accomplishment implies no elevation of the soul and neither evanescence or extinction of it. It is only its ignorance which vanishes. The soul finally ceases to consider itself as independent or relatively independent monad, either without cause (as in Sāṁkhya) or in dualistic relation with its causal Lord (as in Nyāya). It realizes its nature as reflection of the *Brahman* and lives with utter happiness its non-dualistic relation of intimate closeness in complete ontological dependence with this *Brahman* which is its uppermost and innermost *Ātman*. And far from losing the world, it now "enjoys all its desires" in the fullness of its blissful experience:

> The Upaniṣad says, 'The knower of *Brahman* enjoys all desires.' This means that he enjoys all delights procured by desirable objects, without exception. Does he enjoy sons, heavens, etc. alternately as we do? No, he enjoys all delectable things simultaneously, as amassed together in a single moment, through a single perception. This perception is eternal like the light of the sun. It is non-different from the essence of *Brahman* which we have described as Reality-Knowledge-Infinite.... He enjoys all things by that *Brahman* whose nature is omniscience. (*Taitt. Up. Bh.* 2, 1, 1)

6. The Role of Divine Grace

Śaṅkara had no illusion about the success of the liberating discipline. Very few, he said, one in a thousand, reached its goal. Already one upaniṣadic thinker, noticing the apparent inefficacy of the methods proposed by his predecessors, spoke of divine grace and even election as the only sure warrants of success (*Kaṭha Up*. 2, 23; repeated in *Muṇḍ. Up*. 3, 2, 3). This seems to imply that not alone the common inability for highly intellectual pursuits or negligence and failure to persevere are the obstacles to success but above all the opacity of the divine mystery which cannot be pierced by human ingenuity but only revealed from within.

Yet, Śaṅkara does not go all the way to seeing the need for a divine self-revelation "to whom he chooses," as the Upaniṣad said. Perhaps it is his conviction that the *Brahman* is most immediately immanent to every man that hinders him from apprehending its inviolability short of self-disclosure:

> The knowledge which consists in awareness of the *Ātman* is not 'an effect to be achieved' inasmuch as it is invariably coapprehended in every cognition as that illumining consciousness which is distinct from all forms of objects set up by Nescience.... *Brahman* is self-evident: we have only to eliminate what is falsely attributed to *Brahman* by Nescience. (*Bh.Gītā Bh.* 18, 50)

But is the process of *Brahmajijñāsā* in need of no higher grace that the mercy of the teacher? No, says Śaṅkara,

> We must assume that salvation is effected by the discerning knowledge (*vijñānena*) caused by (*hetukena*) His grace (*tadanugraha*), because Scripture teaches it. (*B.S.Bh.* 2, 3, 4)

> [Salvation takes place] "through the obtention of knowledge from the grace of the Lord. (*Bh.Gītā Bh.* 2, 39)

In correspondence to this grace of enlightenment there grows in man a devotion (*bhakti*) which perfects his faith. The latter is now better defined as "the conviction of the truth [of the teaching] accompanied with devotion." (*Bṛh. Up. Bh.* 3, 9. 21) In Śaṅkara, devotion (*bhakti*) is the intellectual love which applies man to his quest, makes his conviction steadfast and focuses him exclusively on the *Brahman-Ātman*. The following is a felicitous explanation of the intricate accord of the Lord's grace and man's *bhakti*-love in the Vedāntic contemplation:

> Out of mercy, anxious that they may attain bliss, I dwell in their internal-organ (*antaḥ-karaṇa*), which is the abode of the *Ātman*, and I destroy the darkness of Nescience, i.e., of that illusory Knowledge which results from the lack of discrimination.
> I do that by the lamp of wisdom, the lamp of discrimination. This lamp is fed by the oil of devotion (*bhakti-prasāda*), fanned by the wind of earnest meditation on Me, furnished with the wick of right intuition, purified by the cultivation of chastity and other virtues, held in an internal-organ completely detached from all worldly concerns, placed in the wind-sheltered nook of that mind (*manas*) which is withdrawn from all sense-objects and untainted by attachment or aversion, and shining with the light of right knowledge generated by the constant practice of concentration and contemplation. (*Bh.Gītā Bh.* 10, 11)

Notes

1 [First published in *Semiotica del Testo Mistico, Atti del Congresso Internazionale per le celebrazioni centenarie di Sant'Ignazio di Loyola (1491/1556), San Giovanni della Croce (1542/1591), Fra Luigi di Leon (1527/1591): L'Aquila, Forte Spagnolo, 24-30 giugno 1991*, ed. Giuseppe De Gennaro (L'Aquila: Edizioni del Gallo Cedrone, 1995) 666-674. Efforts to

trace the current rights holder, Sig. Aristodemo Ferri of L'Aquila, Italy, having failed, this is being reprinted here courtesy De Nobili College, Pune.]

[2] "*Pratyag-ātma-viṣaya jijñāsā*," *Kena Up. Bh.* 1. [Correcting '1, 1'.]

[3] [*Taitt. Up.* 3, 1.]

[4] [Correcting *Māṇḍukya Up. bhāṣya* 2, 1, 7.]

[5] "*citta-vṛtti-nirodha.*" This is the definition of *yoga* given by Patañjali in his *Yoga-sūtra*. It stresses only the self-emptying.

19

FROM THE VEDAS TO RADHAKRISHNAN[1]

When I heard for the first time Dr S. Radhakrishnan at the Calcutta Silver Jubilee session of the All-India Philosophical Congress, in 1950, I realized with what determination he upheld his characterization of Śaṅkara's teachings as "a great example of a purely philosophical scheme."[2] This shocked me as my reading of the *ācārya's* commentaries had convinced me that he was strictly an exegete of the *Śruti* and even the paragon among *śrutivādins*. I had to examine this question thoroughly.

1. The Testimonial Method of Śaṅkarācārya (*śrutivāda*)

It became the object of my doctoral research. I spent many months scrutinizing the Sanskrit text of Śaṅkara's authentic works and compared it especially with Rāmānūja's long endeavour in *Śrī Bhāṣya* to criticize adversely his very method of *śrutivāda*. The result was a doctoral dissertation, 'The Theological Method of Śaṅkara,' which was appraised positively by those among the specialists of that time (1954) to whom I sent it who took the trouble of reacting by letter to its content (men like Olivier Lacombe, Hajime Nakamura, S.K. Belvalkar, Dhirendra Mohan Datta, Paul Hacker, Helmut von Glasenapp, Peter Johanns, A.J. Alston, Louis Renou, A.C. Mukerji, Daniel Ingalls, J.A. Cuttat, H.O. Mascarenhas and J.B. van Buitenen).[3]

I had found Śaṅkara's undertaking to be strikingly similar to the scholastic pursuit of our Catholic theologians in its reliance on and exploitation of an authoritative 'revelation' and tradition (*Śruti* and *Smṛti*). This is why I had called his method theological. However, in the mid-century, the term 'theological' was associated by many Hindus with 'dogmatism' in the sense of 'positive assertion of unwarranted or arrogant opinion' or 'system of ideas based on insufficiently examined premises' whereas it meant '*Śruti*-based *Brahmajijñāsā*.' Consequently I had to explain and defend this in a further article.[4] Recently, I rather speak of the 'hermeneutical' method of Śaṅkara and have examined his hermeneutical pre-dispositions.[5]

His essential task is to explain the 'great sayings' which define *Brahman* and for this he has, since the *Brahman* is inexpressible, to have recourse to the indicative power of words. He arrives at this indicated meaning through the method of *anvaya* and *vyatireka* (agreement and difference)—for instance, between *tat* and *tvam* in *Tattvamasi*. Since this was acknowledged by but a few at that time, I exposed it in diverse writings[6] and showed how one of his first direct disciples, Sureśvara, adhered to this method in his *Naiṣkarmya Siddhi*[7] It is equivalent to the recourse to *lakṣaṇā*, already allowed by Jaimini, as Śaṅkara knew well, or to the later but more precise *jahadajahallakṣaṇā*.

Among the commentaries attributed to Śaṅkara, was the *vivaraṇa* on *Māṇḍ. Up.* and its added *Āgama-śāstra*. Since there were many reasons to refuse it authenticity and reputed scholars like Belvalkar rejected it among spurious works, I excluded it from the sources of my interpretation. Now this was important because the current interpretation upheld by the so-called 'school of Śaṅkara' (but this means the later expositors) in terms of *māyāvāda* (illusionistic acosmism) depended essentially on that *vivaraṇa*. Its authenticity was investigated more and more thoroughly in the course of the last four decades. The most thorough research on it has resulted in the book of Thomas E. Wood, *The Māṇḍūkya Upaniṣad and the Āgama Śāstra*,[8] which has been acclaimed as decisive and deserves serious critical attention.

Briefly, what Wood found is this: the *Āgama Śāstra*, commonly ascribed to Gauḍapāda, is a composite of four separate treatises united as one *Kārikā*; only some of its verses may be ascribed to Gauḍapāda and these are not illusionistic. As to its *vivaraṇa*, it was not the work of Śaṅkarācārya but of a much later Advaitin. The first mention of it occurs around AD 1300 when Ānandagiri composes a *ṭikā* on it and attributes the *vivaraṇa* to the *ācārya* himself. But Ānandagiri is far from reliable on such matters for he wrote another 8 commentaries on works of certainly spurious or very doubtful Śaṅkarian authorship. Wood argues that it is the later (probably by 5 centuries after Śaṅkara) author of the *vivaraṇa* who put together the various pieces of the *Āgama Śāstra*, commented on them and thus introduced his version of Advaita into the teaching of the school. It blends Buddhist with Advaita views. Mahāyāna provides the acosmism of the fourth treatise, the *Ālata-śānti prakaraṇa* according to which nothing arises and nothing perishes. Such teaching contrasts sharply with that of Śaṅkara (especially in his commentaries on *Bṛhad-āraṇyaka-upaniṣad* and the *Brahma-sūtra*) and his direct disciples.

One point which had puzzled me was clarified by Wood: why was it currently held that the concept of *Īśvara* suits only the *saguṇa* and not at all the *nirguṇa Brahman*? In fact, Belvalkar and Ranade had already pointed out in their *History of Indian Philosophy*, p. 325, that "the Prājña [the self of deep sleep], to the author of the Māṇḍūkya, signifies what philosophy calls God. As contrasted with him, stands the Ātman, which is... the Absolute" and that "it is worth noting that God is sundered here from the Absolute as with a hatchet, and ultimate reality assigned only to the Absolute and not to God."[9] Now this sundering did not agree at all with the practice of Śaṅkara in such writings as the *Brahma-sūtra Bhāṣya* which refers the relational term *īśvara* (lord of) indifferently to the one or the other *Brahman*. Wood provides the solution when he established that the first words of the 6th mantra of the *Māṇḍūkya*, *eṣa sarveśvara* (this is the lord of all), have been wrongly referred to the preceding mantra 5 which concerns the deep sleep self or *Prājña* rather than to the so-called *turīya* or fourth self and Absolute of mantra 7.[10]

In answer to the question, is not '*māyā*' a key-term in Śaṅkara's writings, I had to present the reckoning made by the German Paul Hacker of the frequency of that term compared to the frequency of '*avidyā*' and '*ajñāna*' in *B.S.Bh*. The very low frequency of '*māyā*' in the sense of 'illusion' distinguishes the *ācārya* from his late school.[11]

So long as the *māyāvāda* interpretation was reigning, the causality of *Brahman* could not be understood as creation in the sense of free origination of the totality of the universe in all its phases from the *nirguṇa Brahman* alone. But now I could establish it thoroughly in a paper which had to be reprinted several times.[12]

After exposing how cardinal was in Śaṅkara the concept of *Sākṣin* (Witness) as designating the *Paramātman*,[13] it was time to wonder whether the term 'person' in its original and still proper sense as developed in Christianity was applicable to the *nirguṇa Brahman*.[14] Allied questions regarding the definition of 'person,' the history of its development, its application to God, angels and human beings, etc. occupied me much during the seventies because they had begun to appear important to my interlocutors in seminars and congresses.[15]

Naturally the whole progress of Śaṅkara's teaching as a *Sādhanā* had to be investigated carefully. This was done in several papers[16] and the most satisfactorily in an article on "The Dynamics of Contemplation."[17] The allied question of "love versus identity" had been posed early by Prof. Malkani, a die-hard upholder of *māyāvāda*. He read my reply before he died but it was published only when his quarterly was revived in 1980.[18]

In 1987, I was asked to deliver the Śaṅkara special lecture at the Srinagar session of the Indian Philosophical Congress. I made the paper a sort of summing-up in which I included all the salient points which had been the objects of my research.[19]

For the IPC[20] celebration in Delhi of the centenary of S. Radhakrishnan, I was requested to evaluate his interpretation of Śaṅkara in his *Indian Philosophy*. My paper was, I hope, pertinently critical and was published in his *Centenary Volume*.[21] A second paper requested from the BHU[22] treated of his second presentation in the book *Philosophy East and West*.[23]

Finally, I presented this year an answer to the question, why do Śaṅkara and the other Vedāntins differ in their interpretations of the same *Śruti*? My answer attributes this to the diversity of their para-textual understanding of *vākya* (sentence); attention was paid chiefly to the differences of this understanding in Śaṅkara and Rāmānuja.[24]

2. Other Explorations in the Field of Philosophical Hinduism

The course[25] of History of Indian Philosophy, which I began to offer from 1968, was not meant to give only isolated items

(Vedas, Brāhmaṇas, Upaniṣads, darśanas, etc.) but to reveal a development dynamically pursued by way of key-questions, newly discovered methods, options, rejections, preferences and a kind of telefinalism which appeared to betray a divine guidance. Explicit consideration of such factors of development gave rise to several papers.[26]

After the publication in collaboration with nine other Jesuits of *Religious Hinduism*, which contained 2 chapters of mine about the Vedāntins,[27] a criticism was raised concerning the nature of Rāmānuja's doctrine: mitigated pantheism or panentheism? My elucidation implied a rather technical enquiry into Rāmānuja's own basic conceptions and explanations.[28]

Among the other articles which may appear saliently valuable are the following: a study in depth of sacrifice (*yajña*) in the Vedas and Brāhmaṇas;[29] a transphilosophical study of patterns and theories of causality;[30] a search for the elements of permanent value in Sāṁkhya[31] and for Kaṇāda's early teaching on knowledge;[32] a commentary on the Sāṁkhya-Kārikā;[33] a tracing of the philosophers' transition from atheism to theism during AD 400-1000;[34] a re-centering of the *Gītā* on the Gītākāra's reformulation of *karma*[35] and a re-placing of the *Gītā* within its historico-cultural context.[36]

3. The Notion of Person

Because Sanskrit did not develop a philosophical concept of 'person' and, nevertheless Western translators have wrongly interpreted '*saguṇa*' and '*nirguṇa*' as if they meant equivalently 'personal' and 'impersonal,' I felt it indispensable to clarify the denotation and the connotations of the term 'person.' For lack of such clarification, dialogue between Indian intellectuals and Christians was too often running at cross purposes. The essential clarifications will be found in "The Open Person and the Closed Individual," "Towards an Indian View of the Person," and "A Short History of the Person."[37] An earlier article clarifying the notions of 'person,' 'soul,' and '*ātman*' was found enlightening by intellectuals from Bengal.

As to 'man,' its comprehension was described in different contexts, Vedic-Brahmanic-*Gītā*,[38] Aristotelian-Thomistic[39] and Christian.[40]

4. The Christian Side in Philosophico-Religious Dialogue

The whole of my teaching career has been shaped up by a twofold conviction, namely, first, that I could not teach philosophy in India without knowing Sanskrit and understanding the long history of Indian thought, and, second, that I could not do it without frequently encountering and dialoguing with colleagues of the Indian universities. I also made early the option of answering their requests for written contributions rather than pursuing an autonomous course of writing what it would please me to write. Hence, the nature of my bibliography.

Among the many queries from Hindu colleagues regarding Christianity, I note the following: how do you form your priestly students in a way which blends their studies with spiritual growth?[41] What do Christians understand by 'secularism' and 'supernatural'?[42] Could you sketch out the development of Christian monasticism?[43] What is the meaning and importance of theological hope?[44] What is the relation of the Catholic Church with the modern world,[45] with society,[46] with secularization?[47] Which Indian categories can Christianity use to express itself in India?[48] How does the present mutation of values in the West affect the Catholic Church?[49] What is the relation of Jesus with man's freedom?[50] Is not his 'incarnation' to be understood as '*avatāra*'?[51] Is he related to the present transforming growth of religions?[52] Which is the nature of 'Christian' philosophy?[53]

5. Conclusion

Apart from all these items, other pieces of writing are in the hands of editors or being readied for eventual publication. So my bibliographical list, like the future, remains open.

Notes

[1] [A Paper for the Symposium on the Contribution to 'Indian Philosophy' by Contemporary Christian Thinkers of India, Madras: Satyanilayam, 1-3 March 1994, 6 pp. typescript, published here for the first time with permission of De Nobili College, Pune.]

[2] S. Radhakrishnan, *Indian Philosophy*, 2 vols. (Oxford: Oxford University Press, 1923; London: George Allen & Unwin, 1929) 445.

[3] Cf. my bibliography ['Bibliography of Fr Richard De Smet, SJ,' 9 November 1993, 25 pp. typescript, unpublished] I/1: 'The Theological Method of Śaṃkara' (Rome: Pontifical Gregorian University, 1953), unpublished [see "Introduction" note 3 above].

[4] I/4: "Theological Method and Vedānta" = ch. 4 above.

[5] I/37: "Śaṅkara's Perspective on Meaning and Truth" = ch. 16 above.

[6] I/2: "The Correct Interpretation of the Definitions of the Absolute according to Śrī Śaṅkarācārya and Saint Thomas Aquinas" = ch. 21 below; I/6: "Śaṅkara's Non-Dualism (*Advaitavāda*)" (1964/68) = ch. 3 above; I/18: "Chinks in the Armour of *Avidyā*" = ch. 8 above; I/19: "Origin: Creation and Emanation" = ch. 25 below; I/23: "Forward Steps in Śaṅkara Research" = ch. 11 above; I/27: "Radhakrishnan's Interpretation of Śaṅkara" = ch. 13 above; I/33: 'Guidelines in Indian Philosophy,' cyclostyled notes for students (Poona: De Nobili College, 1968-1975), esp. 278-314; I/34: 'A Selection of Texts from Śaṅkarācārya,' cyclostyled notes for students (Poona: Jnana Deepa Vidyapeeth, n.d.) 30 pp.; I/35: 'The Vedāntins' Diverse Conceptions of *Vākya* (Sentence) as Responsible for the Diversity of their Interpretations of the Same Scriptures,' unpublished; I/39: "Langage et connaissance de l'Absolu chez Çaṃkara" = ch. 1 above.

[7] I/5: "The Logical Structure of '*Tattvamasi*' according to Sureśvara's *Naiṣkarmya Siddhi*" = ch. 5 above.

[8] (Delhi: Motilal Banarsidass, 1992).

[9] [S.K. Belvalkar and R.D. Ranade, *History of Indian Philosophy: The Creative Period* (New Delhi: Oriental Books Reprint Corporation, 1974).]

[10] See Wood 2-4 and 8-15. And my I/27: "Radhakrishnan's Interpretation of Śaṅkara" = ch. 13 above; and I/28: "Radhakrishnan's Second Presentation of Śaṅkara's Teaching" = ch. 14 above.

[11] I/7: "*Māyā* or *Ajñāna*?" = ch. 6 above; see also I/18: "Chinks in the Armour of *Avidyā*" = ch. 8 above.

[12] I/19: "Origin: Creation and Emanation" = ch. 25 below; also I/10: "Śaṅkara and Aquinas on Creation" = ch. 22 below; and I/29: "The Creative Word in Śāṅkara Vedānta" = ch. 15 above.

[13] I/15: "The Witness (*Sākṣin*), Source of Thought and Action," *Philosophy: Theory and Practice (Seminar on World Philosophy, Madras, Dec. 7-17, 1970)*, ed. T.M.P. Mahadevan (Madras: University CASP, 1974) 176-185.

[14] I/14: "Is the Concept of Person Congenial to Śāṅkara Vedānta?" = *Brahman and Person* ch. 8.

[15] See the whole section II F: Person, Man.

[16] I/9: "Śaṅkara and Aquinas on Liberation" = ch. 21 below; I/20: "Contemplation in Śaṅkara and Rāmānuja" = ch. 9 above.
[17] I/38: "The Dynamics of Contemplation according to Śaṅkarācārya" = ch. 18 above.
[18] I/8: "Love versus Identity," *Indian Philosophical Quarterly* (Pune) 7/4 (July 1980) 519-526.
[19] I/23: "Forward Steps in Śaṅkara Research" = ch. 11 above.
[20] [Indian Philosophical Congress.]
[21] I/27: "Radhakrishnan's Interpretation of Śaṅkara" = ch. 13 above.
[22] [Benares Hindu University].
[23] I/28: "Radhakrishnan's Second Presentation of Śaṅkara's Teaching" = ch. 14 above.
[24] I/35: 'The Vedāntins' Diverse Conceptions of *Vākya* (Sentence) as Responsible for the Diversity of their Interpretations of the Same Scriptures,' 1994, unpublished.
[25] II B/16: 'Guidelines in [History of] Indian Philosophy' (Pune: De Nobili College, 1968-1975) 314 pp.
[26] II A/3: "Some Governing Principles in Indian Philosophy," *The Philosophical Quarterly* **35** (1963) 249-258; II A/8: "The Lag Between *Sanātana Dharma* and Darshanic Wisdom," *Transactions of the Indian Institute of Advanced Study* (Simla) **1** (1965) 105-108; II A/12: "Stumbling-Blocks or Stepping-Stones," *Western and Eastern Spiritual Values of Life*, ed. Swami B. H. Bon Mahārāj (Vrindāban: Institute of Oriental Philosophy, 1962) 68-75; II A/19: "Hindu and Neo-Hindu Exegesis," *Indian Theological Studies* **21** (1984) 225-240; II A/23: "The Indian Ascertainment of the Godhead (From the Vedas to Udayānācārya)," *Indica* **16** (1980) 59-73; II A/27: "The Hindu *Dharma*: Permanence and Change," *E. Ugarte Felicitation Volume: Philosophy and Human Development*, ed. A. Amaladass (Madras: Satyanilayam, 1986) 3-26; II A/28: "Notes on Hinduism versus the Plurality of Religious Traditions," *Boletin de la Asociación Española de Orientalistas* **21** (1985) 289-300; and especially II A/30: "The Status of the Scriptures in the Holy History of India," *Research Seminar on Non-Christian Scriptures*, ed. D.S. Amalorpavadass (Bangalore: NBCLC, 1975) 280-299 and II A/31: "Dynamics of Hinduism and Hindu-Christian Dialogue," *Communio: International Catholic Review* **15** (Winter 1988) 436-450.
[27] [See chs. 3 above and 20 below.]
[28] II A/22: "Rāmānuja, Pantheist or Panentheist?" *Annals of the Bhandarkar Oriental Research Institute (Diamond Jubilee Volume)* (1977-78) 561-571.
[29] II B/2: "Fleeting Time and Sacrificially Produced Continuity in Vedic Brahmanism and in Early Christianity," *Boletin de la Asociación Española de Orientalistas* **17** (1981) 147-166; also in *Indian Theological Studies* **19/2** (1982) 1-26.
[30] II B/5: "Patterns and Theories of Causality," *Essays in Philosophy Presented to Dr. T. M. P. Mahadevan on his 50th Birthday* (Madras: Ganesh, 1962) 347-367; also in *Indian Ecclesiastical Studies* **2** (1963) 169-190, and *Philosophy Today* 9/2-4 (1965) 134-146.

[31] II B/8: "Elements of Permanent Value in Sāṃkhya," *Oriental Thought* (Nashik) **3**/2-4 (1957) 135-156.
[32] II B/9: "Kaṇāda's Teaching on Knowledge," *Indian Antiquary* (3rd series) **1** (1964) 13-30.
[33] II B/17: 'Notes on the Sāṃkhya-Kārikā: Ad mentem M. Ledrus, S.J.,' cyclostyled notes for students, 64 pp. (Poona: De Nobili College, 1954).
[34] II B/12: "The Philosophers' Transition from Atheism to Theism from the Fourth to the Eleventh Century A.D.," *Challenges of Societies in Transition*, ed. M. Barnabas, P.S. Jacob and S.K. Hulbe (New Delhi: Macmillan, 1978) 310-338; also as "Arjun Meditates on the Philosophers' Transition from Atheism to Theism from the Fourth to the Tenth Century A.D," *When Two Great Hearts Meet*, ed. E. De Meulder (Allahabad: St Paul Publications, 1976) 164-191.
[35] II C/5: "A Copernican Reversal: The Gītākāra's Reformulation of *Karma*," *Chinmaya Mission Silver Jubilee Volume*, ed. S. Barlingay (Poona, 1976) 34-41; also in *Philosophy East and West* **27**/1 (1977) 53-63.
[36] II C/3: "Gita in Time and Beyond," *The Bhagavad Gita and the Bible. Proceedings of the Seminar under the Auspices of the Christian Retreat and Study Centre, Rajpur, Dehradun. May 5-9, 1972*, ed. B.R. Kulkarni (Delhi: Unity Books, 1972) 1-30.
[37] II F/4: "The Open Person and the Closed Individual" = *Brahman and Person* ch. 6; II F/6: "Towards and Indian View of the Person" = *Brahman and Person* ch. 9; II F/11: "A Short History of the Person" = *Brahman and Person* chs. 3-5.
[38] II F/5: "The Early Indian Understanding of Man" = *Brahman and Person* ch. 7.
[39] II F/7: "The Aristotelian-Thomist Conception of Man" = *Brahman and Person* ch. 11; II F/13: "The Concept of Man in Thomism and Neo-Thomism" = *Brahman and Person* ch. 13.
[40] II F/12: "The Christian Conception of Man" = *Brahman and Person* ch. 12.
[41] III A/6: "Training in Spiritual Life," *Silver Jubilee Commemoration Volume, Nowrosjee Wadia College* (Poona, 1958) 1-11.
[42] III A/19: "Is there an Order of the Supernatural?" *Transactions of the Indian Institute of Advanced Study* **1** (1965) 119-122; III A/75: "Secularism and the Supernatural," Exchange of letters between Prof. Mrs Saral Jhingram and De Smet, *Indian Theological Studies* **29** (1992) 55-67.
[43] III A/20: "The Adaptive Development of Christian Monasticism," *Transactions of the Indian Institute of Advanced Study* **1** (1965) 191-202.
[44] III A/23: "Theology of Hope and the Meaning of Mission," *Reflection* (Rajpur, Dehradun) **3** (1969) 3-10; III A/27: "The Marxist-Protestant-Catholic Rediscovery of Hope," *Bethany Golden Jubilee Souvenir* (Trivandrum: Bethany Ashram, 1969) 121-126.
[45] III A/28: "The Catholic Church and the Modern World," *Islam and the Modern Age* **1**/2 (July 1970) 59-67.
[46] III A/69: "Christianity and Society," *The Viśva-Bhārati Journal of Philosophy* **21**/1 (1984) 89-99; also in *Indian Theological Studies* **22**/4 (1985) 325-337.

[47] III A/43: "Secularization as a Dimension of Christianity" (A summary by D. Rodrigues) *Aumol* **19** (September 1972) 124-126; also in *Ateismo e Dialogo* (Bollettino del Segretariato per i non-credenti) **8**/2 (1973) 24(84)-29(89); III A/50: "The Challenge of Secularization," *Present Day Challenges to Religion*, ed. Thomas Paul (Alwaye: PITP, 1973) 83-98.

[48] III A/14: "Categories of Indian Philosophy and Communication of the Gospel," *Religion and Society* **10**/3 (1963) 20-26; III A/15: "Towards an Indian Christology," *The Clergy Monthly Supplement* 7/6 (1965) 254-260; also in *Religion and Society* **12** (1965) 6-15.

[49] III A/22: "Mutation of Values in Present-Day Europe," *Quest* **60** (Jan.-Mar. 1969) 21-27; III A/65: "The Catholic Church in the Crucible," *Religious Situation in the Present-Day World: Seminar Papers*, ed. Taran Singh (Patiala: Punjabi University, 1980) 49-57.

[50] III A/33: "Jesus and the Freedom of Man," *The Call Divine* **19**/11 (July 1971) 582-583.

[51] III A/60: "Jesus and the Avatāra," *Dialogue and Syncretism: An Interdisciplinary Approach*, ed. J.D. Gort, H.M. Vroom, R. Fernhout, A. Wessels (Grand Rapids: W.B. Eerdmans / Amsterdam: Editions Rodopi, 1989) 153-162.

[52] III A/59: "Christ and the Transforming Growth of Religions," *Vidyajyoti: Journal of Theological Reflection* **55** (1991) 449-457.

[53] III A/30: "The Nature of Christian Philosophy," *World Perspectives in Philosophy, Religion and Culture: Essays presented to Prof. Dhirendra Mohan Datta* (Patna: Bihar Darshan Parishad, 1968) 362-368; III A/57: "Stretching Forth to Eternity: The Mystical Doctrine of Gregory of Nyssa," *Prayer and Contemplation*, ed. C.M. Vadakkekara (Bangalore: Asian Trading Corporation, 1980) 331-348; III A/70: "The Medieval Inheritance of Dante," *Journal of the Department of English* (University of Calcutta) **23**/1-2 (1986-1987) 37-49; III B/4: "Method and Doctrine of Saint Thomas Aquinas," *Bulletin of the Ramakrishna Mission Institute of Culture* (Calcutta) **10**/10 (1959) 217-224; III B/5: "Philosophy and Science as Integral Parts of Wisdom," *The Philosophical Quarterly* **33**/1 (1960) 31-39; III B/10: "The Problematics of the Knowledge of God," *Indian Ecclesiastical Studies* **10**/2 (1971) 92-96; also in *Indian Philosophical Annual* 7 (1971) 121-125; III B/13: "Man's Integral Dynamism and his Quest for Values," *Reality, Knowledge and Value: Felicitation Volume in Honour of A.G. Javadekar*, ed. S.R. Bhatt (Delhi: Bharatiya Vidya Prakashan, 1985) 133-142; III B/3: "The Point of Departure of Metaphysics," *The Philosophical Quarterly* **28**/4 (1956) 265-271.

20

ŚAṄKARA'S NON-DUALISM (*ADVAITAVĀDA*) (1997)[1]

The restoration of upaniṣadic Brahmanism was the work of the Vedānta school, whose basic text was the *Brahma-sūtra* compiled by Bādarāyaṇa to harmonise the teachings of the Upaniṣads. Of the first Vedāntins we know hardly more than a few names. But the masterful commentary written by Śrī Śaṅkarācārya on that *Sūtra* as well as his commentaries on nine Upaniṣads and on the *Gītā* together with some minor works set such a high standard of rigorous teaching that they immediately commanded the whole further development of the Vedānta school.

The dates of his life are uncertain. After exploring the whole question again during the last fifty years, specialists now agree to place him in the eighth century AD and more probably in the first half of that century. A Brahmin, he was probably born at Kāladi (Malabar) and spent many years in the monastery which he founded in Śṛṅgeri (Mysore). He is generally reported to have died relatively young either in Kedarnāth (Himālaya) or perhaps in Kāñci. The other traditional details of his life are legendary.

What set him above all previous Vedāntins was his success in synthesizing for the first time the elements of pure wisdom scattered in the Upaniṣads and, through selection, adaptation or downright rejection, relating to that synthesis the variety of contrasting currents and doctrines which had developed up to his time. Before him, this variety had engendered bewilderment and scepticism or a sort of resigned conformism. This situation had been aptly summarised in *Mahābhārata,* Vana-parvan 312, 115:

Tārko 'pratiṣṭhāḥ śrutayo vibhinnāḥ
Naiko ṛṣir yasya vacaḥ pramāṇam
Dharmasya tattvam nihitaṁguhāyām
Mahājano yena gataḥ sa panthāḥ.

Reasoning is unstable and sacred texts diverge;
There is not one Sage whose word carries authority;
The essence of Religion is kept bound in a cave;
The path trod by the great ones is the path to follow.

1. The Current Interpretation of Śaṅkara's Teaching

The young *saṅnyāsin* who was to release the essence of the Religion from the cave of confusion appeared around 700 AD endowed with the best gifts which nature and *sādhana* could provide: metaphysical genius, faultless acumen, dexterous logic, incomparable erudition and unshakable faith. Because of his exclusive faith in *Śruti* he was to be a *śrutivādin:* his writings would be commentaries (*bhāṣya*) following the order of his basic texts, rather than systematic treatises. Due to his readiness to accommodate himself to the traditional modes of thought, he would use the predominantly Sāṁkhya language of speculation and fail to create many new terms to express his novel conceptions. Finally, the greatness of his name would induce paler imitators and even opponents to ascribe to him hundreds of spurious works which would not influence his immediate disciples but would falsify the interpretation of his doctrine by later followers.

On account of these three main factors: unsystematic presentation, inadequate vocabulary, influence of spurious works, there has arisen in India an interpretation of Śaṅkara which distorts his authentic teaching but has unfortunately been accepted by many. According to this *current interpretation,* the chief tenets of *Advaitavāda* (Non-Dualism) are the following:

(1) *Brahma satyam jagad mithyā jīva brahmaiva nāparah.* This line, which is not from Śaṅkara but from *Bālabodhini,* a later short work falsely ascribed to him, means: "*Brahman* is reality, the world is false, the soul is only *Brahman*, nothing else." This is incessantly repeated in the belief that it expresses in a nutshell the whole teaching of Śaṅkara. According to it, the world is *māyā* i.e., a purely illusory manifestation of *Brahman*,

caused by transcendental Nescience *(Avidyā or Ajñāna)*. Hence, *advaita* means strict monism and implies acosmism. The statements of identity, such as "Verily, this whole world is *Brahman*" *(Sarvaṃ khalv-idaṃ Brahma),* or "I am *Brahman*" (*Aham Brahmāsmi*), must be understood literally as they stand.

(2) *Brahman* is the material cause of the world; this would imply that it is a sort of unconscious stuff which becomes modified according to the variety of 'names and forms.' But this causal self-modification is illusory (*vivarta*).

(3) *Brahman* is *nirguṇa*, which would mean 'impersonal.' Hence, there is no possibility of establishing interpersonal relationships with it.

(4) The *jīvātman* or soul which, in the state of *avidyā*, appears to itself as a finite principle of consciousness, activity and passivity, is really identical with *Brahman*, the *Ātman* of all. Senses and body are mere *upādhis* or superimpositions due to Nescience. The *Śruti*-revelation of Advaita is alone capable of freeing (*mokṣa*) the *jīvātman* from the bond of Nescience. It cancels all other evidence and its realisation is absolute Bliss.

2. Śaṅkara's Teaching in his Authentic Writings

The teaching of Śaṅkara has generally been interpreted in the light of the later advaitic tradition. However, in recent times, critical scholarship has been seeking more and more decisively to discover his original views through a fresh and unbiased study of his genuine works.

The list of the writings in his name comprises 433 titles, 107 of which merely duplicate for another 69; 219 do not enjoy unanimous recognition by his school whereas 214 do. Modern scholars, however, reject most of them as spurious. Today, they usually agree that the following are genuine:

(1) the commentaries (*bhāṣya*) on nine Upaniṣads: *Bṛhadāraṇyaka*, *Chāndogya*, *Aitareya*, *Taittirīya*, *Īṣa*, *Kena*, *Kaṭha*, *Praśna*, *Muṇḍaka*;

(2) the commentary on the *Bhagavad Gītā*;

(3) the commentary on the *Brahma-* or *Vedānta-sūtra*.

(4) a non-commentarial treatise, the *Upadeśasāhasrī*.

The attribution to Śaṅkara of a commentary on the *Māṇḍūkya* (actually a *vivaraṇa* on its *Āgama-śāstra*) continues to be disputed and cannot be used safely.

There exist a *Śaṅkara Dig-vijaya* and other 'Lives' of Śaṅkara, but they date from at least five centuries after his time (he flourished probably during the first half of the eighth century AD) and are too legendary to be trusted as history.

It is, therefore, only from his writings that we can attempt to derive an informed idea of Śaṅkara's personality. The modern development of hermeneutics provides a fruitful way of doing this: we shall distinguish in his writings the textual and the para-textual. The 'textual' is all that depends directly on the texts he commented upon; the 'para-textual' comprises his personal predispositions, opinions, principles which are at work in his commenting but are not commanded directly by his sources. It includes both the manifestations of his temperament, such as his mental clarity, retentive memory and intellectual genius, and the marks of his religious and monastic formation.

After drawing our attention to the para-textual endowment of Śaṅkara, we shall assimilate better the textual substance of his writings.

2.1 Śaṅkara's hermeneutical predispositions

Śaṅkara approached his task of commentator of the *Brahma-sūtra* and the Upaniṣads with some remarkable predispositions. As a religious man, he was a complete renouncer, a *parama-haṁsa saṁnyāsin*. As a scholar, he had given his allegiance to the Vedānta *darśana*, but this did not make his culture exclusive. His writings exhibit a precise acquaintance with the whole landscape of philosophico-religious thinking as developed up to his time and with a very large number of the writings then extant. As a reader, he was a *vivekin*, a discerner, always hunting for the truth, ready to reject but also to accept in accordance with the axiom he quotes on *B.S.* 2, 4, 12, "the teaching of others, if not inconsistent with our own, becomes an accompaniment of our own thinking" (*paramatamapratisiddham-anumatam bhavati*). But what he sought was exclusively the **Excellent**; he shunned the rest:

As [according to Indian folklore] the flamingo sifts milk alone from a mixture of water and milk, so the wise man sifts the excellent from the merely pleasant, going mentally all around these two objects, examining them closely, weighing their respective importance or futility; and, having distinguished them, **he chooses the excellent alone** on account of its superiority (*Kaṭha Up. Bh.* 2, 2)

He was convinced that we are born with a radical sort of ignorance (*naisargika-avidyā*) which makes us superimpose the nature and attributes of the Absolute upon the relative and *vice versa.* It is like taking a rope for a snake, but it means giving a central importance to our little self and treating our transcendent Ground (*pratiṣṭhā*), inner Witness (*sākṣin*) and inner Ruler (*antaryāmin*) as a mere object or correlative entity. It vitiates all our thinking and behaviour. Indeed, we view ourselves and things as so many monads, independent, self-sufficient and valuable by themselves, and if at all we think of the supreme Lord, it is to consider him as a means, a cosmic servant like the *devas,* instead of our Illuminer, inner Ruler and true End.

However, he was also convinced that there is in every human being a desire for knowledge (*jijñāsā*) which cannot be satiated short of intuiting the very *Brahman*:

The direct object of the said desire is a knowledge culminating in intuition (*avagati-paryantam jñānam*)... for this intuition of the *Brahman* **is the end of man** (*brahmāvagati hi puruṣārthah*). (*B.S.Bh.* 1, 1, 1)

And Jaimini had defined *puruṣārtha* as "that object to which human desire is inherently attached because it cannot be disconnected from it" (*M.S.* 4, 1, 2).

Śaṅkara had possibly composed earlier a commentary on the *Yoga-sūtra* (discovered some 25 years ago), so he knew well the difference between knowledge as received from teachers and knowledge as interiorized; the first he sometimes called simple *jñāna* and the second *vijñāna,* truly discerning knowledge:

Jñāna means the enlightenment regarding the *Ātman*, etc. as obtained from the teaching and the teacher; *vijñāna* is the experiencing of that (*tad-anubhava*) in its specificity (*Bh. Gītā Bh.* 3, 41). It means turning it into a personal experience (*svānubhava karaṇa*) (*Bh. Gītā Bh.* 6, 8).

But this could not be done easily unless one had first ascertained (*pūrvasiddhi*) the truth of that teaching through a thorough rational questioning (*manana*) lest one would interiorize untruth (cf. *US* 18, 125 and 126). This prior ascertaining would be the chief aim of his commentaries.

Not only in virtue of his allegiance to Vedānta but as a result of his study of other doctrines and of his self-immersing into the Upaniṣads, he believed that these were the only source of valid knowledge regarding the *Brahman-Ātman*.

> It is only with the help of the *Śruti* that this exceedingly deep *Brahman* can be fathomed, not of [independent] reasoning. (*B.S.Bh.* 2, 1, 31)

In a better way than Jaimini he could justify the belief of all *śrutivādins* (scripturalists) in the eternality of the *Śruti*:

> The *mantras*, etc. are the Consciousness of the *Ātman* as limited by extrinsic adjuncts, namely, the modifications (*vṛtti*) of the inner sense, and as abiding in those *vṛttis* of this inner sense. Thus, of that *Ātman* they are the Knowledge that has neither beginning nor end (*Taitt. Up. Bh.* 2, 3).

He explains the connections between the *Śruti*-texts and *Brahman*: That all-knowing, all-powerful *Brahman*, which is the Cause of the origin, subsistence and dissolution of the world, is known from the Vedānta-part of Scripture. How? Because in all the Vedānta-texts the sentences construe insofar as they have that [*Brahman*] as their purport (*B.S.Bh.* 1, 1, 4).

But they presented difficulties for, speaking of the Transcendent, they could not use language in the manner of everyday usage (*vyavahāra*). Often their words were meaningful only in their supreme sense, as when they said that the *Brahman* alone is [eminently] Existent or is [causally and eminently] All or is One only without a second.[2] Again, at times they spoke of the *Brahman* in terms conforming to its transcendence but at other times in quite anthropomorphic terms. Śaṅkara was ready to face these difficulties with his own conception of intellection and of the sentence (*vākya*), especially the definition (*lakṣaṇa*).

2.2 His conception of the sentence

For Śaṅkara, an assertive sentence is composed of a subject to be differentiated (*viśeṣa*) and predicates which differentiate it. These are not only the *viśeṣaṇas,* which are intrinsic characterizers, but also the *upādhis,* which are extrinsic characterizers. Both of them can define the subject but inequally.

Defining, indeed, has two degrees: (1) setting the subject apart from all the rest, and (2) declaring its nature. Of the first, the *upādhis* are capable (as when a crystal cup standing near a red rose is pointed out as "that red cup") but, of the second, only the *viśeṣaṇas* (as when a certain flower is defined as "big, blue, sweet-smelling lotus"). Cf. *Taitt. Up. Bh.* 2, 1, 1.

Now, even with the help of these intrinsic attributes, a definition cannot always 'express' the nature of the subject. There are cases when it can 'only indicate' it because it transcends the expressive power of all terms. For instance, the metempirical *Brahman*, "it is defined by proper indication (*lakṣ-*) but not expressed (*vac-*)": *tallakṣyate na tūcyate* (ibid.). When interpreting a statement about it, attention must be paid to the nature of its subject and to its context, both proximate and remote.

2.3 His conception of intellection

"Knowledge results from the sources of valid knowing (*pramāṇa*) whose objects are the existent things as they are in reality (*yathā-bhūta vastu*)" (*B.S.Bh.* 1, 1, 4). This objective identity (*yāthātmya*) is not easy to attain. Indeed, things have a physical substantiality, which sense-perception and inference can ascertain, but also a metaphysical depth, namely, their total dependence on their Cause. So long as we ignore, or deny, this dependence, our knowledge has not reached its *yāthātmya;* however correct it may be as far as it goes, it is *Avidyā* for it lacks the complement and finality which the *Śruti* alone can give. The *Śruti* will not cancel its content but only its pretention of having reached exhaustively the *yāthātmya* of things:

> A hundred *Śrutis* may declare that fire is cold or dark; still they possess no authority in the matter. Thus we should in no way attach to *Śruti* a meaning which is opposed to other *pramāṇas* (*Bh. Gītā Bh.* 18, 66).

The *yathā* in *yāthātmya* suggests that knowledge must be similar to the things known. Not a few Indian thinkers held a mirror theory of knowledge as if its complexity reflected the very complexity of things. Śaṅkara had surmounted this naive realism. For him intellection is interpretation, either of the sense-data or of the successive words of sentences. The intellect has the power of "considering them as a whole" (*samasta pratyavamarśinī buddhiḥ: B.S.Bh.* 1, 3, 28).[3] It is dynamically synthetic. It can unify all the indications it receives and it is by the synthetic unity of the resulting knowledge that the latter is similar to the known reality. This is important especially when it results from merely indicative terms.

2.4 His interpretation of the five types of definition of Brahman

Śaṅkara divides the upaniṣadic texts into units of teaching by discovering axial 'great sentences' (*mahā-vākya*) subserved by ancillary sentences called *arthavāda*. These great sayings define the *Brahman* in various ways which can be grouped under five types. They are the negative, the superlative, the world-relational, the ego-relational and the essential definitions (*lakṣaṇa*). Each one corrects a special form of our innate ignorance and by their combination they eradicate it completely.

2.4.1 The negative (neti neti) *definition*

It sets the *Brahman* apart from all the other reals (*satya*) by telling us that "it is not so, not so" and that they are only its *upādhis* or extrinsic denominators:

> *Neti neti* designates the *Brahman* unaffected by its *upādhis,* which is beyond the grasp of speech and mind, undifferentiated and one (*Bṛh. Up. Bh.* 3, 8, 12).

It teaches us that no term and no concept can **express** the *Brahman* because their expressive power is restricted to the empirical, whereas it is metempirical. Does *neti neti* teach us the nothingness of the universe, as asserted by Maṇḍana Miśra?

> If you say, "what is prescribed here by the authority of this sentence is a nihilistic meditation (*nivṛtti*)," the answer is, "(indeed,) the Witness not having been positively established (*aprasiddhatvāt*), a void would result" (*US* 18, 125).

But *neti neti* is complemented by the next and the other definitions.

2.4.2 The superlative definition: Brahman *is* Paramam (*supreme*), Brahman *is* Pūrṇam (*Full*)

This definition gives the reason for the first: it is because *Brahman* is Fullness of being, Supreme in every regard that it is unlike anything finite. It is *beyond* anything within our sphere of experience. Because we observe degrees of being, we have an idea of the maximal Being but no experience of it. Yet all the beings we know directly have a relation of similarity to it and can thus enrich our idea of it on the basis of the next two definitions.

2.4.3 The world-relational definition: Brahman *is that from which* (yataḥ) *these beings are born, that by which* (yena) *once born they live, that into which* (yat), *when departing, they enter (*Taitt. Up. *3, 1, 1).*

i. The absolute nirguṇa *Brahman is the sole Cause of the cosmos*

The full sense of that definition, explains Śaṅkara, is: "That omniscient, omnipotent Cause from which proceed the origin, subsistence and resorption of this world, ... the nature of whose arrangement cannot even be conceived by the mind, is *Brahman*."

> The highest *Brahman* only is the evolving agent.... That the highest Lord is he who evolves the names-and-forms is a principle acknowledged by all the Upaniṣads (*B.S.Bh.* 2, 4, 20).

Brahman is Cause in two ways, as *yataḥ* and as *yena*, i.e., it provides both the reality (as *upādāna*) and the orderly structure and course of the cosmos (as its *nimitta-kāraṇa*). *Brahman* is its total principal Cause; all partial causes are dependent on and subordinated to it. But neither its causality nor its effects result in any change in *Brahman*; to it they are mere *upādhis*. It remains *kūṭastha*, firm as a Himalayan peak, unchanged and unchangeable, truly transcendent. But since it is actively giving reality and order from its own fullness, it is immanent and omnipresent not by external nearness but innermostly. It does this out of no necessity but gratuitously and freely:

> The supreme *Ātman*, due to "his **absolutely complete power**" (*B.S.Bh.* 2, 1, 24), creates "like *devas*, etc. who, without availing themselves of any extraneous means, produce palaces, etc. **by their mere intention** which is effective in virtue of the peculiar power of these beings" (*B.S.Bh.* 2, 1, 25). The *Ātman's* volitions are mere *upādhis*, not additive to his essence. Indeed, "how are they found in *Brahman*? As essentially Reality-Knowledge, and as pure in virtue of being their own *Ātman*" (*Taitt. Up. Bh.* 2, 6, l).

Now the question arises, is the Cause the *saguṇa* or the *nirguṇa Brahman*? Śaṅkara tells us that the first is the *Brahman* wrongly conceived as **having** qualities, etc. as complements of its substance, whereas as *nirguṇa* it is conceived correctly as **being** by essence whatever perfection we have to attribute to it. Being composed of substance plus complements such as qualities (*guṇa*) is proper to finite beings; it is foreign to the true *Brahman* which is free of such internal distinction (*akhanda* / *nirguṇa*). Cf. his commentary on *B.S.* 1, 1, 11 and 3, 2, 21. The highest *Brahman* is the *nirguṇa* and "it is of the highest *Brahman* that ether, etc. are understood to be the effects" (*B.S.Bh.* 2, 4, 1).

But is creating not proper to *īśvara* rather than to *Brahman*? The word '*īśvara*' is the relational term 'lord of' (*B.S.Bh.* 2, 2, 41). Śaṅkara attributes it **indifferently both** to the *nirguṇa Brahman* (for which lordship is a mere *upādhi*) and to the *saguṇa Brahman*, i.e., the *Brahman* as often spoken about in anthropomorphic fashion and thus incorrectly by the Upaniṣads.[4] Wood (1990) has shown that the severance of the concept of *īśvara* from that of the Absolute which is currently taken as the most distinctive feature of *Māṇḍ. Up.* is based on a misreading by the author of its *vivaraṇa*. He read mantra 6, "*eṣa sarveśvara, eṣa sarvajña...*" as referring to mantra 5 and thus to the self in the deep sleep state instead of to mantra 7 and thus to the so-called *Caturtha* (Fourth), namely, the **absolute *Ātman***. This unfortunate misreading has determined the current interpretation of Śaṅkara's teaching.[5]

ii. The relation of the creatures to their creative Cause

There is, he says, between the creatures and the *Brahman* "a relation (*sambandha*) which we reasonably define as *tādātmya*, having That as one's *Ātman*" (*B.S.Bh.* 2, 2, 38). He characterizes it by the following properties:

1. *non-reciprocity*: "Names-and-forms (the finite realities) in all their states have their *Ātman* in *Brahman* alone, but *Brahman* has not its *Ātman* in them" (*Taitt. Up. Bh.* 2, 6, 1). It is their supreme Self because it is their **innermost omniscient and total** Cause.

2. *total dependence*: "It is an accepted principle even in the world that an effect is intimately dependent on its [*upādāna*] cause" (*Bṛh. Up. Bh.* 1, 5, 14).

3. *non-separation*: "An effect is non-separate (*avyatirikta*) from its (*upādāna*) cause" (*Bṛh. Up. Bh.* 1, 6, 1). "The non-separation of the two is possible only if the whole aggregate of things originates from the one *Brahman*; and we understand from the Veda that this assertion can be established only on the [*sat-kārya*] principle, namely, that between the *upādāna* or reality-giving cause and the effect there is non-separation, ... non-division (*abheda*)" (*B.S.Bh.* 2, 3, 6).

4. *indwelling*: "All the created beings abide within the *Puruṣa* for every effect rests within its [*upādāna*] cause" (*Bh. Gītā Bh.* 8, 22).

5. *non-otherness* (*an-anyatva*): This term denotes here complete foreignness. "There exists in the past, present or future not one thing simply other than the *Ātman*, simply non-*Ātman*, separate by space or time, utterly subtle, disconnected and remote" (*Īṣa Up. Bh.* 2, 6, 1). "The effect is non-other than the cause, i.e., apart from the cause, it is absent (*kāraṇa-vyatirekeṇa-ābhāvah* (*B.S.Bh.* 2, 1, 14).

6. *distinction and similarity*: "If [because of non-otherness] absolute equality were insisted on, the distinction of cause and effect would be annihilated.... This relation is based on the fact that there is present in the cause an **excellence** [which the effect is lacking; on the other hand, they are similar since] one feature, namely, beingness (*sattā*), is found in ether, etc. as well as in *Brahman*" (*B.S.Bh.* 2, 1, 6).

7. *extrinsic denominativeness* (*upādhitva*): Since they share in *sattā*, the effects are not illusory but with regard to *Brahman* they are neither intrinsic parts (such as qualities, modes or modifications) nor additive adjuncts but extrinsic indicators (due to their similarity to their Cause). They help us to name it as Lord of all, supreme Cause, inner Ruler, highest Self, etc. (all these creatorship-relations being themselves its *upādhis*).

8. *finitude* (*alpatva*): "That is infinite (*ananta*) which is not divided from anything [but pervades] everything" (*Taitt. Up. Bh.* 2, 1, 1); the *Brahman* alone is thus and may truly be called *bhuman* (infinite); each creature is limited by others and is thus small (*alpa*), and may never be called *Sat* (Being) in the maximal sense.

So long as we fail to discern those properties of the *tādātmya* which relates the world to *Brahman*, we view it incorrectly as a *saṃsāra* of independent entities; the world itself is not false, not illusion (*māyā*) but our view of it is.

*2.4.4 The ego-relational (*Tattvamasi*) definition*

"From ordinary experience, the ego (*jīvātman*) is known to everyone as the agent, enjoyer [and knower]" (*B.S.Bh.* 1, 3, 7). But its *tādātmya* relation with *Brahman* is not thus known. The *Śruti* teaches it through "that thou art" (*Chānd. Up.* 6, 9, 4 sq.) which *US* 18 explains best through the method of agreement and difference:

> Just as in the expression 'the black horse,' 'black' excludes all non-blacks even if they are horses and 'horse' excludes all non-horses even if they are black, so in *Tattvamasi*, the words *Sat* [for *Tat*] and *tvam*, which refer to one and the same entity, function like 'black' and 'horse.' Through being put together with *Sat* which expresses absence of misery, *tvam* [loses its connotation of misery and] is left with the meaning *Sat*. Similarly, *Sat*, through its apposition with a word signifying inner self (*pratyag-ātman*)

> [is left with the meaning 'inmost Self] (*US* 18, 170-171). Without giving up their proper meaning (*svārtha*), *tvam*, and *Tat/Sat* convey a special meaning [namely, innermost and uppermost Self] and they lead to immediate awareness of the inmost *Ātman*. **Apart from this meaning, there can be no other one which would not result in a contradiction** (*US* 18, 173).

Thus "That thou art" defines the *Brahman* as our *Ātman*, but what should we understand the ego or *jīvātman* to be?

> This appropriator [that says 'I' and 'mine'] is the ego-sense which always stands (mirror-like) in proximity to that [*Ātman* which is pure Awareness] and acquires a reflection of it (*tad ābha*). Hence, there arises this intrication of *Ātman* and *ātmiya* (that whose *Ātman* it is) which is the sphere of application of the words 'I' and 'mine'.... It is because the ego-sense bears a reflection (*ābhāsa*) of the *Ātman* that it is designated by words [such as 'I' or 'Thou'] pertaining to the *Ātman*....
>
> The reflection of the *Ātman* in the ego-sense is comparable to the reflection of a face [in a mirror]. As in the case of the face, the *Ātman* is other (*anya*), says the tradition, and the two [*Ātman* and its reflection] are likewise undiscriminated (*US* 18, 27 and 31-33).

Why are they so? Because of the similarity, closeness and intimate dependence of the reflection on its original, the *Ātman*. But it is also on account of the same similarity, etc. that *Tattvamasi* can lead to the correct discerning, the reflection being 'the door' (*dvāra*: ibid.[6]) across which our mind apprehends the Prototype *Tat*, provided *Tattvamasi* be well understood. "There is no other door to its recognition" (*Kena Up. Bh.* 2, 4).

Being only a reflection, the ego is not a product. If it were it would be impermanent and resorbable into its substantive cause (*upādāna*) instead of being releasable from nescience (*B.S.Bh.* 2, 2, 42 and 2, 3, 17).

It has the *Brahman-Ātman* as its 'own form' (*svarūpa*), its fundamental essence (*svabhāva*) but as reflection within its *upādhis* (the inner sense comprising intellect, ego-sense and mind). "It is conditioned and coloured by the core of qualities (*guṇa-sāra*) of the intellect, etc." Due to these extrinsic adjuncts (*upādhi-nimitta*), it appears as an individual thinker, doer and enjoyer existing in the *saṃsāra* (*B.S.Bh.* 2, 3, 29.32.40). This superimposition, we may remember, is innate. It prevents the fundamental nature of the ego to be known without the help of the *Śruti*. How to explain this innate condition?

> It is brought about through the permission of the Lord who is the highest Self, the superintendent of all action, the witness residing in all beings, the cause of all intelligence. And we must therefore assume that final release also is effected through knowledge caused by the grace of the Lord (*īśvara-prasāda-hetukena vijñānena*). Why so? Because the *Śruti* teaches it. (*B.S.Bh.* 2, 3, 41)

That permission of the Lord is itself a favour whose result is our person as a well-integrated individual:

> Just as the milk-testing gem imparts its lustre to milk, so the light of the *Ātman*—which is subtler than the intellect or heart through being within the heart, UNIFIES (*ekī-karoti*) and imparts its lustre to the body and the organs including the heart, etc.... The intellect, being diaphanous and next to the *Ātman*, becomes the reflection (*ābhāsa*) of the Consciousness-light of the *Ātman*.... Then this reflection illumines the mind (*manas*), ... then the senses... and finally the body.... It is always through the favour of the light of the *Ātman* that all our activities take place... for every act of man is referred to his ego which results from that illumination. (*Bṛh. Up. Bh.* 4, 3, 7)

B.S.Bh. 2, 3, 43[7] raises the question, is the connection between the highest *Brahman* and the individual soul only of one sort, namely, as between a master and his servant, or also like that between a fire and its parts, the sparks?

> The soul must be considered a part of the Lord.... But by 'part' we mean 'a part as it were,' since a being not composed of parts cannot have parts in the literal sense. Why, then, do we not view the Lord, who is not composed of parts, as identical with the soul? On account of the declaration of difference. [Three texts are mentioned here.] These texts would be inappropriate if there were no difference. (*B.S.Bh.* 2, 3, 43)

Thus instructed about the two modes of its connection with the highest *Ātman*, its Lord and Whole, the reflection-soul aspires more definitely to know the very divine Essence it reflects.

2.4.5 The essential SATYAM JÑĀNAM-ANANTAM *definition (*Taitt. Up. *2, 1, 1)*

This time the *Brahman* is not defined in relation to its effects but in itself. Its essence (*svarūpa*) is REALITY-KNOWLEDGE INFINITE.

Since *Brahman* transcends genus and difference, "each term is independently connected with the term *Brahman*." But "by virtue of their mutual contiguity, they are controlled by, and controlling, each other, and thus they exclude from that [*Brahman*] their expressive meaning (*vācyārtha*) and become the indicatives (*lakṣyārtha*) of *Brahman*." However, "they certainly do not lose their proper meaning (*svārtha*)."

The proper meaning of SATYAM is being, true and stable reality: "its primary denotation (*mukhyārtha*) is 'existence' as common to all external things." Does it then mean here that *Brahman* is permanent and solid reality, like the earth? No, it is not material reality, because *satyam* is accompanied with *jñānam*.

The proper meaning of *JÑĀNAM* is "knowing (*jñāpti*), awareness (*avabodha*).... Its proper denotation consists of whatever is appropriated by the intellect and expresses the reflections (*ābhāsa*) of that [*Brahman*]. But here "because it determines *Brahman* along with *SATYAM* and *ANANTAM* (INFINITE)" it must be understood in its supreme sense (*paramārtha*) as perfect actuality of its root *jña* (know) [i.e., not as restricted into particular meanings, such as knower, activity of knowing, piece of knowledge, but as infinite 'Know']. Similarly, *ANANTAM* infinitizes *SATYAM* which *JÑĀNAM* has already dematerialized. And, since "that which is infinite is not divided from anything else," the two terms *SATYAM-JÑĀNAM* coalesce to indicate the spiritual essence of *Brahman* as free of any inner distinction and composition.

Thus, through the supreme meaning of *SATYAM-JÑĀNAM*, "the *Brahman* is indicated but not expressed (*lakṣyate na tu+ucyate*)" (all above quotations from Śaṅkara's commentary on *Taitt. Up*. 2, 1, 1).

This is the Upaniṣadic way along which Śaṅkara led his pupils to "the *Brahman* whose essence is KNOWLEDGE-BLISS, the GOAL of the man who stands knowing It" (*Bṛh. Up.*

3, 9, 28). Through the negative definitions, he had raised their minds above all the empirical realities; through the superlative ones, focused them on the transempirical Fullness. Then, through the relational definitions, especially *TAT-TVAM-ASI*, and the essential ones, he made them understand the positive Absolute without whose previous ascertainment the pupils would have had nothing to "interiorize and experience by themselves" (*sva+anubhava-karaṇa*).

This beatifying experience of the divine Essence is a "discerning knowledge" which, as we saw, is "caused (*hetuka*) by the Lord's grace" (*B.S.Bh.* 2, 3. 41; also *Taitt. Up. Bh.* 1, 11, 4). It is not a change of the nature of the soul but a 'change of mind' from nescience to awareness:

> It is in that internal organ once pure that the *Ātman* reveals Himself distinctly (*Muṇḍ. Up. Bh.* 3, 1, 9; *Bṛh. Up.* 4, 4, 19).

For purifying the mind, "hearing and pondering are not enough without hankering (*varaṇena*); not needed, however, is any other means but prayer alone (*prārthanā+eva*) for the *Ātman* is by his nature ever attained [and only to be discerned]" (*Muṇḍ. Up. Bh.* 3, 2, 3).

Discerning the *Brahman-Ātman* directly (*sākṣāt*) satiates our radical desire (*Brahmajijñāsā*)—because it is Fullness—and even every desire; past renunciation becomes enjoyment:

> The knower of *Brahman* enjoys all desires, all delights procured by desirable objects, without exceptions. Does he enjoy sons, paradises, etc. alternately as we do? No, he enjoys all delectable things simultaneously, as amassed together in a single moment, which is eternal... which is non-different from the essence of *Brahman*, and which we have described as REALITY-KNOWLEDGE INFINITE.... He enjoys all things by the *Brahman* whose nature is omniscience (*Taitt. Up. Bh.* 2, 1, 1).

3. Conclusion

Advaita Vedānta is pure transcendentalism. Its only concern is the 'goal of man,' namely, to intuit the very essence of the highest *Brahman*. The truth it distils from the Upaniṣads is that this *Brahman* is the highest Lord and highest *Ātman* of all the beings of the universe because it is their total Cause. In the richness of its unspeakable Fullness it exceeds all that we are or can wish to attain because it is Reality-Knowledge-Infinite and therefore absolute Bliss. Its effects can add nothing to its infinity, they exist through its causal presence within them, they are inseparable from it and cannot be counted apart from it. As to their reality it is neither Being nor Non-being in the supreme sense of those terms (*Sad-Asad-vilakṣaṇa*); it is the reality of a totally dependent effect (*sat-kārya*). Hence, their connection with the *Brahman* is not duality but non-duality (*advaita*) which is not the same as monism (*ekatva*). They are similar to it, its reflections (*ābhāsa*), but cannot be reckoned with it under one common genus, for the *Brahman* transcends any genus and is therefore "One without a second" (*ekam-eva+advitīyam*).

S. Samartha, an outstanding CSI theologian, remarked: "there is no particular reason why the Church in India should be so hesitant to recognize Śaṅkara."[8] Our inculturation into *advaita* categories is more important and less open to misunderstanding by the Hindus than that into *bhakti* categories and the interpretation of Christ as *avatāra*. Śaṅkara "draws together God, world and man in a single conception of (non-dualistic) unity"[9] "within the everlasting process that has its beginning, sustenance and end in *Brahman*."[10] Similar conceptions mark the progress of Christian thought from the Greek and Latin Fathers to the medieval and modern theologians, whether Aquinas, Bonaventure, Rahner or Tillich, not to speak of Robinson and a host of others. Advaita did not develop the non-Sanskritic conception of 'person' which is generally misunderstood by Hindus, but in its authentic and traditional Christian understanding it is quite congenial to Advaita. A more open-minded attention to Śaṅkara's conception of the ego would help us deepen our awareness of our creaturely dependence while his intellectual dynamism toward intuiting the divine Essence would interiorize our faith, vitalize our hope and nourish the hankering of our love. Christ, we believe, is man's saving Lord, both historical and cosmic: this affirmation holds together the Absolute, nature and history in a way which can illuminate and be illuminated by the *advaita* conception provided the latter be grasped in its authenticity.

BIBLIOGRAPHY

Alston, A. *A Śaṅkara Source-Book*, 3 vols. London: Shanti Sadan, 1980-1981.

Atmananda, Sw. *Śrī Śaṅkara's Teachings in His Own Words*. Bombay: Bharatiya Vidya Bhavan, 1960.

Clooney, F.X. *Theology after Vedānta: An Experiment in Comparative Theology*. Albany: State University of New York Press, 1993. [Delhi: Sri Satguru Publications, 1993.]

Dandoy, G. *An Essay on the Doctrine of the Unreality*[11] *of the World in the Advaita*. Calcutta, 1919.

Das, S.K. *A Study of the Vedānta*. Calcutta: Calcutta University Press, 1927.

Deutsch, E. *Advaita Vedānta: A Philosophical Reconstruction*. Honolulu: Hawaii University Press, 1971.

Deutsch, E. & van Buitenen, J.A.B. *A Source-book of Advaita Vedānta*. Honolulu: Hawaii University Press, 1971.

Devanandan, P.D. *The Concept of Maya*. Calcutta: YMCA, 1954.

Iyer, M.K.V. *Advaita Vedānta according to Śaṅkara*. Bombay: Asia Publishers, 1964.

Murty, K.S. *Revelation and Reason in Advaita Vedānta*. Waltair: Andhra University Press, 1959; reprint Delhi: Motilal Banarsidass, 1974.

Pande, G.C. *Life and Thought of Śaṅkarācārya*. Delhi: Motilal Banarsidass, 1994.

Pessein, J.F. *Vedānta Vindicated*. Tiruchirapally: St. Joseph Press, 1925.

Potter, K.H. *The Encyclopedia of Indian Philosophy*, Vol. 3. Advaita Vedānta, Delhi: M. Banarsidass, 1981.

Rambachan, A. *Accomplishing the Accomplished: The Veda as a Source of Valid Knowledge in Śaṅkara*. Honululu: University of Hawaii Press, 1991.

Rao, M.S. *Ananyatva: Realisation of Christian Non-Dualism*. Bangalore, CISRS, 1964.

Roy, S.S. *The Heritage of Śaṅkara*. Allahabad: Udayan Press, 1965.

Samartha, S.L. *The Hindu Response to the Unbound Christ*. Madras: CLS, 1974.

Śaṅkara. *Commentary on the Vedānta Sūtra*. [*Vedānta-Sūtras with the Commentary by Śaṅkarācārya*.] Tr. G. Thibaut, SBE 34 and 38, Oxford: Clarendon Press, 1880-96.

Śaṅkara. *Commentary on the Bṛhadāraṇyakopaniṣad*. Tr. Swami Madhavananda. Almora: Advaita, 1950.

Śaṅkara. *Commentary on Eight Upaniṣads*. Tr. Swami Gambhirananda, 2 vols. Calcutta: Advaita, 1957.

Śaṅkara. *Upadeśasāhasri*. Tr. Swami Jagadananda. [Madras: Sri Ramakrishna Math], 1949.

Śaṅkara. *Commentaries on Isa, Kena, Kaṭha Upanisads*. [*The Word Speaks to the Faustian Man: A Translation and Interpretation of the* Prasthānatrayī *and Śaṅkara's* Bhāṣya *for the Participation of Contemporary Man*. Vol. 1: Īśā, Kena, Kaṭha and Praśna Upaniṣads.] Tr. Som Raj Gupta. Delhi: Motilal Banarsidass, 1991.

Singh R.P. *The Vedānta of Śaṅkara*. Jaipur: Bharat Press, 1945.

Sinha J. *Problems of Post-Śaṅkara Vedānta*. Calcutta: Sinha Press, 1971.

Taber J.A. *A Transforming Philosophy: A Study of Śaṅkara, Fichte and Heidegger*. Honolulu: Hawaii University Press, 1983.

Notes

[1] [First published as "Śaṅkara's Non-Dualism (Advaita-Vāda)," *Religious Hinduism*, ed. R. De Smet and J. Neuner, 4nd rev. ed. (Mumbai: St Pauls, 1997) 80-96. This is a substantially revised edition of ch. 4 above. Published here with kind permission of St Pauls, Mumbai.]

[2] Compare Jesus asking the rich man, "Why do you call me good? Only one is [eminently] Good, God"; or the Jewish scholar in *Mk* 12, 34 telling him, "You said truly that He is [eminently] One and there is no other beside Him."

[3] [Correcting *Taitt. Up. Bh.* 2, 3.]

[4] For instance, he equates *Brahman* or *Ātman* and *īśvara* or *Parameśvara* in commenting on *B.S.* 2, 3, 41, 3, 2, 6, *Bṛh. Up*. 3.7.3, 4.4.15, *Chānd. Up*. 1.1.1, 5.18.1, *Kena Up*. 3.1.2, *Kaṭha Up*. 2.2.13, *Bh. Gītā* 11.36. He explains the *Tat* of *Tattvamasi* as *īśvara* or *Parameśvara* in *B.S.Bh.* 1.2.13, 3.2.6. In *B.S.Bh.* 4.4.19 it is the *Parameśvara* whom he distinguishes as either *nirguṇa* or *saguṇa*.

[5] [Thomas E. Wood, *The Māṇḍūkya Upaniṣad and the Āgama Śāstra: An Investigation into the Meaning of Vedānta* (Honululu: University of Hawaii Press, 1990; Delhi: Motilal Banarsidass, 1992).]

[6] [The 'ibid.' here is probably a reference to *US* 18, 110 (see the references to *dvāra* on pp. 165, 183 and 242 above) rather than to *US* 18, 27 or *US* 31-33.]

[7] [The original reads *B.S.* 2, 3, 43.]

[8] S.J. Samartha, *The Hindu Response to the Unbound Christ* (Madras: CLS, 1974) 167.

[9] Samartha 170.

[10] Samartha 191.

[11] [Correcting 'Causality'.]

II. DIALOGUE

21

THE CORRECT INTERPRETATION OF THE DEFINITIONS OF THE ABSOLUTE ACCORDING TO ŚRĪ ŚAṄKARĀCĀRYA AND SAINT THOMAS AQUINAS[1]

1. Both Śrī Śaṅkara, the Vedāntic theologian, and St Thomas Aquinas, the Christian theologian, have been confronted with the difficult task of interpreting either the *Brahmalakṣaṇas* (definitions of *Brahman*), which, according to the first, constitute the testimony of the *Śruti* and *Smṛti*, or the various designations of God, which are found in the Christian Revelation and Tradition. In their interpretation both have relied principally upon a specific element of the theories of the various meanings of words which they inherited from their respective culture, i.e., *lakṣaṇājñāna* in the Indian culture and *knowledge through analogy* in the Greco-Christian culture. And both, in applying these theories to their subject, have given them their full scope and perfection.

2. In realizing for the first time a complete synthesis of the *Śruti* and *Smṛti*, no longer from the standpoint of *dharma* but from the standpoint of *jñāna*, Śaṅkara had to adapt to his own purpose the exegetic rules of the Pūrvamīmāṃsā Darśana from the standpoint of which he was breaking away. His adaptation of these rules was what may be called, with an anachronism, a 'Copernican revolution' in Mīmāṃsā. Jaimini had classified the manifold texts of the infallible *Śabda* into two main categories: the first, being directly and independently authoritative, comprised all injunctions (*codanā* or *vidhi*) and, secondarily, prohibitions (*niṣedha*); the second, being but dependently and therefore indirectly authoritative, comprised *mantras*, *nāmadheyas* and *arthavādas*, i.e., all the texts not included in the

first category. Hence, according to Jaimini, the assertions of the *jñānakāṇḍa* were authoritative in so far only as they subserved injunctions. The revolution of Śaṅkara consisted in reversing this classification and installing the *Vedānta statements* as authoritative by themselves, instead of the dethroned *codanās*, now reduced to the rank of mere *arthavādas* of these Vedānta statements.

3. After thus attributing primacy to the *Vedānta statements*, Śaṅkara had to determine which passages deserved this appellation and which were their respective *arthavādas*. This he did with the help of the six criteria (*pramāṇa*) and the sixfold indication (*ṣaḍvidhaliṅgāni*) set forth by the Pūrvamīmāṃsā.

4. Once he had singled out the *Vedānta statements*, he classified them according to their purpose: "Vedānta assertions have a twofold purpose: some of them aim at teaching the true nature of the supreme Self, some at teaching the unity with the supreme Self of the Self of Knowledge" (*B.S.Bh.* 1, 3, 25). The second category comprises all statements of the type: *Tattvamasi* (*Chānd. Up.* 6, 8, 7), *Ahaṃ brahmāsmi* (*Bṛh. Up.* 1, 4, 10), *Ayamātmā brahma* (*Bṛh. Up.* 2, 5, 19), etc. They direct man to identify the Absolute correctly. The first category includes all definitions (*lakṣaṇas*) of the Absolute. Now such definitions are of two kinds: either essential (*svarūpa*) and non-relational (*nirapekṣa*), or nonessential (*taṭastha*) and relational (*upalakṣaṇa*). The first kind indicates the true nature of *Brahman*; it comprises all statements of the type: *Satyam jñānamanantaṃ brahma* (*Taitt. Up.* 2, 1). The second indicates the true *Brahman*, but through something indifferent (*taṭastha*) to its true nature, as, for instance, its creatorship or its immanence to this finite world; (*Brahman* is, indeed, the same true *Brahman* whether it posits a world or not). Thus, since it is only with reference to an indifferent *upādhi* that such definitions point to the true *Brahman*, their teaching, though valid, is insufficient to illumine man perfectly.

5. All *Vedānta statements* are meant to remove man's ignorance concerning the Absolute. But since they are necessarily expressed in human language, they perform this task by the means of human words which signify human concepts. Now all human concepts are derived from man's experience of this world of finite beings, and therefore inadequate to express

the Absolute. Direct experience (*anubhava, sākṣātkāra*) of the Absolute could alone remedy this inadequacy, but, as long as he is in *Brahmajijñāsā*, i.e., as long as he still inquires about the true *Brahman*, man, by definition, has not yet directly realized this Absolute. However, in spite of the limitations of human concepts, the *Vedānta statements* are not unable to convey to man their proper meaning, provided he interprets them according to the principles of *lakṣaṇājñāna*.

6. Directly authoritative assertions, such as these *Vedānta statements*, ought always to be understood literally, i.e., according to the primary meaning of the concepts of which they are constructed. But the meaning of a concept can be primary in two ways: either it is that meaning which is first according to our human way of knowing and this is generally called primary (*mukhyārtha*); or it is that meaning which a concept has when it is referred to the reality in which it is realized perfectly, and which therefore is first (*paramārtha*) with regard to all other realities in which the same concept is but imperfectly realized. Although absolutely first, this meaning is secondary with regard to our human way of knowing and is therefore called *gauṇa* (secondary). It is also called *lakṣya* or *lakṣita* (indicated, implied), because we have no right to assume such a meaning unless absolutely compelled by the impossibility of understanding a statement in any other sense; it is indeed the peculiar inter-relationship of the terms within that statement and the relation of the statement itself to its proximate and general concept which indicate or imply that all its terms have to be understood *paramārthataḥ* (absolutely), i.e., according to the second form of literality.

7. *Lakṣaṇā* or implication does not in every case lead us to a *paramārtha* or absolute sense, for *lakṣyārtha* is of three kinds: (a) *jahat*, i.e., exclusive of the primary meaning (*mukhyārtha*), as in the case of '*dvirepha*' (double *r*) which comes to mean 'bee' (*bhramara*) because *bhramara* contains twice the letter *r*; (b) *ajahat*, i.e., inclusive of the *mukhyārtha*, as in the case of 'red' in 'the red runs' for 'the red [horse] runs' ('red,' while directly designating a particular horse, does not exclude the notion, expressed by its primary meaning, that this horse is red); (c) *jahadajahat*, i.e., both including and excluding the primary meaning, as in the case of 'cloth' in 'my cloth is burned' for 'a

part of my cloth is burned.' Because in the interpretation of the *Vedānta statements* the *mukhyārtha* of their terms, i.e., their proper meaning (*svārtha*) according to us, is to be preserved, (for, otherwise, their *paramārtha* would have no contents graspable by us), while, at the same time, the limitations which it connotes in our way of thinking are to be removed, this interpretation is based upon *jahad-ajahal-lakṣaṇā* only, i.e., this form of implication which both excludes and includes what we primarily understand through these terms.

8. A proposition such as '*Tattvamasi*' makes no sense if we pretend to understand it according to that meaning of its terms which is usually called primary. To say, indeed, that "Thou, Śvetaketu, son of Uddālaka, art this universe" is mere absurdity. But the whole context compels us to rely upon *jahad-ajahal-lakṣaṇā* and to understand the sentence according to the *paramārtha* or supreme sense of its terms which alone is adequate to its implications. Indeed, "the term '*tat*' means that which, in the immediate context, has been called Being (*sadākhya*), the most subtle essence (*aṇimāṇubhāva*), the world's root (*jagato mūlam*). This cause of the world is true, absolutely real (*paramārthasat*)" (*Bṛh. Up. Bh.* 1, 4, 7). "It is the *Ātman* of the world, i.e., its inner proper form (*pratyakṣvarūpam*), its very reality (*satattvam*), its truth (*yāthātmya*)" (*Chānd. Up. Bh.* 6, 8, 7). The *paramārtha* of '*tat*' as pointed out (*lakṣya*) by the context, is therefore: "the absolute root-cause of this manifold universe" or simply, "the *Brahman*." Similarly, the context forbids us to understand the term '*tvam*' in its primary sense, according to which "it designates directly that person [Śvetaketu] who had not, before he was taught by his father, reached the true nature of his own Self as Being, the Self of all, distinct from body and senses, which are only its reflections" (*Chānd. Up. Bh.* 6, 16, 3). But the only sense of '*tvam*' which is consistent with the context is: "that person who, now, being enlightened by his father, has understood from the teaching 'That thou art,' that, 'I am Being itself'... because the result brought about by the sentence is the setting aside of the notion that the Self is the actual doer and enjoyer. That the said notion is set aside by the sentence follows from the fact that the two are incompatible" (ibid.). Indeed, "the same identity cannot really be both *Brahman* and non-*Brahman*, just as the sun cannot

be both bright and dark, for these are contradictory features" (*Bṛh. Up. Bh.* 1, 4, 10). Thirdly, the verb '*asi*' cannot here be understood in any of the three figurative senses (*sampat*, *gauṇa*, *stuti*), but only as signifying the perfect actual identity of '*tat*' and '*tvam*' understood in their supreme sense as indicated by the context (*Chānd. Up. Bh.* 6, 16, 3). The true sense of '*Tattvamasi*' is therefore: "*Tat*, the absolute root-cause of the universe, and *tvam*, the absolute principle of thy individual self, are (*asi*) one identical supreme Being" or "The *Brahman* and the *Ātman* are the one identical supreme Being."

It would be most enlightening to study the *lakṣaṇā* method as applied by Śaṅkara in the exegesis of all the *Vedānta statements*, and particularly in *Taitt. Up. Bh.* 2, 1 (exegesis of the definition: *Satyam jñānamanantam brahma*), which is the most elaborate of its kind. But such a study would take us beyond the limits of this short paper.

Let us also notice that the *lakṣaṇā* method proceeds in three steps: (1) *adhyāropa* (false attribution), i.e., understanding the sentence according to the *mukhyārtha* of its terms; (2) *apavāda* (negation), i.e., rejection of this absurd meaning; (3) *lakṣaṇājñāna*, i.e., right knowledge of the sentence according to the *paramārtha* of its terms, as indicated (*lakṣya*) by the interrelationship of these terms and the relation of the whole sentence to the totality of its context.

9. The position of St Thomas Aquinas concerning man's capability of knowing God can be summarized as follows: (1) short of the beatific vision, man cannot know the essence of God positively and expressly, but only negatively and through analogy; (2) knowledge of God through analogy is the result of a threefold process: (a) position of God as the supreme Cause of the universe, hence as possessing at least the whole perfection of his effect, (b) removal from this notion of all finiteness and limitation, (c) elevation of the notion thus purified to its highest degree, which can consist only in absolute simplicity, transcendent unity and infinite perfection; (3) the terms of our definitions of God are therefore never to be understood in their primary meaning, but in that secondary meaning only, which is implied by their function as terms of a definition of the true God.

10. Terms, indeed, are either univocal or analogous or purely equivocal. Purely equivocal terms are ambiguous, because to one

and the same term several different concepts correspond; they ought therefore to be excluded from our subject. Univocal terms are all terms which designate a class (either generic or specific), and are therefore realized in all members of this class according to their full definition and the specific and finite way of being which it signifies. Any application of such terms to objects alien to their class is improper and can at the most be metaphorical. Now God is outside any class, either genus or species, and therefore outside any univocal application of any term, except by the way of metaphor which remains below the level of definition proper. Besides, as I have just pointed out, the definition of any univocal term implies a definite way of being finite. But there exist other terms the definition of which does not imply such a limitation, but abstracts from any way of being, either finite or infinite. Such are all terms designating 'pure' perfections, such as being, one, knowing, willing, good, etc., and these are analogous terms, properly speaking. We, of course, derive them from our finite experience and from objects in which they are but finitely realized. But since their notion does not imply this finiteness, they can be predicated of a subject which realizes them in a perfect and infinite way, if such a subject is ascertained from faith or from reason. According to the teaching of the Catholic Church, the existence of God is ascertained from both faith and reason, and it is therefore possible to define God with the help of such analogous terms. Such definitions of God, explains St Thomas, are valid, (and are the only valid ones), because both 'what' they signify and 'how' they signify it are realized in God, but they remain irremediably negative, because, although we know 'what' each term of the definition expresses, we have no adequate representation of the 'how' according to which the definition affirms it of God. They are able to remove all errors regarding the true nature of God, but not to engender that perfectly positive knowledge which alone can quench man's thirst for the supreme Reality.

11. The possibility of using analogous terms in order to know God depends, as we have seen, upon the fact that some of our concepts abstract from both limitedness and unlimitedness. Indeed, the definitions of pure or unmixed perfections do not include any specific mode or manner of realization and the finite representations which always accompany them in our mental

experience can be distinguished and separated from them without at all impairing these definitions. Such separation is implicit in every true definition of God because, otherwise, the defining terms could not fulfil their function; but the same impossibility would arise if these terms could not be elevated to the mode of infinity; this elevation is also implicit in every true definition of God. Hence, because analogous terms lend themselves to the threefold process of position, negation, elevation, it is possible to designate the true God by means of terms derived from finite experience. But, in order to be valid, such designations must be based upon some ontological similarity between the objects of finite experience and God; otherwise the proper meaning of their terms would not be realized in both God and the finite objects, hence these terms would be purely equivocal, not analogous. Anyone, therefore, who resorts to analogy (or *lakṣaṇā*) in order to know God, implies by the very fact some ontological community between creatures and God. St Thomas established this ontological community on the fact that God is the supreme and total Cause upon which all other beings depend entirely in their very being. (His demonstration of this fact cannot be exposed in this short paper). As effects these beings must be similar to their Cause and, since it is as beings that they are effects, they must be ontologically similar to God, their Cause. A cause, indeed, whatsoever it be, can only produce effects similar to itself. For, on the one hand, the concept of a purely equivocal cause, i.e., of a cause whose effects would be entirely dissimilar from itself, is unthinkable; on the other hand, no effect can be entirely identical to its cause, for their complete identity would destroy the very meaning of both cause and effect and leave perfect unity only instead of the duality of cause and effect which the question itself presupposes. If, therefore, the fact of the ontological dependence upon God of all other beings has been validly established, the conclusion follows that these beings are neither entirely dissimilar from, nor entirely identical with, God, but ontologically similar to Him. Hence, whatever is positive in them is to be referred to him, and in particular, those perfections whose very concept abstracts from any limit and is therefore called transcendental and analogous.

12. In spite of the essential dissimilarity of their theological background, Śaṅkara and Thomas Aquinas have treated the definitions and designations of God or the Absolute according to a strikingly similar method and this is one of the main reasons of the large extent to which their respective theodicies are in agreement. But both have not been equal in following up all the rational implications of this method, which both considered as valid. Because there was nothing in his own conception of theology to prevent St Thomas from trusting pure reason as well as his Christian faith, he has been able to develop, in connection with his theology, the philosophy of ontological participation which establishes the proper status in being of all knowable objects. The same philosophy is implicit in Śaṅkara's *Brahmalakṣaṇā-jñāna* and we naturally wonder why he did not derive it explicitly. I have elsewhere[2] inquired into this question and the conclusion of my research, based upon the explicit declarations of Śaṅkara about his intention and method, is that he considered all purely rational speculation as idle and misleading philosophizing. *Śabda*, i.e., *Śruti* and secondarily *Smṛti*, was the only *pramāṇa* or source of valid knowledge absolutely to be trusted, and in his view it ultimately contradicted all evidences of pure or unaided reason. All the antinomies of his teaching are rooted in this conviction, but it was so fundamental that he could not compromise about it. If his doctrine does not have the comprehensiveness and universal appeal of the doctrine of St Thomas Aquinas, it does not mean that the philosophical insight of the latter was greater than his own, but it means that Śaṅkara's faith was antinomic and not completely reconcilable with the full richness and extent of reality.[3]

Notes

[1] [The archives of Jnana Deepa Vidyapeeth and De Nobili College contain an 8 pp. typescript entitled "The Correct Interpretation of the Definitions of the Absolute according to Śrī Śaṃkarācārya and Saint Thomas Aquinas. Paper to be read in December 1954 Philosophical Congress, Colombo" (cf. Collected Papers A, 5-12 = DNC 73/DES/COL). The paper was published under the title "The Correct Interpretation of the Definitions of the Absolute according to Śaṃkarācārya and Saint Thomas Aquinas," *Proceedings of the Indian*

Philosophical Congress (1954) 1-10. It was republished the following year in *The Philosophical Quarterly* 27/4 (January 1955) 187-194. Reprinted here courtesy De Nobili College, having had no reply from *The Philosophical Quarterly* (Amalner) despite several requests.]

[2] In my Ph.D. Dissertation about "The Methodology of Śaṃkarācārya" (not yet published) [= 'The Theological Method of Śaṃkara,' see above, "Introduction" note 3]. The paragraphs of this paper concerning *lakṣaṇājñāna* in the writings of Śaṅkara summarise a few pages of this work. I have also treated the same subject at length in "Langage et connaissance de l'Absolu chez Çaṃkara," *Revue Philosophique de Louvain* **52** (3e série, no. 33) (Février 1954) 31-74. [= ET ch. 1 above.]

The main references concerning St Thomas' doctrine of analogy are *SCG* 1, 14; 1, 29-36; 3, 18-27 and 50; *S.Th.* I, 12, 12 and I, 13, 1-12; *Quaestio Disputata de Potentia* 7, 5.

[3] [De Smet was attacked by Prof. Chubb probably for this assertion: see De Smet, 'The Trajectory of My Dialogical Activity' (see above, "Introduction," note 5) 6-7, and "Interphilosophical and Religious Dialogue in My Life," *Pilgrims of Dialogue*, ed. A. Pushparajan (Munnar: Sangam Dialogue Centre, 1991) 1.]

22

ŚAṄKARA AND AQUINAS ON LIBERATION (*MUKTI*)[1]

Hearing this [Reality] and comprehending [it], a mortal,
Extracting the Essence (*Dharmya*) and reaching the Subtle,
Rejoices for he has attained the very Source of joy.
(*Kaṭha Up.* 1, 2, 13)

Eye has not seen, nor ear heard,
Nor has it entered into the human heart,
What God has prepared for those who love Him.
(St Paul, *1st Letter to the Corinthians* 2, 9)

Liberation is the all-orienting goal of the teaching of St Thomas Aquinas as it is of the teaching of Śrī Śaṅkarācārya. Both define it as the blissful intellectual experience of the Godhead and the complete cessation of man's ignorance. Each one of them is regarded within his own tradition as a thinker of genius and a standard-bearer of orthodoxy. They are remarkably akin in their leading concern, their exegetico-philosophical method, and in many of their settled conclusions. To the Scriptures, *Śruti* or Bible, which were their home-basis, and to all the significant doctrines which they found in their cultural heritage they gave that kind of illuminating critical treatment which without cancelling faith, places the accent on the elements of truth and casts out untruth and confusion. It is, therefore, of no small interest to devise an encounter between them and to compare their respective teachings on the important subject of liberation.

1. The Desire for Liberation

Mumukṣutva, the desire for final release, is the fourth qualification (*adhikāra*) demanded by Śaṅkara of any prospective pupil. (*B.S.Bh.* 1, 1, 1) It is already implied in the first three in the less precise form of desire for immortality (*Kaṭha Up. Bh.* 4, 1: *amṛtatvam-icchan*). Now it is required explicitly as "the desire of knowing the inner *Ātman*" (*pratyagātma-viṣayā jijñāsā*) (*Kena Up. Bh.* 1, 1). It is, indeed, the immediate disposition to *Brahmajijñāsā*, the "desire to know *Brahman*" through a systematic enquiry. Desire, as is well known, concerns either ends or means (*sādhya-sādhana-lakṣaṇam*: *Bṛh. Up. Bh.* 1, 4, 17). *Brahmajijñāsā* is the desire for the supreme end of man (*parama puruṣārtha*), i.e., for that perfect good (*niḥśreya*) which secures complete liberation.

Hence, "the direct object of the said desire is a knowledge culminating in a direct apprehension (*avagati-paryantam jñānam*), desires having reference to fruits. Knowledge, indeed, constitutes the means (*pramāṇa*) by which *Brahman* is desired to be directly apprehended (*avagantumiṣṭaṁ Brahma*). For the direct apprehension of *Brahman* is the end of man (*Brahmā-'vagatir-hi puruṣārthaḥ*) since it extirpates completely that which is bad, namely, nescience, etc., the seed of the entire *saṃsāra*" (*B.S.Bh.* 1, 1, 1). In other terms, "that knowledge which discerns *Brahman* and discards nescience terminates in intuition (*anubhava-'vasānam*)" (*B.S.Bh.* 2, 1, 4). Śaṅkara has thus distinguished knowledge itself, which is a source or means (*pramāṇa*), from its end (*paryanta*, *avasāna*), *avagati* or *anubhava*, intuition. This is the uppermost object of human desire, whereas the desire for its means is but ancillary to it.

The relation of other human longings to this uppermost desire is somewhat ambiguous. On the one hand, they are subsumed and pervaded by it since "it is for the love of the *Ātman* that husband wife, sons, etc. are dearly loved" (*Bṛh. Up.* 2, 4) but, on the other hand, no one is qualified for *Brahmajijñāsā* if he does not "renounce all desire to enjoy objects both here and hereafter *ihāmutrārthabhoga-virāgaḥ*)" (*B.S.Bh.* 1, 1, 1). This means that our highest desire, though it is the master-spring of our other desires and these are its pale adumbrations, stands over against them as the pursuit of the true final end which cancels all other ends.

The poet Dante, who was a most fervent Thomist, may be called upon to present the thought of St Thomas Aquinas on the desire for liberation. In *The Divine Comedy*, *Paradise*, 4, 124-132, he writes:

> I see well that our intellect can never be satisfied
> but with the truth beyond which there is no other truth.
>
> There it reposes, like a wild beast in its lair,
> as soon as it reaches it; and reach it, it can:
> else all desire would be in vain.
>
> And from this springs up enquiry—
> like a sapling at the foot of truth—
> which is nature driving us from hill to hill.

What Aquinas calls the 'nature' of a created being is not for him a static essence but the radical principle of all its activity. It is totally tendential, purposive, goal-seeking through all the activities it generates. The term 'good' can only be defined as the object of this natural intentionality. For each creature, that is good which corresponds to its natural appetency. And, by searching its good, every creature tends to become more similar to its divine Cause, which is Goodness itself. Indeed, "because all creatures proceed from God considered as good, they are impelled by the very nature they have received from him to search for the good according to their respective capacity" (*In IV Sententiarum* 49, 1, 3). "In every object of desire, God himself is desired; nothing, indeed, can be desired except inasmuch as it participates of the supreme good" (*In De Divinis Nominibus* 10, 1, 1). "All things desire God as their end in whatever good they desire and whatever be the kind of their desire, spiritual, sensuous or devoid of any knowledge and purely material, for nothing is good and desirable except inasmuch as it resembles God" (*S.Th.* I, 44, 4, 3). However, though all creatures tend actively towards God by increasing their ontological goodness, the intellectual creature alone can aim at possessing God himself in his very essence.

Indeed, the intellect alone can transcend materiality, temporality and limitedness. The intellect alone is reflective enough to attain the partless spirit and formally reveal self-identity. The intellectual creature knows its objects as beings, as realities. It measures them. It evaluates their ontological limitation and insatiably ranges further in its attempt to satisfy its unlimited thirst for being, truth, goodness. It endeavours to know not only more but better and to attain not only more numerous realities but more perfect ones. What satisfies it provisionally is the reality it finds, what drives it further on is the finiteness of that reality. It is the limited as limited which it wants to overcome. And Aquinas, therefore, discerns at the very heart of its restless chase an over-all desire of nature for the satiating knowledge of the unlimited Being.

To be satiating, he tells us, this knowledge should be intuitive, direct and positive, immediate and absolute. It must extinguish altogether ignorance or nescience. All other knowledge of God, whether attained through reflection or from sacred scriptures, is but abstract, indirect and negative, mediate and relative. It is knowledge "through ignorance" by which we know what God is not without knowing what he is. (*SCG* 3, 50)

Like Śaṅkara, therefore, Aquinas considers that the true end of man can be found in nothing short of the intellectual realisation of God through direct experience in the form of intuition. The desire for this intuition is a desire which characterises our nature as intellectual. It is superior to every other desire of either nature or will. It is, as it were, their soul and energises them all but it surpasses them and soars beyond their reach to pursue in its own right its proper aim. Being innate, primordial and deep-seated, it is at first implicit only but, through reflection, helped eventually by the intimations of holy scriptures, it can be made explicit and, then, pursued voluntarily through further enquiry and spiritual devotion. It is the form which the natural love for God, which is common to all creatures, takes in intellectual beings and this is its highest form. As such, it sublates by assumption all other loves, even our love for our finite self.

2. The Conditions of Liberation

Although the desire for intuiting the Godhead is natural to every man and implicit in his least hankering after truth, the fulfilment of that desire hardly appears naturally possible. Rather it appears conditioned by certain factors in the absence of which it cannot take place. What are these factors according to our two authors? Intuition being an immediate encounter and communion between knowing subject and object known, such factors may pertain either to the subject or the object.

For Śaṅkara, as well as for Aquinas, no object can properly speaking be intuited unless it is (a) real and (b) present immediately to the knower. Neither of them has any doubt that *Brahman* or God (*Deus*) is the fullness of reality and is intimately present to every being. He is the supreme *Ātman* of all (*sarvātman*, *paramātman*), especially of the knower (*veditur-ātmaiva brahma*: *Taitt. Up. Bh.* 2, 1, 1; *B.S.Bh.* Introd.), says Śaṅkara, while Aquinas proclaims after St Augustine: "O God, Thou art more interior to me than my innermost and superior to my uppermost." However, there is some difficulty regarding this divine omnipresence. The absolute Godhead is surely present to all ontologically (*satyasya satyam*) and energetically, as the all-Cause, both *upādāna* and *nimitta kāraṇa*, the inner all-Activator (*antaryāmin*), Presider (*adhiṣṭhātṛ*, *adhiṣṭhita*) and witness (*sākṣin*) but it does not appear to be so epistemologically. It may be the supreme Knowable (*jñeya*), it may even be known implicitly in the knowledge of every object (cf. *Bh. Gītā Bh.* 2, 16), and especially in the knower's self-knowledge (cf. *B.S.Bh.* Introd.), but surely not explicitly and immediately. This situation might arise either from the unknowability of the Godhead or from the deficiency of the knower. But unknowability can surely not be intrinsic to the very Source of all intelligibility. If it is stressed, and rightly so, by both our authors, it is always in relation to the unenlightened knower. We are therefore thrown back upon a consideration of this knower himself.

Nescience is his native condition. It penetrates even his secular knowledge of objects. He may know them as names-forms (*nāma-rūpa*) but he fails to grasp them down to their deepest *Ātman* (*pratyag-ātman*), as wholly effects (*kārya*) and sheer superimpositions (*upādhi*), totally relative to the universal *Ātman*. Even after becoming somewhat enlightened by correct reflection or, more efficiently, by authoritative scriptures and the teaching of a merciful *guru*, the conceptual correct knowledge he attains continues to pertain to ignorance. Because it is abstract, indirect, analogical, says Aquinas, it is but "knowledge through ignorance." "And this," he says, "is the highest summit of the knowledge of God that we can attain in this life, namely, to know that we do not know him" (*SCG* 3, 49), "to know that God is above all that can be thought by us" (*Expositio in De Divinis Nominibus* [*Pseudo-Dionysii*] 83). But what about mystical knowledge? Can ecstasis not overcome ignorance definitely? This, he says, is only the "most divine" degree of our "knowledge through ignorance" because "it is a union which takes place above the mind-soul (*unitio super mentem*), when the soul has withdrawn from all separate objects and, further, even from itself and is plunged in the inscrutable abyss of the light of Wisdom, overcome by its superdazzling rays" (ibid. 732). Blinded as it were by their excessive brilliance, it abides in the luminous darkness which is night for the senses and night for the mind.

For Aquinas, short of the intuition of the very essence of God, there is no final liberation. And for this intuition to happen, our intellect must be epistemologically 'informed' by that very essence. Information is required for any knowledge; the merely ontological presence of a knowable does not suffice. Images, ideas and words can inform us about the realities of this world from which they are obtained. With regard to the Godhead, they can only be analogical pointers because their very finiteness prevents them from ever signifying it adequately. The divine essence alone can adequately inform our intellect about itself, so that, when we shall see it, "it itself will be both the Reality seen and that by which we see it" (*SCG* 3, 51). This is possible because, on the one hand, our intellect like any intellect is open to every intelligible, whether finite or infinite, and, on the other hand, the divine essence as fullness of intelligibility can inform any intellect without any intermediary. Besides, "since our longing for its intuition is a desire of nature and no such desire can be in vain, it follows that the intuition of the divine substance is possible to any intellect. And since this cannot be had unless the divine essence informs that intellect this information must be possible" (ibid.).

However, no finite power can through any attempt or endeavour cause this information to take place. It is, indeed, a divine self-surrender and self-gift of which nothing created can ever be the sufficient condition. "We can, therefore, attain it only through divine grace and as a divine gift" (ibid. 52). Hence, intuition of the Godhead, though it is the goal of our nature, can never be conquered by our natural power but only received supernaturally as a gift that stands within our capacity but beyond the reach of our grasp.

The same thing can be presented in personalistic terms. The term 'person,' for Aquinas, applies to all beings characterised by intellectual knowledge and will, self-awareness, self-dominion and self-possession. To the Godhead, it applies in the most elevated way. Of all beings persons are the highest. Hence, no person can find its real bliss in the possession of impersonal objects but only in the fusion of love between persons, and, ultimately, with the most personal Being. Now, no person can strictly speaking be conquered as we conquer objects. Personal intimacy cannot be broken into but only revealed willingly. "For who among men knows the thoughts of a man, except the spirit of man dwelling in him? Just so, no one comprehends the secret things of God except the Spirit of God" (*1 Cor*. 2, 11). Hence, mutual personal union can only result from mutual self-surrender and freely granted mutual communication. This applies obviously to man's direct experience of the Godhead. It cannot be enforced upon any man independently of his desiring will, even by divine power, and it cannot be extorted from God independently of His will. It can only arise out of a free self-surrender of God and man.

Coming back to Śaṅkara, we may note, first, that blissful liberation is attained only when, in the words of the *Gītā*, "beholding the *ātman* through the *ātman*, one rejoices in the *ātman*": *ātmanā-'tmānaṁ paśyam-ātmani tuṣyati* (*Bh. Gītā* 6, 20). But Śaṅkara did not feel the need of distinguishing strongly between ontological and epistemological presence or immediacy. He saw that in spite of the immediacy of the *Brahman-Ātman* in everyone, the majority of men were deprived of its blissful intuition. But he considered that a matter of fact, to be explained (if one may say so) by unexplainable Nescience, not a matter depending on the very nature of being and knowledge. The nature of things is rather that *Sat* implies *Cit*, *Ātman* implies *anubhava* and *ānanda*, and this is our deepest *svarūpa*. But the veil of nescience prevents us from experiencing that eternal *anubhava*. In the state of ignorance we rather experience our desire for it, our inability to conquer it, our need for a helping grace. Śaṅkara does not refuse to "assume that liberation is effected through discerning knowledge (*vijñānena*) caused by the Lord's grace (*tad-anugraha-hetukena*), because Scripture teaches it" (*B.S.Bh.* 2, 3, 41) and, in commenting upon *Bh. Gītā* 2, 39 he writes: "Thou shalt sever the bond of action only by attaining to knowledge which is caused by the grace of the Lord" (*īśvara-prasādanimitta-jñānaprāptyā eva*). But, in *Kaṭha Up.* 1, 2, 20, he renders "*dhātuḥ prasādāt*" as "through the tranquillity of the senses" and, in *Muṇḍ. Up.* 3, 1, 8, he explains '*jñāna-prasādena*' as "through the tranquillity or transparency of knowledge [i.e., the intellect]." His understanding of *Kaṭha Up.* 1, 2, 23 (or *Muṇḍ. Up.* 3, 2, 3), which apparently speaks of divine choice: *yam-evaiṣa vṛnute tena labhyaḥ*, is also interesting; he expands it as follows: "that very own *ātman* which this aspirant takes as his goal, by that very *ātman* [which is] the chooser (*tenaivā-'tmanā varitrā*) his own *ātman* is obtained, known" (*Kaṭha Up. Bh.*) or "that supreme *ātman* which the knower chooses, wishes to attain, by that choosing (*tena varaṇena*) the supreme *ātman* is attained, not by any other means, for it is by its very nature ever attained" (*Muṇḍ. Up. Bh.*). Hence the same *ātman* is both the origin and the end of the aspirant's choice. And the commentary goes on saying: "the *ātman* of that seeker after the *ātman* reveals, manifests, its own supreme form, its own true reality": (*tasyātmakāmasyaiṣa ātmā vivṛṇute prakāśayati pāramārthikīṁ tanūṁ svāṁ svakīyāṁ sva-yāthātmyaṁ* (*Kaṭha Up. Bh.* 1, 2, 23).

We find here an important similarity with Aquinas who also holds that the Godhead immanent in us originates the natural desire for seeing it and itself fulfils it by a direct revelation of its own supreme form or true essence. However, the question whether the divine 'information' or actuation of the intellect, which Aquinas holds to be a necessary condition of that fulfilment, has any correspondent in Śaṅkara's teaching must now be examined.

"This *Brahman* is to be obtained by the mind made ready by the teacher and the scriptures (*ācāryagama-saṁskṛtena manasā*)" (*Kaṭha Up. Bh.* 2, 1, 11). Yet, this intuition of *Brahman,* "although mental, differs widely from meditation, etc., because it is not an activity of the *manas*, i.e., it does not depend on the activity of the *manas* but only on the reality of its object" (*B.S.Bh.* 1, 1, 4). As far as I know, Śaṅkara does not decide absolutely anywhere whether that intuition implies a *mano-vṛtti* or mental modification upon which it would follow immediately. His followers are divided on this question. Vācaspati admits a *manovṛtti* followed immediately by *vijñāna* which sublates it. Sadānanda and Madhusūdana accept similar views. The Vivaraṇa school, on the contrary, admits the possibility of *vijñāna* independent of a corresponding *manovṛtti*.

3. The Effects of Liberation

For Aquinas the blissful intuition of the divine essence frees man from all ignorance, selfishness, sin and all other evils. It fulfils the whole of his desiring dynamism. Thus he enters in the active repose of possession, having attained the absolute Good which is eternal Bliss. He is not a seeker any more but an enjoyer. His ontological status of creature, of effect totally dependent upon his divine, immanent and transcendent Cause remains what it always was, for knowledge does not change reality, but epistemologically he has become the very Godhead. He shares in divine Consciousness itself and, hence, in divine omnipotence.

However, it is a principle of Aquinas, received from Aristotle, that "whatever is received is measured by the capacity of the receiver." Hence, this blissful sharing is qualitatively finite and its degree is not equal in all. The divine essence is partless and all the blessed, therefore, possess it entire but, since each one of them is finite, none of them is comprehending it exhaustively. That possession, which really satiates them completely, is not infinite in every regard. It is not identically the original divine Awareness but a sharing of it in the form of co-consciousness.

For Śaṅkara, *mukti* which is possible even in the course of this life, frees man from nescience and all its consequences: self-attachment, secular desires, joys and sorrows, subjection to duty, rebirth and all the limitations of *saṃsāra*. The *jñānin* is the perfect *saṅnyāsin* and *kevalin*. He has recoiled away from all finite forms into his infinite and transcendent *svarūpa*. In that identity of *sac-cid-ānanda*, he is merged and abides in the pure *Caitanya* and no distinction endures between his blissful knowledge and the divine Bliss-Consciousness. This is an awakening to his deepest reality rather than a fulfilment of his capacity. Yet, in a higher sense, we may speak of fulfilment. Commenting on the text: *So-'śnute sarvān kāmān saha*, Śaṅkara writes: "The knower of *Brahman* enjoys all desires, all delights procured by desirable objects, without exceptions. Does he enjoy sons, heavens, etc., alternately as we do? No, he enjoys all desirable things simultaneously, as amassed together in a single moment, through a single perception, which is eternal like the light of the sun, which is non-different from the essence of *Brahman* and which we have described as Reality, Knowledge, Infinite.... He enjoys all things by that *Brahman* whose nature is omniscience" (*Taitt. Up. Bh.* 2, 1, 1). Presented with this beautiful statement, Aquinas once more would agree with Śaṅkara.

4. Conclusion

The topic of liberation is so central in the writings of Śaṅkara and Aquinas that a short paper cannot be expected to do justice to it. Only the salient points of their teachings could be gathered here but they suffice to show that their doctrines are much less heterogeneous than might be expected from their different backgrounds. I venture to say that their similarities are due to the fact that their metaphysics of the Godhead is largely identical whereas their differences arise from their diverse epistemologies. This suggestion may open the way to further fruitful comparison.

Notes

[1] [First published as "Śaṅkara and Aquinas on Liberation (*Mukti*)," *Indian Philosophical Annual* **5** (1969) 239-247. Reprinted as "A Twofold Approach: Śaṅkara—Aquinas: Śaṅkara and Aquinas on Liberation (*Mukti*)," *Indian Ecclesiastical Studies* **10**/1 (1971) 10-17, and published here with kind permission of the same.]

23

ŚAṄKARA AND AQUINAS ON CREATION[1]

1. The Cause of the Universe

St Thomas Aquinas holds that the only access we can have to the Godhead, short of divine revelation, is divine causality. Neither this finite universe nor any of its beings can be sufficiently explained it its existence, activity and positivity unless there exists an absolute Power and universal Cause of being. In order to be that, this Cause must itself be, not a being, one that shares in existence in a limited way, but pure unrestricted *Esse*. The verbal term '*esse*' (to be) is here used absolutely in preference to the verbal noun '*ens*' (being) which, as a participle, would connote finiteness. As pure *Esse*, the world-cause is obviously the Fullness of all positivity, without any division, ontological distinction, graduation, dependence, negation or defect of any kind. Hence, it is single and simple, *having* nothing, but *being* all that can be thought of without an implication of negativity. In it, truth, goodness, power, consciousness, will, power, bliss etc. are not qualities of a more radical substance but are identically the absolute *Esse* and there is no difference between essence and existence. Further, as the universal Cause, it is most intimately present in all its effects, all-powerful, all-knowing and all-loving. The relationship which these terms imply is real only from the side of its effect; from the side of the Cause itself, it is only logical, i.e., due to the imperfection of our knowledge.

For Śaṅkara also, *Brahman* is first signified and defined as "that omniscient, omnipotent Cause from which proceed the origin, subsistence and dissolution of this world" (*B.S.Bh.* 1, 1, 2). This is its relational definition (*taṭastha-lakṣaṇa*, which is *sāpekṣa* or *upalakṣaṇa*) but it leads immediately to its essential and unrelational definition (*svarūpa nirapekṣa lakṣaṇa*) as pure Power, pure Consciousness, "Reality-Knowledge-infinite" (*Satyam-jñānam-anantam*). Indeed, *Brahman* could not be all-knowing and powerful, were it not the absolute Reality that simply is Knowledge and Power. The idea that *Brahman* is *Esse* is not expressed by using the verb 'to be' as a noun, although Śaṅkara speaks of its 'is-ness' (*astitva*), but by calling it *Sad-eva* (Being only) or *paramārthataḥ Sat* (Being in the most elevated sense of the term), or even *Asat*[2] (Non-being, i.e., the opposite of all participial beings). As single, undivided (*akhaṇḍa*, *advaita*) Perfection, it is Fullness (*pūrṇa*) and, therefore, *nirguṇa* (not having qualities, but being them). As the one Cause of the universe, it is the *Ātman* of all (*sarvātman*), i.e., the Reality-Consciousness-Bliss (*Saccidānanda*) Principle that pervades and energises all and whose innermost presence can only be signified by saying that it is seated in the cave of the heart of every creature. To our ignorant mind, it thus appears to be situated and related, but in reality it remains ever free of any real relationship.

2. Creation according to Aquinas

The term 'creation' is reserved by Aquinas to designate the divine causation of the world. Since this causation is divine it is unique and has no real parallels. We can only define it by borrowing terms from the realm of finite causation on the basis of analogy. Hence, these terms have to be adapted to this unusual function. This adaptation proceeds in three steps: first, the step of confused affirmation which corresponds to *adhyāsa* (superimposition): creation is the production of the universe by God; second, the step of purification or negation (*apavāda*): this production is unlike any secular production; third, the step of elevation (*paramārthāpatti*): creation is the entire emanation of the totality of this universe from the pure *Esse*. Let us examine the last two steps.

The negative definition provided by the second step is as follows: creation is the production by God of a reality that did not exist independently either in itself or in its materials or in any of its elements (*productio rei ex nihilo sui et materiae*: cf. *S.Th.* I, 45). It is a production of reality (*vastu*, *artha*), not of a sheer illusion. It is production in the sense of ontological origination, not of mere manifestation: the thing is produced from previous non-existence (*arthasya prāgabhāvāt*), not from a state of latency, dormancy or concealment. In other terms, it exists only as divinely produced. Further, this production is unlike any production of nature or man in this that it presupposes and employs no previous materials or any other constitutive elements: it is *upādānabhūtānāṁ prāgabhāvāt*. The matter of the universe is itself co-created together with the forms in the very creation which is a total causation and not a transformation. However, this does not mean that nothing at all is presupposed by creation. For it is true for Aquinas as well as for Śaṅkara or the author of the *Gītā* that nothing can arise out of absolute nothing (*nāsato vidyate bhavaḥ*: *Bh. Gītā* 2, 16). Ultimately, for him things can arise only out of the absolute Being. Thus, they pre-exist virtually in the Power of their Cause, just as they are eternally known by it independently of their actual production. "And as such," writes Aquinas, "creatures pre-existing in God are the divine Essence itself" (*Et sic creatura in Deo est ipsa Essentia divina*: *De Potentia* 3, 16, 24). Thus Aquinas is a partisan of *satkāryavāda*. However, this must be well understood. If we ask whether the Godhead is the material cause of the world and has been transformed into it, his answer will be an emphatic no (*S.Th.* I, 41, 3). The Godhead is immutable, without parts, untransformable. It is spiritual and, in that sense, immaterial. For Aquinas matter or material cause (*materia*) is of itself non-spiritual (*jaḍa*) and formless; it is but the counterpart of form in material beings; hence, it can never be identified with the divine. But if we were to ask whether the Godhead is the world-*upādāna* in the sense used by Śaṅkara in the same topic, i.e., the innermost Cause that provides the whole substantial reality of the creature, he would fully answer yes. The creature as created, he writes, "is not the essence of God but its essence is from God" (*non est ex essentia Dei, sed est ex Deo essentia*: *S.Th.* I, 41, 3, 2). "For in Him we live and move and are, since we are His very offspring" (*S.Th.* I, 8, 2; 18, 4; 18, 4, 1). How can the creature be from God without being a part or a modification of God? Because it is produced by the sheer power of His intelligent will, by His almighty command. Since this power is not applied upon any pre-existing material which it would have to shape up, it needs no instrument (*S.Th.* I, 45, 5).

Since it is the power of the most free will, it is not activated by any necessity, internal or external to God, whose divinity implies no necessity to create and is independent of anything else (*SCG* 2, 30; *S.Th. Suppl.* 91, 1, 2). Since it is the power of the most blissful will, eternally in possession of the absolute Good, it does not create in order to satisfy any unfulfilled desire but through sheer gratuitous liberality (*SCG* 1, 100). Thus nothing accrues to the Creator, neither any self-accomplishment nor any accidental adornment such as a real relationship.

In order to reconcile the two ideas of 'divine' and 'production' we have, in this negative step, eliminated the ordinary connections of 'production' with either pre-existing object or pre-existing matter and with instruments, desirable end, need and necessity, agent's mutability or self-improvement and real relationship. We should further remark that creation is not bound with time. Time is co-created with the world since it does not precede but follows from its essential mobility and evolving changeability. Whether the world-duration is without beginning or starts from a first instant depends entirely on the Creator's free decision and cannot be settled by any deductive process (*S.Th.* I, 46, 1).

In our third step we can now define creation absolutely and eminently (*paramārthataḥ*) as the free emanation of the whole reality of the universe from the pure *Esse* (cf. *S.Th.* I, 45, 1). Aquinas uses the term 'emanation': flowing out (from *ex*: out of + Indo-European root *mad-*, to bubble, to flow) which in his time was still free of the pantheistic sense given to it by Leibniz. This emanation is free, voluntary, dependent on the sole free decision of the Godhead which has no unfulfilled desire and, hence, it is purely liberal and gratuitous. It is the emanation of the whole reality of the universe, not excepting matter; and it is from the pure *Esse* whose fullness is its Source. The relation of the universe to its Source is a relation of total ontological dependence. Being ontological, it is not contingent and amissible but pertains to the very being of the universe which is necessarily and in every condition relative and inseparable from its immanent though transcendent Cause. This relation is non-reciprocal: real in the creatures, it is only logical in their Cause which it does not affect in any real way.

3. Creation according to Śaṅkara

From the writings of Śaṅkara we can also cull elements of information which will amount to a parallel definition of creation. We have already recalled that *Brahman* is the one total Source of the universe and, therefore, its most pervading *Ātman*. Since *Brahman* is "that from whence (*yataḥ*) these beings are born," it is their *upādāna* or immanent and reality-giving cause, as indicated by the ablative case '*yataḥ*.' "There is no other substance from which the world could originate" (*B.S.Bh.* 1, 4, 23). "It is at the same time the *nimitta-kāraṇa*, the shaping or determining Cause, of the world because outside *Brahman* as immanent Cause there is no other ruling principle for *Śruti* says that previously to creation *Brahman* was one without a second" (ibid.). How could *Brahman* be the world-*upādāna* and provide its reality? Because, "in the beginning, before creation, when the differences of names-and-forms were not yet manifested, this world was but the one *Ātman*" (*Ait. Up. Bh.* 1, 1, 1). As such, the *nāma-rūpas* pre-existed only in a virtual state (*bhāviṣyena rūpeṇa*), as future effects pre-exist in the present power of their cause. "These *nāma-rūpas*, which are identical with the *Ātman* in their unmanifested state, can become the materials (*upādāna-bhūte*) of the manifested universe. Hence, it is not incongruous to say that the omniscient (*Ātman*) creates the universe by virtue of his oneness with the materials, namely, names-and-forms, which are identical with itself" (*Ait. Up. Bh.* 1, 1, 2). However, the manifestation of distinct names-and-forms through creation does not mean that the partless *Ātman* undergoes a process of diversification. "The case is rather like that of the clever magician who, independent of any materials. transforms himself, as it were (*iva*), into a second man seemingly climbing into space" (ibid.). Further, "What *Śruti* calls *ajā*, i.e., the causal matter of the four classes of beings, has itself sprung from the highest Lord" (*B.S.Bh.* 1, 4, 9). Creation presupposes "no independent matter, unreducible to the *Ātman*, such as the *Pradhāna* of the Sāṁkhyas or the primordial atoms of Kaṇāda" (*Ait. Up. Bh.* 1, 1, 1).

As *nimitta-kāraṇa*, the *Brahman-Ātman* creates through an intelligent decision: "That *Ātman* who, being omniscient by nature, can think without body and thinking organs, being then the only Existent, thought, 'Let me now create worlds, and, having thus thought, i.e., considered or visualized those worlds, he created them after that deliberation" (*Ait. Up. Bh.* 1, 1, 2). "Passages like, 'He wished, may I be many, etc.,' show that the *Ātman* is the agent in the independent activity which follows his reflection" (*B.S.Bh.* 1, 4, 24). This intelligent wishing does not imply any active change (*pravṛtti*) in the *Ātman* himself. "A thing which is devoid of motion (*pravṛtti-rahita*), for instance, a magnet, can nevertheless be a *pravartaka*, i.e., stir other things into activity.... So the Lord also, who is immanent in all, the *Ātman* of all, the all-knower and the all-power, can, although immune of motion, set the whole world into activity" (*evaṁ pravṛtti-rahito 'pīśvaraḥ sarvagataḥ sarvātmā sarvajñaḥ sarvaśaktiś-ca san sarvaṁ pravartayet*: *B.S.Bh.* 2, 2, 2).

This intelligent Source is universally immanent in real existents but the being of the latter is wholly relative; they are neither parts nor modifications of the *Ātman* but only external adjuncts (*upādhis*) of which he is the causal substrate: "the *Ātman* should be realised as Existing, as productive of effects in which existence inheres (*sat-kārya*), namely, *buddhi*, etc., which are his *upādhis*" (*Kaṭha Up. Bh.* 2, 3, 13). "*Prāṇa*, the life-Breath [i.e., the *Ātman*], is equal to all these bodies of white ants, mosquitoes, elephants, etc., in the sense that it is present in them in its entirety (*kartsnyena-parisamāpta*), somehow as cowness (*gotva*) is present in each individual cow. But it cannot be merely of the size of those bodies for it is formless and all-pervading" (*Bṛh. Up. Bh.* 1, 3, 22). It is because of this causal presence of the whole transcendent *Ātman* in each being that they share with him, though altogether differently, the universal *sattā* (real-ity) (cf., e.g., *Taitt. Up. Bh.* 2, 1, 1).

When creating the *Ātman* needs no instruments: "the absolutely complete power of *Brahman* does not require to be supplemented by any extraneous help...; his high power is revealed as manifold, as inherent, acting as force and knowledge" (*B.S.Bh.* 2, 1, 24). He creates "like gods etc., who, without availing themselves of any extraneous means, produce palaces, etc. by their mere intention, which is effective in consequence of those beings' peculiar power" (*B.S.Bh.* 2, 1, 25).

The wish which *Śruti* attributes to the creating *Ātman* must not be understood as alike to the wants and needs which impel us to action. "Desires cannot thus impel *Brahman*. How then [are they found in it?] As essentially Reality-Knowledge, and as pure in virtue of their being their own *Ātman*; and, as such, they do not impel *Brahman*.... Therefore, *Brahman* is independent in its volitions; hence, it does not want things as yet unattained." (*Taitt. Up. Bh.* 2, 6, 1). "We see in everyday life that certain doings of princes or other men of high position who have no unfulfilled desire left have no reference to any extraneous purpose, but proceed from mere sportfulness.... Analogously, the activity of the Lord may be supposed to be mere sport (*līlā*), proceeding from his own nature without reference to any purpose.... And if in ordinary life we might possibly, by close scrutiny, detect some subtle motive even for sportful action, we cannot do so with regard to the actions of the Lord, all whose wishes are fulfilled, as *Śruti* says" (*B.S.Bh.* 2, 1, 33). Yet, though creating is in no way useful to the Creator, it is useful to the creatures since "it is performed for their welfare" (*Bh. Gītā Bh.* 3, 24).

The relation of the effects to their divine Cause is called *tādātmya* (having that as one's *ātman*). "It is an accepted principle, even in the world, that an effect is intimately dependent (*anuvidhāyin*) on its [internal] cause" (*Bṛh. Up. Bh.* 1, 5, 14). This relation must be said to be real in the effects for "as long as an effect subsists, it is impossible to assume the dissolution of its [internal] cause, since on the dissolution of the latter the effect also cannot exist. On the other hand, we may assume a continued existence of the cause although the effect is destroyed; for that is actually observed in the case of clay" (*B.S.Bh.* 2, 3, 14). Hence, that relation is not real in both terms. It is not reciprocal. *Tādātmya* is often thought to mean absolute identity of its two terms but, "if absolute equality were insisted on, the relation of inner cause and effect would be annihilated.... If you were to demand that not only *sattā* but all the characteristics of *Brahman* should be found in the effect if the latter has to be non-different [*ananya* from its cause], this demand would lead to the negation of the relation of cause and effect which is based on the presence in the cause of an excellence [not found in the effect]" (*B.S.Bh.* 2, 1, 6). "Names and forms in all their states have *Brahman* alone as their *Ātman*, but *Brahman* has not its *Ātman* in them [in other words, this *tādātmya* is not mutual]. Since without this [*Brahman*] they simply do not exist, they are said to have their *Ātman* in it (*tad-ātmaka*). And it is because of these two *upādhis* [*nāma* and *rūpa*] that *Brahman* is related to all mundane activities which imply the significations of the words 'knower,' 'knowable,' 'knowledge,' etc." (*Taitt. Up. Bh.* 2, 6, 1). "Of the effect it is understood that in reality it is non-different (*ananyat*) from the Cause, i.e., has no existence apart from the Cause (*vyatirekeṇā-'bhāvaḥ*)." This theory of *tādātmya* "does away with the independent (*svābhāvika*) existence of the embodied *Ātman*... and of the world" (*B.S.Bh.* 2, 1, 14).

On the other hand, it is because *Brahman* is the absolute Existent (*Sat*), what Aquinas would call the pure *Esse*, that it can emanate a full universe freely and without being affected by it. "It is a matter of common experience in this world that anything from which something is produced does exist, as, for instance, clay, the cause of jars, and seed, the cause of sprouts. So *Brahman* does exist, since it is the Cause of space, etc. Nor is any effect perceived in this world as having been produced from nothing at all (*asataḥ*). If effects, such as names-and-forms, had originated from nothing, they could not be perceived for lack of *ātman* (*nirātmakatvāt*); but they are perceived, hence, *Brahman* exists. Should any effect originate from nothing, then, even though perceived, it would be imbued with unreality; but this is not the case, hence, *Brahman* exists." (*Taitt. Up. Bh.* 2, 6, 1).

Such is Śaṅkara's theory of creation. The universe exists only because in all its elements, including matter, it is freely originated from *Brahman* which is the universal *Ātman*. *Tādātmya* signifies that constant ontological dependence which implies the pervading causal presence of *Brahman* in all other beings. These exist by the power of its free command. They neither add to nor do they subtract anything from the fullness of their Cause. Their real relation to it is not reciprocal. And this Cause is not an intermediary *Īśvara* but the one *Brahman-Ātman*, the supreme Existent, that remains *nirguṇa* and *nirapekṣa* even though its creating makes it appear to our ignorant minds as *saguṇa* and *sāpekṣa*. I have been struck by the close similarity between the creation theory of Aquinas and that of Śaṅkara. Their critical acceptance of their respective scriptural authorities and their outstanding metaphysical genius may explain this remarkable encounter of two philosopher-saints who have blazed for us the difficult paths towards wisdom.

Notes

1 [First published as "Śaṅkara and Aquinas on Creation," *Indian Philosophical Annual* **6** (1970) 112-118. Reprinted in *Indian Ecclesiastical Studies* **11/4** (1972) 235-241, and published here with kind permission.]

2 [This should probably read *a-sat*, going by the qualification that follows, as well as above, ch. 10, section 2 and ch. 12, section 3.1. But see ch. 27, section 2 below, which reads: 'Hence, Brahman is *A-sat*, UN-real, i.e., totally unlike what we normally call *sat*, real.']

24

ADVAITAVĀDA AND CHRISTIANITY[1]

The question has been raised recently in the Marathi newspaper Tarun Bharat *whether Christianity could claim to be a type of* advaitavāda *(non-dualism) rather than a pronounced form of dualism as seems to be the opinion of many, even Christians, in this land. The following remarks were meant first for the readers of that newspaper.*[2]

A meaningful reply demands that one ascertain first the nature of Advaita for Śaṅkara and then the nature of God and man in Christianity.

Advaita is neither what the West calls monism nor what it calls pantheism but is strictly the denial of dualism (*a-dvaita*). It rejects the plurality of ultimate parallel absolutes as in Sāṁkhya (and even Mīmāṃsa or Vaiśeṣika) and affirms the unicity of the Absolute (*Brahman-Ātman*) which, alone is Being (*Sat*) in the supreme sense of the term (*paramārthataḥ*). This *Sat* is *akhaṇḍa*, *nirguṇa*, *atīndriya* and, therefore, cannot be expressed by the primary meaning (*mukhyārtha*) of words but only indicated (*lakṣita*) by the secondary meaning (*lakṣyārtha*) of the terms of such upaniṣadic definitions as "*Satyam jñānam anantam Brahma.*" No other being exists or can exist independently of, and apart from, that *Sat* (*tadvyatirekena*). All depend on it for their existence, persistence, orderly experience and activity (*bhoktṛtva-kartṛtva-ca*), and for reaching it as their goal and end. It is their internal cause (*upādāna*) and supreme *Ātman* (*Paramātman*).

What then is man or any *kartṛ-bhoktṛ-jñātṛ*? A *jīvātman* plus inner senses, outer senses and body conjoined (cf. *Kaṭha Up*. 3, 3-9). What is the *jīvātman* and how does it unify (*ekīkṛ*) *buddhi* and the rest? According to *Upadeśasāhasrī* 18, 27 ssq, it is a reflection (*ābhāsa*), in the mirror-like inner sense, of the supreme *Ātman* which is its Prototype. As such it is not an illusion but an ontologically relative and dependent contingent entity for it is unequal to its Cause and Prototype. Though similar to it in imitated centrality, consciousness, freedom, etc., it also shares in its reflector's finiteness, mobility, passibility, etc. It cannot find its truth in itself but only in its Prototype which is its true *vastu*. In this sense it is not *svārtha* but *parārtha*. In its experience and activity it is autonomous insofar as it consciously takes its own decisions as befits a *jñātṛ-kartṛ*. Śaṅkara's tenet is that *Brahman* "is the *Ātman* of this experiencer" (*Ātmā sā bhoktur iti*: *B.S.Bh.* 1, 1, 1 and elsewhere: *kartur-ātmā*, *jñātur-ātmā*, the *Ātman* of the agent, of the knower; note the genitive). The *Brahman* is itself neither *bhoktṛ* nor *kartṛ* nor *jñātṛ*; hence it is not expressed (*vācya*) by the term 'I' (*aham*) although it belongs to the sphere (*gocara*) of *aham* insofar as it is signified indirectly by the *jahad-ajahal-lakṣaṇā* of *aham*.

Man's integration is explained as follows in intimate dependence upon the *Paramātman* which is *svayam-jyoti*: "As an emerald or any other gem, dropped for testing into milk or a similar liquid, imparts its lustre to them, so does this luminous *Ātman*, being finer than even the heart or intellect, unify (*ekīkṛ*...) and impart its lustre to the body and organs including the intellect, etc., although it is within the intellect; for these have varying degrees of fineness or grossness in a certain order, and the *Ātman* is the innermost of all" (*Bṛh. Up. Bh.* 4, 3, 7). Thus the existential unity of man derives absolutely from the innermost *Ātman* through the mediation of its reflection, the individual *ātman*, which diffuses it unto the *buddhi*, *manas*, *indriyas* and *śarīra*. Such a conception overcomes Sāṁkhya *dvaita*. Man is no longer the heterogeneous assemblage of a blind and a lame but an integrated contingent being totally dependent on the Absolute.

Christianity affirms similarly that God is the one absolute Existent whose sole will has produced freely a world of contingent beings totally dependent on Him for their origin, for every moment of their existence and activity, even for their free activity, and for the achievement of their end. They are created from nothing else but Him alone but this modifies Him in no way. He is the partless, undifferentiated fullness of perfect reality. Even the assertion that He is Trinity introduces in Him no ontological plurality of any sort. He is three Persons but in one Essence (*svarūpa*) which is one Consciousness (*caitanya*), one Bliss (*ānanda*), one Power (*śakti*), etc. Through these many concepts we signify through mere analogical predication the one that is in itself *simplex Deus* (*akhaṇḍa Deva*). Even with regard to creation, the Three are One Creator, one Perfect Cause (providing reality, which is the role of *upādāna kāraṇa*, and organisation, which is the function of *nimitta kāraṇa*), one Inner Ruler (*antaryāmin*), hence one Innermost *Ātman*.

As to man he is made in the image and likeness of God especially because his individual soul is spiritual in close dependence upon God who is absolute Spirit. As such his soul is a reflection of God in whom alone it can find its perfect truth and reality. As a reflection, however it does not depend on a reflector though it is conditioned by the matter it informs into a living human body. The will of God being almighty can project into existence subsistent images of Himself without the help of any instrument. Having thus its Source in God who is the absolute Light, the human soul integrates the whole man through a diffusion that makes even his body share in its spiritual nature. As such it has a dignity which makes it ontologically immortal and apt to attain by God's grace the direct experience (*sākṣātkāra anubhava*) of the very essence of God. In this so-called 'beatific vision' it attains its goal and the end of its creaturely ignorance. It returns to its Source, as the Christian theologians are never tired of affirming, and ceases to conceive itself as a being separate from God. This, however, demands no annihilation of its dependent existence but it plunges through an ineffable[3] awareness and love of God into the full realization of the One who is from its origin the Being of its being and the Truth of its nature as image of God.

Comparing the two conceptions set forth above, let us note the following points:

(1) Śaṅkara does not identify the *aham* in its *mukhyārtha* with the *Brahman* but only in its *lakṣyārtha*. Indeed, it is only after denying (*apavāda*) all the finite characteristics of *aham* and after elevating (*paramārtha-lakṣaṇā*) its purified concept to the utmost that its *tādātmya* with *Brahman* becomes the truth and no longer a false imposition (*adhyāropa*). On the level of the primary meaning, *tādātmya* is not a reciprocal and straight identity-relation (remember the genitive in '*bhoktur-ātmā*'):

Brahman is the *Ātman* of *aham*; *aham* is not the *Ātman* of *Brahman* (cf. *B.S.Bh.* 2, 1, 9 and *Taitt. Up. Bh.* 2, 6, 1). Hence, we cannot go on repeating without ado that Śaṅkara professes the identity of the individual soul with the Absolute.

(2) The too little known anthropology which Śaṅkara develops around the notion of the human ego as a reflection of the inner Witness opens up towards a conception of man as a totally dependent and contingent being which is yet strongly integrated.[4]

(3) His conception of *mokṣa* puts an end to all *dvaita* ideas of a separation between *jīva* and *Paramātman* and establishes their unity on the epistemic level of *anubhava*. The question, however, whether their ontological distinction (not separation) as reflection and Prototype is not eternal, is not clearly put and therefore receives no definite reply.

(4) Christianity, on the contrary, decides clearly this question in the affirmative but simultaneously professes the equivalent of the above three points. Hence, its teaching belongs to the same type as *advaitavāda* but with a difference concerning the last question raised.

(5) Besides this basic teaching and always in accordance with it, Christianity further professes other teachings derived directly from Jesus Christ: the Trinity of Father, Son and Spirit in the One (*eka*), partless (*akhaṇḍa*) and undifferentiated (*aviśiṣta*) Deity;[5] the real incarnation (not simply *avatāra*) of the unique Son in a complete and fully integrated human nature through which he acts and suffers as God-man; the efficacy for universal salvation of this incarnation, Christ being "the Way, the Truth and the Life"; the Christ-taught "worship of God in spirit and in truth." These teachings are prominent in the Bible and may be thought by some to have nothing to do with *advaitavāda*. But the latter is present and alive in the tradition of Christianity not only in some sentences of St Paul but even in the early formulations of the creed of the Christian faith.

Notes

[1] [The text presented here is taken from "Does Christianity Profess Non-Dualism?" *The Clergy Monthly* **37**/9 (1973) 354-357, though the title is taken from "Advaitavada and Christianity," *The Divine Life* **35**/6 (1973) 237-239. As

becomes evident from the first paragraph, the piece was originally intended for the readership of *Tarun Bharat*; it seems to have been translated into Marathi by M. Lederle 'and published by him' under the title "Advaita va Khristi Dharma." The piece was also published under the title "Advaitavada and Christianity" in the *Bulletin of the Secretariate for Non-Christians* Year **8**/2, 23-24 (1973) 143-146, and in French translation as "Advaitavada et Christianisme," *Bulletin (Secretariatus pro Non-Christianis)* **8** (1973) 147-150. The article is published here with kind permission of *Vidyajyoti: Journal of Theological Reflection* (earlier *The Clergy Monthly*).]

[2] [In *The Divine Life* version, this first paragraph is replaced by the following: "The question has been raised in some newspapers whether one may legitimately speak of a Christian Advaitavada." See "Advaitavada and Christianity," *The Divine Life* **35**/6 (1973) 237.]

[3] [*The Divine Life* text reads 'indivisible' instead of 'ineffable.']

[4] [For more on this point, see *Brahman and Person* ch. 8: "Is the Concept of 'Person' Congenial to Śāṅkara Vedānta?"]

[5] [Sanskrit equivalents in brackets missing in *The Divine Life* text.]

25

ROBERT DE NOBILI AND VEDĀNTA[1]

Robert de Nobili (1577-1656), the founder of the Jesuit mission of Madurai, has long been known as the first European scholar in Sanskrit. His numerous letters and more than 50 books in Tamil, Telugu and Sanskrit display his truly encyclopaedic knowledge of Hindu literature but till recently we could only guess at the extent of his acquaintance with the Vedānta. Surely, in 1610, four years after his arrival in Madurai, he still knew little about it. In a letter he wrote on 22 November 1610, to his superior Fr A. Laerzio, he first described the programme of the first course (four to five years) of studies in Nyāya (Gaṅgeśa's *Cintāmaṇi* was the textbook) in the university (*Saṅgam*) of Madurai. Then he said:

> In addition... they have the science which they call Vedānta in which they treat of God and his unity but as I am not yet acquainted with it, I cannot give your Reverence an account of the same. I am now completing my Sanskrit studies.... As sciences here are not studied in Tamil... but only in Sanskrit..., I must hurry up learning Sanskrit thoroughly. I believe that in five or six months I shall know it sufficiently to begin my course of lectures.

Earlier he had explained that course as "a course of philosophy, according to your desire, to young men who are intellectually well-gifted; and such young men are not lacking who are most eager to hear our philosophy." As to his further progress in Sanskrit, his writings left us in no doubt; but, how far did he advance in the study of the Vedānta?

A fortunate discovery permits us now to satisfy this query at least with regard to his knowledge of the Vedānta three years later. In 1968, a manuscript was found in Rome which was, though not the autograph, yet either the dictated text or an immediate copy of the treatise he had composed shortly before 28 November 1613, under the title *Informatio de quibusdam moribus nationis indicae*. Promptly, Fr S. Rajamanickam had it deciphered, edited and translated into English, and published with an introduction in 1972.[2]

This treatise, *On Indian Customs*, is replete with Sanskrit quotations. In the Appendix 2 provided by the editor, they run up to 11 pages. Due to the direct purpose of the treatise, they are taken mainly from *Smṛti* (chiefly from *Manu-smṛti* and several *Purāṇas*, besides a number of untraced sources), but they also include literal quotations from *Śruti* as will appear presently. From the point of view of the history of cultural encounters between the West (here Christian Europe and India), this treatise is quite interesting since it thus gives us data which document the very beginning of Western indology. But its interest increases when we realise that it also documents the well-balanced attitude of critical assessment and sympathetic evaluation which characterises all the writings of de Nobili.

In his chapter 3, "Concerning the sciences which the Brahmins pursue professionally," de Nobili provides an able and ample exposition of the nine chief disciplines proper to the Brahmins: (1) *Śabda śāstra*; (2) *Kāvya* and *Alaṅkāra* with its 8 divisions; (3) *Jyoti śāstra*; (4) *Nyāya* or *Tarka śāstra*; (5) *Cintāmaṇi* according to 6 standard texts, beginning with Gaṅgeśa's basic work; (6) *Adhyātmika śāstra* which comprises the 3 schools of Buddhism, Vedānta and Mīmāṁsā; (7) *Dharma śāstra* as the science of the Laws of the various religious sects; (8) *Dharma śāstra* as *Nīti śāstra* which is Civil Law; and (9) *Ayur Veda*.

Thus among the three schools of *Adhyātmika śāstra*, de Nobili describes the second which is that of the Jñānis or Spirituals whose theology is called Vedānta. Vedānta, he says, is taught in three parts: *Vivācanasyotpādyam*, *Sattva* (or *Satya*?) *Vivekam*, and *Bheda Dikkāram*. The first treats abundantly "about the true God as known solely by the light of reason"[3] and refutes polytheism and idolatry; it also treats of the soul and its immortality and all-pervasiveness and refutes many tenets of the *Cintāmaṇi*. The second part "again with many arguments in support dwells on the oneness of God and the soul."[4] The third purports "to exclude multiplicity in God and in the soul."[5]

> Moreover, in these three parts, the Vedānta theologians explain well nigh all the divine attributes stressing their absolute character. For instance, they show that God is the self-subsistent Being, that he is eternal, immaterial, that of his own nature he is good, that he exists everywhere and is the Cause of every being.[6]

There are, de Nobili says, other parts of this theology

> which I have not yet seen, and a plethora of books; indeed, daily new books appear; and in this our own day there lives an eminent author who keeps writing on these subjects with penetrating sagacity.[7]
>
> However, among these theologians there are still differences of opinion. Thus in their statements about God some confine themselves strictly to what they can discover by the light of reason.... Others, on the contrary, reaching out beyond what has been said [above] about the true God, introduce into the essence of God some material element they call *Māyā*, by means of which, they say, God creates all things.[8] The reason underlying this *māyā*-theory is their stout contention that 'nothing can come out of nothing'.[9]

It is well known that the doctrine of *māyā* originated in Śaṅkara's teaching though he generally preferred to speak in terms of *avidyā*, but, in the words of S. Dasgupta:

> In the hands of the later followers of Śaṅkara it gradually thickened into a positive stuff through the evolution or transformation of which all the phenomena of world-appearance could be explained. The Vedāntists held that this *māyā*, though it adhered to *Brahman* and spread its magical creations thereon, was unspeakable, indescribable, indefinable, changeable and unthinkable and was thus entirely different from the self-revealing, unchangeable *Brahman*. The charge of dualism... could be dodged... only by holding that *māyā* was unreal and illusory.... Almost all the followers of Śaṅkara had, however, been interpreting their master's views in such a way that the positive existence of an objective world with its infinite varieties as the ground of perceptual presentation was never denied.[10]

De Nobili's exposition of the *māyā*-conception cited above is obviously based on the teaching of the Śaṅkarites and witnesses the state it had reached in South India about 1600. In the same paragraph, de Nobili also refers to the theory that God "possesses a twofold energy, one by which he creates the souls, the other by which he creates the bodies." This seems to echo a theory of Padmapāda, a direct disciple of Śaṅkara and the founder of the Vivaraṇa school of Vedānta interpretation whose later representatives were Ānandapūrṇa and Nṛsiṃha in the sixteenth century and Rāma Tīrtha in the seventeenth. According to Padmapāda, *māyā* in association with *Brahman* constitutes *Īśvara*, the root-cause of the universe. He regards *māyā* as the stuff in which resides the double power of knowledge and activity (*vijñāna-krīya-śakti-dvayāśraya*), the first determining the psychical processes and the other the physical processes. By undergoing peculiar transformations of these two kinds with God as its support, it produces the individual persons (*jīvatva pādika*). Appāya Dikṣita restates this doctrine of the origin of *jīva* in his *Siddhāntaleśa*. Nṛsiṃha explains in his *Tattva-viveka* that when the pure Consciousness (*Brahmạn*) is reflected through *rajas* and *tamas* which are the impure aspects of *prakṛti* there takes place the manifestation of the individual selves or *jīvas*. Thus the theory of the twofold *māyā*, kept alive by these contemporaries of de Nobili (including Kṛṣṇa Tīrtha, the *guru* of Rāma Tīrtha) who were very much influenced by the Vivaraṇa tradition, could very well be known and alluded to by de Nobili.[11]

In a much earlier document, a letter of de Nobili to Laerzio dated 17 March 1607, he attributes a similar teaching to Śaiva-Siddhānta which posits three general principles of all things: *Pati*, *paśu*, *pāśa*. "They call God *Pati*, and *paśu* is the matter out of which God makes souls, while *pāśa* is the matter out of which he makes bodies, whether simple or composite." But he later corrected his understanding of Śaiva-Siddhānta as proves his exposition of it in his *Āttuma Niruṇayam (Ātma-nirṇaya)*, a Tamil work he wrote in 1630, ch. 11. In any case, in *IC* (dated 1613), his reference is to a Vedānta doctrine, hence, quite probably to that of the Vivaraṇa school. He writes:

> Further, their opinions differ also in the matter of the soul. Some have it, like Plato, that there is one soul common to all, existing from all eternity and present in all men; and that, dependent on the former, there is another soul which is the particular animating principle in each individual and, is yet immortal; this they call *jīvātman*. Again, others have it that all the souls are severally and newly produced by God from the material element I have mentioned above; and that the same matter subserves the purpose of God in working miracles (should he be so minded) and in taking up various bodies (*avatāra*). Moreover, on each of these tenets we have various theological doctrines and not a few books.[12]

De Nobili is aware that while all Jñānis reject sacrifice to the *Devas*, the stricter ones refrain even from sacrifice to the one true God "who, they contend, should be adored only in spirit."[13] They further maintain that salvation cannot be obtained by means of any *karma* but only through knowledge (*jñāna*). (Śaṅkara, indeed, was emphatic on this point.) They rebuke the Mīmāṃsakas by pointing out that the Vedic commands regarding sacrifice are contradicted by such *Śrutis* as the *Taittirīya Āraṇyaka* (of the *Yajur Veda*) 10, 10, 3a: "*Na karmaṇa*, etc." which he quotes and translates, "Not through [sacrificial] action, progeny, wealth or almsgiving do men attain blissful immortality."[14]

When describing the image-worshipping sects, de Nobili ranks the orthodox Māyāvādis as the oldest sect which has "continued in unbroken unity up to the time of that great Master, Śaṅkarācārya."[15] From him there broke away three disciples who set up three new sects: Rāmānuja, who founded the sect of the Vaiṣṇavas, Madhva, who started the sect of the Tattvavādis, and "a third, whose name was Śivan if I am not mistaken, who established the sect of the Śaivas."[16] The Māyāvādis, he says, "hold in equal honour the three gods Brahmā, Viṣṇu, Rudra, in whom all sovereignty abides.... As to the many other gods they also worship, some are described as sons of the supreme gods, others as their servants, others as heroes."[17] He knows well their ancient books, the four *Veda-saṃhitās* and the many books of *Dharma-śāstra*. But his preference goes to the Upaniṣads, especially the *Taittirīya*.

Quoting the middle part of its Invocation (1, 1, 1), *Tvam eva pratyakṣam brahmāsi*, etc., he translates (taking *pratyakṣam* in the sense of *prakāśam*): "Thou art God and very Light resplendent. Thee God I call very Light resplendent. I call Thee true. I call Thee Truth." And he draws attention to the fact that the term used here for God is not Brahmā (with the long final syllable) which properly designates god Brahmā, the first of the *Trimūrti*, but Brahma (with the short final syllable) which is the name most commonly used for God in the true and absolute sense.[18]

He refers to the *Śikṣā Vallī* (*Taitt. Up.* 1, 2, 12) as "discourses about truth, veracity, the practice of virtue, thanksgiving and rendering like for like in doing good."[19] Of the

Brahmānanda Vallī (*Taitt. Up*. 2, 1, 9) he has the highest opinion: it teaches that God is the real Cause of the world's existence and is One.

> Such tenets in fact as might go to enlarge the doctrine of the *Jñāni* sect; such too as may well and should indeed be acceptable even to Christians. Take for instance the following texts of this Upaniṣad where, referring to the nature of God, the author describes him as '*taṃ tva bhaga*' (1, 4, 3), i.e., 'good of his very own nature,' as "*jñānam anantam Brahma*" (2, 1, 1), i.e., 'infinite wisdom,' as "*ākāśa śarīram Brahma*" (1, 6, 2), i.e., 'of an ethereal form' ('ethereal' meaning 'spiritual' for that is how they express spirituality through a positive term... although they more often express it through the negative term *aśarīri*, 'incorporeal'), and as being of his very nature or of himself 'true and Truth itself' (1, 1, 1 quoted above). Finally, God is said to be the true Rewarder of the good in these words "*brahmavid āpnoti param*" (2, 1, 1), i.e., 'he who knows this God will secure glory' (more literally, reaches the Supreme).[20]
>
> But, what is yet more surprising, I discover in this Upaniṣad even an adumbration of the recondite mystery of the most holy Trinity, God most gracious and great vouchsafing no doubt even to these far distant lands some inkling of this most profound secret of our faith through the mouth of One of their sages.... The text runs as follows: *Sa ya eṣo'ntarhṛdaya ākāśaḥ, tasminn ayam puruṣo manomayah..., antareṇa tāluke ya eṣa stana ivā'valambate se'ndra-yoniḥ* (1, 6, 1); i.e., 'He himself is internally, in his own nature, Spirit; in him is he who is himself Spirit existing forth from the Will [of that One] like one who exists forth from [that One's] Mouth [namely, as the Word], adhering to that One's breast [namely, as His Son]. He is both Lord and Cause of [all] things.'[21]

After this, de Nobili refers to two tenets of the Śrutivādis. First, "the contention of some Māyāvādi Brahmins that these scriptures are existing by themselves." This is the well-known doctrine, common to both Mīmāṃsā and Vedānta, that the *Śruti* is *nitya* (eternal) because it is *apauruṣeya* (authorless, originating from no *puruṣa* whether man or god) and is, therefore, *svataḥ-pramāṇa* (authoritative by itself). The contrary doctrine is "the claim of others who ascribe their authorship to Rudra or Viṣṇu or Brahmā." De Nobili objects to both opinions by pointing out that the scriptures themselves have ascribed to designated human authors particular teachings. For instance, to 'Eastern sages' or 'a *ṛṣi*' or 'Triṣaṅka' or 'Viśvamitra,' etc. Besides, "the merit of collecting all those sayings of wise men goes, they say, to a certain Vyāsa; hence, the collection is known as *Veda Vyāsaḥ*." The second *śrutivāda* tenet he objects to is the claim of *samanvaya* (harmony of all *Śrutis*). De Nobili is of the opinion that the *Śruti* is "but a collection of various opinions which a variety of learned men have brought forth on a variety of subjects, each in his own sense... since the sayings it records are in striking contradiction one with another." He knows that the Brahmins are aware of these difficulties but nevertheless uphold those two tenets in order to enforce upon all the authority of the *Śruti*. As in other parts of the world, this attitude of the lawgivers arose "not from an ungodly, but from a religious motivation."[22]

Finally, against his opponents' general rejection of Hindu scriptures, de Nobili concludes:

> They are not to be condemned altogether but can well be retained insofar as they propound moral ideas or social subjects. Much less should we condemn as superstitious and addicted to image-worship all those who have secured the degree of *Śāstri* in this field or who teach that science insofar, as I have said, as it is morally tenable and refers to merely social precepts.... [Besides], are they not saying many things that are compatible with the true religion, some specimens of which I have mentioned above? ... Are the good people among the Brahmins to reject the pearls that are found in those laws, and to throw away those excellent principles they can learn from them? ... As for me, if I have chosen to discourse on them, it is not that I deem it important to defend all that they contain.... My only intention is to caution against extending condemnation beyond what is proper and to allow the truth to have its say in any subject whatsoever.[23]

Conclusion

There is no evidence that de Nobili was personally acquainted with Śaṅkara's writings but he had a good grasp of the state reached by the latter's doctrine in his time and of its sources and general background. As held by the Jñānis, he characterises it as a theology (*Brahma-jñāna* or *Brahma-jijñāsā*) whose chief tenets he briefly mentions. As held by the *Trimūrti*-worshipping Māyāvādis, it has developed a conception of illusion-creating and matter-like, self-immutable *māyā*. He mentions various opinions regarding *ātman* (*Paramātman* and *jīvātman*), then Śaṅkara's contention that the way to *mokṣa* (salvation) can consist in *jñāna* alone in opposition to *karma* (as sacrificial activity). Turning to the scripture he knows as *Yajur Āraṇyaka*, which is the *Taittirīya Āraṇyaka* with its last part called *Taittīriya Upaniṣad* of the Black Yajur Veda school, he gives several textual quotations from its first two *vallīs* in order to exhibit the penetration of its insights into the nature of the one true God and even, he suggests, of the mysterious Trinity. Having explained historically the splitting that divided Vedānta after Śaṅkara's time, he examines the validity of two basic tenets of all Śrutivādis, namely, the *svataḥ-prāmāṇya* and the *samanvaya* of the *Śruti*, and gives his text-founded reasons for rejecting them.

More important still is his discriminative admiration for the 'pearls' of truth and 'excellent principles' inculcated by the Vedānta and the 'moral ideas' prescribed by the *Dharma-smṛti* (whose exposition by de Nobili I could not document in this article) side by side, with unobjectionable 'merely social precepts.' Contrary to many later Christians, he considers that the term '*Brahma*' (*Brahman*) is an adequate equivalent of the Christian term 'God' and, moreover, esteems that such upaniṣadic insights as he records concerning *Brahman* "should be acceptable to Christians." The *Taittirīya Upaniṣad* is to him a precious source-book and he delights in drawing from it theological formulations consonant with Christianity.[24] If Max Müller was right when he called him 'the first European Sanskrit scholar,' the Brahmins of Madurai went even deeper in their appreciation when, prizing his religious teaching beyond his erudition, they named him '*Tattva Bodhakar*,' the Teacher of Reality.[25]

Notes

[1] [First published in *Vidyajyoti: Journal of Theological Reflection* **40/8** (1976) 363-371; reprinted here with kind permission.]

[2] S. Rajamanickam, SJ, *Roberto de Nobili on Indian Customs*, Latin text deciphered by Fr J. Pujo, and English translation by Archbishop P. Leonard. Research Institute, St Xavier's College, Palayamkottai (now transferred to Loyola College, Madras - 34), 1972. This source will be referred to as *IC*.

[3] *IC* 30. *Vivācanasyotpādyam* (reading uncertain) may stand for *vivācanasya* + *utpādya* = (the doctrine) to be brought forth by the arbitrator (or through the arbitration or authority of the Vedānta texts) or for *vivācanasya* + *utpāda* (or *utpatti*) = the arising of the authoritative decision (about the meaning of the Vedānta texts). *Sattva vivekam* or perhaps *satya vivekam* = the discrimination of truth or the discernment of true reality. *Bheda dhikkāram* = the refutation of

duality. It happens to be the name of a work of Nṛsiṃhāśrama Muni (ca AD 1500) which may have been known to de Nobili.

[4] *IC* 30.

[5] *IC* 30. [This note is missing in the body of the *Vidyajyoti* text.]

[6] *IC* 30.

[7] *IC* 31. Appāya Dikṣita (probably 1554-1626) may have been the eminent author referred to by de Nobili although it is only in 1626 that he came to the Pāṇḍya country at the request of king Tirumalai Nayak to settle certain disputes between Śaivas and Vaiṣṇavas. But his fame as a polymath and polygraph had preceded him and some of the 400 works ascribed to him must have been read and admired by de Nobili. Cf. S. Dasgupta, *A History of Indian Philosophy* **2**: 218-219.

[8] *IC* 31.

[9] *IC* 31. This axiom was generally understood by Indian thinkers to mean that no real product can arise except through the self-transformation (*pariṇāma*) of a material cause. Thus understood, it is opposed to the Christian notion of 'creation' as 'the production of the universe out of no material cause, yet not out of no reality-giving cause but rather totally out of God.' Because God is purely Spirit, he can through his absolute Will create all cosmic realities as finite participations of his Essence without any self-immutation and any antecedent matter. Thus he remains unchanged and transcendent yet, as Creator, he is their immanent Ground and preserving Cause, i.e., their *paramātman*.

[10] Dasgupta **2**:220-221.

[11] Cf. Dasgupta **2**:48, 52, 56, 72, 104.

[12] *IC* 31. The first opinion regarding soul rather represents the *viśiṣṭādvaita* doctrine of Rāmānuja whereas the second is roughly Śaṅkarian. Among Śaṅkarites, Sarvajñātma Muni (ca AD 900) held that *māyā* is the instrumental cause, *Brahman* being the material cause of the universe.

[13] *IC* 38.

[14] *IC* 38.

[15] *IC* 39.

[16] *IC* 39. When venturing a founder's name for this sect, de Nobili was quite aware of the obscurity that surrounds the origin of the Śaivas.

[17] *IC* 38.

[18] *IC* 43.

[19] *IC* 42.

[20] *IC* 42-43. The fuller text of *Taitt. Up.* 1, 4, 3 is "*taṃ tvā Bhaga praviśāni*," i.e., "into Thee Thyself, O Bounty (or Bountiful Lord), may I enter." De Nobili retains the idea of inherent Goodness which makes God the most bountiful Lord.

[21] *IC* 43 but as re-translated from the Latin by myself. The accepted translation of *Taitt. Up.* 1, 6, 1 is: "That ether which is within the heart—in it is this Person consisting of mind, immortal, all-gold (= resplendent). That which hangs down between the palates like a nipple, that is the womb of Indra." This text is in later centuries explained in yogic fashion as indicating the path to Indra through

the *suṣumnā nāḍī*, the channel which is said to pass upward from the heart, through the mid region of the throat up to the skull. (Cf. S. Radhakrishnan, *The Principal Upaniṣads* [London: Allen & Unwin, 1953] 533-534.) For de Nobili's rendering of *ākāśa* as spirit, see *Maitri Up*. 7, 11; of *manas* (in *manomaya*) as will, see *Maitri Up*. 6, 30: "desire, conception, doubt, faith, lack of faith, steadfastness, lack of steadfastness, shame, meditation, fear, all this is truly *manas*." As to "*sa indrayoniḥ*" (he is the womb of Indra), grammatically it could also mean, "he is Lord and Cause." Note also that all the subjects in the text (*sa ya eṣa... ayam puruṣo... ya eṣa... sa*) are in the masculine gender and seem to indicate a plurality of persons. *Muṇḍ. Up*. 2, 2, 1-9 is an amplification of this text.

[22] This whole paragraph sums up *IC* 43-45.

[23] *IC* 45-47 passim.

[24] The *Taittirīya* texts quoted and translated into Latin by de Nobili in this *IC* really constitute the first European translation known to us of any upaniṣadic text. Fr Gonçalo Fernandez, SJ, with whom de Nobili lived in Madurai up to 1607, included in his *Tratado sobre o Hinduismo* (critical edition by J. Wicki, Lisboa: Centro de Estudos Historicos Ultramarinos, 1973, ch. 18, pp. 120-121) a Portuguese translation of *Taitt. Up*. 3, 1-6 (*Bhṛgu vidyā*) but from a Tamil translation made for him by one of the paṇdits on whom he had to rely since he did not know Sanskrit. Fernandez composed his treatise in 1616, three years after de Nobili's *IC*. His ch. 18 has been excellently presented by Fr G. Gispert-Sauch, "The Bhṛgu-Vallī of the Taittirīya Upaniṣad: an Early XVII Century European Translation," *Indica* 5/2 (1968) 139-144, but this author's conclusion on p. 140 demands revision in the light of the facts stated above which he could not yet know in 1968.

[25] *Ajñāna Nivāraṇam* (Dispelling of Ignorance) is a Tamil work of de Nobili in the form of four dialogues. Its central figure is a Christian *sannyāsi* called '*Satya Bodhakar*,' i.e., Teacher of Truth.

26

ORIGIN: CREATION AND EMANATION[1]

The topic of this paper is being presented against the twofold background of St Thomas Aquinas' teaching and Śaṅkara's *Brahmajijñāsā*. It hopefully traces their lines of convergency.[2]

1. The Notion of Origin

For the scientist the notion of origin designates the state of affairs which conditions the arising of a new phenomenon. It implies not only the general disposition of the universe and its material energy at the initial moment of this arising but more properly the immediate antecedents, conditions, factors and the decisive instant of the change which initiates that phenomenon. The arising of the latter is an event—*eventus*—an observable novelty but within a basic continuity of matter and time and becoming, generally considered as evolutionary. Such an origination is specific, not universal; and relative, not absolute. Even if the scientist seeks the origin of the whole universe, he can only seek it through a mental journey backwards toward a primary state of matter—as extremely condensed energy, for instance—beyond which he can, nevertheless, assume a prior, though undeterminable state of the same matter.

The metaphysician, on the contrary, undertakes a more radical investigation concerning the very being of the universe and all its components, including matter itself in any of its states. How is it that there exists a universe rather than no universe? This question is forced upon him by the general contingency of all the existents which through their connections make up the universe. Whether our universe has a first instance or is beginningless in its duration—alternatives which both boggle our imagination—it ever appears unable to account for its existence. Hence, we are presented with the question not of its temporal but of its ontological origin. This question is not to be answered through a backward journey in time but through an ecstasis (in the etymological sense of the term), a reaching of the mind beyond itself and the whole universe towards a Reality which cannot be less than Being itself (*Esse*, *Sat*), Self-existent and Self-communicative. This is generally designated as God or the Absolute (the *Brahman* of Vedānta). My purpose is not here to prove its existence but to speak as correctly as possible of the origination of our universe from this Absolute.

2. The Need for *Lakṣaṇā* or Analogy

In all matters regarding the Absolute, language must be adapted and appropriated to a difficult task. Our everyday language is shaped by our experience of the relative which it normally endeavours to express. But besides its power of expressing, it possesses various capacities of evoking, alluding to, indicating, conveying or even signifying indirectly yet correctly enough what it does not or cannot express directly. In India, its power of indirect signification or indication is called *lakṣaṇā* (distinct from *lakṣaṇa*: definition or characteristic mark). Of the three chief types of *lakṣaṇā*, the one directly useful to the metaphysician is the *jahad-ajahal-lakṣaṇā* which corresponds closely to the *intrinsic analogy* of the Christian Schoolmen, which itself originates in Aristotle and Pseudo-Dionysius. It permits making sense of theological language or God-talk.

For instance, when Śaṅkara or some of his disciples explain that "*Satyam jñānam anantam*" (*Taitt. Up*. 2, 1) is a valid definition of *Brahman*, they use that *lakṣaṇā* and display its process. The sentence means that the Absolute is Reality-Knowledge-Infinite. The pupil who naively understands the first term *Satyam* (Reality) in its primary and expressive meaning as 'concrete material substance' such as solid earth, is told that he must correct this misleading superimposition (*adhyāsa*) since the second term *Jñānam* (Knowledge) immediately negates it. Similarly his primary understanding of *Jñānam* (Knowledge) as a contingent activity or quality of the knower is to be corrected because the third term *Anantam* (Infinite) debars such an understanding. *Jñānam*, says Śaṅkara, must be infinitised on the basis of the pure root *Jña* (know), not of any of its derivatives The Absolute is not infinite Know-ledge, Know-ing or Know-er, but pure Know in the most elevated sense of the term. And it is similarly *paramārthataḥ Sat*, i.e., Being in the supreme sense of the term. Here he uses the participle *sat* (be-ing) instead of the verbal root *as* because of an exigency of his Sanskrit language but his intention is similar to that of St Thomas Aquinas when the latter says that God is eminently *Esse* (Be). Although two terms are used, their infinitisation implies that they merge in identity without, however, losing their *svārtha*, the positive meaning of their roots, as Śaṅkara is careful to point out. Thus their *lakṣaṇā* is intrinsic analogy and the divine Absolute which they define as infinite Be and Know is yet simple (*akhaṇḍa* undivided, incomplex). This example shows how in all theological topics our mind must and can transcend the anthropomorphism innate to language through a processing in three steps: *adhyāsa*, superimposition; *apavāda*, negation, removal of all limitations; and *paramārthāpatti*, assumption of the supreme sense which alone is consistent with absoluteness.

3. Application to the Notion of Creation

Let us now start from an 'adhyāsic' assertion of divine creation such as we find in the Upaniṣads or elsewhere. "*Brahman* is the Root of the world" or "*Brahman* is that omniscient, omnipotent Cause from which proceed the origin, subsistence and dissolution of this world" or "God is the Creator of all things, visible and invisible" or "Consider the heaven and the earth and all that they contain; know that God has made all that from nothing and that the race of men is born in the same manner." All such formulations affirm that the one God, the Absolute, is the unique intelligent Source or Cause of the totality and entirety of all other beings. But the terms they are made of are liable to many misinterpretations and a sifting of their anthropomorphism is to be effected by the metaphysician.

Hence, we come to a negative definition of creation, such as the classical one formulated by Aquinas: Creation means a production of reality out of nothing of itself or of any matter (*productio rei ex nihilo sui et materiae*). This will be elaborated and completed presently.

Provided this purification is complete, the mind is ready to climb up to the level of eminence (the Dionysian *Hyperochē* or Śaṅkarian *paramārthāpatti*) and to say, for instance, with Aquinas: Creation is the emanation of the whole universe by and from the universal Cause (*emanatio totius universi a causa universali*).

4. The Step of Purification through Negations: *Apavāda*

All models of production fail to give us an adequate support of representation for the idea of creation. Creation is unique and transcends them all. Like God himself, it pertains to no genus. Hence, we have to ascend to it by way of negations (*apophasis*, *apavāda*). In order to reconcile the two ideas of 'divine' and 'production' we have to eliminate the ordinary connections of 'production' with either pre-existing matter or pre-existing time, with necessity of want, with transformation and instruments of transformation, with mutability of the creator or his self-improvement, and with relationship that would be a reality in the Creator.

4.1 No independent pre-existence of the created

Let us, first, eliminate the weak sense of 'production' as 'mere manifestation.' The created is not produced like the rabbit out of the magician's hat.[3] It does not arise from a state of latency, dormancy or concealedness, but from its own antecedent absence (*prāg-abhāvāt*), for it has no independent pre-existence; it never exists except as divinely produced.[4]

Virtually, however, or, to use Śaṅkara's terminology, as still undifferentiated, it pre-exists in the power of its Cause, just as it is eternally known by it independently of its production. "And so," writes St Thomas, "a creature as pre-existing in God is the divine Essence itself" (*Et sic creatura in Deo est ipsa Essentia divina*: *De Potentia* 3, 16, 24). This is an important application of the theory which the Indians call *satkāryavāda*, namely, of the virtual pre-existence of an effect in the being of its cause. The statement of *Bhagavad Gītā* 2, 16: *Nāsato vidyate bhāvaḥ* (Out of nothing, no thing can arise) is true for an Aquinas or a Bergson as much as for the Indian schoolmen.

4.2 No pre-existence of the matter or of the forms of the created[5]

Unlike any production of nature or man, creation neither needs nor presupposes any pre-existing matter or other constitutive element. This is due to its character of total origination. Neither is there a pool of pre-existing forms from which the creator would draw. What is created is the universe of existents in which and with which their matter is co-created as well as any other possible constituent. Whether matter is energy or something else should not concern us here. What counts is the realization that the totality of the universe derives immediately from the Creator.

This ontological origination of all finite existents[6] *qua* beings does not preclude the temporal originations that take place within the becoming of the universe. Matter is the permanent stuff of all transformations and generations. This prime matter is an ubiquitous component of the beings of the material universe and never a distinct and complete existent apart from them. As a component it is not the term of any special creation but shares in the ontological origination of the material existents of the universe.

A question raised in Vedānta philosophy is whether the Absolute itself is not the 'material cause' of the universe. The term used is *upādāna* which may be rendered etytmologically as 'subdatum' (*upa+a+dāna*). It is indicated by the ablative case '*yataḥ*' and is thus the 'whence' of the effect, that 'from which' the effect derives its substantial reality. On the level of material transformations, that 'whence' is a material stuff, for instance, clay in jars or steel in scissors, etc. On the basis of such examples, some Indian systems have assumed the existence of an eternal stuff, the *Pradhāna* or *Prakṛti* of the Sāṁkhya system or the primordial atoms (*paramāṇu*) of Vaiśeṣika, as the *upādāna* of the universe. Nevertheless, the denotation of the *upādāna* transcends such specific meanings. That which provides the substantial reality of effects need not be a material cause. In Vedānta, it is the *Brahman-Ātman* which is said to be the *upādāna* of the universe and this *Brahman* is surely not material since it is Spirit (*Cit*) or pure 'Know' (*Jña*) as we have seen earlier. If it were the material cause or stuff of the universe, it would have to produce it through self-mutation (*pariṇāma*) or atomic vibration (*spanda*)[7] but any such process is excluded from the Absolute. Yet, as its total Source, *Brahman* is the immanent and reality-giving Cause, i.e. the *Upādāna* of the universe.[8]

Some quotations from Śaṅkara will throw further light on this problem. The causation of the world presupposes "no independent matter, unreducible to *Ātman*, such as the *Pradhāna* of the Sāṁkhyas or the primordial atoms of Kaṇāda" (*Ait. Up. Bh.* 1, 1, 1). "What the *Śruti* calls *ajā*, i.e., the causal matter of the four classes of beings, has itself sprung from the highest Lord" (*B.S.Bh.* 1, 4, 9). *Brahman* alone is "that from whence these beings are born," i.e., their *upādāna*, as denoted by the ablative *yataḥ*; "there is no other substance from which the world could originate" (*B.S.Bh.* 1, 4, 23). But how can this divine *Upādāna* provide the reality of the universe? Because, "in the beginning, before creation, when the differences of names-and-forms (*nāma-rūpa*, the specific essences) were not yet manifested, this world was but the one *Ātman*" (*Ait. Up. Bh.* 1, 1, 1). These *nāma-rūpas* pre-existed only "in the manner of something future" (*bhāviṣyena rūpeṇa*), i.e., virtually, as effects pre-exist in the actual power of their cause.[9] These *nāma-rūpas*, which are identical with the *Ātman* in their unmanifested state, can become the causal elements (*upādāna-bhūte*) of the manifested universe. Hence, it is not incongruous to say that the omniscient (*Ātman*) creates the universe by virtue of his oneness with causal elements, namely, names-and-forms, which are identical with himself" (*Ait. Up. Bh.* 1, 1, 2). Their manifestation, however, does not mean that the partless *Ātman* undergoes a process of diversification: "the case is rather like that of a clever magician who, independent of any materials, transforms himself, as it were (*iva*), into a second man seemingly climbing into space (ibid.).

4.3 No need of instruments or of demiurge

Considering that the creative power need not be applied upon a pre-existing material which it would have to shape, St Thomas concludes that it needs no instruments. Similarly, Śaṅkara asserts that "the absolutely complete power of *Brahman* does not require to be supplemented by any extraneous help" (*B.S.Bh.* 2, 1, 24).

The same reason rules out any demiurge. A demiurge might be required for the function of shaping up, structuring, ordaining and governing the universe according to an intelligible pattern, in the same way as man in his works generally imposes his own plan upon the materials he uses. The Nyāya system which assumes the independent existence of the materials of the world posits a divine Lord to fulfil universally this role of patterning agent or *nimitta-kāraṇa*. It thus professes a dualism (*dvaita*),[10] which accepts two distinct causes of the world, a material *upādāna* and a lordly *nimitta-kāraṇa*. But Śaṅkara, who upholds a strict non-dualism (*advaita*), holds that the one *Brahman* which is the nonmaterial *upādāna* of the world "is at the same time its *nimitta-kāraṇa* because outside *Brahman* as substantial Cause there is no other ruling principle for the *Śruti* says that prior to creation *Brahman* was one only without a second" (*B.S.Bh.* 1, 4, 23). It can pattern the world intelligently, being Intelligence itself; indeed, "its high Power is revealed as manifold, as inherent, acting as force *and knowledge*" (*B.S.Bh.* 2, 1, 24).

4.4 No need of a temporal beginning of creation

Creation-talk is spontaneously mixed up with the notion of a first instant of the universe. But 'ontological origination' does not by itself imply 'temporal beginning' even if the reverse is true. Duration is a property of being; it denotes the 'unity of active existence' of a being. In God, it is eternity which is the strict unity of his perfect active existence. In mutable beings, it is time which is the relaxed unity of their imperfect and developing existence; every such being has its own concrete time or duration. Universal time is rather an abstraction which serves the mathematical purpose of measuring the concrete durations of mutable beings and the concrete duration of the universe itself as the interrelated totality of such existents. It is this abstraction which seems to reign over and above creation and even to precede it. But concrete time is co-created with the universe since, being a property of its being, it does not precede it but rather follows from its essential mobility and evolving changeability. Whether it starts from a first instant or is beginningless depends entirely on the Creator's free decision and cannot be settled by any deductive process. This is the conclusion of St Thomas in *S.Th.* I, 46, 1.

4.5 The end of creation implies no need or desire in the Creator

Is it anthropomorphic to say that creation has an end, a purpose? Men's works are purposeful. Even a madman, Śaṅkara remarks, does not act without some purpose. But can the Absolute have purposes? Would this not imply that it has desires and, hence, wants? But then it would no longer be the perfect *Brahman*, which is Bliss (*Ānanda*) and Peace (*Śānti*) because "all its desires are eternally realized."

An Indian distinction comes here to our help. That between *artha*, goal, purpose, and *kāma-phala*, the fruit that accrues to the doer according to his desire (*kāma*) to satisfy a need which he feels. Creation is a *niṣkāma-karma*, a work prompted by no desire to satisfy a need of the Creator. But, being an intelligent work, it is not devoid of *artha* or purpose. Obviously, this purpose can only be the good of the creatures. It is *loka-saṁgraha*, the maintenance of the cohesion of the world, and more precisely the welfare and the final salvation of man (*Bh. Gītā Bh.* 3, 24).

This assertion raises a problem. For Śaṅkara, man's uppermost desire is to know the *Brahman* (*Brahmajijñāsā*,) not, however, through any inferior kind of knowledge for it is *avagati-paryanta*, i.e., it aspires after a knowledge which "culminates in comprehension." And this most blissful realization (*vijñāna*) is "caused (*hetuka*)[11] by the grace of the Lord since this is asserted by the infallible *Śruti*" (*B.S.Bh.* 2, 3, 41). In the same way, a Christian like St Thomas affirms that the deepest desire of man is for a blissful intuition of the divine essence itself and that this stands beyond the grasp of the natural power of his intellect though well within the reach of its desire and of its receptive capacity. It is at this point that St Thomas articulates his teaching on divine grace and the possibility of a supernatural complementing of nature. His thesis of the natural desire of man's intellect for a beatific vision of God's very essence shows that the highest end of creation depends on the merciful liberality of the Creator. This gratuitous end will, even more than the lower but sufficient end which consists in *loka-saṁgraha*, bring about an extrinsic glory of God as the author of the final goodness of creation. But this, being extrinsic, will not accrue to him as an accidental adornment or self-accomplishment. Nothing, indeed, can be added to the eternal perfection of the Absolute.

4.6 As participated being, the creature is non-Being

Creation is the production of finite existents in the whole measure in which they are be-ings. Obviously, the Absolute cannot produce other Absolutes but only finite participations of itself. But what is the ontological weight and positivity of such be-ings? There are interpretations of Śaṅkara's Vedānta which view it as an acosmism and attribute only illusory being to all effects. What is the verdict of Śaṅkara himself?

Śaṅkara uses the terms 'being' and 'non-being' on different levels which we may clarify with a judicious use of capital and small letters. On the level of ordinary language, creaturely effects and their Cause are beings (*sat*), are imbued with existence (*sattā*). "Should any effect originate from nothing, then, even though perceived, it would be imbued with unreality; but this is not the case, hence *Brahman* exists" (*Taitt. Up. Bh.* 2, 6, 1). Yet, *Brahman* transcends so immensely its effects that compared to them it must be said to be non-being (*a-sat*). This consideration is the root of apophatism. But *Brahman* is not absolute Non-being (*atyanta Asat*) for it is non-being simply because it is absolute Being (*atyanta Sat*), i.e., Being in the supreme sense of the term (*paramārthataḥ Sat*). And now we have to say that compared to it creatures are non-Being (*a-Sat*) although they are not absolute Non-being (*Asat*). They are, he says, *Sad-Asad-vilakṣaṇa*, unable to be denoted by either *Sat* (Being) or *Asat* (Non-being) if these terms are taken in their supreme sense. This is the level of language on which Śaṅkara's teaching moves generally because his centre of reference is the Absolute rather than the relative existent. He is a radical valuationist who measures everything to the absolute Value, the *Brahman*, and declares its unequality to it rather than the degree of its participation of it. This manner of thinking and speaking is legitimate but it has misled many into acosmistic interpretations of his doctrine.

In the West, St Thomas generally prefers the language of participation. A participated being is in its own deficient way what the absolute *Esse* is without any restrictions. This *Esse* or Being is not a logical genus but the ontological Reality of God. And its participations are not parts of that partless Reality, nor accidents, complements, explicitations or developments of it, nor in any way additive to it.

Śaṅkara too considers the effects of creation as mere *upādhis* (external affixes) of *Brahman*. An *upādhi* is an external adjunct, like the mask of an actor or the clothes of a man which only seem to characterise them; it has only the appearance of a *viśeṣaṇa*, i.e., of a real attribute. Thus all names-and-forms (*nāma-rūpa*) are but *upādhis* and in no way affections of their Cause. But like any *upādhi* they need the constant support of this total Cause which pervades (*vyāpin*) them most intimately without any loss of its unalterable transcendence. This is why they are comparable to magical illusions which do not affect the magician but depend entirely on his power while the appearance of their independent subsistence is due to the spectator's ignorance. This comparison together with the concept of *upādhi* does away with pantheism and preserves nevertheless the central notion of the creatures' total dependence on their Creator.

4.7 Creative activity is not additive to the divine Essence

When man produces something he does it not only with the help of materials, instruments and so forth but also through an operation which is distinct from, and additive to, his substantial essence. This, however, is not due to the essential nature of causation but only to the weakness of his power which prevents him from ever being the total cause of his effects. Causing as such only demands to be an ontological communication of the cause to the effect so that what makes us say that this is an effect, whether it be its external form, its internal structure or its substantial reality, derives from the being of its cause. It does not demand necessarily that the cause lose what it gives or that its causing be an operation additive to its own being. The higher the cause, the more immune to change and independent it is in the exercise of its power. The highest power is the power of intelligent volition which in its upmost degree can posit its term freely and without any self-alteration. Thus no other novelty is consequent upon divine volition but the ontological novelty of its effect.

The supreme *Ātman*, says Śaṅkara, due to his "absolutely complete power" creates "like gods, etc. who, without availing themselves of any extraneous means, produce palaces, etc. *by their mere intention* which is effective in consequence of those beings' peculiar power" (*B.S.Bh.* 2, 1, 25). His creative volitions are not additive to, but identical with, his essence. Indeed, "how are they found in *Brahman*? As essentially Reality-Knowledge, and as pure in virtue of being their own *Ātman*" (*Taitt. Up. Bh.* 2, 6, 1). The distinction between creative volition and divine essence is not ontological but logical; it is by 'upādhic,' extrinsic, denomination in regard to its created term[12] that this essence is to be thought of as creative volition.

5. The Positive and Adequate Definition of Creation

After refining the gross notion of creation with the help of negations meant to clear away all anthropomorphic misconceptions, we can now with St Thomas define creation adequately and eminently (*paramārthataḥ*) as the intelligent and freely willed emanation[13] of the whole reality or positivity of the universe from the pure *Esse* (cf. *S.Th.* I, 45, 1).

The term 'emanation' comes from the Indo-European root *mad-*, to bubble, to flow; thus it means the flowing out as from a source. It is in this etymological sense that it is used here by St Thomas. From the time of Leibniz, however, emanation became associated with the diverse brands of pantheism to express a *necessary* flowing of the universe from an Absolute governed by an inner necessity of self-explication, self-development or self-realization. Whether this necessity is conceived as physical, 'vital,' or moral, pantheism destroys the simplicity of fullness and perfection of the subsistent *Esse* which it posits but anthropomorphically; its divine Principle lacks the perfect transcendence of the *Brahman-Ātman* or the absolute God; and its created emanations lack the radical contingency of true creatures. It is, therefore, in no pantheistic sense that the term 'emanation' is to be understood in the above definition.

What emanates from the Creator is the whole reality or positivity of the universe. This includes the existence and essence of each of its beings, their preservation, their activities even of free will, their finalistic gropings and development, the evolution from inorganic matter unto life and from living species unto man, the achievements of his cultures, etc. It includes cosmic matter and spirits, time—whether beginningless or not, space—whether limited or unlimited, the necessary and the contingent, the regularities of law and the coincidences of hazard. Thus creation does not concern only the origins of finite existents but as universal emanation it is also conservation, motion and activation (by the *pravṛtti-rahito-pravartaka*, the Mover devoid of motion of *B.S.Bh.* 2, 2, 2), providential governing and finalisation.

But what about the negativities in the universe? These cannot be the proper effects of the power of the one who is pure Positivity but arise only consequentially from the natures of creatures: finiteness from their contingency; liability to physical evil such as harmful accidents, diseases, destruction or death from the competitiveness of the immense plurality of material existents within the one realm of matter where chance-encounters predominate; error from the imperfection of finite intellects; and moral evils such as vices and sins from the imperfection of created free-wills. All these are tolerated rather than willed by the Creator who can nevertheless accomplish the end of creation and thus overcome its inherent deficiencies.

From the side of the creatures, creation is total ontological dependence. This is a relation inherent in them and whose ground is their very positive reality as emanations from God. According to St Thomas' refined theory of relationship, this relation is not logical only but real because its ground is intrinsic to the related; its reality is co-created with the creature, As to Creatorship, its correlation, it is but a logical relation because it not grounded in anything pertaining to the Creator but in the same reality of his emanations which is extrinsic to him. Thus these paired relationships are unreciprocal.

The name given by Śaṅkara to the relation of the universe to *Brahman* is *tādātmya*, often translated as 'identity' but rendered more correctly as "having that (*tat*) as one's *ātman*." The term *ātman*, which is the reflexive pronoun, does not denote here what we normally call the self but the substantial cause (*upādāna*) as internal to the effect, as in the expression "the jar is *mṛd-ātmaka*, i.e., is internally constituted of mud or clay." In this expression, *ātman* does not connote intelligence but it generally does. The *tādātmya* of creatures is thus their ontological dependence on That (*Brahman*) as on their innermost and transcendent Cause. "It is an accepted principle, even in the world, that an effect is intimately dependent (*anuvidhāyin*) on its [substantial] cause" (*Bṛh. Up. Bh.* 1, 5, 14). This dependence imparts no reality to the cause but only to its effects for "as long as an effect subsists, it is impossible to assume the dissolution of its [substantial] cause, since on the dissolution of the latter the effect also cannot subsist. On the other hand, we may assume the continued existence of the cause although the effect is destroyed; for that is actually observed in the case of clay" (*B.S.Bh.* 2, 3, 14). Hence, that relation is not real in both terms. It is not reciprocal: "names-and-forms in all their states have *Brahman* alone as their *Ātman*, but *Brahman* has not its *Ātman* in them (i.e., *tādātmya* is not mutual). Since without this [*Brahman*] they simply do not exist, they are said to have their *Ātman* in it (*tad-ātmaka*). And it is because of those two *pādhis* or external adjuncts [names-and-forms], that *Brahman* related to all mundane activities" (*Taitt. Up. Bh.* 2, 6, 1). This is another way of saying that the ground of 'creatorship' is found exclusively on the side of the creatures. This theory of *tādātmya* "does away with the independent (*svabhāvika*) existence of the embodied self... and of the world' (*B.S.Bh.* 2, 1, 14). These are not simply different (*anyat*) from the Absolute since in their whole being they depend on it. "The creature, says St Thomas, is no part of the Essence of God but its essence is from God" (*non est ex essentia Dei sed est ex Deo essentia*: *S.Th.* I, 41, 3, 2). And Śaṅkara: "the effect is non-different (*an-anyat*) from the Cause, i.e., is essenceless and absent apart from it" (*vyatirekenā'bhāvah*: *B.S.Bh.* 2, 1, 14). Thus explained, the non-difference implied by *tādātmya* does not eliminate distinction but stresses the ontological character of the creature's dependence as well as the Creator's transcendence. "If absolute equality were insisted on, the relation of cause and effect would be annihilated..., [a relation] which is based on the presence in the cause of an excellence [which is absent in the effect]" (*B.S.Bh.* 2, 1, 6).

All these clarifications do not suppress the mystery of creation. Even on the level of eminence, theological language remains apophatic. It points correctly to the realities it deals with but is unable to express them (*lakṣyate na tū'cyate*: *Taitt. Up. Bh.* 2, 1).[14] Because our experience knows of no exact parallels of creation, our metaphysical thinking about it can never reach the level of experiential language. But "all metaphysics worthy of the name tends to consume itself in the deep silence of mystical introversion" (Pierre Scheuer).[15]

Notes

[1] [First published in *Indian Theological Studies* **15**/3 (1978) 266-279, with the following note: "A paper read at the meeting of the *International Society for Metaphysics* held in Jerusalem, 18-22 August 1977, on the theme 'God and the Universe.' We are grateful to the ISM for permission to make an advance publication of this article." Subsequently published in *Person and God: Studies in Metaphysics*, ed. George McLean and Hugo Meynell (Lanham, MD: University Press of America, 1988) 209-220, with a Comment by Hugo Meynell, "On Richard V. De Smet, SJ, 'Origin: Creation and Emanation,'" 221-225. Published here courtesy *Indian Theological Studies*.]

[2] [This paragraph is omitted in the text of 1988.]

[3] [This line is not present in the 1988 text.]

[4] [The 1978 text reads: 'For it has no independent pre-existence but never exists except as divinely produced.']

[5] [The 1988 text reads: '*No pre-existence of the matter of the created*'.]

[6] [Correcting 'existence' from the 1978 text.]

[7] ['(*spanda*)' missing in 1988 text.]

[8] [1988: 'i.e., its *Upādāna*'.]

[9] [1988: 'as effects to be pre-exist in the actual power of their cause'.]

[10] [1988: 'It is thus a dualism (*dvaita*)'.]

[11] [1988: 'And this most blissful intuition can only be obtained'.]

[12] [1988: 'it is by 'upādhic', extrinsic, relation to its created term'.]

[13] [1988: 'intelligent and free emanation'.]

[14] [Correcting '*Taitt. Up. Bh.* 2, 2' from the 1988 text.]

[15] [Pierre Scheuer (1872-1957), Belgian Jesuit, great influence on the young De Smet, who described him as "a prince among metaphysicians and a mystic": see "Surrounded by Excellence: An Evocation," *Jivan: Jesuits of South Asia: Views and News* 11/10 (December 1990) 10.]

27

ŚĀṄKARA VEDĀNTA AND CHRISTIAN THEOLOGY[1]

This survey of the attitudes adopted by Christian scholars towards Śāṅkara Vedānta in this century is summed up from a monograph (now in the press)[2] in which I have studied the four centuries of encounters between Christians and Vedānta beginning with Robert de Nobili (1577-1656).

1. The Fulfilment Theorists

As viewed by J.N. Farquhar the fulfilment theory applies to religions the principle of evolution and regards Christianity as the highest on the evolutionary scale. Other religions are related to it as the imperfect to the perfect in which alone they can obtain the realization of their deepest aim. But to arrive at this they must die to themselves and accept their conversion into Christianity. This is true in particular of Hinduism, including Vedānta. Farquhar, however, in spite of his greatness, could not display a bright vision of this Hinduism as not only dying but rising with Christ, or of Christianity as enriched in its very life by the resurrection within itself of a Hinduism first accepting to die with Christ. In his book, *The Crown of Hinduism* (1914), chapter 10, he visualised Hinduism converted only as purified of its 'errors' and corrected of its 'deficiencies.'[3]

Soon afterwards, W. Miller objected that Farquhar had failed to apply the concept of evolution to historical Christianity itself. Instead of a supersession of Hinduism by Christianity, he expected a development of all higher religions, Christianity included, to reach their common fulfilment in a World Religion centred on Christ. Christianity would thus reach its own consummation by being furnished with the peculiar contributions of other religions. But Miller did not suggest what would be the development or the contribution of Vedānta under the light of Christ.[4]

A third type of fulfilment theory presided over the undertaking in 1922 of a new monthly, *The Light of the East*, by the Jesuits G. Dandoy and P. Johanns. From 1922 to 1934, the latter was to contribute a vast study of the chief school of Vedānta under the title, *To Christ through the Vedānta.*[5] In the introduction which defines his purpose, there is no reference to an evolutionary scale of religions or to a surrender of Hinduism to Christianity. Johanns' encounter with the Vedāntins takes place on the level of philosophy. It develops as a contribution towards a reconciliation of the opposed schools of Vedānta in the light of Thomism which has the advantage of having synthesized many positive doctrines and being open to assimilating complementary truths. What is meant here by *positive doctrine*? Any experiential insight which does not contradict other experiential insights but is able to enter with them into a truly rational synthesis, is a *positive doctrine.* From the vantage point of Thomism, each Vedāntic system, while historically opposing others, is able to reveal a core of such positive doctrines sufficiently independent of the negative doctrines that accompany it. And all Vedāntic systems can, therefore, be induced to combine their too long separated cores into an organic body of positive doctrine, akin of course to Thomism, but distinct from it. The Vedāntins are not requested to adopt Thomism but, in its harmonizing light, to reconcile their oppositions and, like the Thomists, to pursue in greater harmony their quest for the fullness of truth which stands beyond the reach of philosophy but within the scope of its commanding desire. Illumined by the same Logos, both Vedāntins and Thomists are called to surrender, not however to a rival philosophical system, but in religious faith to the fulfilling Christ who belongs to no man or nation but is of God for all men.

Johanns' treatment of Śāṅkara Vedānta may be summarized as follows:

(1) The positive doctrine constantly upheld by Śaṅkara is the doctrine of the absolute independence of God, self-existent and

free of bonds[6] to the world. This is also the cornerstone of Catholic philosophy.

(2) The Vedas, which Śaṅkara trusts absolutely, teach it: the *Brahman* is *kūṭastha*, free from any change. They also proclaim that it is the efficient and the material cause of the universe. However, insofar as this seems to imply a *pariṇāma*, i.e., a self-mutation of God into the universe, it contradicts the teaching of immutability and is to be rejected. There is no *pariṇāma*, no real evolution of *Brahman*, but only a *vivarta*, the illusion of an evolution. The universe, therefore, does not share the Reality of *Brahman* and, in that sense, is unreal. What it suggests about God, namely, that God is its soul and is related to it as *saguṇa Brahman*, is false.

(3) Similarly, the Vedic passages which echo that suggestion are only stepping-stones to the final doctrine contained in the *mahāvākyas* or 'great sayings,' especially *neti neti* and *Tattvamasi*.

(4) *Tattvamasi* (that thou art) does not assert that the subject as *individual* is the Absolute but that the absolute Subject is identical with the absolute Object: *tvam*, *cit* = *tat*, *sat*. To realize this is to realize the pure absolute awareness without subject and object, in self-being. The error of Śaṅkara is not to say this but to say it in the wrong way, in a way that implies that if you peel off the individuality and the universality of an individual subject, you obtain the absolute Subject.

(5) The identity of Being and Intelligence in the self-completeness of God should imply that he is self-conscious. But Śaṅkara seems to deny this for fear it would presuppose in God an opposition of subject and object as in human consciousness. But perfect self-consciousness does not consist in such an opposition of *I* and *me* but in the perfect identity of both, so that God is, indeed, *Sac-cit*.

(6) This identity is the very ideal towards which our mind is unceasingly moving according to its first law, namely, that the real, in proportion as it is real, is intelligible. If God is not *Sac-cit*, the whole movement of our mind is aimless and its ideal a chimera. It is true, on the other hand, that short of God nothing fulfils that ideal. Contingent beings are not the Truth but only true 'by participation.' Śaṅkara is, therefore, right when he denies that the world has a *right* to exist.

(7) If such is the truth, a first error is at once discarded, that God is an unconscious substance. Second, God's self-luminosity is not mere interiority without content, for in him ideality is identical with reality. Third, God is absolute Truth, for he is the absolute self-affirmation in which the absolute predicate is identical with the absolute subject. Fourth, God is the absolute Goodness, for good is defined as what conforms with its ideal and in God the whole objectivity is the absolute ideality. Fifth, God is absolute Bliss, for he is absolute perfection in absolute self-possession. Sixth, *Tattvamasi* cuts at the very root of pantheism for it lifts God above all self-division, whether objective (cf. Spinoza) or subjective (cf. Fichte).

(8) Finally, God is incomprehensible. If, as *Tattvamasi* implies, God is the absolute Vision which is its own Visibility, it is clear that, as St Thomas teaches, we cannot naturally see God and every proposition is too complex to express the simplicity (*nirguṇatva*) of the divine essence. One word would do it but this would have to be "the Word which is with God and which is God."

This may suffice to indicate the success of Johanns' quest for what he called the positive doctrine of Śaṅkara.

2. The Creative Assimilationists

In the wake of *The Light of the East* we discern a number of endeavours to bring about a closer interpenetration of the Christian and the Hindu traditions most often around the Vedānta as focus. Following a suggestion of Prof. O. Lacombe, whose important book *L'Absolu selon le Vedānta* should at least be mentioned here, we may see in them 'acts of creative assimilation.' He himself, for instance, assimilated to the doctrine of analogy of the Christian schoolmen Śaṅkara's interpretation of the upaniṣadic definitions of *Brahman* by recourse to *lakṣaṇā* (to be explained presently).[7]

Fr J.F. Pessein's *Vedānta Vindicated* (1925)[8] was such an endeavour which drew the admiration and large approval of eminent scholars like Radhakrishnan and S. Vedānta Aiyengar. Pessein is at his best when, by means of a convenient use of capital letters, he clears up the advaitin's understanding of *sat* and *asat*, real and unreal:

(1) *Brahman* is *SAT*, REAL, and it is the only REAL, since there cannot be two or more REALS, i.e., ABSOLUTE EXISTENTS. Hence, *Brahman* is *A-sat*, UN-real, i.e., totally unlike what we normally call *sat*, real. But it is not *a-sat*, un-real, in the manner of a mirage, and neither is it *A-SAT*, UN-REAL, like the 'son of a barren woman' and other impossibilities.

(2) The world is *sat*, real, in the ordinary sense of the term but it is neither *SAT* nor *ASAT* for it is *SAD-ASAD-vilakṣaṇa*, i.e., undefinable by the terms *SAT* or *ASAT* taken in their supreme and perfect sense. Prior to its creation, when it is not yet real in the ordinary sense but only a future (*bhāviṣya-rūpeṇa*) in the power of its divine cause, it is of course identical with *SAT*, the absolute EXISTENT (as St Thomas himself clearly states). After creation, its *sat*-existence is only a totally caused, dependent and relative reality which cannot stand without the constant creative immanence in it of *Brahman* as the supreme *ĀTMAN* of all contingent beings.

(3) Wrong knowledge (*avidyā*) consists in viewing the world either as *asat*, unreal, according to the opinion of the *māyāvādin* Buddhists so firmly refuted by Śaṅkara, or as REAL, *SAT*, i.e., as existing in its own right through the independent and underived reality of its material causes (atoms or primordial stuff) according to Vaiśeṣika or Sāṁkhya which Śaṅkara rejected as well. *Avidyā* may also consist in identifying the world with the soul alleged to be all-pervading or with *Brahman*: this is the error of pantheism, or in failing to see the *Brahman* as the *Ātman* and Ground of every derived reality and seeing it only as Absolute excluding even the possibility of derived existence: this is the error of acosmism. Some interpreters have fallen into the one or the other error. This is due to their failing to clarify the language of Śaṅkara as done by Pessein. For Śaṅkara, the characteristics of *SAT* are *self-existence* and *immutability* and those of *a-SAT dependent existence* and *mutability* (cf. his definitions in his *Gītā Bhāśya* 2, 16). As dependent, *a-SAT* is inseparate and unseparable from its immanent cause, *SAT*.[9]

Further on, Pessein deals also quite ably with the vexed question of the personality of the Absolute. The term 'personal,' he says, may mean here either (1) anthropomorphic, or (2) *saguṇa*, i.e., determined by attributes really distinct from the essence, or (3) according to the Christian conception, it may signify that God "exists in Himself and not as a part of the universe,—that He possesses intelligence and free will, and that at the same time He is absolutely one simple and infinite essence."[10] Modern Hindus are unaware of this third and authentically traditional meaning and call impersonal the very same *nirguṇa* or incomplex Godhead that Christians deem personal. The divergence, he says, is merely verbal: we agree in the thing itself. Indeed, Advaita upholds God's infinite personality in the very same Christian sense exposed above, because it teaches that the *nirguṇa Brahman* is intelligent, free, and distinct from the universe.

Fr H.O. Mascarenhas[11] has presented an equally vigorous interpretation of Śaṅkara in *The Quintessence of Hinduism* (1951).[12] He first explains how, for the Christian, creation is not out of 'absolute nothing' (*atyantābhāva*, Pessein's *A-SAT*) but out of 'previous nothing' (*prāgabhāva*). The infinite *SAT* alone is its Principle (*Tattva*). Thus we can speak of the *principial* dependence of the creature on its absolute Principle (*tattvataḥ*): Such a 'principial' relation is neither convertible nor reversible and every suggestion of pantheism or immanentism is cut at the root. But it can allow perfect *identity in principle*, while affirming the perfect transcendence of the Infinite. The unity which the discriminating advaitin recognises as necessary and internal is the *unity of principle*. If I consider the whole truth about my own self in terms of Infinity, excluding only 'absolute nothing,' then I realize my 'principial' unity and my 'principial' identity-by-cognition with the Infinite. Indeed, India's highest doctrine is that I am 'principially' identical with the Infinite which, however, being what it is, transcends my finite individuality. Yet, we, Christians, have to go further than Advaita in recognizing that the personal relation of Jesus with his Father is not only *principial* unity as to his created human nature but the divinely *essential* unity (*sattvataḥ*) of the trinitarian Son with the trinitarian Father.

The first of a series of ecumenical colloquies sponsored by the Swiss Ambassador J.-A. Cuttat and Swami Abhishiktananda took place in Almora in April 1961. From a report by Fr. J.B. Chethimattam,[13] I cull the following excerpts:

Advaita, through its stress on interiority and metaphysical experience, points in the direction of the meta-rational Christian revelation. It is from the experience of consciousness that Śaṅkara rises to its immutable *svabhāva*, absolute Consciousness subsisting in itself, in comparison to which all forms of dual consciousness are but *avidyā*. But these forms, he writes, "receive their power only by being inspired by the energy of *Brahman*." Hence, as reflections, they lead to it as to their Illuminator.

No similar introspection can discover God as Trinity; still the fact that the advaitin is able to recognize his individual consciousness as a reflection of absolute Consciousness provides a common ground for him and the Christian towards an understanding of the Trinity which we somehow experience in our supernatural life.

In this experimental knowledge the Holy Spirit comes first for the supernatural gifts are directly ascribed to him. Hence, their experience turns us to Him immediately and to his effective presence in us. Here we have a certain analogy with the *advaita* interpretation of conscious experience. Sincere advaitins may be acknowledged to welcome unknowingly the Holy Spirit's gifts and to have an experience of God which is in that regard supernatural. Hence, an exposition of the doctrine of the Trinity will be an explanation of what they already live. It need not be emphasized to the advaitin that such an experience is obscure and subtle. But the above analogy leads to an opening out of the *advaita* experience. For as a glass becomes radiant from the light of the lamp it enshrines, so the soul receives a real similitude to *Brahman*, a real sonship. But the sentiment that this sonship is imperfect gives us at once the experience that we are not Sons in our own right, but are only partakers of a Sonship which subsists in God as a Person, the Son only-begotten of the Father.

Some reflections of Swami Abhishiktananda himself may now be quoted as focussing on the convergence of advaitic experience and trinitarian faith:

The Advaita, he writes, is not a challenge to Christian faith. It is rather the relentless reminder that God can never be wholly contained in our concepts. This inexorable reminder attacks our congenital self-centredness. It allows us to rest content with nothing less than the 'I' which God utters within himself, in the mystery of the procession of the Son and the Spirit. Advaita means precisely this: neither God alone, nor the creature alone nor God plus the creature, but an indefinable non-duality which transcends at once all separation and all confusion.[14]

Advaita and Christianity confront each other, up to a point, on the conceptual level but no longer on the real and existential plane. Advaita does not demand of Christianity a transcendence, a 'going out' towards something beyond itself, any more than Christ's revelation asks the Vedānta to empty itself of itself in order to pass beyond itself. If there must be a transcendence it is an inner transcendence, a discovery by each of the presence in the other of its own most intimate secret.[15]

3. The Apophatists

If, on the one hand, Advaita rightly emphasizes the great upaniṣadic saying, *neti neti*, [*Brahman* is] not thus, not thus, Christian theology, on the other hand, has known very early and developed consistently a strong current of apophatism or negative theology. No wonder, therefore, that Christians branch themselves on this authentically Christian current when they meet Advaita. This is true in a special way of those I am now about to mention.

Let me first recall the importance of Rudolf Otto's works and especially of his *Mysticism East and West* (1932).[16] It is an endeavour to discover both the surprising structural similarity but also the differences between advaitic and Christian mystical experiences as exemplified in the writings of Śaṅkara and of Meister Eckhart. Thus he showed that in contrast with Śaṅkara's mysticism Eckhart's is a mysticism of numinous majesty, demanding humility instead of the exalted feeling of identity with *Brahman*, and also what he calls a 'gothic' mysticism never at rest but ever dynamic and rising like a gothic cathedral. The types of transcendental salvation they aspire to are different: holiness for the Christian, happiness for the Hindu. Further, the ethical Eckhart aspires towards righteousness away from sinfulness, Śaṅkara towards knowledge away from ignorance. Eckhart's peculiar teaching of the 'deified' man embraces an extreme doctrine of grace whereas Śaṅkara rather explains away the upaniṣadic references to divine grace. Finally the two masters differ in their evaluation of the world and of the relation of love to supreme bliss. It is, of course, in explaining the formal similarity of their mysticisms that Otto treated fully of their apophatism.

Father J. Monchanin's *saṁnyāsa* name Svāmi Paramārūpyānanda, 'he whose Bliss is the supreme Formless (*Arūpi*),' marked him immediately as an apophatist.[17]

India's proper way, he wrote, is the way of *apavāda*, of apophatism, of mystery, like that of the Christian mystics of 'negative theology.' In the moment of negativity, the mystic boldly throws away all that he had first dared to affirm concerning God. Seized by his transcendence and at the risk of forgetting his immanence, he affirms—because he knows and experiences negatively—that the Deity stands beyond any positive content of our thought and experience. Only total negation and self-losing thought can befit that One who is beyond essence and number, that Alone (*Kevala*) ever inaccessible, impredicable. This is the level of what India calls *nirguṇa*, of the upaniṣadic *neti neti*, of the *Kevala* of Śaṅkara.

Yet, there is a beyond of apophatism: the way of eminence, of elevation, which opens up indicible visions on a Mystery more hidden even than the 'One' of Plotinus' *Enneads*. Blind alleys are closed but polarisations are postulated. At the focus of the mind's flight to the Infinite, the dazzling, blinding Fullness stands in its inviolable Aloneness. The apophatism of Śaṅkara does not land him in emptiness (*Śūnya*). The Absolute is. By way of *lakṣaṇā* (indirect signification) or inverted symbols, we may affirm that It is by pure identity Intelligence, Infinity, Bliss. The apophatist runs the risk of substituting for the 'concept-idol' the 'anticoncept-idol.' If being does not equate the Living God, non-being even if called 'superessential Nothingness' does not equate him either; and if God does not exist in the manner of beings, he is even less comparable to 'nothing,' that logical monster.

Christian mysticism is trinitarian or it is nothing. Hindu thought, so deeply focussed on the Oneness of the One, cannot be sublimated into trinitarian thought without a crucifying darkness of the soul. It has to undergo a noetic metamorphosis, a passion of the spirit.

However, we must note that Śaṅkara's philosophy is a positive philosophy of the Absolute as Fullness, not a negative philosophy of the ineffable. The *Sat* is indentified to[18] undifferentiated *Cit*, to unqualified *Satyam*, to modeless *Ānandam*, to impredicable *Ekam*, to God. The *Ātman* is not a non-self. It has of the self all the truth but without the limitations, the suchness. Transcendence and immanence have no meaning except by relation to a non-Absolute. Hence, they have no sense in absolute truth where the Absolute only IS. In relative truth, transcendence means (1) the infinite diffusivity of the Fullness, (2) the irreciprocity of the relation of the finite to this Fullness, (3) the very basis of immanence which derives from God's Supereminence. As to *māyā*, it connotes in terms of the 'world' of diffusivity, the Fullness.

About a possible integration of Advaita and trinitarian apophatism, the Svāmi was not over-optimistic. He who dives, he said, into the vertiginous abyss of Advaita may, I am afraid, find himself rather than the living and trinitarian God.

Klaus K. Klostermaier in his *Kristvidyā* answered this doubt from his own perspective.[19] It seems, he wrote, that *turīya* (the transcending state of consciousness) is what the Christian mystics describe as *quietude*, an ultimate in the process of interiorisation and a point of crisis, a borderline. It is the point at which we are told by Christ to 'knock' at the door and it will be opened. The progress is not a continuation of the interiorisation—which is impossible: *Ātman-Brahman* is the ultimate insight of man. It is rather a reversion: being known by God, 'proceeding' and being sent. The Absolute is not a static end-point but relation—the uniqueness of Christ consists in his being subsisting absolute relatedness *within* the Absolute.

Fr Bede Griffiths also gives the greatest importance to apophatism.[20] The Upaniṣads, he writes, first proceed by the way of affirmation, using images and symbols to represent the mystery, then they follow the way of negation, 'not this, not this.' But if negation is the primary way of expressing the mystery, there is yet an affirmation which points to it more clearly than any other. This is *Saccidānanda*. This term is apprehended not merely as a concept but as an experience, a consciousness of Being, not as the object but as the subject of thought, the *Ātman*, the Self, the Person in its ultimate depth.

The Christian tradition also recognises that there are certain terms which are particularly appropriate to indicate the Absolute by analogy. The first is Being, not determined in any way. The second is Consciousness, excluding the duality of subject and object. This aspect is known as *Logos*. The *Logos* is the full and perfect expression of God (within God). We can see how closely the Christian concept of the *Logos* corresponds to the Hindu concept of the *Ātman*. The third aspect of the Godhead is Bliss. We have to conceive by analogy that as God is infinite Being in perfect consciousness of itself so there is in him a delight in being, a pure joy of being, by which in knowing himself he rejoices in himself.

But if there is in God the capacity of self-knowledge, there is also the capacity of self-communication. It was one of the greatest achievements of Vedānta that it was able to receive into itself the current of *bhakti* and so to conceive of God as love. In the Christian tradition this aspect of the Godhead as Bliss is represented by the Holy Spirit in which Father and Son (*Logos*) communicate in love. And yet there is in it no 'duality,' but an identity of nature and consciousness in the bliss of love.

4. Christians in Dialogue with Advaitins

P.D. Devanandan, who had devoted an academic thesis to the concept of *māyā*, outlined in his later writings a constructive Christian approach to this idea.[21] He explained how, despite the 'vanity' of the world, God's *purpose* is constantly at work in it, realizing its new creation. Time, he wrote, is, as it were, shot through with eternity. This is really a way of stating that this is a world of *māyā*, both real and unreal, conditioned by time and shot through with eternity, the scene of human endeavour and the plans of Divine Activity. But here the *sat-asat* nature of world-life is not understood in terms of Ultimate Reality but of Final Purpose. This world of creation acquires a meaningfulness in that what is regarded as 'natural' is now seen to be shot through with a reality which is 'supernatural.' The phenomenal is conditioned by the noumenal; and what is real in it is real because of the dynamic presence in it of the noumenal.

Marc Sunder Rao stands closer to Vedānta.[22] Taking up the notion of *an-anyatva* (non-otherness), he understands it in a dynamic sense as 'at-one-ness,' i.e., as the overcoming of alienation into communion. He sees this as the true focus of the Hindu experience of union with God. But this overcoming of otherness is best illustrated in the Trinity and the Incarnation. They are the pattern and cause of the dynamic union of Man with God through Christ. This union is not ontological or moral but 'pneumatological,' the work of the Spirit. It is not the mere 'I-thou' but the 'I-in-thee; Thou-in-me' relationship through which all egocentricity and alienation is overcome by love in a new type of spiritual *yoga*.

For lack of space I have to neglect here such interesting writers as Fr Panikkar,[23] Dhanjibhai Fakirbhai,[24] Mrs Nalini Devdas[25] and Bishop S. Kulandran.[26] And I will terminate with a few excerpts from Sr Sara Grant who focuses on *tādātmya* as the irreciprocal relation between the *Brahman-Ātman* and the finite being.[27]

This *tādātmya* which grounds every being in dependence to the absolute *Ātman* permits the latter, in the words of Śaṅkara, "to reveal itself in a graduated series of beings and so to appear in forms of various dignity and power."[28] Thus, far from being stunted by this dependence, creatures are constituted in their relative autonomy and perfection precisely by this dependence. This is what is implied by the upaniṣadic expression "I am *Brahman*." It contains a knowledge sufficient to account wholly for our own being but not necessarily an experience of our innermost ground *as it is in itself*. When, however, Christ says, "*Aham Brahmāsmi*," the Reality he identifies as Self of his human self is the ineffable Mystery as expressed or uttered in the inmost reality of its own Being for he is conscious as man of being not only from God but from the Father. In him *Tat*, the self-shining Consciousness, so fully possesses his intelligence and freedom that his every self-determining act is at the same time a perfect though contingent expression of that Mystery. And we must say, "This man is *Brahman* in a unique sense—the self-shining Consciousness expressed in human terms." His sinless humanity is the point of insertion in the human race of the Self-communication of the ineffable Mystery in the innermost reality.

Before I conclude, I may be allowed to refer to one at least of my own contributions to the Advaitin-Christian dialogue, my study of *lakṣaṇā*, a Śāṅkarian tool of interpretation whose explanation I earlier postponed.

The importance of *lakṣaṇā*, especially of the *jahad-ajahad* type which corresponds to the Schoolmen's so-called 'intrinsic analogy,' resides in this that it provides a bridge for our weak intellect to cross over the abyss between the finite and the infinite, or between *avidyā* and *vidyā*. It leads it to take three steps: (1) the step of superimposition (*adhyāsa*) at which terms like 'being,' etc. are attributed to *Brahman* in some sense as to the Cause of beings; (2) the step of negation (*apavāda*), at which they are denied because in their primary sense they connote finitude; (3) the step of indication (*lakṣaṇā*) through their supreme sense (*paramārtha*), which applies to *Brahman* alone. This is possible because their own essential denotation (*svārtha*) has survived the negation of their finite mode. But now it is infinitized, soaring above the level of our own comprehension of reality, yet pointing authentically to the positive Fullness of *Brahman*. The bridge thus thrown over from the very limits of language does not do away with apophatism. Indeed, Śaṅkara, like St Thomas, remarks that since we have no proper experience of the mode of infinity, negativeness continues to affect even our analogical knowledge of God through *lakṣaṇā*. This is why the latter cannot satiate our desire of knowing *Brahman* which is *avagati-paryantam*, i.e., terminable only through an intuitive apprehension.

5. Conclusion

To conclude, let me recall briefly the areas of reflection of the writers we reviewed. Johanns found in *Tattvamasi* the positive doctrine of Advaita. Pessein cleared the vocabulary of *sat* and *asat*. Mascarenhas[29] has focussed on the Principle and the creature's 'principial' relation to it. The Almora colloquy tried to pave the way from absolute Consciousness to the Trinity. Abhishiktananda centred on the convergence of *advaita* transcendence and trinitarian faith. Otto traced up both the similarities and the differences of Advaita and Christian mysticisms. Monchanin, Klostermaier and Griffiths reflected deeply on their apophatism from either a trinitarian or a Christological perspective. Devanandan viewed *māyā* as shot through with divine purpose. M.S. Rao assimilated *ananyavta* with at-one-ness. Sr Grant passed from *tādātmya* to the truth of *aham brahmāsmi* in Christ's consciousness and I myself recalled the importance of *lakṣaṇā*.

Notes

[1] [First published in *Review of Darshana* **1**/1 (1980) 33-48 and reprinted here courtesy De Nobili College, Pune, having had no reply from *Review of Darshana* despite several reminders.]
[2] [This monograph is very probably the article published as "Christianity and Shaṅkarāchārya" in *The St Thomas Christian Encyclopaedia of India*, ed. George Menachery (Thrissur: The St Thomas Christian Encyclopaedia of India, 2010) **3**:22-42 (vols. 1 and 2 having been published in 1998 and 1973 respectively). (References given in the editorial notes below are often drawn from this article.) However, from conversations with De Smet in 1990-91, I recall that he was engaged in 'enriching' a similar, if not the same, work with matter from the Jesuit Archives during his year long residence at the Jesuit *Casa degli Scrittori*, Rome. A 40 page typescript is available with Daniel De Smet, with the title, "The Christian Encounter with Advaita Vedānta: A Survey of Four Centuries," together with another fragment with pagination running from 33 to 65. The latter item, in fact, echoes the subtitles of the present article: The Creative Assimilationists; The Apophatists; Christians in Dialogue with Advaitins.]
[3] [John Nicol Farquhar (1861-1929), *The Crown of Hinduism* (Calcutta 1913, 1914; Oxford 1919).]
[4] [W. Miller, principal of Madras Christian College of the United Free Church of Scotland.]
[5] [See above, "Introduction," note 13.]
[6] [Correcting 'bounds'.]
[7] [O. Lacombe, *L'Absolu selon le Vedānta* (Paris: Geuthner, 1937); on analogy, see 79-86.]
[8] [J.F. Pessein, *Vedānta Vindicated or the Harmony of Vedānta and Christian Philosophy* (Trichinopoly: St Joseph's Industrial School Press, 1925).]
[9] [Pessein 33-36.]
[10] [Pessein 80.]
[11] [Correcting 'Mascaren.']
[12] [H.O. Mascarenhas, *The Quintessence of Hinduism: The Key to Indian Culture and Philosophy* (Bombay: St Sebastian Goan High School, 1951). In 1994 De Smet lists an H.O. Mascarenhas among 'specialists' to whom he sent copies of his doctoral dissertation: see "From the Vedas to Radhakrishnan" = ch. 19 above.]
[13] [J.B. Chethimattam, 'Indian Interiority and Christian Theology,' mimeograph, 48-53.]
[14] [Abhishiktananda, *Hindu-Christian Meeting Point within the Cave of the Heart* (Bombay: Institute of Indian Culture, 1969) 106-107.]
[15] [Abhishiktananda 109, 116.]
[16] [R. Otto, *Mysticism East and West* (New York: Macmillan, 1932).]

[17] [Jules Monchanin (1895-1957), *Mystique de l'Inde, mystère chrétien* (Paris: Fayard, 1974) 271-272.]
[18] [This should probably read: 'identified with'.]
[19] [Klaus K. Klostermaier, *Kristvidya: A Sketch of an Indian Christology* (Bangalore: Christian Institute for the Study of Religion and Society, 1967).]
[20] [Bede Griffiths (1906-1993), *Vedanta and Christian Faith* (Dehra Dun, 1968); *Christ in India* (New York: Scribner's Sons, 1966) 80-82, 100, 169-174, 183-186, 202-205.]
[21] [See P.D. Devanandan (1901-1962), *The Concept of Maya* (Calcutta: YMCA, 1954), and R. Boyd, *An Introduction to Indian Christian Theology* (Madras: CLS, 1969) 186-197.]
[22] [Marc Sunder Rao, *Ananyatva: Realisation of Christian Non-Dualism* (Bangalore: CISRS, 1964), and Boyd 214-216.]
[23] [Raimundo Panikkar (1918-2010), *The Unknown Christ of Hinduism* (London: DLT, 1964), and Boyd 222-226.]
[24] [Dhanjibhai Fakirbhai (1895-1967), author of *Christopanishad, The Philosophy of Love, Hriday Geeta, Prematattva Darshan,* and *Shree Krist Geeta.*]
[25] [Nalini Devdas, *Sri Ramakrishna* (Bangalore: CISRS, 1966), and *Svāmī Vivekānanda* (Bangalore: CISRS, 1968).]
[26] [Sabapathy Kulandran, first bishop of the Jaffna diocese of the Church of South India, author of *Grace: A Comparative Study of the Doctrine in Christianity and Hinduism* (London: Lutterworth, 1964).]
[27] [Sara Grant (1922-2002), "Reflections on the Mystery of Christ suggested by Study of Shankara's Concpet of Relation," *God's Word among Men*, ed. G. Gispert-Sauch (Delhi: Vidyajyoti, 1973) 105-116. See also her *Sankarācārya's Concept of Relation* (Delhi: Motilal Banarsidass, 1999).]
[28] Śaṅkara, *Bṛh. Up. Bh.* 4, 4, 18. Śaṅkara, *Śāriraka bhāṣya* 1, 1, 11.
[29] [Correcting 'Mascaren'.]

28

FROM CATHOLIC THEOLOGY TO ŚĀṄKARA VEDĀNTA AND RETURN WITH FR F.X. CLOONEY[1]

Fr Francis Xavier Clooney, Dept. of Theology, Boston College, is a rare sort of Catholic theologian: an American Jesuit, he has worked in Nepal and India, studied both Sanskrit and Tamil, explored much of Pūrva Mīmāṃsā, Vedānta, Srī Vaiṣṇavism and also of the writings of the Jesuit pioneers of the seventeenth-eighteenth centuries in South India and produced important studies on such salient figures as Jaimini, Śaṅkara, Roberto de Nobili and Satakopan, the poet of Tiruvaymoli. Those studies have been devoted chiefly to the methods and contents of the commentatorial literature of India and he has found in it a solid anchoring for a fruitful Comparative Theology.

In 1926, Mircea Eliade, then a nineteen-year old student, wrote to the already well-known Raffaele Pettazzoni, asking him the radical question: "Does the History of Religions make sense? Has it a sense?" They went on discussing that by letters all along 33 years.[2] A similar question deserves to be put: "Does Comparative Theology make sense?" In 1953, when I was vindicating the fact that the method of Śaṅkara was exclusively commentarial (a fact wilfully ignored by Radhakrishnan and other modernistic Indian professors) I called this method 'theological,' thus hinting that comparative theology might be fruitful and meaningful. When, however, I devoted one chapter of my Ph.D. dissertation to a formal analysis of the polysemy of terms-in-context as familiar to Jaimini and Śaṅkara as much as to Thomas Aquinas and other medieval theologians, my Gregorian University examiners were seized with timidity and asked me not to include that in the published thesis. What had stood to reason to a Calcutta Jesuit because he was the heir of an interfaith approach initiated by Brahmabandhab Upadhyay and ably practised by the Bengal Jesuits W. Wallace, P. Johanns, G. Dandoy, J. Putz, J. Bayart (to mention only the most prominent up to that date)[3] was still unexplored and seemed risky in the Rome of the last days of the Pius XII. Today, on the contrary, Clooney enjoys full liberty to tread any lane or by-lane of comparative theology.

1. Clooney's Approach to Comparative Theology

Clooney approaches his comparative task from the standpoint of his Catholic faith and distances himself from those who rely on the doubtful principle that all religions are equal carriers of the saving truth (4-6).

Rather than being a 'comparative' reading of texts of different traditions, his task will be a '*collectio*,' i.e., a reading together of such texts in such a way that the reader engages and inscribes himself into them in an act of experimental theology by which he inscribes within the Christian theological tradition theological texts from outside it. More precisely, in his case, his writing will reflect how this engagement reconfigures his religious and theological understanding (7-11).

With approbation, Clooney refers here to Lee Yearley's recent *Mencius and Aquinas*. Yearley says that such studies engage us in a process that utilizes the analogical imagination. Does this imply that standards dissolve? No:

> Imaginative processes involve standards for judging interpretations and rules that can be followed well or badly.... They depend, for example, on the interpreter's sensibilities, they may evoke rather than demonstrate, and they produce inventions... these inventions have the power to give a new form to our experiences.[4]

2. Turning to Advaita

What attracted Clooney to the Advaita writings of Śaṅkara seems to have been their commentarial nature even more than their doctrinal contents. When I turned to Śaṅkara fifty years ago, the nature of his undertaking had been obscured and I wanted to rediscover his original purpose, formal object and method. I deemed this a necessary condition to the correct understanding of his doctrine. It became clear to me that he was unrestrictedly a *śrutivādin*, an exegete of the Upaniṣads. This point was no longer in dispute when Clooney began. There was no doubt that "among the schools of Vedānta, Śaṅkara's school is distinguished by its consistent and thorough dependence on exegesis" (16).[5]

Śaṅkara is a *bhāṣyakāra*, a composer of commentaries (on most of the classical Upaniṣads, the *Bhagavad Gītā* and the *Brahma-sūtras*). These must be read and re-read, I may say, very religiously. But what Clooney sees more clearly than I did is the need to read also the subcommentaries of diverse authors on Śaṅkara's works. I was rather afraid that they might lead me astray and I interpreted Śaṅkara through Śaṅkara. Clooney is convinced and shows that recourse to the subcommentators can be very enriching. It is even essential, although subcommentaries are "intricate, often difficult to use and often resistant to the questions modern readers pose to them" (18).

Clooney is, of course, aware that in calling Advaita 'theology' he is out of line with the majority of authors:

> [I]n making the commentarial side of Advaita central and in describing Advaita as primarily theological, I distinguish my work from the mainstream of modern approaches to Advaita, which have used an almost entirely philosophical language in their treatment of Advaita.... (26-27)

But let us first see what he means by 'theology':

> I refer to Advaita as 'theology,' as faith seeking understanding, a salvation-centred explication of the world generated out of an exegesis of sacred texts which seeks to commit the listening... community to specific rituals and ethical practices. (26)

Concerning the frequent reduction of Advaita Vedānta to being a 'philosophy,' Clooney makes these crucial remarks:

> [I]t would be a mistake to isolate [those Advaita] themes [which appear to be philosophical and make sense even if one abstracts them from their scriptural context] and mistake the sum of them for a full understanding of the Advaita....
>
> ... Reason does not operate independently in Śaṅkara's Advaita, though it has a distinctive function; this distinctive role occurs within, and not

apart from, exegetical and scripturally-formed thinking; it operates properly when exercised by properly educated, literate persons. (29)

This is an old teaching for many of us: the same assertion, say, "There is one God, the source of all, innermost in all," or "The supreme *Brahman* is the innermost *Ātman* of all," may be based on a sacred scripture or on independent reasoning, but it will not have the same truth-value and give access to the same understanding in both cases. The formality of the assertion differs when it is either scriptural or purely rational. This is why my first undertaking was to ascertain the formal nature of Śaṅkara's assertions. Clooney's remarks are important especially in our time when some are tempted to blur the differences between independent rational philosophy and revelational theology.

But can we expect to understand *the* meaning of a text? Just as I had to meet the challenge of Paul Valéry's aphorism, "Il n'y a pas de sens d'un texte" ("there is no such thing as the meaning of a text"), Clooney is confronted by the post-modern Derrida affirming that any text has endless meanings. His apt reply is that

Advaita maintains a 'realist' notion of reading, in which texts are not thought to be open to endless meanings, it discovers meaning through the identification and use of a set of intratextual rules of meaning. By these rules a text means without being replaced by that to which it refers.... (214, n 46)

3. The Texture of the Advaita Vedānta Text

There is an "array of possibilities opened up by the upaniṣads as the textual basis on which Advaita composes its interpretative framework" (38).

When Bādarāyaṇa (perhaps fourth century AD) wished to reduce them to such a framework, he did it in the form of a set of terse aphorisms (*sūtra*) variously distributed into topics (*adhikaraṇa*), about 200 of them. As the basic text of the Vedānta exegetes, it is called *Uttara Mīmāṃsā Sūtra* or *Vedānta Sūtra* or *Brahma-sūtra*. They have explained and commented on [it] in the literary form of commentaries (*bhāṣya*).

The first *sūtra* of a topic raises an exegetical doubt born from some upaniṣadic passage. To resolve it, the commentator begins

> by distinguishing and exploring its full set of ramifications. [He] elaborates the initial doubt which is to be explored in all its logical and rhetorical possibilities, and follows through on the set of positions, counter-positions, distinctions, refinements and conclusions, all of which together constitute the adhikaraṇa. (47)

The occasions when Śaṅkara diverges from Bādarāyaṇa's position can help us to perceive the fruitfulness of this complex procedure. For instance, in its analysis of man, *Taitt. Up*. 2, 1-5 teaches a succession of five inner selves consisting of or sharing (*maya*) respectively in food, vital airs, mind, understanding and bliss. Bādarāyaṇa says: "The self consisting of bliss is the highest Self" (*UMS* 1, 1, 12).[6] Śaṅkara reaches first the same conclusion but then states a different interpretation on the following grounds:

(a) since the ending *-maya* means 'consisting in' in the first four cases and thus has a quantitative meaning, it surely keeps that meaning in the fifth so that this *ānanda-maya ātman* cannot be the highest Self which is devoid of quantity;

(b) in the same Up. 2, 1, 5, *Brahman* is said to be the tail / support of that *ānanda-maya ātman*, hence, is deeper and more interior than it.

In this interpretation, Śaṅkara has had recourse to a secondary meaning (*lakṣaṇā*) of 'tail' (*puccha*). His subcommentator Vācaspati wonders whether the other terms also have to be taken in a secondary meaning but confirms Śaṅkara's restriction of that to *puccha* as more economical (53-54). The other subcommentators too discuss, approve and appropriate this interpretation.

It is by entering actively into the *adhikaraṇa* process that the reader becomes a participant. This is the proper gate:

> [A]ll adhikaranas mediate what is outside the Text, including Brahman, through the Text.... [T]he extratextual world is not properly seen or experienced except through the Text, and... this Textual mediation constitutes the only 'world' the Advaitins are interested in.... [E]verything is transformed by its inscription [in the Text], and is relevant only in that inscribed form. (55)

Why does Clooney not restrict 'the Text' to mean the Upaniṣads alone? Precisely because they cannot be grasped and appropriated apart from a well-conducted exegetical process:

> Advaita subsists as this textual composition, what I have termed 'the Text'.... This Text is a complex, literary project—in its practices, in the developments it makes available to us in the form of commentary, and its resultant reinterpretation of the world is a project in writing. The fruits of this Text... can be abstracted only at the great cost of severing the vital connection between a Vedānta philosophy and an Uttara Mīmāṃsā [Exegesis].... One must remain ready to... be educated, and so to become differently skilled by particular acts of reading... [and] learned in the particular refinements by which the discernment of right positions advances. (74)

4. Moving towards Post-Textual Truths

Advaita moves towards post-textual truths that never become purely extra-textual:

> It argues that it is true that reality is nondual, that *Brahman* is devoid of all qualities, that the world has *Brahman* as its cause—material, efficient and final—and that these positions refer to the actual reality in which not only Advaitins live, but everyone as well. (78)

Śaṅkara extends the systematization of the Upaniṣads begun by Bādarāyaṇa but he stands closer to their text. He does not, like him, uncover in them a doctrine about *Brahman*. For him, "the upaniṣads cannot tell us about Brahman [which no word can express], but they fail in so rich, engaging and persuasive a way that we alter our way of living and realize Brahman in a radical revision of our own identities" (78).

Brahman is ineffable because it is perfect Fullness, not quantitative but qualitative; it is simple Substance, not a compound of substance plus accidents; in it there is nothing secondary, i.e., no *guṇa* (whether quality, quantity, form, real relation or any endowment). Śaṅkara gives prominence to this teaching that *Brahman* is *nirguṇa*. In *UMS* 3, 2, 14,[7] he supports Bādarāyaṇa's clear position:

> *Brahman*, we must definitely assert, is devoid of all form, colour, etc.... Why? 'On account of this being the main purport (of scripture).' [In

support of this, he then brings forth five pertinent quotations from the chief Upaniṣads.]

Thus to the tension between the reader and the ineffability of *Brahman* is added the tension between the *nirguṇa* teachings and their contraries, the *saguṇa* teachings. Śaṅkara relaxes the second tension by assigning a different intention to the two kinds of texts. The *nirguṇa* texts intend to teach the true nature of *Brahman*; "but other texts, which have as their topic *Brahman* with figure, ... express injunctions related to meditation."[8]

Another exegetical move by which Advaita organizes the Upaniṣads in order to make their truth evident is the designation of so-called 'great sentences' (*mahāvākya*) which sum up the entire meaning of an upaniṣadic instruction. Such are, for instance, "I am *Brahman*" (*Aham Brahmāsmi*) (*Bṛh. Up.* 1, 4, 10) or "That you are" (*Tattvamasi*) (*Chānd. Up.* 6, 8, 7). Their effect is perhaps greater because they are paradoxical.

> A great saying, such as 'You are That'... upsets our reading of the upaniṣads because, in the Advaita reading, it seems to equate two things that ought not to be equated: the phenomenal, finite self (*tvam*) and Brahman (*Tat*).... It is a truth which has no evident reference or confirmation in the world of ordinary experience. Made uncomfortable..., the reader is made to seek a stance in which nonduality can be perceived as true, and the search for this requires a rereading of the rest of the given upaniṣad.... (86)

The imposition of a philosophical interpretation upon a great saying should not be immediate but come only after rereading it as a skilful textual achievement terminating a highly pedagogical dialogue.

At this point Clooney engages the reader into an active reading of the Text around four key-passages in order to trace the Advaita's construction of the right meaning of the Upaniṣads. These pages 88-102 cannot be summarized here but we can pick out a few illuminating bits.

As we have seen already, it is axiomatic with Śaṅkara that "different texts have different purposes and must be used accordingly" (102). This guides him when explaining the multiplicity of names of *Brahman*. He distinguishes those that apply in every meditation from those that apply only in special ones. The first are meant to teach the true nature of *Brahman* and are thus fundamental, such as "*Brahman* is one without a second, reality, knowledge, bliss," etc.; the second are mere meditational constructs, such as "its head is joy, its right side delight," "uniting all that is pleasant," etc. Vācaspati refines a little this distinction but Amalānanda enriches it by asking why the *Brahman* is better indicated by a series of terms than by just one. It is, he replies, because they co-operate in correcting wrong ideas about *Brahman*.

> [i] Truth, [ii] consciousness, [iii] bliss, [iv] infinity and [v] self are terms which mutually qualify one another, overturn [in turn] the flaws of [i] falsity, [ii] non-consciousness, [iii] sorrow, [iv] limitedness, and [v] lack of self, and so define that single bliss which is the common basis for truth, etc. It is just like when the words 'existent,' 'material thing,' and 'pot' [all define] a single pot (on *UMS* 3, 3, 11).[9]

Clooney could have pointed out that this excellent clarification is just a rephrasing of Śaṅkara's *bhāṣya* on *Taitt. Up*. 2, 1 (towards the end), a precious teaching exploited also by Sāyaṇa.

5. In Defence of Advaita

"Profoundly exegetical and pedagogical, Advaita as a doctrine is also a (re)description of the world. It occurs throughout the Text and its force accumulates in a series of individual defenses against competing views of the world" (102). Let us pay attention, first, to Śaṅkara's defence of the relative reasonableness of Advaita:

> In UMS II.1.11, Śaṅkara agrees with the proposition that reasoning is legitimate, inevitable and necessary for life, and that it is at work even during the practice of exegesis. But... unless it is the reasoning of the scripturally literate person, it cannot provide an adequate view of reality as a whole....
>
> Independent reason is inherently inadequate for several reasons.
> [(a) because] *Brahman* is not an ordinary object of knowledge...
> [(b)] the reasoning of the uneducated person is notoriously unreliable...
> [(c) in this matter even well-grounded reasoning cannot possibly be final and conclusive for, writes Śaṅkara,] 'this extremely sublime subject-matter, concerned with the true nature of being, the basis of liberation, cannot even be guessed at without the help of the scriptures.'

> *Brahman* is an objective extra- and posttextual reality; legitimate, upaniṣadic statements about *Brahman* do not contradict properly exercised reason.... The purpose of argument is to show that there are no reasonable grounds for seeking an explanation of the whole other than that indicated in the upaniṣads. (104-105)

Clooney then examines the attacks of Sāṁkhya and other systems against Vedānta, their rebuff by Śaṅkara and further his direct assaults against the inner contradictions of the *Sāṁkhya Kārikā* (106-113). He concludes:

> In defending its positions, Advaita precludes access to these positions from any neutral position that might appear independent of [the Vedic scriptures].... The truth is available, yet only within the confines of a demanding Text and consequent upon an engagement in it. (114)

It is now important to consider an obstacle which hinders many a reader of Advaita texts: on the one hand, the claims of Advaita "are articulated in and from sacred texts as understood by a believing community;" on the other hand, many readers are outsiders who lack faith in the infallibility of the Upaniṣads. What access can they find to their truth-claims? Clooney's answer is:

> It is precisely here, on the margin of the Text, and not in speculating about the rational claims of Advaita or in a search for the experience to which it points, that a point of access appears. Though demanding, the Text is a teacher. It instructs the interested inquirer in the skills of approach to *Brahman*; it encourages the reader's engagement in it, and if properly learned, it guides the reader to a truth which can be cognized after it. (114)

This is nicely said but is it not a fact that the access to the Text is barred to many by a whole array of exterior and interior limitations imposed by Advaita itself to those who seek access to it?

6. Qualifying for Advaita

Śaṅkara calls his undertaking *Brahmajijñāsā*. Etymologically, *jijñāsā* means a repeated or unflagging (*ji-*) desire (*-sā*) to know (*-jña*). In current usage, it rather means 'enquiry' which is the fruit of such a desire. Thus Jaimini introduces his *Dharma Mīmāṃsā Sūtra* as *dharma-jijñāsā*, the enquiry into the (ritual) duties (of the higher classes), and then provides the principles and rules of exegesis necessary to interpret correctly the Brāhmaṇas. This inquiry, says his commentator Śabara, is made to fulfil the injunction, "One must study one's proper portion [of the Veda]" (*svādhyāyā 'dhyetavyaḥ*). But Śaṅkara insists that his undertaking, though it is an enquiry, is not conditioned by any injunction or by any other antecedent such as a prior practice of Vedic rituals. Its starting source is the very desire to know the *Brahman* not vaguely but most deeply (*avagati-paryantam jñānam*). This desire is innate (*naisargika*), unprecedented, original, yet common to all human beings.

Its goal, however, is most sublime so that not everyone is simply, by birth, qualified to pursue it along the appropriate way. Yet the sole prerequisites, says Śaṅkara, are the following interior qualities:

> [D]iscrimination between things that are eternal and things that are noneternal; a loss of taste for the enjoyment of objects here [in this life] and hereafter [in various possible paradises]; ... control of the mind, control of the senses and organs, etc.; and the desire for liberation. (UMS I.1.1)[10]

In emphasizing these prerequisites, Śaṅkara does not echo any scriptural assertion but rather draws from his experience of renunciation as a *sannyāsin*.

As enquiry, *Brahmajijñāsā* simply extends to new materials (the Upaniṣads) the older *mīmāṃsā* practice, skills and pedagogy. It also restricts itself to students conforming to special conditions of birth, social rank and education which Clooney discusses, pp. 134-140, in terms of a tension between the Text and the grasping of its truth.

I interject here a personal view regarding the problem he had raised, namely, how can people pursue Advaita who do not share Śaṅkara's faith in the dogma (initiated by Jaimini[11]) of the authorlessness and, hence, infallibility of the Vedas? It seems to me that, since they too share innately the desire to know the essence of *Brahman*, they can on that basis become legitimate students of Advaita. Their study will not be "faith seeking understanding" but "desire (for the blissful and liberating knowledge / intuition) seeking fulfilment."

Coming back to those born within the orthodox system of Hindu *dharma* (duties, prohibitions and restrictions), what happens when they begin to seek Advaita liberation? Clooney studies this in *UMS* 3, 4. Normally they continue their ritual practices but change their motivation: instead of performing the usual ritual goals, they perform them now "for the sake of knowledge," namely for the sake of the purifications, detachment and increase of spiritual desire which those rites will produce. These will be at least indirect helps towards the pursuit of knowledge. Only the *Brahma-jña,* the realized knower of *Brahman* is entirely free.

> Just as the ineffable truth of Advaita occurs in practice only after thorough appropriation of the Advaita Text, the state of life in which one is completely free from restrictions occurs only after the inner appropriation of those restrictions. (149)

In conclusion of his ch. 4, Clooney puts the emphasis on the tension between the ultimate simplicity of the Advaita truth and the complex requirements of reading the Text which yields it, a tension which is extreme for those wishing to enter Advaita from outside orthodox Hinduism. But, on the basis of his own self-limitation to its Exegesis, he assures them that this entry is in fact open to them:

> Though the truth of the Text may elusively conceal itself behind the complex demands of proper reading, our (mis)reading nevertheless provides a simple rejoinder to that complexity, and so cooperates with the Advaita to express once more its characteristic tension between the complex requirements of reading and the simple event of insight. (151)

7. Towards a Retrieval of Catholic Theology after Advaita

Catholic Theology is very much embedded in revealed Texts commented upon again and again. The Western commentarial tradition begins with commentaries on Plato from the second century BC. From the third century AD, Greek Christians take over this work and quickly extend it to Biblical writings. The commentaries written by the Byzantine Christians are often outstanding and have been imitated by the Arabs especially after the Muslim conquest of Iran. From Muslim and Jewish workshops in Spain and, later, Sicily, some of those commentarial works reach Western Europe by the late twelfth and early thirteenth century and give rise to the Western Latin commentarial tradition.[12]

In this tradition, St Thomas Aquinas stands out as most similar to Śaṅkara. More than Origen, Augustine, Albert the Great, Bonaventure or Duns Scotus, he resembles him in the clear apprehension of our innate desire to intuit the very essence of God, his reliance on revealed texts and holy traditions, his method of elucidating them and some of the saving truths he unveils to his disciples. It is to him that Clooney turns when he decides to reread a Catholic Text after his appropriation of the Advaita Text—though for no compelling reason but because it pleases him and he may thus reach unexpected possibilities (155). He is now ready to reconceive of Aquinas' *Summa Theologiae* as a 'Text,'

> a series of (written) acts of language which are irreducible to any author's... intention... but which are read as intertextually composed into a larger whole comprised of a series of related texts: e.g., a text along with those which are inscribed in it by citation, and those which exist in the form of commentary upon it. (157)

He will begin with examples in which parts of the *S.Th.* are read differently after the study of Advaita. The first one uses *S.Th.* I, 13, 4 in comparison with *UMS* 3, 3, 11-13 and Amalānanda's commentary thereon. Reading them in parallel shows immediately their common topic: the legitimacy of the scriptural appellations of God although God / *Brahman* is ineffable. The similarities of questioning and replies are striking. But rereading will lead to differences too and, therefore, possible enrichments and a better nourished theology beyond but in a prolongation of both Śaṅkara and Aquinas (159-167).

Some strategies are sketched out for fuller exploitation of this comparative reading: (1) coordination of selected texts, (2) superimposition of one text on another, (3) comparative conversation, (4) attention to what Ph. Wheelwright calls the "semantic motion" of metaphors (the latter operate a transmutation in two possible ways: "epiphor," which is the "outreach and extension of meaning through comparison," and "diaphor," which is "the creation of new meanings by juxtaposition and synthesis"), (5) collage, as strategy [to my mind more hazardous] inspired by J. Derrida: it consists in excising familiar texts from their legitimate contexts in order to read them together without prior warrant; such newly aligned materials destabilize the reader and compel him or her to coördinate and re-contextualize them in novel ways (168-175).

I would add a sixth strategy: the placing of parallel texts within their respective long range historical contexts, say, Thomistic texts as coming at the conclusion of a twelve-century long struggle of Catholic nondualistic monotheism against Gnostic-Manichean dualism, a struggle rooted in the tension born from conflicting Biblical ways of God-talk, either transcendent or anthropomorphic;[13] and, on the other side, Śaṅkara's monotheistic nondualism as opening up a period of many centuries during which his position and his hermeneutic of conflicting upaniṣadic texts will be nibbled and pared by a Rāmānuja or displaced by the dualism of a Madhva.

Are there limits to the possibility of reading together theological Texts of diverse origins? Are there incomparable Texts? Clooney discusses fruitfully *S.Th.* III, 46, 3, a central text of St Thomas on the Passion of Christ, and concludes:

> [T]here is... no persuasive reason to refuse to reread [this text] alongside a selected Advaita text, even if the juxtaposition highlights distance, inappropriateness and apparent incomparability. Since comparative reading does not depend on similarity, extreme dissimilarity is no reason to end such reading. (179)

In the *S.Th.*, we find many Biblical texts being quoted to support or illuminate theological argumentation and likewise many citations from the writings of the Fathers of the Church and later theologians. For similar reasons Śaṅkara's writings are replete with upaniṣadic citations and later texts of the Brahmanic tradition. Clooney remarks:

> The best readers are those who appreciate the actual citations as indications of the larger contexts from which they are drawn... [not] as mere appeals to authority... [or mere embellishments... or mere proof-texts]. (181-182)

This larger context is the one I spoke about when suggesting a sixth strategy which, therefore, Clooney has in fact integrated. And now a further remark drawn from his experience may aptly close this account of his book: In a comparative setting, one acquires a refined sense of discrimination, an appreciation of the subtle linguistic refinements which enhance a Text and amplify its significance.

8. Conclusion

It is comforting, forty years after the completion of my dissertation on the theological method of Śaṅkara, to get from a confrere with better scholarship and discerning insight a confirmation of its truth and an extension of its worth.

During those forty years, the will to reduce Śaṅkara's *Brahmajijñāsā* to a merely rational intuitional philosophy has on the whole remained predominant. K. Satchidananda Murty was an exception with his *Revelation and Reason in Advaita*, published in 1959.[14] In recent years, thanks to the novel interest of Indian scholars in Hermeneutics, one discerns a still timid change towards a recognition of the true nature of Śaṅkara's writings. In 1991, Anantanand Rambachan, trained in Leeds, UK, published a monograph entitled *Accomplishing the Accomplished: The Vedas as a Source of Valid Knowledge in Sankara.*[15] In this he retraces the path of enquiry I had myself followed and reaches the same results. I can but recommend firmly this clear book which readers will find very accessible. (He thinks that he has to damn my work on one point, namely, whether the realization of *Brahmajijñāsā* is obtained by a further *pramāṇa* supplementary to the scriptural enquiry and which would be the final *anubhava*; but in fact I agree with him that there is no such supplementary *pramāṇa*.)

Notes

[1] Francis X. Clooney, SJ, *Theology and Vedānta: An Experiment in Comparative Theology.* Albany: State University of New York Press, 1993, pp. 265. Bracketed numbers in the text refer to page numbers of the book. [This

'review article' was first published in *Vidyajyoti: Journal of Theological Reflection* **58** (1994) 795-807, and is being reprinted here with permission.]

[2] M. Eliade and R. Pettazzoni, *L'histoire des religions a-t-elle un sense? Correspondence 1926-1959*. Paris: Cerf, 1994.

[3] [On the so-called 'Calcutta School' of Catholic Indologists, see above, "Introduction" note 7.]

[4] [Lee Yearley, *Mencius and Aquinas: Theories of Virtue and Conceptions of Courage* (Albany: State University of New York Press, 1990) 197, cited in Clooney 13.]

[5] [Clooney 16 actually reads: "Among the schools of Vedānta, it is distinguished by its consistent and thorough dependence on exegesis....," where 'it' refers to Advaita rather than Śaṅkara. De Smet has substituted 'it' with 'Śaṅkara.']

[6] [De Smet, with Clooney, uses here the abbreviation *UMS* indifferently for both Bādarāyaṇa's *Uttara Mīmāṁsā Sūtra* and Śaṅkara's *Bhāṣya* on it. I have decided to retain this usage in this particular article.]

[7] [Obviously Śaṅkara's *bhāṣya* on the *UMS* = *B.S.Bh.*.]

[8] [Clooney 83-84, citing Śaṅkara on *UMS* 3, 2, 14.]

[9] [As cited in Clooney 91. The reference (De Smet's addition) is to Amalānanda's commentary, the *Vedāntakalpataru*, which is itself a commentary on the *Bhāmati*, which in turn is Vācaspati Miśra's commentary on Śaṅkara's *B.S.Bh.* Clooney uses the *Brahmasūtra Śaṅkara Bhāṣya with the commentaries Bhāmatī, Kalpataru and Parimala*, 2 vols., Parimala Sanskrit Series no. 1 (Ahmedabad: Parimal Publications, 1981).]

[10] [Cited in Clooney 130; reference added by De Smet.]

[11] Cf. my article, "The Presuppositions of Jaimini and the Vedāntins," *Journal of the Indian Council of Philosophical Research* **11**/2 (1994), especially p. 80 [= ch. 17:274-275 above].

[12] This rich commentarial literature is becoming better known thanks to the progress of the project of publishing (chiefly from Germany) critical editions of those Greek and Byzantine commentaries and, through the collaboration of many scholars around Richard Sorabji, London, English translations of them.

[13] See, for instance, the very informative book of G.G. Stroumsa, *Savoir et salut: Traditions juives et tentations dualistes dans le christianisme ancien* (Paris: Cerf, 1992).

[14] [Waltair: Andhra University Press, 1959; reprint Delhi: Motilal Banarsidass, 1974.]

[15] University of Hawaii Press, 1991, 179 pp.

III. REVIEWS

29

REVIEW OF MARIO PIANTELLI, *ŚAṄKARA E LA RINASCITÀ DEL BRĀHMANESIMO*[1]

To the growing but uneven shelf of books on Śaṅkara, the author adds a valuable contribution. It is unusual insofar as it provides much information difficult to come by elsewhere. Its three chapters deal respectively with the life of Śaṅkara, his doctrine, and the sources concerning them. Scholars know the difficulty of ascertaining the age and the dates of Śaṅkara, the circumstances of his life, and the number of his authentic writings, not to speak of the exact content of his original teaching. To the study of these topics, the author brings forth the resources of his remarkably complete erudition and sums up the results of recent critical research without venturing into presumptuous hypotheses or too controversial assertions. Thus adopting a soundly critical attitude, he yet tempers it with an openness to examine with sympathy even very doubtful sources and to expose leisurely their alleged data, especially regarding the life-events of the great *Ācārya*. He is led to this by a laudable but typically Western desire to discover the man beyond the writings. But apart from these writings there are only legendary biographies, later than Śaṅkara by at least five centuries, unsupported by any discernible dependence on an authentic tradition that would link them with the early disciples, and clearly fabricated for the threefold purpose of pious edification, providing a mnemonic framework for enshrining a host of pieces of pseudo-Śaṅkarian literature, and often striving to uphold the claims of one or the other *maṭha* (monastic centre) over its rivals and to link Śaṅkara with a sect like Śaivism or even Tantrism.

In the beginning of his first chapter, the author sets forth in 17 lines the only data that can be considered as certain regarding the life of Śaṅkara: he lived between the end of the seventh century and the first half of the eighth; he was a Brahmin of the Atri clan; be became an itinerant *saṅnyāsin* who won many disciples to his teaching and form of renunciation; the India of his time was no longer a unitary monarchy and society was in a state of confusion regarding the duties of the different *varṇas* and *āśramas*; the places he refers to belong all to North India; none of the five *rājas* he mentions has been identified with certainty; in the course of his career, he disputed with a certain Vināyaka, probably a Buddhist scholar, and defeated him; among his disciples, two are most certain, Sureśvara and Padmapāda. That is all. In the following 100 pages, the author in a very absorbing[2] narration harmonizes the 'data' of the legendary Lives, exposing fairly their mutual conflicts and sifting out manifest historical impossibilities. For this work of comparative hagiography scholars will be grateful but the question remains, will they be richer in reliable information? Piantelli himself is not inclined to dismiss these 'biographies' *in toto*. "Śaṅkara's image, as alive today in the hearts of millions of Indians, cannot prescind from them, and single episodes reveal so much a character both coherent and most plausible that they cannot be discarded rashly. Śaṅkara, who in his works disappears willingly behind his arguments, appears in them with the sweetness, the strength and also the imperfections of one among us and we feel that we can understand and love him as a man and not merely as a thinker" (217). While respecting and even sympathizing with this attitude, we would still question character-coherence and plausibility as sufficient criteria of acceptability in such matters (are they not the marks of fiction more than of real life?) Besides, there is a real danger that such an openness towards legendary materials will, in the eyes of Indian readers, appear to justify the present uncritical bias of even scholarly advaitins towards a ready acceptance not only of the Śaṅkara legends but, less harmlessly, of doctrinal works ascribed to Śaṅkara with little chance of genuineness.

Chapter 3, which treats of the sources, deals first of all with the writings of Śaṅkara. A useful appendix lists 433 titles, 107 of which merely duplicate for another 69. 219 do not enjoy unanimous recognition by the tradition while 214 titles do. Scholars, however, reject most of them. The list of genuine and doubtful works established by S.K. Belvalkar remains a solid basis which Piantelli accepts for discussion. Regarding the *bhāṣya* on the *Bhagavad Gītā*, he remains unconvinced by the arguments of the critics of its authenticity; in my opinion he is right. As to the *vivaraṇa* on the *Māṇḍūkya Upaniṣad*, he takes good note of its rejection by Jacobi, Belvalkar and V. Bhattacarya but finds their arguments undecisive and counterbalanced by Ānandagiri's reference to glosses on that work earlier than his own (thirteenth century). Given the doctrinal importance of this *vivaraṇa* I wish he could have devoted a critical disquisition to the genuineness of this—to my mind, extremely doubtful—work. He refers to the traditional thesis that these two *bhāṣyas* (on *Gītā* and *Māṇḍūkya*) would be the earliest products of Śaṅkara's exegetical activity; for textual reasons I would accept it for the *Gītābhāṣya* but find no compelling reasons to agree with it even as a compromise solution in the case of the *Māṇḍūkyabhāṣya*. Among the minor works, the *bhāṣya* on the *Viṣṇusahasranāmastotra* has in his opinion some probability of being authentic. The *Dakṣiṇāmūrtistotra* which is one of the 8 hymns retained as more probably genuine by Belvalkar is singled out for translation in the closing appendix on account of its doctrinal weight. As to the *Saundaryalaharī* and the *Śivabhujaṅga* which Belvalkar had rejected, the acceptance of the first by Radhakrishnan and Mahadevan, and of the second by Mahadevan, should have called for a serious discussion rising above the level of mere feeling on which these authors seem to have remained. There is no serious ground to doubt the authenticity of the verse part of *Upadeśasāhasrī* but the prose part continues to appear apocryphal. As to the *Vivekacūḍāmaṇi*, Piantelli remains rightly unconvinced by Ingalls's arguments for his rejection and calls for a new investigation which might result in saving its main core of 265 *slokas* in *anusṣṭubh* (apart from a few like 144, 343, 353) out of its total number of 580 *ślokas* as already suggested by Belvalkar. He further suggests reasons for reconsidering the case of *Ātmabodha*, *Pañcīkaraṇaprakrīya* and *Ātmānātmaviveka*.

The rest of ch. 3 deals quite informatively with the works of Śaṅkara's immediate disciples, the documents relating to the succession lines of the heads of the five chief Śaṅkara *maṭhas* (without discussing the legitimacy of their claims to have originated from the Master), the traces of Śaṅkara's influence on the rival schools and references to him in other literary works. At this point, he usefully recalls that the dating of Śaṅkara which the majority of modern writers have unquestioningly accepted, namely 788/820, was determined on a very weak basis by the Dutch scholar C.P. Tiele in his *Outlines of the History of Ancient Religions* (1877). Piantelli exposes the spuriousness of the sources used by Tiele and other attendant documents on pp. 213-214 after presenting, on pp. 209-219, some at least of the solid reasons for bringing back Śaṅkara to about one century earlier. A more precise dating has not yet been attained. In the same chapter, Piantelli examines also the rather scanty archaeological data and the 14 so-called biographies of the *Ācārya*. In the closing appendix, he offers a careful translation of ch. 18 of the verse part of *Upadeśasāhasrī* which is Śaṅkara's best exposition of the *mahāvākya* "*Tattvamasi*".

The author's outline of Śaṅkara's doctrine (ch. 2, pp. 107-187) is solid, personal and uncompromising. He takes his distance from many a modern interpreter: Otto, Zaehner, Radhakrishnan, Lacombe, Hacker, Panikkar, Hoàng-Sy-Quy. He studies successively (1) the human condition, (2) Reality, (3) unreality, (4) liberation and the way which leads to it. This is preceded by a brief setting forth of Śaṅkara's intention and method. What Śaṅkara intends is exclusively liberation (*mokṣa*) through recognition of the nature of Reality as revealed by the Upaniṣads or *Śruti*. Hence, he only claims to be an *Aupaniṣada* or *śrutivādin*, i.e., an exegete of the Upaniṣads according to the tradition of *Uttara Mīmāṃsā*. Their testimony, which is eternal and, hence, infallible, is received as sovereign and independent, not as complementary to any other source of truth within its domain, *mokṣa*. Reliance on it gives Śaṅkara an assurance which underlies his intellectual fervour and courage, his serene objectivity in meeting opponents, and the organic unity of his thought.

The misery of man's condition in the passing world of *saṃsāra* ruled by the law of *karman* and rebirth which makes man the binder of his own shackles is a *locus communis* of Indian culture in Śaṅkara's time. Instead of simply showing that the latter endorses it, the author might profitably have introduced the reader to Śaṅkara's criticism of Jaimini's conception of *karman* in *B.S.Bh.* 3, 2, 38-41 + 2, 1, 34-35 and *Bṛh. Up. Bh.* 3, 8, 9-12. He, however, does not fail to point out Śaṅkara's high estimation of human birth: man alone is capable of intellectual knowledge and infinite desire; this capacity gives every man access to the saving knowledge even though the study of *Śruti* requires qualifications which are the privilege of only few; but man is also free and can refuse to "cut off the tree of *saṃsāra*" and thus miss salvation.

The opposite of *saṃsāra* is Reality, i.e., the unchanging Absolute, the *Brahman-Ātman*. Its mark, indeed, is unchangeableness. Speech, being *saṃsāra*-bound, is radically unable to express it. Hence, Śaṅkara's apophatism is inflexible. It is rooted in the upaniṣadic *neti neti* which prescribes that the *Brahman* can only be attained "through elimination of all differences due to *upādhis*." *Upādhi* means finite and diversifying adjuncts or attributes or relations wrongly superimposed upon the infiniteness and simplicity of the Absolute. The author refers to this notion but without working it out. Śaṅkara's apophatism, however, is not Buddhistic. Though silence—of speech but with a mind entirely focused on the absolute Fullness—would be the most adequate attitude, the Upaniṣads themselves make use, without betraying apophatism, of positive appellations. And one of the most original and helpful contributions of Śaṅkara is justification of this practice through recourse to the theory of *lakṣaṇā*. This theory takes into account the secondary meanings which accrue to words (and concepts) from their function in contexted sentences. Through such a *lakṣyārtha*, a word may 'indicate' (*lakṣ-*) a reality beyond the area (*gocara*) of 'expressive' power of its primary meaning (*mukhyārtha*). In particular, some words whose primary meaning abstracts from both finiteness and infinity can be contextually infinitized so that their 'supreme meaning' (*paramārtha*) becomes 'indicative' of the Absolute. Such, for instance, are the words *satya* (reality) and *jñāna* (knowledge) used with *ananta* (infinite), which infinitizes them, in the definition of *Brahman* provided by *Taitt. Up.* 2, 1. The author is quite aware of this feature of Śaṅkara's exegesis but does not expose its full scope. Further, in denying its affinity with the Thomistic theory of analogy, he is only half-right. This theory, indeed, is primarily a theory of the secondary meanings of terms which differs little from the theory of *lakṣaṇā*, especially in its Śaṅkarian application; but it is prolonged by a theory of ontological participation which is foreign to Śaṅkara.

To the positive capacity of words thus to serve as pointers to the Absolute, Piantelli rightly adds the capacity of human consciousness to discover it at the very heart of its experience: in its experience of the universe (as the internal and transcendent Cause of all), in its awareness of 'I am' (as the innermost Self or *Ātman* of everyone), in its *cogito* (as the absolute and *per se* Light, *svayaṃjyoti*, Witness, *sākṣin*, Seer, *draṣṭṛ*, and Consciousness itself, *cit*, of every thinking). Our transitory vision would be impossible without that eternal Vision or Seer. Thus, in the most elevated sense (*paramārthataḥ*,) of the term *ātman*, there is but the unique *Ātman*. In *Upadeśasāhasri* 2, 18 translated by the author, Śaṅkara explains that our finite 'I' or *ātman* is but a mere reflection of that unique *Ātman* but Piantelli does not take up this important theory in his exposition.

This presence of Reality at the very root of consciousness relativises all the rest into unreality (or un-Reality, as I would prefer). Śaṅkara's loaded definition of these two terms, *sat* and *asat* (loaded inasmuch as it focuses only on the 'supreme sense' of *sat*) in his *Gītābhāṣya* is unfortunately neglected by Piantelli who simply writes, "impermanente—e dunque irreale" (135). Unreality comprises the whole realm of multiplicity, nothing of which—neither knowers nor objects—can ever be identified with the Real. The latter, therefore, is not a distinct object and in that sense is unknowable. It is often said that for Śaṅkara "all this is *māyā*" but Piantelli is careful to recall that Śaṅkara himself (as distinct from later disciples) speaks very little in terms of *māyā* and rather in the sense of marvellous, divine power, than of illusion. The term he affects is *avidyā*, nescience. All that it really implies for him would have been more relevant than the diverse theories of his followers rapidly mentioned by Piantelli. The latter, however, does not fail to quote the masterful text of *Bṛh. Up.* 4, 4, 7 which shows that *avidyā* is eternally surmounted by the *Ātman* which sees it as *avidyā* and is thus unaffected by it. Ordinary knowledge is imbued with *avidyā* but this does not mean that its objects have no reality at all. Rather they are undefinable (*anirvacanīya*) in terms of 'being' or 'non-being' taken in their supreme sense (*sad-asad-vilakṣaṇa*). The independent reality we spontaneously attribute to them vanishes as such at the moment of our awakening to *Vidyā*. Does this mean that ultimate truth negatives all reality apart from the *Ātman*? To this question Piantelli gives, and seems to adhere simply to, the facile answer that acosmism is not justified before awakening but is imposed by it. However, the rather intricate explanations he gives (145-152) are more refined than that. They should be read carefully. What they amount to is a defence of non-dualism against any confusion with monism and any compromise with dualism. The latter would admit that cosmic reality is in some regard or at some time *per se*; the first would uphold that the aseity of the Absolute renders it incapable of any true creativity. Of these two misconceptions the first is very ably refuted by the author but the second receives no proper treatment. Whereas Śaṅkara devotes numerous stretches of his writings to the topic of creative causality, it is nowhere considered seriously in this book.

If non-dualism is true, liberation is not really an aim to be attained but an eternal fact to which man awakens. Only so long as we are under the sway of *avidyā* can we conceive of it as an end to be reached by some way or means. This way is the teaching of the Upaniṣads duly inculcated by a guide who has himself overcome *avidyā*. It proceeds along the classical three steps of audition, reflection and intense meditation. It cannot be entered without proper qualifications, especially total renunciation and desisting from secular and even sacral activity. Śaṅkara's hard polemics against all *karmavādins* is here recalled. The author is aware that it nullifies the very presuppositions of the whole theory of *karman*. Liberation can take place in the very course of one's life (*jīvanmukti*) since it consists in a total awakening to absolute Consciousness which is ever-present. It is infinite Joy and Freedom.

Through Piantelli's book, Śaṅkara becomes alive and we are richly introduced to the profundity of his doctrine. For this and the many helps it provides, including an excellent bibliography, the author deserves all our gratitude.

Notes

[1] [R. De Smet, Review of Mario Piantelli, *Śaṅkara e la rinascità del Brāhmanesimo,* Maestri di Spiritualità, sezione Mondo Orientale (Fossano: Editrice Esperienze, 1974), first published in *Indica* **12**/1 (March 1975) 56-61, and reprinted here with kind permission. The review was also published in *Boletin de la Asociaciòn Española de Orientalistas* **11** (1975) 249-254 and *Indian Philosophical Quarterly* **4**/3 (April 1977) 429-435. After the publication details, the *Indica* version adds: "Review of an outstanding Italian book on Śaṅkara."]

[2] [The *Orientalistas* and the *Indian Philosophical Quarterly* texts read 'attaching' instead of 'absorbing.']

30

REVIEW OF PAUL HACKER, *KLEINE SCHRIFTEN*[1]

Among post-World War II indologists, Paul Hacker quickly won first rank as leader and inspirer. This was mainly due to the promises held by his renovated and ground-breaking method for the exploration of the historical development of ideas, themes and linguistic concepts in the Indian subcontinent, as we as to the results he achieved by it especially by clarifying the hermeneutics of Śāṅkara Vedānta and the history of its school. This is why we welcome with deep-felt gratitude this handy collection of his minor—but by no means unimportant—works. Our only regret is that it is not so complete to include the totality, and not only a few, of his book recensions and his theological articles. However, some of the latter will appear in a separate publication.

In his programmatic articles of 1960 and 1961, à propos of the text-units common with small differences to many Purāṇas which W. Kirfel had collected in his *Purāṇa Pañcalakṣaṇa*[2] and of which he had studied the developmental variations, Hacker proposed a new methodology. Kirfel's method should be extended so as to situate such comparable text-units within the whole of their area of development, not only backwards but also forwards. If this is done, it will appear that text-units which pertained originally to *Svayambhū-Brahmā* theism have passed through four phases of modification: (1) harmonization with Sāṁkhya, notwithstanding its atheistic and mechanistic bent; (2) harmonization with Buddhistic Vijñānavāda; (3) a Viṣṇuisation which corrects atheistic Vijñānavāda into a *bhakti*-theism (not a too difficult process because Viṣṇu is *jñānātmaka*, substantial knowledge); (4) a last modification through which Brahmā and

Śiva appear as mere forms of Viṣṇu (or Brahmā and Viṣṇu as mere forms of Śiva). Such phases have affected equally purāṇic texts concerned with cosmology, eschatology, etc. Their study should help towards an approximative mutual dating of Purāṇas or parts of Purāṇas (1-7).

But how can we infer from the side-by-sidedness of pre-existing, independent, text-units in the compilations of such anonymous literature the successivity of historical events?

(1) The primitive units, which Lüders tried to discover but could not treat sufficiently due to the limitations of his positivistic method, are to be investigated less for their primitive contents but rather for the clues their divergences in the different versions give as to what is earlier and later than them. Not only the contradictions, misunderstandings, corruptions, etc. of the units as compiled have to be noted (as by Lüders) for solving the question of origins, but each unit has to be seen as a 'geistige Gestalt' whose variations have historical 'geistig' motivations. There are in different times different reigning views, ideals and interests in different social-religious-cultural situations or local situations and leading representations, all of which can be reflected in the variations of a text. Hence, the later versions deserve the same attention as the primitive text.

(2) This search for the divergencies, and not only the mutual affinities, of the successive versions stipulates that certain procedures must be eliminated, e.g., speaking of *the* philosophy of the Upaniṣads, *the* philosophy of the Mahābhārata, *the* doctrine of *dharma* of Manusmṛti, or *the* purāṇic Sāṁkhya, etc.

(3) The researcher must take up definite 'geistiger Gestalten,' e.g., a myth or one element of a myth, a doctrine or a complex of teachings, etc. This, of course, gives only partial results. More integral results must await these.

(4) He must attend to the composition (Redaktion) itself. The more or less literal agreements between such units must refer him not only to a primitive state but also to its re-workings; and these have to be explored no longer through purely philological criteria but through inner criteria which pertain to the history of ideas: "why and to what purpose and in which sense is that text-unit integrated in that *purāṇa*?" He should endeavour to find the different times of such integrations and adaptions, their regional locations, and the enlargings, interpolations and word-variants.

There is also the fact that in the literature of compilation the same topic is at times brought forth according to various traditions which are merely juxtaposed, or that a tradition is used in various senses. Attention to the method [of] redaction will often point to a development of topic rather than an interpolation. For instance, in *M.Bh.* 12, 231-232, a development from an old mechanistic cosmology to a *Brahmā*-theistic, then a *Brahman*-mechanistic, and finally a theistic one; noting, however, that different conceptions were often held at the same epoch by different circles (8-17).

The same ideas concerning his method are developed with more precisions [on] pp. 18-32 and to some extent pp. 33-40. They are at work in exemplary fashion in his study, pp. 167-204, of the Sāṁkhyanization of the emanation doctrine through *M.Bh.*, Manu and several Purāṇas. But it is chiefly through his investigations of Vedānta that Hacker became influent.

He attacks, first, the problem of authorship of the mass of works attributed to Śaṅkarācārya or rather, as he shows, Śaṅkarabhagavatpāda (41-58). Then the problem of Śaṅkara's idealism or cryptobuddhism (59-68): here, on the basic of an analysis of *Bṛh. Up. Bh.* 4, 3, 2ff, he is able to show that Rāmānūja's *Śrī Bhāṣya, Mahāpūrvapakṣa*, does not represent the real Śaṅkara but a later development. Contrary to this presentation, Śaṅkara in his theory of knowledge does not go from perception to Self but from Self to perception and produces a metaphysics of knowledge. He remains on the level of [Sāṁkhya] dualism when he opposes Self and non-Self but in other places (*B.S.Bh.* 2, 1, 14) he overcomes this dualism on the ground of the identity between Cause and products. The derivation by later Vedāntins of the unique Reality and the illusory character of objects is omitted by Śaṅkara who abides by his doctrine of the Self as *Sākṣin* and opposes Buddhist illusionism. He never says that the world is *vijñāna-pariṇāma*, a mind-metamorphosis. Contrary to the Vedāntin attacked by Rāmānuja, he does not say that *Sat* (Being) is only *Anubhūti* (Knowledge) but rather, in *B.S.Bh.* 3, 2, 21, that *Sat* is *Bodha* and *Bodha* (Thought) is *Sat*, without seeming interested in the option between idealism and realism. In this discussion I missed a reference of Hacker to *Bh. Gītā Bh.* 2, 16.

Next follows (69-109) the most important study of the particularities of the doctrine and terminology of *Avidyā*, *Nāmarūpa*, *Māyā* and *Īśvara* proper to Śaṅkara. It is too well-known and too rich to be summed up here. The further article on the conception of man brings forth well analyzed materials to the study of this important topic (243-251).

With the help of his method, Hacker advances considerably the history and chronology of Vedānta. For instance, his enquiry concerning the relations of early Advaitins to Vaiṣṇavism (205-212) extends to Śaṅkara's *Upaniṣad-bhāṣyas* the observation made earlier by G.A. Jacob in his study of *Brahma-sūtra-bhāṣya* that Śaṅkara often used theistic terms instead of impersonalistic ones and ignored again and again the (later) distinction between *Param Brahman* and *Īśvara*. He then enquires into the concrete type of theism favoured by Śaṅkara. Surprisingly, and contrary to an opinion first circulated by as late a writer as Vidyāraṇya, the author of the legendary *Śaṅkara-dig-vijaya*, it is not Śaivism but Vaiṣṇavism. Hacker could not find the slightest trace of any partiality for, or even proximity to, Śaivism in any of the indubitably or probably authentic writings of Śaṅkara. On the contrary, he found unambiguous indications that the Vaiṣṇava religion was more familiar and even acceptable to Śaṅkara than Śaivism, whose contemporary theology is rejected without qualification in *B.S.Bh.* 2, 2, 37-41.

For instance, Śaṅkara commenting on *B.S.* 1, 2, 7 says: "The Lord, who is characterized by extreme subtleness, etc. is said to be perceptible, i.e., visible [to the inner sense] in the lotus of the heart, just as Hari [= Viṣṇu] is in the *śālāgrāma* stone.... The Lord, though omnipresent, graciously allows himself to be reverently meditated upon there." What is here compared with Hari is not the *Lower Brahman*, which is an anthropomorphic notion of the Godhead, but the transcendent *Highest Self*, who cannot become the object of meditation except under a symbol, here the token of Viṣṇu. In another 6 passages which refer to this symbolization, Śaṅkara refers to Viṣṇu rather than Śiva to whom he would have alluded spontaneously if he had hailed from a Śaiva environment (and then he would have named the deity Śiva rather than Rudra as he does in 3, 3, 32). The case is similar in his commentaries on *Taitt. Up.* 1, 6, 1; 1, 8, 1; *Muṇḍ. Up.* 2, 1, 4; *Praśna Up.* 5, 2; *Bṛh. Up.* 1, 1, 1; 5, 1, 1; *Chānd. Up.* 6, 16, 3;

7, 1, 4; 8, 1, 1. A particularly revealing case is his explanation of the *Sambuddha* whom Gauḍapāda invokes in *Māṇḍukya-kārikā* 4, 1. There is no reasonable doubt that Gauḍapāda means the Buddha Śākyamuni but Śaṅkara interprets *sambuddha* as *Nārāyaṇa* the *Puruṣottama* (= Viṣṇu). Further, Śaṅkara's rejection of the *Pāñcarātra* theology of Vaiṣṇavism concerns only its theory of divine emanations (*vyuha*) and is mixed with sympathy for its conception of God as both the reality-providing cause (*upādāna*) and the structure-providing cause (*nimitta-kāraṇa*) of the universe, and of the type of worship due to him: "We do not controvert the doctrine that *Nārāyaṇa*, who is... the supreme Self and the Self of all, has multiplied himself through himself into single forms.... Nor do we raise any objection if it is intended to worship this Bhagavān with unceasing concentration of mind by approaching him [probably in his temple] or by other means." No trace of a similar sympathy for Śaiva doctrines or practices is discernible in the *B.S.Bh.* Hacker remarks here:

> We should take due notice of this fact and we should utilize the result of our investigation when examining the problem of the authenticity of other works ascribed to Śaṅkara. We should cease either to repeat, on the authority of some of the innumerable spurious works, the myth of Śaṅkara having had a particular predilection for Śaivism, or to make him the champion of an idea of unity [of all the religions or varieties of Hinduism] which, to judge from all authentic documents, was quite foreign to his thought (210).

He further notes that Śaṅkara's conception of *māyā* tallies with the Vaiṣṇava conception of the term. For instance, in *B.S.Bh.* 1, 1, 20, he uses it to denote the extraordinary power of *Parameśvara*, the Highest Lord. As to the *maṅgālacaraṇas* (initial invocation of a deity at the beginning or the end of a writing) those of Śaṅkara are not revealing but at least 4 of his early disciples address such invocation to Viṣṇu, a fact which places them in a Vaiṣṇava environment. As a contrast, Hacker notes that Maṇḍana Miśra, a contemporary and somewhat rival of Śaṅkara, calls the state of liberation *paramaśivabhāva* which suggests that he hailed from a Śaiva environment.

As we have seen, Hacker had, early in his career, established and repeatedly tested a number of criteria by which he could separate the spurious from the authentic works of Śaṅkara. His list of authentic works comprises *Upadeśasāhasrī,* the commentaries on ten Upaniṣads (including the *Māṇḍūkya* but excluding the *Śvetāśvatara*), on the *Bhagavad Gītā*, on the *Adhyātma-paṭala* of the *Āpastamba-Dharmasūtra*, and on the *Brahma-sūtras*. When in 1952 the *Yoga-bhāṣya-vivaraṇa*, a sub-commentary on the *Yoga-bhāṣya*, was published,[3] he examined the question of the alleged identity of its author with Śaṅkara. This identity, he says, can be established on the assumption that Śaṅkara was first an adherent of Pātañjala Yoga and then turned an Advaitin. Indeed, some features of his authentic Advaita works, especially peculiarities of his doctrines of Nescience and the Self which he explains, distinguish Śaṅkara's thought from that of other known Advaita authors. In the light of this assumption, Hacker advances the following:

> It is conceivable that Śaṅkara was introduced into Advaita by a teacher who interpreted to him Gauḍapāda's *Māṇḍūkya-Kārikās* and he did his work so well that the teacher entrusted him with writing a commentary on that poem. For the *Māṇḍūkyabhāṣya* stands unique among Śaṅkara's writings by coming closest to Yoga, on the one hand, and exhibiting, on the other hand, some traits of monism which Śaṅkara seems to have dropped in his subsequent career. Closely related to the way of thinking of the *Māṇḍūkyabhāṣya* is *Prakaraṇa* 19 of the *Pādyaprabandha* of the *Upadeśasāhasrī*. The *Taittirīyopaniṣad-bhāṣya*, then, marks the transition from Śaṅkara's earlier period to his mature works (p. 241).

This hypothetical reconstruction of Śaṅkara's early career is further used to account for some contradictions which appear to mar his commentary of the *Māṇḍūkya Upaniṣad*. The complexity of this article (252-269) does not lend it to be summarized here but its riches will delight the specialist.

Other important articles are devoted to the Vedānta not only of Śaṅkara but also of his successors. They concern the Vedāntic idea of Person (270-292), Being and Spirit (293-319) and the concept of Spirit in Vedāntism (*Cit*) and in Neoplatonism (*Nous*) (320-337).

Still concerned with Hinduism but less specialized and reaching towards a larger readership are articles on Hindu faith (*śraddhā*) (360-375 and 437-475), on Hindu tolerance and intolerance (376-388), on two Hindu accounts of cosmology (389-403 and 484-495), on magic, God, person and grace (428-

436), on *dharma* (496-509), and on the development of the conception of *avatāra* (404-427),

A criticism of current misconceptions regarding (a) the god Brahmā, (b) Śaṅkara and Advaitism, (c) tolerance, and (d) the unity of Hinduisms (476-483) ought not to be missed by specialists. It is a good starting-point for the reading of a set of articles critically concerned with Neo-Hinduism (510-608). The chief initiators and prominent writers of Neo-Hinduism are Bankim, Vivekananda, Aurobindo, Gandhi, and Radhakrishnan. Their ways of thinking differ markedly from those of modern Hindu traditionalism. In both we find an assimilation of extraneous Western conceptions but whereas traditionalism maintains a living continuity with the past, Neo-Hinduism finds this past inadequate and breaks away from the authenticity of its essential conceptions and ways of behaviour. A Radhakrishnan asks characteristically: "How can we make it somewhat more relevant to the intellectual climate and social environment of our time?" This loyalty to the present actually implies a disloyalty to the past, which has to be reinterpreted.

Hacker shows in [a] well-documented way where reinterpretation becomes betrayal in the neo-hinduistic treatment of such central conceptions as idol-worship, *dharma*, faith, *advaita*, orthodoxy (*sanātana dharma*), *ahiṁsā*, sacrifice (as the various types of gifts: *dāna* demanded by Vinobā Bhāve), experience (especially religious or mystical), revelation, law of *karma* and transmigration. Ancient notions are seemingly retained but reinterpretation fills them with a new content which is Western and often Christian (but of a latitudinarian type). This modernization is an outcome of nationalism (itself a Western notion) which is the chief impulse of Neo-Hindu thinking. This nationalism is essentially more cultural than political and includes the idea that India has a message to proclaim to the world. Neo-Hindus claim that all religions are equal in essence or value and that Hinduism is their all-including unity, an assertion from which they derive their claim of tolerance. Radhakrishnan is the epitome of those claims (580-608). Neo-Hinduism constitutes the 'geistige Situation' against which Hacker visualizes critically today's encounter of Christians with Hinduism (732-737) but his evaluation of this encounter and of the budding 'Indian Christian Theology' is chiefly to be found in articles which will form a supplementary collection. However, among the 15 book-reviews included in the present one, 5 concern this encounter.

The present collection contains also 4 articles on Hindi as the candidate for the status of national language of independent India or on grammatical particularities of this neo-Aryan language (609-731).

The devoted editor, Lambert Schmithausen, has brought his collecting work to perfection by providing an apparently complete bibliography of Hacker's writing and a very complete index (826-914).

To whatever topic of Indian studies Hacker directed his critical investigation, he threw considerable light, especially on Śāṅkara Vedānta and on Neo-Hinduism which were the chief areas of his search. His work on Vedānta is of the highest quality and I wish to record here my gratefulness for the guidance it has given me for the further pursuit of my own study of this subject. Yet, I always regretted that he never really entered into a perspective which I consider fundamental to Śaṅkara's undertaking. I mean Śaṅkara's perception that the theological language of the Upaniṣads is radically analogical or, to say it in Indian terms, *lakṣaṇā*-ic, *lakṣaṇā* designating the process by which we pass from the primary but mundane meaning of terms to some secondary meaning (as required by the context), in this case to their most elevated meaning (*paramārtha*). Thus the decisive terms of the Upaniṣads, i.e., all those which 'indicate' (though they cannot 'express') the *Brahman-Ātman*, have to be focused upon according to their highest possible meaning (*paramārthataḥ*), as Śaṅkara explains so lucidly in his exegesis of the essential definition of *Brahman* as "Reality-Knowledge-Infinite" (*Taitt. Up*. 2, 1: *Satyam-jñānam-anantam*). This type of exegesis commands in Śaṅkara's writings important notations regarding the capacity of the human mind to transcend the primary level of mundane language and concepts. Hacker with his thorough scholarship would have been able to follow up these notations and to give us a really new understanding of Śaṅkara Bhagavadpāda.

After writing this review the sad news reached me that Paul Hacker had passed away to his reward. It is with deep sorrow that I now evoke not only the great scholar but the personal friend and the convinced Christian and express my condolences to his desolate wife and daughter. To us, scholars, his chief books and this collection of his minor writings constitute a legacy whose seminal value will not perish.

Notes

[1] [R. De Smet, Review of Paul Hacker, *Kleine Schriften,* herausgegeben von Lambert Schmithausen. Glasenapp-Stiftung: Band 15 (Wiesbaden: Steiner, 1978), *Boletin de la Asociaciòn Española de Orientalistas* **16** (1980) 267-273. Reprinted here with kind permission of De Nobili College, Pune, all efforts to contact the *Boletin* having failed.]

[2] [W. Kirfel, *Das Purāṇa Pañcalakṣaṇa* (Bonn: K. Schroeder, 1927).]

[3] [*Yoga-bhāṣya-vivaraṇa*, tr. and ed. P.S. Rama Sastri and S.R. Krishnamurthi Sastri (Madras: Government Oriental Publication, 1952). See the recent new translation, *Yogasūtrabhāṣyavivaraṇa of Śaṅkara: Vivaraṇa Text with English Translation and Critical Notes along with Text and English Translation of Patanjali's Yogasūtras and Vyāsabhāṣya*, vols. 1 and 2, by T.S. Rukmani (New Delhi: Munshiram Manoharlal, 2001).]

31

REVIEW OF WILHELM HALBFASS, *INDIEN UND EUROPA: PERSPEKTIVEN IHRER GEISTIGEN BEGEGNUNG*[1]

On the side of Europe, the relationship with India takes from its very outset the form of a *quest.* As early as the fifth century BC, India appears to the Greeks as the fountainhead of philosophical wisdom and becomes the object of an intense curiosity. But their access to the secretive essence of its culture is only peripheric and the sum total of their gleanings is meagre. Nevertheless, their goal remains tantalisingly attractive to the early Christians who take up the same quest but are unable to advance it much and who soon find themselves cut off from India by the barrier of Islam. The Muslims in turn are attracted by India but the information their travellers begin to collect from the ninth century contains little of real value in the domain of religion and philosophy until al-Bīrūnī (973-1048). Al-Bīrūnī studies Sanskrit and seeks to know the sources of Hindu thought. He succeeds in getting acquainted with the Vedas, the *Bhagavad Gītā*, works of *Dharmaśāstra*, several *purāṇas* and various texts of the classical philosophical *darśanas*. He even translates the *Yogasūtras* of Patañjali and parts of one of their commentaries and also some texts of Sāṁkhya. His *Ta'rīkh al-Hind* does not then obtain the success it deserves but is followed by other valuable works of later Muslim enquirers. Yet the Muslims' curiosity about India seems to be of a less intense quality than the Europeans' fascination which is reawakened by Vasco da Gama's successful sea-journey to Calicut in 1498.

Very soon, the Catholic missionaries—Franciscans, Dominicans and, chiefly, Jesuits—endeavour to enter by the few alleys they find open into the hidden mind of Hindu India. By way of letters and reports their discoveries reach Europe and excite a vast interest. In the beginning of the sixteenth century, the Jesuit Roberto de Nobili manages to become the first European Sanskrit scholar and to get directly acquainted with several of the Vedas and Upaniṣads, with the basic texts of the *darśanas* and with the myths of the Purāṇas. At the same time, he opens up to the Catholic Church the largest measure of adaptation to the customs of the caste culture, himself adopts the renouncer's (*saṅnyāsin's*) garb and mode of life, and discerns the important truths and values by which the Hindu tradition is pre-attuned to Christianity. His successors continue this penetration to the heart of Indian culture. Through their reports published in the eighteenth century series of *Lettres édifiantes et curieuses*, particularly those of the Fathers Pons, Bouchet and Calmette,[2] an amount of reliable essential information about Hinduism gets diffused through Western Europe; this is further increased by the published books of Bartholomäus Ziegenbalg (1683-1719) and other Protestant missionaries and by the travel accounts of laymen like Bernier, Tavernier and Sonnerat.[3] All this—together with parallel information regarding China—influences, often more than superficially, the minds of many European thinkers and even the general culture of eighteenth century Europe; and it lays the ground for the growth of the new science of indology from the terminal years of the eighteenth century.

Henceforth, India becomes for the European intellectuals, especially the philosophers, an inescapable sector of their universalist horizon. With astonishing rapidity sanskritist translators publish basic works and masterpieces of its immense literature which permit an evaluation of the vast resources and the depth of its accumulated legacy. This diffusion excites the enthusiasm of the Romantics, the cultural self-criticism of the humanists, and new perspectives of investigation among the philosophers. After Herder, Goethe, Novalis, the chief names here are F. and A.W. Schlegel, G.W.F. Hegel,[4] F.W.J. Schelling, A. Schopenhauer, F. Nietzsche, M. Müller and P. Deussen.

The above presentation is only a sketch of the first part of the book under review. Professor Halbfass's treatment is practically exhaustive, impeccably accurate and sensitive to the differences of phases and the cultural repercussions of this historical development spread over centuries. But what he provides most originally is what it meant for the European mind (*Geist*): not only a search for objective exotic and curious data, but a subjective disquieting, a hopeful expectation of revelations about itself, a self-criticism and a rethinking of its own basic assumptions and conceptions. To the Greek, India appears be pristine, parental, the direct heir of the origin, the guardian of the keys of primordial wisdom. To the Christian, it appears to have preserved in the midst of many adulterating accretions pure fragments of divine revelation. To many a philosopher, it seems to be in possession of large stretches of *philosophia perennis*. To the Romantic, it is an *Urvolk* with its *Ursprache* and its *Urreligion*. To a Hegel, Hinduism is the religion of Fantasy where the universal but still abstract unity of the Absolute Substance "is more closely related to the Spirit since this abstract unity is present as the very ego" (*Hegels Werke* **11**:310). To the European, India is the object of a promising search; he hopes to find in it hidden pieces of his self-identity, prototypes of his concepts, complements of his aspiration. It moves him, but as an immobile mover.

Indeed, the Indian counterpart of this polarization is a stance of incuriosity, disdain and tranquil self-satisfaction. In his study of the traditional Indian xenology, Halbfass says:

> Im traditionellen Hinduismus ist nichts nach Alternativen und Herausforderungen, nach fremde Grenzen oder Ursprüngen der eigenen Identität, nach Gegenständen exotischer Neugier und Zielen der Belehrung oder Bekehrung gesucht worden: Indien hat den Westen dadurch entdeckt, dass es von ihm entdecket und erschlossen *wurde*, ist ihm aus dem Gesucht-und-Entdeckt *werden* heraus begegnet. Die Entdeckung des Westens, die Begegnung mit ihm erscheint nicht als Resultat und Vollendung geschichtlicher Entwicklungen, sondern als plötzlicher, von aussen herbei-geführte Bruch. (191)[5]

Halbfass, however, is aware that in the present state of research, no full-fledged account of the Indian xenology is yet possible. But a broad survey reveals the unequivocal influence of the caste system and the elaborate *dharma* conception towards the self-enclosing of orthodox Hindu society into its own self-sufficiency. The foreigner is excluded as *mleccha* (barbarian) or even *asura* (demon). For a time the Greeks are awkwardly assimilated to the hierarchy of castes and some other invaders become completely included into it though generally with an inferior status. But the ever renewed effort of the orthodox leaders is to keep unsullied the purity—essentially the ritual purity—of the twice-born (*dvija*), Even the languages of the *mleccha* should not be learnt (*na mlecchabhāṣām śikṣeta*). At the outset of the 'Sanskrit Renaissance' in the second century BC, Patañjali, the great grammarian, declares: one should study grammar in order not to become a *mleccha*. Foreigners are worse even than the outcastes (the *Cāṇḍāla*) because they are completely alien to the *dharma* (the integrated system of customs, laws, rituals, conceptions of polity, morality and religion of the Aryas) either due to forfeiture or to natural exclusion. They are impure and any contact with them should be shunned. A widespread tendency is to consider them as devoid of morality and even beastly (*paśudharmin*). No aggressiveness is normally exhibited towards them but they are quietly ignored. Nothing of value (apart from some technical inventions) can be expected from them. No borrowing of ideas is even conceivable. The *dharma* is eternal, perfect, unchangeable and self-sufficient; it provides efficiently for all the goals of man, including the highest, final liberation. Thus there is no tendency at all to look for another 'way' to salvation among the religious beliefs of foreign peoples. Although al-Bīrūnī remarks that in times prior to the eleventh century the Hindus had been ready to learn from the achievements of the Greeks and Arabs in mathematics, astrology, and astronomy, he yet notes the extraordinary ethnocentrism of the Hindus of his time, their inclination to overestimate their own culture, to enclose themselves within it and to take no notice of any foreign science or religion. If India had become totally Buddhist or Jaina, another stance might have dominated. Buddhism is not ethnocentric but universalistic and adaptive. Jainism with its theory of a plurality of complementary viewpoints is open to inclusivism. But Buddhism became extinct in India after the year 1000 and Jainism became confined to a small minority. Thus Hindu India remained static, insulated and self-involved, even under the repeated knockings at its door by the Europeans after Vasco da Gama, until the dawn of the nineteenth century when the leaders of the 'Indian Renaissance' overturned its long isolation.

Halbfass surveys this modern period with the same excellence that characterises his first 220 pages. But now across description of the facts he traces the radical change of mentality of the Indian people from the moment Rammohan Roy opens it to concrete universalism. First, the euphoric phase of the learning of a foreign language, English, by intellectuals avid to get hold of all the offerings of the West and their imbibition of new ideas in religion, philosophy, politics, ethics and the modern sciences. Then, the reaction of the die-hard traditionalists. And, finally, the compromise solution arrived at by the promoters of Neo-Hinduism and Neo-Vedānta. Inspired by the writings of the late Paul Hacker he complements this with enlightening chapters on the traditional concepts of *darśana* and *ānvīkṣikī* as distinct from the Western concept of philosophy, on the Indian appropriation of the concept of philosophy in modern Hinduism, on the metamorphosis of the concept of *dharma* from traditional to modern Hinduism, and on the so-called lack of historical sense of the Hindus, correcting on his way many facile generalizations. Finally, he balances the ambiguities of neo-hinduistic universalism with the uncertainties of the modern West and awakens anew the European inclination to a self-doubting and self-questioning which may prove to be salutary.

Halbfass's book is a gift to his indologist colleagues. Due its comprehensiveness, thoroughness and clear delineation of the characteristic aspects of the encounter between Europe and India, it will become a trusted work of reference. According to his intention, it has prepared the way for a protracted dialogue which should not be historically naive.[6]

Notes

[1] [R. De Smet, Review of Wilhelm Halbfass, *Indien und Europa: Perspektiven ihrer geistigen Begegnung* (Basel/Stuttgart: Schwabe, 1981), *Indian Theological Studies* 19/2 (June 1982) 183-188; reprinted here with permission. The book has since been published in English as *India and Europe: An Essay in Philosophical Understanding* (Albany: SUNY Press, 1988 / Delhi: Motilal Banarsidass, 1990).]

[2] [Charles Le Gobien, et al, *Lettres édifiantes et curieuses écrites des missions étrangères par quelques missionnaires de la Compagnie de Jesus*, 34 vols. (Paris: Chez Nicolas Le Clerc, 1703-1776).]

[3] [Francois Bernier (1620-88), *Un libertin dans l'Inde moghole: Les voyages de François Bernier (1656-1669)* (Chandeigne, 2008), ET *Travels In The*

Mogul Empire A.D. 1656-1668 (Asian Educational Services, 1996); Jean-Baptiste Tavernier (1605-1689), *Suite des Voyages de Mr Tavernier: Ou Nouveau Recueil de Plusieurs Relations et Traitez (1680)* (Kessinger, 2009); Pierre Sonnerat (1748-1814), *Voyage à la Nouvelle-Guinée* (Paris: Ruault, 1776) and *Voyage aux Indes orientales et à la Chine, fait depuis 1774 jusqu'à 1781* (Paris, 1782).]

[4] Halbfass's excellent chapter on Hegel may be usefully compared with M. Hulin, *Hegel et l'Orient* (Paris: Vrin, 1979); R. Leuze, *Die ausserchristlichen Religionen bei Hegel* (Göttingen, 1975); and, most importantly, the thorough dissertation of I. Viyagappa, *G.W.F. Hegel's Concept of Indian Philosophy* (Roma: Università Gregoriana Editrice, 1980).

[5] [Traditional Hinduism does not seek alternatives and challenges, remote shores or sources of one's identity, objects of exotic curiosity and goals of instruction or conversion; India has discovered the West by *allowing itself* to be discovered and accessed, has encountered it by *allowing itself* to be sought and found. The discovery of the West, the encounter with it, appears not as the result and accomplishment of a historical development, but as a sudden irruption induced from the outside.]

[6] The interested reader may also turn to Edward Said, *L'orientalisme: l'Orient créé par l'Occident* (Paris: Seuil, 1980) 398 pp. [ET *Orientalism: Western Conceptions of the Orient*, rev. ed. with new afterword (Penguin, 1995).]

32

REVIEW OF WILHELM HALBFASS, *STUDIES IN KUMĀRILA AND ŚAṄKARA*[1]

These three important studies plus appendix are a welcome by-product of the vast enquiry undertaken by the author for his earlier work, *Indien und Europa* (Basel/Stuttgart, 1981).[2] They display in depth his wide indological scholarship, philological accuracy, intellectual acumen, critical discrimination and, in the appendix, an uncanny sense for detecting clues toward solution of problems of authorship.

Halbfass studies first "Kumārila on *Ahiṁsā* and *Dharma.*" Like all Mīmāṃsakas, Kumārila is a fundamentalist of the Veda. In a non-Vedic time he defends the sole authority of the Veda in matters of *dharma*. Under the influence of Buddhism and Jainism, *ahiṁsā* has generally become accepted as the fundamental virtue in *dharma*, and the retribution of *karma* has been generalized into a universal law. Kumārila rejects this twofold distortion of the Vedic teaching, especially against Sāṁkhya and Yoga. The non-human Veda is positive law and, therefore, specific. It gives specific commands of *ahiṁsā* (e.g., not to kill a Brahmin) and of *hiṁsā* (in respect of sacrificial victims). The latter is only exceptional but, as in Grammar, exceptions are stronger than general rules. Such exceptions cannot issue into painful rewards. The law of *karma* denies this but there is no scriptural, perceptual or inferential ground for it. Pleasure and pain cannot be the criterion of right and wrong. Like a sword, *hiṁsā* is morally neutral. But the dhārmic precept of *hiṁsā* is not to be extended any more than the command of *ahiṁsā*. Kumārila condemns the *saṁsāra mocakas* (deliverers from this world of changes) who used to practise a sort of (ritualistic?) mercy-killing. Halbfass wonders who they were: a

Śaiva sect? Thugs? Mlecchas? Pārsi Māgas? In any case, Kumārila rejects all attempts to define *dharma* in terms of altruism. Further, he endeavours to refute the Buddhist accusation that the Veda is no better than Mleccha customs. As presented by the Buddhists, *ahiṁsā* is like milk offered in a dog's bladder! And there is no need of apologetics for Vedic ritual *hiṁsā*. Halbfass brings forth echoes of Kumārila's polemics or parallel teachings in Prabhākara, Śālikanāthamiśra, Udayana, etc. He also tones down H.P. Schmidt's thesis about the Vedic origin of *ahiṁsā*.[3]

His second study concerns the relations of reason and Vedic revelation in Śaṅkara. This was a focus of my own research and it has not ceased to occupy my mind for almost 40 years; yet my comprehension of it has been both confirmed and enriched by the author's penetrating and sensitive study.

For the two Mīmāṃsās, the *Śruti* is eternal and not the utterance of any individuals (*apauruṣeya*). It is a special *pramāṇa* (valid source of truth) either for *dharma* or for *Brahmavidyā*. It is distinct from all other *pramāṇas* which are powerless in its domain. Against this traditional assertion, the Neo-Vedāntins, beginning with Ram Mohan Roy, have tried to interpret *Śruti* either as a privileged sort of reason or as supra-rational experience or as superior intuition. Similarly, Radhakrishnan and many others (and even some Western scholars) have exposed Śaṅkara's 'philosophy' as if it were something like Plato's or any other Western system based on autonomous reason. Śaṅkara himself, however, always upheld the *apauruṣeyatva* axiom and the distinction between *Śruti* and *yukti* (human reasoning). But his formulation of their relations is more elaborate, complex and refined than that of Pūrva Mīmāṃsā. First, he reverses its view which gave primacy to the Vedic commands and ranked even the Upaniṣads as mere ancillary statements (*arthavāda*); he gives primacy to the upaniṣadic 'great sayings' (*mahā-vākya*) and does not even consider the commands (*vidhi*) as presupposed by, or useful to, the pursuit of the truth about the *Brahman-Ātman* (*Brahmajijñāsā*). Similarly, he upholds the sovereignty of the upaniṣadic *Śruti* in this, it exclusive domain, which is inaccessible to autonomous, unguided reasoning. But he accepts reasoning guided by *Śruti*. There is an 'alliance' between *Śruti* and the human mind. Not only is *Śruti* pedagogical, the prototype of good teaching, but it provides middle terms for legitimate inferences. The second step of the method it prescribes (*śravaṇa manana nididhyāsana*) demands the utmost effort of the mind to understand rationally the contents ascertained exegetically in *śravaṇa*. But it would be too much to demand that every *Śruti* assertion be supported by an example (*dṛṣṭānta*) from common experience. Just as *Smṛti* is valid insofar as it conforms to *Śruti*, reasoning is valid if it is grounded in *Śruti*. This is the *Vedamūlatva* principle. Once understood, it permits to explain away the alleged inconsistencies denounced by some recent scholars, especially T. Vetter and H. Brückner. Śaṅkara may present an entire 'argumentative' section, such as the prose ch. 2 of *Upadeśasāhasrī*, without abandoning the *Vedamūlatva* principle or contradicting his numerous explicit assertions of the authority of *Śruti* in its own domain. Yet Śaṅkara's teaching is not totally without oscillations and ambiguities.

Halbfass points out some in his exposition of the method of *anvaya-vyatireka* (coordinate presence and absence or continuity-and-discontinuity). To its earlier study by Hacker,[4] Van Buitenen,[5] Mayeda,[6] Vetter[7] and Cardona,[8] he adds important precisions and even corrections for which there is unfortunately no room in this review.

His third study is about Śaṅkara and Kumārila on the plurality of religious traditions. Vivekananda and other neo-Vedāntins tried to reconcile all religions into 'the infinite of Vedānta' as in an all-inclusive meta-religion. Radhakrishnan extended to all faiths the conception of *samanvaya* (harmony). But for Śaṅkara, *samanvaya* is of the Upaniṣads only, although he may say almost casually that the one *Ātman* is the ultimate referent of all human views and teachings. He rejects the pretention of Sāṁkhya, Vaiśeṣika, etc. to have issued 'omniscient' teachers and thus reliable teachers of liberation and in general, any reliability of 'unguided' reasoning or intuition. He is aware of the danger of relativism and his approach is conservative and restrictive like that of Mīmāṃsā. The 'qualifications' (*adhikāra*) are determined by Veda; their list should not be extended. A man's intelligence is no *adhikāra*.

Unlike Rāmānuja and other Vaiṣṇava Vedāntins, Śaṅkara admits no revelation besides the Veda.

Kumārila, who accepts the idea of 'lost Vedas', nevertheless rejects the idea that Buddhist teaching is a lost Veda, because it contradicts the known Veda. Yet he traces Jaina and Buddhist *ahiṁsā* to some Vedic rules, and some of their philosophy to *arthavādas* or Upaniṣads. While criticizing them, he is willing to credit them with a relative and pedagogical usefulness and to find a value in the confrontation of different views. But, on the ground of *Vedamūlatva*, he rebukes the objection that, if variety is acceptable, one should include all possible variations. The similar objection that the 'word of the Lord' (as Nyāya views the Veda) may be found in other traditions is refuted by Jayantabhaṭṭa on the ground of the restrictive rule *mahājana parigṛhītatva* (accept only what the majority—or the great—accept). Kumārila rejects this criterion as well as *loka-prasiddhi* (common acceptance). Around AD 500, the *Brahmaśabda* Vedāntin, Bhartṛhari, had taught that the Speech-*Brahman* differentiates itself into all human views and teachings! (In connection with this topic I draw attention to a recent article of K.K. Gopal in *Purāṇa* **26**/1 [1984] 21-32.)

The Appendix presents notes towards the elucidation of the Śaṅkara or Pseudo-Śaṅkara authorship of *Yoga-sūtra-bhāṣya-vivaraṇa*. Halbfass, through a careful analysis of portions of it, shows the uncertainty of Hacker's assumption (of a young Śaṅkara authorship) too blindly trusted by Vetter.[9]

Notes

[1] [R. De Smet, Review of Wilhelm Halbfass, *Studies in Kumārila and Śaṅkara. Verlag für Orientalistische Fachpublikationen* (Reinbeck, 1983), *Indian Theological Studies* **22**/2 (1985) 205-209 and *Journal of the American Oriental Society* **105**/2 (1985) 373-374. Reprinted here courtesy *Indian Theological Studies*.]

[2] [See ch. 31 above, note 1.]

[3] [H.P. Schmidt, "The Origin of *ahiṁsā*," *Mélanges d'Indianisme à la mémoire de Louis Renou* (Paris: Boccard, 1968) 625-655.]

[4] [Paul Hacker, *Untersuchungen über Texte des frühen Advaitavāda, 1. Die Schüler Śaṅkaras* (Mainz: Verlag der Akademie der Wissenschaften und der Literatur, 1950).]

[5] [J.A.B. van Buitenen, *Rāmānuja's Vedārthasaṃgraha* (Poona, 1956) 62-64.]
[6] [See S. Mayeda, "An Introduction to the Life and Thought of Śaṅkara," *Śaṅkara's Upadeśasāhasrī* (Delhi: Motilal Banarsidass, 2006) **2**:50-53.]
[7] [Tillmann Vetter, "Zur Bedeutung des Illusionismus bei Śaṅkara," *Wiener Zeitschrift für die Kunde Süd- und Ostasiens* 12-13 (1969) 407-423, and *Studien zur Lehre und Entwicklung Śaṅkaras* (Vienna: De Nobili Research Library, 1979).]
[8] [George Cardona, "*Anvaya* and *Vyatireka* in Indian Grammar," *Adyar Library Bulletin* **31-32** (1967-68) 313-352, and "On Reasoning from *Anvaya* and *Vyatireka* in Early Advaita," *Studies in Indian Philosophy: A Memorial Volume in Honour of Pandit Suklaji Sanghvi*, ed. D. Malvania and N.J. Shah (Ahmedabad: L.V. Institute of Indology, 1981) 87.]
[9] [P. Hacker, "Śaṅkara der Yogin und Śaṅkara der Advaitin: Einige Beobachtungen," *Beiträge zur Geistesgeschichte Indiens: Festschrift für Erich Frauwallner*, ed. G. Oberhammer, *Wiener Zeitschrift für die Kunde Süd- und Ostasiens*, parts XII-XIII (1968-69) 119-148, also published in Hacker, *Kleine Schriften* 213-242. Vetter: see note 7 above.]

33

REVIEW OF *DOCTRINE DE LA NON-DUALITÉ (ADVAITA-VĀDA) ET CHRISTIANISME*[1]

For forty years, both the author and this reviewer have, unknown to each other, pondered over the doctrine of non-dualism in Śāṅkara Vedānta and Christianity with similar positive results. It is, therefore, without hesitation that I vouch for the general accuracy and depth of insight which mark this book as an outstanding publication.

It is essentially a Christian presentation of non-dualism keeping close to some central points of the Christian faith but ordered according to the hard form of Śaṅkara's teaching as it has emerged from the developments brought about by his successors. It is not a documented study of this doctrine. The chief reference is the *Vivekacūḍāmaṇi*, whose attribution to Śaṅkara is doubtful but which has the advantage of exposing succinctly all his important themes with substantial fidelity though in a hardened form. The Christian authorities which command the exposition are of the most orthodox: texts of St Bernard and St Thomas Aquinas rather than of Pseudo-Dionysius or Meister Eckhart, though citations from Nicholas Cusanus, a deep but more controversial scholar, are also prominent.

From St Bernard, we are given a key-text: [*Deus est*] *qui suum ipsius est, et omnium esse*: God is He who is His own being and the being of all (*De consideratione* 5, 6, 13). This most advaitic statement is echoed by Aquinas where it joins such arresting assertions as *Creatura in Deo est ipsa divina essentia*: the creature in God is the very divine essence (*De potentia* 3, 16). This is of course, true because, for Aquinas as well as for Śaṅkara, the divine essence is creative because it contains in its fullness (*pūrṇatā*) the similitude of all things that can be created.

Concerning creation, the author first repeats after many that its concept is absent from Vedānta but his further exposition demonstrates quite rightly that its substance is taught by Śaṅkara though with an insistence on the *nihil de se* or *a-Sat* character of the creature.[2] Śaṅkara asserts above all its lack of aseity; he also affirms its substantiality but in the Vaiśeṣika sense of being a support of accidents (*guṇas* and *karmas*), not in the sense of subsistentiality which is unknown to Indian thinkers.

The author exposes rightly that the non-aseity of creatures is expressed by Śaṅkara as well as by the Christian schoolmen in terms of reflection (as of the sun in lakes, etc. or of the face in a mirror). He could have paid more attention to *Upadeśasāhasrī* 18, where the *jīvātman* is explained as being totally a reflection, the closest reflection, of the supreme *Ātman*.

Further, he considers Śaṅkara's other comparisons: of the snake-rope, of the dreams and the sleeper, of the awakened man for whom the images of his dream have vanished. All these comparisons form a progression which points more and more precisely to the total dependence and un-Reality of the creatures and the supreme Identity of the *Ātman*. Man is thus led progressively to deepen and interiorize his viewing and ultimately merge it with the *Brahman's* own viewing. The latter is exhaustive Self-awareness, integral knowledge of its Plenitude and, therefore, omniscient knowledge of all its effects. For Śaṅkara as for St Thomas, to be, when it applies to the Deity, means to know: *Brahman* is *satyam jñānam anantam*.

The author prefers [not] to translate *Brahman* by Absolute and opts for Infinite. This is because by saying Absolute we seem to exclude totally the relative, and this would lead to pure acosmism. But the term Absolute simply denotes plenitude of essence, unicity and immutability and connotes absence of any extrinsic real relation. It does not exclude the finite since this essence is not simply *esse ipsius* but *esse omnium*. The relations of *Brahman* to finite beings are not realities added to its essence but *upādhis*, extrinsic denominators or, as St Thomas said, only logical relations.

Krempel's masterly study of the concept of relation, especially in St Thomas, seems not to have been sufficiently assimilated by the author.[3] This weakens his understanding of 'person' and its possible application in Vedānta.[4] Like many contemporary Christian writers, he includes 'relation' within the very definition of 'person' without wondering why St Thomas did not do that. Specific definitions of the term, when applied to specified persons, such as those of the Trinity, have to include it for special reasons. But 'relation' is not a *definiens* of 'person in general' which only connotes 'capacity for interpersonal relationships.'

While rejecting the idea of a God beyond the three Persons, the author is thus nevertheless led to write: "Since, according to Vedānta, the true Self is the Infinite, i.e., *essentially the non-relative*, we are led to say, in spite of the deep obscurity of this affirmation 'for the ego,' that 'Person' still falls short of 'Identity,' that one has to reach beyond it to find 'Identity'." I do not think this statement is theologically good. It must be depending on the fact that '*saguṇa Brahman*' or '*Īśvara*' is usually rendered in English by 'personal *Brahman*' and this vitiates the author's understanding of it. For Śaṅkara himself, to whom the notion of person was unknown, '*saguṇa Brahman*' is propaedeutic but still pertaining to *avidyā* (nescience) as anthropomorphic.

The author is not the first Christian to have been tempted by the idea that *tādātmya*, the supreme Identity, might be the same as 'hypostatic union' which would then not be proper to Christ. But he treats this question in depth and in an enlightening way which should interest every theologian. His conclusion is that they are not identical.

This book is not simply to be perused but to be read attentively. The author remains constantly close to the essence of his subject. Each one of his paragraphs is substantial. He has made a breakthrough which is not only of interest to students of Vedānta but which may bring back Christian thinkers to the non-dualistic core of Christian theology.

Notes

[1] [R. De Smet, Review of *Doctrine de la Non-dualité (Advaita-vāda) et Christianisme* by 'Un Moine d'Occident,' Collection "Mystiques et Religions," Dervy-Livres, 6 rue de Savoie, Paris – 6, 1982, *Indian Theological Studies* **23**/1 (1986) 65-68. Reprinted here courtesy *Indian Theological Studies*. De Smet provides the information that the 'Moine d'Occident' is Fr Elie of La Trappe; in fact, De Smet was later invited to give a series of lectures on 'The Dynamics of Hinduism' at La Trappe, Soligny-La-Trappe, France, 11-12 June 1988. H. Oldmeadow notes that the civil name of the author was Alphonse Levée, and that he sometimes also used the pseudonym Elie Lemoine (Elias the monk). The book is now available in English translation: *Christianity and the Doctrine of Non-Dualism*, by 'A Monk of the West' (Hillsdale, NY: Sophia Perennis, 2004). See Harry Oldmeadow, *A Christian Pilgrim in India: The Spiritual Journey of Swami Abhishiktananda (Henri Le Saux)* (Bloomington, IN: World Wisdom Books, 2008) 150-151.]

[2] Cf. my article, "Origin: Creation and Emanation," *Indian Theological Studies* **15** (1978) 266-279 [= ch. 26 above.]

[3] [A. Krempel, *La doctrine de la relation chez saint Thomas: Exposé historique et systématique* (Paris: J. Vrin, 1952).]

[4] Cf. my "Is the Concept of 'Person' Suitable in Vedānta?" *Indian Ecclesiastical Studies* **12** (1973) 155-162 [= *Brahman and Person: Essays by Richard De Smet*, ch. 8.]

34

NOTICE OF SOM RAJ GUPTA, *THE WORD SPEAKS TO THE FAUSTIAN MAN*[1]

Although the majority of the teachers of philosophy in India seem to be concerned mainly with problems of linguistic analysis, the desire of many of their students and of the cultured Hindus is for guidance into the classical philosophies and religious traditions of their country, particularly the systems of Śaṅkara and the other Vedāntins. The same desire is also strong in many intellectuals from other countries. The book under review promises to satisfy their common thirst. It is the first volume in a project which will extend to all the commentaries on the Upaniṣads attributed to Śaṅkara and to those he wrote on the *Brahma-sūtra* and the *Bhagavad Gītā*. I hope it will finally include his *Upadeśasāhasrī* as well. The translator and interpreter is not only a master of Sanskrit and a disciple of a traditional guru, Srī Mangratrām, but also a teacher of English in the University of Delhi. His versatility with the language is remarkable. He keeps at a long distance from the 'pandits' English' without any loss of accuracy. His translations are refreshing in a language both modern and innovative.

They are interspersed with an interpretation of his own which is addressed to the Faustian man present in us and many of our contemporaries. It expands the upaniṣadic wisdom according to Śaṅkara but in a medium that integrates the values and highlights of the Western, especially English, culture. Poets like Milton, Blake, Keats and Wordsworth are aptly quoted, philosophers like Descartes, Hume, Hegel, Wittgenstein, Frege, Derrida or the Deconstructionists referred to, Tolstoy, Freud, Spengler also appear but, curiously, Goethe does not, whereas the permanent influence of Plato, Aristotle and Plotinus, Jesus and the Gospel of St John, Homer, Dante and Shakespeare, Nietzsche, Husserl and Heidegger on the modern Western culture is present to Gupta's cultured mind. However, he does not indulge in the kind of harmonization of Vedānta with the religious conceptions of the West which was the mark of Radhakrishnan's presentations of Vedānta; on the contrary, he reveals it in its authentic tenor, idiom and original context.[2]

Notes

[1] [R. De Smet, Notice of Som Raj Gupta, *The Word Speaks to the Faustian Man: A Translation and Interpretation of the Prasthānatrayi and Śaṅkara's Bhāṣya for the Participation of Contemporary Man* (Delhi: Motilal Banarsidass, 1991), Vol. I: Īśā, Kena, Kaṭha and Praśna Upaniṣads. First published in *Boletin de la Asociaciòn Española de Orientalistas* **28** (1992) 282; reprinted here courtesy De Nobili College, Pune, all efforts to contact the *Boletin* having failed. De Smet published a somewhat different notice of the same book in *Indian Theological Studies* **29/3** (1992) 274, the text of which is given in note 2 below.]

[2] [The text of the *Indian Theological Studies* notice, reproduced here with permission:

> It seems important to bring to our readers' notice this new translation of all the commentaries written by Śaṅkara on the Upaniṣads, the *Brahma-sūtra* and the *Bhagavad-gītā*. This is the first volume of it in a project which may take up to some ten volumes. It is accompanied with the translator's own interpretation which is solidly rooted in the texts, really clarifies them and brings them up to the understanding of cultured people of our time without indulging in a facile harmonization which would conceal the particularity of their views and their belonging to a quite distant past and cultural context.
>
> Professor Gupta is a teacher of English (in the University of Delhi) as well as a sanskritist. This is why he could attempt this work written in an English nurtured from the writings of the best authors and made into an adequate tool for translation through the resource of a rich vocabulary. The presentation and printing are excellent and in no need of a table of errata.]

35

REVIEW OF JOSE THACHIL, *THE UPANIṢADS: A SOCIO-RELIGIOUS APPROACH*[1]

This book will be very useful to students and other beginners rather than to specialized indological scholars. It first introduces its user to the Vedas and Vedānta corpus. Then it focuses on the essential teachings of the Upaniṣads, interpreting them according to Śaṅkarācārya. This may be regrettable since the Upaniṣads are not a unified system but a corpus of chronologically disparate though allied texts and they would have deserved to be exposed in their own right (and then hopefully as a development from the sacrificial dimension which I expounded in *ITS* **19** [1982] 119-144).[2] But the author aims at vindicating the socio-ethical value of their diverse Vedāntic interpretations, including that of Śaṅkara which is often viewed as acosmistic and devoid of such value. This is why he starts with a Śaṅkarian view of those texts and centres his undertaking on it.

In his ch. 4, he presents the Vedānta as interpreted by Śaṅkara, Rāmānuja and Aurobindo. These presentations are well researched and quite penetrating. In presenting Śaṅkara's teaching, he is attentive to those declarations regarding the ontological status of the world which tend to show that this *ācārya* is not an acosmist. He, however, says on p. 110 that the world is *anirvacanīya*, 'unexplicable' (not simply 'not self-explanatory') with a reference to *B.S.Bh.* 2, 1, 27. This calls for some precision:

Does Śaṅkara say that the world is *anirvacanīya*? Unlike Bhartṛhari and Maṇḍana Miśra, he never uses the phrase *sadasadbhyām-anirvacanīya* (undefinable as either being or

Nonbeing) but only *tattva+anyatvābhyām anirvacanīya* (undefinable as 'that' or 'other than that') and what is thus qualified is never the universe but only its objective potentiality in the *Brahman*. Thus in *B.S.Bh.* 1, 1, 5 the question being put, "what was the object of *Brahman's* thinking before the creation?" he replies, "The object of its thinking is unevolved names and forms (*nāmarūpe avyākṛte*) which are not definable as 'that' or 'other' (*tattvānyatvābhyām anirvacanīya*) and which are going to be manifested. Of them he says in *Ait. Up. Bh.* 1, 1, 2: "These *nāma-rūpas*, which in their unmanifested state are identical with the *Ātman*, can become the causal elements (*upādāna-bhūte*) of the manifested universe." In *B.S.Bh.* 1, 4, 3, it is the undifferentiated creative energy (*māyā*) which is said to be *tattvānyatva nirūpanasya*, an equivalent expression. In 2, 1, 27, referred to by the author, the phrase is again connected with the unevolved names-and-forms. As to the manifested world, Śaṅkara has declared it to be 'totally effect' and negatively as *sad-asad-vilakṣaṇa*, not definable as either being or Non-being. These two terms, *sat* and *asat* have to be understood here "in their supreme meaning" (*paramārthataḥ*) as signifying either the Absolute Being or the absolute Non-being, i.e., the contradictory, such as 'the son of a barren woman.'

In his last chapter, professor Thachil gathers from his multipronged enquiry the results regarding the ethical teachings of the Upaniṣads and their implications. He asserts that the basic doctrine of non-dualism has acted in the minds of the great men of the Indian Renaissance as the integrator for their reforms. No doubt these men were much influenced by the teachings of Christ and the socio-political doctrines of the West. "But all these influences were integrated into the basic Upaniṣadic teaching from which emerges a healthy and harmonious attitude which enables a person to dedicate himself, without selfish interest, for the welfare of the whole society" (185). This is a view made fashionable by the Ramakrishna Mission. Scholars dispute its correctness. It is not sure that Dr Thachil has fully vindicated it for the style of his assertions appears finally more forceful than his arguments.

Notes

[1] [R. De Smet, Review of Jose Thachil, *The Upaniṣads: A Socio-Religious Approach* (New Delhi: Intercultural Publications, 1993), *Indian Theological Studies* **30**/2 (1993) 175-177; reprinted here with permission.]

[2] [R.V. De Smet, "Fleeting Time and Sacrificially Produced Continuity in Vedic Brahmanism and in Early Christianity," *Indian Theological Studies* **19**/2 (1982) 1-26.]

36

REVIEW OF SRINIVASA RAO, *ADVAITA: A CRITICAL INVESTIGATION*[1]

This book is slight in size but has justly been hailed by many eminent indologists because it reopens the discussion about the validity of the Advaita doctrine. Actually it concerns the tenets of its post-Śaṅkara version rather than those of Śaṅkara himself. However, it is not a critical study of any text belonging to the historical development of the Advaita tradition, but a purely logical discussion starting from the basic distinction between the two kinds of experience. These are the ordinary empirical experience, coded 'experience' of 'reality,' and the *Śruti*-born transempirical one, coded 'Experience' of 'Reality' and consisting in *Brahmānubhava* (intuition of the *Brahman*). All Advaitins agree that there cannot be any 'experience' of 'Reality' but the question raised by Professor Rao is whether there cannot be an 'Experience' of "reality.' Advaita, he says, rejects this possibility but this rejection surely deserves to be investigated anew.

The rejection is linked with the idea that 'reality' is illusory and, hence, cancelled by 'Experience.' This idea was formulated by Padmapāda, the author of the *Pañcapādika* (ninth century) and implies acosmistic monism. The teaching of Śaṅkara himself regarding our congenital Ignorance as superimposition of the *Brahman-Ātman* upon the non-*Ātman* and vice-versa does not reduce 'reality' to 'Non-reality.' On the contrary, Śaṅkara declares that 'reality' cannot be defined as either 'Reality' or 'Non-reality' for, being entirely 'effect' (*kārya*) of that cause which is 'Reality' (*Sat-Kāraṇa*), it is *Sad-Asad-vilakṣaṇa*, unable to be signified by either *Sat* or *Asat* if these two terms are taken in their supreme sense (*paramārthataḥ*). According to [him,] knowledge is valid within its proper limits ("no *Śruti* may declare the sun to be black or cold"); it is imbued with ignorance but only insofar as it fails to grasp this reality as totally dependent and thus erroneously superimposes absoluteness on it. When reality is known with the help of the *Śruti*, this superimposition is removed but this does not cancel the basic validity of the other sources of right knowledge (*pramāṇas*).

Professor Rao addresses his criticisms to what he calls 'the Advaita doctrine,' as is indeed done by many others, but this is not the authentic doctrine of the *ācārya*. In 16 sequences of pertinent arguments, Rao pursues mercilessly the numerous fallacies which follow from the basic view of the *Sad-Asad-vilakṣaṇa* as illusory (cf. his 1.7). He says rightly:

> If it is not recognized that falsity is a matter of thought, the price one has to pay metaphysically is the postulation of the existence of an illusory world and of *anādi avidyā* as the cause of its manifestation. (5.18)

> After 'Experience' it is not the ontological status of the world that undergoes a radical revision but its epistemological configuration in one's knowledge. (9.2)

In connection with this excellent remark, let me quote Śaṅkara: The knower of *Brahman* enjoys all desires, all delights procured by desirable objects, without exception. Does he enjoy sons, heavens, etc. alternately as we do? No, he enjoys all desirable things simultaneously, as amassed together in a single moment, through a single perception which is eternal like the light of the sun, which is nondifferent from the essence of *Brahman*, and which we have described as Reality-Knowledge-infinite.... He enjoys all things by that *Brahman* whose nature is omniscience. (*Taitt. Up. Bh.* 2, 1, 1)

Obviously the 'Experience of reality' cannot be another 'Experience' than the 'Experience of Reality' since the effects of *Brahman* can never be simply other than It and to be knowable apart from It. Rather it is by knowing their total Cause that we shall know them as they really are.

A review cannot provide a summary of such a book which is a masterpiece of dialectics. All details of its argumentation must be left to the reader to discover. But it can mark well the kind of Advaita which is the butt of its attacks and nurture in him a keen desire to have his mind cleaned up from centuries of misrepresentation of Śaṅkara's teaching.

Notes

1 [R. De Smet, Review of Srinivasa Rao, *Advaita: A Critical Investigation* (Bangalore – 560056: Indian Philosophical Foundation 1985), *Indian Theological Studies* 30/2 (1993) 179-181; reprinted here with permission.]

APPENDIX 1

UPADHYAY'S INTERPRETATION OF ŚAṄKARA[1]

The biography of Brahmabandhab Upadhyay prepared by Animananda and published recently by Fr Turmes cannot fail to arouse in all concerned with the planting and growing of the Church in India, a deep sympathy and a still deeper reflection on the nature of their task.[2]

It confronts us with a Bengali Brahmin who, after his own surrender to Christ in the Catholic Church, sets himself decisively the work of evangelizing his countrymen. Leaving aside any other care, remaining unmarried, practising Christian poverty as a begging *sannyāsi*, he attempts by every means in his power, by education, by lectures, by monthly, weekly, daily papers, by the foundation of a monastery, to bring about that synthesis of the Indian culture around the Christian Revelation which will one day be a bright jewel in the crown of the universal Church.

His idea is simple; he takes it from the Gospel and from the life of the Church, and he clings to it unflinchingly: Christ is the Fulfiller not the destroyer of man; His Church is the transformation of mankind into His Mystical Body, not the destruction of any authentically human value. She is the judge and supreme arbiter of these values, but whenever a Christian takes on himself to destroy one of them, or even to oppose certain relative values of a civilization while they are not endangering his main task of evangelising, in so far he is not faithful to his Christian mission. Much more, members of Christ who do not strive towards the achievement of His Incarnation by bringing unto Him and submitting to Him whatever riches and value mankind has been developing, are restricting Christ's action and limiting His universal message.

More precisely the task of missioners and Christians in this country is not to foist a Western Church into the Indian commonwealth, not even an adult and nineteenth or twentieth century Church, but to fertilize the Hindu world with the golden germ of the universal revelation of Christ so that it may develop and thrive in, and from, that Indian soil as it did in other cultures.

This, for us, is not only a matter of opportunity, a question of efficiency of the missionary effort, as Upadhyay seems to have believed in the beginning of his action, but it is a matter of faithfulness to the fact of the Incarnation fully understood. If we narrow it down to our own views we are not faithful witnesses of Christ.

The supreme decision whether this or that initiative can really bring about the intended result rests of course with the authority of the Church and Upadhyay acknowledged it by his heroic obedience to this authority, but the principle: *Christus Consummator, non destructor* remains the criterion of our action as the last Popes have clearly stated in their Encyclicals concerning the planting of the Church in missionary countries.

In that work of fulfilment a point of utmost importance is our concern for the thinking traditions of the different peoples; because it is an undeniable fact that civilizations are moulded on, and develop according to, complex bodies of ideas more or less systematized. In dealing with them one ought always to remember the saying of the Fathers: "Whatever is true, by whomsoever it be said, comes from the Holy Ghost."

In India that thinking tradition is at the same time philosophical and religious. Most of her great thinkers were even subjectively convinced that they were building up a theology, elaborated upon the revealed foundation of the Vedas; they not only made full use of all the resources of natural reason of which too it has been written that "in Christ all things hold together" (*Col.* 1, 17), but their very methods are closely similar to those of our own theology. Hence we owe them not only respect but an enlightened sympathy.

As it is natural for all converts Upadhyay did not at first grasp all the implications of his principle and he was ready to burn a big part of what he had previously worshipped. But even then his keen sense of the Christian reality led him to burn only the chaff of the Hindu culture of his time while neglecting for a time the good grain in it. Taking a firm stand upon Catholic theology he launched merciless attacks against whatever system was then spreading atheism or false conceptions about God: the Sāṁkhya System, the Arya Samaj and the Brahmo Samaj, the Hegelian and Spencerian philosophies, and above all Theosophy. If Hindus were not returning to the pure theism of their main tradition, it was useless to try to make Christians out of them.

But pure theism could hardly be taught without at the same time explaining the true relation of the world to God, as expressed in the Catholic notion of Creation. And he soon realised that this mystery was difficult for the Hindus to accept because in the rational garb we had given it, it appeared to them as something extraneous and foreign..

Hence he was forced to go back to the best Hindu philosophers and to borrow from their writings the same doctrine regarding Creation which could not but be there, although in an Indian garb, if they had really been teaching pure theism.

During the heroic time of his forty days' fast and prayer on the banks of the Nerbudda[3] in the Monastery he had just opened, his long wandering had crystallized an interpretation of the Vedānta which to him appeared inclusive and destined to be the intellectual foundation of the Christian religion in India. Instead of ridiculing *Māyā* as he had done before when Śaṅkara's statement of the unreality of the world seemed to his mind to be absolute and therefore to lead to a vague theopanism, he henceforward adopted it, identifying it, more faithfully to Śaṅkara's tenets, with the transcendental relation of the creature to the Creator, or the "*creatio passive sumpta*" of the Schoolmen.

His friend, Father Hegglin, who later opposed this interpretation in the *Bombay Examiner*, contended that it was not to be found in Śaṅkara and that Śaṅkara's theory was in truth that absurd conception of the absolute unreality of all creatures, so often indeed attributed to him. We have no time to spend in the examination of Fr Hegglin's long array of arguments. Suffice it to say that he himself held a very unrefined conception of Creation and that he was hardly a philosopher as a single sentence of his will show: Commenting on Stanza 241 of the *Vivekacūḍāmaṇi*, a lengthy poem of Śaṅkara: "The wise know the Supreme Being to be without subject, object and act of knowledge, but to be mere unbroken Intelligence," Fr Hegglin declares: "the meaning is that the Supreme Being is a mere mass of abstract thought or knowledge in which there is no distinction whatsoever." Let us at once remark that the word 'abstract' is surely not to be found in the stanza. But Fr Hegglin goes on: "This is of course," he says, "a thing utterly inconceivable to us. A thought, we should hold, requires a subject who makes it, an object which forms its contents, an act by which it is produced." Such a statement shows sufficiently that although unconscious of it, Fr Hegglin was a perfect rationalist, unable to grasp that our own mode of knowing can in no way be attributed to God. His conception of God was at bottom that of a Super-man, not of a transcendent God.

This last remark brings us closer to Śaṅkara's mind. God is indeed, for him as for us, absolutely self-sufficient and endowed with all the transcendental perfections, such as Being, Intelligence, Bliss, in an infinite degree. "The fundamental tenet," he writes in the IInd *Adhyāya*, 1st *pāda*, 14, of his commentary on the *Vedānta-sūtras*, "which we maintain is that the creation, sustentation and reabsorption of the world proceed from an omniscient, omnipotent Lord, not from a non-intelligent *Pradhāna* or any other principle." He is fond of quoting the description of *Brahman* as given in the *Taitt. Up*. 2, 1 ff, where it is said: "Truth, Knowledge, infinite is *Brahman*." Thus God alone is Pure, Necessary Being.

It is however an undeniable fact for Śaṅkara as for us that we ourselves and the world are existing. What is the meaning of this existence? Being (*sattā*) is indeed the one characteristic feature of the world as well as of *Brahman* (*B.S.Bh.* 2, 1, 6), but they are irremediably distinct and different because existence in the creatures cannot receive the attributes of absolute substantiality and infinity as in *Brahman*. Created existence is only an image, a reflection of the absolute existence, and as such a dependent participation, not an existence by right. Of such an existential reflection the only possible operative cause is the Supreme *Brahma*; but is God also its material cause? Yes, says Śaṅkara, "*Brahma* is to be acknowledged as the material cause as well as the operative cause (*B.S.Bh.* 4, 23) on account of the principle of the non-difference between the effect and the material cause (ibid.).

In order to understand this much-controverted statement we ought to remember that the term 'material cause' can be understood in two ways: either it means that inner principle of a finite being which is potential with regard to the act, or it means the Being of whose substance the effect—i.e. both the potency and its act in their substantial union—is made. Now it follows from Śaṅkara's very conception of God that the latter can in no way be a material principle in the first sense, a part as it were of His effect. But He can very well, by communicating Himself, be the very stuff His creatures are made of. As His reflections they *have* in their finite way a share in that being which He alone *Is*. Our doctrine of analogical participation does not teach anything else. The Infinite can, just because He is infinite, make without any change, decrease or increase in His own being, finite participations of Himself, so much so that by knowing them we can somehow know Him, and by knowing Him as He is we can know everything (*B.S.Bh.* 1, 4, 23). This might be impossible if He were only the operative cause because effects are not necessarily non-different from their operative cause, but they cannot but be non-different from their material cause (ibid.). Again if we look only at this statement of the non-difference between effects and their material cause, we might be mistaken concerning Śaṅkara's real position. But simultaneously with this we have to take into account his other statements: that God is simple and infinite in nature and perfections; that consequently nothing can be added to, or subtracted from, His substance; that creatures, while being identical to God in so far as being is common to both, are also radically different from Him because the same attributes of perfection can never be predicated in the same way of both; that creatures therefore cannot be parts of, or emanations from, God, but only reflections or participations, at the same time identical with, and different from, Him. (*B.S.Bh.* 3, 2, 5)

The 'what' of the mystery is thus neatly delineated but not yet its 'how.' This can only be suggested. We have *our* ways of suggesting it, Śaṅkara has *his* own. In the parts of his works which provide such hints, the notion of *Māyā*, which incidentally is hardly to be found in the Upaniṣads, is given prominence. The word itself conveys the idea of glamour, illusion, dazzle and by using it Śaṅkara wishes to stigmatize our congenital error of believing ourselves and the world to be self-sufficient beings, while compared with the Infinite Being, the only adequate measuring-rod of all beings, we are like nothing.

Hence to say that the world is *Māyā* means that the world has no right to exist; it is not absolute but contingent being and entirely dependent on the Supreme.

To say that we ourselves are under the spell of *Māyā* means that our superimposition of independent reality on ourselves and on objects which possess only communicated existence is blindness.

To say that God possesses the great power of *Māyā* (*B.S.Bh.* 2, 1, 37) means that, as a necessity in God, creative causality exists only as a mysterious non-manifest power which He has not to actuate in order to be Himself, but may use or not use according to His absolute free will (*B.S.Bh.* 1, 4, 3), and that therefore it is blindness to conceive Him as a Creator by necessity.

To say that *Īśvara*, i.e. the Creator conceived as connected to His creation by a mutual and real relationship, is *Māyā* means that such a conception does away with the absolute transcendence of the one true God and is therefore a product of our ignorance and stupidity.

To say that God's activity *ad extra* is *Māyā* means that to conceive His creative action as really and absolutely *ad extra*, i.e. real of a reality distinct and different from His eternal Being, is again falsity and blindness.

Śaṅkara's conception of *Māyā* will further be understood by drawing our attention to the similes he invented or adopted from the Upaniṣads when commenting on the *Sūtras* referring to Creation:

The world is like a rope which in the dark is mistaken for a snake or like a post which at the dusk of night appears to be a man (*B.S.Bh.* 1, 1, 4; 1, 3, 19; etc.). Thus the apparent self-sufficiency of this world ought to be discarded and we should discover its utter nakedness and absolute contingency of being (*B.S.Bh.* 2, 1, 14).

The world is like a mirage of which the blue expanse of water "is really not different from the surface of the salty steppe, for the nature of that water is that it is seen in a moment and has vanished in the next, and moreover it is not to be perceived by its own nature [apart from the surface of the desert]; so this manifold world... has no existence apart from *Brahman*" (*B.S.Bh.* 2, 1, 14).

The world is like a heap of clay which the potter kneads successively into a pot, a god or any other form. These names and forms do not change the nature of the clay but only limit it to representing this or that figure. So also beyond the individual nature of the creatures is their being which they possess in common with the Creator but only in a finite and contingent way (*B.S.Bh.* 2, 1, 14).

The world is like a shell of mother-of-pearl mistaken for silver (*B.S.Bh.* 1, 1, 4), or like a bowl of pure crystal which appears to be red on account of the presence of a peony rose nearby (*B.S.Bh.* 1, 3, 19). We thus mistake the individuality of the object or the personality of our own selves for a purely independent existence, an absolute '*aseitas*.'

The similes of the illusory sights produced by a magician (*B.S.Bh.* 2, 1, 28) and of the dream-world of a sleeping man (*B.S.Bh.* 3, 2, 3) can be misleading and must be explained strictly according to Śaṅkara's use of them. The tricks of the magician and the world of dreams are, as such, mere illusions of course, but the real objects or the perceptions upon which these illusory ones are superimposed retain their own reality once true knowledge has discriminated fiction from actual facts. Moreover the tricks or the dreams testify to the activity of an actual magician or of a dreaming self. "We only maintain," says Śaṅkara, "that the world in dreams is not real in the same sense as the world of the waking state is real. On the other hand we must remember that also the so-called real creation... is not absolutely real" (*B.S.Bh.* 3, 2, 4). Śaṅkara therefore does not say that our phenomenal world is a world of dreams but that compared with the absolute being of God it is in a relation of unreality analogous to the relation of unreality of the dreams when compared to the objects of the waking state.

What is now that relation of unreality which affects our real world? We may try to characterize it by another simile which, to my knowledge, is not to be found in Śaṅkara's writings, but keeps in conformity with his own comparisons:

When a mathematician forms in his mind the idea of a geometrical figure, let us say, of the circle, that idea has a quite determined nature which distinguishes it from all other notions, and it can receive a very precise definition. Its efficient cause is the person of the mathematician, its material cause his intellect. Its essence is intellectual or intentional being borrowed from that intellect. Most mathematicians will agree that, although in practice it is preceded by the experience of concrete and imperfect circles, it is however in itself purely *a priori*, i.e., produced from nothing but the mind of the thinker. With regard to the latter it is *ad extra*, i.e., it is in no way implied by necessity in the mathematicians' nature but has been produced by a free activity of the intellect.

We have thus here an excellent analogy of our own way of existing: "We are in the mind of God," said Father Scheuer, a well known Jesuit metaphysician, "exactly like the circle in the mind of the mathematician."

Suppose now the circle to be endowed with self-consciousness. It would quite naturally believe itself to be self-existent and self-sufficient. Possessing its own perfect definition, its own relationships and possibilities of combining with other figures, it would think itself completely independent; till at last, under the instruction of some wiser geometrical being, or under a revelation made by the mathematician himself, it would discover its own mistake and realize the "*Tattvamasi*," its own absolute dependence on the mathematician. Starting a regressive reflection on itself, it would discover that it is indeed a conscious self but limited inside its own precise definition, contingent self that would lead it to another discovery, that of the higher Self completely immanent to, but absolutely transcendent to, its own little self, and which alone could be the explanatory cause of its own springing into existence. That, it would say, is my own higher Self, not my own in the sense of my individual self, but my true Self in the sense of the type, of the original of which I am only a reflection, of the being of which I am a participation different and non-different, real and not absolutely real.

Such is our own situation with regard to God. We exist in Him from all eternity like the potential contingent products of His mind. At His wish, out of no necessity in Him but by a kind of sportfulness (*B.S.Bh.* 2, 1, 33) we come to be real in time. But henceforth we are under the spell of *Māyā*. If we centre everything around our individual self and construct a world of self-sufficiency, we are doomed to blindness. But if we recognize our true relationship to God and keep ourselves open to Him, then we may hope for a complete sharing in His eternal Bliss.

We have patiently followed up the direction pointed out to us by Upadhyay towards the great Vedāntin and we have discovered a doctrine which, far more than the teachings of the Greek Philosophers, provides an intellectual body for the Christian Spirit. Let us hope that this lead will in the future be followed with more and more decision and let us wait with confidence for the day when the Christian Mysteries will shine more convincingly to everyone in this land in an authentically Indian garb.

Notes

[1] ["Upadhyay's Interpretation of Śaṅkara," typescript, Kurseong, Ascension Day, 1949. Collected Papers D, 1-6. Published here for the first time, with kind permission of De Nobili College, Pune.]

[2] B. Animananda, *The Blade: Life and Work of Brahmabandhab Upadhyay*, preface by P. Turmes, SJ (Calcutta, 79/25 D, Lower Circular Road: Roy & Son, 1949).

[3] [Narmada.]

APPENDIX 2

A NOTE ABOUT ŚAṄKARA'S DOCTRINE OF CREATION[1]

According to Śaṅkara, *Brahman* is the supreme, infinite being; He is absolutely simple, intelligent and changeless.

> Here nothing is eternal. All activity only helps that which is perishable. But I am a seeker after perfection, which is eternal, undying, fearless, unchanging, unmoving and constant. (*Muṇḍ. Up. Bh.* 2, 21)

> From Non-Being lead me to Being.
> From darkness lead me to light.
> From death lead me to deathlessness. (*Bṛh. Up.* 1, 3, 28)

This perfection, this light is:

> Brahman, without beginning, without end, imperishable, deathless, quenching fear, pure and transparent and nothing but Being. (*Muṇḍ. Up. Bh.* 2, 10)

Brahman is the infinite Being, Intelligence, Bliss (*Satcitānanda*). It follows that He is the supreme Person, "knowing Himself through Himself" (*Bh. Gītā Bh.* 10, 14, 16). He alone is absolutely real.

> His being is by nature eternal, pure, wise and free, all-knowing and endowed with omnipotence. (*B.S.Bh.* 1, 1, 1)

> They teach Him as the eternal, omniscient, omnipresent, complete, eternally pure, wise free Being, as Knowledge and Joy, as Brahman. (*B.S.Bh.* 1, 1, 4)

> The absolutely real Being, exalted, eternal, all-penetrating as the ether, free from all change, all-sufficient, indivisible, self-luminous. (*B.S.Bh.* 1, 15, 4)

> The one identical, all-highest, eternal spirit. (*B.S.Bh.* 1, 1, 4)

The eternal pure God. (*B.S.Bh.* 1, 1, 5)

The eternal, perfect, highest God. (*B.S.Bh.* 1, 1, 20)

The category of reality is always conceived by Śaṅkara as the category of the absolute reality; consequently God alone is real because the co-existence of two absolute realities would be mere absurdity (*ekam eva advitīyam*. *Chānd. Up*. 6, 2, 1).

This singleness of God as absolute reality does not however imply any monism or theopanism; it only means *a-dvaita*: non-duality. All realities other than *Brahman*, although they possess a specific existence (*B.S.Bh.* 2, 1, 22) do not constitute another absolute and self-existent reality but they are one with *Brahman* from Whom, by Whom and in Whom they exist. (Cf. St Paul in the *Acts* 17, 28: "In Him we live and move and are.") Śaṅkara strongly denies the existence of anything *apart, independently from Brahman* (*B.S.Bh.* 2, 1, 14).

It is indeed one of his cardinal theses that *Brahman* alone must be held as the one supreme Cause of all other beings. As such He is of course a purely transcendent (*atiśaya*) cause. Causing implies no change in Him and He does not need anything else in order to be able to cause: no instruments, no *materia circa qua*, no *materia ex qua*. No instruments,

> because causation is possible in consequence of a peculiar constitution of the causal substance, as in the case of milk turning into curds; ... its turning is merely accelerated by the co-operation of an extraneous agent, v.g. heat.... The absolutely complete power of Brahman, on the other hand, does not require to be supplemented by any extraneous help. Thus Scripture also declares, 'There is no effect and no instruments known of Him, no one is seen like unto Him or better.' (*Śvet. Up*. 6, 8) (*B.S.Bh.* 2, 1, 24).

> As gods, etc.... all of intelligent nature, are seen to create many and various objects, such as palaces, chariots, etc., without availing themselves of any extraneous means, *by their mere intention*, which is effective in consequence of those beings' peculiar power... —and as the spider emits out of itself the threads of its web; and as the female crane conceives without a male; and as the lotus wanders from one pond to another without any means of conveyance; so the intelligent Brahman also may be assumed to create the world by itself without any extraneous means.... [By using these illustrative examples] we mean to show merely that the case of Brahman is different from that of potters and similar agents. For while potters, etc., on the one side, and gods, etc., on the other side, possess the

common attribute of *intelligence*, potters require for their work *extraneous* means and gods *do not*. Hence Brahman also, although intelligent, is assumed to require no extraneous means. So much only we wanted to show by the parallel instance of the gods, etc. (*B.S.Bh.* 2, 1, 25, emphases added)

These texts, by insisting on the all-powerfulness of the causative intention, also show that no pre-existing *materia* is required.

Created beings, if they have no absolute reality, must needs find outside themselves an absolute basis upon which their being may be founded and from which they can derive that positivity without which they are unconceivable. Such a basis must be one after which no other is required and therefore it must be supremely intelligent and free, i.e., it must be a self (*ātmā*) or person. That is why *Brahman* who alone is able to verify the conditions required for the basis, is called and is in truth our supreme substantial Self. He is never to be viewed as an *object*, as a thing divided from the knowing subject and opposed to it; but we must conceive Him by regressing along the line of our own subjectivity till we reach that supreme Subject or Self (*Paramātman*) in which alone we can at last find consistence and being.

The *Ātman*, to know whom is salvation, not to know whom is bondage to the world, who is the root of the world, who is the basis of all creation, through whom all exists, through whom all is conceived,—the Unborn, the Deathless, the Fearless, the Good, without second,—He is the Real. *He is thy Self.* And therefore that art thou. (*Chānd. Up. Bh.* 6, 16)

All the attributes of a Person are given to Him:

He who has known me, Nārāyaṇa, the receiver of all sacrifice and all penance, both as their instigator and their end, Lord of all the world, who benefits all being without reward, who *dwells in the heart* and controls all works and their fruits, who witnesses all thoughts,—he attains *śānti* (rest), the cessation of all *saṃsāra*. (*Bh. Gītā Bh.* 5, 29)

We can never find Him by developing our 'objective' knowledge of things, however far we extend it.

The purpose of all words is to illuminate the meaning of an object. When they are heard they should enable the hearer to understand this meaning, and this according to the four categories of substance, of activity, of quality and of relationship. For example, cow or horse belong to the

> category of 'substance.' Or 'he cooks, he prays' belongs to the category of activity. White, black belong to the category of quality. Having money, possessing cows, belong to the category of relationship. Now there is no class of 'substances' to which then Brahman belongs, no *genus commune*. It cannot therefore be denoted by words, which, like 'being' in the usual sense, signify a category of things. Nor can it be denoted by quality, for it is without qualities; nor yet by activity because it is without activity according to the Scriptures, 'at rest, without parts or activity.' Neither can it be denoted by relationship, for it is 'secondless,' is *not the object of anything*, but is *its own self*. It is therefore true that it cannot be defined by word or idea; it is the One as the Scripture says: 'Before whom words recoil.' (*Taitt. Up.* 2, 4, 1)—But it might be falsely supposed that because the Brahman cannot be denoted as Being (*Sat*), it is to be described as Non-Being (*Asat*). [To prevent this supposition our text teaches the '*astitvam*' of Brahman—we might translate: 'is-ness'—figuratively attributing to Him all the organs of the living: hand, foot, hearing, etc; and it states that Brahman should not be said to be '*sat*' or '*asat*'.] (*Bh. Gītā Bh.* 13, 12-13)

The way to *Brahman* is therefore to be found in a deep and regressive development of the precious core of intuitional knowledge (*darśana*) which underlies and substantifies any concrete knowledge of ours. "*Ātmani ātmānam ātmanā*": "Know the *Ātman* in the *ātman* alone through the *ātman*." *Know the Ātman*: means the *Ātman-Brahman*. *In the ātman*: in the depth of man's own *ātman*. *Alone through the ātman*: that means not by the power of the *indriyāni* or of the *manas* or the *buddhi*, not through the senses, or by common sense or by the activity of the discursive understanding but dispensing with all these organs and mediators, directly through the *Ātman* itself.

> The royal knowledge, the kingly secret is here knowledge of Brahman. And this is not scripture knowledge, but *pratyakṣagamanam*: an immediate self-knowledge; 'just as one feels one's own weal or woe,' i.e., in immediate self-perception. (*Bh. Gītā Bh.* 9, 2)

> When the confusing play of ideas (*cittam*) has come to rest, and he thus through himself [without the senses], through the purified 'inward organ' apprehends the Highest, which is wholly spirit, essentially light, then he wins through to Joy. (*Bh. Gītā Bh.* 6, 20)

Of course such a transcendental and intuitional metaphysics requires a painful purification of the intellect and is hard to reach. The mysterious, wonderful, entirely suprarational essence which is thus sought for is as difficult to plumb as the mighty ocean (*Māṇḍ. Up*. 4, 100), its path is as little to be traced as that of birds in the sky:

> He who is the self of all being and the salvation of all beings,
> About whose path even the heavenly powers are in confusion,
> Seeking the track of the trackless,
> As one cannot find the path of the birds in the air. (*Mānd. Up*. 4, 95)

In his *Bhāṣya* on the *Brahma Sūtras* 2, 1, 1, Śaṅkara neatly summarizes all what precedes:

> It has been shown in the first adhyāya that the omniscient Lord of all is the cause of the origin of this world...; that by His rulership He is the cause of the subsistence of this world once originated...; and that he, lastly, is the cause of this emitted world being finally reabsorbed into his essence.... It has further been proved, by a demonstration of the connected meaning of all the Vedānta-texts, that the Lord is the Self of all of us. Moreover, the doctrines of the pradhāna, and so on, being the cause of this world have been refuted as not being scriptural.

Brahman being thus the total Cause of this world, His causality has to be a perfect one. Whatever perfection of causality is needed in order to explain the ontology of this world must be attributed to His causality.

Now causality is generally distinguished in efficient, final, formal (exemplary), and material causality. Instrumental causality does not concern this case as it cannot refer to the supreme cause.

Efficient or operative causality is the causality of an intelligent and free agent. When this causality is transcendent and perfect, it follows that the agent is supremely active through his infinite intelligence and infinite freedom, that he therefore creates not on account of any inner necessity but merely at his wish (*saṅkalpa*) and by a kind of sportfulness (*līlārūpaḥ*) (*B.S.Bh.* 2, 1, 33) and that he does so by a simple intention (which implies intelligence and freedom), having no need of any instrument or pre-existing matter.

To speak of a *sportive* impulse of the *intelligent Brahman* is to explain away two mistaken conceptions of His activity: First, concerning His action *ad extra* as springing from inner necessity; second, conceiving it as orderless, merely fanciful, illogical and absurd. On the contrary we see that the result is a wise, just, well-regulated, finalised world; it embodies the omniscience, super-intelligence, all-powerfulness of the Creator. But just as its very being depends on *Brahman* and has no explanation apart from Him, so also its inner intellectuality becomes mere absurdity when separated from *Brahman's* intelligence. The notion of sport is most adequate to characterise such a causality.

The notion of *final causality* connotes that the world is self-evolving, dynamic and polarized upon a specific end. Observation indeed shows a world in motion and self-reflection reveals the dynamic nature of the self. According to the principle of finality the last end must needs be able to fulfil the whole tendency of the mobile. Now in our case self-reflection reveals the finite nature of our desire and movement. We come therefore to the conclusion that our end must be possible, ultimate, supreme and absolutely quenching our striving. Unitive merging into *Brahman* as the absolute Bliss (*ānandamaya*) appears thus as the only possible last end, the very possibility of which makes itself possible the whole reality of our becoming and evolutive activity.

First the regularity and purposefulness of the movements of nature point out a true finality which in turn presupposes an intelligent guide:

> The wind fulfils its function, namely to blow, regularly. But such regularity presupposes a guide [who wills and realises this regularity]. (*Taitt. Up. Bh.* 3)

> Houses, palaces, beds, chairs, and pleasure-gardens are built by *judicious* artists for the purpose of furthering pleasure or dispelling ennui. It is the same with the whole world. See for instance how the earth is arranged for the enjoyment of the fruits of manifold works, and how bodily form both outwardly and inwardly possesses a disposition of parts fitting to the different creatures even in detail, and thus forms the basis of the enjoyment of the fruits of manifold works. Even intelligent and highly trained artists are not able to comprehend it with their reason—how then should this disposition of the world come from a non-spiritual primary material, since clods of earth, stones, etc. are not capable of achieving this? (*B.S.Bh.* 2, 2, 1)

> This movement, namely toward a goal, is impossible with a non-spiritual cause. For instance, clay or a wagon, because they are non-spiritual,

> cannot of themselves move toward a definite end unless they are directed by potters or horses. (*B.S.Bh.* 2, 2, 2)

Our own inner movement is also a true finality directed by a self-existent and intelligent '*telos*':

> All the elements or the conglomeration of the physico-psychic elements, which make up the finite self of man, borrow their activity and consciousness from the true and the transcendental self that is at the back of the finite self. (*Kena Up. Bh.* 1, 4)
>
> The restraining of the first natural activities one after the other and thereby the gradually inducing fresh and higher activities serves to create an aspiration to reach the innermost self. (*Bh. Gītā Bh.* 18, 66)
>
> The supreme Self is revealed in the spirit of man in a higher and superior form. *It is for this presence that man ever wants to know more and more and by mundane means ever to reach what is supra-mundane*. (*Taitt. Up. Bh.* 2, 1)
>
> (Cf. also *Kaṭha Up. Bh.* 4, 3)

The derivative affix *maya* in the word *ānandamaya* is used in the sense of modification but also in the sense of·abundance. Thus *Brahman* is called *ānandamaya* because He is "abounding in bliss." That He does abound in bliss follows from the passage (*Taitt. Up.* 2, 8) where, after the bliss of each of the different classes of beings, beginning with man, has been desired to be a hundred times greater than the bliss of the immediately preceding class, the bliss of *Brahman* is finally proclaimed to be absolutely supreme (*B.S.Bh.* 1, 1, 13). It follows also for that reason that scripture declares *Brahman* to be the cause of bliss, "For He alone causes bliss" (*Taitt. Up.* 2, 7). For he who causes bliss must himself abound in bliss (*B.S.Bh.* 1, 1, 14).

The texts speak figuratively of "going upwards" (*Chānd. Up.* 8, 6, 5), "proceeding on a path" (*Chānd. Up.* 4, 15, 6) of "being led to the worlds of *Brahman*" (*Bṛh. Up.* 6, 2, 15) of "entering the hall of Prajāpati" (*Chānd. Up.* 14, 1) but these expressions should not be taken literally, they are fitting only the lower knowledge of *Brahman*, i.e., the anthropomorphic and propaedeutical stage of knowledge; in the higher stage of pure metaphysical or mystical knowledge, they are no more appropriate. "The highest Self cannot be assumed to possess any differences depending on time or space or anything else, and cannot therefore become the object of going." (*B.S.Bh.* 4, 3, 14). "Omnipresent and eternal like the ether" the *Brahman* which is visible, not invisible, the Self that is within all" (*Bṛh. Up.* 3, 4, 1) "Self only is all this" (*Chānd Up.* U, 25, 2) "*Brahman* only is all this, it is the best" (*Muṇḍ. Up.* 2, 2, 11): from all these passage we ascertain that the highest *Brahman* is present everywhere, within everything, the Self of everything, and of such a *Brahman* it is altogether impossible that it ever should be the goal of going, for we do not go to what is already reached." (*B.S.Bh.* 4, 3, 14) Going or reaching therefore "denotes only the obtainment of realisation of one's own nature, in so far as (through true knowledge) the expanse of names and forms which science (*Avidyā*) superimposes is dissolved. (*B.S.Bh.* 4, 3, 14) There is no difficulty about this doctrine which follows from the omnipresence of *Brahman*, the absolute Spirit (*Ātman*), and from the spiritual nature of our individual self; we are never outside God but it is true that to realise, and to become beatified by, that '*a-dvaitic*' presence in Him, requires the removing of all figments of nescience (i.e., according to Śaṅkara, of our human knowledge when we take our standpoint as the absolute one; only God's standpoint is the true one) and of all the attachments engendered by selfish actions.

True finality would be impossible if the transcendent End be not immanent too to the evolving world of the souls and also to this world of ether, earth, etc. As the inner guide of that evolution, *Brahman* is called the *Antaryāmin*.

This God-led evolution being a passing from non-absolute reality to absolute reality appears as a process of salvation, the success of which depends simultaneously on our own instrumental, if we may call it so, activity and on the principal and supremely causative attraction of the End. Now just because this End is *sat-cit-ānanda*, it can only rescue us as a person does, by a powerful and gracious help, in other words by grace.

> Whoever comes thus by stages to the Brahman, and has attained to the grace of the supreme Ātman (*adhyātman*) is free from sorrow. (*Bh. Gītā Bh.* 18, 54)

Let us notice that saving grace is here attributed not to *Īśvara* the lower and māyic *Brahman*, but is an act of the highest *Brahman-Ātman*. That Śaṅkara proposes *bhakti* or personal love of the highest *Brahman* is indubitable when we read his commentary on *Gītā* 11, 55 (called the *parama-śloka*, i.e., the most important passage of the *Gītā*):

> 54. Through *Bhakti*, directed to nothing else, that is, through faithful love which is directed toward nothing save Bhagavat Himself and which does not turn for a moment from Him and which with all its faculties perceives only Vāsudeva and nothing more. By this sort of devotion, He can be known, not only as He is declared in the *śāstras*, but He can be intuitively seen in essence and in truth.
>
> Now the essential teaching of the whole book of the *Gītā* which conduces to highest Bliss will be summed up here, the teaching being such as everyone should follow:
>
> 55. Who, what he does, does for me only, is inclined towards me only, and true to me. Free from envy, free from dependence on the world, he goes to me, O Pāṇḍava.
>
> A servant [comments Śaṅkara,] carries out the work of his lord but he does not say of his lord that he is the highest goal to which he hopes to attain one day after his death. But he who has surrendered to me, who does my work, he attains to me as his highest goal. He who cleaves to me, in all things with his whole soul and with utmost zeal, he has surrendered to me. He comes to me; that is: I alone am his highest goal.

But for length's sake, we might like to quote *Chānd. Up. Bh.* 6, 14, where is told most forcefully the story of a man, lost in the misery of the world, yet longing to return 'home' to eternal salvation. Thus he is confused and blinded and "thus he cries, caught in a hundredfold and monstrous way. [...] Until in one way or another he meets one who—conscious of true being that is the *Brahman-Ātman*, free from bondage and truly blessed—is also by reason of his abundant merit full of deepest sympathy. He teaches the wanderer the way to knowledge and the failure of all worldly things...." The text finishes: "To such a one the delay seems long and weary until—as he says—'Ultimately I shall be set free. Then I shall arrive'." We see here clearly how for Śaṅkara the saving help comes to man from somebody else, and how he is longing for a perfect and sinless Guru.

The nature of *formal causality* can be understood in two ways:

- the internal principle of perfection of a 'māyic' nature.

- the external causality of the Archetype upon its copy, image or reflection. In other words as exemplary causality.

The first sense cannot apply directly to *Brahman* for it would reduce Him to being a part as it were of His creature and it would make both one single being (monism instead of *a-dvaita*). Śaṅkara is emphatic in his rejection of whatever would destroy the pure transcendence of *Brahman*. He has no ear for a cosmic God, except as a transitory and erroneous but propaedeutic stage of human knowledge. Such a God is *māyā*, i.e., no absolute reality. And as only absolute reality suits God, it is no God at all.

Indirectly this formal internal causality may be referred to God because it is a constituent of māyic being and whatever is positive in created being should be referred to God. It is indeed only by starting from the world that we acquire some conception of God, namely by removing (*avritti*: *remotio*) from finite reality all imperfections (*via negativa*) and by making all perfections thus obtained and purified qualitatively infinite and transcendent (*via eminentiae*):

> 'This great *un*born Self, *un*decaying, *un*dying, *im*mortal, fear*less*, is indeed Brahman' (*Bṛh. Up*. 4, 4, 25); 'That Self is to be described by *No, no*' (*Bṛh. Up*. 3, 9, 26); 'It is *neither* coarse *nor* fine' (*Bṛh. Up*. 3, 8, 8). Such scriptural passages, by denying all modification of Brahman, teach it to be *absolutely changeless* (kūṭastha). For to the one Brahman the two qualities of being subject to modification and of being free from it cannot both be ascribed. And if you say, 'Why should they not be both predicated of Brahman (the former during the time of the subsistence of the world, the latter during the period of reabsorption) just as rest and motion may be predicated (of one body at different times)?' we remark that the qualification, 'absolutely changeless' (kūṭastha) precludes this. For the changeless Brahman cannot be the substratum of varying attributes. And that, on account of the negation of all attributes, Brahman really is eternal and changeless has already been demonstrated. (*B.S.Bh.* 2, 1, 14, emphases added)

In the second sense *Brahman* is for Śaṅkara the Archetype of the māyic selfs or created persons (*ātmans* not *ahaṁkāras*)—and through them of nature—because they are His reflection and there is nothing perfect in them which could ultimately be referred to anything different from Him. The world is His glory:

> What is the glory of Brahman? By its command the earth is maintained and the heaven endures; by its command the sun and the moon run their course as flaming fire; by its command the rivers and the seas do not overflow their boundaries. Its command is obeyed alike by all which moves and all which does not move; the seasons, the solstice, the years do not overstep its command; by its command all Karma and actors under Karma and the fruits they bring forth, do not continue beyond their allotted time.... That is His glory. (*Muṇḍ. Up. Bh.* 1, 17)

The world "shines through Him." It is created according to the eternal Veda which is the Wisdom of *Brahman* and which contains within itself eternally the primary types of all classes of things.

> That which is posterior, namely the effect, is declared by Scripture to have, previous to its actual beginning, its Being in the cause, by the self of the cause merely. For in passages like, 'In the beginning, my dear, this was that only which is' (*Chānd. Up.* 6, 2, 1); and, 'Verily, in the beginning this was Self, one only' (*Ait. Ār.* 2, 4, 1, 1), the effect which is denoted by the word 'this' appears in grammatical coordination with (the word denoting) the cause (from which it appears that both inhere in the same substratum). A thing, on the other hand, which does not exist in another thing by the self of the other thing is not produced from that other thing; for instance, oil is not produced from sand. Hence as there is non-difference before the production (of the effect), we understand that the effect even after having been produced continues to be non-different from the cause. (*B.S.Bh.* 2, 1, 16)
>
> But, an objection will be raised, in some places Scripture speaks of the effect before its production as that which is not; so, for instance, 'In the beginning this was that only which is not' (*Chānd. Up.* 3, 19, 1); and 'Non-existent indeed this was in the beginning' (*Taitt. Up.* 2, 7). Hence being (*sattvam*) cannot be ascribed to the effect before its production.
>
> This we deny. For by the Non-existence of the effect previous to its production is not meant absolute Non-existence, but only a different quality or state, viz. the state of names and forms being unevolved, which state is different from the state of names and forms being evolved. With reference to the latter state the effect is called, previous to its production, non-existent although then also it existed identical with its cause. (*B.S.Bh.* 2, 1, 17)

We shall find back this doctrine and its consequences when we speak of the material cause of the world. However "the origination of the world from the 'word' [from the Vedas] is not to be understood in that sense, that the word constitutes the material cause of the world, as *Brahman* does; but while there exist the everlasting words, i.e., the words whose essence is the power of denotation in connection with their eternal sense (i.e., the *ākṛtis* denoted), the accomplishments of such individual things as are capable of having those words applied to them is called an origination from those words."—"For, although the individuals of the [species denoted by the word] have an origin, their species (*ākṛtis*; best translated by *eidos*) does not have an origin, since of [the three categories] substances, qualities and actions the individuals only originate, not the species. Now it is with the species that the words are connected, not with the individuals, which, as being infinite in number, are not capable of entering into that connection." (*B.S.Bh.* 1, 3, 28) Therefore "the eternity of the word of the Veda has to be assumed for this very reason, that the world with its definite (eternal) species, such as gods and so on, originates from it." (*B.S.Bh.* 1, 3, 29)

These types are external (i.e., transcendent though immanent) to the individual copies made after them; in themselves they are identical with *Brahman* in whom there is no division (*abheda*) whatsoever. To conceive Him as *Saguṇa Brahma* or as "a collection of all noble qualities" is human enough, but we must at once deny all multiplicity thus involved and speak of Him as *Nirguṇa Brahma* or mere actuality.

The doctrine of the pre-existence of all created beings in the eternal '*eidê*' identical with *Brahman* is subject to the objection that from it there follows the result "that the activity of causal agents is together purposeless. For if the effect were lying already fully accomplished in the cause and were non-different from it, nobody would endeavour to bring about effects....—Your objection is refuted, we reply, by the consideration that the endeavour of the causal agent may be looked upon as having a purpose in so far as it arranges the causal substance in the form of the effect (i.e., the cause remained unchanged while the whole change exists only in the effect)" (*B.S.Bh.* 2, 1, 18).

Material causality is also to be understood in two ways. [First,] as the internal principle of imperfection and undetermination of the māyic being (the *upādāna* of the Sāṁkhya System). To apply the notion in this sense to *Brahman* would again be equivalent to making of Him a cosmic god, substantially immanent to his creatures and therefore it must be rejected.

But it can also mean that from whence (*yataḥ*), that out of which māyic Beings are made. Provided such a causality remain '*vivartavāda*' kind of causality (which implies no changes whatsoever in the cause) and does not become '*pariṇāmavāda*' (continuous transformation of the cause into the effect) it may and must be applied to God.

Śaṅkara says that out of nothing nothing can emerge. To affirm the opposite would be equivalent to interpreting the '*creatio ex nihilo*' as creation through the medium of a pre-existing matter which would itself be identical with nothingness; it would amount to mere absurdity.

'*Creatio ex nihilo*' is on the contrary a negative expression which helps in bringing out the truth that there is absolutely nothing, no matter, no instrument, no secondary agent, pre-existent and necessary to the transcendent causation of the world by God.

> 'Others say, in the beginning there was that only which is not, but how could it be thus, my dear? How could that which is, be born of that which is not?' (*Chānd. Up.* 6, 2, 1; 2) (cf. *B.S.Bh.Bh.* 1, 4, 14)

But the positive assertion implicit in the negative expression is that God is the one total cause of all māyic beings.

> In the passage, 'He created all this whatever is,' it represents the Creator as the Cause of the entire world, and thereby declares Him to have been without a second previous to the creation.... 'Being only, my dear, was this in the beginning, one only, without a second....' (*Sat eva idam agre āsit, ekam eva, advitīyam*) (*Chānd. Up.* 6, 2, 1). 'It thought, may I be many, may I grow forth. It sent forth fire, etc.' (*Chānd. Up.* 6, 2, 3), and 'In the beginning all this was Self, one only; there was nothing else blinking whatsoever. He thought, shall I send forth worlds?' (*Ait. Ār.* 2, 4, 1, 1; 2) (*B.S.Bh.* 1, 4, 14)

No positivity of being exists therefore in the world which He is not the Source of (*yoni*—cf. *B.S.Bh.* 1, 4, 28); thus He is not only the one operative but even the one material Cause of all beings (*B.S.Bh.* 1, 4, 25).

The Sāṁkhya System held the primeval material cause (*Pradhāna*—nature) to be an absolute reality different from *Brahman* (of whom they had nothing to say, neither denying, nor affirming His existence) and in itself undifferentiated and non-developed. Out of it all natural beings should have originated and evolved. Now Śaṅkara strongly opposed their exclusive thesis; he denied that *Pradhāna* is an absolute reality apart from *Brahman*, that it is in itself non-intelligent and mere potentiality, and that it is the source of beings. But he does not deny that in order to explain the world some material cause should be found. Only he transfers it into the infinite actuality of the Supreme. The whole being of the world is pre-contained eminently in God. With regard to the world it can be said to be potentially in God. But with regard to God Himself it is pure actuality identical with His very being. And God does not by creating pass from non-activity to activity, only the world passes from non-existence to existence. (Cf. *B.S.Bh.* especially the whole 4th *Pāda* of the *Adhyāya*).

The simile of clay (*B.S.Bh.* 1, 4, 28) being the material cause of the pots, gods, and other 'names and forms' induced from it is adduced by Śaṅkara only in order to inculcate the notion of the material cause: that primordial entity from which, out of which, particular things are made, and which gives them to be, by participation, identical with itself (i.e., the same nature as itself). He supposes the clay to be infinite (i.e., be all the clay possible, or the clay as such) and in that connection brings in the other comparison of the ether as such (*ākāśa*—sky, space) and the ether in the jar (i.e., the space limited by the capacity of the jar). The infinity of ether indeed, the least differentiated of primary substances, seems somehow closer to the infinity of a spiritual entity, and it helps in understanding how a spiritual infinite can communicate itself and originate a reflection of the same nature as itself but dependent, without losing anything of its own infinity and transcendence. The knowledge of Kapila or of Manu undergoes no decrease or increase in originating a reflected knowledge in the mind of the disciples.

For gross minds unable to conceive a transcendental material causality but only that gross material causality of clay, ether and the like, to say that *Brahman* is the material Cause of the world means nothing but that the effect is a part, an emanation, or a self-evolution of *Brahman* and that there is univocity and continuity (*pariṇāmavāda*) between God and the world. (*B.S.Bh.* 2, 1, 14) We have already seen Śaṅkara's answer to them: "This objection is without a force, because a number of scriptural passages, by denying all modification of *Brahman*, teach it to be absolutely changeless (*kūṭastha*)." (*B.S.Bh.* 2, 1, 14) Śaṅkara holds *vivartavāda* asserting simultaneously the ontological identity and the absolute discontinuity of Cause and effect. The springing into existence of the effect does not bring about any change, increase or decrease in the infinite Cause. Such a mode of causing is of course beyond the range of our imagination, although within the suggestion of well-chosen analogies, but can be conceived without any contradiction and it must be affirmed on the ground of our previous metaphysical certainties about the nature of *Brahman* and His creatures.

It is a general principle that the effect is somehow identical with its material cause; they cannot be merely equivocal. On the contrary neither the operative nor the final cause implies of necessity such identity. A potter or a mover can very well be of another nature than that of their effects; and one can strive towards a goal that has only accidental connection with oneself. But if the cause is one and total and if it originates the whole being of its effect, it is impossible that there be nothing in common between them. Being, here participated and reflectional, there absolute and original, is indeed the common ground of identity.

In a lengthy and rational (not merely exegetical) discussion (*B.S.Bh.* 2, 1, 18) Śaṅkara meets with 13 objections against the thesis of the fundamental identity of the material cause and of its effect and refutes their merely philosophical grounds one after the other. His argumentation might be summed up like this: Either the nature of the cause and the nature of the effect are not fundamentally different or they are absolutely heterogeneous. In the latter case in order to explain the relationship we apprehend between both, we must have recourse to some *atiśaya* as the causal substance, i.e., some capacity of the cause reaching beyond self for some particular effect only and not for other effects—or some *samavāya* connection of both, i.e., some inherence or intimate relation like that connecting a whole and its parts, a substance and its qualities, etc. If we resort to *atiśaya*, it may mean either the antecedent condition of the effect in the cause—then we come to our doctrine that the effect exists in the cause—or it means a certain connection of the cause with the effect—then we fall back into our second hypothesis. If it is thus assumed that a *samavāya* connects cause and effect, we have to admit that the *samavāya* itself is joined by a certain connection to the two terms which are connected by the *samavāya*, and then that connection will again require a new connection joining it to the two terms which it binds together and we shall thus be compelled to postulate an infinite series of connections. But *anavasthā* (*regressus ad infinitum*) never leads anywhere. Therefore the only solution possible is the one of the first hypothesis, namely that the effect is of the same nature as its material cause.

This highly technical argumentation is but the development of a simple but important principle: when one thing, for instance an effect, an object, etc. is never apprehended except in connection with something else, for instance a cause, or a subject, etc., it cannot be ultimately explained by using the analytical method, i.e., by supposing the two related beings to be at first separate and heterogeneous, for then a third entity, namely some kind of connection, will have to be called for in order to bridge the opened gulf and this third entity will in its turn require other connecting entities, and so on *ad indefinitum*. The only adequate explanation therefore is to admit the unity as our starting point and, while trying to characterize it, never to stray from it.

This principle, being universal, must apply to *Brahman* and His creatures, unless it can be proved that He cannot be, on account of His nature, their material cause.

Śaṅkara examines the point in commenting on the *sūtra*: "(Brahman is) the material cause also on account of (this view) not being in conflict with the promissory statements and the illustrative instances" (*B.S.* 1, 4, 23).

The *pūrvapakṣin* [opponent] maintains that *Brahman* is only the operative cause of the world and brings several arguments for his position: *Brahman*'s creative energy is, according to Scripture (v.g. *Praśna Up.* 6, 3; 4: 'He reflected, he created *prāṇa*') preceded by reflection. Now only the action of operative causes, such as potters and the like, is preceded by reflection. (*B.S.Bh.* 1, 4, 23)

Observation shows also that the effect is generally brought about by the concurrence of several factors. That is to say, the operative cause and the substantial cause always appear as separate things. It is therefore appropriate that we should view the prime creator in the same light. (*B.S.Bh.* 1, 4, 23)

He is known as '*Īśvara*' (Lord). "Now lords such as kings and the son of Vivasvat are known only as operative causes and the highest Lord must on that account be viewed as operative cause only." (*B.S.Bh.* 1, 4, 23)

"Further the effect of the Creator's activity, viz. the world, is seen to consist of parts, to be non-intelligent and impure; we therefore must assume that its cause also is of the same nature; for it is a matter of general observation that cause and effect are alike in kind. But that *Brahman* does not resemble the world in nature, we know from many scriptural passages such as: 'It is without parts, without actions, tranquil, without fault, without taint' (*Śvet. Up.* 6, 19)." (*B.S.Bh.* 1, 4, 23)

"Hence there remains no other alternative but to admit that in addition to *Brahman* there exists a material cause of the world of impure nature, such as is known from the [Sāṁkhya-] *Smṛti*, and to limit the causality of *Brahman*, as declared by Scripture, to operative causality only." (*B.S.Bh.* 1, 4, 23)

To these objections Śaṅkara makes the following reply:

> Brahman is to be acknowledged as the material cause as well as the operative cause; because this latter view does not conflict with the promissory statements and the illustrative instances.
>
> The promissory statement chiefly meant is the following one, 'Have you ever asked for that instruction by which that which is not heard becomes heard; that which is not perceived, perceived; that which is not known, known?' (*Chānd. Up.* 6, 1, 3) This passage intimates that through the cognition of one thing everything else, even if (previously) unknown, becomes known. Now the knowledge of everything is possible through the cognition of the material cause, since the effect is non-different from the material cause. On the other hand, effects are not non-different from their operative causes; for we know from ordinary experience that the carpenter, for instance, is different from the house he has built.
>
> The illustrative example referred to is the one mentioned (*Chānd. Up.* 6, 1, 4), 'My dear, as by one clod of clay all that is made of clay is known, the modification being a name merely which has its origin in speech, while the truth is that it is clay merely;' which passage again has reference to the material cause.
>
> The text adds a few more illustrative instances of a similar nature, 'As by one nugget of gold all that is made of gold is known; as by one pair of nail-scissors all that is made of iron is known.'

> Similar promissory statements are made in other places also, for instance ... *Muṇḍ. Up.* 1, 1, 3; 1, 1, 7. *Bṛh. Up.* 4, 5, 6; 4, 5, 8. [...] [All] are to be viewed as proving, more or less, that Brahman is also the material cause of the world.
> The ablative case also in the passage, 'That from which (*yataḥ*) these beings are born,' has to be considered as indicating the material cause of the beings, according to the grammatical rule, *Pāṇ.* 1, 4, 30. (*B.S.Bh.* 1, 4, 23)

Śaṅkara's main argument to substantiate his thesis appears therefore to be the possibility of a knowledge of God such that it brings along with itself the true knowledge of everything. If it is asserted that nothing is common between God and His effects but all is equivocal, this knowledge becomes impossible. But if, starting from the effects and guided by the assertions of Scripture, we are able to obtain a true knowledge of Him, it follows that whatever is positive in the effects is to be found in Him in an eminent and transcendent way, that therefore there is an analogical identity between the Cause and its effects, and that God is really "that from whence (*yataḥ*) these beings are born."

This argument is stated again and again by Śaṅkara as the ground-argument for his thesis:

> We declare that the reason for assuming the non-difference of cause and effect is the fact of the internal organ (*buddhi*) being affected (impressed) by cause and effect *jointly*. (*B.S.Bh.* 2, 1, 15)

> On any other assumption it would not be possible to maintain that by the knowledge of one thing everything becomes known. We therefore must adopt the following view. In the same way as those parts of ethereal space which are limited by jars and waterpots are not really different from the universal ethereal space, and as the water of a mirage is not really different from the surface of the salty steppe—for the nature of that water is that it is seen in one moment and has vanished in the next, and moreover, it is not to be perceived by its own nature (i.e., apart from the surface of the desert)—; so this manifold world with its objects of enjoyment, enjoyers and so on has no existence apart from Brahman. (*B.S.Bh.* 2, 1, 14)

> This doctrine of the individual soul having its Self in Brahman... does away with the independent existence of the individual soul, just as the idea of the rope does away with the idea of the snake (for which the rope had been mistaken). And if the doctrine of the independent existence of the individual soul has to be set aside, then the opinion of the entire phenomenal world—which is based on the individual soul—having an independent existence is likewise to be set aside. (*B.S.Bh.* 2, 1, 14)

The doctrine here hinted at of *Māyā* as a tentative explanatory theory of the 'how' of the creation has been explained elsewhere and moreover we do not wish to give it an importance and a prominence which are not to be found in Śaṅkara's writings; it is but a complementary theory and its value is one of suggestion rather than of assertion.

The absolute identity of the operative and of the material causality of *Brahman* is also set up by Śaṅkara, as we have already seen:

> That Brahman is at the same time the operative cause of the world, we have to conclude from the circumstance that there is no other guiding principle. Ordinary material causes, indeed, such as lumps of clay and pieces of gold, are dependent in order to shape themselves into vessels and ornaments, on extraneous operative causes such as potters and goldsmiths; but outside Brahman as material cause there is no other operative cause to which the material cause could look; for Scripture says that previously to creation Brahman was one without a second. (*B.S.Bh.* 1, 4, 23)

Now that the unity of God and His creatures is not an absolute identity is clear from texts such as these:

> *Sarvam ca nāmarūpādi vikārajātam sad-ātmanā eva satyam, svatas tu anṛtm* (*Chānd. Up. Bh.* 6, 3, 2): The whole multiplicity which exists by being produced under names and forms and so on is true *only in as far as it is Being itself* (literally: only—*eva*—by the Being—*Ātman-Sad-ātmanā*) but of itself (*svatas tu*) it is untrue.

Or:

> *Sad-āspadam sarvam sarvatra* (*Bh. Gītā Bh.* 13, 14): The all is everywhere a storehouse of being (*Sad-āspadam*).

The formula "*Aham Brahma asmi*": I am Brahma, is of course not of a logical but of a mystical nature, says Rudolf Otto. The word 'is' in the mystical formula of identification has a significance which it does not contain in logic. It is no copula as in the sentence: S is P; it is not a sign of equality in a reversible equation. It is not the 'is' of a normal assertion of identity.... One might try to indicate this by forcing the language and making the word 'be' into a medium of higher unity of intransitive and transitive. For instance instead of "I am Brahma," one might say: "I am existed by Brahma" or "essenced" by Brahma, or "Brahma exists me." If Śaṅkara builds the form '*āstitvam*' and '*āstikata*,' the form "to exist somebody" would be permissible.[2]

> In the same way [says Śaṅkara,] as Scripture speaks of the origin of the world from Brahman, it also speaks of Brahman subsisting *apart* from its effects (*Chānd. Up.* 3, 12, 6 and other texts).... Those texts declare on the one hand, that not the entire Brahman passes over into its effects and, on the other hand, that Brahman is without parts. Even certain ordinary things such as gems, spells, herbs, and the like possess powers which... produce various opposite effects, and nobody unaided by instruction is able to find out by mere reflection the number of these powers, their favouring conditions, their objects, their purposes, etc.; how much more impossible it is to conceive without the aid of Scripture the true nature of Brahman with its powers unfathomable by thought! As the *Purāṇa* says: 'Do not apply reasoning to what is unthinkable! The mark of the unthinkable is that it is above all material causes.' ...
>
> The break [between Brahman and its creatures is not an absolute one] but merely an apparent one. By a break of that nature a thing is not really broken up into parts, not any more than the moon is really multiplied by appearing double to a person of defective vision. By that element of plurality which is the fiction of *Avidyā* [not absolutely true knowledge; not knowledge from the absolute standpoint of God], which is characterized by name and form, which is evolved as well as non-evolved, which is not to be defined either as the Existing (*Sat*) or the Non-existing (*Asat*), Brahman becomes the basis of this entire apparent world with its changes, and so on, while in its true and real nature it at the same time remains unchanged, lifted above the phenomenal universe. (*B.S.Bh.* 2, 1, 27)

Before putting an end to this short study it might be good to examine a few objections against the doctrine exposed and to have a look at Śaṅkara's answers to them.

(a) "If we acquiesce in this doctrine, the ordinary means of right knowledge, perception, etc. become invalid because the absence of manifoldness has deprived them of their objects; just as the idea of a man becomes invalid after the right idea of the post has presented itself." (*B.S.Bh.* 2, 1, 14)

> [This objection], we reply, [does] not damage our position because the entire complex of phenomenal existence is considered as absolutely true as long as the knowledge of Brahman being the Self of all has not arisen; just as the phantoms of a dream are considered to be true until the sleeper wakes. (*B.S.Bh.* 2, 1, 14)

(b) The objection that the doctrine is equivalent to monism, the creatures being either a modification, or an emanation, or a self-evolution, or a part of *Brahman* has already been refuted enough. (cf. *B.S.Bh.* 2, 1, 14; 2, 1, 26 and ff.)

(c) To the objection that a mutual relationship between God and His creatures follows from the doctrine, Śaṅkara replies:

> The *Bhagavad Gītā* [5, 14; 15] declares that in reality the relation of Ruler and ruled does not exist. That, on the other hand, all those distinctions are valid, as far as the phenomenal world is concerned, Scripture as well as the *Bhagavad Gītā* states; compare *Bṛh. Up.* 4, 4, 22 … and *Bh. Gītā* 18, 61…. The *Sūtrakāra* [Bādarāyaṇa] also asserts the non-difference of cause and effect only with regard to the state of Reality; while he had, in the preceding *Sūtra* [*B.S.Bh.* 2, 1, 13], where he looked to the phenomenal world, compared Brahman to the ocean, etc., that comparison resting on the assumption of the world of effects not yet having been refuted. (*B.S.Bh.* 2, 1, 14)

(d) If that doctrine is accepted, certain faults, as, for instance, doing what is not beneficial, will attach to [the intelligent cause, i.e., *Brahman*]. (*B.S.Bh.* 2, 1, 21)

> We rather declare that that omniscient, omnipotent Brahman, whose essence is eternal pure cognition and freedom, *and which is additional to, i.e., different from the embodied self,* is the creative principle of the world. The faults specified above, such as doing what is not beneficial, and the like, do not attach to Brahman; for as eternal freedom is its characteristic nature, there is nothing either beneficial to be done by it or non-beneficial to be avoided by it. Nor is there any impediment to its knowledge and power; for it is omniscient and omnipotent. The embodied self, on the other hand, *is of a different nature*, and to it the mentioned faults adhere.
>
> But then we do not declare it [Brahman] to be the creator of the world [to be the same as Īśvara, the Lord conceived as essentially related to the world] [but to be the transcendent Creator of the world] and this, on account of 'the declaration of difference.' For scriptural passages (such as, … 'The Self we must search out…,' *Chānd. Up.* 8, 7, 1; 'Then he becomes united with the True,' *Chānd. Up.* 6, 8, 1; 'This embodied self mounted by the intelligent Self,' *Bṛh. Up.* 4, 3, 35) declare differences founded on the relations of agent, object, mobile, end, etc., and thereby *show Brahman to be different from the individual soul.*
>
> And if it be objected that there are other passages declaratory of non-difference (for instance, 'That are thou'), and that difference and non-difference cannot co-exist because contradictory, we reply that the possibility of the co-existence of the two is shown by the parallel instance of the universal ether and the ether limited by a jar….

> With regard therefore to the state in which the appearance of plurality is not yet sublated, it follows from passages declaratory of difference that Brahman is superior to the individual soul; whereby the possibility of faults adhering to it is excluded. (*B.S.Bh.* 2, 1, 22, emphases added)

The last quotation is of such a density that it summarizes the whole doctrine and might serve as a conclusion. It adds important shades to that doctrine of non-difference (*advaita*) rather than of identity of God and His creation. God is the total cause but His causality is not of the same order as the mundane causalities known to us. Even while causing He remains absolutely untouched by His action; the whole reality of the change is in the effect alone. His causality is the perfection of all our causalities, efficient, final, formal, material, but it is above all a transcendent one. All our speculations about its mode of activity are deficient and, after all, not of the utmost importance for us. What is important is to acknowledge the supreme Beingness of God and our participating beingness, for in that knowledge lies the principle of our salvation. Simultaneously to exalt man up to asserting that he is a reflection of God, and to humiliate him down to stressing that he is only a reflecting participation and as nothing in himself, this is indeed Śaṅkara's imperishable greatness.

Notes

[1] ["A Note about Śaṅkara's Doctrine of Creation," typescript dated 13 June 1949. Collected Papers D, 7-23. Published here for the first time with kind permission of De Nobili College, Pune. For the *B.S.Bh.* De Smet uses the Thibaut translation for the most part, modifying it at times.]

[2] Cf. Rudolf Otto, *Mysticism East and West* (London: Macmillan, 1932) 84-85.

APPENDIX 3

PARALLEL ARGUMENTS FOR THE EXISTENCE OF GOD IN AQUINAS AND ŚAṄKARA[1]

For both Aquinas and Śaṅkara causality is the only gateway to the existent God short of infallible revelation or perfect knowledge.

Śaṅkara knows of two types of cause: *upādāna* and *nimitta-kāraṇa*. Hence, he proposes two types of arguments: those which prove that *Brahman* is the fundamental *upādāna*, and those which prove that *Brahman* is the supreme *nimitta-kāraṇa* of the whole universe. He further shows their convergence by establishing that one and the same *Brahman* verifies these two functions which are not opposed but complementary. Indeed, on the one hand, *upādāna* transcends materiality or immateriality and can in fact be either material, like clay, or spiritual, like consciousness; it should simply be understood as inner or immanent cause, that "from which, in which, and into which" the effect arises, endures and returns, and without which it cannot subsist; it may be either an intrinsic constituent part of the effect, or a deeply immanent and necessary but altogether transcendent and independent principle of that effect. Hence, *upādānas* form an ascending series. As to *nimitta-kāraṇa*, it is always connected with consciousness (intellectual or at least sentient) whether it means the principal operative cause or the instruments which the latter directs. It is generally extrinsic to the effect but nothing precludes that some *nimitta-kāraṇa* be immanent. Hence, operative causes too form an ascending series. Now, since *anavasthā* or infinite regress is excluded from all ascending or vertical series, it is but logical that all *upādāna-* and all *nimitta-kāraṇas* series end in a supreme Cause which is innermost Consciousness (and thus

Paramātman) as well as transcendent and uppermost Perfection (*Pūrṇa*, *Parabrahman*).

Examples of Śaṅkara's arguments

1. From order to Ruler: "The sun and the moon must have been created **for the purpose** of giving light by a **universal Ruler who knows** of what use they will be to all...; just as an ordinary lamp; therefore, that exists which has made the sun and the moon and compels them, although they are powerful and independent, to rise and set, increase and decrease, according to fixed place, time and causes. Thus there exists their mighty Ruler, the Immutable (*Akṣara*), as the lamp has its maker and regulator.... The unfailing sign of this is the fact that **heaven and earth obey a fixed order**; this would be impossible were there not a conscious, transcendent Ruler" (*Bṛh. Up. Bh.* 3, 8, 9ff)

Cf. Aquinas' fifth way: "We see that things which lack knowledge... act for an end, and this is evident from their acting... nearly always in the same way, so as to obtain the best results. Hence it is plain that they achieve their end, not fortuitously, but designedly. Now whatever lacks knowledge cannot move towards an end, unless it be directed by some being endowed with... intelligence; as the arrow is directed by the archer. Therefore some intelligent being exists by whom all natural things are directed to their end; and this being we call God" (*S.Th.* 1, 2, 3, c).

Cf. also Śaṅkara's reduction of *karma* to Providence: *phala* cannot be produced directly by *karma*, which no longer exists; nor by *apūrva*, which neither *pratyakṣa* nor *anumāna* nor *arthāpatti* can establish. Indeed, *apūrva* is neither a sufficient condition of *phala*, since it is devoid of knowledge, nor a necessary one, since the Lord suffices to requite all actions, due to his omniscience and omnipotence. Requiting is but one aspect of his total Causality, to which all *karmas*, even if their series has temporal beginning, are reduced as effects. (Cf. *B.S.Bh.* 3, 2, 38-41; 2, 1, 34-35 and *Bṛh. Up. Bh.* 3, 8, 9ff)

2. From lower to Highest Ātman: "Outer senses are nothing but gross. Their objects... are **subtle, and great, and their inner** ***ātmās***. And *manas* is more subtle and great than they and is their inner *ātman*.... And *buddhi*, being superior to *manas*, is more subtle and great and inner *ātman*... (Higher than) *buddhi* is the 'great *ātman*,' called '*ātman*' because it is the inner principle or *ātman* of all *jīvas*, *buddhis*, and 'great' because it is most pervasive; it is the first-born of *Prakṛti*, called *Hiraṇyagarbha*.... Being superior to it, the undifferentiated (*Prakṛti*) is more subtle, inner *ātman*, and greater than all... it is the condensation of all powers of causes and effects... it abides in the supreme *Ātman*... The latter is more subtle, since He is the innermost *Ātman* and is, indeed, called '*puruṣa*' because He fills up (*pṛ*) everything... This *Puruṣa* is *kāsthā*, the utter limit, the culmination, **the climax of** subtleness, greatness and inner-ātmāhood... Hence, He is *parā gatiḥ*, the supreme goal" (*Kaṭha Up. Bh.* 1, 3, 10-11).

"Since It is arrived at as the root of the world, It indeed exists, because the elimination of effects terminates in Is-ness (*Astitva*). Thus, indeed, this effect (the world), when followed **along the ascending** series of its more and more subtle (inner causes or *ātmās*), leads ultimately to the simple awareness of 'Existent' (*Sad-buddhi*).... If the world had no Cause, this effect, being transfused with *asat* (non-being) only, would at every step be grasped as non-being only.... It is, on the contrary, grasped at every step as being only, just as jars, etc., ... are perceived as permeated with clay, etc. Therefore, the *Ātman*, the root of the universe, must be apprehended as 'It is' only" (*Kaṭha Up. Bh.* 2, 3, 12).

"It is present in its entirety (*kartsnyena parisamāpta*) in all bodies, somehow as 'cowness' is present in each individual cow. But It cannot be merely of the size of these bodies, for It is formless and all-pervading" (*Bṛh. Up. Bh.* 1, 3, 22).

Cf. Aquinas' fourth way from the gradation to be found in things: "Among beings there are some more and some less good, true, noble and the like. But 'more' and 'less' are said of different things according as they resemble in their different ways a corresponding Maximum.... Now the Maximum in any genus is the cause of all in that genus.... Hence, there must be something which is to all beings the Cause of their being, goodness, and every other perfection, and this we call God" (*S.Th.* I, 2, 3, c).

3. From affirmation to its necessary Object: "Whatever we perceive or infer is not permanently real (*vastusat*), since it is change, and change fails to be always...; so, it cannot be apprehended apart from its inner cause.... Indeed, it would be wrong to conclude that nothing at all is *sat*, for in every affirmation we are aware of a twofold cognition, namely of *sat* and *asat*. *Sat* means that object whose knowledge never fails; *asat*, that whose knowledge fails. Their double notion is present in every affirmation of jar, cloth, elephant, etc. (*san-ghaṭaḥ, san-paṭaḥ, san hastī*).... Now, the knowledge of jar, etc., happens to fail, but never the knowledge of 'existing.' Hence, jars, etc., are *asat*, whereas the object of the cognition of 'existing' is indeed *sat* since it never fails... even in the illusory affirmation of a mirage.... Hence we conclude that... *sat*, i.e., *ātman*, is never inexistent, because it never fails anywhere" (*Bh. Gītā Bh.* 2, 16).

Cf. Aquinas' proof of God's infinity: "Our intellect extends to the infinite in understanding; and a sign of this is that, given any finite quantity, our intellect can think of a greater one. But this ordination of the intellect would be in vain unless an infinite intelligible Reality existed. Such a Reality must therefore exist and be the greatest of beings. This we call God, God is therefore infinite." (*SCG* 1, 42, 10)

And Aquinas' third way from changeable to Necessary: "We find in the world beings that can either be or not be, namely those subject to generation and corruption. But what is such has a cause since, being equally related to the two contraries, being and non-being, it must be owing to some cause that being accrues to it. Now one cannot proceed to infinity among causes. We must therefore posit something that is a necessary being.... But one cannot proceed to infinity among necessary beings the cause of whose necessity lies in an outside source. We must therefore posit a first necessary being, which is necessary through itself, i.e., God." (*SCG* 1, 15, 5)

4. Aquinas's first way from motion to unmoved Mover and his second way from secondary operative cause to unaffected

Effector are also paralleled by Śaṅkara's scattered arguments from changing activity to its *pravṛtti-rahito Pravartaka*: cf. especially *B.S.Bh.* 2, 2, 2.

Notes

[1] [Lecture to the Poona Philosophy Union, 26 August 1965. Typescript, Collected Papers D, 74 (2 typed pp). Published for the first time with kind permission of De Nobili College, Pune.]

BIBLIOGRAPHY

Alston, A. *A Śaṅkara Source-Book.* 3 vols. London: Shanti Sadan, 1980-1981.

Alston, A.J. "Introduction." *Naiṣkarmya Siddhi of Śrī Sureśvara.* Tr. A.J. Alston. London: Shanti Sadan, 29 Chepstow Villas, W. 11, 1959.

Animananda, B. *The Blade: Life and Work of Brahmabandhab Upadhyay.* Calcutta: Roy & Son, 1949.

Anscombe, G.E.M. *An Introduction to Wittgenstein's Tractatus.* London: Hutchison, 1959.

Atmananda, [Swami]. *Śrī Śaṅkara's Teachings in His Own Words.* Bombay: Bharatiya Vidya Bhavan, 1960.

Belvalkar, S.K. *Shree Gopal Basu Mallik Lectures on Vedānta Philosophy*, pt. 1. Poona, 1929.

Belvalkar, S.K. and R.D. Ranade. *History of Indian Philosophy: The Creative Period.* New Delhi: Oriental Books Reprint Corporation, 1974.

Bhattacharya, V. "Śaṅkara's Commentaries on the Upaniṣads." *Sir Asutosh Mookerjee Silver Jubilee Volume*, vol. III, part 2. Calcutta, 1925. 103-110.

Boyd, R. *An Introduction to Indian Christian Theology.* Madras: CLS, 1969.

Cardona, George. "*Anvaya* and *Vyatireka* in Indian Grammar." *Adyar Library Bulletin* **31-32** (1967-68) 313-352.

Cardona, George. "On Reasoning from *Anvaya* and *Vyatireka* in Early Advaita." *Studies in Indian Philosophy: A Memorial Volume in Honour of Pandit Suklaji Sanghvi.* Ed. D. Malvania and N.J. Shah. Ahmedabad: L.V. Institute of Indology, 1981.

Chakrabarti, Samiran Chandra. *The Paribhāṣās in the Śrautasūtras.* Calcutta: Sanskrit Pustak Bhandar, 1980.

Chethimttam, J.B. 'Indian Interiority and Christian Theology.' Mimeograph.

Chintamani, T.R. "Śaṅkara—The Commentator on the Māṇḍūkya Kārikās." *Proceedings of the Third Oriental Conference.* Madras, 1924. 419-421.

Clooney, Francis X. *Thinking Ritually: Rediscovering the Pūrva Mīmāṃsā of Jaimini.* Vienna: Institut für Indologie der Universität Wien, 1990.

Clooney, F.X. *Theology after Vedānta: An Experiment in Comparative Theology.* Albany: State University of New York Press, 1993. Delhi: Sri Satguru Publications, 1993.

Coelho, Ivo. "Fr. Richard V. De Smet (1916-97): Reminiscences." *Divyadaan: Journal of Philosophy and Education* **8**/1 (1997) 3-15.

Coelho, Ivo. 'Person and Subject in Lonergan: A Methodical Transposition.' Paper presented at the 36th Annual Lonergan Workshop, "Ongoing Collaboration in the Year of St Paul," 21-26 June 2009, Boston College, Boston. To be published in *Lonergan Workshop.*

Coelho, Ivo. 'Retrieving Good Work: De Smet on Śaṅkara.' Paper presented at the 37th Annual Lonergan Workshop, "Reversing Social and Cultural

Decline 'in a Friendly Universe'," 20-25 June 2010, Boston College, Boston. To be published in *Lonergan Workshop*.

Dandoy, Georges. *An Essay on the Doctrine of the Unreality of the World in the Advaita*. Calcutta: Catholic Orphan Press, 1919.

Dandoy, Georges. *L'ontologie du Vedānta: Essai sur l'acosmisme de l'Advaita*. Paris, 1932.

Das, S.K. *A Study of the Vedānta*. Calcutta: Calcutta University Press, 1927.

Dasgupta, S. *A History of Indian Philosophy*. Delhi: Motilal Banarsidass, 1975.

Datta, D.M. *The Six Ways of Knowing*. London: Allen & Unwin, 1932.

De Nobili, Roberto. *Roberto de Nobili on Indian Customs*. Ed. S. Rajamanickam. Latin text deciphered by Fr J. Pujo, and English translation by Archbishop P. Leonard. Palayamkottai: Research Institute, St Xavier's College, 1972.

De Smet, Richard. 'A Selection of Texts from Śaṅkarācārya,' cyclostyled notes for students (Poona: Jnana Deepa Vidyapeeth, n.d.) 30 pp. Unpublished.

De Smet, Richard. 'Bibliography of Fr Richard De Smet, SJ.' 9 November 1993. 25 pp. typescript. Unpublished.

De Smet, Richard. 'Guidelines in Indian Philosophy.' Pune: De Nobili College, 1968-1975. Cyclostyled notes for students. Unpublished.

De Smet, Richard. 'Indian Contribution to General Metaphysics.' Typescript. Collected Papers B, 342-360 = DNC 73/DES/COL 342-360.

De Smet, Richard. 'Notes on the Sāṃkhya-Kārikā: Ad mentem M. Ledrus, S.J.' Cyclostyled notes for students. 64 pp. Poona: De Nobili College, 1954. Unpublished.

De Smet, Richard. 'The Christian Encounter with Advaita Vedānta: A Survey of Four Centuries.' Typescript of 40 pp. + notes, and pp. 33-65 + notes. Written for St Thomas Christian Encyclopedia of India. N.d.

De Smet, Richard. 'The Theological Method of Śaṃkara.' Rome: Pontifical Gregorian University, 1953. Unpublished.

De Smet, Richard. 'The Trajectory of My Dialogical Activity.' Autobiographic text for Bradley J. Malkovsky, Rome, 23 April 1991. Unpublished.

De Smet, Richard. 'The Vedāntins' Diverse Conceptions of *Vākya* (Sentence) as Responsible for the Diversity of their Interpretations of the Same Scriptures.' 1994. Unpublished.

De Smet, Richard. "A Copernican Reversal: The Gītākāra's Reformulation of *Karma*." *Chinmaya Mission Silver Jubilee Volume*. Ed. S. Barlingay. Poona, 1976. 34-41. Also in *Philosophy East and West* **27**/1 (1977) 53-63.

De Smet, Richard. "Ancient Religious Speculation." *Religious Hinduism: A Presentation and Appraisal*. Ed. J. Neuner and R. De Smet. Allahabad / Bombay: St Paul Publications, 1964, 1968. Ch. 3, 41-51.

De Smet, Richard. "Categories of Indian Philosophy and Communication of the Gospel." *Religion and Society* **10**/3 (1963) 20-26.

De Smet, Richard. "Christ and the Transforming Growth of Religions." *Vidyajyoti: Journal of Theological Reflection* **55** (1991) 449-457.

De Smet, Richard. "Christianity and Shankarāchārya." *The St Thomas Christian Encyclopaedia of India*. Ed. George Menachery. Thrissur: The St Thomas Christian Encyclopaedia of India, 2010. **3**:22-42.

De Smet, Richard. "Christianity and Society." *The Viśva-Bhārati Journal of Philosophy* **21**/1 (1984) 89-99; also in *Indian Theological Studies* **22**/4 (1985) 325-337.

De Smet, Richard. "Dynamics of Hinduism and Hindu-Christian Dialogue." *Communio: International Catholic Review* **15** (Winter 1988) 436-450.

De Smet, Richard. "Elements of Permanent Value in Sāṃkhya." *Oriental Thought* (Nashik) **3**/2-4 (1957) 135-156.

De Smet, Richard. "Fleeting Time and Sacrificially Produced Continuity in Vedic Brahmanism and in Early Christianity." *Boletin de la Asociación Española de Orientalistas* **17** (1981) 147-166; also in *Indian Theological Studies* **19**/2 (1982) 1-26.

De Smet, Richard. "Gita in Time and Beyond." *The Bhagavad Gita and the Bible. Proceedings of the Seminar under the Auspices of the Christian Retreat and Study Centre, Rajpur, Dehradun May 5-9, 1972*. Ed. B.R. Kulkarni (Delhi: Unity Books, 1972) 1-30.

De Smet, Richard. "Guidelines in Indian Philosophy, ch. 2: The Growth of Speculation in the Brahmanas and Aranyakas." *Divyadaan: Journal of Philosophy and Education* **20**/3 (2009) 467-472.

De Smet, Richard. "Guidelines in Indian Philosophy, ch. 3: The Upaniṣadic Discoveries. 1. The Quest for the Brahman." *Divyadaan: Journal of Philosophy and Education* **21**/2 (2010) 257-289.

De Smet, Richard. "Guidelines in Indian Philosophy, ch. 3: The Upaniṣadic Discoveries. 2. The Other Upaniṣadic 'Great Sayings' (*Mahā-vākya*-s)." *Divyadaan: Journal of Philosophy and Education* **21**/3 (2010) 407-424.

De Smet, Richard. "Guidelines in Indian Philosophy. Introduction. Ch. 1: The Birth of Philosophical Reflection among Vedic Aryans." *Divyadaan: Journal of Philosophy and Education* **20**/2 (2009) 259-282.

De Smet, Richard. "Hindu and Neo-Hindu Exegesis." *Indian Theological Studies* **21** (1984) 225-240.

De Smet, Richard. "Indiens Beitrag zur allgemeine Metaphysik." *Kairos* (Salzburg) **3**/4 (1961) 161-182.

De Smet, Richard. "Interphilosophical and Religious Dialogue in My Life." *Pilgrims of Dialogue*. Ed. A. Pushparajan. Munnar: Sangam Dialogue Centre, 1991.

De Smet, Richard. "Is there an Order of the Supernatural?" *Transactions of the Indian Institute of Advanced Study* **1** (1965) 119-122.

De Smet, Richard. "Jesus and the Avatāra." *Dialogue and Syncretism: An Interdisciplinary Approach*. Ed. J.D. Gort, H.M. Vroom, R. Fernhout, A. Wessels. Grand Rapids: W.B. Eerdmans / Amsterdam: Editions Rodopi, 1989. 153-162.

De Smet, Richard. "Jesus and the Freedom of Man." *The Call Divine* **19**/11 (July 1971) 582-583.

De Smet, Richard. "Kaṇāda's Teaching on Knowledge." *Indian Antiquary* (3rd series) **1** (1964) 13-30.

De Smet, Richard. "Love versus Identity." *Indian Philosophical Quarterly* (Pune) 7/4 (July 1980) 519-526.

De Smet, Richard. "Man's Integral Dynamism and his Quest for Values." *Reality, Knowledge and Value: Felicitation Volume in Honour of A.G.*

Javadekar. Ed. S.R. Bhatt. Delhi: Bharatiya Vidya Prakashan, 1985. 133-142.

De Smet, Richard. "Method and Doctrine of Saint Thomas Aquinas." *Bulletin of the Ramakrishna Mission Institute of Culture* (Calcutta) **10**/10 (1959) 217-224.

De Smet, Richard. "Mutation of Values in Present-Day Europe." *Quest* **60** (Jan.-Mar. 1969) 21-27.

De Smet, Richard. "Notes on Hinduism versus the Plurality of Religious Traditions." *Boletin de la Asociación Española de Orientalistas* **21** (1985) 289-300.

De Smet, Richard. "Patterns and Theories of Causality." *Essays in Philosophy Presented to Dr. T. M. P. Mahadevan on his 50th Birthday.* Madras: Ganesh, 1962. 347-367. Also in *Indian Ecclesiastical Studies* **2** (1963) 169-190, and *Philosophy Today* **9**/2-4 (1965) 134-146.

De Smet, Richard. "Philosophy and Science as Integral Parts of Wisdom." *The Philosophical Quarterly* (Amalner) **33**/1 (1960) 31-39.

De Smet, Richard. "Rāmānuja, Pantheist or Panentheist?" *Annals of the Bhandarkar Oriental Research Institute (Diamond Jubilee Volume)* (1977-78) 561-571.

De Smet, Richard. "Secularism and the Supernatural." Exchange of letters between Prof. Mrs Saral Jhingram and De Smet, *Indian Theological Studies* **29** (1992) 55-67.

De Smet, Richard. "Secularization as a Dimension of Christianity." (A summary by D. Rodrigues). *Aumol* **19**.(September 1972) 124-126; also in *Ateismo e Dialogo* (Bollettino del Segretariato per i non-credenti) **8**/2 (1973) 24(84)-29(89).

De Smet, Richard. "Some Governing Principles of Indin Philosophy." *The Philosophical Quarterly* (Amalner) **35**/4 (1963) 249-258. Also in *Philosophy Today* **9**/3-4 (1965) 192-199.

De Smet, Richard. "Stretching Forth to Eternity: The Mystical Doctrine of Gregory of Nyssa." *Prayer and Contemplation.* Ed. C.M. Vadakkekara. Bangalore: Asian Trading Corporation, 1980. 331-348.

De Smet, Richard. "Stumbling-Blocks or Stepping-Stones." *Western and Eastern Spiritual Values of Life*. Ed. Swami B. H. Bon Mahārāj. Vrindāban: Institute of Oriental Philosophy, 1962. 68-75.

De Smet, Richard. "Surrounded by Excellence: An Evocation," *Jivan: Jesuits of South Asia: Views and News* **11**/10 (December 1990). 8, 10-11.

De Smet, Richard. "The Adaptive Development of Christian Monasticism." *Transactions of the Indian Institute of Advanced Study* **1** (1965) 191-202.

De Smet, Richard. "The Catholic Church and the Modern World." *Islam and the Modern Age* **1**/2 (July 1970) 59-67.

De Smet, Richard. "The Catholic Church in the Crucible." *Religious Situation in the Present-Day World: Seminar Papers*. Ed. Taran Singh. Patiala: Punjabi University, 1980. 49-57.

De Smet, Richard. "The Challenge of Secularization." *Present Day Challenges to Religion*. Ed. Thomas Paul. Alwaye: PITP, 1973. 83-98.

De Smet, Richard. "The Hindu *Dharma*: Permanence and Change." *E. Ugarte Felicitation Volume: Philosophy and Human Development*. Ed. A. Amaladass. Madras: Satyanilayam, 1986. 3-26.

De Smet, Richard. "The Indian Ascertainment of the Godhead (From the Vedas to Udayānācārya)." *Indica* **16** (1980) 59-73.

De Smet, Richard. "The Lag between *Sanātana Dharma* and Darshanic Wisdom." *Transactions of the Indian Institute of Advanced Study* (Simla) **1** (1965) 105-108.

De Smet, Richard. "The Marxist-Protestant-Catholic Rediscovery of Hope." *Bethany Golden Jubilee Souvenir.* Trivandrum: Bethany Ashram, 1969. 121-126.

De Smet, Richard. "The Medieval Inheritance of Dante." *Journal of the Department of English* (University of Calcutta) **23**/1-2 (1986-1987) 37-49.

De Smet, Richard. "The Nature of Christian Philosophy." *World Perspectives in Philosophy, Religion and Culture: Essays presented to Prof. Dhirendra Mohan Datta.* Patna: Bihar Darshan Parishad, 1968. 362-368.

De Smet, Richard. "The Philosophers' Transition from Atheism to Theism from the Fourth to the Eleventh Century A.D." *Challenges of Societies in Transition.* Ed. M. Barnabas, P.S. Jacob and S.K. Hulbe. New Delhi: Macmillan, 1978. 310-338. Also "Arjun Meditates on the Philosophers' Transition from Atheism to Theism from the Fourth to the Tenth Century A.D." *When Two Great Hearts Meet.* Ed. E. De Meulder. Allahabad: St Paul Publications, 1976. 164-191.

De Smet, Richard. "The Point of Departure of Metaphysics." *The Philosophical Quarterly* **28**/4 (1956) 265-271.

De Smet, Richard. "The Problematics of the Knowledge of God." *Indian Ecclesiastical Studies* **10**/2 (1971) 92-96; also in *Indian Philosophical Annual* **7** (1971) 121-125.

De Smet, Richard. "The Status of the Scriptures in the Holy History of India." *Research Seminar on Non-Christian Scriptures.* Ed. D.S. Amalorpavadass. Bangalore: NBCLC, 1975. 280-299.

De Smet, Richard. "The Witness (*Sākṣin*), Source of Thought and Action." *Philosophy: Theory and Practice (Seminar on World Philosophy, Madras, Dec. 7-17, 1970).* Ed. T.M.P. Mahadevan. Madras: University CASP, 1974. 176-185.

De Smet, Richard. "Theology of Hope and the Meaning of Mission." *Reflection* (Rajpur, Dehradun) **3** (1969) 3-10.

De Smet, Richard. "Towards an Indian Christology." *The Clergy Monthly Supplement* **7**/6 (1965) 254-260; also in *Religion and Society* **12** (1965) 6-15.

De Smet, Richard. "Towards Re-orienting Indian Philosophy: Hints from a Thomist." *The Philosophical Quarterly* **29**/4 (1957) 237-243.

De Smet, Richard. "Training in Spiritual Life." *Silver Jubilee Commemoration Volume, Nowrosjee Wadia College* (Poona, 1958) 1-11.

De Smet, Richard. *Brahman and Person: Essays by Richard De Smet.* Ed. Ivo Coelho. Delhi: Motilal Banarsidass, 2010.

Deshpande, M.M. "The Changing Conceptions of the Veda: From Speech-Acts to Magical Sounds." *The Adyar Library Bulletin* **54** (1990) 1-41.

Deutsch, E. and J.A.B. van Buitenen. *A Source-book of Advaita Vedānta.* Honolulu: Hawaii University Press, 1971.

Deutsch, E. *Advaita Vedānta: A Philosophical Reconstruction.* Honolulu: Hawaii University Press, 1971.

Devanandan, P.D. *The Concept of Maya*. Calcutta: YMCA, 1954.
Devdas, Nalini. *Sri Ramakrishna*. Bangalore: CISRS, 1966.
Devdas, Nalini. *Svāmī Vivekānanda*. Bangalore: CISRS, 1968.
Dharmarāja Adhvarīndra. *Vedāntaparibhāṣā*. Ed. S.S.S. Shastri. Adyar, Madras, 1942.
Doyle, Sean. *Synthesizing the Vedānta: The Theology of Pierre Johanns, S.J.* Oxford, etc.: Peter Lang, 2006.
Eliade, M. and R. Pettazzoni. *L'histoire des religions a-t-elle un sense? Correspondence 1926-1959*. Paris: Cerf, 1994.
Fakirbhai, Dhanjibhai. *Christopanishad*. Bangalore: CISRS, 1965.
Fakirbhai, Dhanjibhai. *Hriday Gita*. Surat, 1956.
Fakirbhai, Dhanjibhai. *Prematattva Darshan*. Ahmedabad, 1963.
Fakirbhai, Dhanjibhai. *Shree Krist Geeta: Song of the Lord Christ*. Delhi: ISPCK, 1969.
Fakirbhai, Dhanjibhai. *The Philosophy of Love*. Delhi: ISPCK, 1966.
Farquhar, John Nicol. *The Crown of Hinduism*. Calcutta 1913, 1914; Oxford 1919.
Fernandez, Gonçalo. *Tratado sobre o Hinduismo*. Critical ed. By J. Wicki. Lisboa: Centro de Estudos Historicos Ultramarinos, 1973.
Gadamer, Hans-Georg. *Philosophical Hermeneutics*. Tr. and ed. David E. Linge. Berkeley: University of California Press, 1976.
Gadamer, Hans-Georg. *Truth and Method*. 1st ET Garrett Barden and John Cumming. New York: Seabury, 1975. 2nd ET J. Weinsheimer and D.G. Marshall. New York: Crossroad, 1989.
Gauḍapāda. *The Āgamasastra of Gauḍapāda*. Ed., tr. and annotated by Vidhushekara Bhattacharya. Calcutta: Calcutta University, 1943.
Gispert-Sauch, G. "The Bhṛgu-Vallī of the Taittirīya Upaniṣad: an Early XVII Century European Translation." *Indica* **5**/2 (1968) 139-144.
Gopal, K.K. *Purāṇa* **26**/1 (1984) 21-32.
Grant, Sara. *Śaṅkarācārya's Concept of Relation*. Delhi: Motilal Banarsidass, 1999.
Griffiths, Bede. *Christ in India: Essays towards a Hindu-Christian Dialogue*. Templegate, 1967, 1984.
Griffiths, Bede. *Vedanta and Christian Faith*. Dehra Dun, 1968.
Gupta, Som Raj. *The Word Speaks to the Faustian Man: A Translation and Interpretation of the Prasthānatrayi and Śaṅkara's Bhāṣya for the Participation of Contemporary Man*. Vol. I: Īśā, Kena, Kaṭha and Praśna Upaniṣads. Delhi: Motilal Banarsidass, 1991.
Hacker, Paul. "Eigentumlichkeiten der Lehre und Terminologie Śaṅkaras: *Avidyā, Nāmarūpa, Māyā, Īśvara*." *Zeitschrift der Deutschen Morgenländischen Gesellschaft* **10** (1950) 246-286. Reprinted in his *Kleine Schriften* 69-109.
Hacker, Paul. *Kleine Schriften*. Ed. Lambert Schmithausen. Glasenapp-Stiftung: Band 15. Wiesbaden: Steiner, 1978.
Hacker, Paul. "Śaṅkara der Yogin und Śaṅkara der Advaitin: Einige Beobachtungen." *Beiträge zur Geistesgeschichte Indiens: Festschrift für Erich Frauwallner*. Ed. G. Oberhammer. *Wiener Zeitschrift für die Kunde Süd- und Ostasiens*, parts XII-XIII (1968-69) 119-148. Also published in Hacker, *Kleine Schriften* 213-242.

Hacker, Paul. *Untersuchungen über Texte des frühen Advaitavāda, 1. Die Schüler Śaṅkaras*. Mainz: Verlag der Akademie der Wissenschaften und der Literatur, 1950.

Halbfass, Wilhelm. *Indien und Europa: Perspektiven ihrer geistigen Begegnung*. Basel/Stuttgart: Schwabe, 1981. ET: *India and Europe: An Essay in Philosophical Understanding*. Albany: SUNY Press, 1988 / Delhi: Motilal Banarsidass, 1990.

Halbfass, Wilhelm. *Studies in Kumārila and Śaṅkara*. Reinbeck: Verlag für Orientalistische Fachpublikationen, 1983.

Herbert, Jean. "Védantisme et vie pratique." *Mélanges sur l'Inde*. Paris: Cahiers du Sud, 1941. 150-184

Hideki, Kiyoshima. "The Concept of *anirvacanīya* in Early Advaitavedānta." *Acta Asiatica* (Tokyo: The Tōhō Gakkai) **57** (1989) 45-60.

Hulin, M. *Hegel et l'Orient*. Paris: Vrin, 1979.

Ingalls, Daniel H.H. "Śaṅkara's Arguments against the Buddhists." *Philosophy East and West* **3** (1953-54) 291-306.

Inge, W.R., L.P. Jacks, M. Hiriyanna, E.A. Burtt, and P.T. Raju. "[Editors'] Introduction." *Radhakrishnan: Comparative Studies in Philosophy Presented in Honour of His Sixtieth Birthday*. Ed. W.R. Inge, L.P. Jacks, M. Hiriyanna, E.A. Burtt, and P.T. Raju. London: Allen & Unwin / New York: Humanities Press, 1951, 1968. 9-15. Also, unattributed, in *Radhakrishnan Reader: An Anthology*, ed. K.M. Munshi, R.R. Diwadkar, P. Nagaraja Rao, K. Gopalaswami, and S. Ramakrishnan (Bombay: Bharatiya Vidya Bhavan, 1969) 607-614.

Iyer, M.K.V. *Advaita Vedānta according to Śaṅkara*. Bombay: Asia Publishers, 1964.

Jacobi, H. "On Māyāvāda." *Journal of the American Oriental Society* **33** (1913) 51-54.

Jaimini. *Mīmāṃsā Sūtra: Pūrvamīmāṃsāsūtra*. Ed. G. Jha. *Sacred Books of the Hindus*, vols. 10-11. Allahabad, 1911.

Johanns, P. *A Synopsis of 'To Christ through the Vedānta': 1 – Śaṅkara*. Pamphlet no. 4 of The Light of the East series. Calcutta, 1930.

Johanns, Pierre. "To Christ through the Vedānta." *The Light of the East*. **1-13** (1922-34).

Johanns, Pierre. *To Christ through the Vedānta: The Writings of Reverend P. Johanns, S.J.* 2 vols. Ed. Theo de Greeff. Bangalore: The United Theological College, 1996.

Johanns, Pierre. *Vers le Christ par le Vedānta*. 2 vols. Louvain: Museum Lessianum, section philosophique, 1932-33.

Kirfel, W. *Das Purāṇa Pañcalakṣaṇa*. Bonn: K. Schroeder, 1927.

Klostermaier, Klaus K. *Kristvidya: A Sketch of an Indian Christology*. Bangalore: Christian Institute for the Study of Religion and Society, 1967.

Krempel, A. *La doctrine de la relation chez saint Thomas: Exposé historique et systématique*. Paris: J. Vrin, 1952.

Kulandran, Sabapathy. *Grace in Christianity and Hinduism*. Cambridge: James Clark, 2004.

Lacombe, Olivier. *L'Absolu selon le Vedānta: Les notions de Brahman et d'Ātman dans les systèmes de Çankara et de Rāmānoudja*. Paris: Geuthner, 1937; reimpression augmented with notes in 1966.

Le Gobien, Charles, et al. *Lettres édifiantes et curieuses écrites des missions étrangères par quelques missionnaires de la Compagnie de Jesus.* 34 vols. Paris: Chez Nicolas Le Clerc, 1703-1776.

Leuze, R. *Die ausserchristlichen Religionen bei Hegel.* Göttingen, 1975.

Lonergan, Bernard. *Insight: A Study of Human Understanding.* Collected Works of Bernard Lonergan 3. Ed. F.E. Crowe and R.M. Doran. Toronto: University of Toronto Press, 1992.

Lonergan, Bernard. *Method in Theology.* Toronto: University of Toronto Press, 1990.

Madhusūdana. *Siddhāntabindu.* Tr. P.M. Modi. Bhavnagar, 1929, 1938.

Malkovsky, Bradley J. "Introduction: The Life and Work of Richard V. De Smet, S.J." *New Perspectives on Advaita Vedanta: Essays in Commemoration of Professor Richard De Smet, S.J.* Ed. Bradley J. Malkovsky. Leiden / Boston / Köln: Brill, 2000. 1-17.

Maṇḍanamiśra. *Brahmasiddhi by Maṇḍanamiśra and commentary by Sankhapāni, with introduction, appendices and indexes.* Ed. S. Kuppuswami Sastri. Madras Government Oriental Series, 4. Madras: Government Press, 1937. Delhi: Sri Satguru Publications, 1984.

Mascarenhas, H.O. *The Quintessence of Hinduism: The Key to Indian Culture and Philosophy.* Bombay: St Sebastian Goan High School, 1951.

Mayeda, Sengaku. "Introduction." *Śaṅkara's Upadeśasāhasrī.* Vol. 1: Introduction, Text and Indices. Tr. and ed. Sengaku Mayeda. Delhi: Motilal Banarsidass, 2006. 1-68.

Mayeda, Sengaku. "An Introduction to the Life and Thought of Śaṅkara." *Śaṅkara's Upadeśasāhasrī.* Vol. 2: Introduction and English Translation. Tr. and ed. Sengaku Mayeda. Tokyo: The Hokuseido Press, 1973. Delhi: Motilal Banarsidass, 2006. 1-97.

Mayeda, Sengaku. "On the Author of the *Māṇḍūkyopaniṣad* and the *Gauḍapādīya-Bhāṣya.*" *The Adyar Library Bulletin* **31-32** (1967-68) 73-94.

Meynell, Hugo. "On Richard V. De Smet, SJ, 'Origin: Creation and Emanation'." *Person and God: Studies in Metaphysics.* Ed. George McLean and Hugo Meynell. Lanham, MD: University Press of America, 1988. 221-225.

Monchanin, Jules. *Mystique de l'Inde, mystère chrétien.* Paris: Fayard, 1974 / Fata Morgana, 1999.

Mukerji, A.C. "Idealistic Trends of Contemporary India." *The Philosophical Quarterly* (Amalner) **32** (July 1960) 111-121.

Murty, K. Satchidananda. *Revelation and Reason in Advaita Vedānta.* Waltair: Andhra University Press, 1959; reprint Delhi: Motilal Banarsidass, 1974.

Namboodiry, Udayan. *St Xavier's: The Making of a Calcutta Institution.* New Delhi: Viking / Penguin Books India, 1995.

Oldmeadow, Harry. *A Christian Pilgrim in India: The Spiritual Journey of Swami Abhishiktananda (Henri Le Saux).* Bloomington, IN: World Wisdom Books, 2008.

Otto, R. *Mysticism East and West.* New York: Macmillan, 1932.

Pande, G.C. *Life and Thought of Śaṅkarācārya.* Delhi: Motilal Banarsidass, 1994.

Panikkar, Raimundo. *The Unknown Christ of Hinduism: Towards an Ecumenical Christophany*. London: DLT, 1964, 1968, 1977. Rev. and enlarged ed. London: DLT, 1981 / Bangalore: ATC, 1982.

Pessein, J.F. *Vedanta Vindicated or the Harmony of Vedanta and Christian Philosophy*. Trichinopoly: St Joseph's Industrial School Press, 1925.

Piantelli, Mario. *Śaṅkara e la rinascità del Brāhmanesimo*. Maestri di Spiritualità, sezione Mondo Orientale. Fossano: Editrice Esperienze, 1974.

Potter, K.H. *The Encyclopedia of Indian Philosophy*, Vol. 3. Advaita Vedānta, Delhi: M. Banarsidass, 1981.

Radhakrishnan, S. "Fragments of a Confession." *Radhakrishnan Reader*. Ed. K.M. Munshi, R.R. Diwakar, P.N. Rao, K. Gopalaswami and S. Ramakrishnan. Bombay: Bharatiya Vidya Bhavan, 1969.

Radhakrishnan, S. "*Indian Philosophy*: Some Problems." *Mind*, New Series 35/138 (1926) 154-180.

Radhakrishnan, S. "Religion and Society." *Transactions of the Indian Institute of Advanced Study* 1 (1965) 39-42.

Radhakrishnan, S. *Indian Philosophy*. 2 vols. London, 1929.

Radhakrishnan, S. *The Principal Upaniṣads*. London: Allen & Unwin, 1953.

Radhakrishnan, S., ed. *History of Philosophy Eastern and Western*. London: G. Allen & Unwin, 1952.

Radhakrishnan, S., tr. and intro. *The Brahma Sūtra: The Philosophy of the Spiritual Life*. London: George Allen & Unwin, 1960.

Rāmānuja. *Śrībhāṣya*. Bombay Sanskrit and Prakrit Series, LXVIII. Bombay, 1914.

Rambachan, A. *Accomplishing the Accomplished: The Veda as a Source of Valid Knowledge in Śaṅkara*. Honululu: University of Hawaii Press, 1991.

Rao, Marc Sunder. *Ananyatva: Realisation of Christian Non-Dualism*. Bangalore: CISRS, 1964.

Rao, Marc Sunder. *Concerning Indian Christianity*. Delhi: YMCA Publishing House, 1973.

Rao, Srinivasa. *Advaita: A Critical Investigation*. Bangalore: Indian Philosophical Foundation, 1985.

Renou, Louis. "The Enigma in the Ancient Literature of India." *Diogenes* 29 (Spring 1960) 32-41.

Robinson, Richard. "Some Methodological Approaches to the Unexplained Point." *Philosophy East and West* 22 (1972) 309-323.

Roy, S.S. *The Heritage of Śaṅkara*. Allahabad: Udayan Press, 1965.

Rukmani, T.S. "Dr Richard De Smet and Śaṅkara's Advaita." *Hindu-Christian Studies Bulletin* 16 (2003) 12-21.

Said, Edward. *L'orientalisme: l'Orient créé par l'Occident*. Paris: Seuil, 1980. ET: *Orientalism: Western Conceptions of the Orient*, rev. ed. with new afterword. Penguin, 1995.

Samartha, S.J. *The Hindu Response to the Unbound Christ*. Madras: CLS, 1974.

Śaṅkara. *Brahmasūtra Śaṅkara Bhāṣya with the commentaries Bhāmatī, Kalpataru and Parimala*. 2 vols. Parimala Sanskrit Series no. 1. Ahmedabad: Parimal Publications, 1981.

Śaṅkara. *Brahmasūtraśaṅkarabhāṣyam*, with Vācaspati Miśra's *Bhāmati*. Ed. Mahadeva Sastri Bakre, rev. W.L. Shastri Panshikar. 3rd ed. Bombay: Nirnaya Sagar Press, 1934.

Śaṅkara. *Bṛhadāraṇyakopaniṣad with Śaṅkara's Bhāṣya*. Tr. Swami Madhavananda. 3rd ed. Almora, 1950.

Śaṅkara. *The Word Speaks to the Faustian Man: A Translation and Interpretation of the* Prasthānatrayī *and Śaṅkara's* Bhāṣya *for the Participation of Contemporary Man*. Vol. 1: Īśā, Kena, Kaṭha and Praśna Upaniṣads. Tr. Som Raj Gupta. Delhi: Motilal Banarsidass, 1991.

Śaṅkara. *Commentary on Eight Upaniṣads*. Tr. Swami Gambhirananda, 2 vols. Calcutta: Advaita, 1957.

Śaṅkara. *Commentary on the Bṛhadāraṇyakopaniṣad*. Tr. Swami Madhavananda. Almora: Advaita, 1950.

Śaṅkara. *Śaṅkara's Upadeśasāhasrī*. Vol. 1: Introduction, Text and Indices. Vol. 2: Introduction and English Translation. Tr. and ed. Sengaku Mayeda. Tokyo: The Hokuseido Press, 1973. Delhi: Motilal Banarsidass, 2006.

Śaṅkara. *Śrīmadbhagavadgītāśrīśaṅkara... bhāṣyena sahitā*. Ed. D.V. Gokhale. 2nd rev. Ed. Poona: Oriental Book Agency, 1950.

Śaṅkara. *The Vedānta-sūtras with the Commentary of Śaṅkarācārya*. Tr. G. Thibaut. Sacred Books of the East, vols. 34 and 38. Oxford: Clarendon Press, 1890 and 1896.

Śaṅkara. *Upadeśasāhasrī*. Tr. Swami Jagadananda. 2nd ed. Madras, 1949.

Śaṅkara. *Upaniṣadbhāṣyam*. 2 vols. Ed. H.R. Bhagavat. 2nd ed. Poona: Ashtekar, 1927, 1928.

Śaṅkara. *Yoga-bhāṣya-vivaraṇa*. Tr. and ed. P.S. Rama Sastri and S.R. Krishnamurthi Sastri. Madras: Government Oriental Publication, 1952.

Śaṅkara. *Yogasūtrabhāṣyavivaraṇa of Śaṅkara: Vivaraṇa Text with English Translation and Critical Notes along with Text and English Translation of Patanjali's Yogasūtras and Vyāsabhāṣya*. 2 vols. Tr. and ed.T.S. Rukmani. New Delhi: Munshiram Manoharlal, 2001.

Satyanand, J. *Nimbārka: A Pre-Śaṁkara Vedāntin and His Philosophy*. Varanasi: Vishwa Jyoti Gurukul, 1994.

Schmidt, H.P. "The Origin of *ahiṁsā*." *Mélanges d'Indianisme à la mémoire de Louis Renou*. Paris: Boccard, 1968. 625-655.

Singh, R.P. *The Vedānta of Śaṅkara*. Jaipur: Bharat Press, 1945.

Singh, Ram Pratap. "Radhakrishnan's Substantial Reconstruction of the Advaita of Śaṅkara," *Philosophy East and West* **16** (1966) 5-32. See excerpts in "Śaṃkara and Radhakrishnanm" *Radhakrishnan Reader: An Anthology*, ed. K.M. Munshi, R.R. Diwadkar, P. Nagaraja Rao, K. Gopalaswami, and S. Ramakrishnan (Bombay: Bharatiya Vidya Bhavan, 1969) 615-628.

Sinha, J. *Problems of Post-Śaṅkara Vedānta*. Calcutta: Sinha Press, 1971.

Stroumsa, G.G. *Savoir et salut: Traditions juives et tentations dualistes dans le christianisme ancient*. Paris: Cerf, 1992.

Taber, J.A. *A Transforming Philosophy: A Study of Śaṅkara, Fichte and Heidegger*. Honolulu: Hawaii University Press, 1983.

Thachil, Jose. *The Upaniṣads: A Socio-Religious Approach*. New Delhi: Intercultural Publications, 1993.

Un Moine d'Occident [= Elie of La Trappe / Elie Lemoine / Alphonse Levée]. *Doctrine de la Non-dualité (Advaita-vāda) et Christianisme*. Collection "Mystiques et Religions." Dervy-Livres, 6 rue de Savoie, Paris – 6, 1982. ET: *Christianity and the Doctrine of Non-Dualism*, by 'A Monk of the West.' Hillsdale, NY: Sophia Perennis, 2004.

Van Buitenen, J.A.B. *Rāmānuja's Vedārthasaṃgraha*. Poona, 1956.

Vattanky, J. "Fr Richard De Smet, S.J.: Friend, Scholar, Man of Dialogue." *Vidyajyoti: Journal of Theological Reflection* 71/4 (2007) 241-261.

Vetter, Tillmann. "Zur Bedeutung des Illusionismus bei Śaṅkara." *Wiener Zeitschrift für die Kunde Süd- und Ostasiens* **12-13** (1969) 407-423.

Vetter, Tillmann. *Studien zur Lehre und Entwicklung Śaṅkaras*. Vienna: De Nobili Research Library, 1979.

Viyagappa, I. *G.W.F. Hegel's Concept of Indian Philosophy*. Roma: Università Gregoriana Editrice, 1980.

Weber, Ed. H. "Mystique parce que theologien: Maitre Eckhart," *La Vie Spirituelle* (Paris: Éditions du Cerf) **136**/652 (1982) 730-749.

Wood, Thomas E. *The Māṇḍūkya Upaniṣad and the Āgama Śāstra: An Investigation into the Meaning of Vedānta*. Honululu: University of Hawaii Press, 1990; Delhi: Motilal Banarsidass, 1992.

Yearley, Lee. *Mencius and Aquinas: Theories of Virtue and Conceptions of Courage*. Albany: State University of New York Press, 1990.

INDEX

abādhitatva: upheld by Śaṅkara, 6, 105, 144
abaleity, 14
ābhāsa, 164, 242, 257, 354; as door, 182
Abhishiktananda (Henri Le Saux), 388, 389, 395
Absolute: does not exclude the finite, 443; found through regression from effects to Cause, 136; implicitly affirmed in every judgment, 134; not known by ordinary *pramāṇas*, 45
acosmism: and the Absolute, 443; and Padmapāda, 451; contemporary dissatisfaction with, 159; elimination of, 205; exclusion even of derived existence, 387; implied by Advaita, 84; imposed by awakening, according to Piantelli, 420; in Gauḍapāda, 12; in Maṇḍana Miśra, 290; in Radhakrishnan's interpretation of Śaṅkara, 210; of Advaita, 32, 307; of Mahāyāna origin in *Māṇḍ. Up. Āgama Śāstra*, 297; Śaṅkara not concerned with directly rejecting, 168
acosmist interpretation of Śaṅkara: 1, 8, 10, 16, 17, 202, 296, 377, 378; in Radhakrishnan, 22; not rejected by Calcutta School, 5; not rejected by De Smet in doctoral dissertation, 5-7; not rejected by Lacombe, 5; rejected by De Smet under influence of Upadhyay, 2-4; rejection of, 17, 169, 448; upheld by Johanns, 5
adhyāropa, 39, 55, 117, 160, 330, 356. *See also adhyāsa*; superimposition
adhyāsa, 15, 39, 141, 160, 187, 371, 395. *See also adhyāropa*; superimposition
Advaita: and Catholic theology, 398-411; and Christianity, 354-7; as theology, 400; as faith seeking understanding, 400; as philosophy, 400; not monism, not pantheism, but non-dualism, 354
Aham Brahm'āsmi, 181, 327, 394, 404, 481; indicates absolute unity of *Brahman* and *Ātman*, 53
ahiṁsā: as fundamental virtue in *dharma*, 437; in Buddhism, 438; Kumārila on, 440; Vedic origin of, 438
Aiyengar, S. Vedanta, 386
ajahallakṣaṇā, 40
ajñāna: belief in absolute and independent reality of effect 6; epistemological category, 122; favoured in Śaṅkara's usage, 122; frequency of, in Śaṅkara, 122-8; in *B.S.Bh.*, 297; technical term in *B.S.Bh.*, 122. *See also avidyā*
ākaṃkṣā: *see* expectation, 43
akhaṇḍārthaka: another name for *nirapekṣa lakṣaṇa*, 58
ākṛti, 250, 474
Albert the Great, negativism of, 198
Al-Bīrūnī, 431, 434
All-India Philosophical Congress: De Smet's first participation in, 173; silver jubilee session, 208, 295
Almora Colloquy, 388
Alston, A.J., 295; and Sureśvara's two stages of *Brahmajñāna*, 115; and three peculiarities in *NS*, 112
Amalānanda, 405, 409
ambivalence: of upaniṣadic pairs of terms, 18

Brahman, double form of, 261, 474; misunderstood by Radhakrishnan, 19, 234-5; proper understanding of, 236
Brahman: arguments for existence of, 14; as absolute and as related to world, 167; as Real, 10; *Ātman* of the experience, 355; better indicated by plurality of terms, 405; does not belong to common genus, 466; impersonal, 85, 307; no self-transformation, 216; equivalent to God, according to De Nobili, 366; indicated, not expressed, 175, 277; ineffability of, 263, 276-7; lack of *viśeṣaṇas*, 278; needs no instrument, 247; *nirguṇa*: 91, 277, 346, 352, 403; no extraneous help, 217; no real relationship to effects, 175, 346; as Non-Being (*Asat*), 466; not object of anything, 466; not univocal with effects, 216; ontological Absolute, 245; ontological simplicity of, 277; personal, 1, 222, 298, 388; reality of, defended by Śaṅkara, 230; sole universal Cause, 245, 246, 252, 349; universally immanent in effects, 350; non-material *upādāna*, 216; verbal, 245. *See also* causality of *Brahman*; causality; cause, supreme / universal
Brahmānubhava, 451
Brahmātmaikatva: absolute unity of *Brahman* and *Ātman*, 52
Brahma-vidyās: in Rāmānuja, 154
Brückner, H., 439
Buddha vacana: *pauruṣeya*, 275, 276
Buddha, 96
buddhi: link with *sat* static, for Śaṅkara, dynamic for Aquinas, 136; mirror-like, 130; permanently anchored in *sat*, 136. *See also* intelligence
Buddhism: universalistic and adaptive, 434; teaching on unreality of world rejected by Śaṅkara, 11
Bulcke, Camille, 26n28
Calcutta School of indology, 2; De Smet's debt to, 26n28; did not reject Śaṅkara as acosmist, 5
Calmette, Jean, 432
capacity: and grasp of synthesis, 43
capital letters, use of, 10, 14, 16, 17, 23, 85, 139-46, 163, 169, 186-7, 203, 232, 377, 443. *See also* Pessein, J.F.
Cardona, G., 439
Cārvākas, 97
caste, as pre-condition for *Brahmajijñāsā*, 89, 109
categories, Indian: and expression of Christianity, 300, 462
Catholic missionaries, and India, 431-2
Catholic theology, and Advaita, 398-411
causality of *Brahman*: by mere intention, 314; material and operative, 457, 475; misunderstood by Radhakrishnan, 19, 221, 234; no change, 314; omniscient, all-powerful, 59, 314; purification of, 236; total sufficiency of, 236; universal, 215; *upādāna* and *nimitta*, 485;
causality: and arguments for existence of God, 485; and creation, 15-17, 22, 297-8; and Dharmakīrti, 19, 238; ascending series, 144; creative, neglected by Piantelli, 420; divine, imprecision of Śaṅkara's theory of, 94-5; efficient and material, 385; efficient or operative, 467-8; exemplary, 472; final, 468-71; formal: —internal, 427; —two conceptions of, 471-4; inadequacy of Sāṁkhya doctrine of, 95; material, 373, 458, 474-82; —two conceptions of, 474; —as internal principle of imperfection, 474; —in addition to *Brahman*, 479; patterns and theories of, 299;

intellect: dynamically synthetic, 43, 312; dynamic and interpretative, 188; not mirror but synthesizer, 21, 188, 279; open to every intelligible, 340; polarized on Being, 199. *See also* dynamism, intellectual
intellectio: equivalent to *manana*, 105
intellection, conception of, 310; 311-2
intellectual creature: alone capable of possessing divine essence, 337
intention of author, 268; and grasp of synthesis, 43, 44
intentionality: breaks through limits of effability, 189. *See also* dynamism, intellectual
interpretation of Śaṅkara: *see* Śaṅkara interpretation
intuition, 309, 336; blissful, 343; comprehensive and penetrating, 291; mystic, given to all, 212; mystic, given only to chosen spirits, 212; supreme, misconceived by Śaṅkara, 94, 129; misunderstood by Radhakrishnan, 212, 224-5, 233; comes at end of *Brahmajijñāsā*, 225
intuition, direct, 273, 336, 451; extrinsically, not causally, dependent on *Brahmajijñāsā*, 69; goal of *Brahmajijñāsā*, 47; in Rāmānuja, 154; not result of human effort, 34; prepared for but not caused by *yoga*, 34; through recollection and meditation, 69; awakening, 69. *See also* *anubhava*; *avabodha*; *dhyāna* experience; experience
intuitive penetration, 285. *See also* *avagati paryantam jñānam*
Īśvara: applied only to *saguṇa Brahman*, 297; applied to *Brahman* as object of both *Vidyā* and *a-Vidyā*, 237; as operative cause, 479; attributed to both *nirguṇa* and *saguṇa Brahman*, 314; *māyā* in association with *Brahman*, 362; not distinct from *param Brahman*, 425
Īśvarakṛṣṇa: as pre-Śaṅkara, 97
iti: indicates formula as analogical, 52
Jacob, G.A., 425
Jacobi, H., 210, 416; rejects authenticity of *Māṇḍ. Up. Bh.*, 18
jahadajahallakṣaṇā, 14, 22, 40, 41, 53-56, 60, 81, 119, 185, 296, 329; and intrinsic analogy, 370-1, 394-5; equivalent to *anvaya vyatireka*, 182; method for elucidating *svarūpalakṣaṇa* of *Brahman*, 59; Śaṅkara conscious of his use of, 55
jahallakṣanā, 40
Jaimini, 78, 96, 188, 259, 274, 326, 327, 398, 406; and *lakṣaṇā*, 280, 296; conception of *karman* criticized by Śaṅkara, 418; definition of *puruṣārtha*, 285, 309; hermeneutical presuppositions of, 271-6
Jainism: inclusive, 434
Jayantabhaṭṭa, 440
jijñāsā: and desire for liberation, 144. *See also* dynamism, intellectual
jīvan-mukti, 242-3, 291, 420; and service to humanity, 243
jīvātman, 240-2; animating principle in individual, 362; distinct from *Ātman*, 165, 240, 241; door, 164; epistemic unity with *Ātman* in *anubhava*, 357; error of endowing with divinity, 94; indirectly indicates *Ātman*-Consciousness, 165; integrator, 165; not cause of world, 124; not simply identical with Absolute, 357; really identical with *Brahman*, 10, 85, 307; recovers eternal form in *mukti*, 156; reflection of *Ātman*, 15, 64, 170, 317, 354; unity with *Paramātman*, 327
jñāna: salvation through, 363; supreme, 77; theoretical

knowledge, 147. *See also* knowledge
jñāna-kāṇḍa: primacy of, 89
jñānam, meaning of, 370-1, 319; role of, in definition of *Brahman*, 63
Johanns, Pierre, 26n28, 95, 98, 295, 384, 395, 399; influence on De Smet, 2, 21-22; pantheism foreign to Śaṅkara, 7, 94; acosmist interpretation of Śaṅkara, 5
kāma-phala, 376
Kaṇāda: early teaching on knowledge, 299; pre-Śaṅkara, 96
kāraṇa: *upādāna-* and *nimitta-*, 124
karma: as universal law, 437; reduced to providence, 486
Kautsa, 273
Kenghe, C.T., 99
kevalalakṣaṇa, 39
Kirfel, W., 422
Klostermaier, Klaus K., 392, 395
knowable: only sense objects as, 46
knower: immediately apprehended as thinking subject, 47
knowledge: always partial, according to Vallabha, 283; empirical, not possible without superimposition, 161; linked with being by its dynamism, 134; metaphysics of, 424; mirror theory of, 312; mystical, 340; polarized on being, 134; primacy of, 86; result of *bimbapratibimba*, 130; secular, valid within its own realm, 139; similarity or identity between objects and subject, 129; sphere of I and non-I, 161; theory of, attempt by Śaṅkara to overcome defects, 135; true, and *avidyā*, 36; valid within proper limits, 452
Krempel, A.: study of relation in Aquinas, 444
Krishna, Daya, 271, 273, 276
Kṛṣṇa Tīrtha, 362
Kulandran, S., 394
Kumārila Bhaṭṭa: pre-Śaṅkara, 96. *See also* Bhāṭṭa school
Lacombe, Olivier, 211, 295, 386, 417; and method of indirect indication, 23; recognition of *lakṣaṇā* in Śaṅkara, 4-5; and acosmist interpretation of Śaṅkara, 5
Laerzio, A., 359, 360
lakṣaṇa, 92, 310; *akhaṇḍārthaka* and *nirapekṣa*, 63; negative, 92
lakṣaṇa and *lakṣaṇā*: direct and indirection indication, 57
lakṣaṇajñāna, 326, 328, 330, 334n2; always attractive to philosophers, 120; developed as ancillary requirement of *Brahmajijñāsā*, 120.
lakṣaṇā method, 13; *adhyāropa*, *apavāda*, *paramārtha*, 117, 330; in Sureśvara, 118-20
lakṣaṇā, 78, 241, 328, 332, 402; acceptance by indologists and Vedāntins, 26n27; allowed by Jaimini, 296, 280; and interpretation of *svarūpalakṣaṇas* of *Brahman*, 92; De Smet's contribution to Advaitin-Christian dialogue, 26n26; De Smet's study of, 394, 395; in De Smet's doctoral dissertation, 4; need for, 370-1; neglect of Śaṅkara's use of, 94; not akin to Aquinas' analogy, 419; not fully exposed by Piantelli, 419; phase of elevating transmutation, 56; possible because of dynamism of intellect, 189; power of, 80-1; used to interpret *Tattvamasi*, 15. *See also* implication, theory of; *jahadajahallakṣaṇā*; meaning
lakṣitalakṣaṇa, 39
lakṣyārtha, 144, 241, 319, 354, 356; given primacy by Śaṅkara, 280; *jahat*, *ajahat*, *jahadajahat*, 328.
language: anthropomorphism of, 36; commentatorial, 187; cribwork of Śaṅkara's writing, 162, 202-4, 203-4t; hermeneutical or śrutivādic, 203; indicative power of, and Radhakrishnan, 223; of

extremes, 202; ordinary (*vyavahāra*), 186, 310; powers of expressing and indicating, 201, 223, 264, 370; three levels of, 17, 23, 162, 186-8; upaniṣadic, 186; utilitarian, 202
Lederle, M., 358
Ledrus, M., 26n28
Leibniz, G., 379
Leuze, R., 436n4
liberation, 335-44, 417; as blissful intellectual experience of God, 335; as cessation of ignorance, 335; conditions of, 338-43; desire for, 335-8; —and other human desires, 336; effects of, 343-4; eternal fact to which man awakes, 420; as intuition of divine essence, 340; not an annihilation, 356; as simultaneous enjoyment of all things in *Brahman*, 344. *See also mokṣa*
like is known by like: principle governing early Greek philosophy, 129; overthrown by Aristotle, 129; and Thomas Aquinas, 129; and Śaṅkara, 134
līlā, activity as, 247-8
Logos, and *Ātman*, 393
Lokāyatikas, 97
Lonergan, Bernard, 24; cognitional theory as aid to interpretation, 29n97
Lord: innermost Self of enjoyer, 259
lotus, blue, 45, 62, 65, 79, 118, 186, 223, 277; as example of *svarūpalakṣaṇa*, 58
love: and identity, 298; reciprocity of, 156
Lüders, Heinrich, 423
Madhusūdana, 343
Madhva, 363, 410; conception of *vākya*, 283; interpretation of *Śruti*, 20; not aware of analogy of 'one', 283
magic: always sustained by an underlying reality, 123; as comparison, 184-5, 220, 249, 349, 378; *māyā* as, 211; Śaṅkara familiar with Buddhist usage, 123
Mahadevan, T.M.P., 416; acceptance of *lakṣaṇā* in Śaṅkara, 26n27
mahāvākyas, 59, 177, 179, 232, 287, 296, 312, 385, 404; bridge between *a-Vidyā* and *Vidyā*, 145; distinction between primary and secondary meanings, 111; five types of, 19, 215, 215, 233; indicating but not expressing *Brahman*, 77; infallible only as to purified meaning, 19, 234; interpretation of, 264; meaning discovered through exegesis, 19; not identity- but identifying- or identification-statements, 115; primacy of, 24, 91, 438; role of, 233
Mahāvīra Jina, 96
Malkani, G.R., 298
man: Christian idea of, 356; integration of, 355, 357; nature of, 354; Śaṅkara did not intend to produce a philosophy of, 93; various understandings of, 300
manana, 105, 147, 176-7, 289; and *fides quaerens intellectum*, 103; presupposed by *vijñāna*, 310
manas: material sense, 46
Maṇḍana Miśra, 113, 313, 426, 448; apophatism, 280, 290; only negative *Śrutis* authoritative, 177; *dhyāna-yoga* needs only negative teaching of Upaniṣads, 149; interpretation of supreme experience not determined positively by *Śruti*, 133; uses *sadasadbhyām anirvacanīya*, 19
Māṇḍūkya Kārikā Bhāṣya: attribution to Śaṅkara, 230
Māṇḍūkya Kārikā: combination of Buddhism and Upaniṣads, 230
Māṇḍūkya Upaniṣad and *Āgama Śāstra*: blending of Buddhism with Advaita, 297; decisive study by Wood, 296; not completely attributable to Gauḍapāda, 296

nimitta-kāraṇa, 180, 356, 375, 426; always connected with consciousness, 485; ascending series, 485; *Brahman* as, 13, 215, 349

nirapekṣa definition: non-relational, 58, 61, 327

nirodha: Buddhist, Patañjali, Śaṅkara, 132

nirvāṇa: not absolute nothingness, 198

niṣkāma-karma: pre-Śaṅkara teaching, 96

nityānitya-vastu-viveka, 85, 113, 144, 260

non-aseity: of creatures, 443

non-contradiction, principle of: and *arthāpatti*, 50

non-difference (*advaita*), doctrine of, 484

non-dualism: Christian religion as, 23; in Aquinas, 442; in Bernard of Clairvaux, 442; monotheistic, 410

non-otherness, 183, 205, 315; of effects and inner cause, 166-7

non-reciprocity, 315. *See also* unreciprocality

non-separateness, 183, 204, 315; of effects and inner cause, 166

nothing: in Buddhism, 191-8; in Eckhart, 198-202; in Śaṅkara, 202-6

Novalis (G.P.F. Freiherr), 432

Nṛsiṃha, 362

object of intuition: real and immediately present, 339

objectivity: and *pramāṇas*, 159

omnipresence, divine: ontological and epistemological, 339, 341

one: analogy of, and Madhva, 283

ontic permanence: inbuilt norm of intellectual valuation, 144. See also *abādhitatva*

ontology: *prakārin-prakāra* type, 281; *śarīra-ātman* type, 282

Origen, 253

origin, ontological, 375; scientific and metaphysical, 369-70

origination: from words, 473-4

Otto, Rudolf, 390, 417, 481

Padmapāda, 361-2, 415; and acosmistic monism, 451; first to introduce *vivarta*, 9, 127

panentheist: Rāmānuja as, 299

Panikkar, R., 394, 417

Pāṇini, 274

pantheism: and emanation, 379; elimination of, 17, 205, 250, 378, 386, 388; foreign to Śaṅkara, according to Johanns, 94; identification of world with *Brahman-Ātman*, 387; of Neo-Vedānta, 32-3, 94; of Rāmānuja, 8, 299; rejected by Śaṅkara, 17; Śaṅkara's doctrine as not, 7, 10, 17, 18, 23, 168, 169

paramārtha, 117, 328, 329; *lakṣaṇā*, 187, 356; primacy of, 92; *sattā*, 6

paramarthāpatti, 15, 371, 372

paramārthataḥ Sat, 249-50, 346

Paramārūpyānanda (J. Monchanin), 391

Paramātman: nature of, 327

paramhaṁsa, 260

para-textual factors, 308

pariṇāma: accepted by Śaṅkara, 8, 12, 13; effort to de-Sāṁkhyanize, 126, 211, 239

pariṇāmavāda, 475, 476; cancelled by *vivartavāda*, in Sarvajñātman, 9; rejected by Śaṅkara, 8, 12, 13; rejected by Sureśvara, 9; upheld by Śaṅkara from point of view of effect, 5

Parmenides, 129

participation, 377-8, 484; and Aquinas, 16, 199, 378, 419; and Śaṅkara, 8, 419; created existence as, 3, 377, 457, 458; doctrine of analogical, 458; in *Brahman*, 16; indicates 'what' of relationship between Absolute and world, 3; man as, 4; ontological, 8, 333; prolongs theory of analogy, 419; true by, 385

Patañjali, 434; as pre-Śaṅkara, 97

patiens divina, 150

perfections, pure, 331, 457

Buddhist position rejected by Śaṅkara, 17; as ontologically and intrinsically dependent on Cause, 20, 238; as *Sat*, Sāṁkhya and Vaiśeṣika position rejected by Śaṅkara, 17; as totally effect, 238, 239; as un-Real, 10; glory of *Brahman*, 472-3; *mithyā*, according to Radhakrishnan, 237; not *atyanta Asat*, 24; not *mithyā*, 239; not nothing, 237; not phenomenal, 239; not self-sufficient, 3; not *vijñāna-pariṇāma*, 424; ontological status of: 236-40; —not Śaṅkara's concern to elucidate, 10; pervaded by Cause, 250; relatively unreal, 4; Śaṅkara did not intend to produce a philosophy of, 93; *sat*, but *a-Sat*, 20; unreal, 385; viewed as self-existent thanks to *a-Vidyā*, 238

xenology, Indian, 433

Yāska, 273

yāthātmya, 169, 262, 311-2; and ignorance of *Brahman* as supreme *Ātman*, 159; succession of increasing approximations, 159. *See also* objectivity

Yearley, Lee, 399

yoga, 290

Yoga-bhāṣya-vivaraṇa: author of, 427; Śaṅkara authorship rejected by Halbfass, 440

Yoga-sūtra Bhāṣya, 309

yogyatā: *see* capacity

Zaehner, R.C., 417

Zen: and sudden illumination, 148-9

Ziegenbalg, Bartholomäus, 432